COUNSELLING YOUNG PEOPLE

Practical and clearly written, this new book from best-selling author Louise Porter equips mental health professionals with the knowledge and skills they need to provide insightful guidance and support to children and adolescents.

The book introduces exciting new models for thinking about young people's needs, self-esteem and resilience that will invigorate counselling. It outlines the most common presenting difficulties for young people and provides clear, practical guidance on how professionals in a counselling environment can respond to these in an effective way. Offering a coherent blend of theories and practices, chapters address a wide range of emotional, social, behavioural and learning difficulties with which young people may present to counselling, such as experiences of grief and loss, anxiety and depression, disordered eating, and dealing with adversity. With an aim to empower, the book presents a non-pathologising approach to counselling that respects the skills that young people bring to working through their challenges.

Accessible for professionals and trainees alike, this book is a must-have for anyone working in a counselling capacity with children and adolescents.

Louise Porter is a child psychologist with 40 years' experience working with young people with social, emotional, behavioural and developmental challenges. She is a university lecturer, national and international speaker, and author of many books on parenting, children's needs, and behaviour guidance.

COUNSELLING YOUNG PEOPLE

A Handbook for Trainees and Practitioners

Louise Porter

Routledge
Taylor & Francis Group
LONDON AND NEW YORK

Designed cover image: © Getty Images

First published 2024
by Routledge
4 Park Square, Milton Park, Abingdon, Oxon OX14 4RN

and by Routledge
605 Third Avenue, New York, NY 10158

Routledge is an imprint of the Taylor & Francis Group, an informa business

British Library Cataloguing-in-Publication Data
A catalogue record for this book is available from the British Library

Library of Congress Cataloging-in-Publication Data
Names: Porter, Louise, 1958- author.
Title: Counselling young people : a handbook for trainees and practitioners / Louise Porter.
Description: Abingdon, Oxon ; New York, NY : Routledge, 2024. | Includes bibliographical references and index. | Identifiers: LCCN 2023036510 (print) | LCCN 2023036511 (ebook) | ISBN 9781032348094 (hardback) | ISBN 9781032348087 (paperback) | ISBN 9781003323938 (ebook)
Subjects: LCSH: Youth--Counseling of. | Counselors--Training of.
Classification: LCC HQ796 .P627 2024 (print) | LCC HQ796 (ebook) | DDC 362.7--dc23/eng/20230902
LC record available at https://lccn.loc.gov/2023036510
LC ebook record available at https://lccn.loc.gov/2023036511

ISBN: 978-1-032-34809-4 (hbk)
ISBN: 978-1-032-34808-7 (pbk)
ISBN: 978-1-003-32393-8 (ebk)

DOI: 10.4324/9781003323938

Typeset in Interstate
by SPi Technologies India Pvt Ltd (Straive)

I wrote this book on the land of the Gubbi Gubbi and Ningy Ningy peoples, who are part of the Undambi peoples.
I acknowledge and respect their continuing culture and contributions to land, waters and communities.

I acknowledge that their connection to country was never relinquished.

I recognise those whose ongoing effort to protect and promote Aboriginal and Torres Strait Islander cultures will leave a lasting legacy for future generations.

I venerate past and present Elders on whose protection and care the new generation relies.

In loving memory of Stephen (1994 - 2022)
and those who love, miss and cherish him.

When the person who has died should still be with us,
this can leave us not knowing where to look,
not knowing where to go or who to turn to.
At times like this, all we have left are questions:
Why did this happen?
What is going wrong if our young people
are having such a hard time?
How can we support other young people?
What steps can be put in place
to make sure this doesn't happen to others?

These are important questions.
They show respect for the person who has died.
They show respect for all young people.
They show respect for life.

Members of the Port Augusta Aboriginal Community,
in Denborough et al. (2006, p. 21)

Used with permission

Denborough, D., Koolmatrie, C., Mununggirritj, D., Marika, D., Dhurrkay, W., & Yunupiingu, M. (2006). Linking stories and initiatives: A narrative approach to working with the skills and knowledge of communities. *The International Journal of Narrative Therapy and Community Work*, *2*, 19–51. https://dulwichcentre.com.au/linking-stories-and-initiatives.pdf

CONTENTS

FIGURES

BOXES

FOREWORD

In this book, I outline the principles and practices for forming partnerships with children and adolescents in counselling. These young people typically do not refer themselves, and even when they attend voluntarily, they drop out of counselling at high rates. This means that we need methods that engage them by allowing them to tell their own story and by respecting the strengths and resilience they bring to surviving adversity or challenges in their lives.

The methods I present recognise that young people are rational, which is to say that their behaviours are an attempt to meet their needs - that is, they have reasons for what they do. When we start with this assumption - rather than its opposite, that young people are in some way incompetent, damaged or malicious - then we can see them at their best and help them build an identity based on their strengths, rather than seeing themselves in terms of their 'problems'.

This book begins by outlining three post-modern theories that share this aim: solution-focused therapy, narrative therapy and Acceptance and Commitment Therapy. It applies these to emotional and social issues with which young people often present for counselling, such as stress, anxiety, depression, disordered eating, self-harm, suicidal ideation and attempts, drug and alcohol use, bullying, and aggressive outbursts.

To guide counsellors' thinking about these issues, I present models for understanding human needs, self-esteem and resilience in young people, and I discuss how young people experience grief - not only at losses such as the death of a family member, but the losses that their presenting issues bring into their lives, such as the loss of rich friendships and educational opportunities.

Valuable inclusions within this book are how to support young people who have endured traumatic experiences, who have been the targets or perpetrators of violence, and who themselves sexually abuse other young people. I also discuss the emotional and social well-being of gender and sexual minority youth.

I frame my recommendations within a context of addressing the ethical challenges inherent in working with young people, how to care for oneself in this work, to collaborate with young clients' parents or other caregivers, to consult with outside experts such as teachers and other practitioners, and to work across diversity.

Each issue I discuss here is backed by comprehensive research and my own four decades of experience in working with young people. I hope that this integration of theory and practice will expand your knowledge and skills in the service of supporting young people to achieve their goals for their lives.

PART I

Philosophy, theory and practice of working with young people

1 Philosophy and theories of counselling young people

In this chapter I describe my philosophy for working with young people, before introducing the theories that align with it. I start here because, as the saying goes, *If you don't stand for something, you will fall for anything* - that is, we need to be clear about our philosophy so that we can select theories and practices that align with our principles.

Philosophy of counselling theories

In selecting a theory or theories to guide our work, we need to consider what they believe - that is, their philosophy. Counselling theories differ on four dimensions which themselves shape the quality of the relationship between counsellor and client (see Figure 1.1).

Modernism versus postmodernism

First of these dimensions is that some theories adopt a *medical* model whose core assumption is that the 'doctor knows best'. Under medical approaches such as psychoanalysis, practitioners are objective observers of clients' experiences, identifying their deficits and labelling and diagnosing these (as appropriate/inappropriate; functional/dysfunctional; rational/irrational, etc.). Assessment is a top-down process where the expert seeks out client deficits and delivers a verdict or diagnosis, imposing a 'normalising' judgement about whether individuals measure up to norms (White, 2007). From this perspective, clients - or in fact 'patients' - need the expert to instruct them and to manage the reduction of their symptoms.

This approach arose with the discovery of microbes which implied that every disease has a cause, and every cause a treatment. This is termed *modernist* by way of contrast to previous beliefs that evil spells or the wrath of God caused plagues or natural disasters. Although science and rationality are an improvement on superstition, this model has amplified the voice of psychiatry, giving practitioners the power to name clients' pain and take over their rights to tell their own story (Marsten et al., 2016, p. 159).

A second problem is that diagnoses (like beauty) are often in the eye of the beholder - that is, they are unreliable. Even especially trained diagnosticians seldom agree on the general, let alone specific, nature of an individual client's psychiatric condition (Duncan et al., 2003).

DOI: 10.4324/9781003323938-2

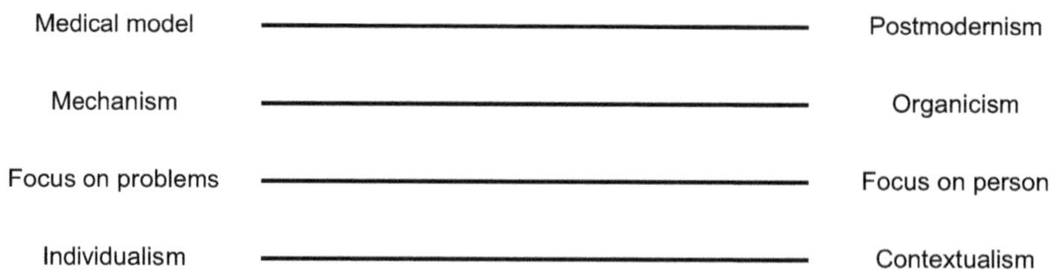

Figure 1.1 Philosophical dimensions of counselling theories

Third, psychiatric diagnoses are not as valid as we assume. We treat them with reverence in the belief that they are explanatory when instead they are only descriptive. The distinction is that an explanatory diagnosis is *sequential*, as in:

> Why does your child have developmental delays?
> Because she has Down syndrome.
> How do you know that she has Down syndrome?
> Because her 21st chromosome is fractured.

In contrast, descriptive diagnoses are *circular*, as in:

> Why does your child have difficulties paying attention?
> Because he has an attention deficit disorder.
> How do you know that he has an attention deficit disorder?
> Because he has difficulties paying attention.

When we treat descriptive diagnoses as if they are explanatory and we append the word 'disorder', we give diagnoses more credibility than they deserve, at the same time depriving labelled individuals of responsibility for their own actions and – because labels are static – disempowering them and stripping them of hope that they can improve their predicament in life.

Fourth, the medical model is fine for crises such as emergency surgery for a broken limb, but cannot sustain a collaborative relationship in the long term. Fifth, this model raises ethical issues about the power differentials between counsellors and their clients, and about the disempowering effects on clients of having an expert diagnose them and determine the best course of treatment for them. Under the guise of scientific objectivity, modernist theories impose on clients experts' definition of what is normal or abnormal, rational or irrational, sane or otherwise (Besley, 2001). In exalting scientific knowledge, our theories subvert clients' own knowledge of their lives, when 'No one is in a position to be an objective expert on someone else's experience' (Combs & Freedman, 2012, p. 1036).

This medical (modernist) model is in contrast to a *postmodern* approach which upholds that there is no one objective way of looking at human experience and that we all perceive things differently. This means that the facts are not necessarily relevant – because we act *as if* our perceptions are the truth. From this stance, the role of the counsellor is not to quantify or diagnose clients' experiences, but to be sensitive to the perspective that clients bring to their own lives (Ward & Reuter, 2011). Individuals will know more about themselves than

Box 1.1 Modernism versus postmodernism in counselling

Modernism	*Postmodernism*
A therapist-driven hierarchical relationship.	A client-driven collaborative relationship.
A dualist relationship between an expert and non-expert.	A collaborative partnership with clients possessing insider knowledge
Therapists collect data and diagnose clients' difficulties.	Counsellors listen to clients' perspectives about their presenting concerns.
Therapists know how others should live their lives.	Counsellors create space for clients to gain clarity about their goals.
Therapists are certain of what they know.	Counsellors adopt a 'not knowing' or curious stance about their clients' lives.
Therapists attempt to provoke change.	Change evolves through dialogue.

Source: adapted from Anderson (1997, pp. 4-5)

even trained outsiders because their experience is nearer to the problem than anyone else's (Lock et al., 2004).

Postmodernism differs from a strengths-based approach, in which counsellors assess and highlight clients' strengths. Despite being a big improvement on assessing their deficits, strengths-based counsellors are still engaged in assessment - of whether clients are ready for change, their social supports, their resilience skills and emotion regulation skills, for example. Although the goal is to empower clients, this is still a top-down, expert-driven approach.

Mechanism-organicism

The second philosophical element on which counselling theories differ is the mechanistic-organic dichotomy. The mechanistic model says that when people are in distress, something has gone wrong with the mechanism (in this case, their mind). Like fixing an overheated car by repairing its radiator, mechanism links cause and effect in a linear fashion. This leads to a search for a cause, in the belief that this will imply a solution.

The problems with this model are first, that even if counsellors know a diagnosis, that implies little about the best course of intervention. Moreover, solution-focused theorists argue that a mechanistic search for causes is pointless - because what started it might not be the same thing that is maintaining it now. As Kennerley et al. (2017, p. 71) note, 'If you want to put out a fire, then you had better tackle what keeps it going (heat, fuel, oxygen, etc.) rather than look for the match that started it'.

Third, even when you *can* find a cause, you still might not find a solution. For example, the cause might be in the past - and we don't have a time machine to go back and undo it. Looking for causes can lead to 'analysis paralysis' which traps counsellors and their clients in the past, when the past should be a place of reference, not a place of residence.

Furthermore, the cause and the solution might not be linked. For example, I might take paracetamol for a headache even though the pain was not caused by a lack of paracetamol. That is, in many cases, effective solutions are unrelated to the initial cause of a problem. The solution itself (not a theory of cause) is the best explanation for what works (de Shazer, 1988).

At other times, as outsiders, we do not have enough information about what is happening in our clients' lives to be able to identify a cause. Meanwhile, the search for the cause could take up so much time and resources that there is little time left over for intervention. Accordingly, I believe that we need to question the justice of delaying the delivery of appropriate treatments in search of an understanding of past causes (as seen in psychoanalysis) or of waiting for clients' self-discovery (as seen in person-centred counselling).

Finally, we assume that if only we could find the right diagnosis, that would imply what to do about it. However, the principle of equifinality (colloquially known as 'There is more than one way to skin a cat') says that there is more than one single correct solution. And the most relevant might be an everyday remedy such as getting more sleep or exercise, eating healthier foods, getting some extra tuition, or improving relationships with others (Murphy, 2015).

The contrasting belief is termed *organicism*, which argues that human beings are organic (living beings interacting with their world) and non-linear. They are more complex than a simple linear equation that cause A leads to effect B. Their interactions are often circular, with one person reacting to another, who responds back ... and so on. When the issue is circular in this way, the search for a cause is both fruitless and unnecessary, because there *is* no beginning or end in a circle. This concept of circularity implies that what an observer regards as a cause and what as an effect is purely arbitrary.

Focus on problems versus on people

The third dimension on which counselling theories vary is whether they focus on *problems*, or on the *person*. The deficit model contends that human problems stem from deficiencies either within individuals or their environment (Ward & Reuter, 2011). This, however, limits our descriptions of people to a litany of their problems, leaving counsellors feeling pessimistic about the potential for client improvement (Daniels & Shumow, 2003).

Meanwhile, the view of clients as a collection of defects is likely to undermine their sense of self-efficacy and self-esteem, diminishing their view of themselves and of the possibilities for their future (Murphy, 2015). It imposes a spoiled or damaged identity on clients, locates disorders within their own bodies and judges them if, in the eyes of outsiders, they do not measure up to norms (White, 2007). This dismisses clients' own knowledge and discredits cultural wisdom (Marsten et al., 2016).

Therefore, solution-focused practitioners assume that people have many skills, competencies, beliefs, values, commitments and abilities that will assist them to reduce the influence of problems in their lives. Rather than looking for what is wrong with people and trying to fix that, these methods *choose* to look for what is working in clients' lives and to make use of that. Accordingly, the task of solution-focused counsellors is not to assess and diagnose problems, but to listen out for individuals' accounts of what they currently do that works well for them (Murphy, 2006).

This is especially vital for working with young people because they have often been chastised, reprimanded, lectured to, preached and moralised at, blamed, scapegoated, humiliated and punished for the issues that bring them to counselling. For this reason, more than for any other population, when working with young people we need a guiding theory that does none of these things. That is, we need to abandon a deficit model.

Individualism versus contextualism

Finally, many early theories were *individualistic*, focusing on what clients experience, feel, or think and thus locating the problem within them. Consequently, clients' presenting problems come to be explained by their personal - rather than their social - circumstances.

Critics contend that in their resolute focus on minute details, individualistic theories overlook the social circumstances of individuals which might be giving rise to clients' difficulties and, in doing so, mirror, legitimise and perpetuate the inequalities of society (Akom, 2001). This individualistic philosophy is in contrast, then, to *contextualism*, which acknowledges that people live in a social context that affects both how they function and how they see themselves. In concert with a deficit approach, individualism blames people for their predicament rather than seeing them as possessing extraordinary strength at enduring social disadvantage.

Theories of counselling

A theory is an orderly set of beliefs, concepts and models (that is, links between ideas) which is used to describe, explain or predict behaviour. Although theories might sound too abstract to be of practical use, they describe why and how things work as they do (Chibucos et al., 2005). As Gehart (2018, p. 5) notes, 'Theories provide the means for quickly sifting through the tremendous amount of information clients bring'.

Although we all eventually develop theories about our practice through experience and reflection, this process of personal theory building is more efficient and comprehensive when informed in advance by theoretical knowledge. Accordingly, counsellors' theory base needs to be coherent so that they know where to go next, and their conceptualisation of what is happening for clients needs to make sense to them, so that they 'buy in' to counselling, in the belief that the counsellor has a solid plan.

At the same time, we have to be cautious about our theories, so that we don't take them too literally and believe them to be a higher form of Truth, rather than just one interpretation of reality. An inflexible theory can bias our observations. (This is the principle that *If you're a hammer, everything looks like a nail.*) We need to use theory to understand our subject, without ourselves being subject to the theory. A useful theory, then, is one that provides focus and direction without blinding us to other issues and to the individuality of each case (Young, 1992).

Stance of the counsellor

Michael White (in Morgan, 2006) identifies that our theory shapes our relationship or 'stance' with respect to clients, as illustrated in Figure 1.2. In some theories - such as person-centred counselling - the counsellor is (mainly) non-directive, and accordingly, less influential, with the client at centre stage; postmodernists such as solution-focused, narrative and Acceptance and Commitment Therapy practitioners are more directive but still consider that clients know more about themselves than outsiders will, and therefore these counsellors are 'decentred' whereas modernist practitioners - such as those employing psychoanalysis, behaviourism,

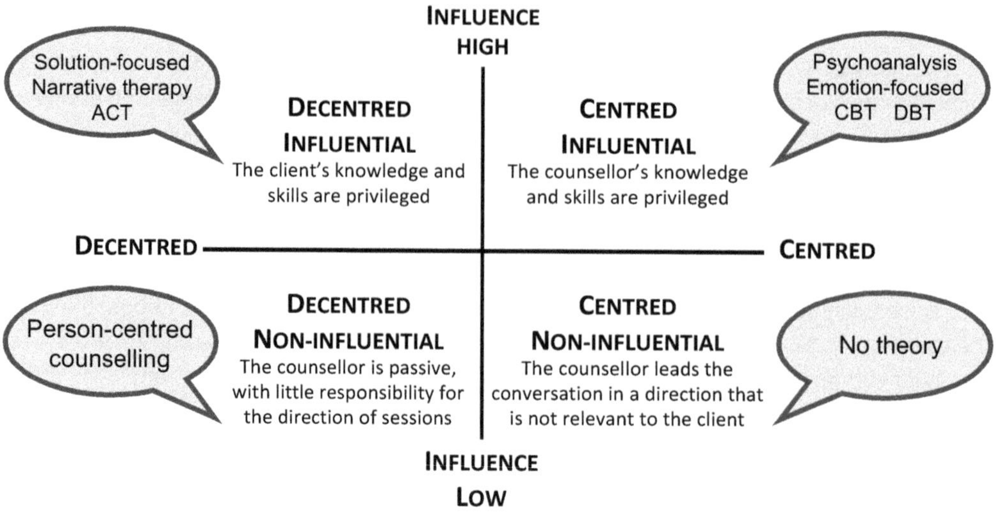

Figure 1.2 The stance of the counsellor

Source: adapted from White (2005, in Morgan, 2006, p. 59).

classic cognitive-behaviour therapies, dialectical behaviour therapy and many others - see the counsellor as the sage on the stage who, as the expert, influences the course of therapy.

Eclecticism

The model in Figure 1.2 implies that when we draw ideas from a range of theories, it is important that their underlying philosophies are compatible. Otherwise we end up with a blend that lacks a coherent theory base, resulting in using practices whose only justification is that they 'seemed like a good idea at the time'. This is known as atheoretical eclecticism, which Corey (1996) contends is merely a justification for picking and choosing ideas that support our preconceived notions and biases.

A second form of eclecticism is technical. This utilises one organising theory but borrows in some supplementary methods which may or may not be compatible with the core theory. The result is that the practices can contradict and undermine each other.

The third and highest form of eclecticism is integrative. This is the synthesis or integration of congruent approaches, resulting in a more complex and comprehensive blend than any of the original components alone. The advantage of integrating approaches is that we can employ effective techniques originating from a range of schools in response to client needs and preferences. However, referring to Figure 1.2, I believe that while it is possible to blend theories that are to the left of the vertical (*y*) axis, it is difficult to blend those theories that are above the horizontal (*x*) axis ... and even more difficult to blend diagonally across the centre, because their philosophy is incompatible. One cannot be a little bit authentic ... and counsellors cannot believe in clients' capacities but adopt modernist, deficit-focused approaches.

Theory selection

In the next chapters, I describe my integration of three key theories that I employ in my work with young people: solution-focused therapy, narrative therapy and Acceptance and Commitment Therapy. You are free, of course, to add in your own theories - but any resulting blend must have a consistent theoretical base.

Mine is a philosophical, ethical and pragmatic blend. Taking each element in turn, as Hayes et al. (1999, p. 17) state, 'The goal of philosophizing is nothing more than clarity and responsibility. It is to say, *This is what I assume. Precisely this. I cannot justify it, but I can own it*'. Accordingly, although other theories have relevance for young clients, and you, my reader, will have allegiances to other theories, these are the ones from which I work because their philosophy suits my politics of valuing young people and because they allow me to adopt my preferred collaborative stance as a practitioner.

Ethically, I choose them because of the reality that resources are limited and that young people can - and often do - drop out of counselling and therefore we need to make quick progress to inspire their ongoing commitment; and because I have found that the theories' focus on solutions relieves clients' suffering more quickly than methods which favour analysis of causes or insight about the past or about the 'subconscious'.

Pragmatically, on the grounds that a positive explanation is just as likely to be true as a negative one, my guiding theories are positive and generate hope that things can improve. They allow us to focus on how to change the presenting problem, rather than on diagnosing (or blaming) those involved. They suggest what to do, rather than what to think, by focusing on actions that could improve the problem. In other words, my selected theories have the capacity to impel us towards change rather than immobilise us in despondency (Haley, 1980; Molnar & Lindquist, 1989).

Evidence

In each of the coming chapters, I will give an overview of the evidence for the effectiveness of each theory. However, the first criticism of such research is raised by Chomsky (1998, in Kohn, 2004), who notes that when we debate which practices work best in which circumstances, we give the appearance of a lively and scholarly debate, but all the while fail to question the assumptions behind our methods.

Second, most studies compare one brand of therapy with 'treatment as usual' or 'no treatment' - and one would hope that doing something would indeed be better than doing nothing. Concluding that these treatments work, therefore, is not saying much.

Third, research cannot possibly span the myriad of presenting issues, cannot control for clients having multiple issues, and cannot claim that the findings are generalisable across diverse populations.

Fourth, in applied psychology and counselling, we cannot do 'double blind' studies where neither the client nor the clinician knows what treatment they are receiving or delivering. Instead, in a quest for an alternative form of rigour, most research studies investigate pure approaches based on circumscribed or standardised interventions (such as cognitive behaviour therapy and its variants). It is easy to train practitioners in the use of these manualised approaches (Chorpita et al., 2011), making their adherence to the manual more likely. However, while this is vital for the credibility of the research findings, the resulting practice would not be competent if it were unresponsive to clients (Davies, 2019). In real life, counsellors use a range of methods and engage in a 'dance' with clients in which they respond to client needs, rather than parroting back a practice manual (Duncan et al., 2004). That is, counselling is organic, which quantitative research cannot capture. This makes findings into manualised treatments not generalisable to actual practice, while outcome measures of less structured treatments might not be replicable (Davies, 2019).

Finally, even with our present state of knowledge, it is still not possible to disentangle which elements of each theory are responsible for generating any reported gains. Without this information, as a practitioner, you cannot select components from the various theories in any confidence that you have chosen the most effective features.

One possible conclusion is suggested by Hubble et al. (2010), who claim that our theoretical model and its practices are actually less vital to therapeutic outcomes than the counsellor-client alliance and consequent client expectations of success. Therefore, they claim, researching which methods work best is futile. This is not to say that the theory which we adopt is irrelevant, however: It just tells us that the coherence of the counsellor's thinking allows clients to have faith in the process, hope for a beneficial outcome, and belief in the therapist and themselves (Hubble et al., 2010).

Therefore, Hubble et al. (2010) argue for a shift from evidence-based practice to *practice-based evidence* - that is, monitoring client progress by asking clients how their counselling is working for them. Gaining client feedback, these authors report, substantially improves outcomes, halves drop-out rates, and ensures that therapy is tailored to the individual - rather than rigidly adhering to some techniques imposed by a particular theoretical model.

Conclusion

Given that our philosophy will underpin our practice, it is better to scrutinise our beliefs than for them to remain beneath our awareness (O'Hara & O'Hara, 2014). In this chapter, I have made a case for a combination of three theories that share a postmodern philosophy, whose stance towards clients is decentred but influential and for which there is evidence of their effectiveness. In the next three chapters, I detail these theories.

References

Akom, A. A. (2001). Racial profiling at school: The politics of race and discipline at Berkeley High. In W. Ayes, B. Dohrn, & R. Ayers (Eds.), *Zero tolerance: Resisting the drive for punishment in our schools* (pp. 51-63). The New Press.

Anderson, H. (1997). *Conversation, language and possibilities: A post-modern approach to therapy*. Basic Books.

Besley, T. (2001). Foucauldian influences in narrative therapy: An approach for schools. *The Journal of Educational Enquiry*, *2*(2), 72-93.

Chibucos, T. R., Leite, R. W., & Weis, D. L. (2005). *Readings in family theory*. SAGE.

Chorpita, B. F., Daleiden, E. L., Ebesutani, C., Young, J., Becker, K. D., Nakamura, B. J., ... & Starace, N. (2011). Evidence-based treatments for children and adolescents: An updated review of indicators of efficacy and effectiveness. *Clinical Psychology: Science and Practice*, *18*(2), 154-172. https://doi.org/10.1111/j.1468-2850.2011.01247.x

Combs, G., & Freedman, J. (2012). Narrative, poststructuralism, and social justice: Current practices in narrative therapy. *The Counseling Psychologist, 40*(7), 1033–1060. https://doi.org/10.1177/0011000012460662

Corey, G. (1996). *Theory and practice of counseling and psychotherapy* (5th ed.). Brooks/Cole.

Daniels, D. H., & Shumow, L. (2003). Child development and classroom teaching: A review of the literature and implications for educating teachers. *Journal of Applied Developmental Psychology, 23*(5), 495–526. https://doi.org/10.1016/S0193-3973(02)00139-9

Davies, B. (2019). Critique of manualized therapies: Systemic family therapy manual for adolescent self-harm. *Systemic Practice and Action Research, 32*(4), 403–409. https://doi.org/10.1007/s11213-018-9462-y

de Shazer, S. (1988). *Clues: Investigating solutions in brief therapy*. Norton.

Duncan, B. L., Miller, S. D., & Sparks, J. A. (2003). Interactional and solution-focused brief therapies: Evolving concepts of change. In T. L. Sexton, G. R. Weeks & M. S. Robbins (Eds.), *Handbook of family therapy: The science and practice of working with families and couples* (pp. 101–123). Brunner-Routledge.

Duncan, B. L., Miller, S. D., & Parks, J. A. (2004). *The heroic client: A revolutionary way to improve effectiveness through client-directed, outcome-informed therapy* (rev. ed.). Jossey-Bass.

Gehart, D. (2018). *Mastering competencies in family therapy: A practical approach to theories and clinical case documentation* (3rd ed.). Cengage.

Haley, J. (1980). *Leaving home: The therapy of disturbed young people*. Jossey-Bass.

Hayes, S. C., Strosahl, K. D., & Wilson, K. G. (1999). *Acceptance and commitment therapy: An experiential approach to behavior change*. Guilford.

Hubble, M. A., Duncan. B. L., Miller, S. D., & Wampold, B. E. (2010). Introduction. In B. L. Duncan, S. D. Miller, B. E. Wampold & M. A. Hubble (Eds.), *The heart and soul of change: Delivering what works in therapy* (2nd ed., pp. 23–46). American Psychological Association.

Kennerley, H., Kirk, J., & Westbrook, D. (2017). *An introduction to cognitive behaviour therapy* (3rd ed.). Sage.

Kohn, A. (2004). *What does it mean to be well educated?* Beacon Press.

Lock, A., Epston, D., Maisel, R., & Faria, N. D. (2004). Resisting anorexia/bulimia: Foucauldian perspectives in narrative therapy. *British Journal of Guidance and Counselling, 33*(3), 315–332. https://doi.org/10.1080/03069880500179459

Marsten, D., Epston, D., & Markham, L. (2016). *Narrative therapy in wonderland: Connecting with children's imaginative know-how*. Norton.

Molnar, A., & Lindquist, B. (1989). *Changing problem behavior in schools*. Jossey-Bass.

Morgan, A. (2006). The position of the therapist in working with children and their families. In M. White & A. Morgan (Eds.), *Narrative therapy with children and their families* (pp. 37–84). Dulwich Centre Publications.

Murphy, J. J. (2006). *Solution-focused counseling in middle and high schools*. Pearson Merrill Prentice Hall.

Murphy, J. J. (2015). Solution-focused approaches. In H. T. Prout & A. L. Fedewa (Eds.), *Counseling and psychotherapy with children and adolescents* (5th ed., pp. 279–316). Wiley.

O'Hara, D. J., & O'Hara, E. F. (2014). The identity of counselling and psychotherapy and the quest for a common metatheory. *Psychotherapy and Counselling Journal of Australia, 3*(1). https://research.usc.edu.au/discovery/delivery/61USC_INST:ResearchRepository/12126187720002621?l#13126915330002621

White, M. (2007). *Maps of narrative practice*. Norton.

Ward, C. C., & Reuter, T. (2011). *Strength-centered counseling: Integrating postmodern approaches and skills with practice*. Sage.

Young, M. E. (1992). *Counseling methods and techniques: An eclectic approach*. Merrill.

2 Solution-focused theory

When we meet young people with difficulties serious enough to bring them to counselling, it is easy to notice what is not working for them and to try to fix that. In contrast, the solution-focused approach *chooses* to look for what is working in people's lives and to use that. As seen in Box 2.1, this focus on solutions is in contrast to the deficit models which focus on problems (Ward & Reuter, 2011). The title of this approach does not mean that counsellors suggest solutions to clients' problems, nor is it a strengths-based approach (see Chapter 1), but is an 'exceptions-focused' approach, where we examine occasions when the problem is less severe than usual and discover what brings this about.

Box 2.1 Distinctions between problem solving and solution building

Problem solving	*Solution building*
Attempts to understand what is going wrong and how to fix it.	Focuses on what is working and how to use it.
Focuses on weaknesses and deficits.	Focuses on strengths and resources.
Examines instances of problems.	Examines exceptions to difficulties.
Asks why people do things.	Asks how people do things.
Focuses on the past.	Emphasises future possibilities.
Sees people as sick.	Sees people as stuck.
Regards people as flawed.	Sees people as capable.
The adviser aims to diagnose.	The adviser aims to uncover solutions.
The adviser is responsible for providing a solution.	The person experiencing the problem is the source of its solution.
The adviser is the expert.	The individual with the problem is the expert.
The client follows the expert's lead.	The counsellor follows the client's lead.
The adviser tells.	The counsellor asks and listens.
The adviser is certain.	The counsellor is curious.
The adviser takes the credit for progress.	Individuals take credit for their own progress.

Causes versus solutions

Being post-modernists, the task of solution-focused counsellors is not to assess and diagnose problems, but to listen out for individuals' accounts of what they currently do that works

DOI: 10.4324/9781003323938-3

well for them (Murphy, 2006). Solution-focused listening aims to understand the client's own account of what is happening, without filtering this through a problem-focused lens that looks to diagnose reasons or causes. We have to suspend our own frame of reference (De Jong & Berg, 2013) - not least because clients bring their own frame of reference and regard it as the only logical one. Therefore, it is not necessary to establish the facts of any particular problem: It is merely enough to understand how those involved *perceive* the problem, because they act on these perceptions *as if* they are reality.

The shift from problem-focused to solution-oriented language in solution-focused practice raises clients' awareness of their existing skills and transforms how they understand themselves, their relationships and their future possibilities (Bolton et al., 2017). This increases their self-efficacy, their belief that they have the power to make changes in their own lives.

Philosophy of a solution-focused approach

The solution-focused approach is based on social constructionism, which argues that meaning is created (or constructed) in the process of interaction or conversation (O'Connell, 2012). The process of questioning and answering aims to create new awareness in clients and, in turn, new possibilities for their future (De Jong & Berg, 2013, p. 24).

Principle 1. People know more about themselves than outsiders ever will (Selekman, 2010). Just as the orchestra conductor trusts the musicians to know their instrument (Banks, 2005), so too the solution-focused counsellor trusts clients to know their own minds. Those experiencing the problem are the experts on how the problem affects their lives and, often unbeknownst to themselves, are the experts on how they can change it.

Principle 2. The person is not the problem: *the problem is the problem* (Winslade & Monk, 2007, p. 2). Our focus has to be on solving the difficulty, not finding who is to blame for it. In other words, we will look for a solution, not a culprit.

Principle 3. Problems signal that people are stuck, not sick. The theory takes little interest in how they got stuck in the first place, but focuses instead on how solutions can be developed (Nichols & Schwartz, 1995). As such, it has a future orientation, rather than an interest in the past (De Jong & Berg, 2013; Molnar & de Shazer, 1987; Murphy, 1994).

Principle 4. All individuals, no matter how stuck, are doing *something* to prevent their problems deteriorating. Therefore, we need to direct our focus onto those things that *are* working.

Principle 5. All environments, no matter how bleak, provide some resources to support individuals to be effective in their lives. Even families enduring adversity draw on internal resources and external supports to help them to function.

Principle 6. These internal and external resources ensure that no problem occurs all the time: There are always instances when it could have occurred but did not, or was less severe than usual. These instances are known as *exceptions*. They are the source of the solution.

Principle 7. The problem is not the dancers: *It is the dance*. That is to say, people respond to each other, both believing that their actions are justified in light of the other's behaviour. This circularity means that we can intervene at any point of this cycle because there *is* no beginning or end in a circle.

Therapeutic questioning

Like a detective, solution-focused counsellors use persistent questioning and listening to explore what clients want in their lives and what strengths and resources they can call on to make these goals a reality (Berg & De Jong, 1996; Winslade & Monk, 2007). Respondents' answers (rather than our own assumptions) will provoke our next question.

In the decentred but influential position (see Chapter 1), the role of the counsellor is one of 'skilfully scaffolding questions and responses in ways that enable the skills and knowledges of [clients] to become more richly known' (Morgan, 2000, p. 71). Solution-focused counsellors ask questions with genuine curiosity, respecting that clients are experts in their own lives and that they know how their current problem affects them.

Morgan says that she notices when she is reverting to centre stage when she asks questions to which she thinks she already knows the answer. Steve de Shazer called the decentred stance being 'reader focused' rather than 'text fo 51489 cused' - that is, we listen to the person, not to our book-originated theories about this type of presenting problem. Another way of thinking about this is that, as the counsellor, you are leading from one step behind. This simply means that, although you do lead the conversation, you do so from a curious standpoint, with all your evaluations and knowings left behind.

Phases of solution-focused therapy

Berg and Steiner (2003) give an overview of the phases of solution-focused work, illustrated in Figure 2.1.

- *Discuss pre-session change*. In first sessions, counsellors will ask clients about what has changed since they made the appointment for counselling. In subsequent sessions, the discussion will involve asking about what has changed since the last appointment.
- *Problem-free talk*. Particularly in the first session, you will talk with clients about their interests and passions, prior to talking about the problem. As well as creating rapport by not focusing iimmediately on their difficulties, this will allow you to get to know the strengths and skills that they bring to problem solving.
- *Describe the problem* and if the problem as described is not amenable to change, reframe it so that it is.
- *Develop goals*. Through questioning, the counsellor helps clients to describe how their life would be if the problem were not present. *This* is their goal.
- *Identify exceptions*: Those instances when the problem is absent or not as severe as usual tell you that a solution is already in place, however partially. This is a clue about how clients can solve their current predicament.
- *Highlight strengths and resources*: These are the inner strengths and outer resources that support these partial solutions and which can be harnessed for future solutions.
- *Give feedback* comprising some statements ('compliments' or 'messages') about clients' strengths and resilience.
- *Homework*. Counsellors will suggest some homework tasks to build on the exceptions.
- *Review progress*. In follow-up sessions, you will review progress.

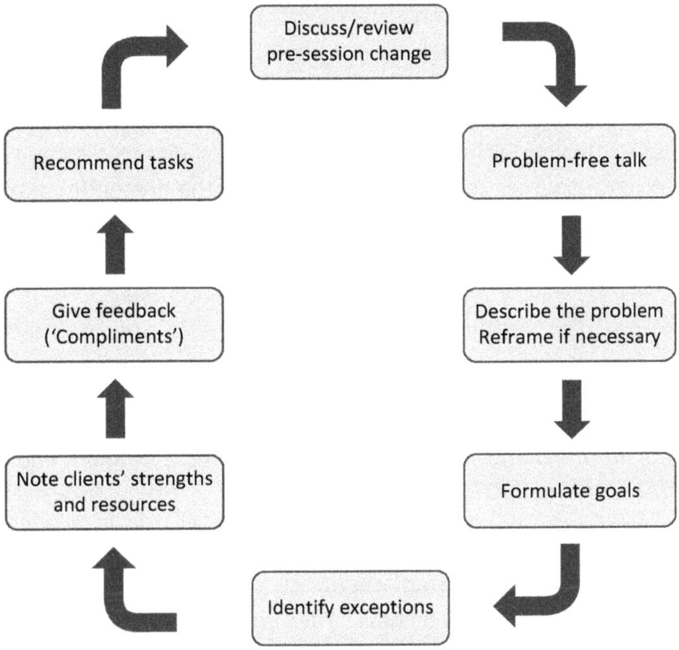

Figure 2.1 Phases of solution-focused sessions

Source: adapted from O'Connell (2012).

Discuss pre-session change

For first sessions, counsellors will ask clients about what has changed since they made the appointment to consult you: We all clean up before our cleaning lady comes (Lang & Lang, 1986). In subsequent sessions, it will involve asking about what has changed since your last appointment.

> **Box 2.2 Questions to elicit information about pre-session change**
>
> - What has changed since you made the appointment to see me?
> - What is better already since you decided to come here?
> - What has been working for you?
> - How is that new for you?
> - What has been better for you recently?
> - What's better since the last time we talked?

Problem-free talk

Especially when working with young people who, up till coming to see you, have frequently been blamed and criticised for having or even 'being' a problem, it is vital that you begin a session with problem-free talk. You can say that you'll get to talking about why they are here shortly but, first, you would like to get to know them. I start by asking about their favourite things, or their passions.

This takes the pressure off those who are feeling defensive in the expectation that they will be humiliated for having difficulties and allows you to discover something about their internal and external resources that will support solving the presenting problem. That is, a focus on aspects other than the problem is not merely to help everyone feel better, but to gather information about clients' skills and personal attributes that can become part of the solution.

Describe the problem

Once clients move on to describing the problem, solution-focused counsellors are interested in a description of who is doing what, how that constitutes a problem and to whom it is a problem (Murphy & Duncan, 2007).

- Can you describe a recent example of the problem?
- If I were a fly on the wall, what would I see?
- What happens first? What happens next? Then what?
- How often does this happen?
- Who is usually involved?
- What are they doing or saying?

When clients frame their problem in ways that make it difficult to solve, before proceeding, solution-focused practitioners might reframe the problem.

Reframing the problem

Winbolt (2011, p. 137) quotes Jay Haley that 'therapy starts with negotiating a solvable problem'. Sometimes, however, clients come to counselling with a view of the problem that suggests that it cannot change. These explanations often blame the present difficulties on a past event (such as an attachment disorder), the personality of the client (such as a mental illness), or something that cannot be undone (such as a disability). True though these explanations might be (in a modernist sense at least), they are not helping, as evidenced by the fact that the problem is still occurring. Clients are stuck.

In order to get unstuck, they will need a new way of looking at or thinking about the problem, one that suggests how it can be solved. A new way of seeing the problem will become our 'map' that will help us plan our route from how things are now, towards how we want them to be. Some maps are more - or less - useful for a given purpose. For example, consider some of the various maps of Australia: an elevation map, mineral deposits, rainfall map, Aboriginal lands, magnetic map, or road map.

Looking at these various maps, we can ask ourselves which one is the most true or correct. Obviously, none of them - because Australia is much bigger than these tiny pictures and is not the colour of them. So, instead we could ask which one is best. However, to answer that question, we need to know our purpose. If we wanted to climb a mountain, we would use the elevation map; if we wanted to pan for gold, a map of mineral deposits would be most useful; if we wanted to locate the lands of an Aboriginal tribe, that map would be useful. ... But if we want to get from Adelaide to Darwin, we will need a road map.

Similarly, if clients want to get from where they are now, to where they want to be, they will need a map that depicts a route. Rather than a pictorial map, however, in counselling we will be using a verbal map. To initiate change for clients who are stuck, our 'map' has to provide a view of the problem that suggests that change is possible. Solution-focused therapists call this reframing. This title alludes to the fact that an old picture can take a new lease on life when we put it into a fresh frame. On the grounds that a positive explanation is just as likely to be true as a negative one, and that change is less likely when people feel blamed or criticised, any theory aimed at encouraging change should be positive and generate hope that things can improve (Haley, 1980; Molnar & Lindquist, 1989). This idea is built on Einstein's observation that we cannot solve problems with the same kind of thinking that created them.

As an example of reframing a problem, I was referred a ten-year-old for not completing his schoolwork, with his teacher's explanation for his problem being that he needed to learn to persist because he gave up easily. This focuses on what is wrong with him and therefore will not lead to a solution.

During our problem-free talk, he disclosed that his great passion in life was soccer and that he was the goalkeeper on his team. I asked him if he attended practice sessions and he reported that he never missed one. I asked him if he attended all the games and, again, he and his mother confirmed that he never missed one of those. I asked how come he was so persistent at soccer, to which he replied that he didn't want to let his team down. (This, then, uncovered a strength of loyalty.) He also wanted to get better at soccer through practice. (These indicate strengths of commitment and hard work.) I also pointed out that his role was the most vital on the field, so asked if this meant that his team trusted and depended on him. He agreed. (This is the strength of dependability.)

Then I confessed that I knew little about soccer but, it seemed to me, that as a goalkeeper there was a lot of waiting around until the goal needed defending. He agreed. So then I feigned confusion: His teacher said that he needed to learn persistence, yet he attended all the team practice sessions, attended all the games and attended throughout each game until his role was needed. I said that it didn't seem to me that he needed to learn persistence. He already knew how to persist. (The problem had been reframed.)

So then I asked what would it take to transfer that persistence from the soccer field to his school work. The rest of the session was spent uncovering that he believed that he could not do the work and that, by avoiding it, he was trying to avoid seeing himself as a failure. He had been defending his self-esteem, just as fiercely as in soccer he would defend his goal from the opposition's incursions.

This led to arranging extra tutoring, on the understanding that he did not have to become first in class (schoolwork was not his passion, after all) but that he could use his team of skills at persistence, commitment and hard work to ensure that he was making progress academically so that he could come to feel proud of himself for the progress he was making.

As seen in this example, any new explanation does not have to be 'The Truth' (just as one map of Australia is no more True than the others), but it does have to fit the facts at least as well as any competing views do; be sufficiently different from current views to make a difference; and be sensible and acceptable to the client. If it does not, you will just generate another explanation.

At other times, clients come to counselling with a sense that there is something wrong with *them* for having the problem. In that case, the problem does not need reframing, but the meaning that they attach to it does. This is an identity issue. To reframe this, we could ask questions designed to help clients reflect on the meaning that they are extracting from their difficulties, such as, 'If someone at a bus stop was describing the same events as you have been through, would you feel compassion for them, or would you think that they were over-reacting?' (or some other adjective that clients have used to dismiss their feelings).

Sometimes, people have been given a diagnosis that is keeping them stuck. To provoke a shift, we can ask whether they agree with the label and then, 'Is there some other label that fits your situation better than these descriptions?' (Murphy, 2015, p. 286).

Formulate goals

After the problem description phase, solution-focused counselling takes time to clarify clients' goals. Given that it is always easier to reach a destination when you know where you are going, it pays to have a destination or goal in mind. Through questioning, the solution-focused counsellor helps clients to describe how their life would be if the problem were not present. *This* is their goal. To achieve this, you can ask clients three types of questions: outcome questions, future-oriented questions and hypothetical questions (Sharry et al., 2012).

Clients' answers to these questions will uncover what is important to them in life, what they value and how they would like to live. *This* is their goal. After clients have described their goal, you can expand on this by asking 'What else will happen after the miracle has occurred?... And what else?' so that they elaborate on their picture of life without the problem (Sklare, 2014).

Box 2.3 Questions for formulating goals

Outcome questions

- What are your best hopes for coming here today?
- What would be the most helpful issue to talk about today?
- What needs to happen to make our meetings useful for you?
- How were you hoping I could be of use to you?
- What will be the first small sign that things are getting better?
- What are your thoughts about why you're here today?
- Is there anything else you would like to get out of coming here?

Future-oriented questions

These allow clients to consider alternatives to current patterns.

- When in the future, this is no longer happening, what will be happening instead?
- What will life be like without this problem?
- Imagine that it is three months from now, and this problem has been solved. As you look back from that future time to today, what do you reckon you would have been doing differently to solve the problem?
- Suppose that our work here is successful. What will be different in your life that tells you that our sessions have worked for you?
- Letter from the future. Write a letter to yourself, pretending that it is two months (or years) from now and life is just as you want it to be. The letter details how you achieved this.

Hypothetical questions

- The miracle question asks: 'If, while you were sleeping tonight, a miracle/some magic happened and your best hopes had been realised, what would have changed? Who will be doing what differently?' (de Shazer, 1988). This question arose when a client had said that she needed a miracle to overcome her problems and, hence, the question was framed in the client's own language (De Jong & Berg, 2013). However, for those who declare 'I don't believe in miracles' it can instead be framed in *their* language, such as (Kayrouz and Hansen, 2020):
  - If tomorrow, your wise self was awakened, what would have changed?
  - If tomorrow could be a completely fresh start, what would be different?
  - If tomorrow some magic happened and your problems were completely solved, what would be different?
  - If this problem vanished overnight, how would the morning be different for you? (Murphy, 2015)

  For individuals from cultures other than the dominant one, counsellors can adjust the goal, using words clients have already raised in sessions, such as, 'If tomorrow, you woke and were in complete harmony with people and things, what would be different?' (Kayrouz and Hansen, 2020).
- Crystal ball: Imagine that I'm holding a crystal ball here in my hands. It helps you to see yourself in the future, when things are working out for you. What do you see in the crystal ball?
- Time machine: Imagine that there is a time machine here. It can propel you into the future to a time when things are going the way you'd like: What do you see happening in the future? (Bertolino & Schultheis, 2002).
- Pretend that there are two movies of your life, one with the problem as it is now, and one without the problem: What does the second movie look like? (Murphy, 2006). How would that make a difference to (each person involved)?

Types of goals

To provide a clear direction for change, goals must be meaningful to those having to make changes so that they are motivated to do so; and they must be measurable, framed in positive terms and be realistic. They might arrive at a range of potential goals.

Outcome goals

Some clients frame goals in terms of outcomes, such as that they want to get better grades at school. In this case, we need to help them identify the strategies or things they will do to make that outcome happen. Therefore, you will ask questions (in a process called *detailing*) to get specific details of what they plan to do to achieve the outcome.

Box 2.4 Translating outcome goals into specific strategies

Outcome goal	*Concrete action*
I want to be less depressed.	If I were watching a movie of you being less depressed, what would that look like?
I don't want to get detention anymore.	What needs to happen for you to get detention less?
I want to get into less trouble at school.	What will you be doing instead of getting into trouble?
I don't want to fail this subject.	What can you do to help yourself to pass?
I want to stop worrying so much.	What will you be doing when you are worrying less?

Source: Murphy (2008, p. 58)

Vague goals

When clients describe their problem in vague terms such as wanting someone to 'show them respect' or 'not lose their temper', you need to help them to translate this into 'action talk' (Bertolino & Schultheis, 2002):

- If I were a fly on the wall, what would I see her doing when she loses her cool?
- If I had a video recorder, what would it record?
- What have you done that tells you that you have a problem with anger?
- What is she doing at those times when you feel that she does not respect you?
- When your daughter is being irresponsible, what is she doing?
- What do other people do which tells you that you cannot trust them?

Negative goals

Negative goals are framed in terms of what clients want to stop happening, such as wanting to stop feeling so depressed. However, this has to be translated into actions they will be taking because the cessation of something is hard to detect, just as we fail to notice when our headache has gone (De Jong & Berg, 2013; Sklare, 2014). Second, negative goals have been termed 'dead person goals' because a dead person could do them: Dead people do not feel anxious, fight with their friends, or feel depressed.

The opposite of the negative behaviours will be their goals. They can be translated into actions by asking, 'If you weren't feeling depressed, what would you be doing?'; or 'If you weren't losing your temper, what would you be doing instead?'. The next step will be to find out what it will take for them to do that.

Emotional goals

Emotional goals include wanting to feel better, or wanting unpleasant feelings to stop. In this case, counsellors will ask what they would like to feel or do instead of having the emotional symptoms.

Insight goals

Solution-focused counsellors do not believe that insight will lead to change. (Every smoker knows that 50 per cent of them will die from smoking and 100 per cent will be unwell as a direct result of it, but this insight does not necessarily lead to change.) Therefore, when clients want to understand why they feel as they do, we can ask, 'Once you have that understanding, what do you want to do differently?'.

Wanting others to change

De Jong and Berg (2013) say that, when young clients claim that other people have or *are* the problem, counsellors can ask about what the clients are able to do to have a positive role in change. For example, when a child complains that a teacher is 'always picking on me', we can gently ask what clients themselves could do that might put the teacher in a better mood. That is, their complaint will have to be translated into something that *they* can do (e.g. 'If your teacher were being nicer to you, what would you be doing differently to make that happen?').

Unrealistic goals

Young people might identify impossible goals, such as for their parents to remarry (when the relationship has broken down completely); you can respond to these wishes by asking, 'That means a lot to you because ...?' or 'What difference would that make to you?' (Sklare, 2014). In other words, their goal (of having their parents reunite) is a *strategy* for meeting a need, and the follow-up question invites them to focus on other potential (less impossible) ways to meet the same need.

Harmful goals

When clients nominate a goal that is likely to be harmful, such as wanting to be left alone to keep taking drugs, or losing more weight when they are already demonstrably under-nourished, again these are just strategies for meeting a need. Therefore, you can ask a client with disordered eating, 'How would losing more weight be good for you?' This will identify the underlying need. The client might answer that it would give them more confidence. In that case, you can discuss what other (less harmful) strategies the client could use for gaining more confidence (Sharry et al., 2002).

Multiple goals

When clients list multiple problems and corresponding goals, there is a risk of feeling overwhelmed and not knowing where to begin. Having acknowledged how tough their situation is, you would simply ask (De Jong & Berg, 2013, p. 65):

- Which of those issues is most important for you to work on first?
- What is happening in your life that tells you it is important to work on that first?

'I don't know' responses

Involuntary clients plus those who are just genuinely confused can find it difficult to articulate what they want counselling to achieve for them. They often respond to questions about their goals with 'I don't know'. In response, you can ask (Sklare, 2014, pp. 35-36):

- If you did know...?
- If you had to take a guess, what might it be?
- If I asked (your mother, best friend) what would she say?
- What would your friend tell me was the most important thing to you?

'I don't care' responses

Clients sometimes respond to questions about their goals with 'I don't care'. In response, you can ask them to suppose, imagine or pretend that they did care, and in that case, what they would be doing differently (Sklare, 2014, p. 37).

Process goals

When there is no specific goal but instead clients want support to work through a process such as grieving, it is vital to identify small manageable steps. Doing so will help the client to recognise signs of progress rather than a complete solution (Sharry et al., 2002).

- What will be the first sign that you are making progress?
- How will you know when you are starting to come to terms with what happened?
- What will be the smallest sign that progress is happening?
- And what else?

Scaling

Once goals are framed in achievable terms, scaling questions can ask those involved to rate how close they are to achieving those goals (with 1 being the worst that the problem has ever been and 10 being the day after the miracle). You can follow their rating with, 'What does that number stand for?' (Bannink, 2010, p. 162). Being concrete, using numbers suit children particularly well (Berg & Steiner, 2003) especially when, for young children, you draw a ladder or numbered stepping stones on the floor, so that they can signal which station they are at by moving to stand on the corresponding number.

You can use scaling questions during the problem definition and goal setting stages, and then again during a review session, when you can compare the two ratings and ask your clients to account for any improvement: 'Last week you rated your depression at 4 and now it's a 6 ... How did you get the number to go higher? What did you do?'. By making the idea of incremental change concrete, these questions also undermine clients' all-or-nothing thinking (that the problem is either dreadful or perfect) and increase clients' sense of control over their progress.

The following questions can be useful (Kral & Kowalski, 1989; Rhodes, 1993; Wagner & Gillies, 2001):

- *Scaling*. On a scale of 1 to 10, with 1 being dismal and 10 ideal (or the day after the miracle), at what number is your life at the moment?
- *Motivation*. How happy are you with that number? (This will tell you how motivated they are to change.)
- *Goal*: What number would you prefer to be at? This is the goal number (*x*). ... Suppose that you felt just a little better and had been able to move from 3 to 4.... What would things be like then for you? ... For your family?
- *Hope*: What will life be like at (*x* + 1)? What will you be doing differently? ... When was the last time you were at (*x* + 1)?
- *Examine exceptions*: Tell me about a time when you have been at (*x* + 1) before: What was happening then? ... What were you doing differently? ... What were other people doing? ... What is different about being at 3 compared with being at 2? ... What else is different? ... What would other people notice?
- *Confidence*: What do you think are the chances that you will reach *x* (the goal number)?
- *Progress*: How will you know that you are making progress? What will be the first sign?
- *Concrete objective*: When you reach (the goal number), what will be happening that is different from what is happening now? ... What needs to happen so that you can move to (*x* + 1) again?

Box 2.5 Using scaling to identify a solution

A student has thrown scissors in class and is sent to the principal. This behaviour, of course, is completely unacceptable because it is dangerous and intimidating to the target and to onlookers. However, rather than asking why the student did it, after greeting the student, the principal can ask the following series of questions:

- 'At the time when you threw the scissors, on a scale of 1 to 10, how furious were you?'. (Let's say that the student nominates a rating of 9.)
- 'It's taken you a couple of minutes to get from your classroom to my office ... On a scale of 1 to 10, how angry are you now?'. (Let's say that the student nominates 7.)
- 'How did you get from 9 to 7?'.

This supplies the principal with three pieces of information. First, the student has the skill to calm down (to go from a rating of 9 to a 7). Second, we do not have to think up a new solution, because the student is already using one. Third, if the student can go from 9 to 7 on the scale, they can equally go from 7 to 5, from 5 to 3 and from 3 to 1. Therefore, the principal does not need to impose a solution, just enquire about what the student needs in order to employ the solution earlier in future so that their feelings do not escalate into violence.

Source: Porter (2014, p. 306)

Identify solutions

To get a behaviour to change, we have to change the current solution on the grounds that, if it were going to work, it would have by now. Again, trusting young people to know their own minds, we will ask them about solutions that have been tried, listening out for those that have failed, those that have worked, those that they considered but rejected; and those that others have advised (Murphy & Duncan, 2007).

Finding out what has failed tells you what not to try again, while finding out what has worked even partially gives you a clue about what might work again. It also tells you what strengths those involved have already brought to bear on the problem and hence could use again.

Box 2.6 Questions that unlock solutions

- What ideas do you have about what needs to happen for this to change?
- What's your hunch about how to solve this?
- Everyone has made changes in their lives. How do you usually get change to happen in yours?
- What's one small thing that you did in the past that seemed to help a little?
- Who needs to do what to make that happen again?
- What have your tried so far? Did it help? How did it help? Why didn't it help?
- What have you thought about trying?
- What have you thought about doing, but haven't yet?
- Of all the things that you and others have done, what has worked best? What has worked least?
- What have other people said you should try? Of all those ideas, which one do you think has the best chance of working?
- You've seen other counsellors about this before: What did they suggest? (so that you avoid making the same mistake because, given that they are now seeing you, the previous intervention did not work).
- Invite them to act as your consultant, asking questions such as, 'When I work with another young person with a problem like this, what do you think I could do to help that person?' (Murphy, 2006).
- Enquire about their fictional or real-life heroes and then ask: 'What do you think (their hero's name) would do if faced with this problem? Would that be something you'd be willing to try?' (Murphy, 2006).

Unique possibility questions

A second category of questions to unlock solutions focuses on moving forward or crafting next steps (Combs & Freedman, 2012; Freedman & Combs, 1996).

- What will you do instead of ... (getting angry with your teacher)?
- What small change will be the first thing you notice when this begins to turn around?

- What will be a small sign that ... (you are less sad)?
- What will you notice about yourself when this improves? What will others notice?
- How could you do more of that this week?
- If you think of these events as creating a new direction for your life, what do you think the next step would be?

Future-oriented questions

These ask those involved to picture a time a few months hence when this problem is resolved, and looking back from this hypothesised future time, to imagine what they did to achieve the improvement.

- How did you solve it?
- What have you been doing differently to achieve this success?
- What have you (or others) been doing that contributed to the improvement?

Relationship questions

These contextualise clients' perceptions.

- Of everyone involved in your life, who is the most/least concerned about this?
- On the scale of 1 to 10, which number would your mother say you were at?
- Who in your life would be most surprised that you were able to do that?
- What about you would have told them that it was a possibility for you?

Sources: Murphy (2008, 2015); Murphy & Duncan (2007); Selekman (2010)

Identify exceptions

No problem occurs all of the time (Murphy, 2008). Therefore, a crucial source of solutions is to examine the times when the problem could have occurred but did not, when it happened less often, or was less intense than usual. These occasions are called *exceptions*. They are solutions that are already in place. They save us from having to invent a new solution, because we can use one that is already activated.

Identify strengths

Having examined the times when the problem is less severe than usual, you will naturally move onto asking clients what they did to bring about these exceptions and about the history of these solutions. To do this, you can ask questions such as those listed in Box 2.8. In listening to their answers, you will look out for examples of the following skills (De Jong & Berg, 2013; Sklare, 2014).

- *actions* that indicate courage, healthy risk taking (adventurousness)
- *effort* that demonstrates strength, growth, application, impulse control
- *commitments* that show loyalty, dedication, devotion, follow-through, persistence, diligence

Box 2.7 Questions that identify exceptions

- When is the problem absent or less noticeable?
- When is this problem not a problem?... What's happening at those times?
- When didn't you have this problem? Even a little bit?
- Is the problem always with you?
- What stops it?
- Tell me about a time when the problem tried to get the upper hand, but you were able to resist its influence.
- Suppose you *could* think of an exception. What might it be?
- In which class do you get into least trouble?
- What is your best class?
- What's different about that class compared to your other classes?
- In what ways is that teacher different from your other teachers? What else?
- What difference does that difference make to you?
- At what time in the past week have things been a little better than usual?
- Tell me about a time recently when (the problem) wasn't happening.
- Tell me about a time in the past month when you were above a 3 (reflecting the client's rating on the scaling question).

Sources: Murphy (2008); Murphy & Duncan (2007); Selekman (2010)

- *attitudes* that reflect tolerance, acceptance, flexibility, enthusiasm, confidence, patience
- *social orientation*, including empathy, caring, cooperation, loyalty, independence, compromise, negotiation, listening, assertiveness, problem solving
- *thoughts* that are creative, imaginative, positive, realistic, sensitive, insightful
- *goals* that are healthy, sensible, realistic, strategic, or growth producing
- *decisions* based on wise judgement, morality, self-awareness, maturity, planfulness.

The decision to focus on aspects other than the problem is not merely to help everyone feel better, but to gather information about children's skills and personal attributes that can become part of the solution. If clients are not able to name some strengths or cannot locate exceptions, you can ask what their best friend would tell you about their personal qualities.

Highlight strengths

Once you have detected instances where young people have been able to apply these skills and qualities either to the problem itself or even in a different domain altogether, you can highlight their strengths so that they and everyone else involved become more aware of possibilities for change. This is powerful, because it implies that you see them as having the capacity to make things happen and gives them hope about their future (De Jong & Berg, 2013). Nevertheless, listening out for clients' strengths does not mean ignoring their pain or flattering them; instead, we listen to both the pain and the resilience (Murphy & Duncan, 2007).

Box 2.8 Questions that elicit strengths

Once those involved can recount instances when the problem was absent or less severe than usual, you can ask 'positive blaming' questions to help them identify what they did to generate these exceptions.

- How did you do that?
- How did you get that to happen?
- What did you do to pull that off?
- What did you tell yourself that helped you do that?
- What steps did you take leading up to it?
- How did you manage to get your work done in that class?
- How do you resist the urge to muck around?
- Can you tell me about other times you've tried something useful like that?

A second set of follow-up questions implies something about the client's identity:

- What does it tell us about what is important to you in life that you were willing to do that?
- What does this tell you about yourself and your ability to solve this problem?
- What did the problem have you thinking about yourself before? What do you think about yourself now?
- Did you know you could do that?
- Is that something different for you?

Sources: Carey & Russell (2003); Selekman (2010, p. 184)

A standard practice in solution-focused work is to congratulate or give clients compliments about their use of their strengths, not as a form of flattery or to make them feel better, but to remind them about what is important to them. Nevertheless, I think this is risky – especially with young people – because they will have received so much praise to date in an effort to get them to repeat behaviours that adults approve that compliments can sound manipulative; and there is also a risk that compliments will sound patronising or disingenuous. Instead, we can (De Jong & Berg, 2013):

- Use *'positive blame' questions* that ask them to account for how come they achieved a positive change. For example, 'How did you get that to happen?'... 'Did you know beforehand that you could do that?'.
- Employ *indirect compliments* that imply something positive about the client such as, 'What would (your best friend) say about that achievement (of, say, walking away when you were angry)?'.
- *Respond to clients' self-compliments*, such as 'Where did you get the strength to do that?' or 'Did it surprise you that you could do that?'.

- *Ask identity or meaning questions*. These ask clients to consider the implications of the exceptions - that is, what these mean for their understanding of themselves and their relationships. The questions invite clients to notice how their decisions reflect larger life values, beliefs, projects, or knowledge. For example, one client told me that he never used drugs in front of children, to which I asked, 'What does this tell you about how much effort you are willing to put in, to live out your values?'. (Follow-up questions will be about what he can do to live out his value of getting clean.) Other examples could be:
  - So you're the sort of person who is diligent about doing your best for your team. Not letting your team down must mean a lot to you that you're prepared to practise so hard.
  - What other things do you work hard at?
  - What helps you to keep at it when you feel like giving up?
  - What does it say about you that you're willing to do that?

Homework tasks

Between sessions, counsellors might allocate behavioural tasks for those clients who are clear about their goals and who have been able to identify exceptions. These tasks can be behavioural or observational (or *notice*) tasks (O'Connell, 2012).

Behavioural tasks

- *Randomised tasks*. These are useful when clients are torn between conflicting solutions. You can suggest that they alternate from one solution to the other every second day and observe what happens. (The illogic of this is likely to incite them to dream up their own, better, solution.)
- *Pretend tasks*. Clients are invited to act *as if* the miracle had happened, or their goal has been achieved (Durrant, 1995). For example, you could invite children who are often aggressive to *pretend* that they feel friendly. You can then conspire with them that, each day their parents or teacher have to guess whether they are pretending or are 'for real'. (They enjoy trying to trick adults.)
- *Experimental tasks*. If they doubt their ability to repeat an exception, invite them to experiment with ways to get it to happen again.
- *More of the same tasks* are used for clients who are already doing what they have to do to make exceptions happen. We just recommend that they do more of it.
- *Do something different tasks*. The counsellor invites the client to do something different to break out of old patterns; the client decides what this different action will be.

One example of the 'Do something different' category of behavioural tasks is *doing the opposite* of current solution attempts, despite not knowing in advance how it might help (Selekman, 1997). This is particularly useful when life with the problem has become earnest. The parents can simply do a haka or the Highland Fling when the concerning behaviour happens again. If it doesn't change the behaviour, at least they have had some fun.

A second example is *pattern interruption*. This is based on the premise that a troublesome behaviour persists because it is working - at least in part. On this basis, pattern interruption permits the problem to continue, while insisting that it be less disruptive to surrounding individuals.

The key to this strategy is to identify the chain or sequences of events. Given that a chain is only as strong as its weakest link, the task is to disrupt the sequence or pattern to see if that will change how it is expressed. Possibilities for pattern interruption include (Durrant, 1995):

- changing the location of the behaviour
- changing who is involved
- changing the sequence of the steps involved
- interrupting the sequence in its initial stages ('derailing'). (For example, before a child starts to refuse to do a particular activity, say 'I bet you don't feel like doing this right now')
- introducing random starting and stopping
- increasing the frequency of the behaviour (not to be used for aggression).

Box 2.9 Pattern interruption: Increasing the frequency of a behaviour

I worked with a Year 6 student who was often violently disruptive in class. The typical sequence was that Martin disrupted; a teacher tried to calm him; and, if that did not work, his mother (who lived nearby) was summoned to school to calm him down. We had reframed this sequence as allowing Martin to check that his mother (who had experienced mental health problems) was okay.

To interrupt the pattern, we could impose the checking up, by insisting that Martin call his mother at every recess and lunch time, until he realised for himself that it was no longer necessary. This is increasing the frequency of the behaviour. Or we could invite his mother to call into the school on her way past, perhaps when walking the dog. This is random starting and stopping. Or we could give Martin permission to go home every lunch time (and miss out on play time!) to check in on his mother, again until he realised for himself that it was no longer necessary.

Observational tasks

Notice tasks are useful for clients who have struggled to identify exceptions or goals or who have few ideas about how to improve things. The goal is for them to notice something positive that happens, when the problem doesn't occur at times when it normally would, or when something in their life happens that they would like to see continue.

- When clients think only other people can solve the problem, have them pay attention to what is happening in their life that tells them that they can have some influence over the problem.
- Ask them to think about how it has come about that the problem is not more serious than it is (Molnar & de Shazer, 1987).

Box 2.10 Pattern interruption: Derailing

Over the course of a week, I observed two year-10 students repeatedly in physically rough (not quite violent) disputes with each other. They would usually desist once I entered the room but it was clearly upsetting for them and disruptive for everyone else. I didn't have enough information to know what was going on and I knew they wouldn't tell me. So, when I walked into the room at the end of lunch time to observe it happening again, I told one that I wanted to talk to him after class. Amid protests of how unfair it was to pick on him when they were both involved, I just repeated that I would see him after the lesson.

At the end of the lesson, we moved to the corridor outside the classroom. I am short. (Vertically challenged be damned: I'm just short.) He was 16 and taller than me and was able to laud it over me - so I sat down. Now he felt ridiculous, so had to sit too.

Then I said, 'I've been watching the two of you and it seems to me that you're getting picked on. And I need to ask if there is anything I can do to help you?'. The bluster went out of him instantly. He took pains to assure me that he was fine. After a brief discussion, I concluded, 'Well I'm still concerned. So if I see it happening again, I'll step in to help'. The last thing this young man wanted was some slip of a female standing up for him, so the fighting stopped.

Given the concept of circularity, it would not have mattered which one of the pair I had chosen to speak with. If I had spoken instead with the other protagonist, he too would have agreed with me that he was getting picked on. Given that they were both involved, I needed only one of them to make it stop.

- If they see exceptions as mere flukes, you will need to raise their awareness that these are not mere accidents, but happen as a result of something they do. Therefore, you could assign the task of observing the exceptions to see who does what to make them happen.
- If they doubt their abilities to repeat a success, merely have them observe between now and your next session what is different about those times when they do manage to create an exception (de Shazer, 1988).
- When they blame their personality, (e.g. obsessive-compulsive disorder) have them notice what is different about those times when they overcome their urges.

Review

In subsequent sessions, you would ask clients about the homework task but, unlike homework in other modes of therapy, it will not really matter whether they do it or not. If they do not, they will have found something else to do instead.

As you talk about what has worked for them since your last meeting, starting with the question 'What's better?', there will be four scenarios (Selekman, 2010). First, when there have been improvements, highlight these and ask what each person has done to bring them about and ask what it would take for them to continue to use these strategies.

Second, when there appears to all those involved to have been no change in the presenting problem, you could externalise the problem (see Chapter 3) or recommend pattern interruption. Giving adults the task of observing children for any signs of non-problematic behaviour can also be a way to help them notice small improvements that otherwise they might overlook in their discouragement.

Third, when the problem seems worse than before, begin by listening to and empathising with their despondency (Freeman et al., 1997), asking what it tells them about how important getting relief from the problem is to them. Then move on to asking coping and resilience questions from Box 2.11.

The fourth possible scenario is when progress reports are mixed, with some individuals reporting improvement while others still feel pessimistic. In this event, begin by highlighting the improvements. This can help sceptics to rise above their pessimism. At the same time, however, acknowledge their caution, agreeing that it is only sensible, given how long they have been living with the problem.

Box 2.11 Questions that identify resilience and coping skills

- How have you prevented things from getting worse?
- Everyone has tough times but not everyone has the strength to do what you've been doing to hang in there. How come you haven't given up?
- When you think of other tough times in your life, what helped you to get through them?
- What tells you that there is hope?
- What is it about you that keeps you hanging in there?
- How do you resist the urge to just give up?
- Where do you find the strength to keep trying?
- What does your persistence tell you about your faith in yourself?

Source: Murphy (2008, 2015)

Plan for overcoming obstacles to change

Behaviours persist because they work. Therefore, if a behaviour changes, clients will need to replace it with another strategy for meeting the same need. We also need to prepare them for new or unfamiliar experiences that occur as a result of the change. For example, when young people are unsuccessful in school, chances are that they will be friends with similarly disenchanted students. If they suddenly start to be conscientious, old friends are likely to desert them. Meanwhile, a negative reputation might mean that they are shunned by the more prosocial students. In an effort to avoid loneliness, therefore, they might revert to being unsuccessful.

This means that, ahead of time, we need a plan for overcoming the obstacles that could block change. Planning for obstacles helps clients to be realistic about the work that is ahead of them, and prevents their being caught off guard by unforeseen challenges (Sklare, 2014).

Relapses

When there has been a relapse in the presenting problem, we can explain to clients that relapses:

- are a way of telling you that some of what you are doing is working and some is not
- are a reminder to keep doing what works
- are a reminder to resume using the strategies that you originally used to overcome the problem (Kowalski, 1990)
- are ways that the problem tests you to see if you can 'get back on track'
- provide extra information about the tricks and tactics the problem uses to take over your life (Morgan, 1999).

We can choose to focus on the setback, or to search within it for evidence of a success, however partial. For example, when young people have been verbally abusive towards a peer or teacher, they did something to stop themselves lashing out physically as well. In other words, we can highlight the successes and reframe the setback as an interruption to (or a hiccup in) the overall trend of improvement.

Checking back

During the session, after there has been some conversation, you can check back with clients by asking process questions (Bertolino & Schultheis, 2002, p. 17):

- Do we seem to be talking about what you want to be talking about?
- Are there other things that you'd like to be discussing instead?
- Are we moving in a direction that seems right for you?
- Has our conversation so far been helpful to you?
- Is there something you would like me to be doing differently?

Evidence

Evaluation of the effectiveness of solution-focused therapy is made difficult by the wide range of methods it spawns and how the research defines and then measures therapeutic effectiveness (Nicholson, 1989). Many studies have methodological inadequacies and lack rigour (Corcoran and Pillai, 2009; Gingerich & Eisengart, 2000; Zhang et al., 2018). Nevertheless, in their meta-analysis of 251 published studies, Neipp and Beyebach (2022) found that solution-focused therapy produced superior outcomes compared with control groups in almost nine out of ten studies.

A growing body of studies has demonstrated positive benefits of solution-focused interventions for a range of difficulties (De Jong & Berg, 2001; Duncan et al., 2003; Franklin et al., 2017; Gingerich & Eisengart, 2000; Kim et al., 2019). A key outcome has been symptom reduction. Beyebach (2014) found that at termination, between 65 and 76 per cent reported their complaint was completely or partially solved and between 82 and 88 per cent reported that they had totally or partially achieved their therapy goals. Similar results (of 77 per cent full or partial success) were reported by Berg and De Jong (1996) for diverse clients receiving an average of just three solution-focused sessions. Other outcomes have been improved quality of life, lowered medical costs (Vogelaar et al., 2011), improved sleep, improved self-esteem and parenting (Eads & Lee, 2019) and improvement of prisoners' psychological well-being, relationships with others and self-appraisal (Sucipto et al., 2020).

Specifically, in adults, it has shown effectiveness with substance use (Kim et al., 2018); depression (Gingerich & Peterson, 2013); trauma symptoms (Eads & Lee, 2019); recidivism of criminality (Lindforss & Magnusson, 1997); and reduced fatigue and improved quality of life for individuals with Crohn's disease (Vogelaar et al., 2011) and improved psychological and social well-being of individuals with certain health conditions (Zhang et al., 2018).

With respect to children's difficulties, in their meta-analytic review, Gingerich and Peterson (2013) found improvements in young people's behaviour, academic outcomes and adolescent delinquency. Specific childhood problems to which solution-focused methods have been successfully applied span behavioural difficulties (Bond et al., 2013; Conoley et al., 2003; Franklin et al., 2008; Hsu et al., 2021; Newsome, 2005), childhood stealing (Seymour & Epston, 1989); emotional difficulties (Franklin et al., 2008; Gong & Hsu, 2017; Schmit et al., 2016); and behavioural difficulties, learning problems, psychosomatic problems, impulsivity and hyperactivity (Corcoran & Stephenson, 2000). Solution-focused methods achieved significant emotional and academic outcomes for children with reading difficulties, with intervention superior to tutoring (Daki & Savage, 2010).

The conclusion from a meta-analysis of eight meta-analytic studies is that there is now a strong evidence base that this treatment approach is effective across settings, with diverse populations and age groups, and across emotional, social and behavioural difficulties (Kim et al., 2019). Brief therapy has been found to be considerably cheaper than other treatments (Gingerich and Peterson, 2013), with a low dropout rate (Vogelaar et al., 2011) and high engagement by clients and families (Corcoran, 2006). It is also applicable across cultures, with Gong and Hsu (2017) commenting for example that the approach's focus on successes rather than problems is compatible with Chinese culture's emphasis on the need to save face.

Conclusion

The solution-focused approach is a brief therapy approach, aimed at getting clients unstuck in the quickest way possible on the grounds that this is more humane than longer-term therapy. In contrast to approaches where the practitioner is the hero while those with problems are regarded as fragile and ineffective, the solution-focused approach chooses to see young people as the heroes in their own story, the creators of their own solutions (Murphy and Duncan, 2007).

Together, its key concepts imply the following recommendations (de Shazer et al., 1986; de Shazer et al., 2007; Murphy, 2008, 2015):

When something is working, *do more of it*.
If something isn't working, stop it.
If something isn't working, do something else.

References

Banks, R. (2005). Solution-focused group therapy. In T. S. Nelson (Ed.), *Education and training in solution-focused brief therapy* (pp. 17–21). Haworth Press.

Bannink, F. (2010). *1001 Solution-focused questions*. Norton.

Berg, I. K., & De Jong, P. (1996). Solution-building conversations: Co-constructing a sense of competence with clients. *Families in Society, 77*(6), 376–391. https://doi.org/10.1606/1044-3894.934

Berg, I. K., & Steiner, S. (2003). *Children's solution work*. Norton.

Bertolino, B., & Schultheis, G. (2002). *The therapist's notebook for families: Solution-oriented exercises for working with parents, children, and adolescents*. Haworth.

Beyebach, M. (2014). Change factors in solution-focused brief therapy: A review of the Salamanca studies. *Journal of Systemic Therapies, 33*(1), 62–77. https://doi.org/10.1521/jsyt.2014.33.1.62

Bolton, K. W., Hall, J. C., Blundo, R., & Lehmann, P. (2017). The role of resilience and resilience theory in solution-focused practice. *Journal of Systemic Therapies, 36*(3), 1–15. https://doi.org/10.1521/jsyt.2017.36.3.1

Bond, C., Woods, K., Humphrey, N., Symes, W., & Green, L. (2013). Practitioner review: The effectiveness of solution focused brief therapy with children and families: A systematic and critical evaluation of the literature from 1990–2010. *Journal of Child Psychology and Psychiatry, 54*(7), 707–723. https://doi.org/10.1111/jcpp.12058

Carey, M., & Russell, S. (2003). Re-authoring: Some answers to commonly asked questions. *The International Journal of Narrative Therapy and Community Work, 2003*(3), 60–71.

Combs, G., & Freedman, J. (2012). Narrative, poststructuralism, and social justice: Current practices in narrative therapy. *The Counseling Psychologist, 40*(7), 1033–1060. https://doi.org/10.1177/0011000012460662

Conoley, C. W., Graham, J. M., Neu, T., Craig, M. C., O'Pry, A., Cardin, S. A., Brossart, D. F., & Parker, R. I. (2003). Solution-focused family therapy with three aggressive and oppositional-acting children: An N=1 empirical study. *Family Process, 42*(3), 361–374. https://doi.org/10.1111/j.1545-5300.2003.00361.x

Corcoran, J. (2006). A comparison group study of solution-focused therapy versus 'treatment-as-usual' for behavior problems in children. *Journal of Social Service Research, 33*(1), 69–81. https://doi.org/10.1300/J079v33n01_07

Corcoran, J., & Pillai, V. (2009). A review of the research on solution-focused therapy. *British Journal of Social Work, 39*(2), 234–242. https://doi.org/10.1093/bjsw/bcm098

Corcoran, J., & Stephenson, M. (2000). The effectiveness of solution-focused with child behaviour problems: A preliminary report. *Families in Society, 81*(5), 468–474. https://doi.org/10.1606/1044-3894.1048

Daki, J., & Savage, R. S. (2010). Solution-focused brief therapy: Impacts on academic and emotional difficulties. *Journal of Educational Research, 103*(5). https://doi.org/10.1080/00220670903383127

De Jong, P., & Berg, I. K. (2001). Co-constructing cooperation with mandated clients. *Social Work, 46*(4), 361–374. https://doi.org/10.1093/sw/46.4.361

De Jong, P., & Berg, I. K. (2013). *Interviewing for solutions* (3rd ed.). Brooks/Cole Thomson.

de Shazer, S. (1988). *Clues: Investigating solutions in brief therapy*. Norton.

de Shazer, S., Berg, I. K., Lipchik, E., Nunnally, E., Molnar, A., Gingerich, W., & Weiner-Davis, M. (1986). Brief therapy: Focused solution development. *Family Process, 25*(2), 207–222. https://doi.org/10.1111/j.1545-5300.1986.00207.x

de Shazer, S., Dolan, Y., Korman, H., Trepper, T., McCollum, E., & Berg, I. K. (2007). *More than miracles: The state of the art of solution-focused brief therapy*. Haworth.

Duncan, B. L., Miller, S. D., & Sparks, J. A. (2003). Interactional and solution-focused brief therapies: Evolving concepts of change. In T. L. Sexton, G. R. Weeks & M. S. Robbins (Eds.), *Handbook of family therapy: The science and practice of working with families and couples* (pp. 101–123). Brunner-Routledge.

Durrant, M. (1995). *Creative strategies for school problems*. Eastwood Family Therapy Centre/Norton.

Eads, R., & Lee, M. Y. (2019). Solution Focused Therapy for trauma survivors: A review of the outcome literature. *Journal of Solution Focused Practices, 3*(1), 9. https://digitalscholarship.unlv.edu/journalsfp/vol3/iss1/9

Franklin, C., Moore, K., & Hopson, L. (2008). Effectiveness of solution-focused brief therapy in a school setting. *Children and Schools, 30*(1), 15–26. https://doi.org/10.1093/cs/30.1.15

Franklin, C., Zhang, A., Froerer, A., & Johnson, S. (2017). Solution focused brief therapy: A systematic review and meta-summary of process research. *Journal of Marital and Family Therapy, 43*(1), 16–30. https://doi.org/10.1111/jmft.12193

Freeman, J., Epston, D., & Lobovits, D. (1997). *Playful approaches to serious problems: Narrative therapy with children and their families*. Norton.

Freedman, J., & Combs, G. (1996). *Narrative therapy: The social construction of preferred realities*. Norton.

Gingerich, W. J., & Eisengart, S. (2000). Solution-focused brief therapy: A review of the outcome research. *Family Process*, *39*(4), 477–498. https://doi.org/10.1111/j.1545-5300.2000.39408.x

Gingerich, W. J., & Peterson, L. T. (2013). Effectiveness of solution-focused brief therapy: A systematic qualitative review of controlled outcome studies. *Research on Social Work Practice*, *23*(3), 266–283. https://doi.org/10.1177/1049731512470859

Gong, H., & Hsu, W. (2017). The effectiveness of solution-focused group therapy in ethnic Chinese school settings: A meta-analysis. *International Journal of Group Psychotherapy*, *67*(3), 383–409. https://doi.org/10.1080/00207284.2016.1240588

Haley, J. (1980). *Leaving home: The therapy of disturbed young people*. Jossey-Bass.

Hsu, K. S., Eads, R., Lee, M. Y., & Wen, Z. (2021). Solution-focused brief therapy for behavior problems in children and adolescents: A meta-analysis of treatment effectiveness and family involvement. *Children and Youth Services Review*, *120*, 105620. https://doi.org/10.1016/j.childyouth.2020.105620

Kayrouz, R., & Hansen, S. (2020). I don't believe in miracles: Using the ecological validity model to adapt the miracle question to match the client's cultural preferences and characteristics. *Professional Psychology: Research and Practice*, *51*(3), 223. https://doi.org/10.1037/pro0000283

Kim, J. S., Brook, J., & Akin, B. A. (2018). Solution-focused brief therapy with substance-using individuals: A randomized controlled trial study. *Research on Social Work Practice*, *28*(4), 452–462. https://doi.org/10.1177/1049731516650517

Kim, J., Jordan, S. S., Franklin, C., & Froerer, A. (2019). Is solution-focused brief therapy evidence-based? An update 10 years later. *Families in Society*, *100*(2), 127–138. https://doi.org/10.1177/1044389419841688

Kowalski, K. (1990). The girl with the know-how: Finding solutions to a school problem. *Family Therapy Case Studies*, *5*(1), 3–14.

Kral, R., & Kowalski, K. (1989). After the miracle: The second stage in solution focused brief therapy. *Journal of Strategic and Systemic Therapies*, *8*(2), 73–76. https://doi.org/101521jsst198982373

Lang, T., & Lang, M. (1986). *Corrupting the young and other stories of a family therapist*. Rene Gordon.

Lindforss, L., & Magnusson, D. (1997). Solution-focused therapy in prison. *Contemporary Family Therapy*, *19*(1), 89–103.

Molnar, A., & de Shazer, S. (1987). Solution-focused therapy: Toward the identification of therapeutic tasks. *Journal of Marital and Family Therapy*, *13*(4), 349–358. https://doi.org/10.1111/j.1752-0606.1987.tb00716.x

Molnar, A., & Lindquist, B. (1989). *Changing problem behavior in schools*. Jossey-Bass.

Morgan, A. (Ed.) (1999). *Once upon a time... Narrative therapy with children and their families*. Dulwich Centre Publications.

Morgan, A. (Ed.) (2000). *What is narrative therapy? An easy-to-read introduction*. Dulwich Centre Publications.

Murphy, J. J. (1994). Brief therapy for school problems. *School Psychology International*, *15*(2), 115–131. https://doi.org/10.1177/0143034394152002

Murphy, J. J. (2006). *Solution-focused counseling in middle and high schools*. Pearson Merrill Prentice Hall.

Murphy, J. J. (2008). *Solution-focused counseling in schools* (2nd ed.). American Counseling Association.

Murphy, J. J. (2015). Solution-focused approaches. In H. T. Prout & A. L. Fedewa (Eds.), *Counseling and psychotherapy with children and adolescents* (5th ed., pp. 279–316). Wiley.

Murphy, J. J., & Duncan, B. L. (2007). *Brief intervention for school problems: Collaborating for practical solutions* (2nd ed.). Guilford.

Neipp, M. C., & Beyebach, M. (2022). The global outcomes of solution-focused brief therapy: A revision. *American Journal of Family Therapy*, 1–18. https://doi.org/10.1080/00220670903383127

Newsome, W. S. (2005). The impact of solution-focused brief therapy with at-risk junior high school students. *Children and Schools*, *27*(2), 83–90. https://doi.org/10.1093/cs/27.2.83

Nichols, M. P., & Schwartz, R. C. (1995). *Family therapy: Concepts and methods* (3rd ed.). Allyn and Bacon.

Nicholson, S. (1989). Outcome evaluation of therapeutic effectiveness. *Australian and New Zealand Journal of Family Therapy*, *10*(2), 77–83. https://doi.org/10.1002/j.1467-8438.1989.tb00745.x

O'Connell, B. (2012). *Solution*-focused therapy (3rd ed.). Sage.

Porter, L. (2014). *A comprehensive guide to classroom management: Facilitating engagement and learning in schools*. Routledge.

Rhodes, J. (1993). The use of solution-focused brief therapy in schools. *Educational Psychology in Practice*, *9*(1), 27–34. https://doi.org/10.1080/0266736930090105

Schmit, E. L., Schmit, M. K., & Lenz, A. S. (2016). Meta-analysis of solution-focused brief therapy for treating symptoms of internalizing disorders. *Counseling Outcome Research and Evaluation*, *7*(1), 21–39. https://doi.org/10.1177/2150137815623836

Sklare, G. B. (2014). *Brief counseling that works: A solution-focused therapy approach for school counselors and other mental health professionals* (3rd ed.). Corwin.

Selekman, M. D. (1997). *Solution-focused therapy with children: Harnessing family strengths for systemic change*. Guilford.

Selekman, M. D. (2010). *Collaborative brief therapy with children*. Guilford.

Seymour, F., & Epston, D. (1989). An approach to childhood stealing with evaluation of 45 cases. *Australian and New Zealand Journal of Family Therapy*, *10*(3), 137–143. https://doi.org/10.1002/j.1467-8438.1989.tb00757.x

Sharry, J., Darmody, M., & Madden, B. (2002). A solution-focused approach to working with clients who are suicidal. *British Journal of Guidance and Counselling*, *30*(4), 383–399. https://doi.org/10.1080/0306988021000025690

Sharry, J., Madyden, B., & Darmody, M. (2012). *Becoming a solution detective* (2nd ed.). Routledge.

Sucipto, A., Purwanto, E., Japar, M., & Ilendo-Milewska, A. (2020). Improving the psychological well-being of prisoners through group counseling with solution-focused brief therapy (SFBT) approach. *Psikohumaniora: Jurnal Penelitian Psikologi*, *5*(2), 155–168. http://doi.org/10.21580/pjpp.v5i2.6036

Vogelaar, L., Van't Spijker, A., Vogelaar, T., van Busschbach, J. J., Visser, M. S., Kuipers, E. J., & der Woude, C. J. V. (2011). Solution focused therapy: A promising new tool in the management of fatigue in Crohn's disease patients: Psychological interventions for the management of fatigue in Crohn's disease. *Journal of Crohn's and Colitis*, *5*(6), 585–591. https://doi.org/10.1016/j.crohns.2011.06.001

Wagner, P., & Gillies, E. (2001). Consultation: A solution-focused approach. In Y. Ajmal & I. Rees (Eds.), *Solutions in schools* (pp. 147–162). BT Press.

Ward, C. C., & Reuter, T. (2011). *Strength-centered counseling: Integrating postmodern approaches and skills with practice*. Sage.

Winbolt, B. (2011). *Solution focused therapy for the helping professions*. Jessica Kingsley.

Winslade, J., & Monk, G. (2007). *Narrative counseling in schools: Powerful and brief* (2nd ed.). Corwin Press.

Zhang, A., Franklin, C., Currin-McCulloch, J., Park, S., & Kim, J. (2018). The effectiveness of strength-based, solution-focused brief therapy in medical settings: a systematic review and meta-analysis of randomized controlled trials. *Journal of Behavioral Medicine*, *41*, 139–151. https://doi.org/10.1007/s10865-017-9888-1

3 Narrative therapy

Originally conceptualised by Michael White from Adelaide and David Epston from Auckland, narrative therapy is a respectful, non-blaming approach to counselling which centres people as the experts in their lives. Its approach is in contrast to those therapies which 'do' things to people, such as diagnose, assess or formulate a case conceptualisation, offer interpretations, psychoeducate, challenge dysfunctional thinking, prescribe treatments and reflect feelings (Semmler & Williams, 2000). Instead, particularly for chronic problems that have come to define individuals, narrative therapy aims to disentangle the person from the problem (Lock et al., 2004). It views problems as separate from people and assumes that people have many skills, competencies, beliefs, values, commitments and abilities that will assist them to reduce the influence of problems in their lives. In other words, it refuses to pathologise people (Semmler & Williams, 2000).

Unique to narrative therapy is the assumption that people construct stories or 'narratives' that shape their identity, or how they see themselves. They make meaning from the events in their lives to construct a story about who they are. Problems arise when their dominant story is saturated with many negative experiences, memories, images, and judgements. Accordingly, they come to see themselves as damaged, broken and irredeemable. This is the story - or 'narrative' - that brings them to counselling - see Figure 3.1.

In response, narrative practice employs re-authoring conversations that highlight the resistance that clients have mounted to this identity (White, 2007). Thus, whereas in solution-focused therapy the choice is to look for what is working in people's lives, in narrative therapy, the choice is between creating identities that are defined and limited by our causal thinking, diagnoses and labels - or to support identities that can resist these efforts to marginalise and discount individuals (Lock et al., 2004). We help them to find ways of thinking about their lives that contribute to their self-efficacy and allow *them* - not health practitioners - to be the authority on their own life (Lock et al., 2004). The goal is for clients to change the meaning they extract from their problems, which is easier than asking individuals to change who they are (Combs & Freedman, 2012).

The job of the narrative therapist is to listen for 'spaces, gaps, hidden meanings or conflicting stories' (Besley, 2001, p. 75) that contradict the problem-saturated version of clients'

DOI: 10.4324/9781003323938-4

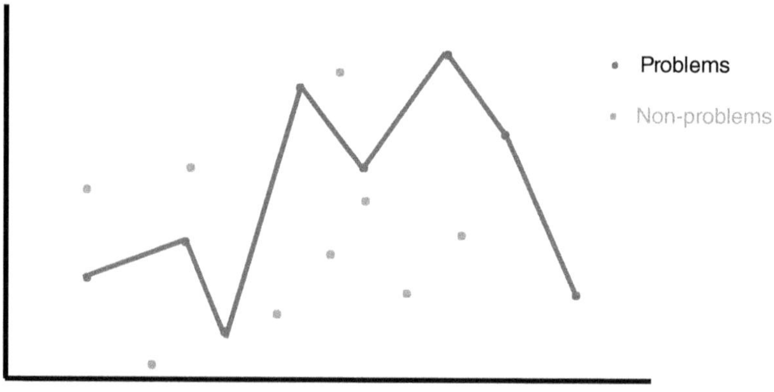

Figure 3.1 The dominant, problem-saturated story

lives, and to describe these alternative stories richly (Morgan, 2000). These alternative stories are the stories that the client does not pay attention to, has selected out or has dismissed. By creating a counter-narrative, clients will be able to resist limiting accounts of who they have been, are, and might become (Madigan, 2019).

Restorying allows the ownership of individuals' story-telling rights to return to themselves, rather than being held by 'experts' who define, diagnose and treat them as abnormal (Madigan, 2019). This will restore their dignity (Marsten et al., 2016).

Questions

Like solution-focused therapy, narrative therapy encourages counsellors to maintain a stance of abundant, genuine curiosity, and to ask questions to which we genuinely do not know the answers (which is termed a 'not-knowing' stance). Freedman and Combs (1996, p. 121) refer to questions as 'mutual puzzling'. They are not designed to give predetermined answers, but instead to allow people to deconstruct the problematic stories that have amassed about themselves, to identify their preferred directions in life and to develop alternative stories that support these preferred directions (Freedman & Combs, 1996).

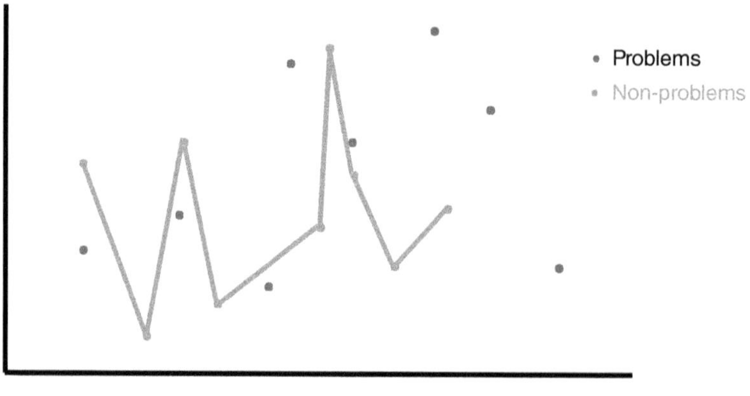

Figure 3.2 The counter-narrative

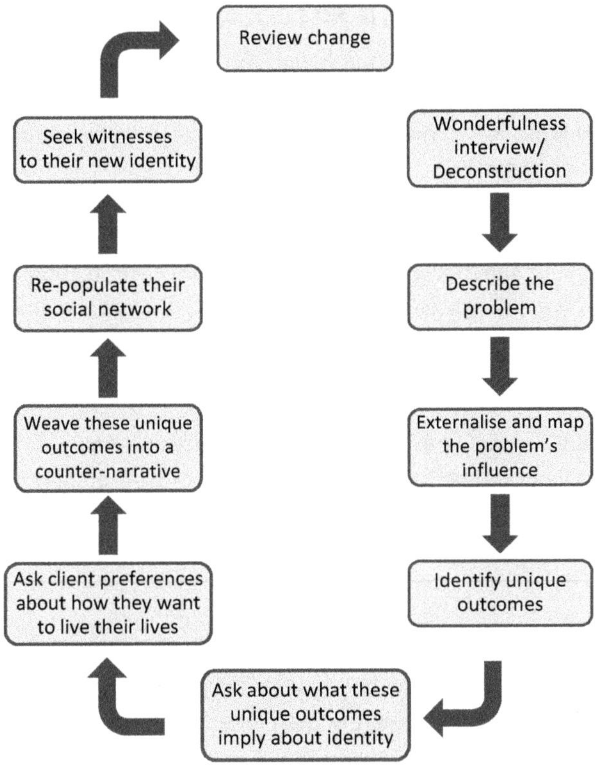

Figure 3.3 Phases of narrative sessions

Narrative therapy employs three core types of questions about the content of problems, which they refer to as *landscape of action, landscape of identity* and *preference* questions. They also employ relationship and 'unique circulation' questions.

Although of necessity I list the question types in a sequence and draw the steps of narrative therapy in Figure 3.3 as if they are linear, there will always be an organic dance in which clients' answers to previous questions will provoke counsellors' next question and counsellors will zig-zag between question types (White, 2007). Landscape of action and landscape of identity questions will be interspersed where relevant with preference questions, both so that the session does not turn into an inquisition and also to highlight clients' reasons for wanting to change. There is no script for these questions and no manual for learning questions by rote and when to ask them - just the imaginative application of enquiry (White, 2007).

The wonderfulness interview

The first step towards undoing clients' negative identities is to start by saying that you will get to the problem shortly but that you first need to learn about the young person's 'wonderfulness' (Marsten et al., 2016). Their difficulties are a message to children about themselves, and also a message to parents about their skill as a parent. Therefore, at the same time that these questions aim to restore parents' pride in their children, they equally aim to restore parents' own dignity.

To those ends, Marsten et al. (2016, p. 32) suggest:

- (To the young person): Jaxon, would it put you on the spot if I asked you about your wonderfulness? Or would you prefer me to ask your Mum and Dad?
- (To the parents) What is it about your daughter that serves to remind you that you are a wonderful mother to her?
- Could you tell me about some of your son's qualities that I might come to admire as I get to know him better?
- What is it about your son that would cause you to want to brag about him to your friends?
- What is it about your daughter that warms your heart when you think of it?

Counsellors will ask for detailed stories that illustrate these wonderful qualities and trace them through time to elaborate on them, with questions such as (Marsten et al., 2016, pp. 43-45):

- (To the parents) When did you first notice this quality in them?
- Who in your family would be the most appreciative of this talent?
- (To the young person) Do your friends see you in this way as well? How might they describe it?
- (To the father) By any chance, does his wonderfulness come from his mother and her family?
- (To the mother) By any chance, does her wonderfulness come from her father and his family?
- (To each parent) By any chance, do you consider that having your son in your life has inspired you to live your life differently than if he weren't here?
- (To the young person) Were you aware before we got talking about this, that you have been an inspiration to your Mum/Dad and that they have had so much more happiness in their lives since you came along?

Describe the problem

White (in Combs & Freedman, 2012) said that people do not generate problems; instead, they are recruited into ways of thinking and acting that create problematic identities for themselves. As counsellors ask questions to obtain a clear description of the problem, they will be interested not only in generating a simple statement about events, but also listening out for who was involved in creating the story about the problem, and how clients came to think of themselves in a problematic way (Madigan, 2019). Denborough (2014) asks:

- When did (the problem) first come into your life?
- When is it most likely to visit?
- Does it come unannounced, or announced?
- What are the times and places when it is most powerful?
- What do you understand about what's going on for you?
- What conclusions have you drawn about yourself because of this problem?

As we listen to clients' accounts of the problem, they will be contrasting it to an alternative experience that they prefer or treasure (Combs & Freedman, 2012). That is to say, to report that they feel depressed means they know that there is a state called 'not-depressed' which they would prefer. Using what White (2004) calls 'double listening', narrative counsellors will listen out for something important that has been frustrated or betrayed (Combs & Freedman, 2012). For example, when clients report on an abusive childhood, the implication is that they value justice and treating children kindly. This opens the door to discussing their values which, so far have been 'absent but implicit' (Combs & Freedman, 2012, p. 1046). It also introduces the need to deconstruct or challenge social forces that oppress and marginalise individuals - and to explore how the condition itself oppresses individuals.

Externalising the problem

Externalisation is the practical application of the core idea that people and problems are separate (Combs & Freedman, 2012). It rests on the knowledge that the words that surround us and which others use to describe us get mapped onto our psyches, or define our identities. The descriptions acquire the status of 'truth' and become irrefutable. Moreover, they are totalising: They take over such that no other view of the individual can penetrate (Winslade & Monk, 2007). Despite the fact that labels reflect only *some* of the characteristics of individuals, the descriptions come to dominate outsiders' and recipients' own concept of their *whole* self and, furthermore, highlight their deficits rather than their competencies.

Externalising, then, is a way of speaking about the problem as if it were external to clients or a separate entity. In this way, we avoid locating blame *within* individuals. This reverses the internalising logic of guilt, embarrassment and shame (Winslade & Monk, 2007). It sets the problem up as the antagonist and the client as the hero within their story (Freedman et al., 1997) in order to reverse a narrative of failure. The rationale is that if you believe that you are the problem, all you can do is act against yourself, whereas if you believe that the problem is external, you can reduce its effects on your life (Denborough, 2014).

The method can be particularly useful when the problem seems to have a life of its own (as with self-harming behaviours) or when young people report feeling helpless to control it. It centres on naming the problem, using language that clients have used to describe it, or asking them what is the best name for it. Being a proper noun, it is given a capital letter.

Deconstruction

Unlike individualist approaches that privatise clients' presenting problems, narrative therapy believes that social and political influences contribute to clients' predicaments (Nylund & Temple, 2017). What is defined as 'bad' is dictated by those in authority, and individuals adopt these norms and police themselves accordingly (Lock et al., 2004). They come to see themselves as 'the naughty child, the difficult student, the all-round screwup, the crazy one' and so on. Not only are these descriptions disrespectful by overlooking positive aspects of the self and are limiting because they affect how individuals will act in the future, but they also overlook the social oppression that many individuals suffer and which is instrumental in their lives.

Deconstruction questions are designed to expose oppression that supplants individuals' voice with the voices of those in power. For any marginalised individual, we can externalise the prejudice and discrimination they endure with questions such as:

- How much has racism played a part in your being bullied?
- What has living in disadvantaged circumstances caused you to think about your ability to be a good parent?
- How has transphobia infiltrated your life?
- In what ways have you committed to living your life in opposition to this prejudice?
- What do you do to keep homophobia from taking its grip on you?
- How do you manage to distance yourself from the negating messages that you hear about who you are?
- Did you know that you have it in you to survive such injustice?
- Do you think that it is easier for mothers to be recruited into a view that they have failed their children, than it is for fathers?
- How were you recruited into the belief that you were inferior (e.g. to White people/heterosexuals)? (Semmler & Williams, 2000, p. 56).
- What was the training ground for your feelings of inferiority? (Semmler & Williams, 2000, p. 56).
- How did feeling different alienate you from your goals?
- How was Racism able to make its claim on your life? (Semmler & Williams, 2000, p. 57).
- How did transphobia trick you into believing you lack courage and competence? (Semmler & Williams, 2000).
- As a mother, how does it feel to have Jesse exposed to legal and education systems that treat him differently because of the colour of his skin? (Madigan, 2019, p. 66).
- What gets in the way of your preferred way of being?
- If this problem is a protest against something, what would you say that something is?

Investigate the problem's strategies and pattern of entry

During the conversation, the counsellor will be asking what strategies the problem uses to take over clients' lives. This will entail examination of its tricks, tactics, ways of operation, ways of speaking, intentions, beliefs and ideas, plans, likes and dislikes, rules, purposes, desires, motives, techniques, dreams, deceptions and lies:

- When does it make an appearance?
- When is it most likely to strike and catch you off guard?
- Does it sneak up on you, or burst out of you?
- Does it boss you around?

Sometimes, Problems have Allies that team up with them and cause further oppression, such as Self-doubt or Self-criticism (Morgan, 2000). In that case, you can ask:

- What are the friends of (the problem)?
- Does it work in tandem with Racism, Self-criticism (or other forms of oppression)?

Map its influence

In order to know the story well and to do clients the justice of hearing them thoroughly, counsellors will ask about the losses that the problem has brought into their lives; what effects it has had on their school life, on their relationships with family and friends, and on their dreams for the future (De Jong & Berg, 2013; Madigan, 2019).

- In what ways is it a problem? For you? For your parents/your teachers?
- How have the Squirmies affected your relationship with your teacher?
- In what way is Shame a problem for you?
- What effect has Fighting had on your friendships at school?
- Does the problem introduce or encourage particular feelings in your life? (Freedman & Combs, 1996).
- What is missing from your life as a result of this problem?
- What does it want for you?

Map clients' influence on the problem

People are never passive in response to their circumstances: They always do *some*thing to survive. To find out about clients' actions, counsellors will ask them about the times when they resisted the power of the problem to take over their lives - even a little bit. These instances when they have resisted the limiting description of themselves are 'points of entry' for developing an alternative narrative.

In narrative therapy, these are known as unique outcomes or 'sparkling moments'. The aim is to make space for a new story to emerge about the problem and clients' influences over it. These re-authoring conversations help clients to flush out areas that the dominant story overlooks, such as their achievements, survival skills and personal qualities such as persistence, generosity or loyalty (Madigan, 2019).

Landscape of action questions

To discover unique outcomes or exceptions, you will ask landscape of action questions. In addition to those given in Box 2.7 (page 26), the focus is clients' actions that contribute to sparkling moments.

- What's one small thing that you did in the past that seemed to help a little?
- How did you get yourself ready to take this step?
- Just prior to trying that, did you nearly turn back? If so, how did you stop yourself from doing so?
- What did you tell yourself that pulled you through on this occasion?
- What would the important people in your life say was different about you then?
- Looking back from where you are now, what did you notice yourself doing that contributed to this achievement?
- What were you thinking at the time? Were you advising yourself differently from usual?

These new stories are then woven into a different description of their identity (Madigan, 2019; White, 2004). This will change how they see themselves from someone without hope, to someone who has done exceptional things, and increases their sense of agency (or self-efficacy) in their lives (Bolton et al., 2017).

Landscape of identity questions

Clients' answers to the landscape of action questions expose a *landscape of identity*: (or landscape of *meaning*) which uncovers what meanings they derive about their identity or who they are as a result of the problem. In response to counsellor questioning, clients will examine what the events disclose about their own motives, attributes, personality, strengths, resources, needs, drives, intentions, purposes, values, beliefs, hopes, dreams and commitments (White, 2004).

- What does this say about what you treasure?
- What does this tell you about yourself that you didn't know otherwise?
- When you think back, what events from your past might you be building on to use these skills?
- What does it tell us about what is important to you in life that you were willing to do that?
- What does it say about you as a (friend, son/daughter, partner) that you were willing to do that?
- What does this tell you about yourself and your ability to solve this problem?
- What did the problem have you thinking about yourself before? What do you think about yourself now?
- Suppose you were going to give yourself a compliment for your effort, what would you say?

This questioning transforms clients' past from being troubled, into having the potential to be useful in the future (Bolton et al., 2017).

Relationship questions

Relationship questions are aimed at introducing a new validating perspective to support clients' reclaimed identity (Bolton et al., 2017). They invite clients to notice things about themselves from the perspective of a dear relative or friend, as in:

- What would your mother say was the biggest change in you?
- What effect has this change had on your friendships?
- Who was the first to notice this new thing about you?'.
- Who else in your life will notice that you are functioning better?
- If they were here right now, what might they say about the times when you are on top of this? (Martin et al., 2012).
- What do (other people in your life) think about this new you?
- If your (deceased grandmother) could see you now, what would she be most proud of for you?
- If I asked (a parent, friend, grandparent) who has known you all your life, who might have predicted that you would accomplish this?
- What do they know about you that would have led them to predict this?

This form of questioning is useful for highlighting how the changes will affect clients' relationships, which will motivate them to do something different (De Jong & Berg, 2013). It also fits within clients' own cultural frame of reference.

Unique circulation questions

Relationship questions can be formalised by asking clients who they would like to tell about their new direction in life, who might be most pleased with the changes, who might be most proud for them. In Madigan's terms (2019), this fastens the personal changes that clients have made by linking them to their broader relationships.

Metaphors for responses to the problem

White (2007, pp. 32-33) lists many metaphors that clients might choose for how they want to respond to the problem: walk out on it, dispel it, go on strike against its influence, set themselves apart from it, defy its requirements, disempower it, educate it, reject its influence, reclaim their life from it, decline its invitations to cooperate with it, come out of its shadow, disprove its claims about their identity, reduce its grip on their life, repossess their life from the problem, take their life out of its hands, resign from working for it, salvage their life from it, commence a comeback from it, or tame it. Marsten et al. (2016) suggest that young clients could ask an imaginary friend for advice on how to live with Turbo energy in a world that did not always appreciate it.

You will note that none of these metaphors mentions warring with the problem, conquering it or beating it because fight metaphors can contribute to a fortress mentality, to a sense of being under siege and set up a battle which clients have typically already been fighting and losing (White, 2007).

Preference questions

Throughout the session, you will be interspersing questions about what clients prefer for their lives. Some examples include the following (Combs & Freedman, 2012; Freedman & Combs, 1996; Madigan, 2019; Winslade & Monk, 2007).

- How well does it suit you to have Fighting make you lonely?
- How do you feel being bossed around by Trouble?
- Are you happy about that?
- Do you want your reputation to speak for you, or would you prefer to speak for yourself?
- Would you like a Bad boy reputation, or a Good boy reputation?
- Would you prefer Anger to run your life, or for you to run your life?
- Can you tell me what it is about Anger that doesn't suit you?
- What does this tell you about how you wish your life to be?
- Could we say that your naming this as problematic means that you don't go along with it?
- In not going along with it, are you standing for something else?

Re-membering conversations

White (2016) uses the analogy of a 'Club of life' whose members are recognised as having authority to speak of clients' identity. As an antidote to isolation, this analogy is used for clients to re-engage purposively with what others appreciate about them, and to identify how they have contributed to others' lives (White, 2007). Clients might choose to write letters to thank people, pets, fictional characters or their stuffed toys who have helped them in the past, or ask to meet with them again. The team that stands with them can even be a virtual team of heroes whom clients have never met (Combs & Freedman, 2012).

In reverse, the rights of some people (such as an abuser's) to define their identity will be rescinded and their membership in the Club of life downgraded or revoked. Denborough (2014) describes how a client drew up a constitution for her Club, with clauses specifying that certain abusive actions disqualified individuals from membership, such that their voices on matters of her identity would no longer get a hearing.

Documentation

Both solution-focused and narrative therapy use documents to amplify exceptions and celebrate the changes that clients achieve. Whereas conversations are ephemeral, documents possess a staying power that might otherwise fade after the counselling session ends (Marsten et al., 2016). As White (2007) observes, documents rescue progress from obviousness.

Sometimes, the documents are letters that clients write to the Problem to give it fair warning that they now have a team on their side and the Problem needs to know what it is up against (Marsten et al., 2016). It could be a letter of invitation daring the Problem to attend counselling meetings. Or it might be a letter from outside witnesses to affirm clients' stand against a problem. The documents can be photos of children's achievements, such as a formerly isolated child playing alongside others, counsellors' letters to them, certificates of achievement, or positive stories about a child. David Epston sent letters to a client allegedly from his favourite fictional character, while denying that he had written them himself (Marsten et al., 2016).

The documents can be for the client's personal use, or can be circulated to family members or trusted friends, or (with clients' permission) to outsiders (such as teachers) to help them notice the children's efforts (Combs & Freedman, 2012). The audience can even be hypothetical (such as deceased or absent relatives or friends, the family pet or, for younger children, a stuffed toy or imaginary friend).

It will be vital, however, that the intent of these is to celebrate and congratulate and, therefore, that the documents are not tinged with praise or any other reward - because these can be seen to be patronising and an attempt to manipulate clients into repeating their new behaviours. Instead, the documents are to punctuate their achievements, to serve as a concrete reminder for them of what they are achieving.

Evidence

Narrative therapy has demonstrated effectiveness with children's social and emotional skills (Beaudoin et al., 2016); encopresis (soiling) (Silver et al., 1998); self-esteem, depression and disruptive behaviour (Jørring & Jensen, 2018); and the classroom behaviour of pre-adolescent girls with attention deficits (Looyeh et al., 2012).

For adults, it has improved the self-esteem and stress levels of inpatient alcoholics (Park & Kim, 2021); improved disordered eating (Conti et al., 2022; Weber et al., 2006); reduced parent-child conflicts (Etchison & Kleist, 2000); and achieved significant gains with major depression (Vromans & Schweitzer, 2011). Moreover, it shifted long-standing problems for which other therapies had not been effective (Silver et al., 1998).

In terms of process, clients appreciate the non-blameful approach inherent in the externalisation of problems (Etchison & Kleist, 2000; Silver et al., 1998). As for outcomes, Conti et al. (2022) concluded that clients experienced identity shifts, which is the core goal of this therapy.

Conclusion

Miles Davis, the jazz musician, said that when playing jazz, you don't play what's there on the music sheet, you play what isn't there. Epston (2016) compared Michael White's narrative practice to this craft of musicianship. In the same way, I implore you not to limit yourself to what I write here in such a necessarily brief overview of these theories - but to discover what I don't write. Seek out the masters in books, Youtube and in training courses. There is such creativity in you that, armed with the idea of trusting clients and refusing to see them as damaged, the richness of a narrative approach will inspire both you and your clients.

References

Beaudoin, M. N., Moersch, M., & Evare, B. S. (2016). The effectiveness of narrative therapy with children's social and emotional skill development: An empirical study of 813 problem-solving stories. *Journal of Systemic Therapies*, *35*(3), 42–59.

Besley, T. (2001). Foucauldian influences in narrative therapy: An approach for schools. *The Journal of Educational Enquiry*, *2*(2), 72–93.

Bolton, K. W., Hall, J. C., Blundo, R., & Lehmann, P. (2017). The role of resilience and resilience theory in solution-focused practice. *Journal of Systemic Therapies*, *36*(3), 1-15. https://doi.org/10.1521/jsyt.2017.36.3.1

Combs, G., & Freedman, J. (2012). Narrative, poststructuralism, and social justice: Current practices in narrative therapy. *The Counseling Psychologist*, *40*(7), 1033-1060. https://doi.org/10.1177/0011000012460662

Conti, J., Heywood, L., Hay, P., Shrestha, R. M., & Perich, T. (2022). Paper 2: A systematic review of narrative therapy treatment outcomes for eating disorders—bridging the divide between practice-based evidence and evidence-based practice. *Journal of Eating Disorders*, *10*(1), 1–9. https://doi.org/10.1186/s40337-022-00636-4

De Jong, P., & Berg, I. K. (2013). *Interviewing for solutions* (3rd ed.). Brooks/Cole Thomson.

Denborough, D. (2014). *Retelling the stories of our lives: Everyday narrative therapy to draw inspiration and transform experience*. Norton.

Epston, D. (2016). Re-imagining narrative therapy: A history for the future. *Journal of Systemic Therapies*, *35*(1), 79–87. https://doi.org/10.1521/jsyt.2016.35.1.79

Etchison, M., & Kleist, D. M. (2000). Review of narrative therapy: Research and utility. *The Family Journal*, *8*(1), 61-66. https://doi.org/10.1177/1066480700081009

Freedman, J., Epston, D., & Lobovits, D. (1997). *Playful approaches to serious problems: Narrative therapy with children and their families*. Norton.

Freedman, J., & Combs, G. (1996). *Narrative therapy: The social construction of preferred realities*. Norton.

Jørring, N. T., & Jensen, K. G. (2018). Treatment efficacy of narrative family therapy for children and adolescents with diverse psychiatric symptomatology. *Scandinavian Journal of Child and Adolescent Psychiatry and Psychology*, *6*(2), 107–114. https://doi.org/10.21307/sjcapp-2018-012

Lock, A., Epston, D., & Maisel, R. (2004). Resisting anorexia/bulimia: Foucauldian perspectives in narrative therapy. *British Journal of Guidance and Counselling*, *33*(3), 315–332. https://doi.org/10.1080/03069880500179459

Looyeh, M. Y., Kamali, K., & Shafieian, R. (2012). An exploratory study of the effectiveness of group narrative therapy on the school behavior of girls with attention-deficit/hyperactivity symptoms. *Archives of Psychiatric Nursing*, *26*(5), 404–410. https://doi.org/10.1016/j.apnu.2012.01.001

Madigan, S. (2019). *Narrative therapy* (2nd ed.). American Psychological Association.

Marsten, D., Epston, D., & Markham, L. (2016). *Narrative therapy in wonderland: Connecting with children's imaginative know-how*. Norton.

Martin, C. V., Guterman, J. T., & Shatz, K. (2012, March 21–25). *Solution-focused counseling for eating disorders*. Paper presented at the American Counseling Association, San Francisco.

Morgan, A. (2000). *What is narrative therapy? An easy-to-read introduction*. Dulwich Centre Publications.

Nylund, D., & Temple, A. (2017). Queer informed narrative therapy: Radical approaches to counselling with transgender persons: Discourse in practice. In C. Audet & D. Paré (Eds.), *Social Justice and Counseling* (pp. 159–170). Routledge. https://doi.org/10.4324/9781315753751-16

Park, J. W., & Kim, H. S. (2021). The effects of group counseling utilizing narrative therapy on self-esteem, stress response, and insight for individuals with alcohol dependency. *Journal of Creativity in Mental Health*, 1–30. https://doi.org/10.1080/15401383.2021.1972885

Semmler, P. L., & Williams, C. B. (2000). Narrative therapy: A storied context for multicultural counseling. *Journal of Multicultural Counseling and Development*, *28*(1), 51–62. https://doi.org/10.1002/j.2161-1912.2000.tb00227.x

Silver, E., Williams, A., Worthington, F., & Phillips, N. (1998). Family therapy and soiling: An audit of externalizing and other approaches. *Journal of Family Therapy*, *20*(4), 413–422. https://doi.org/10.1111/1467-6427.00096

Vromans, L. P., & Schweitzer, R. D. (2011). Narrative therapy for adults with major depressive disorder: Improved symptom and interpersonal outcomes. *Psychotherapy Research*, *21*(1), 4–15. https://doi.org/10.1080/10503301003591792

Weber, M., Davis, K., & McPhie, L. (2006). Narrative therapy, eating disorders and groups: Enhancing outcomes in rural NSW. *Australian Social Work*, *59*(4), 391–405. https://doi.org/10.1080/03124070600985970

White, M. (2004). Working with people who are suffering the consequences of multiple trauma: A narrative perspective. *International Journal of Narrative Therapy and Community Work*, *1*, 44–75.

White, M. (2007). *Maps of narrative practice*. Norton.

White, M. (2016). *Narrative therapy classics*. Dulwich Centre Publications.

Winslade, J., & Monk, G. (2007). *Narrative counseling in schools: Powerful and brief* (2nd ed.). Corwin Press.

4 Acceptance and commitment therapy (ACT)

Acceptance and Commitment Therapy (ACT, pronounced act) is a third wave therapy, with the first wave being pure behaviourism which upheld that every action we perform (except for reflexes) has been learned through rewards and punishments, and the second wave being cognitive theory which says that to relieve psychological pain, individuals need to unlearn dysfunctional thinking patterns (Hayes, 2004).

Representing the third wave, ACT upholds that our thoughts lead to an emotion or an action, to which we ascribe a meaning - and it is these meanings that govern how we respond to them. No meaning is true or false, simply useful or unhelpful. This aligns with narrative therapy, which says that it is our relationship to - or interpretation of - the problem that is the problem. We give the problem meaning and allow it to become part of our identity.

Philosophy of ACT

Behaviourism and cognitive theory are mechanistic: That is, they try to fix the mechanisms of either our actions or our thoughts (Hayes, 2004). Unlike these first two waves, ACT is contextual. That is to say, it examines the function of thinking patterns within their historical and situational contexts (Hayes, 2004). The underlying philosophy of ACT - functional contextualism - upholds that we interpret the world depending on our experience, while its underlying theory - relational frame theory - says that it is possible to interpret (that is, use language to think about) events in many different ways (Vilardarga et al., 2007). Hence, thinking is a process that is arbitrary, constructing our realities, to which we then respond *as if* they are real.

Like solution-focused and narrative therapies, ACT is not interested in symptom reduction because this would imply that symptoms are pathological and need to be suppressed, managed or struggled with (Harris, 2006). Psychological pain is not abnormal: It is the inevitable accompaniment of living a rich and meaningful life. Indeed, so many people at one time or another during their lives experience depression, anxiety, or suicidal ideation, for

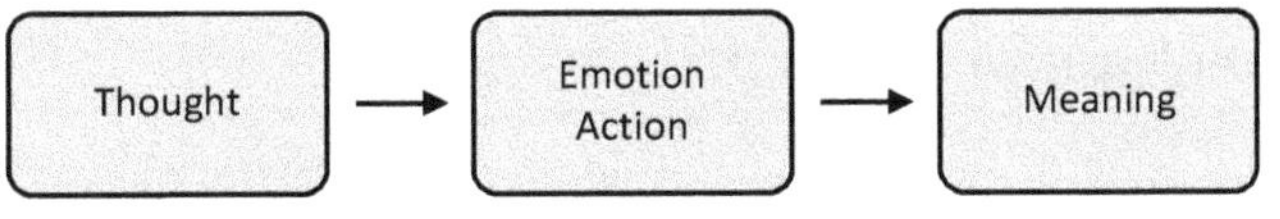

Figure 4.1 The sequence from thought to meaning

DOI: 10.4324/9781003323938-5

example, that the law of large numbers says that they can't all be abnormal - just human (Harris, 2006). Given our evolutionary history, our minds are built to anticipate danger and therefore they generate a pessimistic stream of thoughts that is not always helpful. Therefore, the aim of ACT is to transform individuals' relationship to their thoughts and feelings (Harris, 2006).

ACT practitioners believe that our difficulties - or 'symptoms' - come about because of three ineffective but natural processes: avoiding or escaping feelings, struggling with feelings, or fusing with our thoughts (Hayes, 2004). First - trying to avoid or escape from our feelings - is an attempted solution which can work in the short term but, in the long term, can increase the occurrence and intrusiveness of distressing thoughts and magnify their behavioural impact (McLean & Follette, 2016). (Being told not to think of a pink elephant immediately brings one to mind.)

Second is struggling with our feelings - that is, trying to control or suppress them. ACT believes that we cannot control our thinking by avoiding thoughts, distracting ourselves, or challenging our thoughts as cognitive theory suggests - because the brain doesn't work that way. It is built to keep producing thoughts, and we have much less control over this process than we think. Furthermore, when we challenge our thoughts (e.g. by looking for evidence to dispute them), we are still focusing on them and thereby giving negative thoughts more oxygen or attention than they deserve, prolonging their life and increasing rather than reducing their influence in our lives.

Moreover, when we try to control our thinking: We discover that we can't do it; we criticise ourselves for not being able to do it (on the grounds that we 'should' be capable of self-control); and we then obsess about not being able to do it - and the thought becomes more rather than less intrusive and more rather than less self-critical (Harris, 2007).

More than this, when we suppress part of our experience, we cannot be whole (Walser & Hayes, 2006). And because one situation can remind us of a prior negative experience and because self-talk can happen at any time anywhere, our attempt to avoid unpleasant feelings by avoiding situations can progressively expand the types of situations that we evade (Walser & Hayes, 2006). Our solution, then, actually becomes the problem (Harris, 2007). We are attempting to control our thoughts and actions, when what we seek - and need - is control of our lives (Walser & Hayes, 2006).

Without struggle, we achieve a natural level of emotional discomfort, called *clean discomfort*, that is not inflamed by buying into unhelpful thinking (Harris, 2006).

The third cause of emotional problems is fusing with our thoughts, or taking them to be The Truth. Instead of regarding our thoughts as stories that we are telling ourselves, we believe that (Harris, 2007, pp. 52-53):

- Thoughts are reality.
- Thoughts are the truth.
- Thoughts are important and need to be taken seriously.
- Thoughts are orders to be obeyed.
- Thoughts are wise.
- Thoughts can be threatening.

Instead, we need to know that *We can't believe everything that we think*. Most of our thoughts are reflexive, like shutting our eyes when we sneeze (Harris, 2007). They are just stories, strings of words or 'bits of language' that may or may not be true, important or wise ... and are certainly never threatening (Harris, 2007).

The six aspects of acceptance and commitment therapy

ACT interventions focus on two processes: developing acceptance of painful feelings and taking committed action towards living a valued life (Harris, 2006). To that end, it relies on six processes (see Figure 4.2) that overlap and are inter-related, all of which promote psychological flexibility (Hayes et al., 2006):

- being mindful and aware of our experiences
- acceptance, which is a willingness to accept unpleasant thoughts, emotions and memories rather than struggling with or trying to avoid them
- cognitive defusion, which is being able to step back from our thinking so that it does not trap us into believing unhelpful thoughts
- maintaining perspective about ourselves so that we monitor our own thinking
- values: staying connected to and acting in accord with our personal values
- committed action: engaging in actions that propel us towards what we value in life.

Mindfulness

Mindfulness means contacting the present moment and being aware of our present experience with openness, curiosity, receptiveness and kindness (Harris, 2011). It is about noticing emotions and experiences without being 'drawn in' by them or actively trying to change them (Laifer et al., 2017). Our mind will never stop generating stories, but we neither have to extinguish them nor believe them, just recognise that they are there. It is about watching our mind do its work with a sense of distance and dispassionate curiosity. This demonstrates that unpleasant thoughts and feelings are not threatening, making them more bearable.

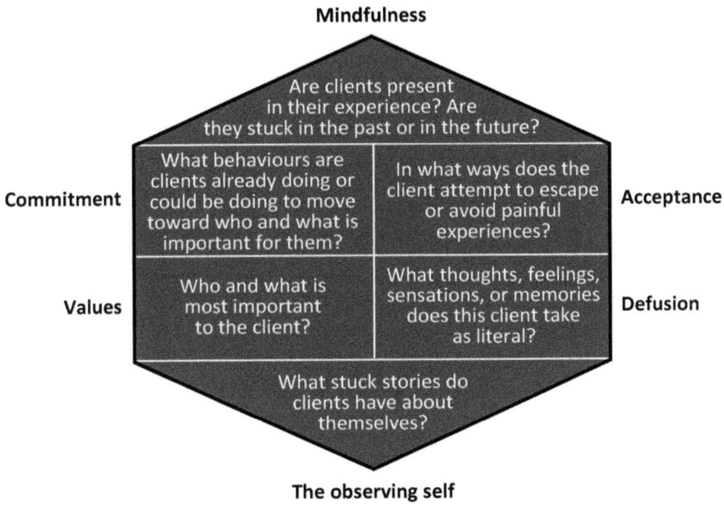

Figure 4.2 The six processes of ACT

Source: adapted from Gordon & Borushok (2017).

If we avoid being in the present moment by focusing on past hurts, anticipating future threats or distracting from current pain we lose touch with what is important to us *now*. We need to be aware of now, because only then can we change our current behaviours in the service of living a meaningful life.

Acceptance

In place of avoidance, we need acceptance, which is the second aspect of ACT. Germer (2009, in Briere & Scott, 2015, p. 216) defined it as, 'a conscious choice to experience our sensations, feelings, and thoughts, just as they are, moment to moment'. It means coming in full contact with experiences, even the painful ones - for no other purpose than to actively experience life fully (Hayes, 2004).

Acceptance does *not* mean liking or wanting painful experiences, but simply making space for them, rather than struggling with them. Emotions are chemicals. When we try to suppress them or tighten around them, there is no circulation to clear out the chemical from the tissue. Instead, therefore, we need to breathe into the pain and make space for it. Or we could examine it like a scientist who has never seen such a thing before, examining its edges, shape, weight, colour and temperature so that it becomes an object of curiosity rather than a threat (Harris, 2006). Then, when we are not working to suppress it, we can engage in the world around us. The feeling won't have gone: We have just stopped fearing it. The result will be that even though noxious feelings might be unpleasant, they are not distressing. This is the difference between experiencing *pain* versus *suffering*.

Defusion

ACT is based on the belief that the good thing about our minds is that they are constantly churning out thoughts that help us plan for the future and learn from the past (Harris, 2011). But the downside is that our minds evolved to anticipate danger and, therefore, are wired to be pessimistic and judgmental of ourselves and others (Harris, 2009). Unhelpful thoughts are not the problem: Their believability is the problem.

In other words, negative thoughts are normal, because in past eras, caution and pessimism kept us alive in a dangerous environment. But negative thoughts become a problem when we believe them and allow them to control us (Harris, 2011). The issue is not whether our thoughts are true or false, but whether they help us to live a full and enriched life.

Therefore, ACT says that we have to distance or 'unhook' ourselves from our thinking, so that we can choose to believe it if it is helpful to us, or let it go if it's not. I describe this method next.

The observing self

You will be familiar with the distinction between cognitive (thinking) skills and metacognitive skills (our capacity to scan and manage our own thinking). In ACT language, this distinction is referred to as two parts of the mind:

- the thinking self: the part that is constantly generating thoughts
- the observing self: the part that observes and is aware of these.

The part of the mind that is constantly generating thoughts is useful, but it also makes self-criticism or self-avoidance almost inevitable (Hayes et al., 1999). Therefore, we need to use the observing self to put the brakes on thinking that is unhelpful to us. This allows us to manage our thinking without becoming attached to it (Hayes et al., 2006).

Instead, when the observing self is disengaged, we fuse with our thoughts about who we are, which is to say that we believe the stories that we tell about ourselves, whether these are objectively true or not, or harmful or not (Eifert & Forsyth, 2011). More than this, we assume that our past experiences and our thoughts define who we are, for which Hayes (2004, p. 24) delivers the punchline: 'the things you've been struggling with and trying to change are not *you*'. For those who have been traumatised, separating their history from their identity is especially vital (McLean & Follette, 2016).

Values

In order to judge actions to be effective, we have to clarify what we aim to achieve by them (Vilardarga et al., 2007). These aims will be defined by our values. These are what we stand for in life, which act as an inner compass that keeps our lives on track (Harris, 2011). They inspire and motivate us to do what it takes to achieve our goals and sustain us as we live our lives (Harris, 2011).

Clients' values determine whether their actions are effective for them (Hayes et al., 2006). Questions to discover these might be:

- What do you want your life to stand for? (Clients might focus on domains such as family, relationships, health, spirituality or other aspects.)
- If taking your life in the direction of these values means you need to make room for (feelings of anxiety), are you willing to do that (Harris, 2006, p. 75)?
- Are you sure? Lots of people find it easier to just give in to the feelings and stay at home where they are safe.
- Is it more important for you to be right that child abuse has caused you so much pain, or to be living your life now the way you want it to be?

One activity is for clients to imagine that they can take all of the values that are important to them in a boat to a deserted island (McKay et al., 2010). Now, imagine that during the journey the boat starts taking on water, weighed down by the load. They have to throw one of their values overboard. Which one would they toss away? Now imagine that the boat continues to take on water because the load is still too much. Which value would they discard this time? Repeat this until they are left with just one. Which one is it? Why did they choose it? *This* is their passion.

Commitment

Commitment is a conscious choice to take action to engage in a meaningful life, to do what it takes to live by our values. This involves asking clients preference questions about whether their actions move them closer to what and who matters most to them and helping clients plan for barriers to committed action and how to overcome these (McLean & Follette, 2016).

Box 4.1 A menu of values

Acceptance	Forgiveness	Order
Achievement	Freedom	Passion
Adventure	Friendliness	Patience
Altruism	Fun	Persistence
Assertiveness	Generosity	Pleasure
Authenticity	Genuineness	Power
Autonomy	Gratitude	Rationality
Beauty	Growth	Realism
Caring	Health	Reciprocity
Challenge	Helpfulness	Respect
Change	Honesty	Responsibility
Compassion	Honour	Risk taking
Conformity	Humility	Romance
Connection	Humour	Safety
Considerateness	Independence	Self-awareness
Contribution	Industry	Self-care
Cooperation	Integrity	Self-development
Courage	Intimacy	Self-regulation
Courtesy	Justice	Service
Creativity	Kindness	Sexuality
Curiosity	Knowledge	Simplicity
Dependability	Leisure	Skilfulness
Encouragement of others	Love	Spirituality
Equality	Mastery	Stability
Excitement	Mindfulness	Supportiveness
Fairness	Moderation	Tolerance
Fitness	Non-conformity	Tradition
Flexibility	Open-mindedness	Trust

Sources: David & Congleton (2015); Harris (2011)

Goals

ACT identifies clients' goals by asking them how the problem interferes with their life, such as (Gordon & Borushok, 2017, p. 46; Harris, 2006):

- What thoughts, feelings, sensations or memories do you struggle with the most?
- What have you tried before? How has it worked?
- When you're in pain like this, what do you usually do?

- In that moment, what would I see you doing, if I were there?
- Has this strategy reduced your symptoms in the long term?
- What does this strategy cost you, in terms of time, energy, health, vitality, your relationships?
- What is the price you pay for attempting to avoid or get rid of your pain?
- This struggle hurts for a reason. What about this is important to you?
- What is it like to be present with your pain now, even just talking about it?
- If you weren't busy trying to avoid or escape your pain, what would you be doing instead?

In response, clients' answers will typically fall into three categories:

- I can't stand feeling like this: This response indicates avoidance.
- I just want to be normal: This signals clients' belief that they are 'abnormal'.
- It stops me from doing x, y or z: This points to clients' values or goals.

Ending the struggle with feelings

As far as we know, we are the only species that has feelings *about* our feelings. For example, we might be nervous about speaking in public and embarrassed that we cannot hide our nervousness. One feeling spawns a second. We see this in children who are in meltdown mode - and then a switch flips, as it were, and they become hysterical. The problem now is not the original complaint, but that they have become scared by the intensity of their own feelings. Adults have the same experience when we have lost someone we love through death or desertion. During grief we feel so intensely sad, that our feelings scare us. However, although feelings can be painful, they cannot threaten us.

When we allow our feelings to dictate how we live our life, we are like a puppet on a string, being jerked around by our emotions. Being out of control like this feels dangerous, which teaches us that strong feelings are dangerous. Getting stressed about our feelings activates the fight-flight response - not to deal with an external stressor, but to fight our own feelings. We do this because we judge certain emotions to be bad - when all they are is a stream of thoughts and sensations. In short, we are turning ourselves into victims of ourselves - of our own feelings.

Our sadness, anger and anxieties become the enemy (Gordon & Borushok, 2017). As a result, we begin to fear them and try to avoid or control them. And when this doesn't work we get down on ourselves by telling ourselves that we shouldn't feel this way, that there is something wrong with us for feeling like this, and that we cannot handle it (Harris, 2007).

To rid ourselves of a sense of threat, Harris (2006, 2007) asks us to imagine that in our mind is a 'struggle' switch that, when turned on, acts like an emotional amplifier. In turn, struggling adds to our original feeling by, for example, piling guilt on top of anxiety ('I shouldn't let myself get so worked up') and anger on top of the guilt ('I'm sick of feeling like this. It's not fair that I feel so awful').

To help with this second layer of feeling (our feelings *about* our feelings), Harris likens our mind to the sky, with our thoughts and feelings being the storm clouds that appear now and again (Harris, 2007). He reminds us that, once these clouds (our thoughts and feelings) pass, the sky (our mind) is the same as it always was. This implies that we do not need to be frightened of or fight our own thoughts or emotions. Like storm clouds, they have a limited life span and will go away by themselves if we give them time and don't give them airplay that they don't deserve. Emotions are like the weather: constantly changing (Harris, 2007).

Defusing from thoughts

The thoughts that we are likeliest to get stuck ruminating about are the ones that are scary or shameful (Haidt, 2006). These will not be helpful to us. Therefore, ACT says that we have to distance or 'unhook' ourselves from our thinking, so that we can choose to believe it if it is helpful to us, or let it go if it's not (Harris, 2011).

Having decided that a thought is unhelpful, instead of fighting it or trying to correct it, we need to stop believing it as strongly as we do. Rather than regarding them as a threat, we can rob thoughts of their power over us by treating the words and images in our heads as mere stories. To do this, clients can choose one of the metaphors given in Box 4.2. You will need to make sure to suggest them with compassion and a sense of humour, without making light of clients' pain.

Box 4.2 Metaphors for defusion from unhelpful thinking

Create distance between the thought and yourself

- Regard your thoughts as being like music playing in the background or like cars driving past your house. You can pay attention to them if they are interesting, but let them slide on past if they are not helpful.
- Think of your thoughts as bubbles in champagne: They rise to the top and then disappear.
- Preface the thought with, 'I'm thinking that ... (I'm stupid)'. Or, 'I'm noticing that I'm having the thought that ... (I'm useless)'. Adding this preface reminds us that we can't believe everything we think: We would not believe ourselves if we declared, 'I'm thinking that ... I'm a banana'.
- Think of your self-statements as being read by actors in a play. You don't have to get on stage and perform the script.
- Imagine your thoughts on placards on the floats of a passing parade. The floats will pass on by, without your having to climb on board.
- They can be pictured as clouds floating by, or birds flying across the sky.
- Visualise the thought on a leaf, floating down the stream, or in space floating away into distant infinity.
- Picture your thoughts as luggage on an airport conveyor belt: It passes by without you having to pick it up.

Be playful

- Set the thought to music (*Jingle Bells*, *Happy Birthday*, or the Muppet song, for example) and sing it to yourself.

- Repeat the thought in a humorous voice (e.g. Homer Simpson's or Yoda's).
- Repeat the word (such as *stupid* or *idiot*) out loud for one minute, until only its sound remains, devoid of its meaning.
- Visual learners might enjoy seeing the thought on a computer screen in their mind's eye, and adjusting the font and the colours of the text. They can change the font size and spacing and bounce the words up and down.

Manage your mind

Your mind is an imp that keeps producing thoughts whether they are useful or not. We have no control over this, but we can control which thoughts we invite in and entertain. Some ways of putting the brakes on the mind's chatterbox are the following.

- Give your mind a name, and respond with, 'Thanks (mind), for that thought. But I *have* heard it before'.
- When you detect an unhelpful thought, tell yourself, 'Meh, that's the *I'm stupid* story again'. Maybe followed by 'BOR-ing .... Heard it before .... Whatever.... Tell me when you've got something new'.
- Think of your thoughts as junk email: You can't stop it from arriving in your Inbox, but you don't have to read it.
- Think of your ongoing commentary as *Radio Triple F*, with regular bulletins on everything you need to *fear*, updates on all your *flaws*, and around-the-clock reminders of your *failures* (Harris, 2011). Once you notice this commentary going on in your head, you can remind yourself, 'Aha, here's Radio Triple F again'.

Sources: Harris (2007, 2011); Hayes et al. (2006); Nash (n.d.); Turrell & Bell (2016)

When clients find themselves believing the doom and gloom of their mind's chatterbox, they need to avoid self-blame for thinking these thoughts in the first place - because it's just the way the human mind works (Harris, 2007; McLean & Follette, 2016; Turrell & Bell, 2016) - and instead tell themselves that they got hooked again (like a fish being reeled in on the angler's line): 'Oops, hooked again' (Harris, 2011). Remind them not to berate themselves for getting hooked, but just to notice it and let the thought go.

Neutralise painful memories

Individuals who are suffering as a result of childhood trauma can imagine what life would have been like without this experience and yearn for a different history in order not to be someone with these types of memories (Walser & Hayes, 2006). Instead, acceptance prevents our history from defining us because, despite traumatic experiences, we can still live a full and meaningful life (McLean & Follette, 2016). We do not first have to win a war with our own history (Hayes, 2004).

When the mind is constantly dredging up painful memories, nothing will ever take these away (because our brain's memory centre does not have a delete button) - but clients can allow them to have less impact over them today. Harris (2009, p. 64) gives an analogy for this:

> When these memories show up, it's like watching a terrifying horror movie late at night, all alone by yourself, in a rickety old house, with all the lights off. Now suppose you have exactly the same movie playing, but this time the TV's in the corner of the room, it's broad daylight, sunlight's streaming in through the windows, your house is full of friends and family, and you're all interacting together - talking, laughing, eating, having fun. The movie hasn't changed one bit - it's still playing on the TV in the corner of the room - but now it's having much less effect on you.

The goal for clients is not to avoid unpleasant emotions or to replace these with 'good' feelings, but to learn new ways of handling emotions that work for them. This will entail refusing to think of their memories as threatening, embracing the aspects of themselves that prior traumas might have cut off, and holding their history for what it is: a memory or a thought (Walser & Hayes, 2006). They do not have to act on these: Their history can inform them rather than drive them (Walser & Hayes, 2006).

Externalising ACT metaphors

Two practices need to be refined to allow ACT to fit neatly within the postmodern ethos of solution-focused and narrative therapies. First, the psychoeducational element puts the practitioner in centre stage. To undo this power differential, I ask if clients would like me to teach them about their mind so that they can find ways to feel better. For young children, I would simplify the ACT acronym to stand for Accept, Choose, and Take action (Walser & Hayes, 2006). Then I might explain the three unsuccessful ways of dealing with feelings (avoidance, struggling with feelings, and fusing with thoughts), then will focus mainly on defusion. I will show them a list of defusion metaphors, from which they can choose any that make sense or are fun for them, or I will ask them to generate their own strategies.

Second, treating clients' self-talk as internal is risky because they can then criticise themselves for getting hooked by the same old unhelpful stories. Failure and self-blame can be powerful adversaries. To avoid this, we can externalise the ACT metaphors. For example:

- For unassertiveness: What does Rules (about not speaking up) want for you? To have a voice, or to be intimidated into silence?
- For depression: When the Storm Clouds descend on your mind, what lies do they tell you about the possibilities for your life and your future?
- For social anxiety: When Anxiety tells you that you're boring and no one will want to talk to you, what stunts does it pull in your body to convince you that it's right?
- For low self-esteem and its behavioural sequalae: When the 'I'm stupid' story is grabbing your attention, what tricks does it use to try to suck you into believing it?
- When the Pathological Self-critic is harassing you, what does it want for your life?
- When Junk email arrives in your mind's inbox, what disguises does it use to hide from you that it's junk?
- When Radio triple F is blaring, what does it take to turn its volume down?

These can be followed with preference questions employing words clients have used in their previous answers, such as 'Are you happy that (Metaphor) does this to your body / talks to you so rudely / wants you to have no future / be all alone?'. Then would follow landscape of action questions about exceptions (or unique outcomes, in narrative terms):

- Tell me about a time when (social) Anxiety tried to keep you from having company but you managed to shut it down and chat to some classmates?
- Tell me about a time when the 'I'm stupid' story tried to convince you that you were hopeless at schoolwork, but you tried again and got the answer?
- Tell me about a time when Pathological Self-critic was screaming for your attention but you did something you wanted for yourself anyway?
- What did it take for you to hit 'delete' on Junk mail without reading it first?

Then would follow preference questions about the counter-narrative:

- Is the 'I'm stupid' story your friend? Why not?
- Do you think it's fair that 'I'm boring' stops you from having friends?
- Is closing down Pathological Self-critic something that will help you (make friends) or something that will make it harder? Why?
- Does Radio triple F broadcast anything interesting to you, or have you heard it all before?

Last would be landscape of identity questions that ask about what these exceptions mean for who clients are, such as:

- What does it say about you that you are able to turn the volume down on Radio triple F?
- What did the 'I'm boring' story have you believing about yourself before? What do you believe about yourself now?

Evidence

ACT is not manualised, but rather organic. This means that it is less easy to measure its outcomes than it is for its more structured cousins, cognitive behaviour therapy and dialectical behaviour therapy. Nevertheless, Hayes et al. (2006) and Vilardarga et al. (2007) report on numerous small studies verifying the relevance of psychological flexibility to various outcomes such as quality of life and pain tolerance, while micro-studies of specific aspects of ACT, especially the acceptance, defusion and values aspects, have demonstrated their workability for the likes of pain management (McCracken et al., 2005), deliberate self-harm (Gratz & Gunderson, 2006) and anxiety (Roemer & Orsillo, 2007).

ACT has been demonstrated to be effective for adults with a range of presenting issues, such as depression (A-Tjak et al., 2015; Bai et al., 2020; Forman et al., 2007; Gloster et al., 2020; Ruiz, 2012), social anxiety (Dalrymple & Herbert, 2007; Ossman et al., 2006), coping with psychotic hallucinations (Bach et al., 2006), post-traumatic stress symptoms (Molavi et al., 2020; Wharton et al., 2019), the management of diabetes (Gregg, 2004) and other conditions, including substance abuse, disordered eating, chronic pain and various somatic complaints (Gloster et al., 2020).

Similarly, in adolescents it has achieved significant improvements in a variety of presenting difficulties (Swain et al., 2015) and specifically depression and stress (Livheim et al., 2015;

Petts et al., 2017), anxiety (Petersen et al., 2022), post-traumatic stress symptoms (Woidneck et al., 2014), behavioural difficulties such as impulsivity and aggression (Gómez et al., 2014), the behavioural difficulties of children with chronic pain (Ghomian & Shairi, 2016), and depression and anxiety in children with special health care needs (Parmar et al., 2021). It has achieved clinically meaningful changes in disordered eating, body image and hospital admissions of people with anorexia (Fogelqvist et al., 2020; Juarascio et al., 2013a; Manlick et al., 2013; Onnink et al., 2022).

ACT has also been applied across many cultural groups, with good success (Woidneck et al., 2012). In addition to symptom reduction, outcomes include improved life satisfaction (A-Tjak et al., 2015) and a decrease in the believability (but not the frequency) of unhelpful thoughts (Hayes, 2004), while the ACT sessions were popular with clients (Juarascio et al., 2013b; Petersen et al., 2022).

Conclusion

With only a few minor refinements, ACT fits neatly within the decentred-influential quadrant of Figure 1.2 (see page 8), justifying its placement there alongside solution-focused and narrative therapies. All three theories take no interest in diagnoses, labels or causes, because these will not imply a solution. Instead, clients' own solutions are their own answer to their predicament. When we respect and trust clients' knowledge by asking questions rather than teaching, we capitalise on their own skills, maintain their engagement and allow their own voice to gain ascendancy.

References

A-Tjak, J. G., Davis, M. L., Morina, N., Powers, M. B., Smits, J. A., & Emmelkamp, P. M. (2015). A meta-analysis of the efficacy of acceptance and commitment therapy for clinically relevant mental and physical health problems. *Psychotherapy and Psychosomatics*, *84*(1), 30–36. https://doi.org/10.1159/000365764

Bach, P. A., Gaudiano, B., Pankey, J., Herbert, J. D., & Hayes, S. C. (2006). Acceptance, mindfulness, values, and psychosis: Applying acceptance and commitment therapy (ACT) to the chronically mentally ill. In R. A. Baer (Ed.), *Mindfulness-based treatment approaches: Clinician's guide to evidence base and applications* (pp. 93–116). Elsevier Academic Press. https://doi.org/10.1016/B978-012088519-0/50006-X

Bai, Z., Luo, S., Zhang, L., Wu, S., & Chi, I. (2020). Acceptance and commitment therapy (ACT) to reduce depression: A systematic review and meta-analysis. *Journal of Affective Disorders*, *260*, 728–737. https://doi.org/10.1016/j.jad.2019.09.040

Briere, J. N., & Scott, C. (2015). *Principles of trauma therapy: A guide to symptoms, evaluation, and treatment* (2nd ed.). Sage.

Dalrymple, K. L., & Herbert, J. D. (2007) Acceptance and commitment therapy for generalized social anxiety disorder: A pilot study. *Behavior Modification*, *31*, 543–568. http://dx.doi.org/10.1177/0145445507302037

David, S., & Congleton, C. (2015). Emotional agility. In *HBR's 10 must reads: On Emotional intelligence* (pp. 119–126). Harvard Business Review Press.

Eifert, G. H., & Forsyth, J. P. (2011). The application of acceptance and commitment therapy to problem anger. *Cognitive and Behavioral Practice*, *18*(2), 241–250. https://doi.org/10.1016/j.cbpra.2010.04.004

Fogelkvist, M., Gustafsson, S. A., Kjellin, L., & Parling, T. (2020). Acceptance and commitment therapy to reduce eating disorder symptoms and body image problems in patients with residual eating disorder symptoms: A randomized controlled trial. *Body Image*, *32*, 155–166. https://doi.org/10.1016/j.bodyim.2020.01.002

Forman, E. M., Herbert, J. D., Moitra, E., Yeomans, P. D., & Geller, P. A. (2007). A randomized controlled effectiveness trial of acceptance and commitment therapy and cognitive therapy for anxiety and depression. *Behavior Modification*, *31*(6), 772–799. https://doi.org/10.1177/0145445507302202

Ghomian, S., & Shairi, M. R. (2016). The effectiveness of acceptance and commitment therapy on externalizing symptoms in 7 to 12 year-old children with chronic pain. *Caspian Journal of Internal Medicine*, *2*, 97–102. http://research.shahed.ac.ir/WSR/WebPages/Report/PaperView.aspx?PaperID=43101

Gloster, A. T., Walder, N., Levin, M. E., Twohig, M. P., & Karekla, M. (2020). The empirical status of Acceptance and commitment therapy: A review of meta-analyses. *Journal of Contextual Behavioral Science*, *18*, 181–192. https://doi.org/10.1016/j.jcbs.2020.09.009

Gómez, M. J., Luciano, C., Páez-Blarrina, M., Ruiz, F. J., Valdivia-Salas, S., & Gil-Luciano, B. (2014). Brief ACT protocol in at-risk adolescents with conduct disorder and impulsivity. *International Journal of Psychology and Psychological Therapy*, *14*(3), 307–332. http://www.redalyc.org/articulo.oa?id=56032544001

Gordon, T., & Borushok, J. (2017). *The ACT approach: A comprehensive guide for acceptance and commitment therapy*. PESI Publishing and Media.

Gratz, K. L., & Gunderson, J. G. (2006). Preliminary data on an acceptance-based emotion regulation group intervention for deliberate self-harm among women with borderline personality disorder. *Behavior Therapy*, *37*(1), 25–35. https://doi.org/10.1016/j.beth.2005.03.002

Gregg, J. A. (2004). *A randomized controlled effectiveness trial comparing patient education with and without acceptance and commitment therapy for type 2 diabetes self-management* [Doctoral dissertation]. University of Nevada, Reno.

Haidt, J. (2006). *The happiness hypothesis: Finding modern truth in ancient wisdom*. Basic Books.

Harris, R. (2006). Embracing your demons: An overview of acceptance and commitment therapy. *Psychotherapy in Australia*, *12*(4), 70–76.

Harris, R. (2007). *The happiness trap: Stop struggling, start living*. Exisle.

Harris, R. (2009). *ACT made simple: An easy-to-read primer on Acceptance and Commitment Therapy*. New Harbinger.

Harris, R. (2011). *The confidence gap: A guide to overcoming fear and self-doubt*. Trumpeter.

Hayes, S. C. (2004). Acceptance and commitment therapy, relational frame theory, and the third wave of behavioral and cognitive therapies. *Behavior Therapy*, *35*(4), 639–665. https://doi.org/10.1016/S0005-7894(04)80013-3

Hayes, S. C., Luoma, J. B., Bond, F. W., Masuda, A., & Lillis, J. (2006). Acceptance and commitment therapy: Model, processes and outcomes. *Behaviour Research and Therapy*, *44*(1), 1–25. https://doi.org/10.1016/j.brat.2005.06.006

Hayes, S. C., Strosahl, K. D., & Wilson, K. G. (1999). *Acceptance and commitment therapy: An experiential approach to behavior change*. Guilford.

Juarascio, A., Shaw, J., Forman, E., Timko, C. A., Herbert, J., Butryn, M., Bunnell, D., Matteucci, A., & Lowe, M. (2013a). Acceptance and commitment therapy as a novel treatment for eating disorders: An initial test of efficacy and mediation. *Behavior Modification*, *37*(4), 459–489. https://doi.org/10.1177/0145445513478633

Juarascio, A., Shaw, J., Forman, E., Timko, C. A., Herbert, J. D., Butryn, M., & Lowe, M. (2013b). Acceptance and commitment therapy for eating disorders: Clinical applications of a group treatment. *Journal of Contextual Behavioral Science*, *2*(3–4), 89–94. https://doi.org/10.1016/j.jcbs.2013.08.001

Laifer, A. L., Wirth, K. A., & Lang, A. J. (2017). Mindfulness and acceptance and commitment therapy in the treatment of trauma. In *APA handbook of trauma psychology: Trauma practice*, Vol. 2 (pp. 253–273). American Psychological Association.

Livheim, F., Hayes, L., Ghaderi, A., Magnusdottir, T., Högfeldt, A., Rowse, J., & Tengström, A. (2015). The effectiveness of acceptance and commitment therapy for adolescent mental health: Swedish and Australian pilot outcomes. *Journal of Child and Family Studies*, *24*, 1016–1030. https://doi.org/10.1007/s10826-014-9912-9

Manlick, C. F., Cochran, S. V., Koon, J. (2013). Acceptance and commitment therapy for eating disorders: Rationale and literature review. *Journal of Contemporary Psychotherapy*, *43*, 115–122. https://doi.org/10.1007/s10879-012-9223-7

McCracken, L. M., Vowles, K. E., & Eccleston, C. (2005). Acceptance-based treatment for persons with complex, long standing chronic pain: A preliminary analysis of treatment outcome in comparison to a waiting phase. *Behaviour Research and Therapy*, *43*(10), 1335–1346. https://doi.org/10.1016/j.brat.2004.10.003

McKay, M., Forsyth, J. P., & Eifert, G. H. (2010). *Your life on purpose: How to find what matters and create the life you want*. New Harbinger.

McLean, C., & Follette, V. M. (2016). Acceptance and commitment therapy as a nonpathologizing intervention approach for survivors of trauma. *Journal of Trauma and Dissociation*, *17*(2), 138–150. https://doi.org/10.1080/15299732.2016.1103111

Molavi, P., Pourabdol, S., & Azarkolah, A. (2020). The effectiveness of acceptance and commitment therapy on posttraumatic cognitions and psychological inflexibility among students with trauma exposure. *Archives of Trauma Research*, *9*(2), 69–74. https://doi.org/10.4103/atr.atr_100_19

Onnink, C. M., Konstantinidou, Y., Moskovich, A. A., Karekla, M. K., & Merwin, R. M. (2022). Acceptance and commitment therapy (ACT) for eating disorders: A systematic review of intervention studies and call to action. *Journal of Contextual Behavioral Science*, *26*, 11–28. https://doi.org/10.1016/j.jcbs.2022.08.005

Ossman, W. A., Wilson, K. G., Storaasli, R. D., & McNeill, J. W. (2006). A preliminary investigation of the use of acceptance and commitment therapy in group treatment for social phobia. *International Journal of Psychology and Psychological Therapy*, *6*(3), 397–416. http://www.redalyc.org/articulo.oa?id=56060308

Parmar, A., Esser, K., Barreira, L., Miller, D., Morinis, L., Chong, Y. Y., & Orkin, J. (2021). Acceptance and commitment therapy for children with special health care needs and their parents: a systematic review and meta-analysis. *International Journal of Environmental Research and Public Health*, *18*(15), 8205. https://doi.org/10.3390/ijerph18158205

Petersen, J. M., Davis, C. H., Renshaw, T. L., Levin, M. E., & Twohig, M. P. (2022). School-based acceptance and commitment therapy for adolescents with anxiety: A pilot trial. *Cognitive and Behavioral Practice*. https://doi.org/10.1016/j.cbpra.2022.02.021

Petts, R. A., Duenas, J. A., & Gaynor, S. T. (2017). Acceptance and commitment therapy for adolescent depression: Application with a diverse and predominantly socioeconomically disadvantaged sample. *Journal of Contextual Behavioral Science*, *6*(2), 134–144. https://doi.org/10.1016/j.jcbs.2017.02.006

Roemer, L., & Orsillo, S. M. (2007). An open trial of an acceptance-based behavior therapy for generalized anxiety disorder. *Behavior Therapy*, *38*(1), 72–85. https://doi.org/10.1016/j.beth.2006.04.004

Ruiz, F. J. (2012). Acceptance and commitment therapy versus traditional cognitive behavioral therapy: A systematic review and meta-analysis of current empirical evidence. *International Journal of Psychology and Psychological Therapy*, *12*(3), 333–358.

Swain, J., Hancock, K., Dixon, A., & Bowman, J. (2015). Acceptance and commitment therapy for children: A systematic review of intervention studies. *Journal of Contextual Behavioral Science*, *4*(2), 73–85. http://dx.doi.org/10.1016/j.jcbs.2015.02.001

Turrell, S. L., & Bell, M. (2016). *ACT for adolescents: Treating teens and adolescents in individual and group therapy*. Context Press.

Vilardarga, R., Hayes, S. C., & Schelin, L. (2007). Philosophical, theoretical and empirical foundations of acceptance and commitment therapy. *Anuario de Psicología/The UB Journal of Psychology*, *38*(1), 117–128. https://raco.cat/index.php/AnuarioPsicologia/article/view/71750

Walser, R. D., & Hayes, S. C. (2006). Acceptance and commitment therapy in the treatment of posttraumatic stress disorder: Theoretical and applied issues. In V. C. Follette & J. I. Rusek (Eds.), *Cognitive-behavioral therapies for trauma* (2nd ed., pp. 146–172). Guilford.

Wharton, E., Edwards, K. S., Juhasz, K., & Walser, R. D. (2019). Acceptance-based interventions in the treatment of PTSD: Group and individual pilot data using acceptance and commitment therapy. *Journal of Contextual Behavioral Science*, *14*, 55–64. https://doi.org/10.1016/j.jcbs.2019.09.006

Woidneck, M. R., Pratt, K. M., Gundy, J. M., Nelson, C. R., & Twohig, M. P. (2012). Exploring cultural competence in acceptance and commitment therapy outcomes. *Professional Psychology: Research and Practice*, *43*(3), 227–233. https://doi.org/10.1037/a0026235

Woidneck, M. R., Morrison, K. L., & Twohig, M. P. (2014). Acceptance and commitment therapy for the treatment of posttraumatic stress among adolescents. *Behavior Modification*, *38*(4), 451–476. https://doi.org/10.1177/0145445513510527

5 Principles of working with young people

From our vantage point in history, it seems strange that the concept of childhood as a separate – and vulnerable – developmental stage did not emerge until the late 1800s. The likes of Charles Darwin described in literature the impact of early life experiences on the young characters in his stories, which was a new concept at that time. Prior to that, children were considered to be miniature adults and were held accountable for their actions to the same extent as adults were (Peterson, 2014).

As for adolescence, G. Stanley Hall was the first psychologist (in 1904) to acknowledge adolescence as a psychologically important stage of human development, although he highlighted the 'storm and stress' of this period of life (Gullotta et al., 2000). However, much of what has been written about adolescent problems is based on clinical populations – those who are in contact with the mental health or justice systems – and this taints perceptions of this stage of life (Porteous, 1979; Rutter et al., 1976). In Rutter and colleagues' classic study, they found that emotional difficulties generally arise during childhood (in response to family adversities) rather than during adolescence, and that any difficulties that emerge in adolescence are already brewing (Rutter et al., 1976).

Core beliefs about young people

In this section, I discuss the founding beliefs on which I base my interactions with young people. The first of these is a belief in human nature.

Belief in human nature

Our species has a long history of distrust of our own nature, remnants of which remain in the language that we use about young people today. We continue to make statements that signify that we suspect children of evil intentions, such as that they are attention seeking, manipulative, 'out to get us' and that if we spared the rod, we would spoil the child. We cannot make statements like this about people of different races from ourselves, which signals that these are stereotypes – and if racism is offensive, ageism must be too.

Kohn (1992) rejects what he calls this 'sour' view of human nature. He notes that the qualities which we attribute to human nature are almost always the unsavoury ones – such as competitiveness or aggression – whereas we seldom blame 'human nature' for heroism or

DOI: 10.4324/9781003323938-6

altruism. Instead, we interpret heroic actions as evidence of the rare occasion when individuals triumph over their own base instincts. But everyday life is full of heroism: parents who attend a tedious job day after day to provide for their families; individuals who help each other in a crisis; people who visit the elderly and infirm; individuals who rescue others from natural disasters.... These acts of selflessness do not rate a mention on the nightly news or Twitter precisely *because* they are so commonplace.

My theories for counselling children all share the same trust that children want to learn skills that are useful in their lives, they want to surprise us with their achievements and want us to be proud for them (Holt, 1983). Yet, we do not trust children - perhaps, says Holt, because we were taught as children that we ourselves could not be trusted.

An extension of our suspicion of children is the recent phenomenon of criticising adolescents for being 'narcissistic'. However, self-absorption is essential during adolescence as young people adjust to the rapid physical, socioemotional and existential changes that cause a continual revision of their identity. Older critics were like that too, but they were too self-absorbed at the time to notice. (They were too busy wanting to live in a yellow submarine.)

Belief in children's competence

My second core principle is based on the constructionist view that children actively *construct* their understandings of their world. This view is in contrast to the philosopher John Locke, who saw children as bereft of useful knowledge, as 'blank slates', irrational and ignorant and, accordingly, in need of shaping, training, controlling and schooling (Lee, 2001; Montgomery, 2003).

My belief in children's competence means that I do not base my practice on developmental theory. This is because its focus is often on what young people can*not* do, rather than on what they *can*. My assumption has always been that young people are cleverer than we think. Therefore, I talk with them at a higher level than might be usual for their age and adjust my language only if they show that they do not understand.

It does, however, inform practice to know some developmental milestones, such as that renewed toileting accidents at the age of three are not a sign of an emotional problem but of the fact that children's brains can now concentrate for longer - but cannot yet alternate between their focus on their now-prolonged activity and the signals of a full bladder, and therefore they do not interrupt themselves in time to avoid toileting accidents. And it can help to know that three-year-olds are not being oppositional when they cannot follow a command: They simply cannot withdraw their focus instantaneously. Or that children do not achieve reliable emotion regulation until the ages of eight to 10 years, particularly for the hot emotions of anger and frustration (Gilliom et al., 2002). And it can pay to know that adolescents do not have immature executive control (which has been thought to underpin the likes of risk taking and impulsivity at this age), but instead their exercise of control is more flexible and variable, depending on the task demands and how salient the task is to them (Crone & Dahl, 2012). This type of knowledge allows us to be compassionate towards children rather than censuring them for their behaviours.

One adjustment, of course, is that children's attention span can be limited. (For adult-led activities, I use the equation of three minutes multiplied by their age in years, up to a maximum of 20 minutes.) Young people also need to move more than adults do and to eat more often than us, because their brain draws more glucose than does an adult's (Glaser, 2000). And, like adults, they might need time for a breather in which to process the conversation to that point. Therefore, we could have to 'drip feed' content for them more than we might for adults and allow them to digress off a topic to give them processing time. We might also need a larger room with more opportunity for movement; we might supplement talk therapy with the use of creative media; and might even leave the room to take a walk so that we can talk in parallel with young people if face-to-face conversation could seem confronting for them.

Children matter now

My third core principle is in opposition to the proclamations (often by politicians) that children are worth investing in, because they are 'our future'. This focus on the future leads to the concept of adults as gardeners, who intervene at each stage of children's growth, taking deliberate control over the types of plants (children) that flourish, training and feeding them in order to 'maximise their potential'. The focus is not on children's present needs, but on how they will turn out in the future. This perspective sees children as only *becoming* human. In comparison with adults who are regarded as being full human *beings*, children are seen as being incomplete and therefore unworthy of respect until they have grown up (Buckingham, 2000; Lee, 2001).

Instead, my belief is that children matter *now*, not for what they might become later in life. I recognise that young people have current needs and rights that deserve to be met. Coincidentally, when we meet children's needs, they will flourish not only at the time but also in later life.

Practices for counselling young people

Based on these three core principles, there are some practices that are unique to working with young people.

Power

More than any other client population, children are prone to having their perspectives discounted in favour of what others say about them (Madigan, 2019). It is vital, therefore, that counsellors do not adopt power over them but instead base our authority on being skilled at what we do - that is, we need to gain our authority from our *expertise*, from being wise, and from being connected to children, rather than from having power *over* young people (Gordon, 1991). This goes one step beyond a leadership role, to the role of facilitation. The distinction here is that, 'Leadership requires followers, but facilitating requires standing among others rather than standing apart' (Rogers & Freiberg, 1994, p. 103).

Communication with young people

I will not be detailing here communication skills or generic counselling skills relevant to clients of all age groups. For one thing, I assume that you have expertise in these already. Second, because we are all human, we each know the qualities of communication that we appreciate, and those that shut us down. That is, we already have a wellspring of knowledge about compassionate communication.

We also know what helps and what does not. To identify this knowledge, you might think about an occasion in the past when someone helped you. (Those of you who cannot identify such an occasion, breathe deeply ... and give yourself a moment to grieve before reading on.) Then consider the skills that your helper used, what effect they had on you and what this tells you about what might be useful to those who want your help.

The only communication change that I adopt for children is to lose the upward inflection at the end of each sentence that we call mother-ese (which I think of as 'squeaking' at children); instead, I just slow down the pace of my speech. I find that this allows younger children to understand what I am saying and also conveys that I am taking them seriously.

Involuntary clients

We must always keep in mind that young people are likely to be involuntary clients. They are often referred by adults and will commonly declare that they don't have a problem, but someone else has a problem with them. They believe that 'the system' has conspired against them and does not have their interests at heart (De Jong & Berg, 2001). Involuntary clients usually believe that they have not been given a choice to attend, a choice of goal, or a choice about how to achieve it (De Jong & Berg, 2013). This robs them of their dignity and can cause them to be reluctant to commit to counselling.

Starting by listening out for the successes in their lives via a wonderfulness interview is therefore a pleasant surprise and one that helps them to engage (De Jong & Berg, 2001). Subsequent solution-focused questioning is aimed at reinstating them as the expert in their lives, by asking what the referring person expects to be different and what clients think about those expectations (De Jong & Berg, 2001; Sklare, 2014):

- What makes (the referrer) think you should come here?
- Do you think (the referrer) is right to be concerned about you?
- In your opinion, how is that a problem for him/her?
- How is that a problem for you?
- What does (the referrer) think you should do differently?
- What would have to happen here for (the referring person) to come to believe that you don't need to come here anymore?
- What do you need to do to convince (the referrer) that you don't have to come back here?
- What would it take to reassure them that you don't have a problem?
- Knowing yourself, which of those things would you be willing to do?
- When was the last time you did that?
- What needs to come out of this so that you can say, 'Hey this wasn't my idea, but this turned out to be useful for me?'.

Authenticity

Adolescents highly value authenticity in relationships (Holliman & Foster, 2016) and especially with their health care professionals (Stige et al., 2021). Young clients particularly value their counsellor being a 'real person' and being interested in them as a person rather than a case on legs (Stige et al., 2021). To me, being real means not adopting a 'Holier than thou' stance, but neither a 'Jollier than thou' attitude - because when you are superficially nice, people don't respect you: They suspect you (Bryson, 2004). Being 'real' will also require admitting to and apologising for mistakes (Holliman & Foster, 2016).

Trust

It can be more difficult to develop trust with young people, especially those who have been traumatised or abused by adults. As a result of being mistreated, not listened to, misunderstood, treated with suspicion, regarded as 'naughty', manipulated with rewards and punishments and otherwise judged negatively, young people often have an 'enemy image' of adults, having come to see adults as controlling, judgmental and - indeed - 'the enemy'. Remember that this attitude, however, is not a reflection of you. You might explain that you plan to give them time to figure out if they can trust you, which, paradoxically, is likely to hasten the process. And being good at what you do, refusing to judge them and externalising their problem will build trust.

Neutrality

When counselling young people, we are even more than usually moved to want to protect them from the outcomes of their actions that, with their limited life experience, they do not realise would be harmful for them. However, humans' survival - both as individuals and as groups - demands that we achieve a balance between having to deal with too much change, and being so inflexible that we cannot adapt to new circumstances. This tension means that if an outside force demands that we change, we will attempt to maintain balance by favouring staying as we are.

Therefore, to avoid activating this rebalancing manoeuvre, you will have to be careful not to argue that clients should change their behaviour. That is, on the issue of whether they should change or not, you must be *neutral*. Amongst your preference questions, you will ask young people their reasons for wanting to change, but will not try to talk them into it.

This, however, is not the same as having no bias. In the fervent belief that they are making a mistake (say, with self-destructive behaviours), you can point out how gravely concerned you are about their ultimate decision. But, at the same time, you can add that you are aware that only they know what they want for their life.

Neither is neutrality the same as reverse psychology. With reverse psychology, you do not believe the suggestion and are trying to arrange for the other person to behave in a certain way; the principle of neutrality requires that you believe that no one can convince anyone to do anything.

Resistance

As just mentioned, change is difficult for humans - because some measure of stability is necessary for our survival. Therefore, when clients come to counselling saying that they want a change, they will also be frightened of changing. Sometimes, they are cautious and taking things slowly (Murphy, 2015). This, however, is not 'resistance'. Clients are just cooperating with their own rules.

Similarly, if clients are not going along with something counsellors say, it is because what we say has not captured their frame of reference or experience of the problem. We will need to change our approach instead of asking them to change (Molnar, 1986).

Engaging children playfully

Problems are always earnest and serious but are threatened by playfulness and humour. Therefore, we can employ open-ended play materials to enhance our work with young children (Berg & Steiner, 2003). Cloths can become veils, a river, or a cape; hand puppets can speak for the children when they cannot; and soft toys can bear witness to the changes they are making or be used to represent and thus externalise what is going on for them.

Children also need space so that they can move freely, play ball games, or use a stepping-stone or ladder scale that they can stand on as a gauge of their feelings and progress. You can use picture books to open a conversation about difficult topics such as their parents' divorce. You can give children a project of taking photos of places and activities where they feel safe, which they enjoy or which inspire them (for me, it would be the night sky) and together you can build this into a book about their resilience.

Berg and Steiner (2003) detail giving children a large sheet of paper, with six panels in which they can draw solution-building cartoons. In the first panel, they draw the problem; in the second panel they draw the helper (who could be fictional, or the children's counter-narrative identity) who supports them to deal with the problem; the third shows the solution that the child and helper used to create an exception to the problem; the fourth panel shows what is different for the child during an exception; the fifth focuses on the future when the exception becomes the norm; and the final panel is a sign that shows the child's gratitude to the helper.

Another of Berg and Steiner's (2003) suggestions is for you both to create a book about a child. Page one details their name, description, date of birth and favourite activities, food or people. On page two, the child lists simple things they have learned (such as to walk and talk), social skills and skills they have learned at school and at home. Page three includes what they would like to achieve next, and which abilities from page two will help them to do that.

When reviewing children's progress, you can give young children a bag of wooden blocks, and for every positive achievement that the children or their parents remember since your last meeting, the children can add a block to a stack, to build a tower of success (Berg & Steiner, 2003).

Trauma-informed practice

Our work with young people must be based on awareness that they are reactive to their circumstances, and that many of their emotional, social and behavioural difficulties have their roots in early adversity and trauma. This requires us to be:

- Trauma aware: understand the impact of trauma on young people.
- Trauma sensitive: practise in ways that do not re-traumatise them.

- Trauma responsive: enable clients to identify their internal resilience skills and external protective factors.
- Trauma informed: instil a culture throughout schools or other organisations that understands the effects of trauma on young people.

Conditions needed for change

Last in this chapter, I find it useful to keep in mind the four factors that need to be in place for people to be able to make changes their lives.

- Discomfort. This *motivates* change. Given that change is difficult for us (because we need stability), we only undertake it when we are in pain. (We do not get a divorce while our marriage is blissful: We divorce when we are miserable.) It is clear that anyone who comes to counselling voluntarily already experiences enough discomfort to want to change.
- Information about options. This *informs* change.
- Self-efficacy – the belief that we can make those alternatives a reality *empowers* change.
- Self-esteem. The conviction that we deserve better sparks the *courage* to make changes.

It is our job as counsellors to allow clients to sit with their discomfort when their antisocial actions warrant it, to use questions that invite them to explore their options, to assume that they can be powerful forces in their own lives and to treat them with dignity so that their deep sense of self-worth ignites a passion for change in the belief that they deserve it.

Conclusion

Given young people's powerlessness in their own lives, they will be especially sensitive to counsellors who adopt power over them and who purport to know more about them than they do themselves. In order to be authentic in our work, we need to scrutinise our assumptions, including our assumptions about the nature and competence of children.

References

Berg, I. K., & Steiner, S. (2003). *Children's solution work*. Norton.
Bryson, K. (2004). *Don't be nice, be real: Balancing passion for self with compassion for others* (rev. ed.). Elite Books.
Buckingham, D. (2000). *After the death of childhood: Growing up in the age of electronic media*. Polity Press.
Crone, E. A., & Dahl, R. E. (2012). Understanding adolescence as a period of social-affective engagement and goal flexibility. *Nature Reviews Neuroscience*, *13*(9), 636–650. https://doi.org/10.1038/nrn3313
De Jong, P., & Berg, I. K. (2001). Co-constructing cooperation with mandated clients. *Social Work*, *46*(4), 361–374. https://doi.org/10.1093/sw/46.4.361
De Jong, P., & Berg, I. K. (2013). *Interviewing for solutions* (3rd ed.). Brooks/Cole Thomson.
Gilliom, M., Shaw, D. S., Beck, J. E., Schonberg, M. A., & Lukon, J. L. (2002). Anger regulation in disadvantaged preschool boys: Strategies, antecedents, and the development of self-control. *Developmental Psychology*, *38*(2), 222–235. https://doi.org/10.1037//0012-1649.38.2.222
Glaser, D. (2000). Child abuse and neglect and the brain – A review. *Journal of Child Psychology and Psychiatry*, *41*(1), 97–116. https://doi.org/10.1017/S0021963099004990
Gordon, T. (1991). *Teaching children self-discipline at home and at school*. Random House.

Gullotta, T. P., Adams, G. R., & Markstrom, C. A. (2000). *The adolescent experience* (4th ed.). Academic Press.

Holliman, R. P., & Foster, R. D. (2016). Embodying and communicating authenticity in adolescent counseling. *Journal of Child and Adolescent Counseling, 2*(1), 61–76. https://doi.org/10.1080/23727810.2016.1160353

Holt, J. (1983). *How children learn* (rev. ed.). Merloyd Lawrence.

Kohn, A. (1992). *No contest: The case against competition* (rev. ed.). Houghton Mifflin.

Lee, N. (2001). *Childhood and society: Growing up in an age of uncertainty*. Open University Press.

Madigan, S. (2019). *Narrative therapy* (2nd ed.). American Psychological Association.

Molnar, A. (1986). A systemic perspective on solving problems in the school. *NASSP Bulletin, 70*(493), 32–40.

Montgomery, H. (2003). Childhood in time and place. In M. Woodhead & H. Montgomery (Eds.), *Understanding childhood: An interdisciplinary approach* (pp. 45–83). Open University Press.

Murphy, J. (2015). Solution-focused approaches. In H. T. Prout & A. L. Fedewa (Eds.), *Counseling and psychotherapy with children and adolescents* (5th ed., pp. 279–316). Wiley.

Peterson, C. (2014). *Looking forward through the life span: Developmental psychology* (6th ed.). Pearson.

Porteous, M. A. (1979). A survey of the problems of normal 15-year-olds. *Journal of Adolescence, 2*(4), 307–323. https://doi.org/10.1016/S0140-1971(79)80037-8

Rogers, C. R., & Freiberg, H. (1994). *Freedom to learn* (3rd ed.). Merrill.

Rutter, M., Graham, P., Chadwick, O. F. D., & Yule, W. (1976). Adolescent turmoil: Fact or fiction? *Journal of Child Psychology and Psychiatry, 17*(1), 35–56. https://doi.org/10.1111/j.1469-7610.1976.tb00372.x

Sklare, G. B. (2014). *Brief counseling that works: A solution-focused therapy approach for school counselors and other mental health professionals* (3rd ed.). Corwin.

Stige, S. H., Barca, T., Lavik, K. O., & Moltu, C. (2021). Barriers and facilitators in adolescent psychotherapy initiated by adults: Experiences that differentiate adolescents' trajectories through mental health care. *Frontiers in Psychology, 12*, 633663. https://doi.org/10.3389/fpsyg.2021.633663

6 Collaboration and consultation

When working with young people, we will often need to collaborate with their parents or other carers. The processes of collaborating with families and consultation with other professionals give us an opportunity to change the worlds to which children are reacting, instead of simply changing their reactions to those worlds (Ungar, 2015).

Models of collaboration with families

A key impediment to working in a collaborative fashion with parents is the modernist or 'clinical' model of service delivery which sees professionals as the experts, while parents and young people are seen as dysfunctional. This clinical model of intervention has been described as paternalistic, undermining and deficit-based (Dunst, 1985). It ignores valuable information that parents could supply about their child's and family's needs and overlooks the broader social and familial context in which the young person's needs are experienced and dealt with. Furthermore, discounting parents' views can lead to parents' ignoring professional advice or withdrawing from services. Disrespected parents simply 'vote with their feet'.

As discussed in Chapter 1, when professionals drive relationships with parents, it is assumed that they are exclusively qualified to apply a specialised body of knowledge, and that this is the only information relevant to the issue at hand (Osher & Osher, 2002; Thompson et al., 1997). They are the ones to assess young people's needs, interpret these to parents in a one-way flow of communication and formulate a program, with parents expected either to defer to advisers' diagnoses and comply with their recommendations, or clear the scene to allow the professionals to get on with their job. Parents must either passively accept professionals' advice, or go elsewhere (Osher & Osher, 2002).

This expert body of knowledge is a source of what has been termed *normalisation power*, in which advisers uphold a norm for how parents should behave, and then judge parents critically if they fall short of this ideal (Lasky, 2000). From their elevated position, professionals often regard parents as the source of their children's problems, particularly when their family is socially disadvantaged or has a structure other than the idealised nuclear family (Fylling & Sandvin, 1999). This deficit orientation criticises parents and leaves advisers feeling pessimistic about their ability to counteract family 'inadequacies' (Daniels & Shumow, 2003).

DOI: 10.4324/9781003323938-7

A more respectful option is a parent-driven model. This recognises that, more than being mere consumers or even equal participants in a partnership with you, parents are actually your employers. Their function is not to help you treat their children, but the reverse: They employ you to assist them in raising skilled, knowledgeable and well-adjusted children. They hire you for your expertise, much as they might employ doctors, naturopaths or dentists to support their children's health. Hence, in a parent-driven model, you are accountable to parents: They are not accountable to you.

This means that parents are the ones to steer their children's upbringing, and when searching for solutions to their children's difficulties, can be our consultants. This liberates counsellors from being responsible for fixing problems that they are not living with and therefore have no inside knowledge about.

Principles of solution-focused parental collaboration

Solution-focused interactions with parents recognise that they may have been co-opted somewhat involuntarily into discussing their child's difficulties with you. They would prefer not to have the problem in the first place, and if previous attempts at resolving it have been unsuccessful, will not relish the prospect of yet another encounter with professionals about their child's difficulties. Previous failed efforts can mean that parents' self-efficacy has been undermined and they might feel sceptical and lack hope about the chances of success of any new intervention.

Nevertheless, you both want what is best for the child. And all parents from all backgrounds want to be proud and have hope for their children (Berg & Steiner, 2003). When collaborating with parents, it is our task, therefore, to restore parents' pride in their children.

Finally, it is self-evident that you will be working with parents at times when there is a problem to be solved, rather than when all is going well. At such times of stress, it could be easy to fall into a trap of judging parents or assuming that their alleged personal or parenting deficiencies are the cause of their children's difficulties. However, children's difficulties can stress even a well-functioning family and can add intolerable pressure to one that is already strained. The stressor can be beyond the family's influence - as with poverty - or even be a product of the problem itself. This implies that the final key ingredient of collaborating with parents is to bear in mind that the child (or family) is not the problem: *The problem is the problem* (Winslade & Monk, 2007, p. 2).

Recruit parents' expertise

Given that they see their children in a wide variety of contexts and over a longer time period than anyone else, that children behave differently at home versus elsewhere, and that parents have intimate knowledge of their children's emotional well-being, parents will be more accurate than outsiders at describing their child's characteristic behaviours (Lindsay & Dockrell, 2000). This expertise will inform solutions. Using a solution-focused approach, the counsellor will adopt a curious stance, asking questions that draw out the child's and parents' own expertise. This, say Sokoly and Dokecki (1995, p. 191), gives the professional 'double vision' - that is, information from two perspectives - which will enrich the information on which solutions will be built. You will begin with the wonderfulness interview and problem description (see Chapters 2 and 3) and then ask consultancy questions about parents' views of how the problem can be solved, a sample of which are listed in Box 6.1. These explicitly capitalise on parents' knowledge.

Box 6.1 Consultancy questions

- Given that you know your child better than anyone else, what suggestions do you have for us to help him/her at school? (Murphy, 2006).
- You've spoken to your child's teachers about this in the past. What have we all missed so far that could help?
- If there was one useful question about your child that I could ask, what would that question be? (Selekman, 2010, p. 47).
- What have you witnessed (your child) doing recently that tells you she/he/they can overcome this problem?
- What can you tell me about (the child's) history that would help me understand how she/he/they managed to take this step?
- It seems that this accomplishment reflects some behind-the-scenes thinking that (your child) has been doing about what they want for their life. Were you aware of any signs that they were thinking this way? If so, what were the signs?
- If I meet another adolescent with similar issues in future, what could you tell me about how I might help that young person?
- (To the young person): What are your suggestions of how your parents/teachers could help with this?

Landscape of identity questions

- What do these problems with your son/daughter have you believing about yourselves as parents?
- What do these difficulties that you're enduring right now tell you about your strengths and survival skills?
- What will life be like when Failure no longer speaks to you of your identity as a parent?
- What does your being here tell you about your resistance to losing hope for your child?
- Who in your life would be least surprised that you continue to hold onto hope that there is something you can do to help your child, and resist the view of yourself as a failure?

Preference questions

- Is this description of your family how you want it to be?
- How would you prefer that others see you?
- Is the havoc that your guilt as a parent is wreaking on your life and relationship with your child acceptable to you? Or would you prefer to break free of the tyranny of this guilt? (White, 2016).

Despondency questions

- What does your worry for your son/daughter tell you about your feelings for them?
- What is it about him/her that tells you she/he/they can do better? (Berg & Steiner, 2003).
- What is going well for (name the young person)?
- What needs to happen to encourage more of that success?

Next, you will highlight exceptions or, for more entrenched difficulties, might externalise the problem and examine its pattern of entry, its allies, how it affects the child and family and how they affect it (see Chapter 3). The discussion will then centre on how the young person and parents could influence the problem in future.

Collaboration with families in adversity

A solution-focused approach is the same for families experiencing multiple problems as for those who are more advantaged: Find out from parents which problem is their priority and assist them in solving that (Fisch & Schlanger, 1999). This will relieve the most stress and might open the way for spontaneous improvement of other troubling aspects of their lives, or their early success will bolster their self-efficacy for solving their next problem.

Although you are powerless to control external factors that undermine parents' self-efficacy, you can challenge the message they often convey to parents about their worth. You can ask marginalised parents what it is like for them to have to function under oppression: Does poverty, violence or racism cause them to believe that they cannot raise healthy children? Do they feel criticised and believe that they have to be perfect to counter stereotypes about single parents (say), or about members of their culture? How do they manage to raise their children in a loving way in an environment characterised by poverty, prejudice, disadvantage or violence? (De Jong & Berg, 2013)

Consultation

Often, the role of counsellor of young people will involve consulting with those who work directly with them - such as teachers, school counsellors or special educators. Your joint efforts can help generate new solutions to chronic difficulties. Successful consultation involves having mutual goals, sharing problem solving and decision making, and valuing each party's expertise (Friend, 2020).

When acting as a consultant within schools, you need to keep in mind that the parents or classroom teachers employ you for your specialist knowledge and, therefore, being your employers, they are the ones who drive the interaction. The consultant is accountable to the teacher and responsible for suggesting appropriate and feasible solutions (Friend, 2020), which requires familiarity with the teacher's setting and its constraints. For their part, teachers will also be responsible for generating potential solutions, but they have the ultimate authority to determine which are practicable in their classrooms. They are also expected to be open to being innovative and incorporating adjustments to their practices.

The typical expectation of consultants in schools is that they adopt a clinical style of assessment to diagnose a cause for students' difficulties in order to generate a prescription detailing what teachers and parents can do about them (Wagner & Gillies, 2001). Instead, solution-oriented case conferences will not yield a 'laundry list' of what is going wrong but can follow the same format as used with the young people themselves (Harker, 2001). That is, they will describe and, if necessary, re-define the problem, formulate goals, discuss and highlight exceptions, note the skills employed by those involved to bring these exceptions about, and then plan to do more of what is working.

Useful questions that consultants can ask teachers, parents or students include (Murphy, 2015; Wagner & Gillies, 2001):

- When faced with this kind of issue before, what did you do that worked?
- How can your experience of similar challenges help you with solving this one?
- What effects did you notice?
- How do you explain those?
- How did you turn that into something that was useful?
- How might you do that again?

Each person involved can rate the behavioural problem on a scale of 1 to 10 before, during and after the planned intervention. The different ratings by various stakeholders and by the same person over time help identify what contributes to the higher ratings, can clarify what goal is realistic ('What rating would you settle for?') and, later, can document progress (Harker, 2001).

The first meeting can close on questions such as the following (Wagner & Gillies, 2001, p.156).

- How close are we to making a plan?
- What else do we need to consider?
- What would it take to put these ideas into action?
- If you were to do this as an experiment, where would you start?

When acting as a consultant, it pays to be clear who your client is. If you are employed by and work in the school, the school is often the client. This makes it difficult to advocate for students' needs without jeopardising your relationships with school staff. In contrast, if you are an outside consultant, it is easier for the young person to be your client, particularly when you are being paid by that child's parents. This difference can make a difference.

Advocacy

Perceived injustices at the hands of teachers and feelings of being 'picked on' rank high in students' list of school-based problems that affect their emotional and behavioural adjustment at school (Farrell et al., 2006). Young people are still often treated as the object of adults' actions, rather than being the subjects in their own lives, with the result that they seldom have opportunities to participate in making decisions that affect themselves (Johnny, 2006). When students lack a voice, it can be necessary for counsellors to advocate for them.

Advocacy is about removing external barriers to equal opportunities for all, in the service of clients' well-being. It involves four sets of knowledge (Tarhan, 2022):

- of resources that can support clients
- of the system, such as the school, child welfare or the justice systems
- of dispute resolution mechanisms
- of what systems need in order to change.

Meanwhile, advocates need skills for communicating, consulting and problem resolution, plus the dispositions to think and act autonomously and to take risks for those in need (Tarhan, 2022). A strong sense of justice and honouring of diversity underpin the exercise of this knowledge and these skills and dispositions.

While achieving social justice is beyond the capabilities of a single practitioner, it is possible to advocate for distributive justice within schools (where opportunities and resources are equitably allocated according to need) and for procedural justice, which is students' right to voice their point of view and to appeal decisions made about them (Sanches et al., 2012). When students experience their teachers as fair, they are likely to remain committed to the school, to education and to their own learning (Adams & Forsyth, 2009; Roeser et al., 1998).

Advocacy for teachers who, for example, are treated unfairly by aggrieved parents, is not the role of school counsellors but of school administrators. However, when teachers are being treated unfairly by students, counsellors' role will be to discover students' grievance and to ask them which other ways they could express their dissatisfaction without violating the rights of their teachers to feel safe.

Conclusion

When working with families, above all, it is crucial to ensure that parents maintain their confidence in their own skills for meeting their child's needs and retain their ability to act as leaders in their family. Therefore, you will need to consider the impact of your work on the whole family. Professionals are only ever small stakeholders in children's lives compared with their parents. This means that you will need to be a resource and source of support to families, but not a decision maker or a substitute family leader. You will need to resist professional dominance, so that families see that you trust their judgement and stand by their knowledge.

References

Adams, C. M., & Forsyth, P. B. (2009). The nature and function of trust in schools. *Journal of School Leadership*, *19*(2), 126–152. https://doi.org/10.1177/105268460901900201

Berg, I. K., & Steiner, S. (2003). *Children's solution work*. Norton.

Daniels, D. H., & Shumow, L. (2003). Child development and classroom teaching: A review of the literature and implications for educating teachers. *Journal of Applied Developmental Psychology*, *23*(5), 495–526. https://doi.org/10.1016/S0193-3973(02)00139-9

De Jong, P., & Berg, I. K. (2013). *Interviewing for solutions* (3rd ed.). Brooks/Cole Thomson.

Dunst, C. J. (1985). Rethinking early intervention. *Analysis and Intervention in Developmental Disabilities*, *5*, 165–201. https://doi.org/10.1016/S0270-4684(85)80012-4

Farrell, A. D., Sullivan, T. N., Kliewer, W., Allison, K. W., Erwin, E. H., Meyer, A. L., & Esposito, L. (2006). Peer and school problems in the lives of urban adolescents: Frequency, difficulty, and relation to adjustment. *Journal of School Psychology*, *44*(3), 169–190. https://doi.org/10.1016/j.jsp.2006.02.001

Fisch, R., & Schlanger, K. (1999). *Brief therapy with intimidating cases: Changing the unchangeable*. Jossey-Bass.

Friend, M. (2020). *Interactions: Collaboration skills for school professionals* (9th ed.). Pearson.

Fylling, I., & Sandvin, J. T. (1999). The role of parents in special education: The notion of partnership revised. *European Journal of Special Needs Education*, *14*(2), 144–157. https://doi.org/10.1080/0885625990140205

Harker, M. (2001). How to build solutions at meetings. In Y. Ajmal & I. Rees (Eds.), *Solutions in schools* (pp. 30–44). BT Press.

Johnny, L. (2006). Reconceptualising childhood: Children's rights and youth participation in schools. *International Education Journal*, *7*(1), 17–25.

Lasky, S. (2000). The cultural and emotional politics of teacher-parent interactions. *Teaching and Teacher Education*, *16*(8), 843–860. https://doi.org/10.1016/S0742-051X(00)00030-5

Lindsay, G., & Dockrell, J. (2000). The behaviour and self-esteem of children with specific speech and language difficulties. *British Journal of Educational Psychology*, *70*(4), 583–601. https://doi.org/10.1348/000709900158317

Murphy, J. J. (2006). *Solution-focused counseling in middle and high schools*. Pearson Merrill Prentice Hall.

Murphy, J. J. (2015). Solution-focused approaches. In H. T. Prout & A. L. Fedewa (Eds.), *Counseling and psychotherapy with children and adolescents* (5th ed., pp. 279–316). Wiley.

Osher, T. W., & Osher, D. M. (2002). The paradigm shift to true collaboration with families. *Journal of Child and Family Studies*, *11*(1), 47–60. https://doi.org/10.1023/A:1014715527823

Roeser, R. W., Eccles, J. S., & Sameroff, A. J. (1998). Academic and emotional functioning in early adolescence: Longitudinal relations, patterns, and prediction by experience in middle school. *Development and Psychopathology*, *10*(2), 321–352. https://doi.org/10.1017/S0954579498001631

Sanches, C., Gouveia-Pereira, M., & Carugati, F. (2012). Justice judgements, school failure, and adolescent deviant behaviour. *British Journal of Educational Psychology*, *82*(4), 606–621. https://doi.org/10.1111/j.2044-8279.2011.02048.x

Selekman, M. D. (2010). *Collaborative brief therapy with children*. Guilford.

Sokoly, M. M., & Dokecki, P. R. (1995). Ethical perspectives on family-centred early intervention. In J. A. Blackman (Ed.), *Working with families in early intervention* (pp. 186–198). Aspen.

Tarhan, S. (2022). School counsellors' perceptions of justice and awareness of advocacy duties. *Journal of Qualitative Research in Education*, *29*, 33–55. https://doi.org/10.14689/enad.29.2

Thompson, L., Lobb, C., Elling, R., Herman, S., Jurkiewicz, T., & Hulleza, C. (1997). Pathways to family empowerment: Effects of family-centered delivery of early intervention services. *Exceptional Children*, *64*(1), 99–113. https://doi.org/10.1177/001440299706400107

Ungar, M. (2015). *Working with children and youth with complex needs: 20 skills to build resilience*. Routledge.

Wagner, P., & Gillies, E. (2001). Consultation: A solution-focused approach. In Y. Ajmal & I. Rees (Eds.), *Solutions in schools* (pp. 147–162). BT Press.

White, M. (2016). *Narrative therapy classics*. Dulwich Centre Publications.

Winslade, J., & Monk, G. (2007). *Narrative counseling in schools: Powerful and brief* (2nd ed.). Corwin Press.

7 Ethics of working with young people

Ethics are principles of conduct that direct us to act in a manner consistent with our professed values (Mattison, 2000). Our response to ethical dilemmas reflects how we have learned to think about ethical issues (Mattison, 2000), which requires us to be attuned to dilemmas, aware of our own values and how we prioritise these, considerate of clients' social context, willing to sit with ambiguity, and open to critical reflection about our decisions.

In previous chapters I have outlined some evidence for my ways of working with young people. However, for methods to be of value, they need to do more than simply work: They also need to be ethical - in not just an individual sense as I will be discussing here, but in a social and cultural sense. Here I am referring to the ethical imperative to question the dominant views of children as incompetent, of young people with emotional, social or behavioural difficulties as sick or damaged, and of counselling itself as being a neutral process, when it often (along with its predecessors, psychiatry and psychology) entrenches a medicalised view of clients as the source of their own difficulties, disregarding social constraints on them (Besley, 2001). This means that counselling is inherently a political endeavour, which is to say that it is based within social systems of power (Madigan, 2019).

Power

The history of civilisation is a history of the abuse of the power of the privileged over the marginalised. Hence, the responsible use of power is a key dimension of professional ethics in counselling. It is particularly vital when working with young people because of the difference between adults' and young people's 'psychological size'. Youth live in a world where adults have the power over every aspect of their lives and even their bodies, including their food intake, their posture at their school desk, and their sleeping patterns. As a result, young people are sensitised to adults' efforts to impose power over them.

The social science disciplines pronounce that they have access to the 'truth' about individual psychology, and permit practitioners 'to speak with authority beyond the range of their personal experience' (Parker & Shotter, 1990, in White, 2016, p. 46). Yet other people's lives will always be beyond counsellors' personal experience and, therefore, we must trust clients to know and tell their own story. Ethically, we need to make it our business to collaborate with them as they reclaim their story-telling rights in the service of recapturing agency in their own lives (White, 2016).

DOI: 10.4324/9781003323938-8

Types of power

Power includes hard power, role (or status) power, soft power, and personal power - see Figure 7.1. Hard power emanates from and is legitimatised by federal or state laws, and is then further authorised by professional organisations that regulate counsellors' actions (Zur, 2007). Examples of hard power are that counsellors are often in a position to recommend the removal of children from their families, or to report any illegal behaviour of their clients. Counsellors also have the power to generate progress or compliance reports that reflect on young clients and influence the systems around them, such as the courts (Barstow, 2008).

A second type of power, role or status power, is the status conferred by one's professional standing. Counselling theories allow professionals the power to diagnose what is happening with someone else's life, defining them and depriving them of the rights to tell their own story (White, 2016). Professionals get to define what is normal and to scrutinise and even police those who do not measure up (White, 2016). Females, parents - and mothers in particular - minority group members, and young people are the most likely to be silenced.

In helping professions, the third type of power - soft power - is an inherent element of the therapeutic relationship. The three forms of soft power are expert, referent and connection power. Well used, *expert* power has tremendous value in giving clients confidence in the expertise of their counsellor, providing for clients a safe space to be themselves, giving them clarity about their goals, and providing resources to support their attainment of these. One potential outcome of this is that young clients will confer *referent* power on their counsellors, in which they identify with their counsellors and wish to emulate their best qualities. The third form of soft power, *connection* power, is achieved through an affirming alliance between counsellors and their clients.

Finally, personal power is the ability to have an effect on and to influence others. I think of this as power *with*, rather than power *over*. This type of power underpins the decentred stance of the counsellor (see Chapter 1).

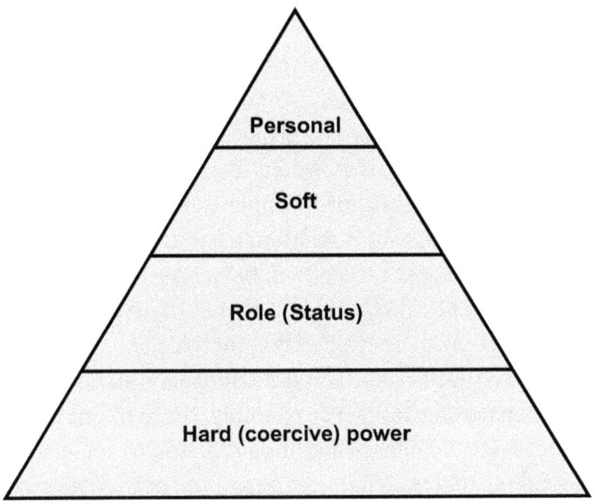

Figure 7.1 Types of power

Source: adapted from Laverack (2009).

An ethic of care

Work with young people needs to be guided by an ethic of caring. This is a choice to place a premium on children's well-being over control (McLaughlin, 1991). It represents fidelity to adults' moral obligation to be responsive to children's needs. An ethic of care is underpinned by an ethic of compassion towards others, which entails being aware of their suffering, being emotionally or cognitively moved by it, and being motivated to respond to it (Hiatt, 2022).

Ethical dilemmas

An ethical dilemma is not a case of choosing right from wrong. That would be easy. Instead, dilemmas occur when all potential courses of action could have negative outcomes. Dilemmas can arise in a number of circumstances, such as the following (Johnson et al., 2022; Scaturo, 2002).

- Conflict between guidelines, where ethical codes, the law or organisational policy are in conflict with each other. For example, in Queensland, counsellors are not mandated notifiers of child abuse, but the counsellor's employer might require that counsellors make reports of suspected child maltreatment.
- Conflict of principles, where one or more ethical principles are competing. For example, the principles of autonomy and nonmaleficence (see below) can be in conflict with each other when the counsellor wants to avoid harm to suicidal clients by involuntarily committing them to hospital.
- Conflict of one's own values. One's own values might conflict with professional ethics or the law. To repeat the previous example, even if not mandated in one's state to report child abuse, our personal ethics would demand that we do so.
- Conflict of values with clients. Our ethics can also conflict with clients' values. Corey et al. (2019) claim that this is a simple dilemma to resolve in that counsellors must work within clients' value system, not their own. This is a relativist stance: that practices are relative to their culture. However, I am an absolutist in that I contend that, regardless of culture, some practices – such as child marriage or genital mutilation – are absolutely unethical because they do not uphold the innate dignity and physical integrity of individuals (Mitchell, 1993). Given that these are criminal acts, they would require notification to the police.
- Competing interests. The interests of multiple parties can be in conflict. A common instance of this is where adults want children's behaviour to be managed, whereas the traumatised child needs support rather than behaviourist interventions.
- Competing loyalties. It can be difficult to know what to do when a supervisor or manager advises or even orders counsellors to behave unethically.
- Compromise dilemmas. These occur when a counsellor struggles between ideal versus pragmatic interventions with clients. For example, there might be insufficient resources to provide an ideal service. Or clients might be reacting to social injustice, in response to which counsellors might feel impelled to engage in social justice advocacy despite this role being outside the scope of their employment conditions.
- Boundary dilemmas. The counsellor is confronted by a choice as to whether or not to cross boundaries, such as when suicidal clients need after-hours support.

- Dilemmas of allegiance. The counsellor has an allegiance to a particular school of thought and believes that branching into other therapeutic modalities might cause a loss of support from their original peer group.
- Dilemmas of responsibility. The counsellor struggles between accepting a certain degree of responsibility for young clients' welfare versus respecting their autonomy and accountability for their own life choices.
- Impasse dilemmas. Counsellors become uncertain about what to do when clients' difficulties are intractable and progress is frozen: Should they discontinue treatment, or is this phase merely a plateau and progress will resume with persistence?
- Competence dilemmas. If counsellors are not qualified to deal with a particular presenting problem, should they refer to someone with the expertise, or would the client experience this as rejection or, perhaps having already formed a bond with their counsellor, might not attend the new service and thereby receive no professional support at all?

Influences on ethical practice

In resolving ethical dilemmas, we need to consider many influences (see Figure 7.2): relevant legislation, our professional codes of ethics, the ethical principles they enshrine, ethical lenses, organisational policies, and the particular needs of especially vulnerable clients. All of these will be influenced by our work setting.

The law

The law represents minimum standards of conduct in society. It emphasises order, rationality, stability, and fact-finding ('beyond reasonable doubt'). Created by government and enforced by law enforcement agencies, it applies common standards for all citizens. It specifies what *not* to do (which are legal imperatives).

At the time of writing, in Australia, counsellors and psychotherapists are not subject to Health Practitioner Regulation National Law (2009). In this vacuum, a National Code of

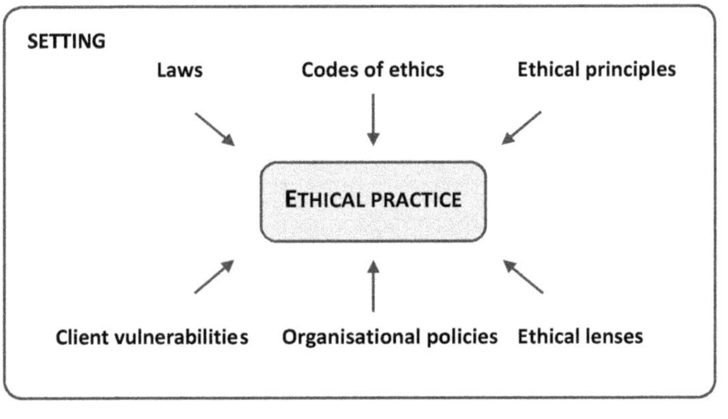

Figure 7.2 Influences on ethical practice

Conduct for Healthcare Workers is being developed. For public protection, some states have developed their own Code of Conduct for unregistered health practitioners.

The onus is on counsellors to know the legislation in their state or territory. However, when providing online counselling, the applicable legislation is that in the clients' state or territory, which might be different from legislation in the counsellors' location (Bolton, 2017).

Codes of ethics

A second source of guidance when resolving ethical dilemmas is professionals' codes of ethics. In Australia, these are provided by the Australian Counsellors' Association (ACA, 2022) and the Psychotherapy and Counselling Federation of Australia (PACFA, 2021). These codes are designed to protect recipients of professional services by helping to define professionals' responsibilities to their clients and guiding professionals in their conduct of that service. Many codes of ethics also specify penalties for violations and, in this way, make practitioners accountable for their practices.

The purpose of codes is not for practitioners to arrive at a predetermined outcome for an ethical dilemma, but one that is particular to the client and context but which adheres to the core principles (Thannhausser et al., 2021). Nevertheless, codes of ethics enshrine broad expectations and can serve only as starting points for making decisions. Like legislation, codes of ethics often specify minimum standards of conduct only, which Barnett (2019) refers to as an *ethical floor*, a level below which practitioners must not fall.

Ethical principles

The next influence on ethical practice is the core ethical principles, which Kitchener (1984) was the first to detail. These principles are binding, which is to say that they impose an obligation on professionals to uphold them, except in special circumstances (Kitchener, 1984).

Autonomy. Counsellors' principles and practices in word and deed will support clients' freedom to be autonomous or self-determining because individuals' dignity rests on their ability to choose freely what they will do with their lives (Kant, 1785/1996). Freedom requires that clients are free *to* choose how *to* live their life and are free *from* unnecessary constraints.

Nonmaleficence (pronounced non-mal-*eff*-i-sense). This is the principle that counsellors must do no harm to clients. Our practices must be respectful of clients and in no way 'degrade, endanger, exploit, intimidate or harm them psychologically or physically' (AECA, 1991, p. 4). This implies that practitioners have a responsibility to be competent, which includes knowing theories, being familiar with a range of treatment options, and being aware of their own limitations and how to refer clients to other practitioners as needed. This principle also requires that we reflect on and evaluate our practices and their outcomes.

But at a deeper level than technique, we need to be aware of the harm caused when we impose expert power on clients, especially when our diagnoses come to define them by their problems, dehumanise them (Kitchener, 1984) or excuse them from taking responsibility for their own actions, which disadvantages both them and those who are the targets of their behaviour.

Beneficence. This third ethical principle is that counsellors must promote clients' health and welfare. At the same time, however, we must understand that it is not up to us to determine what is in their best interests, and that such a paternalistic (or parentalistic to be gender-neutral) stance would violate clients' right to autonomy.

Justice. Counsellors will be fair and equitable in their treatment of all clients. Nevertheless, an equal right to treatment does not mean the right to equal treatment, because individuals are diverse and therefore will need different things. Corey et al. (2019) note that if interventions are not available to some segments of society, the principle of justice is being violated. Therefore, in practice, we might need to consider whether devoting considerable resources to one individual or a particular group of clients could deprive others of the possibility of receiving any service at all.

Fidelity. This principle involves faithfulness, which requires counsellors to make realistic commitments and do their best to keep their word. It is at the core of a trusting alliance between counsellor and client, of informed consent, and of our duty to maintain client confidentiality except in exceptional circumstances (Kitchener, 1984).

These principles are typically presented as an holistic set of discrete and equally valued ideals yet, at times, upholding one principle can undermine others. Nevertheless, our principles do not disappear, but some can become a higher priority than others, depending on the circumstances. This is like dice: Although all faces are constant, the one that is uppermost will drive our actions in any given situation.

Ethical lenses

When having to choose between various potential actions, ethical lenses are the criteria by which we make our selection. In choosing how to respond to a dilemma, we could select one of six ethical lenses (Velasquez et al., 2015).

First is the *deontological* lens (or principle ethics). This approach maintains that fixed moral rules or laws should define the rightness or wrongness of actions (Mattison, 2000). Hence, principle ethics are grounded in concepts of duty and obligation - the ethics of 'should' and 'ought' (Duffy et al., 2018). Focusing on which rules, principles or duties apply in the situation, the deontological approach asks, 'What is intrinsically the right or wrong thing to do?'. Adherence to rules, laws and principles is central. Accordingly, this approach is inflexible and absolutist.

Second is the *teleological* (or 'consequentialist') approach. This asks, 'What is the most beneficial thing to do in this circumstance?'. It focuses on assessing potential outcomes of the various options. This, however, is difficult because not all outcomes can be predicted. This is a relativistic or flexible perspective, in which the ends can (at times) justify the means. This is based on the 19th-century utilitarian philosophers, Jeremy Bentham and John Stuart Mill, who contended that laws which were morally best were those that worked best (had greatest *utility*) in that the most ethical action will be the one that produces the greatest good for the greatest number of people.

Third, the *virtue* approach to ethics assumes that there are certain ideals towards which we should strive. Hence, the virtues or moral character of the counsellor are the most important element of ethical practice. Accordingly, this approach calls on counsellors to reflect on and examine their values, as well as other aspects such as unresolved emotional issues that could influence their decision. Under this approach, the selection of a course of action relies on an answer to the question, 'Who do I want to be in this circumstance?'. Nevertheless, professionals cannot simply rely on our own ethical standards because these are not all equally valid (Cottone et al., 2021). Therefore, we will need a structured framework for decision making, as discussed shortly.

The fourth ethical lens is the *rights* approach. It asks, 'Whose rights are at stake, and whose should be paramount?'. Through this lens, actions are judged to be wrong if they violate the rights of individuals; the more serious the violation, the more wrongful the action (Velasquez et al., 2015).

The fifth ethical lens is the fairness or *justice* approach. It asks, 'What is just for all concerned?'. This has its roots in the teachings of the ancient Greek philosopher, Aristotle, who said that 'equals should be treated equally and unequals unequally'. The basic moral questions in this approach are, 'How fair is a proposed action? and 'Does it treat everyone in the same way, or does it show favouritism and discrimination?' (Velasquez et al., 2015). Favouritism gives benefits to some individuals without a justifiable reason for singling them out; discrimination imposes burdens on people who are no different from those on whom burdens are not imposed (Velasquez et al., 2015). According to this approach, both favouritism and discrimination are unjust and wrong.

The final ethical lens is *relational* ethics, which asks, 'What is the social and political context?'. This approach affirms the 'inseparability of the ethical and the political' (Duffy et al., 2018, p. 322) – that is, the power relationships between individuals and the various sectors of society.

Organisational policies

Another influence on counsellors' ethical decision making is the policies of their employer. Sometimes, organisational policies plug gaps in the law or codes of ethics. For example, although in Queensland counsellors are not mandated notifiers of child abuse or neglect, the policy of counsellors' employers might require them to report. On the other hand, policies can sometimes work against the interests of clients, favouring instead the needs of the institution. For example, when organisations have a religious sponsor whose beliefs and counselling practices might conflict with clients' lifestyles, their values must be made explicit if client consent is to be fully informed (Mitchell, 1993).

Client vulnerabilities

Next, our ethical decision making needs to take account of particularly vulnerable clients. In addition to being discriminated against on the basis of their age, young people can be marginalised in other ways, such as having a disability or being a cultural or sexual minority. This will change their needs and hence our ways of supporting them.

Settings

Finally, all of these outside influences have differing effects depending on where one practises. In private practice, lines of accountability are clearer, compared with working within a multi- or trans-disciplinary team. On the other hand, it can be less clear in private practice settings about who is the client, given that parents will be paying for the service and usually need to consent to it. In this setting, confidentiality and privacy will also have their limits, as the parents might be seen to be a joint client with the child.

School counselling and chaplaincy have a distinct advantage that young people see school-based practitioners around the school, in which case they might drop in casually to sound out the counsellor or be more willing to see the counsellor for a planned consultation. On the other hand, this informality can blur the lines of when parental consent is needed. (Some schools avoid this dilemma by requiring parents to consent at enrolment to their children's consulting a counsellor.)

In contrast to external child psychologists, in many respects for school-based counsellors, the school is the client, not the child. It can be difficult for school counsellors to advocate for changes to the culture of a school for fear of alienating school staff, on whose goodwill they rely for collegiality and continued support for clients.

Frameworks for decision making

With so many aspects to consider, we need a systematic process for ethical decision making. To that end, ethical decision-making models aim to provide a structure for decision making, so that elements are not overlooked and professionals can be accountable for their ultimate decision. Models provide scaffolding - particularly for novice practitioners - towards ethical competence (Johnson et al., 2022). Research has shown that the use of a model to guide decision making produces better decisions than the application of ethical principles and codes alone, although intuition and experience also contribute to competent decision making (Johnson et al., 2022).

I present one of many potential models in Figure 7.3, where the first, preparatory, steps involve identifying a dilemma and the stakeholders and being familiar with any laws, codes, principles and policies that need to be brought to bear on the dilemma. Subsequent steps involve consulting with clients and colleagues.

In the active problem-solving phase, you will consider your options, apply ethical principles to choose between these, enact your choice and document the process. Documentation is

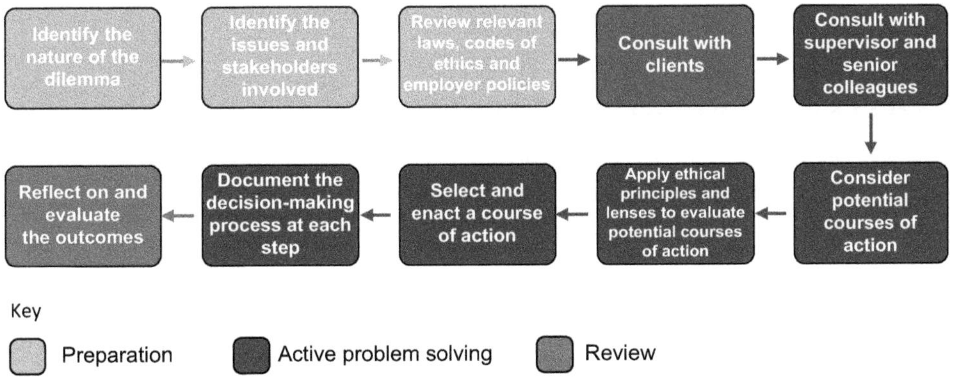

Figure 7.3 A framework for ethical decision making

vital because, 'If it isn't written down, it didn't happen' (Welfel, 2016, p. 54). To ensure accountability, documentation must happen at the time decisions are being made, rather than after the event.

Finally, counsellors will review and reflect on the outcomes of their decision. Accountability involves being willing to give account of what we have or have not done. It will take into consideration how the decision aligns with external guidelines or expectations. It will include a full assessment of what we had to work with (without making excuses), and what we brought to the situation (without self-deception or rationalisation) (Carroll & Shaw, 2012).

Consultation with supervisors and trusted colleagues will occur throughout the decision-making process to provide a wide view of the problem and provoke reconsideration of your options by answering questions such as (Welfel, 2016, p. 50):

- Which facts of the case seem most important?
- What have I not considered?
- What sociocultural considerations am I overlooking or misunderstanding?
- How is my background and sociocultural context affecting my thinking?
- Is my interpretation of the Codes of ethics and relevant laws accurate?
- Does my analysis of the ethical principles appear sound?

While the process of decision making illustrated in Figure 7.3 appears linear, McAuliffe and Chenoweth (2008) and Cottone et al. (2021) add additional 'essential dimensions' that must be applied at each step:

- Critical reflection: to recognise how one's own values affect one's decisions.
- Cultural sensitivity: involving respect for the world views of others and balancing others' perspectives with one's own.
- Consultation with clients and others who might assist us to uphold important values (Johnson et al., 2022).
- Attending to the social context. This has two elements: The first is regarding decision making not as a psychological process, but as occurring in interactions with others. To ensure that counsellors do not monopolise power in the decision-making process, clients are as fully engaged as possible in arriving at a resolution of an ethical dilemma (Cottone et al., 2021). Second, this aspect considers the effects of the decisions on relationships with clients, colleagues and the profession.

The ethics of counselling practices

In this section, I discuss practices that carry ethical obligations: counselling contracts, consent, privacy and confidentiality, maintaining boundaries, exchanging gifts, self-disclosure, multiple relationships, the use of touch, and sexual contact with clients.

The counselling contract

The contract for therapy services is a legal agreement, that is, enforceable by law. It is based on a fiduciary relationship, which is a relationship of trust that invokes the duty to act in the best interests of client. It is also a financial agreement, with fee schedules and payment options clearly specified. Third, the contract for therapy services is also an ethical agreement, informed by ethical principles of the profession. Therefore, it must specify the measures to safeguard privacy and privileged communication and the limits of confidentiality. It must communicate clearly what is involved in the counselling process so that consent is informed.

When writing a contract, particularly for young clients, we need to consider its readability, given their literacy levels, how clearly it explains key terms (e.g. confidentiality and privacy), and ensure that clients have an opportunity to ask questions and seek clarification about its terms and conditions.

Informed consent

Seeking clients' consent conveys respect for their decision-making skills; increases their sense of ownership of the counselling process; and, by demystifying the process, can reduce their anxieties (Fisher & Oransky, 2008). Given that consent is achieved in collaboration with clients, consent procedures establish counsellor and client as partners working towards a common goal and, in so doing, can improve the effectiveness of therapy.

Information to which clients will need to consent includes (Carnes-Holt et al., 2016; Fisher & Oransky, 2008):

- the duration of each session
- the anticipated length of treatment, with clarification that this might be reassessed as counselling evolves
- therapeutic techniques
- whether any of these techniques are new or experimental
- whether the counsellor is qualified to use them (e.g. is a trainee)
- who will be supervising the counsellor
- criteria for termination
- the limits of confidentiality
- fees and payment options
- whether information will be exchanged with other involved professionals.

Consent comes in four types (Rekers, 1984). First is *legal* consent, in which one person (such as a parent) might give consent as a surrogate for another (such as their child). Although legal consent is given by an adult, it is still important to explain issues such as limits to confidentiality with children in a way that they can understand. One challenge with legal consent is that for children whose parents have divorced, unless one parent has sole custody and care, the consent of both parents is the ideal. With adolescents, unless they are legally emancipated, a challenge can be that, although they might be underage, they might not wish you to contact their parents to gain parental consent. This is complicated by the mature minors doctrine which requires that we grant mature young people the right to autonomous decisions (Thannhauser et al., 2021).

Second is that the person must be *competent* enough to be capable of giving consent. Individuals who might not be able to give informed consent include those with intellectual disabilities or very young children. These clients will be capable instead of giving 'assent' in that they trust that adults will work in their best interests, complemented by consent from a legally recognised surrogate (a parent or guardian) (Lambert & Glacken, 2011).

Third, consent must be *informed*. It is vital that clients' consent is with understanding (Corey et al., 2019). This means that a range of viable interventions are considered and discussed with clients. Informed consent is in one sense more difficult with young children in that they might not understand what they are consenting to; on the other hand, the younger they are, the more willing they are to *assent*.

Fourth, consent must be *voluntary*. This means that counsellors must not threaten unfair outcomes for withholding consent, nor make extravagant claims about the benefits of participating in counselling. Clients' desperation or professionals' status can mean that they are subtly pressured into giving consent. Therefore, the onus is on us to ensure that what clients are agreeing to represents best practice.

Lambert and Glacken (2011, p. 783) use the following acronym to define consent:

C Consider the person's competence or capacity to give consent.
O Offer sufficient and appropriate information to make a decision, both verbally and, where the young people can read, in writing.
N No pressure is applied for clients to give their consent.
S Search for subtle signs of refusal.
E Evidence of clients' understanding is sought and demonstrated via questions and feedback.
N Negotiate consent continually because consent is an ongoing process that is designed around the clients' evolving needs (Fisher & Oransky, 2008).
T Clients have time to think about their decision.

Privacy

Privacy is clients' legal right to control their personal information (Corey et al., 2019). All health professionals in Australia are governed by national privacy legislation which upholds that personal information must be collected only when it is necessary for a specific function, obtained by lawful and fair means and is accurate. In practice, this implies the duties to safeguard files and other records by storing hard copies in locked cabinets and electronic copies on password-protected devices; keeping these records accurate, unbiased and fair; avoiding gossip about clients; and giving clients access to their records.

Note taking might seem to be a challenge to privacy, given that the counsellor's notes can be subpoenaed by the courts. However, the purposes of note taking are for accountability, service review and case planning (PACFA, 2021); to document the quality of care; for continuity or consistency across sessions; and to give evidence of competence and ethical conduct by practitioners.

The information to include in notes are the clients' identifying data; the date and time of the session; presenting issues, needs and goals of clients; observations (as relevant); progress made to date; summary of the session, including key phrases clients might have used; outcomes and priorities for the next session. Meanwhile, it will be important not to record your opinions, judgements or feelings about clients or any information that would be counterproductive if clients gained access to your notes or if the information became public. These notes should be retained for seven years after the last professional contact with clients, or until they reach the age of 18 years, whichever is the later.

Limits on confidentiality

As is the case for clients of all ages, confidentiality does not apply when clients intend to do harm to themselves or others. With young people, confidentiality must be violated when counsellors become aware that the children are being abused. This is a legal obligation, as is reporting clients' serious illegal behaviour. Therefore, clients need to know about your legal obligations in advance.

When working with children, the second limit on child confidentiality is that parents need to be able to retain a leadership role in their family, which is impaired when they are not fully informed about issues with their child. They cannot function as executives in the family if they do not have the information they need to do so.

A third challenge is how to preserve young people's privacy at the same time as communicating enough to their teachers for them to be able to meet the children's needs (Glosoff & Pate, 2002).

Boundaries

The term *boundaries* describes structural (e.g. time of service, place of service, fees and agreements) and interpersonal dimensions (e.g. physical contact, sexual contact, relationship limits and giving or receiving gifts) of the professional-client relationship (Simon, 1992). Boundaries (as illustrated in Figure 7.4) demonstrate respect for ourselves and our clients and clarify our respective roles so that the relationship is transparent. They set a context for unambiguous communication between counsellor and client; decrease the potential for misinterpretations of the counsellor's messages, motives, and behaviours; and ensure that the professional's judgement is not impaired by fearing damage to any personal aspect of the relationship (Simon, 1992).

When the boundaries between ourselves and clients are blurred (as illustrated in Figure 7.5), this places the therapeutic alliance in peril because it can impair our professional judgement, create confusion for ourselves and clients and thereby introduce 'noise' into the counselling relationship and - particularly for clients whose boundaries have been breached by abuse - can mirror their prior maltreatment.

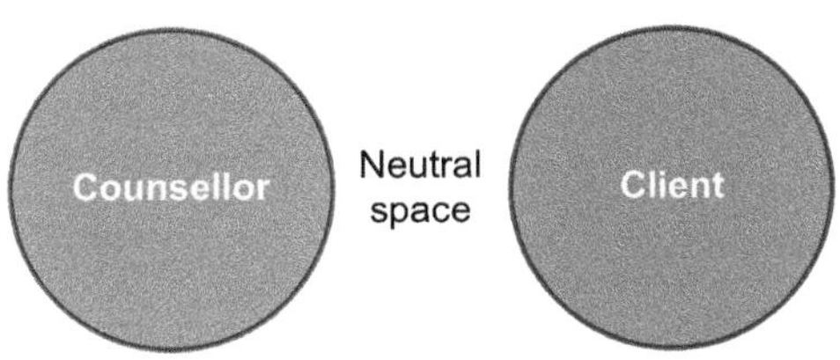

Figure 7.4 Healthy boundaries

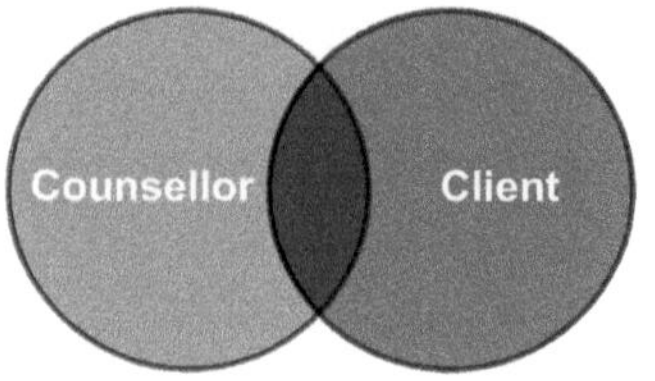

Figure 7.5 Blurred boundaries

Nevertheless, engaging with children and young people can require some blurring of personal and professional boundaries in order to develop authentic relationships. For example, celebrating birthdays and achievements can be helpful for building rapport. Similarly, when working with clients who could be suicidal, it might be necessary to be more flexible about boundaries, perhaps by allowing after-hours contact, reaching out to clients if they do not attend a scheduled session, or (with prior client consent) ringing them between sessions to check on them. This will need to be decided on a case-by-case basis.

Multiple relationships

It is important to avoid having dual relationships with young clients, such as having a social relationship with them or their family at the same time as being their counsellor. These multiple relationships are confusing to both client and counsellor; introduce challenges to confidentiality; and can affect client welfare - because, when you have a second relationship, you have different stakes in each one.

Sometimes, however, dual relationships are unavoidable, such as in regional or rural areas, where it might be impossible not to encounter clients in social settings. In that case, you will need to discuss this possibility ahead of time. One example could be, 'If we see each other at my daughter's swimming lessons, we will say 'Hello' and move on. We won't tell other people how we know each other'.

Gifts

Gift giving is problematic because it can lead to the expectation of reciprocity (DeJong, 2014). However, young clients in particular will commonly develop affection for their counsellors and might want to give them something to show their appreciation. In that case, you can thank them and say that you will share it with your colleagues. Paintings or other art can be put in your 'special folder' but cannot be displayed in your counselling room as it could identify clients to others or subtly pressure others to similarly give you gifts.

In reverse, young children might expect gifts for their birthdays as these are a big deal for them. To mark the special occasion, you might choose to make them something of little value, such as a card or a cupcake.

Self-disclosure

This is a contentious topic within counselling. Self-disclosure about the therapeutic process (as in, 'It seems to me that you don't want to be here today') will be appropriate. When it is about the person of the counsellor outside of the sessions, such as their family or events in their lives, the best rule to apply is the WAIT rule: Why Am I Telling? (Hall, 2021). Self-disclosure can validate clients' experience, help them feel less alone and help to build trust, whereas refusal to tell clients anything at all about yourself can communicate that you do not trust them. On the other hand, counsellors' self-disclosure can divert the focus from the client and cause clients to be concerned that you might be over-invested in their lives, or about whether they need to offer you support.

Use of touch

Outside of touch-based therapies, the Zur Institute (2022) identifies some appropriate forms of deliberate touch including a handshake as a greeting, to console or reassure clients, playful touch (such as a shoulder shuck), for celebration or congratulation (such as a 'high-five'), to ground or reorient clients, when demonstrating an action, to prevent someone from hurting themselves, or in self-defence.

Whereas we might be clear about the use of touch, young people will not always be. In all relationships with clients, we are friendly - but we are not their friends. This can be a difficult concept for young children or adolescents with intellectual disabilities to understand, who might naturally give hugs to trusted adults. How counsellors respond to a child's expressed affection can affect the relationship. As a general guideline, counsellors might not initiate hugs with clients, but discretion can be used as to whether they accept one once a therapeutic relationship has been established.

Touch must be used only with clients' consent and in light of their presenting issues and personal history. It is usually contraindicated for clients who are actively hostile or aggressive, highly sexualised or who have experienced assault (Zur Institute, 2007). With young children, touch can be essential to soothe their distress, but counsellors will have to protect themselves from charges of inappropriate contact.

Sexual contact with clients

Sexual relationships with clients are expressly forbidden in every code of ethics in every jurisdiction. In Australia, a sexual relationship is prohibited throughout a counselling relationship and for two years afterwards (ACA, 2022) or five years afterwards (PACFA, 2021).

No rationalisations - not even that this is 'true love' - excuse violating this prohibition (Pope, 1988). The profession is negatively affected by a loss of public confidence in its members as a result of the sexual abuse of clients, while the harm to clients includes their subsequent inability to trust; hesitation about seeking further help from professionals; and the classic emotional reactions to rape such as depression, suicide, feelings of guilt, isolation, suppressed rage and post-traumatic stress (Pope, 1988).

Assessing for risk of harm to others

Therapists faced with potentially dangerous clients should take specific steps to protect the public and to minimise their own liability by taking careful histories, advising clients of the limits of confidentiality, keeping accurate records of threat and of the steps they have taken to protect others, and seeking consultation with supervisors (Corey et al., 2019). Negligence lies in the practitioner's failure to conduct an assessment for potential violence or failure to warn a third party of imminent danger, not in failing to predict any violence that might be committed.

If clients threaten to harm others, practitioners' duty to warn requires that they make a reasonable effort to contact the identified victim or notify the police (Welfel et al., 2009). A duty to protect adds options in addition to these steps, including hospitalisation; referral for medication changes by a doctor or psychiatrist; referral to specialists in violence perpetration; or informing child protection services (Jensen, 2012).

Knowing the law in your jurisdiction is crucial when clients have contagious diseases such as HIV that are a threat to the well-being or life of their sexual partner. In these cases, the duty to protect can override confidentiality. Counsellors should consult with a supervisor or a lawyer about their duty to disclose this information both for public safety and because they could be subject to legal liability for failing to notify those in harm's way.

Mandatory reporting

Mandatory reporting is a legal obligation to report reasonable suspicions that a person aged under 18 (or, in some jurisdictions, under 16) is suspected of being subjected to child abuse or neglect. This is not discretionary: In the interests of child safety, the counsellor has no choice, even when a report would breach confidentiality.

Categories of mandatory reporters differ between the Australian states and territories, but professionals who are responsible for children are generally considered mandatory reporters. (At the time of writing, Queensland is the only state where counsellors are not mandated notifiers, although psychologists are.)

If you are making a report, you will need to advise your clients and spend some time helping them to understand the process and validate any feelings they might have about it. It will be important to reassure children who have disclosed abuse that they have not done anything wrong. They might fear what will happen as a result of this disclosure. Answer their questions as well as you can, but do not make any promises about the outcome. Throughout the process, consult your supervisor. And do not interview children to discover the details of alleged incidents. This is best left to specialists so that in any subsequent court trial, defence lawyers for the accused cannot claim that the child was coached.

Referrals

Counsellors must practise within their scope of competence. However, sometimes clients refer themselves for an issue that is within this scope but then, as therapy evolves, an issue that is beyond the counsellor's competence arises. This raises the questions:

- Do I refer this client to a specialist and risk their feeling abandoned ... or do I continue to see them and risk their being treated incompetently?
- If the issue is that my values clash with their lifestyle, do I have the right - or even an obligation - to refer them on to someone else who is in tune with their values? Is this just indulging my own views, at the expense of clients?

- Can counsellors be expected to be competent (and comfortable) handling all difficulties with which clients might present?
- What about for rural or regional clients, for whom there may be no one else?

For counsellors to know where to refer clients, they need to amass a list of specialists in the locality, which is more challenging when consulting at a distance, as with online counselling.

Termination

Ethically, we must terminate counselling when clients no longer require therapy because the presenting issue has been resolved, if they are no longer deriving any benefit from therapy, or when they are being harmed by the therapy (for example, by becoming dependent on the counsellor). These issues are less pronounced when counsellors position clients as the experts in their own lives who, at the outset, identify specific goals, so that it is clear when these have been reached.

Definitional ceremonies (see Chapter 15) can punctuate the progress that clients have made and provide a natural and deliberative end to sessions (Lenz et al., 2012). Other possibilities for termination include:

- Contract for a specific number of sessions, with a clear review date at which time continuation or termination can be decided upon jointly.
- Wean clients from therapy by reducing the frequency of sessions or taking a temporary break from sessions (Dobson & Dobson, 2017).
- Provide occasional top-up, maintenance or booster sessions to replace regular scheduled appointments.

Ethics of collaboration with families

When young people have difficulties, often they are scapegoated within the family as 'the problem'. That person is less likely than other family members to consent voluntarily to counselling. Despite their lack of consent, externalising or renaming the problem will reverse the logic of blame, which in itself will improve their circumstances.

Issues of confidentiality with family work mainly arise around secrets (Corey et al., 2019). One way to avoid secrets is not to see family members separately, for fear of engaging in unproductive alliances or of being placed in a position of having to collude with secrets.

The ethics of supervision

Supervision provides a mechanism for upholding the integrity and professionalism of the profession. It is a recognised resource for ethical decision making, specifically referred to in all ethical decision-making models. Whereas the goal of counselling is to facilitate client growth, supervision is aimed both at facilitating the counsellors' growth and protecting clients (Wong & Wong, 2020). It is a mandatory requirement of most human service organisations and is typically written into employment contracts. Counsellors in private practice are required to organise their own supervision.

According to PACFA (2021), the ethical responsibilities of supervisors include ensuring that clients are the primary focus of supervision sessions; monitoring the welfare of the supervisee; ensuring compliance with the relevant legal, ethical and professional practice standards; and monitoring the achievements and the professional development of supervisees.

In school settings, a lack of time is often cited as a reason that school counsellors receive insufficient supervision. However, failing to offer supervision can lead to role ambiguity and counsellors performing duties that are not within their role (Miserentino & Hannon, 2022; Wambu & Meyers, 2019). A second barrier is the lack of training on the part of school personnel to offer supervision, which involves a set of skills that is distinct from counselling skills. Therefore, supervisors need training for the role: It is not enough simply to be an experienced counsellor (Wambu & Meyers, 2019).

Supervision and the law

Supervisors are legally responsible for the competent practice of their supervisees and therefore rely on their supervisees to provide clear and truthful reporting of client progress and associated clinical issues (Corey et al., 2019). To safeguard themselves, supervisors should practise risk management in supervision much as they would in working with their own clients, by maintaining accurate and timely documentation of the performance of their supervisees and the steps they have taken to ensure their competence.

Just as therapists are vulnerable to clients who launch malpractice actions, supervisors are open to malpractice litigation against them by the supervisees' clients. In 2010, the Health Care Complaints Commission prosecuted two psychologists - one the counsellor for not disclosing that her client was sexually molesting his daughter and the other her supervisor who was aware of the abuse and who also failed to report it. The Tribunal found both psychologists guilty of professional misconduct (HCCC, 2010).

Unethical behaviour by supervisors

Ethical breaches by supervisors include inadequate performance evaluation and monitoring of supervisee activities, breaches of confidentiality in supervision, and culturally insensitive supervision (Cimino et al., 2013; Wong & Wong, 2020). Unethical supervisor behaviour outside of sessions can include when their drinking impairs their performance or they bully clients or colleagues, pressure counsellors to provide substandard services, or have a relationship with the supervisee's client (Cimino et al., 2013). Such behaviours raise a dilemma of what to do. Cimino and colleagues indicate that, for one-off events, the supervisee should discuss the issue with the supervisor but that for ongoing issues, they will need to report the supervisor to management. If administrators do not respond adequately, a resulting assessment that the organisation is corrupt might lead to the decision to resign (Cimino et al., 2013).

Complaints

Even though counsellors practise prudently and follow ethical guidelines, they still might be sued. Complaints can be of four types: errors of judgement or genuine mistakes; poor practice or carelessness; negligence, which is a failure to act or giving advice that resulted in harm; and malpractice - knowingly breaching or violating a code of conduct.

When practitioners act in the best interest of the client and can demonstrate this through a process of consultation and documentation, they are less likely to be sanctioned for negative outcomes of therapy. The risk of complaints against practitioners can be reduced when (Jobes & O'Connor, 2009):

- an assessment was thorough and reasonable
- documentation was thorough and contemporaneous
- appropriate methods of clinical assessment and triangulation of data were employed - that is, information is sought from multiple sources such as parents and teachers as well as clients themselves
- reasonable treatments or interventions were made available to the client
- professional supervision was sought
- appropriate clinical referrals were made.

Conclusion

Professional ethics represents a deep personal commitment to be a virtuous clinician who strives for the ethical ideal. The task is to integrate the values of the profession into one's personal values. This will enable you to navigate the many daily ethical dilemmas that surface in counselling. The ultimate aim of ethical decision making is to reach conclusions that are justifiable and defensible (Carroll & Shaw, 2012). Although a challenge to resolve, making an informed professional decision can improve your sense of professionalism and self-efficacy, and your pride in your allegiance to high principles (Welfel, 2016).

References

Australian Counselling Association. (2022). *Code of ethics*. https://www.theaca.net.au/documents/ACA-Code-of-Ethics-and-Practice-Ver16

Australian Early Childhood Association. (1991). Australian Early Childhood Association code of ethics. *Australian Journal of Early Childhood*, *16*(1), 3–6.

Barnett, J. (2019). The ethical practice of psychotherapy: Clearly within our reach. *Psychotherapy*, *56*(4), 440–441. https://doi.org/10.1037/pst0000272

Barstow, C. (2008). *Right use of power: The heart of ethics*. Many Realms Publishing.

Besley, T. (2001). Foucauldian influences in narrative therapy: An approach for schools. *The Journal of Educational Enquiry*, *2*(2), 72–93.

Bolton, L. (2017). The ethical issues which must be addressed in online counselling. *Australian Counselling Research Journal*, *11*(1), 1–15. http://www.acrjournal.com.au/resources/assets/journals/Volume-11-Issue-1-2017/Volume-11-Issue-1-2017-FULL.pdf

Carnes-Holt, K., Maddox, R. P. II, Warren, J., Morgan, M., & Zakaria, N. S. (2016). Using bookmarks: An approach to support ethical decision making in play therapy. *International Journal of Play Therapy*, *25*(4), 176–185. https://doi.org/10.1037/pla0040380

Carroll, M., & Shaw, E. (2012). *Ethical maturity in the helping professions: Making difficult life and work decisions*. PsychOz Publications.

Cimino, A. N., Rorke, J., & Adams, H. L. (2013). Supervisors behaving badly: Witnessing ethical dilemmas and what to do about it. *Journal of Social Work Values and Ethics*, *10*(2), 48–57.

Corey, G., Corey, M. S., & Corey, C. (2019). *Issues and ethics in the helping professions* (10th ed.). Cengage.

Cottone, R. R., Tarvydas, V., & Hartley, M. T. (2021). *Ethics and decision making in* counseling *and psychotherapy* (5th ed.). Springer.

DeJong, S. M. (2014). Blogs and tweets, texting and friending. *Science Direct*, https://www.sciencedirect.com/topics/psychology/boundary-crossing

Dobson, D., & Dobson, K. S. (2017). *Evidence-based practice of cognitive-behavioural therapy* 2nd ed.). Guilford.

Duffy, J., Gallagher, J., & Holmes, S. (2018). Virtue ethics: Introduction. *Rhetoric Review*, *37*(4), 321-327. https://doi.org/10.1080/07350198.2018.1497882321

Fisher, C. B., & Oransky, M. (2008). Informed consent to psychotherapy: Protecting the dignity and respecting the autonomy of patients. *Journal of Clinical Psychology in Session*, *64*(5), 576-588. https://doi.org/10.1002/jclp.20472

Glosoff, H. L., & Pate, R. H. Jr (2002). Privacy and confidentiality in school counseling. *Professional School Counseling*, *6*(1), 20–27. https://www.jstor.org/stable/42732386

Hall, L. (2021). *Five golden rules for using self-disclosure in counselling*. https://www.opencolleges.edu.au/careers/blog/self-disclosure-in-counselling

Health Care Complaints Commission. (2010). *HCCC vs Dene and Donnelly*. https://www.hccc.nsw.gov.au/decisions-orders/media-releases/2010/Kerri-Dene-and-James-Donnelly---deregistered-by-Psychologists-Tribunal

Hiatt, K. (2022). Compassion-supported development: A humanistic approach to counseling supervision. *The Journal of Humanistic Counseling*, *61*(3), 211–223. https://doi.org/10.1002/johc.12181

Jensen, D. G. (2012). ›The Tarasoff two-step. *The Therapist*, *24*(5), 44–51.

Jobes, D. A., & O'Connor, S. S. (2009). The duty to protect suicidal clients: Ethical, legal, and professional considerations. In J. L. Werth, Jr., E. R. Welfel, & G. A. H. Benjamin (Eds.), *The duty to protect: Ethical, legal, and professional considerations for mental health professionals* (pp. 163–180). American Psychological Association.

Johnson, M. K., Weeks, S. N., Peacock, G. G., & Domenech Rodíguez, M. M. (2022). Ethical decision-making models: A taxonomy of models and review of issues. *Ethics and Behaviour*, *32*(3), 195–209. https://doi.org/10.1080/10508422.2021.1913593

Kant, I. (1785/1996). Groundwork of the metaphysics of morals. In M. J. Gregor (Ed.), *Practical philosophy* (pp. 49–93). Cambridge University Press.

Kitchener, K. S. (1984). Intuition, critical evaluation, and ethical principles: The foundation for ethical decisions in counseling psychology. *The Counseling Psychologist*, *12*, 43–55. https://doi.org/10.1177/0011000084123005

Lambert, V., & Glacken, M. (2011). Engaging with children in research: Theoretical and practical and implications of negotiating informed consent/assent. *Nursing Ethics*, *18*(6), 781–801. https://doi.org/10.1177/0969733011401122

Laverack, G. (2009). *Public health: Power, empowerment and professional practice*. Palgrave Macmillan.

Lenz, A. S., Zamarripa, M. X., & Fuentes, S. (2012). A narrative approach to terminating therapy. *Journal of Professional Counseling: Practice, Theory and Research*, *39*(2), 2–13. https://doi.org/10.1080/15566382.2012.12033883

Madigan, S. (2019). *Narrative therapy* (2nd ed.). American Psychological Association.

Mattison, M. (2000). Ethical decision making: The person in the process. *Social Work*, *45*(3), 201–212. https://doi.org/10.1093/sw/45.3.201

McAuliffe, D., & Chenoweth, L. (2008). Leave no stone unturned: The inclusive model of ethical decision making. *Ethics and Social Welfare*, *2*(1), 38–49. https://doi.org/10.1080/17496530801948739

McLaughlin, H. J. (1991). Reconciling care and control: Authority in classroom relationships. *Journal of Teacher Education*, *42*(3), 182–195. https://doi.org/10.1177/002248719104200304

Miserentino, J., & Hannon, M. D. (2022). Supervision in schools: A developmental approach. *Journal of Counselor Preparation and Supervision*, *16*(1), 3. https://digitalcommons.sacredheart.edu/jcps/vol16/iss1/3

Mitchell, D. L. (1993). When the values of clients and counsellors clash: Some conceptual and ethical propositions. *Canadian Journal of Counseling*, *27*(3), 203-211. https://cjc-rcc.ucalgary.ca/article/view/58934

Pope, K. S. (1988). How clients are harmed by sexual contact with mental health professionals: The syndrome and its prevalence. *Journal of Counseling and Development*, *67*, 222–226. https://doi.org/10.1002/j.1556-6676.1988.tb02587.x

Psychotherapy and Counselling Federation of Australia. (2021). *Code of ethics*. https://pacfa.org.au/Portal/Prac-Res/Code-of-Ethics.aspx

Rekers, G. A. (1984). Ethical issues in child behavioral assessment. In T. H. Ollendick & M. Hersen (Eds.), *Child behavioral assessment* (pp. 244–262). Pergamon.

Scaturo, D. J. (2002). Fundamental dilemmas in contemporary psychotherapy: A transtheoretical concept. *American Journal of Psychotherapy*, *56*(2), 115–133. https://doi.org/10.1176/appi.psychotherapy.2002.56.1.115

Simon, R. I. (1992). Sexual exploitation of patients: How it begins before it happens. *Psychiatry Annals*, 19, 104–122. https://doi.org/10.3928/0048-5713-19890201-13

Thannhauser, R. E., Morris, Z. A., & Gamble, N. (2021). Informed consent, confidentiality, and practitioner disclosure in therapeutic work with youth: A systematic review of practitioners' perspectives. *Adolescent Research Review*, *7*, 355–382. https://doi.org/10.1007/s40894-021-00173-2

Velasquez, M., Andre, C., Shanks, T. J. & Meyer, M. J. (2015). *Thinking ethically*. Markkula Centre for Applied Ethics. https://www.scu.edu/ethics/ethics-resources/ethical-decision-making/thinking-ethically/

Wambu, G. W., & Meyers, C. E. (2019). School counselor site supervisors' perceptions of preparedness and training needs. *Journal of School Counseling*, *17*(14), 1–30. https://files.eric.ed.gov/fulltext/EJ1217460.pdf

Welfel, E. R. (2016). *Ethics in counseling and psychotherapy: Standards, research and emerging issues* (6th ed.). Brooks/Cole.

White, M. (2016). *Narrative therapy classics*. Dulwich Centre Publications.

Wong, P. T., & Wong, L. C. (2020). Assessing multicultural supervision competencies. In D. L. Dinne, D. K. Forgays, S. A. Hayes & W. J. Lonner (Eds.), *Merging past, present, and future in cross-cultural psychology* (pp. 510–519). Garland Science.

Zur Institute (2022). *Guidelines for clinically appropriate and ethical touch in therapy*. https://www.zurinstitute.com/clinical-updates/touch-in-therapy/

8 Taking care of yourself

Counsellors have an ethical responsibility to look after themselves to safeguard their own well-being for its own sake and also so that they can continue to be of use to others (PACFA, 2021). The code of ethics specifies that counsellors need to ensure that they do not put their well-being at risk, that they seek professional support as needed, and withdraw from their role if their functioning is significantly impaired. This means that not only is it important to care for ourselves but also to be aware if our functioning is degraded (Barnett, 2014).

Fitness to practice

The concept of fitness to practise aims to balance practitioners' rights to pursue their occupation of choice, their right to well-being, and the rights of the clients whom they will be serving. Fitness to practise entails not only having a strong theoretical knowledge base and working within one's scope of expertise, maintaining appropriate boundaries with clients, and having a refined system of personal and professional ethics, but it also involves having the physical and emotional robustness required for the safe and effective provision of health services (Lo et al., 2018; Sofronoff et al., 2011). This means not just taking time to relax when stressed but building in a daily routine of self-care.

A continuum of stress syndromes

In addition to taking care of yourself, being fit also requires that you structure your work and seek the external supports necessary to avoid succumbing to a range of stress syndromes. These syndromes are labelled variously, often with interchangeable terms, so for simplicity I have arranged them on a continuum of seriousness, ranging from occupational stress to vicarious traumatisation - see Figure 8.1.

These syndromes come about from prolonged exposure to primary, secondary and tertiary stressors. Primary stressors include direct victimisation from violence by clients; secondary stress is when we are overwhelmed by the emotional content of clients' experiences; and tertiary stress is when we ourselves become traumatised by the graphic detail of human cruelty to which we are exposed through clients' stories (Geoffrion et al., 2016).

Worker stress has an impact both on individual workers, their colleagues and the workplace. Stressed workers become more concerned with ensuring their own survival than with

DOI: 10.4324/9781003323938-9

Figure 8.1 A continuum of stress syndromes

supporting colleagues or producing high-quality work. Stress can lead to devaluing of and resentment towards clients, apathy towards 'the system', and a deterioration in one's personal life. Accordingly, burnout is both a personal threat to our well-being and a professional threat to our capacity to be of use to our clients. At an existential level, each of these syndromes undermines professional ideals, disrupts hope and meaning, affects practitioners' physical health and leads to emotional distress (see Box 8.1), while also impairing our capacity to be useful to clients (Yang & Hayes, 2020).

With respect to their colleagues, exhausted staff tend to blame their job dissatisfaction on other people. They are less able to contribute to a positive working environment, are more likely to experience conflict with colleagues, and might even model negative behaviours such as emotional venting (Groeneveld et al., 2012; Lambert et al., 2009; Whitaker et al., 2015). In turn, their colleagues, clients, and the whole workplace suffer from a negative emotional climate (Friedman-Krauss et al., 2014a, 2014b; Santavirta et al., 2007).

As for the organisation, worker stress results in high staff turnover - which in child welfare organisations, for example, ranges from 14 to 60 per cent annually (Salloum et al., 2015). This raises the workload of remaining staff, leads to hiring less experienced workers, and is expensive for employers (Salloum et al., 2015).

Occupational stress

The first stress syndrome, occupational stress, arises when we believe that the demands of our work exceed the available personal and external resources to support our coping (Brackett et al., 2010; Lambert et al., 2009) - see Figure 8.2. Resilience (resisting stress) is

Box 8.1 Signs of stress syndromes

Physical signs	*Emotional signs*	*Cognitive signs*	*Relationship signs*	*Spiritual signs*	*Behaviours*
Appetite change	Temper outbursts	Loss of humour	Isolation	Feeling of emptiness	Restlessness
Headaches	Anxiety	Dulled senses	Defensiveness	Apathy	Swearing
Fatigue	Nightmares	Lethargy	Intolerance	Holding grudges	Substance abuse
Insomnia	Irritability	Boredom	Resentment	Cynicism	Inactivity
Indigestion	Depression	Indecisiveness	Loneliness	Loss of direction	Slumped posture
Illness	Frustration	Forgetfulness	Blame of others	Doubt	Hypervigilance
Weight change	Oversensitivity	Poor concentration	Lowered sex drive	Need to prove self	Risk aversion
Teeth grinding	Mood swings	Personality changes	Aggression	Negative outlook	Disordered eating
Tension	Fearfulness	Stuck in past	Abuse	Gloom	Giving up

Source: adapted from De Janasz et al. (2015, p. 96)

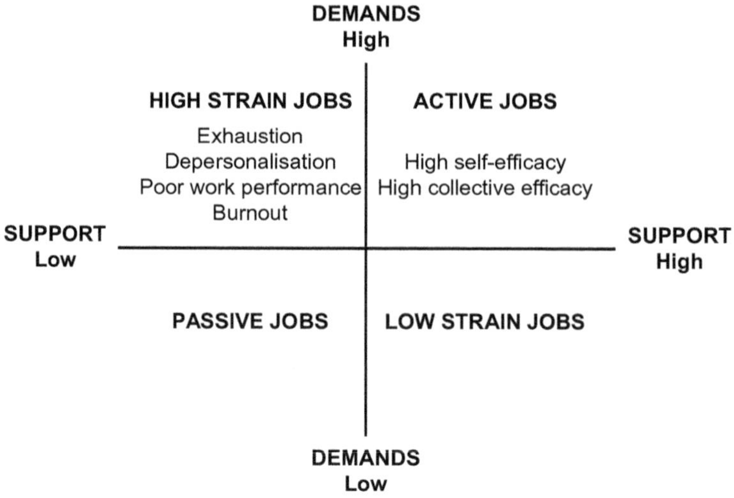

Figure 8.2 Contributors to occupational stress

not simply a matter of the resourcefulness and coping skills of the individual worker, but is closely tied to how much support workers receive within the workplace. Even the most robust person can buckle under extreme pressure. We might think that we can push through, but our body can become symptomatic despite our attempts to tough it out. As Cunningham (2016) notes, 'Your brain and your body do not poll for your opinion'.

Compassion fatigue

At the next level of seriousness on the continuum of stress syndromes is compassion fatigue. This is a sense that we have no more empathy left to give and are overwhelmed and exhausted by the demands of our work, particularly the emotional demands. It comes about when practitioners have empathic ability (awareness of the suffering of others); empathic concern (motivation to help); an empathic response; and compassion stress, which is the residue of emotional energy that arises from the other three elements (Figley, 2002). Workers who are vulnerable to experiencing compassion fatigue are not the ones who do not care, but those who do. This means that, while our capacity to empathise is our greatest asset as counsellors, it is also a point of vulnerability (Lambie, 2006).

Burnout

The third stress syndrome is burnout, which is a state of physical, emotional and mental exhaustion arising from long-term exposure to demanding work (Figley, 2002). A cumulative sense of fatigue and dissatisfaction, burnout is largely a reaction to systemic stressors within the work setting (Thompson et al., 2014). It is characterised by emotional exhaustion and venting, depersonalisation (cynicism) and reduced feelings of effectiveness (a lack of professional efficacy) (Collins & Long, 2003; Green et al., 2014; Kokkinos, 2007; Lambie, 2006; Puig et al., 2014; Skaalvik & Skaalvik, 2007). Emotional depletion results in reduced emotional energy to devote to clients, while depersonalisation refers to feelings of alienation and estrangement, and adopting negative, cynical, callous and detached attitudes towards clients.

Vicarious traumatisation

The most severe stress syndrome is secondary or vicarious traumatisation. This mostly refers to the cognitive changes that occur in professionals' views of themselves, others and the world, as a result of cumulative exposure to the graphic and/or traumatic stories of their clients (Baird & Kracen, 2006; Canfield, 2005; Jordan, 2018; Salloum et al., 2015). As a result of bearing witness to human cruelty, counsellors can suffer from grief, rage and outrage on behalf of their clients, especially those who are young. They can also be traumatised when a client dies by suicide (Sakinofsky, 2007).

As with other stress syndromes, traumatised practitioners experience a loss of faith in themselves (low self-efficacy) and changes in their values and beliefs, such that their work no longer gives meaning or purpose to their life. This is an existential crisis (Lambie, 2006). In addition, symptoms can parallel acute or post-traumatic stress disorder, such as flashbacks, nightmares and intrusive thoughts. Simple self-care measures are unlikely to be enough to overcome these symptoms (Salloum et al., 2015), in which case traumatised counsellors will themselves need to recruit professional support.

Risk factors

There are three categories that make practitioners either vulnerable or resilient to a stress syndrome: our own history, the nature of the work itself, and the nature of the organisation where we work. These contribute in various amounts to the differing syndromes, with organisational factors and job satisfaction more significant in burnout, whereas personal factors are more relevant to compassion fatigue (Thompson et al., 2014). Overall, however, the nature of the work and of the workplace appear to be more influential than personal factors in generating worker stress (Hensel et al., 2015; Regehr et al., 2004).

Personal factors

Many people enter the helping professions after encounters with their own pain (Bager-Charleson, 2010). Given this history, there is an increased risk that counselling others could trigger distress for counsellors themselves and compromise the therapeutic process (Mallioux, 2014). Personal risk factors include having unrealistic and punitive expectations of ourselves, fearing that others will judge us if we declare that we need support, and letting our work impinge on our personal time (Figley, 1995, in Geoffrion et al., 2016). Our personal history of trauma, current life circumstances, sense of being in control, coping strategies, and length of work experience also influence our vulnerability to stress (Geoffrion et al., 2016; Hensel et al., 2015; Regehr et al., 2004). In terms of years of experience, it is possible that novices and mid-career workers are more prone to work-related stress, whereas those experienced workers who have not already succumbed are either more personally resilient or else have moved up the organisational hierarchy to a position where they are more in control of their work, or less on the front lines (Salloum et al., 2015).

Self-efficacy

Compassion satisfaction decreases the risk of succumbing to stress (Salloum et al., 2015). This is the gratification that we derive from helping others (Geoffrion et al., 2016). It is an experience of professional self-efficacy - that is, of being able to make a contribution to the lives of others. Counsellors with high self-efficacy believe that they can design and deliver appropriate services to clients, can adapt to clients' individual needs, can recruit support from colleagues and friends, and can cope with change and challenges (Friedman, 2003; Klassen & Chiu, 2010). In contrast, professionals with low efficacy are more likely to become overwhelmed by their job and to feel helpless. Accordingly, there is a strong link between professionals' self-efficacy and their job satisfaction, stress and outcomes for clients (Klassen & Chiu, 2010; Morris-Rothschild & Brassard, 2006; Skaalvik & Skaalvik, 2007).

On the other hand, helping others can be an addiction (Berry, 1989). Berry notes that some who enter the helping professions learned during difficult childhoods to connect their self-worth to their capacity for helping. These 'helpaholics' get trapped by two deceptive statements: 'If I don't do it, it won't get done' and 'Everyone else's needs take priority over mine'.

Berry (1989) describes a number of helpaholic types - see Box 8.2. She argues that all of these 'types' try to earn a sense of worth by acting worthily, let others dictate their actions, are driven to endless activity, are attracted to helping those with similar pain to themselves, and stop only when they drop. Many are accused of having poor time management skills, when their time management is excellent: They just consent to doing too much.

Box 8.2 Types of helpaholics

- *Pleasers* are nice but not authentic or 'real'. They are hooked by those who appear dependent and unhappy.
- *Rescuers* promote helplessness in others and gravitate towards those who appear in need.
- *Crusaders* are angry with others who are not as dedicated to the cause as themselves and are hooked by anyone who appears to have been treated unjustly.
- *Givers* attempt to control others by caring for others. They get hooked by people who seem to be in need.
- *Protectors* believe that others are fragile and therefore they will hide information from them. They are susceptible to others who appear inadequate, vulnerable or in danger.
- *Counsellors* promote one-sided intimacy and are attracted to those who appear troubled and confused.
- *Teachers* avoid intimacy by being 'the sage on the stage'. They respond to those who are searching for the truth or looking for a hero.

Source: Berry (1989)

Berry (1989) advises that when we have learned this pattern - usually from having to look after our own parents during childhood - we need to heal by mourning over the experiences that conditioned us to help, and to manage the perfectionism, guilt and shame that entrenched our parent-watching. Affected counsellors need to acknowledge that they are addicted to helping and instead allow themselves to *choose* whether to help or not. Last, we need to learn to ask for help to meet our needs on that grounds that, 'It's my turn, and I deserve it'.

Work-related factors

The second category of factors that place workers at risk of stress are, in a dose-related manner, aspects of the work itself. Work overload is the aspect most consistently found in research. Work demands span onerous administrative and bureaucratic tasks, an excessive workload, time constraints or inadequate time for planning and preparation, a lack of control over working conditions, a negative work climate, low salary and high levels of organisational uncertainty (Albrecht et al., 2009; Friedman, 2003; Griffith et al., 1999; Klassen & Chiu, 2010; Kokkinos, 2007; Lambert et al., 2009; Nelson et al., 2001; Salloum et al., 2015; Santavirta et al., 2007). Other sources include experiencing conflict with clients or colleagues, and feeling obliged to work in ways that violate our principles (Skaalvik & Skaalvik, 2007).

Accordingly, six qualities of the workplace reduce workers' vulnerability to stress (Canfield, 2005; Yang & Hayes, 2020):

- A sustainable workload in terms of working hours, the number of clients one sees, and the complexity of their presenting issues.
- Feelings of choice and control, and the extent to which workers can make autonomous decisions about how best to fulfil their responsibilities.
- Recognition for one's efforts.
- Support from colleagues, leadership and supervisors.
- Being treated with fairness, respect and justice.
- Performing meaningful, valued tasks.

Organisational environment

A third category of risk is the nature of the organisation where we work. Workplace negativity and general unhappiness, constant restructuring, a lack of support for practitioners, low collective efficacy, role conflict, ineffective leadership, compromised team work, and a culture of silence about the demands of the job all undermine practitioners' effectiveness and satisfaction with their work (Geoffrion et al., 2016; Green et al., 2014; Regehr et al., 2004).

The setting itself is also significant, with those in private practice typically experiencing more autonomy than counsellors in public service (Thompson et al., 2014). Child protection work and working with disadvantaged or stigmatised sectors of the community add to the strain (Geoffrion et al., 2016), while negative public perception of certain types of community work also contribute (Regehr et al., 2004).

A wellness model

In order to maintain your own well-being, Barnett (2014) recommends that counsellors see the ongoing practice of self-care as both a necessity and an ethical obligation, rather than a special treat that you give yourself every now and then when you have achieved everything on your *to do* list. In other words, it is vital to prevent exhaustion rather than to wait for symptoms to develop before taking corrective action.

Personal measures

Personal measures for coping include appraising a stressful situation more positively and using coping mechanisms and problem solving, all of which rely on our self-efficacy or belief that we can make a difference to how we are feeling about our work (Thompson et al., 2014). We can distance ourselves from clients' misery by practising mindfulness, relaxation or other trauma-reducing and self-care methods that are personally revitalising (Figley, 2002; Thompson et al., 2014). Writing a list of *things not to do today* is one of my favourites. We also need to recruit social and professional support.

Self-compassion

Just as we offer compassion to clients, we need to turn this towards ourselves. Self-compassion comprises engaging in self-kindness as opposed to self-judgement; recognising that failure and suffering are universal - that is, having a sense of common humanity, rather than seeing ourselves as defective; and being able to acknowledge our emotions without being overtaken by them - that is, being accepting and mindful (Neff, 2021; Nelson et al., 2018).

Nelson et al. (2018) note that, whereas self-esteem about our competence (see Chapter 11) is vulnerable to negative feedback, self-compassion is protective in the face of negative outcomes. These writers report on a strategy of thinking about a stressful event and saying (mindfully) 'This is a moment of suffering. ... Suffering is a part of life (common humanity). ... How may I be kind to myself?'. Or, 'This is painful. I am not alone in feeling pain like this. May I be gentle with myself during this struggle?'. Externalising the pathological self-critic could also be useful.

Distancing

The same measures that help our clients to distance from unhelpful thinking can help us to do likewise. Pakenham (2015) found that the Acceptance and Commitment Therapy measures of acceptance, defusing (see Chapter 4) and committing to act in accord with our values all contributed to practitioners' adjustment and life satisfaction.

Maintain boundaries

Whereas *concern* causes us to focus outwardly on others' suffering, *distress* causes us to focus inward and on trying to feel better ourselves (Zaki, 2016). Our well-being as helpers depends on being able to experience concern, without experiencing contagious distress (Zaki, 2016). To achieve this, we need clear boundaries between ourselves and our clients.

Supervision

Supervision is a key method for facilitating counsellors' competence (Hiatt, 2022) and for preventing stress syndromes (Miserentino & Hannon, 2022). In addition to providing emotional support, supervision helps counsellors to use their skills and knowledge effectively in the service of clients and to deepen their understanding of their beliefs and values (Vallance, 2005).

For these aims to be achieved, supervisors need to give priority to establishing a working alliance (Bordin, 1983) that provides a balance between challenge and support, so that supervisees feel safe enough to risk growing and learning (Hiatt, 2022). This will entail establishing a collaborative relationship, being clear about what is expected of whom (through clarification of roles and tasks), having clear goals defining what should be accomplished and monitoring whether these are being achieved.

Supervision must be responsive to the developmental stages of the counsellor (Jordan, 2006; Miserentino & Hannon, 2022). Novices, for example, are likely to be highly motivated but dependent and insecure and therefore could respond to a directive expert (see Figure 8.3). With increasing experience, practitioners are likely to strive for more independence (when a supportive teacher might suit their needs) until ultimately they will become master practitioners who might look for their supervisor to be more of a consultant or mentor.

It is important that supervisors are experienced counsellors with expertise with the particular client group - in our case, young people - and in their typical presenting difficulties. This can include expertise in trauma-informed practice (Jordan, 2018) and in multicultural competence, both to support supervisees who are from a culture other than their own, and also to support counsellors to be competent with diversity themselves (Wong & Wong, 2020).

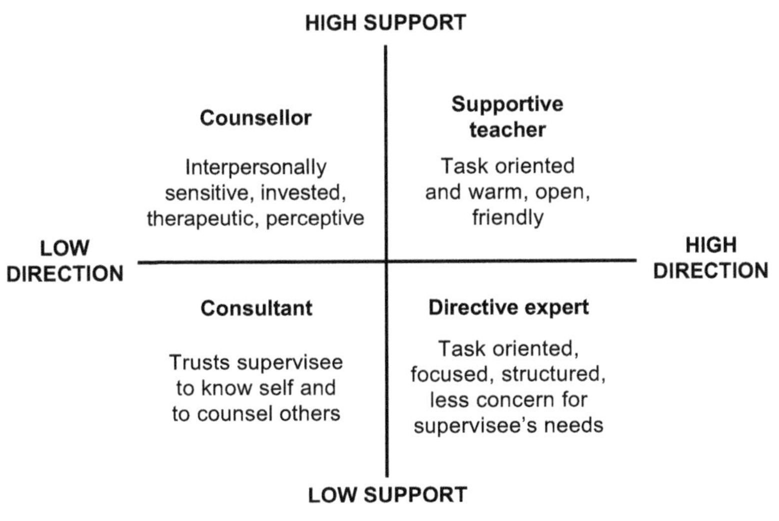

Figure 8.3 Supervisor styles

Source: Hart & Nance (2003)

Professional development

We can maintain resilience as counsellors by participating in professional development. With openness to new learning, professional development 'widens the space' so that different views can bring about a shift in thinking and practice (Krieg et al., 2014). This can renew our enthusiasm for our work, improve our confidence in our abilities, and allow us to continue to grow professionally. In turn, this can increase compassion satisfaction (Geoffrion et al., 2016).

Ensure a healthy work-life balance

We often think of a 'good worker' as one who stays late, goes the extra mile and puts work ahead of all other commitments. However, this leads to burnout and resentment. Practitioners whose work is their sole purpose self-righteously demand equal commitment from colleagues and attempt to induce guilt in those who do not share their obsession (Jeffers, 2007). When workers sacrifice themselves to the job in this way, they have one main aspect to their lives. As a result, their life looks like Figure 8.4.

Then, if they lose their job or their exhaustion becomes insurmountable and they have to go on stress leave, self-sacrificing workers are miserable, because their life now looks like Figure 8.5. (Although I have labelled each box, what titles you put in your own boxes is up to you, as long as you can fill in all nine boxes in the grid.)

Instead, our lives need to have multiple aspects spanning love, work, education and fun. In that way, we can achieve balance and satisfaction. And the loss of one aspect (such as a job or a relationship), while being an occasion for mourning, will not leave us with nothing. This is shown in Figure 8.6.

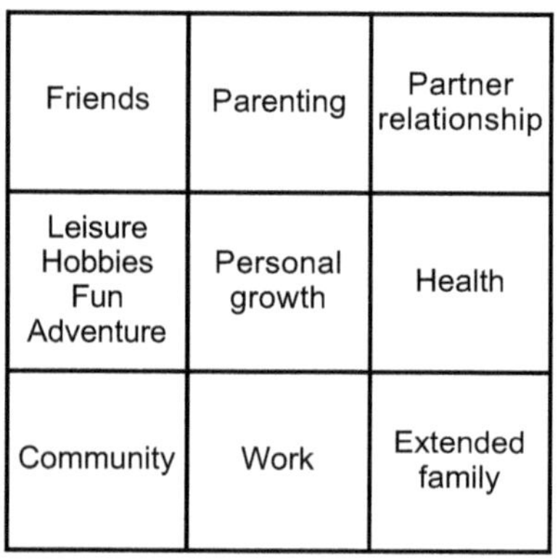

Figure 8.4 Aspects of a full life

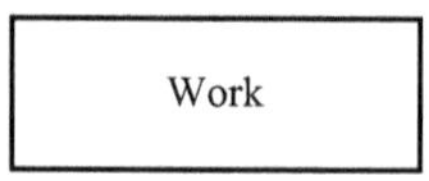

Figure 8.5 Aspect of life of the over-committed worker

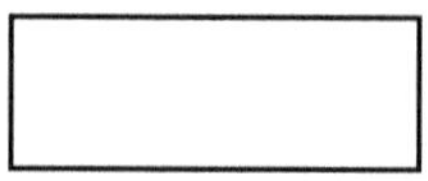

Figure 8.6 Aspects of a full life

> **Box 8.3 A balance of fillers and drainers**
>
> If during the day we progressively drained an electric kettle without refilling it, we would eventually expose its element and it would burn out. So it is with people. To avoid burn-out or exhaustion, we need to top up our energies throughout the day.
>
> What fills us versus what drains our energy differs for each person. It can help, therefore, to take an inventory of your own 'fillers' and 'drainers' and aim to spend more time doing the things that give you energy and vitality. Note, however, that sometimes the things that we *think* are relaxing are not. For example, browsing through fashion magazines with their airbrushed models can lower our self-esteem and therefore drain rather than fill us with energy.

Workplace culture

A successful workplace culture is open about the challenges the team faces, is willing to give time and support to team members to resolve these, has strong relationships with the team leader and among the team members, involves everyone in making decisions, and appreciates individuals' efforts (Gamman, 2003; Nelson et al., 2001). This respect carries over into respectful relationships with clients.

Collective efficacy

In order for workers to feel personally able to make a difference in their work lives, the whole team must have a shared or collective sense of efficacy (Gibbs & Powell, 2011; McGinty et al., 2008; Skaalvik & Skaalvik, 2007). This is grounded in joint decision making that gives all individuals a sense that, as a whole, they have the capacity to operate collectively to achieve their mission (Caprara et al., 2003; Skaalvik & Skaalvik, 2007). This is vital because a strong sense of collective efficacy contributes to the prestige of the workplace and is a potent source of workers' job satisfaction (Caprara et al., 2003; McGinty et al., 2008). It emboldens workers to accept challenging goals, and to expend effort and persist in achieving them. This is likely to produce better outcomes while, in turn, success strengthens both individual and collective efficacy (Goddard et al., 2000).

Leadership

According to research by Kouzes et al. (2015), there are five core leadership tasks: modelling values, inspiring a shared vision, challenging processes, enabling others to act, and 'encouraging the heart'. In terms of modelling values, the foundations of leadership are trust and credibility, which come when others see leaders steadfastly acting in tune with their values. This gives rise to the first law of leadership: *To believe the message, people must believe in the messenger* (Kouzes et al., 2015, p. 33).

Second, leaders must steer the culture of the organisation (or 'the way we do things around here') by co-creating with other stakeholders a shared vision for the agency (Kouzes et al., 2015). This vision is a statement of what you are trying to accomplish together, why that matters, and how everyone's efforts contribute to a better future. It has to appeal to people's heads in that they must understand it logically; to their heart in that it is emotionally elevating and compelling; and to their hands, which means that they know what they can do to make it happen (Kouzes et al., 2015).

Third, leaders must be contagiously enthusiastic about challenging how things can meaningfully be done better, rather than accepting the way they've always been done (Kouzes et al., 2015). The key question here is 'Why?'.

Fourth, a core responsibility of effective leaders is to develop team members' confidence to take initiative and to shine. Leaders do this by building trust, facilitating relationships among team members and developing individuals' competence.

Finally, at heart, leadership is a personal relationship: It's about all team members knowing that they are valued and are doing something significant that matters and is appreciated. Therefore, effective leaders balance the need for task attainment with a concern for the individuals who make that happen (Nupponen, 2006; Rodd, 2013).

Team work

In order to build a spirit of community, Lencioni (2002) proposed that teams need five qualities, the first of which is trust. This is the faith that one's colleagues' intentions are good, which makes open debate (the second quality) possible. With robust debate comes the third quality, commitment and buy-in to the group's decisions because (as Lencioni puts it) people have to weigh in before they can buy in. Fourth, having committed to a certain course of action, team members next need to be accountable for achieving the group's vision. With each member of the team accountable for achieving the vision, the last quality of an effective team will be achieved: that is, attention to results.

The goal of effective leadership and team work is to provide support to our work colleagues both in an everyday sense and during stressful episodes. In the immediate aftermath of a stressful event or crisis, workers can support their colleagues during three phases of recovery: release, reflect and rebuild (Gamman, 2003). During the *release* phase, workers might need to release some emotional energy, with the opportunity to vent to colleagues being a useful part of this; next, they will need to talk through the incident to *reflect* on what happened and why; and finally, in the *rebuilding* phase, the team will need to plan how to prevent or deal with such incidents in future (Gamman, 2003).

Conclusion

Our training as counsellors does not immunise us against the distressing effects of our work; therefore we need to extend to ourselves the same compassion that we give our clients (Canfield, 2005). We need to take seriously the potential impact of our own life stressors and of client distress on our well-being and how the two sets of demands affect each other. We also need to be realistic about our goals, workload, financial expectations and personal needs.

Barnett (2014) advises that we must not rely on our own self-assessment and judgement about when we are succumbing to stress and need instead to structure our practices to safeguard our own well-being and, in turn, our usefulness to clients. Nevertheless, self-care is not just an individual responsibility, but a responsibility of the professional community, of a group of colleagues who look out for and support each other (Barnett, 2019).

References

Albrecht, S. F., Johns, B. H., Mounsteven, J., & Olorunda, O. (2009). Working conditions as risk or resiliency factors for teachers of students with emotional and behavioral disabilities. *Psychology in the Schools*, *46*(10), 1006–1022. https://doi.org/10.1002/pits.20440

Bager-Charleson, S. (2010). *Reflective practice in counselling and psychotherapy*. Sage.

Baird, K., & Kracen, A. (2006). Vicarious traumatization and secondary traumatic stress: A research synthesis. *Counseling Psychology Quarterly*, *19*(2), 181–188. https://doi.org/10.1080/09515070600811899

Barnett, J. E. (2014). Distress, burnout, self-care, and the promotion of wellness for psychotherapists and trainees: Issues, implications, and recommendations. Retrieved from: http://www.societyforpsychotherapy.org/distress-therapist-burnout-self-care-promotion-wellness-psychotherapists-trainees-issues-implications-recommendations

Barnett, J. E. (2019). The ethical practice of psychotherapy: Clearly within our reach. *Psychotherapy*, *56*(4), 431–440. https://doi.org/10.1037/pst0000272

Berry, C. R. (1989). *When helping you is hurting me*. Harper and Row.

Bordin, E. S. (1983). A working alliance based model of supervision. *The Counseling Psychologist*, *11*(1), 35–42. https://doi.org/10.1177/0011000083111007

Brackett, M. A., Palomera, R., Mojsa-Kaja, J., Reyes, M. G., & Salovey, P. (2010). Emotion-regulation ability, burnout, and job satisfaction among British secondary-school teachers. *Psychology in the Schools*, *47*(4), 406–416. https://doi.org/10.1002/pits.20478

Canfield, J. (2005). Secondary traumatization, burnout, and vicarious traumatization: A review of the literature as it relates to therapists who treat trauma. *Smith College Studies in Social Work*, 75(2), 81–101. https://doi.org/10.1300/J497v75n02_06

Caprara, G. V., Barbaranelli, C., Borgogni, L., & Steca, P. (2003). Efficacy beliefs as determinants of teachers' job satisfaction. *Journal of Educational Psychology*, *95*(4), 821–832. https://doi.org/10.1037/0022-0663.95.4.821

Collins, S., & Long, A. (2003). Working with the psychological effects of trauma: Consequences for the mental health-care workers – A literature review. *Journal of Psychiatric and Mental Health Nursing*, *10*, 417–424. https://doi.org/10.1046/j.1365-2850.2003.00620.x

Cunningham, A. (2016). *Drowning in empathy:The cost of vicarious trauma*. https://youtu.be/ZsaorjIo1Yc

De Janasz, S. C., Dowd, K. O., & Schneider, B. Z. (2015). *Interpersonal skills in organizations* (5th ed.). McGraw Hill Education.

Figley, C. R. (2002). Compassion fatigue: Psychotherapists' chronic lack of self care. *Journal of Clinical Psychology*, *58*(11), 1433–1441. https://doi.org/10.1002/jclp.10090

Friedman, I. A. (2003). Self-efficacy and burnout in teaching: The importance of interpersonal-relations efficacy. *Social Psychology of Education*, *6*(3), 191–215. https://doi.org/10.1023/A:1024723124467

Friedman-Krauss, A. H., Raver, C. C., Morris, P. A., & Jones, S. M. (2014a). The role of classroom-level child behavior problems in predicting preschool teacher stress and classroom emotional climate. *Early Education and Development*, *25*(4), 530–552. https://doi.org/10.1080/10409289.2013.817030

Friedman-Krauss, A. H., Raver, C. C., Neuspiel, J. M., & Kinsel, J. (2014b). Child behavior problems, teacher executive function and teacher stress in Head Start classrooms. *Early Education and Development*, *25*(5), 681–702. https://doi.org/10.1080/10409289.2013.825190

Gamman, R. (2003). Sharing the load, supporting the staff: Collaborative management of difficult behaviour in primary schools. *Emotional and Behavioural Difficulties*, *8*(3), 217–229. http://dx.doi.org/10.1080/13632750300507020

Geoffrion, S., Morselli, C., & Guay, S. (2016). Rethinking compassion fatigue through the lens of professional identity: The case of child-protection workers. *Trauma, Violence, and Abuse*, *17*(3), 270–283. https://doi.org/10.1177/1524838015584362

Gibbs, S., & Powell, B. (2011). Teacher efficacy and pupil behaviour: The structure of teachers' individual and collective beliefs and their relationship with numbers of pupils excluded from school. *British Journal of Educational Psychology*, *82*(4), 564–584. https://doi.org/10.1111/j.2044-8279.2011.02046.x

Goddard, R. D., Hoy, W. K., & Hoy, A. W. (2000). Collective teacher efficacy: Its meaning, measure, and impact on student achievement. *American Educational Research Journal*, *37*(2), 479–507. https://doi.org/10.3102/00028312037002479

Green, A. E., Albanese, B. J., Shapiro, N. M., & Aarons, G. A. (2014). The roles of individual and organizational factors in burnout among community-based mental health service providers. *Psychological Services*, *11*(1), 41–49. https://doi.org/10.1037/a0035299

Griffith, J., Steptoe, A., & Cropley, M. (1999). An investigation of coping strategies associated with job stress in teachers. *British Journal of Educational Psychology*, *69*(4), 517–531. https://doi.org/10.1348/000709999157879

Groeneveld, M. G., Vermeer, H. J., van IJzendoorn, M. H., & Linting, M. (2012). Caregivers' cortisol levels and perceived stress in home-based and center-based childcare. *Early Childhood Research Quarterly*, *27*(1), 166–175. https://doi.org/10.1016/j.ecresq.2011.05.003

Hart, G. M., & Nance, D. (2003). Styles of counselor supervision as perceived by supervisor and supervisees. *Counsellor Education and Supervision*, *43*(2), 146–158. https://doi.org/10.1002/j.1556-6978.2003.tb01838.x

Hensel, J. M., Ruiz, C., Finney, C., & Dewa, C. S. (2015). Meta-analysis of risk factors for secondary traumatic stress in therapeutic work with trauma victims. *Journal of Traumatic Stress*, *28*(2), 83–91. https://doi.org/10.1002/jts.21998

Hiatt, K. (2022). Compassion-supported development: A humanistic approach to counseling supervision. *The Journal of Humanistic Counseling*, *61*(3), 211–223. https://doi.org/10.1002/johc.12181

Jeffers, S. (2007). *Feel the fear... and do it anyway*. Ballantine.

Jordan, K. (2006). Beginning supervisees' identity: The importance of relationship variables and experience versus gender matches in the supervisee/supervisor interplay. *The Clinical Supervisor*, *25*(1–2), 43–51. https://doi.org/10.1300/J001v25n01_04

Jordan, K. (2018). Trauma-informed counseling supervision: Something every counselor should know about. *Asia Pacific Journal of Counseling and Psychotherapy* *9*(2), 127–142. https://doi.org/10.1080/21507686.2018.1450274

Klassen, R. M., & Chiu, M. M. (2010). Effects on teachers' self-efficacy and job satisfaction: Teacher, gender, years of experience, and job stress. *Journal of Educational Psychology*, *102*(3), 741–756. https://doi.org/10.1037/a0019237

Kokkinos, C. M. (2007). Job stressors, personality and burnout in primary school teachers. *British Journal of Educational Psychology*, *77*(1), 229–244. https://doi.org/10.1348/000709905X90344

Kouzes, J., Posner, B., & Bunting, M. (2015). *Extraordinary leadership in Australia and New Zealand: The five practices that create great workplaces*. Wiley.

Krieg, S., Davis, K., & Smith, K.A. (2014). Exploring the dance of early childhood educational leadership. *Australasian Journal of Early Childhood*, *39*(1), 73–80. https://doi.org/10.1177/183693911403900110

Lambert, R. G., McCarthy, C., O'Donnell, M., & Wang, C. (2009). Measuring elementary teacher stress and coping in the classroom: Validity evidence for the Classroom Appraisal of Resources and Demands. *Psychology in the Schools*, *46*(10), 973–988. https://doi.org/10.1002/pits.20438

Lambie, G. (2006). Burnout prevention: A humanistic perspective and structured group supervision activity. *Journal of Humanistic Counseling, Education and Development*, *45*, 32–44. https://doi.org/10.1002/j.2161-1939.2006.tb00003.x

Lencioni, P. (2002). *The five dysfunctions of a team: A leadership fable*. Jossey-Bass.

Lo, K., Curtis, H., Francis-Cracknell, A., Maloney, S., Nickson, W., Bearman, M., & Keating, J. L. (2018). Physiotherapy clinical educators' perspectives on a fitness to practice initiative. *Physiotherapy Theory and Practice*, *34*(1), 41–53. https://doi.org/10.1080/09593985.2017.1370752

Mallioux, S. (2014). The ethical imperative: Special considerations in the trauma counselling process. *Traumatology*, *20*(1), 50–56. 10.1177/1534765613496649

McGinty, A. S., Justice, L., & Rimm-Kaufman, S. E. (2008). Sense of school community for preschool teachers serving at-risk children. *Early Education and Development*, *19*(2), 361–384. http://dx.doi.org/10.1080/10409280801964036

Miserentino, J., & Hannon, M. D. (2022). Supervision in schools: A developmental approach. *Journal of Counselor Preparation and Supervision*, *16*(1), 3. https://digitalcommons.sacredheart.edu/jcps/vol16/iss1/3

Morris-Rothschild, B. K., & Brassard, M. R. (2006). Teachers' conflict management styles: The role of attachment styles and classroom management efficacy. *Journal of School Psychology, 44*(2), 105–121. https://doi.org/10.1016/j.jsp.2006.01.004

Neff, K. (2021). *What self-compassion is.* https://self-compassion.org/the-three-elements-of-self-compassion-2/

Nelson, J. R., Maculan, A., Roberts, M. L., & Ohlund, B. J. (2001). Sources of occupational stress for teachers of students with emotional and behavioral disorders. *Journal of Emotional and Behavioral Disorders, 9*(2), 123–130. https://doi.org/10.1177/106342660100900207

Nelson, J. R., Hall, B. S., Anderson, J. L., Birtles, C., & Hemming, L. (2018). Self-compassion as self-care: A simple and effective tool for counselor educators and counseling students. *Journal of Creativity in Mental Health, 13*(1), 121–133. http://dx.doi.org/10.1080/15401383.2017.1328292

Nupponen, H. (2006). Leadership concepts and theories: Reflections for practice for early childhood directors. *Australian Journal of Early Childhood, 31*(1), 43–50. https://doi.org/10.1177/183693910603100107

Pakenham, K. I. (2015). Investigation of the utility of the acceptance and commitment therapy (ACT) framework for fostering self-care in clinical psychology trainees. *Training and Education in Professional Psychology, 9*(2), 144. https://doi.org/10.1037/tep0000074

Psychotherapy and Counselling Federation of Australia. (2021). *Code of ethics.* https://pacfa.org.au/Portal/Prac-Res/Code-of-Ethics.aspx

Puig, A., Yoon, E., Callueng, C., An, S., & Lee, S. M. (2014). Burnout syndrome in psychotherapists: A comparative analysis of five nations. *Psychological Services, 11*(1), 87–96. https://doi.org/10.1037/a0035285

Regehr, C., Hemsworth, D., Leslie, B., Howe, P., & Chau, S. (2004). Predictors of post-traumatic distress in child welfare workers: A linear structural equation model. *Children and Youth Services Review, 26*(4), 331–346. https://doi.org/10.1016/j.childyouth.2004.02.003

Rodd, J. (2013). *Leadership in early childhood* (4th ed.). Allen and Unwin.

Sakinofsky, I. (2007). The aftermath of suicide: Managing survivors' bereavement. *Canadian Journal of Psychiatry, 52*(6), 129S–136S.

Salloum, A., Kondrat, D. C., Johnco, C., & Olson, K. R. (2015). The role of self-care on compassion satisfaction, burnout and secondary trauma among child welfare workers. *Children and Youth Services Review, 49*, 54–61. http://dx.doi.org/10.1016/j.childyouth.2014.12.023

Santavirta, N., Solovieva, S., & Theorell, T. (2007). The association between job strain and emotional exhaustion in a cohort of 1,028 Finnish teachers. *British Journal of Educational Psychology, 77*(1), 213–228. https://doi.org/10.1348/000709905X92045

Skaalvik, E. M., & Skaalvik, S. (2007). Dimensions of teacher self-efficacy and relations with strain factors, perceived collective teacher efficacy, and teacher burnout. *Journal of Educational Psychology, 99*(3), 611–625. https://doi.org/10.1037/0022-0663.99.3.611

Sofronoff, K., Helmes, E., & Pachana, N. (2011). Fitness to practice in the profession of psychology: Should we assess this during clinical training? *Australian Psychologist, 46*, 126–132. https://doi.org/10.1111/j.1742-9544.2011.00031.x

Thompson, I., Amatea, E., & Thompson, E. (2014). Personal and contextual predictors of mental health counselors' compassion fatigue and burnout. *Journal of Mental Health Counseling, 36*(1), 58–77. https://doi.org/10.17744/mehc.36.1.p61m73373m4617r3

Vallance, K. (2005). Exploring counsellor perceptions of the impact of counselling supervision on clients. *Counselling and Psychotherapy Research, 5*(2), 107–110. https://doi.org/10.1080/03069880412331303330

Whitaker, R. C., Dearth-Wesley, T., & Gooze, R. A. (2015). Workplace stress and the quality of teacher-child relationships in Head Start. *Early Childhood Research Quarterly, 30*(1), 57–69. https://doi.org/10.1016/j.ecresq.2014.08.008

Wong, P. T., & Wong, L. C. (2020). Assessing multicultural supervision competencies. In D. L. Dinne, D. K. Forgays, S. A. Hayes & W. J. Lonner (Eds.), *Merging past, present, and future in cross-cultural psychology* (pp. 510–519). Garland Science.

Yang, Y., & Hayes, J. A. (2020). Causes and consequences of burnout among mental health professionals: A practice-oriented review of recent empirical literature. *Psychotherapy, 57*(3), 426–436. http://dx.doi.org/10.1037/pst0000317

Zaki (2016). *How to avoid empathy burnout.* http://nautil.us/issue/35/boundaries/how-to-avoid-empathy-burnout

9 Diversity and social justice

Diversity is any characteristic that creates the perception that individuals are different from others (De Janasz et al., 2015). Within any society, individuals differ on many dimensions, encapsulated by the acronym *ADDRESSING* (Hays, 2001):

*A*ge and generational differences
*D*evelopment
*D*isability
*R*eligion or spirituality
*E*thnicity
*S*ocioeconomic status
*S*exual orientation
*I*ndigenous heritage
*N*ational origin
*G*ender

Some of these characteristics are primary to individuals' identity and others are less central, or are secondary – see Figure 9.1.

Some key terms

- Stereotypes are assumptions that individuals will possess particular attributes as a result of their group membership. It is a set of beliefs that we apply universally to all members of the group, overlooking their individuality.
- Prejudice is literally a pre-judgement (negative or positive) about those attributes, groups or their individual members. In the acronym of ABC, it comprises three aspects: affect (feelings), behaviour and cognitions (beliefs).
- Discrimination is negative behaviour, often excluding individuals from full participation on the grounds of their group membership. It arises from prejudicial attitudes.
- Xenophobia is discrimination against people because of their country of origin.
- Hegemony is the dominance of one social group over another.
- Ethnocentrism is the belief that our own culture, gender or nation is superior to all others, with our own rituals and values the correct ones to adopt.

DOI: 10.4324/9781003323938-10

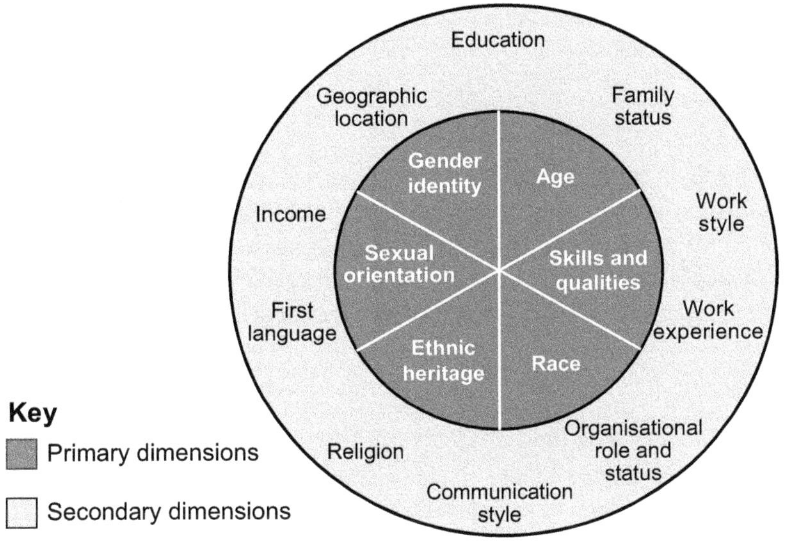

Figure 9.1 Primary and secondary aspects of diversity

- Sexism and racism are institutional practices that discriminate, resulting in unfair and avoidable disparities in power, resources and opportunities (Babacan et al., 2021).
- Paternalism is a form of sexism based on the belief that women are special and should be protected and adored; misogyny is the hostile belief that women are inferior to men.

Theories that inform diversity competence

Five key theories inform our competence across diversity: decolonisation, feminism, queer theory, minority stress theory and intersectionality.

Decolonisation

The repeated and cumulative loss of whole Australian Aboriginal tribes to genocide, displacement, disease and indenture (the Australian equivalent of slavery), of languages, culture and country over many generations could be termed a First Nations holocaust (St Vil & St Vil, 2019). While today many First Nations peoples have attained middle class status, a disproportionate number are subjected to poverty, unemployment, an incomplete education, poor health care, high infant mortality, a 20-year shorter lifespan than other Australians and elevated incarceration rates. This is why 'Get over it' is not only scornful but dismissive – because the human rights violations of First Nations peoples are not yet in the past (St Vil & St Vil, 2019).

Therefore, for First Nations peoples, counselling must acknowledge intergenerational trauma, in order to 'promote the healing of the souls, spirits and minds of persons suffering the continuing influences of colonisation' (Heath, 2018, p. 51). Heath (2018, p. 52) asks how counsellors can frame their questions in ways that 'do some measure of justice to ancestral trauma sitting with us in the room'. For example, whereas I might start an interview asking how I can be of use to clients today, we could instead ask, 'How can I be of service to you so that your spirit can soar?'.

Feminism

Originally focusing on gender inequality alone, modern feminism wants to give all people - but especially those on the margins - the option of an educated choice. This agenda has expanded to include all forms of inequality, which this theory sees as an issue of domination and subordination. In that case, the solution is not only to end discrimination, but also to alter the power dynamics within society that suppress and silence marginalised groups (Kymlicka, 2002).

Queer theory

Queer theory challenges how individuals are 'conceptualised, labeled and positioned in society' (Rivera, 2022). It rejects binary thinking and fixed boundaries between gay/straight, male/female, masculine/feminine and instead contends that identities are constructed, multiple and fluid (Nylund & Temple, 2017). Queer theory extends this non-binary thinking to other categorisations such as Black/White and rich/poor. (I discuss the needs of sexual minorities in Chapter 21.)

Minority stress theory

Minority stress theory acknowledges that individuals' emotional problems are not just due to their own psychology but can have a social cause (Meyer, 1995; Price et al., 2019). It states that there are both distal and proximal factors that influence the emotional well-being of minority group members. Distal factors are their experiences of discrimination, bullying and violence; while proximal factors are those that are internal to the individual, such as the expectation of rejection, concealment of their identity, and internalised racist, sexist or homophobic attitudes (Jadva et al., 2021). In other words, those who are marginalised internalise negative social, cultural or institutional cues that they are an outsider, which leads to psychological distress arising from their negative view of self and a view that their identity is deviant (Meyer, 1995). Stress occurs as a result of constant vigilance or expectation of prejudice, discrimination and rejection (Meyer, 1995). In turn, this can lead to fear and mistrust of others.

Intersectionality

The concept of intersectionality identifies that discrimination on the basis of membership of one disadvantaged social group can be compounded by persecution based on membership of other marginalised groups (Elze, 2019). This produces unique patterns of discrimination and oppression (Price et al., 2019). The use of an intersectional lens does not attempt to isolate one particular aspect of a person's identity nor prioritise one form of oppression over another, but instead treats various forms of oppression and privilege as 'interactive and mutually reinforcing' (Hulko & Hovanes, 2017). The concept recognises that individuals who are members of multiple groups can find themselves subjected to a combination of racism, sexism, ageism, classism, heterosexism, transphobia and xenophobia (Lewis & Gadson, 2022). A female high school student of colour could experience the additive or even multiplicative effects of sexism, racism, ageism and class oppression, for example. This requires counsellors to recognise that individuals can be discriminated against for being female *and* poor; being young *and* having a disability; being a member of a cultural minority *and* being gay.

Box 9.1 Open-ended questions for youth with intersecting minority culture membership

Cultural identity

- What would you like me to know about your cultural identities that will help me better understand you?
- Tell me about your various cultural identities.
- Which identity or identities are most important to you?
- Is there more than one identity that you feel most comfortable with?
- How do your identities influence your current concerns?
- How do you prioritise your various cultural identities?
- How does religion or spirituality fit into your life, if at all?
- Are there aspects of your identities that influence (your presenting issue)?

Cultural conceptualisations of distress

- Have you experienced distress about embracing dissimilar values from your identified cultural groups?
- How do you think your family would describe your (presenting issues)?
- Are any of your family members' descriptions of what you are experiencing different from yours?
- How do you think your religious leaders would describe your concerns?

Cultural stressors

- What has been your experience of discrimination because of your identities?
- Have you been treated unfairly as a result of being a member of (a cultural or sexual minority)?
- Have you experienced personal challenges as a result of societal biases against any of your identities?
- Have you experienced feeling isolated because of your identities?
- Has it been difficult for your voice to be heard as a result of your identities?

Culturally protective factors

- Who in your family can you trust to talk with about your (presenting issues)?
- Who in your community can you trust to talk with about your (presenting issues)?
- Are there friends or family members who accept who you are? If so, how does that affect your (presenting issue)?
- Are there some other communities that you believe could provide you with support to whom you could reach out?

Cultural features of the relationship between the client and counsellor

- Are you comfortable to work with me, given that we have different cultural backgrounds?
- I notice that you've seen a counsellor in the past. How was that experience?
- What was it like for you to experience discrimination within a counselling relationship?
- What can I do differently in order to be helpful to you?

Sources: Chaney et al. (2020, pp. 292–293); Oh et al. (2019)

More than this individual level, the concept of intersectionality is based in social justice. It goes beyond the individual level of discrimination that marginalised individuals experience, to examine, question and push back against the interlocking social and political systems of oppression and privilege that affect their lives (Lewis & Gadson, 2022; Moffitt et al., 2020).

Disadvantaged groups

Because of their young age, children and adolescents are frequently marginalised and their views discounted. In addition, they can face challenges because of their gender, disability or culture.

Girls and women

Kymlicka (2002, p. 381) observes that, despite advances in women's rights, still 'In every society across the world, females remain disadvantaged relative to males economically, socially, occupationally and politically – and consequently become dependent on men for their security'. Females' elevated rates of emotional difficulties are related to the facts that they are still evaluated by their appearance; they are sexually harassed from the age of 4 (Harter et al., 1997); more than half of Australian women experience some form of sexual harassment in their lifetime (Barlow et al., 2021); and 75 per cent experience sexual objectification once every two days (Holland et al., 2017). Gendered violence results in one police report every two minutes in Australia (and most violence is unreported), and women are the biggest group of homeless Australians (Norris, 2016).

Educationally, because their behaviour is typically less disruptive, girls with learning difficulties such as attention deficits get overlooked and are less likely than boys to receive remedial support (Arnold, 1996; Hallahan & Kauffman, 2006). Meanwhile, patriarchal values impose a compliance on girls that allows them to do well in their schoolwork but produce a conventionality that disadvantages them in adult life (Kerr, 1996; Kline & Short, 1991; Loeb & Jay, 1987). As for those who are gifted, many young women with exceptional skills have to contend with greater alienation from their families, culture and peers than do boys because high achievement – particularly in certain fields – is considered unfeminine (Kerr, 2000; Noble et al., 1999).

Young people with disabilities

In discussing disability, it will be helpful to distinguish between a cluster of terms (Pope, 1992):

- an *impairment* is a discrete loss of mental or physical functioning, such as damage to the brain
- a *disability* refers to the effect of this on the individual, such as the movement difficulties associated with cerebral palsy
- a *handicap* is the social stigma and environmental restrictions that are often imposed on those with disabilities but which are not an inevitable feature of their condition.

Compared to the general population, adolescents with learning disabilities are at double the risk of distress, depression, anxiety, low self-efficacy, suicidal ideation and overall poor mental well-being, with their quality of life difficulties increasing into adulthood (Costello & Stone, 2012; Wilson et al., 2009). Individuals with physical or intellectual disabilities are compared (and compare themselves) to others with similar disabilities, in which case their self-esteem is largely intact, whereas students with learning disabilities are compared to their nondisabled cohort, against whom they are seen as failing and, therefore, they can suffer low self-esteem (Higgins et al., 2002).

These difficulties seem to arise both from academic and social problems, such as neglect or rejection by peers (Higgins et al., 2002; Myers, 2005; Wilson et al., 2009). For some, the physical fatigue from having to put in extra effort to navigate an environment built for able-bodied individuals or teaching methods aimed at the more able students can take its toll on their ability to engage in academic work.

The biomedical model of disability pathologises differences and sets about conferring diagnoses (Smart & Smart, 2006). In the understandable desire to access educational funding to support young people who are struggling in schools, there is a trend to label any quirky learning style as a disability. On the one hand, this can provide comfort to and take pressure off those who have been struggling for some time with school achievement (Higgins et al., 2002) but is concerning because the label can come to define and limit them. With one in five school students being diagnosed as having a learning disability (Bell et al., 2022), we could conclude that there is a strong need for advocacy for this group - but could also query how come such a large proportion of the population is defined as departing from the norm. Surely these large numbers mean that having difficulty learning is common, if not normal.

In contrast, the sociopolitical model of disability proposes that the stigma and prejudice to which individuals with disability are often subject is more of a problem for their daily life than are their actual impairments (Smart & Smart, 2006). This view concludes that the issue is that the education system is not geared to cater for the broad range of learning styles of the student population (Bell et al., 2022). Ableism within the system allows the lack of appropriate accommodations for diverse students to be obscured (Bell et al., 2022).

In terms of how a diagnosis informs their identity, some individuals respond by simply choosing the least stigmatising label or by compartmentalising - that is, attaching the label to a specific skill that is difficult for them, while seeing the rest of their self as 'normal' (Higgins et al., 2002). Some see their disability not as something tragic or limiting, but as a valued part of their identity (Smart & Smart, 2006). After some time, many come to see their difficulties as having taught them some skills for circumventing obstacles, for being tolerant of diversity, and for carving a different path in life (Higgins et al., 2002). Therefore, counsellors cannot assume that there is a straight line between having an impairment, a disability and a handicap and must recognise that clients who have disabilities want respect, not pity.

Time is a limitation with any service delivery, but individuals with disabilities may already be being pulled out of class for special tutoring, speech pathology, physiotherapy, occupational therapy or general medical appointments, all of which make less time available for attending counselling (Myers, 2005). And coordinating among these services can become a role of the counsellor, which detracts from the time available to support the young people's emotional and social well-being directly (Myers, 2005).

Culture

In Australia, 29 per cent of the population are born elsewhere, while in Aotearoa/New Zealand, this figure is 23 per cent (Lee et al., 2021). Australia's rich cultural diversity spans more than 300 languages spoken in homes, more than 300 different ancestries and the many cultures of Aboriginal and Torres Strait Islander peoples (Sisko, 2021a) and, in Aotearoa, of the New Zealand Māori peoples. This means that these two countries are amongst the most racially diverse in the world (Lee et al., 2021). It also means that clients and counsellors will often come from different backgrounds.

The term *culture* refers to 'webs of significance' or patterns of meaning that are historically transmitted (Geertz, 1973, in Miller, 2014). Observable aspects will include customs, practices and language whereas unobservable aspects will include values and beliefs (Ridley et al., 2021). Culture also refers to the norms and customs of institutions such as schools or churches.

White privilege

Being a White person in a dominantly White society means chronic exposure to ethnocentric monoculturalism in which Whiteness is the norm against which other races are judged (Sue & Sue, 2016). There is a 'contract' which denotes some people as 'White' and all the remainder as 'non-White' and, by implication, inferior. As Mills (1997, in Matias & Boucher, 2022, p. 69) states: 'All whites are beneficiaries of the Contract, though some whites are not signatories to it'.

Beneath a discussion of culture there is often a presumption of either innocence or ignorance on the part of the white, dominant society (Matias & Boucher, 2022). If there were true ignorance, there could be neither racism nor racists. Matias and Boucher (2002, p. 63) state: 'Clearly, folks do know about race and how it operates and strategically use it to feign innocence ... so as to not be held accountable'.

As members of the majority are increasingly sensitised to avoid overt discrimination, nevertheless, they might unconsciously deliver a contemporary form of oppression in the form of micro-aggressions (Sue & Sue, 2016). These are brief, subtle, everyday exchanges that send denigrating messages that are meant to demean the group identity of minority individuals.

They are often produced and received unconsciously and comprise micro-assaults (behaviours) that intimidate or exclude; micro-insults that convey stereotypes, perhaps disguised as humour; and micro-invalidations that ignore or negate the thoughts, feelings or reality of marginalised groups (Sue & Sue, 2016).

These micro-aggressions can be quite complex to deal with because they are ambiguous. They can be essentially invisible to perpetrators so confronting them can lead to defensiveness, claims that the person who is protesting is 'reading too much into it', that there was no harm in it, or that the target is overreacting or being hypersensitive. This is known as gaslighting, which refers to psychological manipulation intended to make targets question their own judgement (Knutson et al., 2019).

Racial identity

Traditionally, counselling and psychology have been shaped by an etic (culturally universal) approach which views psychological processes as universal and proposes that Western concepts of normality and deviance (and associated treatments) are applicable across cultures. In contrast, there has been a growing push for counsellors to adopt an emic (or culturally relative) approach, which considers the impact of cultural differences on clients' world views, values and lifestyles.

Meanwhile individuals of mixed-race heritage are often ignored, neglected and considered nonexistent in our educational materials, media portrayals and psychological literature (Sue & Sue, 2016). These individuals often face racial or ethnic ambiguity. The 'What are you?' question almost asks bi-racial individuals to justify their existence in a world rigidly built on the concepts of racial purity and monoracialism. They exist between the margins, often viewed as fractionated people, composed of fractions of a race, culture or ethnicity (Root, 1990).

Components of diversity competence

Both counsellors and their clients are cultural beings, which makes incorporating clients' worldviews and backgrounds (cultural and otherwise) an integral part of all counselling (Ridley et al., 2021). Responsiveness is about routinely incorporating diversity into the process of counselling, gaining salient cultural data from clients and integrating it into a respectful therapeutic alliance with them (Ridley et al., 2021). This is more than making cosmetic changes to counselling processes but infusing an inclusive ethos throughout the process (Ridley et al., 2021; Smith et al., 2021). It incorporates the elements in Figure 9.2, which are illustrated as overlapping because each aspect informs the others.

Self-awareness

In an attempt to understand the effects on individuals' lives of social power and privilege (or lack thereof), counsellors who are competent at working across diversity are actively engaged in becoming aware of their class and cultural identity, assumptions, values, biases, preconceived notions and limitations (Sisko, 2021b). They can explore these through professional

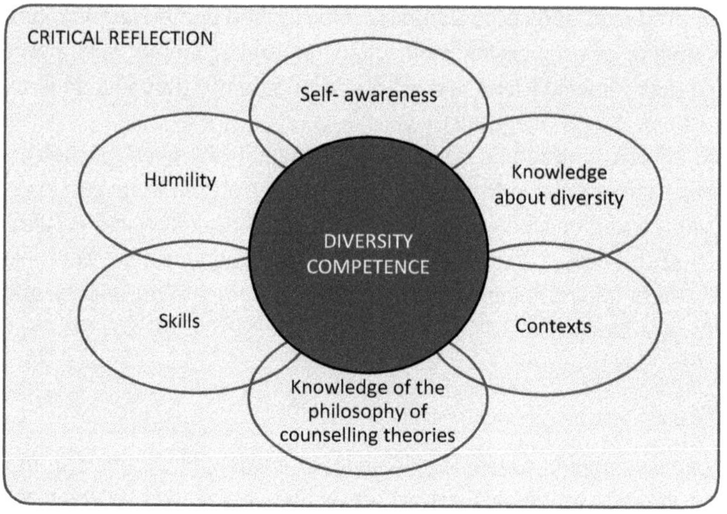

Figure 9.2 Elements of competence across diversity

Source: adapted from Lago (2010, p. 79).

development, engaging with multicultural mentors or community representatives and adopting a self-reflective stance.

Although self-awareness is the key to competence, strong emotions such as anger, sadness, guilt, shame, defensiveness and helplessness can be potential roadblocks for counsellors from the dominant culture (Matias & Boucher, 2022; Sue & Sue, 2016). If these intense feelings are left unexplored, they can greatly reduce counsellors' effectiveness when working with diverse clients.

Knowledge about diversity

Cultural sensitivity entails not only how we interact with people across differences, but also how we frame our perceptions of them in the first place. Our interpretations can render diverse clients unsafe by assessing a young person's issues as problematic within the dominant culture's frame of reference, whereas they might be appropriate within the child's culture (Ramirez et al., 1998) or be a natural reaction to social disadvantage or marginalisation. Hence, while self-awareness asks us to question, 'What do I believe?', the next step of knowledge about diversity expands this reflection to ask, 'What meaning am I attaching to the other person's actions?' (Barrera & Corso, 2002). This allows us to bridge cultural differences.

Knowledge about diversity will entail learning (by asking them) how clients define wellness, how they react to seeking outside help, and how helpful this 'help' has been to them in the past. At a deeper level, though, it is not a matter of content knowledge, of knowing the cultural beliefs, values and communication styles of every culture on the planet (Ridley et al., 2021). Not only would this be impossible, but it assumes that any given individual adopts all of the beliefs and values of their culture, which is patronising and homogenising. And it is a simple cognitive exercise (Smith et al., 2021). Instead, deep knowledge is a critical consciousness of the processes of discrimination and oppression, of power and privilege and of access to opportunity, and about the effects of colonisation, minority stress, intersectionality and intergenerational trauma on individuals' well-being (Sisko, 2021b).

Contexts

The third aspect of diversity competence is awareness that human dilemmas are manufactured and maintained within social contexts and that, in turn, cultural messages can be internalised (Semmler & Williams, 2000). This is a cornerstone of the solution-focused and narrative approaches. These counsellors will help clients to challenge how their economic, gender, social and individual contexts (and the intersectionality of these) shape their current predicament. The goal will be to enable clients to rediscover their identity, strengths and voice, framing their responses to adversity not as a personal defect but as resilience (Corcoran, 2000).

Knowledge of the philosophy of counselling theories

Fourth, and as discussed in previous chapters, diversity competence requires awareness of the sociopolitical aspect to counselling theories and their practices, in that the standards used to judge normality and abnormality come from a predominately Euro-American perspective (Brammer, 2012). If these standards are imposed upon diverse groups without regard for differences, counsellors can be unwittingly engaging in oppression, invalidating clients' life experiences and failing to affirm their resistance to colonisation (Neville et al., 2001; Sue & Sue, 2016).

The solution-focused and narrative approaches are ideal for navigating across diversity because clients' stories emerge from counsellor-client interactions (Akinyela, 2014; Miller, 2014). In having clients generate their own definitions of problems, determine their own goals and design action plans based on their own past successes, necessarily these will match their perspectives (cultural and otherwise).

Skills

Next in the model of diversity competencies is the employment of the following core therapeutic skills for conveying respect for clients' worldview (Bernal et al., 1995; Ratts et al., 2016; Sue & Sue, 2016).

Language is the carrier of culture. It might be possible to deliver counselling in clients' native language, or adapt communication styles to match client preferences and use terms that are salient for them, such as: 'If you weren't fighting as much, how would you be instead?' (replacing the verb *doing* with *being*) (Blakeslee & Jordan, 2014).

Person. This considers how differences can affect the counselling relationship (Ratts et al., 2016) and, in turn, the safety of clients (Smith et al., 2021). Self-reflexivity describes the process of taking account of the self and the impact that our attitudes, beliefs and biases on another person's self (Holland, 1999; Sisko, 2021a). This call on us to take account not only of the personal but also how power and privilege affect our relationships with clients (Aron, 2000; Smith et al., 2022).

We could attempt to match client and counsellor cultural backgrounds, use interpreters, or ask clients if they wish to bring along a member of their own community or extended family. This has to be their choice entirely because in some cultures the presence of an outsider would be experienced as supportive, whereas in others it would cause clients to lose face.

Counsellors can also engage in a dialogue about difference: 'It must be difficult talking to a White person who isn't from your tribe. How might I be helpful, given that I am not (from your mob)?' (Blakeslee & Jordan, 2014). Madigan (2019, p. 67) related to a Black mother with, 'I am sad that this story is going on for you. I'm saying that as a person here with you, and I'm also saying that as a White person'.

Metaphors. Counsellors can use symbols and concepts and tailor questions or metaphors to be culturally relevant. For example: On a scale from 1 to 10, where 10 is things as good as they can be while living outside of the tribe/off country and 1 was furthest from that, where would you be on the scale right now? (Blakeslee & Jordan, 2014).

Goals. Solution-focused and narrative therapists value self-determination whereby clients select their own goals. In the service of this aim, we can adjust the miracle question to take in the cultural orientation of First Nations peoples – for example, such as:

> If an elder or animal appeared in a vision and they let you know that the problems you have been talking about today are no longer a problem.... So you wake up tomorrow to start your day but things are different. What are the first things you would notice that are different?
>
> (Blakeslee & Jordan, 2014, p. 114)

For Australian Aboriginal and Torres Strait Islander peoples, their goals will be framed within an awareness of the interconnectedness of the body, mind and emotions, family and kinship, community, culture, country, spirituality and ancestors (Smith et al., 2021).

For many Chinese (and others), the miracle question for identifying clients' goals is too fanciful, but can be made pragmatic by imagining that 'something big is possible' or by linking it to clients' sense of a higher power (the faerie):

> Imagine ... you visit Wong Tai Sin temple today, and you worship at Wong Tai Sin. Your effort impresses the faerie. At night, while you are sleeping, he removes all of your troubles and stressors by his super-power. On the next morning, how is your world different, what does it look like, and what changes do you discover?
>
> Moir-Bussey (2014, p. 42)

Methods (such as questioning, being directive, using play, music or art, visualisation, homework tasks, or using psychoeducation) are in tune with clients' diverse preferences. For Aboriginal and Torres Strait Islander peoples, this will include affirming both traditional and contemporary healing models (Gee et al., 2014).

Moir-Bussey (2014) notes that some cultures value humility and do not like to receive compliments. This can be easily accommodated by asking them questions that imply a strength. Counsellors can also ask about their efforts or virtues (such as patience, or contributing to the well-being of others) rather than their accomplishments (Moir-Bussey, 2014).

Cultural humility

The last element of my model of competence across diversity is cultural humility. This requires practitioners to be willing to 'step out of the culture of the self in order to understand the culture of the other' (Smith et al., 2021, p. 448). It suspends any notion of superiority of one's worldview, values or beliefs (Smith et al., 2022). This is in tune with the solution-focused theory's posture of 'not-knowing' (Berg & Steiner, 2003) which entails asking clients specifically about their values and preferred practices (Phoenix, 2002). Cultural humility reflects an openness to cultural multiplicity and a commitment to self-reflection and lifelong learning (Zhu et al., 2021).

Critical reflection

Catering to diversity requires engaging in critical reflection. This involves reflecting on surface issues such as our practices in the moment. But also, at a deeper level, we can look back on and reflect on what these practices say about who we are (Gardner, 2014). It requires a deeper look at the premises on which our thinking, actions and emotions are based (Gardner, 2014).

Social justice advocacy

Social justice advocacy broadens counsellors' role from working reactively with distressed clients, to challenging inequity at the organisational and societal levels (Ratts et al., 2016; Singh et al., 2020; Sue & Sue, 2016; Sue & Torino, 2005). Counsellors based in schools are particularly well placed to transform the structure, policies and practices of their school to promote greater equity (Ratts & Greenleaf, 2018). They can lead school personnel to consider how diversity issues and intersectionality affect the access and engagement of all students and to consider students' presenting issues within the context of discrimination at school and the wider culture (Ratts & Greenleaf, 2018).

Conclusion

The need to promote social justice for all requires an understanding of the complex and intersecting identities that contribute to individuals' sense of self, recognising the negative effects of marginalisation and oppression on individuals' well-being, seeing individuals as embedded in their social and cultural contexts and raising questions about the inclusivity of counselling theories and their practices (Ratts et al., 2016).

References

Akinyela, M. M. (2014). Narrative therapy and cultural democracy: A testimony view. *Australian and New Zealand Journal of Family Therapy*, *35*(1), 46–49. https://doi.org/10.1002/anzf.1041

Arnold, L. E. (1996). Sex differences in ADHD: Conference summary. *Journal of Abnormal Child Psychology*, *24*(5), 555–569. https://doi.org/10.1007/BF01670100

Aron, L. (2000). Self-reflexivity and the therapeutic action of psychoanalysis. *Psychoanalytic Psychology*, *17*, 667–689. https://doi.org/10.1037/0736-9735.17.4.667

Babacan, A., Jacobs, R., Kemp, A., Paradies, Y., Piyarathne, A., Wang, C., Zwi, K., Woodland, L., & Hutton, V. (2021). Racism. In V. Hutton & S. Sisko (Eds.), *Multicultural responsiveness in counselling and psychology: Working with Australian populations* (pp. 53–102). Springer. https://doi.org/10.1007/978-3-030-55427-9_3

Barlow, F. K., Vickers-Jones, R., Alba, B., Williamson, E., & Hutton, V. (2021). Sexism. In V. Hutton & S. Sisko (Eds.), *Multicultural responsiveness in counselling and psychology: Working with Australian populations* (pp. 125–151). Springer. https://doi.org/10.1007/978-3-030-55427-9_5

Barrera, I. & Corso, R.M. (2002). Cultural competency as skilled dialogue. *Topics in Early Childhood Special Education*, *22*(2), 103–113. https://doi.org/10.1177/02711214020220020501

Bell, T., Remley, T. Jr, & Hill, T. (2022). Counseling clients with learning disabilities: Counselor perceived competencies. *Review of Disability Studies: An International Journal*, *18*(1 & 2), 1–32.

Berg, I. K., & Steiner, S. (2003). *Children's solution work*. Norton.

Bernal, G., Bonilla, J., & Bellido, C. (1995). Ecological validity and cultural sensitivity for outcome research: Issues for the cultural adaptation and development of psychosocial treatments with Hispanics. *Journal of Abnormal Child Psychology*, *23*(1), 67–82.

Blakeslee, S. & Jordan, S. S. (2014). Solution-focused approach with American Indian clients. In J. S. Kim (Ed.), *Solution-focused brief therapy: A multicultural approach* (pp. 106–121). Sage.

Brammer, R. (2012). *Diversity in counseling*. Cengage.

Chaney, M. P., Dubaybo, F., & Chang, C. Y. (2020). Affirmative counseling With LGBTQ+ Arab Americans. *Journal of Mental Health Counseling*, *42*(4), 281–302. https://doi.org/10.17744/mehc.42.4.01

Corcoran, J. (2000). Solution-focused family therapy with ethnic minority clients. *Crisis Intervention*, 6(1), 5–12. https://doi.org/10.1080/10645130008951292

Costello, C. A., & Stone, S. L. (2012). Positive psychology and self-efficacy: Potential benefits for college students with attention deficit hyperactivity disorder and learning disabilities. *Journal of Postsecondary Education and Disability*, *25*(2), 119–129.

De Janasz, S. C., Dowd, K. O., & Schneider, B. Z. (2015). *Interpersonal skills in organizations* (5th ed.). McGraw Hill Education.

Elze, D. E. (2019). The lives of lesbian, gay, bisexual, and transgender people: A trauma-informed and human rights perspective. In L. D. Butler, F. M. Critelli & J. Carello (Eds.), *Trauma and human rights: Integrating approaches to address human suffering* (pp. 179–206). Springer.

Gardner, F. (2014). *Being critically reflective: Engaging in holistic practice*. Macmillan Education.

Gee, G., Dudgeon, P., Schultz, C., Hart, A., & Kelly, K. (2014). Aboriginal and Torres Strait Islander social and emotional wellbeing. In P. Dudgeon, H. Milroy & R. Walker (Eds.), *Working together: Aboriginal and Torres Strait Islander mental health and wellbeing principles and practices* (2nd ed., pp. 55–68). Commonwealth of Australia.

Hallahan, D. P., & Kauffman, J. M. (2006). *Exceptional learners: Introduction to special education* (10th ed.). Pearson Allyn & Bacon.

Harter, S., Waters, P., & Whitesell, N. R. (1997). Lack of voice as a manifestation of false self behavior among adolescents: The school setting as a stage upon which the drama of authenticity is enacted. *Educational Psychologist*, *32*(3), 153–173.

Hays, P. A. (2001). *Addressing cultural complexities in practice: A framework for clinicians and counselors*. American Psychological Association. https://doi.org/10.1037/10411-000

Heath, T. (2018). Moving beyond multicultural counselling: Narrative therapy, anti-colonialism, cultural democracy and hip-hop. *International Journal of Narrative Therapy and Community Work*, *3*, 50–55.

Higgins, E. L., Raskind, M. H., Goldberg, R. J., & Herman, K. L. (2002). Stages of acceptance of a learning disability: The impact of labeling. *Learning Disability Quarterly*, *25*(1), 3–18. https://doi.org/10.2307/1511187

Holland, E., Koval, P., Stratemeyer, M., Thomson, F., & Haslam, N. (2017). Sexual objectification in women's daily lives: A smartphone ecological momentary assessment study. *British Journal of Social Psychology*, *56*(2), 314–333. https://doi.org/10.1111/bjso.12152

Holland, R. (1999). Reflexivity. *Human Relations*, *52*, 463–484. https://doi.org/10.1177/001872679905200403

Hulko, W., & Hovanes, J. (2017). Intersectionality in the lives of LGBTQ youth: Identifying as LGBTQ and finding community in small cities and rural towns. *Journal of Homosexuality*, *65*(4), 427–455. http://dx.doi.org/10.1080/00918369.2017.1320169

Jadva, V., Guasp, A., Bradlow, J. H., Bower-Brown, S., & Foley, S. (2021). Predictors of self-harm and suicide in LGBT youth: The role of gender, socio-economic status, bullying and school experience. *Journal of Public Health*, 1–7. https://doi.org/10.1093/pubmed/fdab383

Kerr, B. A. (1996). *Smart girls two: A new psychology of girls, women and giftedness*. Hawker Brownlow Education.

Kerr, B. A. (2000). Guiding gifted girls and young women. In K. A. Heller, F. J. Mönks, R. J. Sternberg & R. F. Subotnik (Eds.), *International handbook of giftedness and talent* (2nd ed., pp. 649–657). Pergamon.

Kline, B. E., & Short, E. B. (1991). Changes in emotional resilience: Gifted adolescent females. *Roeper Review*, *13*(3), 118–121. https://doi.org/10.1080/02783199109553333

Knutson, D., Koch, J. M., & Goldbach, C. (2019). Recommended terminology, pronouns, and documentation for work with transgender and non-binary populations. *Practice Innovations*, *4*(4), 214–224. https://doi.org/10.1037/pri0000098

Kymlicka, W. (2002). *Contemporary political philosophy: An introduction* (2nd ed.). Oxford University Press.

Lee, E., Greenblatt, A., & Hu, R. (2021). A knowledge synthesis of cross-cultural psychotherapy research: A critical review. *Journal of Cross-Cultural Psychology*, *52*(6), 511–532. https://doi.org/10.1177/00220221211028911

Lewis, J. A., & Gadson, C. A. (2022). Applying intersectionality to school psychology: Implications for research, practice and advocacy. In S. L. Proctor & D. P. Rivera (Eds.), *Critical theories for school psychology and counseling: A foundation for equity and inclusion in school-based practice* (pp. 3–16). Routledge.

Loeb, R. C., & Jay, G. (1987). Self-concept in gifted children: Differential impact in boys and girls. *Gifted Child Quarterly*, *31*(1), 9–14. https://doi.org/10.1177/001698628703100102

Madigan, S. (2019). *Narrative therapy* (2nd ed.). American Psychological Association.

Matias, C. E., & Boucher, C. (2022). Toward a critical study of whiteness. In S. L. Proctor & D. P. Rivera (Eds.), *Critical theories for school psychology and counseling: A foundation for equity and inclusion in school-based practice* (pp. 63–81). Routledge.

Meyer, I. H. (1995). Minority stress and mental health in gay men. *Journal of Health and Social Behavior*, *36*(1), 38–56. https://doi.org/10.2307/2137286

Miller, G. (2014). Culture in solution-focused consultation: An intercultural approach. *Journal of Solution Focused Practices*, *1*(2), 4. https://digitalscholarship.unlv.edu/journalsfp/vol1/iss2/4

Moffitt, U., Juang, L. P., & Syed, M. (2020). Intersectionality and youth identity development research in Europe. *Frontiers in Psychiatry*, *11*, 78. https://doi.or/10.3389/fpsyg.2020.00078

Moir-Bussy, A. (2014). Using SFBT in Hong Kong: Initiatives from Hong Kong Master of Counselling psychology students and implications for cultural contexts in Australia. *Journal of Solution-Focused Practices*, *1*(1), 30–45. https://digitalscholarship.unlv.edu/journalsfp/vol1/iss1/5

Myers, H. N. F. (2005). How elementary school counselors can meet the needs of students with disabilities. *Professional School Counseling*, 8(5) 442–450. https://www.jstor.org/stable/42732487

Neville, H. A., Worthington, R. L., & Spanierman, L. B. (2001). Race, power, and multicultural counseling psychology: Understanding White privilege and color-blind racial attitudes. In J. Ponterotto, J. M. Casas, L. A. Suzuki & C. M. Alexander (Eds.), *Handbook of multicultural counseling* (pp. 257–288). Sage.

Noble, K. D., Subotnik, R. F., & Arnold, K. D. (1999). To thine own self be true: A new model of female talent development. *Gifted Child Quarterly*, *43*(4), 140–149.

Norris, M. (2016). *Look what you made me do: Fathers who kill*. Echo.

Nylund, D., & Temple, A. (2017). Queer informed narrative therapy: Radical approaches to counseling with transgender persons. In C. A. Audet & D. Paré (Eds.), *Social justice and counseling: Discourse in practice* (pp. 159–170). Routledge.

Oh, S., Kim, N., Bennett, C. M., & Taylor, D. D. (2019). Multiculturally competent intake interview with LGBTQI++ clients. *Journal of Gay and Lesbian Mental Health*, *23*(2), 186–204. https://doi.org/10.1080/19359705.2019.1568943

Phoenix, A. (2002). Working with diverse communities. In S. Roffey (Ed.), *School behaviour and families* (pp. 125–139). David Fulton.

Pope, A. M. (1992). Preventing secondary conditions. *Mental Retardation*, *30*(6), 347–354.

Price, M., Polk, W., Hill, N. E., Liang, B., & Perella, J. (2019). The intersectionality of identity-based victimization in adolescence:A person-centered examination of mental health and academic achievement in a U.S. high school. *Journal of Adolescence*, *76*, 185–196. https://doi.org/10.1016/j.adolescence.2019.09.002

Ramirez, S. Z., Lepage, K. M., Kratochwill, T. R., & Duffy, J. L. (1998). Multicultural issues in school-based consultation: Conceptual and research considerations. *Journal of School Psychology*, 36(4), 479–509. https://doi.org/10.1016/S0022-4405(98)00014-4

Ratts, M. J., Singh, A. A., Nassar-McMillan, S., Butler, S. K., & McCullough, J. R. (2016). Multicultural and social justice counseling competencies: Guidelines for the counseling profession. *Journal of Multicultural Counseling and Development*, *44*(1), 28–48. https://doi.org/10.1002/jmcd.12035

Ratts, M. J., & Greenleaf, A. T. (2018). Multicultural and social justice counseling competencies: A leadership framework for professional school counselors. *Professional School Counseling*, *21*(1b), 2156759X18773582. https://doi.org/10.1177/2156759X18773582

Ridley, C. R., Sahu, A., Console, K., Surya, S., Tran, V., Xie, S., & Yin, C. (2021). The process model of multicultural counseling competence. *The Counseling Psychologist*, *49*(4), 534–567. https://doi.org/10.1177/0011000021992339

Rivera, D. P. (2022). Queering school psychology: A queer theory for school-based practice. In S. L. Proctor & D. P. Rivera (Eds.), *Critical theories for school psychology and counseling: A foundation for equity and inclusion in school-based practice* (pp. 48–62). Routledge.

Root, M. P. (1990). Resolving 'other' status: Identity development of biracial individuals. *Women and Therapy*, 9(1-2), 185–205. https://doi.org/10.1300/J015v09n01_11

Semmler, P. L., & Williams, C. B. (2000). Narrative therapy: A storied context for multicultural counseling. *Journal of Multicultural Counseling and Development*, *28*(1), 51–62. https://doi.org/10.1002/j.2161-1912.2000.tb00227.x

Singh, A. A., Nassar, S. C., Arredondo, P., & Toporek, R. (2020). The past guides the future: Implementing the multicultural and social justice counseling competencies. *Journal of Counseling and Development*, *98*(3), 238–252. https://doi.org/10.1002/jcad.12319

Sisko, S. (2021a). Cultural responsiveness in counselling and psychology: An introduction. In V. Hutton & S. Sisko (Eds.), *Multicultural responsiveness in counselling and psychology: Working with Australian populations* (pp. 3–21). Springer. https://doi.org/10.1007/978-3-030-55427-9_1

Sisko, S. (2021b). Key principles for multicultural perspectives and responsiveness in counselling and psychology. In V. Hutton & S. Sisko (Eds.), *Multicultural responsiveness in counselling and psychology: Working with Australian populations* (pp. 287–296). Springer. https://doi.org/10.1007/978-3-030-55427-9_11

Smart, J. F., & Smart, D. W. (2006). Models of disability: Implications for the counseling profession. *Journal of Counseling and Development*, *84*(1), 29–40. https://doi.org/10.1002/j.1556-6678.2006.tb00377.x

Smith, P., Rice, K., Usher, K., & Schutte, N. (2021). Cultural responsiveness for mental health professionals working with Aboriginal and Torres Strait Islander clients: A concept analysis. *Australian Psychologist*, *56*(6), 446–457. https://doi.org/10.1080/00050067.2021.1974281

Smith, P., Rice, K., Schutte, N., & Usher, K. (2022). Reflexivity: A model for teaching and learning cultural responsiveness in mental health. *Australian Psychologist*, *57*(4), 209–214. https://doi.org/10.1080/00050067.2022.2078648

St Vil, C., & St Vil, N. M. (2019). Black trauma in the US and the pursuit of human rights: A brief history. In L. D. Butler, F. M. Critelli & J. Carello (Eds.), *Trauma and human rights: Integrating approaches to address human suffering* (pp. 99–124). Palgrave Macmillan. https://doi.org/10.1007/978-3-030-16395-2

Sue, D. W., & Sue, D. (2016). *Counseling the culturally diverse: Theory and practice* (7th ed.). Wiley.

Wilson, A. M., Deri Armstrong, C., Furrie, A., & Walcot, E. (2009). The mental health of Canadians with self-reported learning disabilities. *Journal of Learning Disabilities*, *42*(1), 24–40. https://doi.org/10.1177/0022219408326216

Zhu, P., Liu, Y., Luke, M. M., & Wang, Q. (2021). The development and initial validation of the cultural humility and enactment scale in counseling. *Measurement and Evaluation in Counseling and Development*, *55*(2), 98–115. https://doi.org/10.1080/07481756.2021.1955215

PART II

Emotional issues

10 Emotions and emotion regulation

It is vital that we understand the role emotions play - and do not play - in generating clients' presenting problems and in locating solutions to these. In this chapter I distinguish emotions from thoughts, and frame emotions as messengers about unmet needs. This means that the emotion is not the problem, but its message about a need requires attention.

Emotions are like colours in that, just as there are a few primary colours, there are also a few primary emotions. All newborn babies are capable of experiencing the primary emotions of joy, love, hurt, sadness, fear and disgust/recoiling (Adler et al., 2020). And, just as most hues are blends of the three primary colours, from infancy, most of our emotions are a combination of thoughts and feelings. These are known as secondary emotions, and include the likes of suspicion, surprise or excitement.

Purposes of emotion

Emotions serve many vital purposes. The most important is to ensure our survival. We recoil in disgust from contaminated food and thereby avoid food poisoning; and falling in love (or in lust) ensures the survival of the species (Smith, 2015).

Second, our emotions signal whether our needs are being met (Ashiabi, 2000). This motivates a response from us. Our feelings can change rapidly and (like colours) can be bright and intense, or muted (Adler et al., 2020). This, in turn, affects how strongly or weakly we are activated to do something about them. In this sense, our emotions (perhaps especially the unpleasant ones) are our allies because they impel us to meet our needs.

Third, our emotions fundamentally drive our motivation, engagement and satisfaction with our everyday tasks (Eynde & Turner, 2006; Pekrun, 2006; Pintrich, 2003). If we did not care about our daily activities, nothing would get done. We think about how we feel about doing a task beforehand, our experience of it as we do it, and reflect on our satisfaction with it after it is completed (Pekrun, 2006; Wigfield & Cambria, 2010).

Fourth, our emotions serve a vital communicative function of letting other people know what we need, in the hopes that they will be moved to help us. This is not just a mere kindness: Babies would die if they could not communicate that they were in pain, hungry, frightened and so on - and receive attuned care from an adult.

Fifth, feelings allow us to maintain optimal levels of arousal (Mikulas & Vodanovich, 1993), which is fundamental to our physiology. Insufficient arousal is termed *boredom*. This is more

DOI: 10.4324/9781003323938-12

than a mere lack of interest (which is emotionally neutral and unpainful) but comprises low-intensity unpleasant emotions such as dissatisfaction, emptiness and impatience.

Finally, our emotions quite simply enrich our lives. Imagine how dull life would be if we never felt anything.

Box 10.1 Key points about feelings

- Emotions cannot be controlled by rules, any more than breathing can (Miller, 2005).
- Feelings simply *are*: They do not need to be judged.
- What you feel now is exactly what you should be feeling, given your history and whatever you are doing or not doing.
- Your thoughts and feelings are not the main problem. The problem is getting caught up in them and avoiding or struggling with them.
- Difficult or unpleasant feelings are a necessary part of life and of struggling to live your values.
- Your thoughts and feelings do not control your actions.
- Feelings have a natural life span: they do not have to be fixed or controlled because they will go away by themselves.
- Feelings cannot harm you. If your feelings are clouds and your mind is the sky, once the clouds disperse, the sky is the same as it always was.
- Difficult feelings are your allies: They alert you to your unmet needs.
- Difficult emotions teach you what matters enough in your life to hurt for.
- Accepting that pain is inevitable gives you the freedom to do what matters, and dignifies the effort you put into living your life.

Sources: Harris (2007, 2009); McKay et al. (2010)

Emotions as signals about needs

The second purpose of emotions is to let us know whether our needs are being met. Needs differ from desires in four ways: First, we do not *learn* that we require food, for example - whereas we do learn that we 'need' a device with an *i* in front of its name. Second, needs are universal: Every person everywhere requires them. Third, needs are vital in that we are happiest when our needs are being met and, conversely, we experience distress when they are not (Baumeister & Leary, 1995). Finally, needs are constant across the life span, from childhood to old age. (What meets those needs can differ across the lifespan, but the need itself is permanent.)

As illustrated in Figure 10.1, the most basic of our needs is to survive. As infants, this is threatened by a lack of basic care or separation from a parent. Next, we need emotional and physical safety and well-being, which can be threatened by any form of maltreatment or adversity. Next in the model are the three emotional needs for belonging, which means that we suffer when emotionally isolated (Sommer & Baumeister, 2002); for self-esteem, which is compromised when our worth is conditional on our achievements (see Chapter 11); and for autonomy, which is our need to be self-governing (Ryan & Deci, 2000, 2017) and is threatened when others try to control us. Then come the two luxury needs for happiness (or fun)

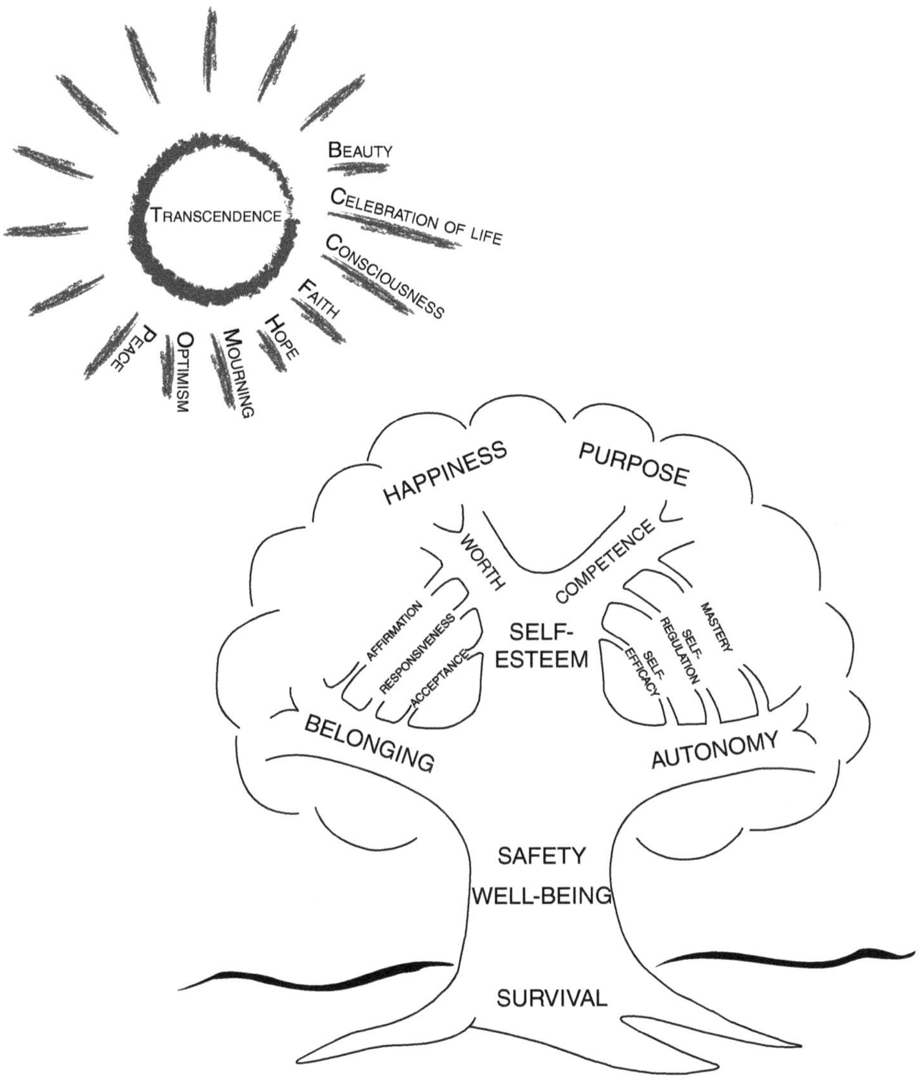

Figure 10.1 A model of human needs

Source: Porter (2014, p. 121).

and purpose, which go hand in hand in that humans are happiest when we are pursuing goals in life that are meaningful to us (Seligman, 2011), rather than when we adopt 'second-hand' goals of trying to be what someone else wants for us.

Last is transcendence, depicted in Figure 10.1 as the sun shining on and invigorating the whole organism. This is the uniquely human need to transcend day-to-day experience by appreciating the beauty and possibilities of life. We need optimism or faith in ourselves and others, and to have hope that we can achieve our goals (Brown, 2012; Seligman, 2011). We also need to be able to mourn or grieve over unmet needs so that we can heal old wounds (Rosenberg, 2003).

Box 10.2 Human needs

Survival

Air
Clothing
Food
Movement/exercise
Sexual expression
Shelter
Sleep
Touch
Water

Safety

Fairness
Justice
Order
Predictability
Privacy
Reliable care
Security
Stability
Support
Trust

Well-*being*

Awareness
Clarity
Comfort
Communion
Ease
Harmony
Health
Nurturance
Relaxation
Rest
Space

Belonging

Acceptance
Affection
Closeness
Communication
Community
Companionship
Compassion
Connection
Consideration
Cooperation
Empathy
Home
Inclusion
Intimacy
Love
Loyalty
Mutuality
Warmth

Self-esteem: Competence

Achievement
Competence
Independence
Learning
Mastery
Stimulation

Self-esteem: Worth

Affirmation
Appreciation
Equality
Mattering
Presence
Respect
To be understood
Validation
Visibility (to see and be seen)

Autonomy

Choice
Creativity
Discovery
Effectiveness
Efficacy
Freedom
Integrity

Purpose

Authenticity
Challenge
Contribution
Fulfilment
Growth
Inspiration
Participation
Self-expression

Happiness

Celebration
Contentment
Enjoyment
Fun
Humour
Joy
Pleasure
Spontaneity

Transcendence

Appreciation of beauty
Celebration of life
Consciousness
Faith in self and others
Hope
Mourning
Optimism
Peace

Sources: Porter (2014, 2015)

Our emotions are messengers about whether these needs are being met. When they are, we experience a range of emotions that we find 'pleasant', as listed in Box 10.3. When they are not being met, we experience noxious emotions, as listed in Box 10.4. Although we would prefer not to have these unpleasant feelings, they actually protect us by motivating us to do something to meet our needs.

Box 10.3 Feelings in response to fulfilled needs

Affection

adoring
affectionate
caring
charmed
compassionate
desirous
fond
friendly
loving
moved
open hearted
sympathetic
tender
touched
trusting
warm

Calmness

calm
carefree
centred
clear headed
comfortable
composed
contented
fulfilled
mellow
peaceful
pleasant
quiet
relaxed
relieved
rested
sated
satisfied
serene
settled
still
tranquil

Confidence

adamant
adept
adventurous
assured
bold
brave
capable
certain
confident
definite
determined
empowered
encouraged
firm
open
optimistic
safe
secure
skilled
sure
vital

Delight

amused
animated
bubbly
buoyant
cheerful
delighted
ecstatic
elated
enchanted
euphoric
glad
happy
joyful
jubilant
overjoyed
playful
pleased
positive
rapture
thrilled
upbeat

Engagement

absorbed
alert
attentive
aware
captivated
challenged
committed
curious
dedicated
eager
energetic
engaged
engrossed
enthralled
enthusiastic
entranced
fascinated

fervent
immersed
intent
interested
intrigued
involved
keen
lively
motivated
passionate
rapt
riveted
spellbound
stimulated

Excitement

amazed
animated
ardent
aroused
dazzled
energetic
excited
giddy
invigorated

Exhilaration

blissful
ecstatic
elated
electrified
exhilarated
exuberant
fervent
pleased
radiant
thrilled

Gratitude

appreciative
grateful
gratified
honoured
pleased
thankful
touched

Hope

expectant
encouraged
hopeful
optimistic

Inspiration

admire
amazed
astonished
astounded
awe
enthused
impressed
inspired
invigorated
marvel
respect
wonder

Refreshed

enlivened
recharged
rejuvenated
renewed
rested
restored
revitalised
revived

Sources: Porter (2014, 2015)

Box 10.4 Feelings in response to unmet needs

Anger

angry
enraged
fuming
furious
incensed
infuriated
irate
livid

Annoyance

annoyed
bothered
cross
disgruntled
disillusioned
dismayed
displeased
dissatisfied
exasperated
frustrated
impatient
irked
irritated
peeved
piqued
thwarted

Anxiety

anxious
cranky
distraught
distressed
edgy
fidgety
frazzled
irritable
jittery
jumpy
nervous
on edge
overwhelmed
restless
stressed
tense
uptight
worried

Aversion

abhor
animosity
dislike
hate
hostile
loathe
repulsed

Confusion

ambivalent
baffled
bemused
befuddled
bewildered
confounded
confused
dazed
deceived
diffident
disoriented
divided
doubtful
dubious
hesitant
lost
mystified
perplexed
puzzled
questioning
stupefied
tentative
tenuous
torn
uncertain
unconvinced
undecided
unsure
vague

Disconnection

alienated
aloof
apathetic
bored
cold
conspicuous
detached
different
distant
distracted
estranged
indifferent
lethargic
listless
lonely
longing
numb
remote
removed
reserved
uninterested
withdrawn

Disquiet

agitated
alarmed
disconcerted
disturbed
flustered
frantic
jumpy
nervous
perturbed
rattled
restless
startled
surprised
overwrought
tense
troubled
turbulent
turmoil
uncomfortable
uneasy
unnerved
unsettled
upset
wary

Embarrassment

apologetic
ashamed
contrite
culpable
embarrassed
foolish
guilty
humiliated
mortified
penitent
regretful

remorseful
repentant
self-conscious
shamed
sorry

Fatigue

beat
burnt out
defeated
depleted
drained
empty
enervated
exhausted
helpless
lethargic
listless
sleepy
tired
weary
worn out

Fear

afraid
anxious
apprehensive
cautious
concerned
delicate
dread
fearful
foreboding
fragile
fretful
frightened
frustrated
guarded
insecure
leery
mistrustful
nervous
panicked
petrified
scared
sensitive
shaky
suspicious
tense
terrified
threatened
uneasy
vulnerable
wary

Pain

agonised
anguished
bereaved
crushed
devastated
distraught
distressed
disturbed
heartbroken
hurt
lonely
pained
regretful
sore
tormented
troubled

Sadness

bereft
bleak
blue
dejected
desolate
despairing
despondent
disappointed
discouraged
disheartened
dismal
down
forlorn
gloomy
glum
grieving
heavy hearted
hopeless
hurt
inconsolable
low
maudlin
melancholy
miserable
morose
sad
sorrowful
suffering
unhappy
wretched

Yearning

aching
brooding
grief-stricken
homesick
longing
nostalgic
pining
wistful

Sources: Porter (2014, 2015)

Implications of the needs model for counselling

This model has five implications for counselling. First, before we assume what might be behind young people's presenting issues, we need to explore whether their basic needs are being met. Tyrrell (2019) suggests that this is like making sure that, before we ring for a tow truck, we check whether our broken-down car hasn't simply run out of fuel. He lists some basic questions, as given in Box 10.5.

Box 10.5 A focus on needs

As we gather information about clients' presenting issues, we need to ask some obvious questions about how well their needs are being met (Tyrrell, 2019):

- How are you sleeping these days? (Survival, well-being)
- Are you happy with your diet? (Survival, well-being)
- How much exercise are you getting? (Survival, well-being)
- How often do you get to meet up with friends? (Belonging)
- Can you and your partner really talk together? (Belonging, intimacy)
- Is there anyone who you feel really understands you, and is close to you? (Belonging)
- What involvement do you have with people around you? (Belonging, community)
- What choice do you have about what happens in your life? (Autonomy)
- Do you have a clear sense of where you want to take things in life? (Purpose)
- Do you feel excited by stuff in your life? (Purpose, transcendence)

Second, despite being trained as counsellors to reflect clients' feelings, I find that this seldom progresses the discussion. To the child who is being bullied at school, the reflection, 'You're feeling sad about that' will lead to confirmation and perhaps some tears - but little else. Instead, on the basis that every emotion is a communication about a need, you can reflect the underlying need, as in: 'You're feeling sad because you need to be accepted and to belong'. Cate Crombie gives examples of some colloquial ways to reflect young people's needs - see Box 10.6.

Not only does this reflection touch clients more deeply, but it opens up a discussion about what they can do to meet their needs. For young people, you could talk about needs as if they are 'cups' that require filling, as proposed in the Phoenix Cups model (Phoenix, 2021). This says that humans will be impelled to fill their cups in circumstances that are emptying them (that is, not meeting their needs). But children do not necessarily have the skill to fill their cups in ways that do not inconvenience others. The result can be that, if they are feeling victimised, they might lash out at their tormenter. This can get them into trouble - but all they were trying to do was to fill their safety cup. Our discussion with them, then, can be how else to fill it in ways that do not make problems for themselves or others.

Box 10.6 Colloquial reflection of needs

Need	*Reflection*
Acceptance	You'd like people to accept you just as you are?
Autonomy	You'd like some choice about what you do?
Belonging	You want to be part of the group?
Consistency, order	You want to be able to count on things happening when you need them to?
Contribution	You'd like to be able to help/share?
Ease	You need this to be easier for you?
Grief	You need to show how sad you're feeling?
Inclusion	You want to be part of what's happening?
Purpose	You want something worthwhile to do?
Security	You need to know that you're going to be okay?
Self-esteem	You want to feel good about yourself?
Validation	You want to be heard about how special/hard/ scary this is for you?

Source: Cate Crombie (downloaded from www.metacommunicate.com)

Third, clients will express that they have a 'need' when in fact it is just a strategy for meeting a need. You can know this because the 'need' cannot be located anywhere on the tree model (in Figure 10.1) or on the list of needs in Box 10.2. In counselling, this confusion can get us stuck. Therefore, it will help to translate their statement from a strategy to a need (see Box 10.7), and guide them find other strategies if the one they seek is not available to them.

Box 10.7 Translating outcomes into needs

Outcome	*Potential needs*
I need Mum and Dad to get back together again.	Safety Belonging
I need less homework.	Well-being (time to rest). Fun/relaxation time.
I need an iPad.	Belonging (with peers, who play games on their iPads). Fun.
I need to drop maths.	Self-esteem (to avoid failure at maths). Purpose (to spend time doing something else which one values more).
I need them to let me go to bed later at night.	Autonomy (self-determination). Fun/relaxation time.

Fourth, solution-focused approaches do not focus on emotions, because these are not the problem: They are simply messengers about the problem. People will feel better when their needs get met. Therefore, emotions have a different place in solution-focused theory than in other forms of counselling. Walker et al. (2022) accuse this neglect of 'staying on the surface' and risking moving too quickly for clients. The assumption behind this criticism is the hydraulic (or 'pressure cooker') theory of emotions which states that feelings get put under more and more pressure until eventually we have to 'blow off steam' (as it were). Expressing the emotion is thus supposed to take the pressure off. This is known as 'catharsis'.

In contrast, I employ the opposing theory of emotion, which I term the 'hippopotamus rolling in mud' theory. This states that the more you roll in mud, the more it sticks. That is, the more you express a feeling, the stronger it grows. Murphy (2015) reports findings that, indeed, the more people talk about their distress, the more discouraged they get.

Nevertheless, solution-focused counsellors do not callously ignore feelings and will signal that we have understood clients' predicament by using their own feeling words to reflect that it has been tough for them, for example (Lipchik, 2002). In this way, clients will know that they have been heard. Counsellors might follow this by asking clients whether they would like to talk more about their feelings, or would they prefer to talk about how to solve their issues. Or we could ask resiliency questions that imply a respect for their feelings, such as: 'Wow! How have you managed to hold it all together with all this going on / while feeling as you do?'. Then we would move on to asking about their goal and, by examining exceptions, how they have achieved this in the past (see Chapter 2).

The fifth and final implication of the needs model is that it works interculturally by placing emotional and social well-being within a wide context. This suits Aboriginal and Torres Strait Islander peoples, for example, who see well-being as holistic, encompassing a recognition of human rights (survival); the right to self-determination (autonomy); their experience of trauma and loss (safety); the impact of racism and stigma (self-esteem); the centrality of kinship and a strong relationship to heritage (belonging); resilience and a spiritual connection to country (transcendence) (Gee et al., 2014).

Two fallacies about feelings

In order to manage our emotional lives, we need to dispel two common myths about our feelings. The first occurs when we believe that outside events cause our feelings, and the second is when we put our feelings in charge of us instead of controlling them.

The fallacy of external control

This fallacy states that events cause us to feel things. This is known as having an *external locus of causality* - that is, we *locate* the *causes* of our feelings outside of or *external* to ourselves. You can hear this fallacy at work when people say 'She *made* me do it. ... That *makes* me sad. ... How does that *make* you feel?'. This is based on a 'common sense' notion about feelings that we can illustrate as seen in Figure 10.2.

However, cognitive theory upholds that what we *think* about events is what generates the emotion. This generates the mediation concept of emotions, wherein our thoughts mediate the link between an event and our feelings about it - see Figure 10.3.

When we think that other people or outside events make us unhappy, we believe that we can't feel better until those events cease. Therefore, we demand that other people do our

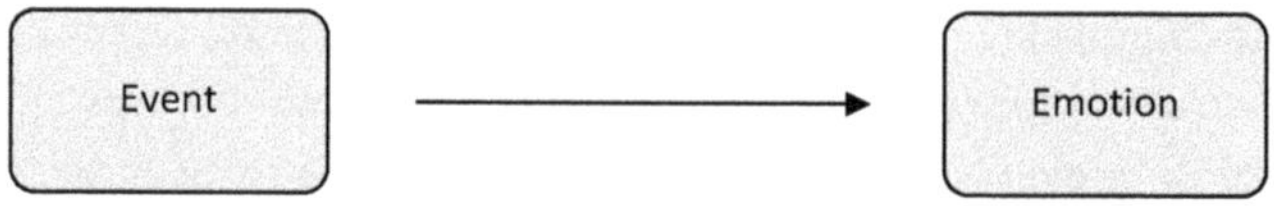

Figure 10.2 The 'commonsense' concept of emotion

Source: Kennerley et al. (2017).

Figure 10.3 The mediation concept of emotion

Source: Kennerley et al. (2017).

bidding. If our attempts to make them do things our way fail, we become angry. Beneath this fallacy of external control are three potential sub-fallacies:

- *Victim fallacy*. We feel at the mercy of other people, oppressed by them and helpless to do anything about it.
- *Fallacy of influence*: We believe that we can make other people change how they act if we just nag and cajole enough. (Our desire to do this is driven by the victim fallacy.)
- *Guilt fallacy*. This false belief makes us responsible for everyone else's well-being. It tells us that if others are unhappy, we are to blame.

In contrast, people with an *internal* locus of causality believe that, although life events can happen that are beyond our control, we are still responsible for how we respond to these. We are in command of what we think and do about events. This has two implications. The first is that no one else can make us think, feel or do anything. (If you kick a stone, it has to move; but if you kick humans, they get to choose what to do about that.) The second implication is that we cannot make other people do anything.

Implications of an internal locus of causality in counselling

So that we do not lose sight of our own agency, it is vital that we tell ourselves and others the truth about our choices. Instead, we often deny responsibility when we blame our actions on (Rosenberg, 2003, p. 20):

- Vague, impersonal forces: 'I tidied up because I had to'.
- Our condition, personality or history: 'I can't help it. I've always been like that.'
- The actions of others: 'He started it'.
- The dictates of authority: 'I was only following orders'.
- Group pressure: 'Everyone else does it'.
- Policies, rules and regulations: 'That's just policy. My hands were tied'.
- Gender, age or social roles: 'I have to cook because I'm the female'.
- Uncontrollable impulses: 'I couldn't help myself'.

Blaming outside forces disguises our choices and implies that we are helpless and not responsible for our own behaviour. Therefore, we have to challenge our own and others' denials of accountability, as seen in statements such as: 'I couldn't help it. ... They made me do it. ... It's not my fault. ... She got me angry. ... It's all your fault. ... I'd behave better if you weren't so mean'.

To heighten accountability in our young clients, we can subtly translate their denials of accountability into statements that highlight their agency. As the examples in Box 10.8 detail, you can do this by (Bertolino & Schultheis, 2002):

- reflecting back the statement, without the non-accountability part
- raising counterexamples
- using the word 'and' to link feelings with accountability.

Box 10.8 Translating denials of accountability

Denial of accountability:	He teased me so I hit him.
Reflection without the non-accountability element:	You hit him.
Denial of accountability:	She didn't give me my medication, so I couldn't concentrate.
Reflection without the non-accountability element:	You couldn't concentrate.
Denial of accountability:	I couldn't help it.
Supplying a counter-example:	And yet last time you got angry, you were able to go off quietly by yourself until you felt better.
Denial of accountability:	He made me angry so I hit him.
Linking feelings with accountability:	It's okay to be angry. It's not okay to hit people.
Denial of accountability:	She wouldn't let me play, so I told on her.
Reflection without the non-accountability element:	She wouldn't let you play. And you told on her.
Linking feelings with accountability:	You were sad and you told the teacher.

The fallacy of emotional reasoning

The second false belief about feelings is the fallacy of emotional reasoning. This tells us that we cannot do something - (such as going outside when we are agoraphobic) until we *feel* better about doing so. (And the agoraphobic never feels better, so does not make it outside.) This turns us into prisoners of our own feelings, as if we belong to our emotions, instead of them belonging to us (Smith, 2015). It gives our feelings the power to yank us around like a puppet on a string, making us their victim - and no one enjoys being victimised, even by ourselves.

Instead, Glasser (1998) notes that there are four parts to our behaviour: thoughts, actions, feelings and our physical state. He likens these to the four wheels of a front-wheel-drive car (see Figure 10.4). The front two (or driving) wheels are our thoughts and our actions, and these pull along behind them our feelings and our physical well-being.

Glasser explains that when we want to drive somewhere, we do not wait in our driveway for our car's rear wheels to 'get in the mood' to move - but instead we engage the front, driving, wheels to pull the rear ones along. Likewise, if we want to feel better, we have to change what we think and do. In turn, this will change our feelings and our physical state.

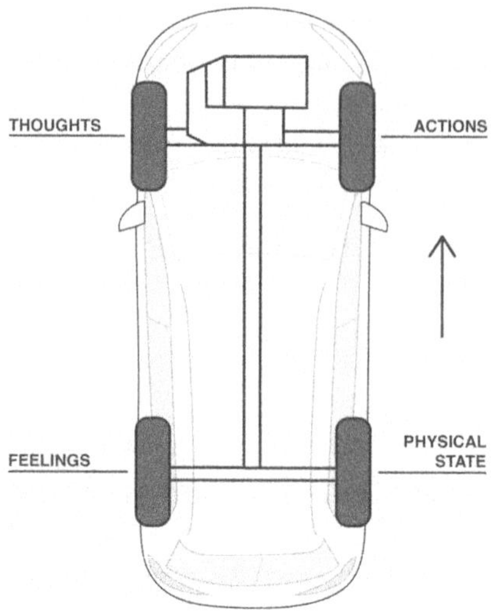

Figure 10.4 The four aspects of behaviour

Source: Illustration by Samantha Bruce.

Figure 10.5 The four aspects of behaviour (young children's version)

Source: Illustration by Peter MacMullin, in Porter (2015, p. 166).

An alternative view of this concept of the front-wheel drive vehicle that might appeal to young children is the concept of elephants pulling each other along - see Figure 10.5.

Fake feelings

These two fallacies give rise to statements that we believe are about our feelings, when in fact they are thoughts. Rosenberg (2003) termed these 'fake feelings'. When we give these the status of feelings, we believe that we are justified to act on them and to make others suffer for 'causing' them. Instead, we must realise that these are only thoughts, which we have chosen to invite in and entertain. Fake feelings come in three forms: demanding thinking, *I-feel* statements and victim language.

Demanding thinking

The first type of fake feeling is generated by demanding thinking. This uses words such as *should, should not, ought, ought not, have to* and *must* to demand that we or someone else act in particular ways. (Albert Ellis provocatively called this *must*urbating!) This type of thinking generates inflamed emotions, which we blame on the original trigger, when the cause is actually our own thinking. The result is that our emotions become inflamed and more intense than the circumstances warrant. In addition to the *should* family of words, others which indicate that we are adding demands to feelings include:

aghast	appalled	bitter
contemptuous	depressed	disgusted
envious	horrified	indignant
jealous	offended	outraged
resentful	revolted	scornful
shocked	sickened	spiteful

In comparison, thoughts that accurately express our desires are less likely to provoke exaggerated emotions and, therefore, will make it easier for us to focus on what we need. We could still have unpleasant emotions such as sadness, regret, sorrow, annoyance or frustration - but these are healthy, balanced, realistic or 'workable', in that they are more likely to propel us towards solutions. These two pathways to our feelings are depicted in Figure 10.6.

I-feel statements

Rosenberg (2003) identifies the second type of fake emotion as 'I-feel' statements that are followed by *that, as if* or *like*, or by *pronouns* (she, he, you) or *nouns* (people's names):

I feel *that* I'm being asked to do too much.
I feel *as if* I'm the only one willing to go the extra mile.
I feel *like* I'm under pressure.
I feel *she's* lazy.

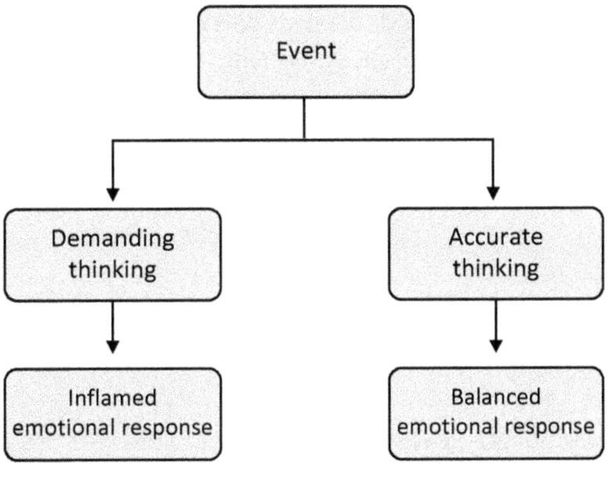

Figure 10.6 Differing pathways to emotion

One way to tell that these are not feelings is that we could not mime them or act them out in a game of charades. Another is that they would make just as much sense if we said:

I *believe* that I'm being asked to do too much.
I *consider* that I'm the only one willing to go the extra mile.
I *am* under pressure.
I *think* that she is lazy.

Being clear that these I-feel statements are actually thoughts allows us, first, to own our own thoughts and, in turn, to be responsible for changing what we think.

Victim language

The third type of fake emotion is victim language, provoked by the victim fallacy (as already outlined). This language focuses on how others 'should' be treating us. These thoughts place us in the role of victim and give others power by placing them in the role of our enemy or oppressor. Victim language makes us a prisoner of our own thinking and includes words such as:

abandoned	abused	attacked
betrayed	bullied	cheated
coerced	condemned	cornered
deserted	distrusted	dominated
ignored	imposed upon	intimidated
invisible	isolated	left out
let down	manipulated	misunderstood
neglected	overworked	patronised
persecuted	pressured	provoked
put down	rejected	rushed
taken for granted	threatened	trapped
unappreciated	unfair	unheard
unseen	unwanted	used

This victim language deceives us into thinking that other people 'make' us feel as we do and, therefore, are to blame for our misery. When we believe this, we try to make them stop it; we believe that they deserve to be punished for what they are doing; and we exaggerate the outcomes if they don't stop. Instead, no one can *make* anyone do anything and how we *feel* about others' actions depends on what we *think* about these. We have a choice about the thoughts we invite into our heads. This choice is liberating and will not breed resentment of others.

Self-regulation

In order to be able to manage their emotional lives, individuals need to able to regulate. Self-regulation has four aspects:

- *Physical state*: Managing our level of alertness so that we are not so aroused that we become disorganised, nor so lethargic that we cannot focus.
- *Thinking skills*: Using meta-cognitive skills to monitor and regulate our thoughts.

- *Emotions*: Up-regulation of our positive emotions, and down-regulation of noxious feelings (Shanker, 2013).
- *Behaviour*: Regulation of our impulses or ideas to suit the context and task, and increasing behaviours that will bring joy to our lives.

Emotion regulation

Emotion regulation is the ability to manage and modify if, when, how and how intensely we experience emotions. Although every emotion serves a useful function and can nourish our lives, feelings become debilitating when they are too intense or too prolonged. Whereas babies' survival demands that they express everything they feel, adults' healthy adjustment requires that we do not, because impulsive actions can get in the way of meeting our goals (Moffitt et al., 2011). Therefore, although at birth we are programmed to communicate our feelings, from the age of $3^1/_2$ we must start to develop skills for regulating or managing our emotions. Learning this capacity for self-regulation is the most important emotional task of early and middle childhood (Eisenberg et al., 2004; Mortensen & Barnett, 2015).

To be able to regulate our feelings, we need to be aware of our own emotional states and use that information to exercise choices about how we express our feelings (Roth et al., 2009). This gives us a 'dimmer switch' on our emotions (as it were), rather than only an on-off button (Thompson et al., 2002). This ensures that our feelings are not so dysregulated that they are explosive, but neither do we have to repress or deny what we feel, because that is not healthy. People are best adjusted when on occasion we can be spontaneous and express ourselves (Kohn, 2014; Letzring et al., 2005; Polivy, 1998).

In short, self-regulation is not a question of having an optimal amount of self-control, but of having *choice* over how we express our feelings (Roth et al., 2009). Using a driving analogy, we neither want to press too hard on the accelerator, nor too hard on the brakes (Shanker, 2013).

Box 10.9 Components of emotion regulation

- Being open to but not overwhelmed by emotions.
- Being able to engage with or detach from emotions as appropriate.
- Being able to suspend judgement, to think before acting on our feelings.
- Managing emotions flexibly in order to choose a measured response that best fits the circumstances and need.
- Self-soothing so that we can recover from strong emotion to restore emotional balance.
- Maintaining boundaries between our own and others' feelings so that these are not contagious.

Purposes of emotion regulation

The first purpose of emotional regulation is for our own well-being. Managing our feelings ensures that our dysregulated emotions do not upset our own emotional balance and disrupt our ability to solve problems. Second, self-regulation allows us to cope with life's setbacks, and ensures that our emotions nourish our lives, rather than blocking our achievement of our goals. Third, our ability to self-regulate protects surrounding individuals from enduring our emotional outbursts. The aim is for us to be able to express ourselves without infringing on others. In this way, self-regulation safeguards our relationships by ensuring that we can balance others' needs and values with our own and with the demands of the situation (King, 1996; Letzring et al., 2005; Polivy, 1998).

Upregulation of pleasant feelings

Some children become so sensitised to threat that they lose sight of the positive aspects of life and need support to up-regulate positive emotions. To help them get back in touch with life's positive possibilities, you might comment on their stories about their week that something they did sounded fun. You can use children's books to introduce themes where people similar to themselves conquer adversity, and coach children to use optimistic self-talk, such as, 'This is tricky, but I can do it' (Kostelnik et al., 2015).

The bottom-up theory of emotion

So far, I have discussed the top-down theory of emotion, which upholds that our feelings are driven by our thoughts. (That is, they work from the brain down to the body.) However, a second theory tells us that many emotions occur in a 'bottom-up' process, whereby the brain centre, the amygdala (pronounced much as it looks: a-*mig*-da-la) assesses stimuli that enter it from the outside or from within our bodies. When stimuli arrive, the amygdala then sends a cascade of instructions to cells to produce hormones (such as adrenaline), constrict blood vessels and direct blood flow to the muscles so that we can fight or flee from a source of stress.

Feldman Barrett (2020) explains that, based on our memory of past experience, our brain predicts what incoming sensations mean. It asks: 'The last time I encountered a similar situation, when my body was in a similar state, what did I do next?' (Feldman Barrett, 2020, p. 67). When our last encounter was unsafe, our brain will infer that the current one is too, because our body is feeling the same as it did then - even when our present circumstances contradict this. Having generated the emotion that we are not safe, our hormonal, metabolic and immune systems kick into action.

Implications of emotion regulation for counselling

The top-down and the bottom-up theories imply that there are two routes to emotion regulation: managing our thinking; and calming the body in order to quieten distressing physical sensations. For those who have been traumatised, Herman (2015) believed that counsellors need to focus first on clients' agitation so that clients can gain a sense of empowerment and control over their own bodies as a first step to emotion regulation.

The top-down method is exemplified by Acceptance and Commitment Theory's methods of acceptance, mindfulness and defusion - see Chapter 4. The core bottom-up methods are breathing exercises and progressive muscle relaxation. Slowing the breath can serve as a manual feedback mechanism to the body to begin to reduce arousal, while progressive relaxation involves the sequential clenching and relaxing of muscles in the body, from head to toe, until a state of relaxation is achieved. Although beneficial for many, some clients can have an anxious response to such exercises while relaxation alone rarely leads to a long-term reduction in distress and instead will need to be included as a part of a wider 'toolbox' of distress reduction techniques.

Conclusion

Without emotions, we would not know if our needs are being met. Without getting our needs met, we cannot flourish. At the same time, we need to be able to listen to our feelings without being overwhelmed by them, which requires a measure of self-regulation so that our emotions enhance rather than detract from our lives. Learning this is the core emotional task of the childhood years and its non-achievement the core business of counselling.

References

Adler, R. B., Rosenfeld, L. B., & Proctor, R. F. II (2020). *Interplay: The process of interpersonal communication* (15th ed.). Oxford University Press.

Ashiabi, G. S. (2000). Promoting the emotional development of preschoolers. *Early Childhood Education Journal*, *28*(2), 79–84. https://doi.org/10.1023/A:1009543203089

Baumeister, R. F., & Leary, M. F. (1995). The need to belong: Desire for interpersonal attachments as a fundamental human motivation. *Psychological Bulletin*, *117*(3), 497–529. https://doi.org/10.1037/0033-2909.117.3.497

Bertolino, B., & Schultheis, G. (2002). *The therapist's notebook for families: Solution-oriented exercises for working with parents, children, and adolescents*. Haworth.

Brown, B. (2012). *Daring greatly*. Gotham.

Eisenberg, N., Spinrad, T. L., Fabes, R. A., Reiser, M., Cumberland, A., Shepard, S. A., Valiente, C., Losoya, S. H., Guthrie, I. K., & Thompson, M. (2004). The relations of effortful control and impulsivity to children's resiliency and adjustment. *Child Development*, *75*(1), 25–46. https://doi.org/10.1111/j.1467-8624.2004.00652.x

Eynde, P. O. T., & Turner, J. E. (2006). Focusing on the complexity of emotion issues in academic learning: A dynamical component systems approach. *Educational Psychology Review*, *18*(4), 361-376. https://doi.org/10.1007/s10648-006-9031-2

Feldman Barrett, L. (2020). *Seven and a half lessons about the brain*. Picador.

Gee, G., Dudgeon, P., Schultz, Hart, A., & Kelly, K. (2014). Aboriginal and Torres Strait Islander social and emotional wellbeing. In P. Dudgeon, H. Milroy & R. Walker (Eds.), *Working together: Aboriginal and Torres Strait Islander mental health and wellbeing principles and practices* (2nd ed., pp. 55–68). Commonwealth of Australia.

Glasser, W. (1998). *The quality school: Managing students without coercion* (rev. ed.). Harper Perennial.

Harris, R. (2007). *The happiness trap: Stop struggling, start living*. Exisle.

Harris, R. (2009). *ACT made simple: An easy-to-read primer on Acceptance and Commitment Therapy*. New Harbinger.

Herman, J. L. (2015). *Trauma and recovery: The aftermath of violence from domestic abuse to political terror* (rev. ed.). Basic Books.

King, L. A. (1996). Who is regulating what and why? Motivational context of self-regulation. *Psychological Inquiry*, *7*(1), 57–60. https://doi.org/10.1207/s15327965pli0701_11

Kohn, A. (2014). *The myth of the spoiled child: Challenging the conventional wisdom about children and parenting*. Da Capo Press.

Kostelnik, M. J., Soderman, A. K., Whiren, A. P., Ripiper, M., & Gregory, K. M. (2015). *Guiding children's social development and learning: Theory and skills* (8th ed.). Cengage.

Letzring, T. D., Block, J., & Funder, D. C. (2005). Ego-control and ego-resiliency: Generalization of self-report scales based on personality descriptions from acquaintances, clinicians, and the self. *Journal of Research in Personality*, *39*(4), 395–422. https://doi.org/10.1016/j.jrp.2004.06.003

Lipchik, E. (2002). *Beyond technique in solution-focused therapy: Working with emotions and the therapeutic relationship*. Guilford.

McKay, M., Forsyth, J. P., & Eifert, G.H. (2010). *Your life on purpose: How to find what matters and create the life you want*. New Harbinger.

Miller, A. (2005). *The body never lies: The lingering effects of hurtful parenting*. Norton.

Mikulas, W. L., & Vodanovich, S. J. (1993). The essence of boredom. *The Psychological Record, 43*(1), 3–12.

Moffitt, T. E., Arseneault, L., Belsky, D., Dickson, N., Hancox, R. J., Harrington, H., ... & Caspi, A. (2011). A gradient of self-control predicts health, wealth, and public safety. *Proceedings of the National Academy of Science, 108*(7), 2693–2698. http://www.jstor.org/stable/41002200

Mortensen, J. A. & Barnett, M. A. (2015). Teacher-child interactions in infant/toddler child care and socioemotional development. *Early Education and Development, 26*(2), 209–229. https://doi.org/10.1080/10409289.2015.985878

Murphy, J. (2015). Solution-focused approaches. In H. T. Prout & A. L. Fedewa (Eds.), *Counseling and psychotherapy with children and adolescents* (5th ed., pp. 279–316). Wiley.

Pekrun, R. (2006). The control-value theory of achievement emotions: Assumptions, corollaries, and implications for educational research and practice. *Educational Psychology Review, 18*(4), 315–341. https://doi.org/10.1007/s10648-006-9029-9

Phoenix, S. (2021). *Educator toolkit for behaviour*. Phoenix Support for Educators.

Pintrich, P. R. (2003). A motivational science perspective on the role of student motivation in learning and teaching contexts. *Journal of Educational Psychology, 95*(4), 667–686. https://psycnet.apa.org/doi/10.1037/0022-0663.95.4.667

Polivy, J. (1998). The effects of behavioral inhibition: Integrating internal cues, cognition, behavior, and affect. *Psychological Inquiry, 9*(3), 181–204. https://doi.org/10.1207/s15327965pli0903_1

Porter, L. (2014). *A comprehensive guide to classroom management: Facilitating engagement and learning in schools*. Routledge.

Porter, L. (2015). *Parental guidance recommended: How to raise emotionally healthy children*. Small Poppies International.

Rosenberg, M. B. (2003). *Nonviolent communication: A language of life* (2nd ed.). Puddle Dancer Press.

Roth, G., Assor, A., Niemiec, C. P., Ryan, R. M., & Deci, E. L. (2009). The emotional and academic consequences of parental conditional regard: Comparing conditional positive regard, conditional negative regard, and autonomy support as parenting practices. *Developmental Psychology, 45*(4), 1119–1142. https://doi.org/10.1037/a0015272

Ryan, R. M., & Deci, E. L. (2000). Self-determination theory and the facilitation of intrinsic motivation, social development, and well-being. *American Psychologist, 55*(1), 68–78. https://doi.org/10.1037/0003-066X.55.1.68

Ryan, R. M., & Deci, E. L. (2017). *Self-determination theory: Basic psychological needs in motivation, development and wellness*. Guilford.

Seligman, M. E. P. (2011). *Flourish: A visionary new understanding of happiness and well-being*. Free Press.

Shanker, S. (2013). *Calm, alert, and learning: Classroom strategies for self-regulation*. Pearson.

Smith, T. W. (2015). *The book of human emotion: An encyclopedia of feeling from anger to wanderlust*. Profile Books.

Sommer, K. L., & Baumeister, R. F. (2002). Self-evaluation, persistence, and performance following implicit rejection: The role of trait self-esteem. *Personality and Social Psychology Bulletin, 28*(7), 926–938. https://doi.org/10.1177/014616720202800706

Thompson, M., Cohen, L. J., & Grace, C.O.N. (2002). *Mom, they're teasing me: Helping your child solve social problems*. Ballantine.

Tyrrell, M. (2019). *Ten therapy questions to get to the root of the problem*. https://youtu.be/B8G846WVA2I

Walker, C. R., Froerer, A. S., & Gourlay-Fernandez, N. (2022). The value of using emotions in solution focused brief therapy. *Journal of Marital and Family Therapy, 48*(3), 812–826. http://doi.org/10.1111/jmft.12551

Wigfield, A., & Cambria, J. (2010). Students' achievement values, goal orientations, and interest: Definitions, development, and relations to achievement outcomes. *Developmental Review, 30*(1), 1–35. https://doi.org/10.1016/j.dr.2009.12.001

11 A model of resilience

Unlike a theory which explains, a model describes phenomena. In this chapter, I introduce my model of resilience, as various aspects of it will inform interventions with a range of the issues that young people bring to counselling.

Resilience

Resilience is the capacity to bounce back from adversity. It is not built up by never facing a challenge, but by confronting challenge *with support*. I have developed a model of resilience that identifies eight factors that support young people's capacity to bounce back – see Figure 11.1. Although I have listed the eight factors as being characteristics of resilient individuals, for them to use these personal skills and qualities, individuals require access to resources from the families, communities, cultures and institutions of which they are a member (Vindevogel & Verelst, 2020).

Health

The first requirement for resilience is good health and well-being. In order for a brain to produce healthy thoughts, emotions and actions, it has to be healthy itself. Many factors influence brain health: nutrition, methylation, diet, sleep and physical activity.

Nutrition

The brain is greedy for nutrients, making nervous system tissue the most susceptible to nutrient deficiencies, especially those needed to convert amino acids into neurotransmitters – see Figure 11.2. Referring to that Figure 11.2, you will see that zinc and magnesium are vital for converting 5-HTP into serotonin. Yet zinc levels are low in the Australian diet and stores are used up during growth spurts, while stress depletes the body of magnesium in particular (Lyon, 2000), leaving adolescents especially vulnerable to depression and insomnia (from a corresponding lack of melatonin).

A second important nutrient is copper. You will see in Figure 11.2 that it is needed to turn dopamine into norepinephrine (pronounced nor-ep-in-*eff*-rin). If the person has too

DOI: 10.4324/9781003323938-13

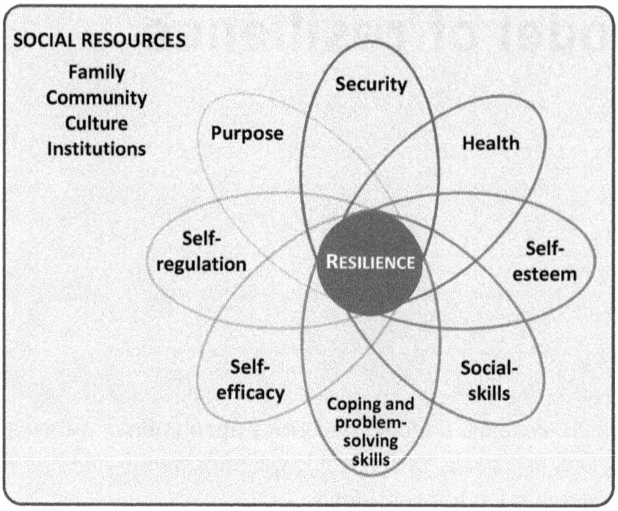

Figure 11.1 Porter's model of resilience

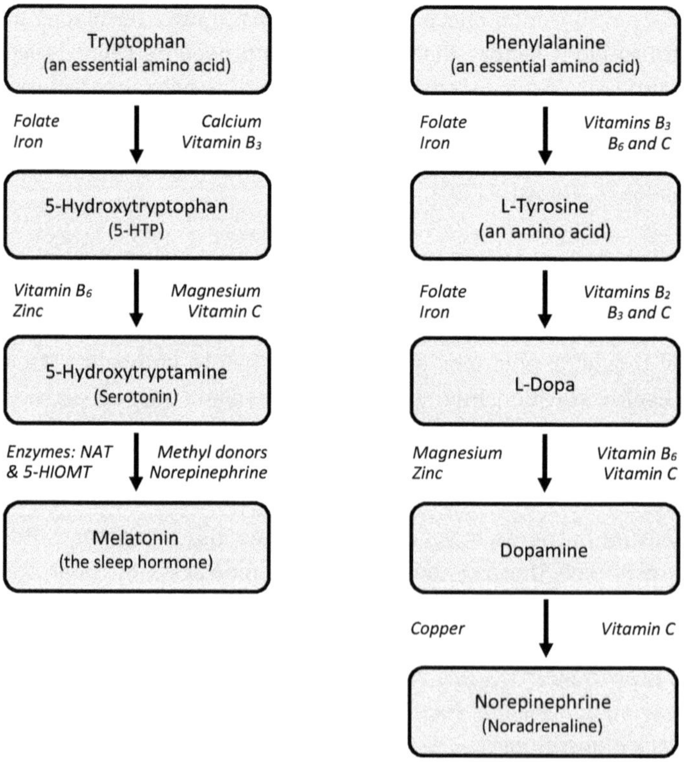

Figure 11.2 Nutrients needed to produce neurotransmitters

Sources: Kharrazian (2013, p. 306); Tabrizian (2003, pp. 18 & 112).

much copper (relative to zinc and magnesium levels), too much dopamine is converted into norepinephrine. Dopamine deficiencies are implicated in the attention deficit disorders and dopamine is responsible for finding life pleasurable; the other name for norepinephrine is noradrenaline, which is the stress neurotransmitter, an excess of which will contribute to high levels of anxiety.

Meanwhile, brains are voracious for energy. In adults, they use 30 per cent of the glucose that's in our bloodstream; children's brains use up to 45 per cent (Glaser, 2000). A roller coaster of high and low blood sugar levels is perilous for us all, but especially for children. It affects not just fuel supply to the brain in general, but disruption to blood sugar levels will impair serotonin pathways in particular (which is implicated in depression) (Kharrazian, 2013).

When our blood sugar levels drop so low that the brain does not have enough glucose to fuel all of its functions, the brain cleverly directs blood flow away from the least vital brain centres to those that ensure survival. The result is that the pre-frontal lobes of the brain can be deprived of sufficient fuel to function (Blum & Mercugliano, 1997). This area of the brain is responsible for self-regulation and executive functions such as planning and attention control. Accordingly, hypoglycaemia has been found to be the underlying cause of one-third of cases of attention deficit disorder (Blum & Mercugliano, 1997).

Further, our body has a backup plan for when we get hungry: It releases adrenaline to alert us that we need to eat. (This is what gives us the shakes at 3 pm when we have skipped lunch.) However, adrenaline - combined with under-functioning pre-frontal lobes arising from hunger - can lead to emotional meltdowns.

Methylation

Methylation is a basic biochemical process that is needed for almost all chemical reactions in the body. Technically, it is a process of transferring a methyl group (which has a carbon atom with three hydrogens attached) to manufacture SAMe (pronounced *sammy*) which, in turn, regulates over 200 other enzymes in our bodies. After ATP (the energy currency in our cells), SAMe is the second most important compound in our bodies.

Our methylation status is governed (in the main) by two pairs of MTHFR genes (Lynch, 2013). Eighty-five per cent of people carry an error on one of the gene pairs (resulting in a 40 per cent decrease in their methylation function); while 5 per cent have two genes affected, which reduces their methylation by 70 per cent (Purser, 2015). This has effects throughout the body, but in the brain weak methylation disrupts the conversion of tryptophan into serotonin and melatonin (Yasko, 2010) - see Figure 11.2. This can disrupt the nervous system in the relatively minor ways of producing irritability, poor sleep, anxiety or depression - or in major ways, as seen in the neurodegenerative disorders such as the autism spectrum, Parkinson's disease or dementia.

Food intolerances

There are three types of reactions to foods: First are food allergies, which occur when B cells of the immune system produce antibodies. Only this type of reaction can be identified by a blood test, yet one estimate is that just 10 per cent of food reactions are allergy-based (Collison & Hall 1989).

Second is an inability to digest a food because of a lack of digestive enzymes. The most common of these is the inability to digest milk after the age of three, which is genetically determined. This leads to lactose (milk sugar) intolerance for one-third of people of Anglo-Saxon descent, and 93 per cent of Asians, for example (Bayless et al., 1975; Collison & Hall, 1989; Wotecki et al., 1977).

Third are food intolerances, where T cells produce histamine and, in turn, inflammation that can target any organ, with the brain being of interest here. An intolerance to dairy protein but especially to gluten (the protein in most grains) is highly suspect in anyone with emotional difficulties such as anxiety or depression, or any neurological condition (Hadjivassiliou et al., 2001; Mäki & Collin, 1997; Percy & Propst, 2008; Perlmutter & Loberg, 2013; St Aubyn Crump, 2009). Brain-based symptoms can occur even without gastrointestinal symptoms; indeed, one estimate is that, for every one person with gastrointestinal symptoms, there are *seven* people with nervous system symptoms (Perlmutter & Loberg, 2013). Because the protein structure of gluten is very similar to the structure of nervous tissue, a gluten intolerance is more damaging to the brain than to any other tissue (Kharrazian, 2013).

Brain effects are borne out by findings that children with celiac disease are at increased risk of developing schizophrenia during adulthood while, in reverse, as many as two-thirds of people with schizophrenia are intolerant to gluten (Mackarness, 1990; Philpott & Kalita, 2000). Furthermore, children whose mothers are intolerant to gluten have an elevated risk of childhood behavioural difficulties and mental illnesses in later life (Karlsson et al., 2012).

Given this link between food intolerances and emotional difficulties, when working with young people, I always enquire into their diet, especially the foods that they 'love' – because we get addicted to foods to which we are intolerant. I will then explain to young children that 'their body is playing tricks on their brain'. Under the supervision of a health care provider, a brief elimination diet can confirm if intolerances are part of the picture. When so, not only do the children's symptoms improve, but they get out from under being blamed for their behaviours.

Viruses

The herpes viruses (cold sores, chicken pox, genital herpes, CMV and Epstein-Barr virus, which is responsible for glandular fever) can all affect brain function (Gesser & Koo, 1996; Spear & Straus, 2007; Tomsone et al., 2001). Influenza is another culprit. There is an increased incidence of schizophrenia in children whose mothers contract the flu during the fifth to seventh months of pregnancy (Barr et al., 1990; Murray et al., 1992), although the cause is not the flu virus itself, but that the antibodies produced by the mother somehow alter fetal brain development. Specifically, dopamine and glutamine receptors are implicated (Shi et al., 2003).

Sleep

Sleep is vital for resilience. It is not merely resting, but falling into a state of unawareness and unresponsiveness to the outside world (Dahl, 1999). It appears that REM sleep fulfils a 'housekeeping' role for the brain, maintaining optimal brain excitability and efficiency (Mallick & Singh, 2011; Palagini & Rosenlicht, 2011). Even small losses (one hour) of REM sleep adversely affect behaviour and almost all physiological processes, and with continued deprivation can even compromise cell survivability (Mallick & Singh, 2011). Sleep deprivation decreases individuals' energy for routine tasks in particular, leads to a two-year decline in intellectual performance (which is equivalent to that caused by lead poisoning) (Bronson & Merryman, 2009), impairs emotion regulation, and is linked to anxiety and depression (Gregory & Sadeh, 2012; Motivala et al., 2005).

In order to sleep, humans need to feel safe. Accordingly, children who are being maltreated or bullied often suffer sleep disturbances (Wang et al., 2022). Adolescents are chronically sleep deprived - partly because they begin to produce melatonin 45 minutes later than they did during childhood and therefore, even if they go to bed at a reasonable hour, they tend to lie awake (Bronson & Merryman, 2009). To compensate for getting to sleep later, they need to sleep longer in the mornings but cannot, given their schedules, and therefore will be constantly sleep deprived (Bronson & Merryman, 2009). As for early childhood, young children are often deprived of sleep not because of their own body clock but because a busy household schedule makes adults unavailable to put them to bed until late in the evening (Snell et al., 2007).

Physical activity

Physical activity gives young people confidence in their ability to control their bodies (self-efficacy), teaches them that they can meet physical challenges, and - as long as it does not become an avenue for competition - offers an outlet for stress. It is beneficial for depression, improves young people's self-esteem (Ekeland et al., 2004; Liu et al., 2015), activates both sides of the brain (which is essential for reading), increases endorphin (natural pain killer) levels, and raises brain levels of three main neurotransmitters: dopamine, norepinephrine and serotonin (Kharrazian, 2013).

Counselling implications of the need for health

In addition to checking that young people are eating well, getting enough rest and exercising sufficiently, those with clinical problems might be prescribed medication and, in crises, might be hospitalised. Although these interventions can seem out of their control, we can use narrative ideas to frame these as transitions, rather than as messages about their identity as failures to 'cope'.

Medication

The need to go onto medications can cause young people to think that they have no control over their symptoms, and can seem to be a failure. Therefore, White (2016, p. 59) advises framing the need for medication within a narrative approach by asking questions such as:

- What will you use to tell if the drug is helping you or not?
- How will you know that the medication is contributing to your quality of life or whether it is subtracting from it?

- How will you notice the effects on your (schoolwork/relationships)?
- What criteria will you use to make your evaluation?
- How can we go about helping you to know whether it is helping, or disabling you?
- How can we go about helping you to monitor the effects of the medications?
- How do the drugs contribute to your seeing yourself as 'sick' or 'disabled', versus how do they open up new horizons for you?
- In your opinion, what does taking the drug tell you about who you are?

Hospitalisation

Individuals in crises that necessitate hospitalisation will typically interpret having to be admitted to hospital as a sign of failure and will be demoralised as a result. Instead, White (2016) suggests that we frame hospital admission as a rite of passage. All rites of passage have a separation phase, an in-between phase, and a reincorporation phase. Being admitted is a separation from a location that is no longer appropriate for clients to occupy because it is unsafe; the inpatient phase is the in-between stage where there is likely to be considerable confusion and disorientation, as accompanies any change in life but which gives them space to review their life and clarify what would support their quality of life; and the reincorporation phase is being discharged from hospital to be reincorporated back into the world, armed with a new vision for their life.

Security

The second personal quality needed for individuals to be resilient is a sense of physical and emotional security. Sapon-Shevin (1999, p. 13) notes that emotional security is 'the safety to be yourself, to be vulnerable, to ask for help, and to be warmly supported'.

We often invoke attachment theory to explain young people's need for security. This model upholds that attachment develops during the first six or so months of life, when children acquire a 'working model' about how the world works, how relationships work, and about their own worth that subsequently shapes their relationships throughout life (Sigelman et al., 2022). This is not the case. Attachment quality in childhood does not reliably predict adjustment in the long term, as the theory expects (Lewis et al., 2000).

Attachment theory adopts a mechanistic view that blames people's current difficulties on the past - which, however, they cannot undo. This disempowers them and deprives them of hope. This is unnecessary, because the evidence is conclusive that children's well-being is related to the quality of parenting that they receive *at the time*, which of course can be changed (Bakermans-Kranenburg et al., 2004; Facompré et al., 2018; Diener et al., 2003; Granqvist et al., 2017; Hamilton, 2000; Koren-Karie et al., 2002; Moss et al., 2005; National Institute of Child Health and Human Development Early Child Care Research Network, 2001, 2006; Posada et al., 1999; Raval et al., 2001; Seifer et al., 2004; Sroufe, 2005; Waters et al., 2000a, 2000b; Weinfield et al., 2000; West et al., 2012). In later life, their attachment style is a result of the quality of their current relationships (Overall & Simpson, 2015; Peterson, 2014). That being the case, we lose nothing and avoid blame by saying simply that children feel secure when their caregivers offer attuned, predictable, sensitive and responsive care.

The need for security is violated for the homeless. Our home is not just a building that shelters the body, but a place that serves an integrating function, where our needs can be met (Noddings, 2003). A home provides comfort, connects us to our environment, houses our family, permits connection to outsiders because it allows people to find us, provides stability, forms part of our identity, is a place for securing our possessions, offers a private sanctuary, is a place where we can be informal, is a venue for daydreaming, is a place where we can become more skilful at activities that we value and 'shelters the imagination' (Noddings, 2003, p. 32). The nest is our refuge.

Women make up the biggest single group of homeless Australians and given that more than half have children in their care, they are homeless too (Norris, 2016). Most who are homeless lack the support of extended family and friends, have been subjected to violence, and are impoverished (Fraenkel et al., 2009). Sleeping rough or repeated change of residence ('couch surfing') make it difficult for children to engage in education, and the accompanying poverty has all its deleterious effects.

One counselling approach from narrative therapy is to use externalisation to 'put homelessness in its place' (Fraenkel et al., 2009). These writers help clients examine exceptions to the effects of homelessness and which skills and values they employ to make those sparkling moments happen.

A second group who are vulnerable to feeling insecure are children in out-of-home care. Their adjustment difficulties relate to the adversity that caused them to be removed from their homes in the first place, the instability of alternative placements (Leve et al., 2012) and the sometimes protracted process of being returned home (Keddell, 2012). Despite their maltreatment, children can experience their removal from home as forced abandonment (Adams et al., 2021). These adversities put children in out-of-home care at risk of low educational attainment, compromised physical and mental health, sexual victimisation, weak connections to the community and a loss of cultural identity (AIHW, 2020; Burns et al., 2004; Holt & Birchall, 2022; McCallion et al., 2004), which are compounded by the lack of appropriate and timely services (Zuchowski et al., 2019). This implies the need to support both children and their carers to promote stable placements.

Grandparents who care for their grandchildren need financial and emotional support to provide adequate care, but are reluctant to ask for help from child welfare agencies for fear of having the children taken away, which would disrupt the children's lives further (Holt & Birchall, 2022; Janicki et al., 2000; Letiecq et al., 2008). For their part, against the background of the stolen generations, Aboriginal and Torres Strait Islanders are reluctant to seek support from child welfare services (Zuchowski et al., 2019).

Self-esteem

The third quality that supports resilience is a healthy self-esteem. This is like having an immune system for our mental health (Branden, 1994): When our self-esteem is robust, we can withstand the challenges that life sends our way.

Our self-concept is our image, description or perception of ourselves, an inventory of our qualities and achievements (Kernis, 2003). It is a series of beliefs we hold about ourselves. You might like to think of it as your identity. To some extent, our self-concept is a fiction that we construct about ourselves to make sense of who we are. This opens the door to narrative therapy, which helps us reconstruct our identity into one that is more appreciative of our qualities.

Young children describe themselves quite simply: by their appearance, what they can do, who is in their family, and what they own. By adolescence, this has expanded into more nuanced and multi-faceted self-description (Bracken et al., 2000; Burns, 1982) comprising the elements illustrated in Figure 11.3.

Whereas our self-*concept* reflects our *thoughts* or a mental list of our skills and qualities, our self-*esteem* reflects how we *feel* about these (Kernis, 2003). It is perfectly possible to have a concept of ourselves that we are no good at a particular skill (such as speaking Latin) but not to *care* about that because speaking Latin is not a skill that we value.

Our self-esteem has two separate aspects (Branden, 2001; Gecas, 1982; Kernis, 2003):

- our *competence*, which is the extent to which we achieve at skills that matter to us (our ideals).
- our *worth*, which refers to how much we like, respect, trust and accept ourselves. Branden (2001) puts it eloquently when he defines self-esteem as the reputation we acquire with ourselves. It is our estimation of our right to be happy, to belong, to assert our needs and to achieve our goals (Branden, 1994, 2001). It is our measure of our value to others (Bos et al., 2006).

There are three vital differences between these two aspects of self-esteem: First, whereas competence has to be *earned* (via putting in some effort to acquire skills), worth (ideally) is *given*. It is our birthright: It must have no prerequisites (Brown, 2012). Second and relatedly, worth matters more to us than competence does. If we want to feel better about our competence, we can lower our expectations or acquire some skills, whereas it is more difficult to convince ourselves about our worth if this has been undermined, especially by abuse or neglect.

Third, the two aspects operate differently in our lives. Our sense of competence is a *result* of our appraisal of our history of successes and failures, whereas our sense of worth is a *cause* of our future approaches to life's tasks. It shapes our willingness to pursue our goals

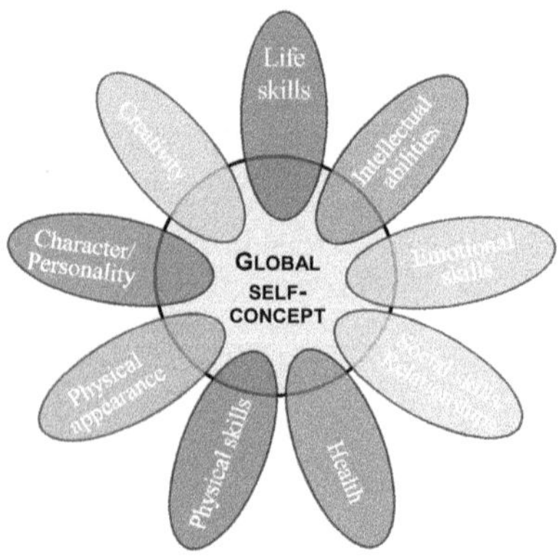

Figure 11.3 The multi-faceted nature of the self-concept

Sources: adapted from Bracken et al. (2000, p. 484).

and surmount obstacles (Marsh & Martin, 2010; Pinxten et al., 2010; Tafarodi & Vu, 1997; Valentine et al., 2004).

These two aspects must inform each other, in that being competent will contribute to a healthy self-respect (or sense of worth) only as long as what we do is worthy of that respect. For example, a person might be an effective bully, but that behaviour should not contribute to a sense of worth, because it is not meritorious.

Types of self-esteem

These two elements can be combined to produce four types of self-esteem: low, defensive, conditional and authentic self-esteem - see Figure 11.4.

Low self-esteem

Approximately 7 per cent of children have been found to have consistently low self-esteem (Birkeland et al., 2012), and during adolescence this figure progressively climbs to the adult rate of 13 per cent (Hirsch & DuBois, 1991). This group has low, unstable or confused evaluations of both their competence and their worth (Kernis, 2003). They are not just ambivalent about themselves but about life in general (Baumeister et al., 2003). (Their self-esteem is illustrated in Figure 11.5.)

Those with low self-esteem are at increased risk for a range of future emotional problems, such as depression (even under benign conditions), poorer physical health, early school exit, worse economic prospects and lower life satisfaction (Baumeister et al., 2003; Birkeland et al., 2012; Diener & Diener, 1995; Mruk, 2006; Murrell et al., 1991; Trzesniewski et al., 2006). Some of these problems could result from the original cause of the low self-esteem, such as abuse or neglect (Waldinger et al., 2001).

Defensive self-esteem

Individuals with a defensive self-esteem measure themselves not in terms of their absolute skilfulness, but in comparison to others. Those who bully will use the criterion of power to

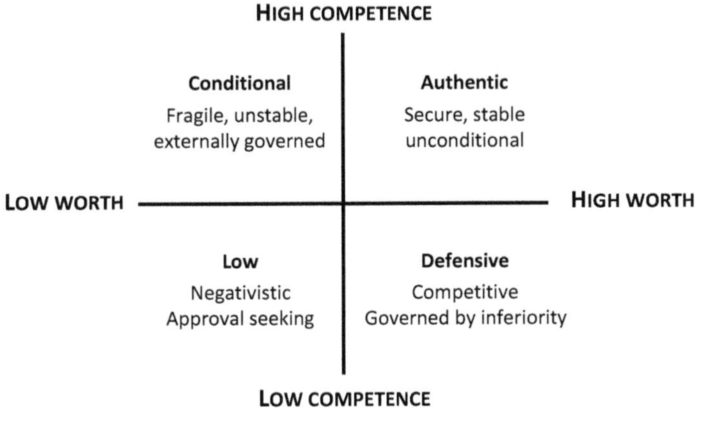

Figure 11.4 Types of self-esteem

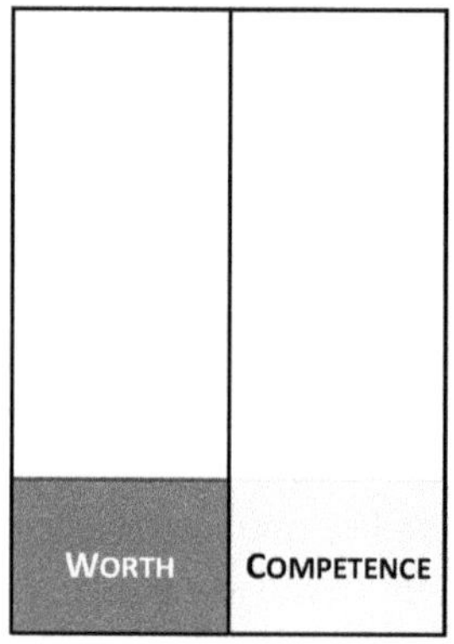

Figure 11.5 Low self-esteem

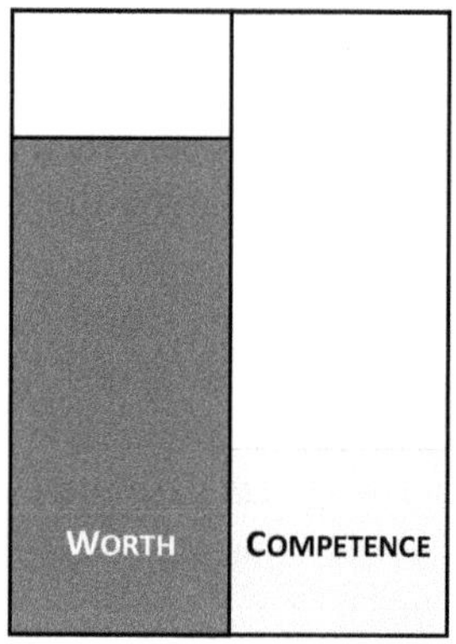

Figure 11.6 Defensive self-esteem

assess if they are better than others; those who have learned that they have to be clever to be good enough feel superior when they are smarter than others; bigots take for granted that their race, skin colour, gender or religion makes them better than others; and elitists believe that they are superior when wealthier than others. (Their self-esteem is illustrated in Figure 11.6.)

With their self-esteem so reliant on winning, in the face of evidence of incompetence, these individuals become defensive. Appearing to be 'tough' they are in fact brittle because when these children detect an unflattering evaluation, they are easily angered and likely to respond with hostility (Baumeister et al., 1996; Diamantopoulou et al., 2008; Kernis, 2003; Kernis et al., 1989; Mruk, 2006; Pauletti et al., 2012; Salmivalli et al., 1999). Their antagonistic style when their pride is injured alienates others (Baumeister et al., 2003). This group is often accused of exaggerating their own importance. However, along with Brené Brown, I believe that this label is mistaken: Their self-worth is not in fact inflated but low, while the feeling behind their obnoxious behaviours is a fear of being ordinary (Brown, 2012). In essence, the feeling is one of shame at not being 'enough'.

Conditional self-esteem

Individuals who doubt their worth strive to *earn* a sense of worth through their accomplishments in the domains that are a priority for them, such as academic results, peer approval, physical appearance, athletic skills and so on (Bos et al., 2006). However, this cannot work: Achievement can only ever contribute to our sense of competence, not to our sense of worth. The resulting failure to achieve a sense of worth leaves a 'hole in the soul' that these individuals attempt to fill with the next achievement which, again, does not work. The downward arrow in Figure 11.7 signifies that because our worth matters more to us than our competence, no matter how competent we become, a lack of self-worth will pull down our overall self-esteem.

This form of self-esteem requires constant validation (Assor & Tal, 2012; Crocker, 2002; Kernis, 2003). Necessarily, then, it is fragile or unstable because fortune is fickle: The next failure or rejection is just around the corner. Individuals with a conditional self-esteem are highly anxious, depressive, and stressed; and they treat themselves harshly when they perceive that they have performed below expectations (Feldhusen et al., 2000; Neumeister 2004a, 2004b; Neumeister & Finch, 2006). In contrast to *self-referenced* perfectionism, where individuals strive to do well for the pleasure of becoming competent (LoCicero & Ashby, 2000; Parker & Adkins, 1995; Siegle & Schuler, 2000; Wood & Care, 2002), these humans are *socially prescribed* perfectionists. This form of perfectionism is a bully that tells them that they *must* do things perfectly, *have* to get things right the first time, *must not* make mistakes and that if they can't do something well instantly, there is no point in trying, so they give up (Harris, 2011). This form involves compulsive striving in an effort to avoid the shame of failure and the rejection that people believe this would attract (Brown, 2010).

In an effort to avoid seeming incompetent (which to them is the same thing as being unworthy), individuals with a conditional self-esteem will avoid challenging tasks where failure is a possibility (Covington & Müeller, 2001) and will often procrastinate on graded tasks for fear of not doing well. This is because they mistakenly believe that:

Ability = Performance = Worth.

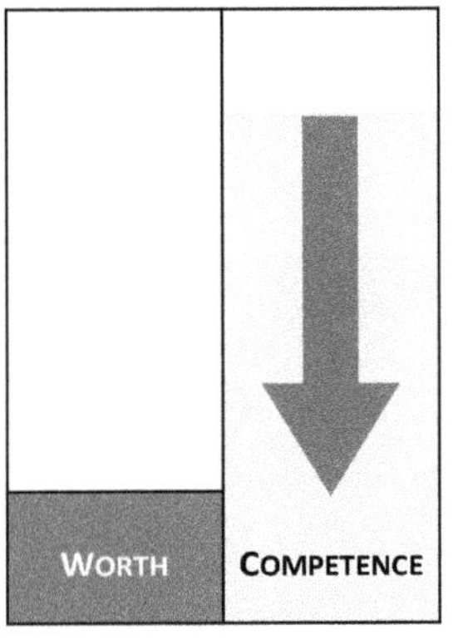

Figure 11.7 Conditional self-esteem

However, we all perform below our ability on occasions, in which case:

Ability ≠ Performance (where ≠ reads, 'is not equal to').

Moreover, our performance tells us about our *competence*, not about our *worth*, in which case:

Performance ≠ Worth.

Therefore:

Ability ≠ Performance ≠ Worth.

Authentic self-esteem

An authentic high self-esteem (illustrated in Figure 11.8) is secure and genuine because it is gained from unconditional love and acceptance. As a result, these individuals' self-worth is well anchored, without the need for constant validation or the compulsion to prove themselves by outdoing others (Kernis, 2003). This is because failure - even at skills that matter to them - will not imperil their sense of worth. Possessors of an authentic self-esteem feel competent to take achievement risks and worthy enough to sustain a failure (Mruk, 2006). Accordingly, although (as indicated by the double-headed arrow in Figure 11.8) there is some minor fluctuation in their esteem about their *competence* in response to successes or failures, on the whole they will use failure not as a message about their worth but as a guide to future action (Kernis, 2003). Over time, their self-esteem will be relatively stable.

Implications of self-esteem for counselling

Performing a critique of one's performances is vital for self-regulation (Bergner, 1995). However, pathological self-criticism is seen in many presenting difficulties such as depression, disordered eating, socially prescribed perfectionism, stress and conditional self-esteem (Kannan & Levitt, 2013). It is more than merely 'beating oneself up' or goading oneself to excel, but instead is allowing failure to define oneself as being ineligible to be loved, respected

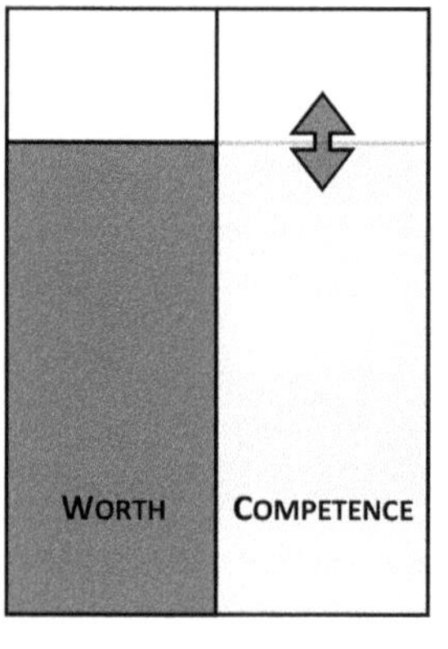

Figure 11.8 Authentic self-esteem

or successful (Bergner, 1995). Overlooking their achievements robs self-critics of satisfaction in life (Bergner, 1995).

One option is to reframe the problem, not of having a pathological self-critic but of having an *inaccurate* self-critic. The job of clients is then transformed into becoming a *competent* self-critic who can deliver and adjust to *accurate* feedback.

Alternatively, narrative therapy would externalise the self-critic, asking clients what it wants for their lives and if they want to put it in its place (or subdue or tame it). Externalisation is ideal for self-criticism, given that most who live with it already experience the self-critic as having a life of its own (Bergner, 1995).

Antidotes to shame

A low sense of worth comes from life scripts that we acquired in childhood that we are not good enough. Brené Brown (2010) says that shame is a fear of disconnection that we develop when not being 'enough' leads to rejection. It comes when others question, 'Who do you think you are?' and we learn to apologise for being ourselves. In short, it comes from the belief, 'I am a mistake'.

The antidotes to these shaming messages are compassion towards ourselves and forging connections to others who accept us unconditionally. In terms of self-compassion, we need to: defuse from shaming messages (see Chapter 4); recognise that the people in our orbit are better off for having us in their lives; learn not to apologise for ourselves; and distinguish our worth from our competencies, so that what we do does not define who we are.

Advocate for an end to reward programs in classroom and schools

Judgemental feedback in the form of praise or other rewards (such as stars, grades or student-of-the-day awards, or end-of-year award ceremonies) has many detrimental effects (Deci & Ryan, 1987; Deci et al., 1991, 1999, 2001; Farson 1963, in Grolnick, 2003; Kamins & Dweck, 1999; Lepper & Greene, 1975; Morgan, 1983; Mueller & Dweck, 1998; Rubinstein, 1977; Ryan & Deci, 1996, 2000, 2017; Vansteenkiste et al., 2008). Rewarding children for their accomplishments teaches them to link their sense of worth to their competence: If they are 'good' for getting things right, this implies that they are 'bad' if they do not. For these and many other reasons (see Kohn, 1999; Porter, 2016), schools need to cease reward systems and instead acknowledge and celebrate children's successes. Acknowledgment differs from praise in that it firsts asks children's evaluations of their performances, does not judge and is a private event that does not show children up in public, compare them with each other or try to manipulate other children into copying a commended child (see www.louiseporter.com.au).

Remediation of learning difficulties

Children with learning difficulties develop low academic self-esteem but, given that academics are the main game in school, this will figure highly in their overall self-esteem and, given that classrooms are generally competitive, will affect their social self-esteem as well (Boyes et al., 2018; Zuppardo et al., 2021). Young people with attention deficits also have a low social self-esteem in reflection of their social skill difficulties (Mazzone et al., 2013). Therefore, if children are accurate in their assessment that they lack important competencies, counsellors can advocate that they receive tutoring to support their academic progress.

Social skills

The next quality that individuals need for resilience is social skills in order to recruit people into their lives as company and support, to enjoy all the benefits of group acceptance and friendship and to avoid loneliness (see www.louiseporter.com.au). Social competence is the ability to accomplish our personal goals while maintaining relationships with others (Santos et al., 2014). This entails a prosocial disposition of being positive, agreeable, empathic, altruistic and affectionate (LaFontana & Cillessen, 2002); and the interpersonal skills of sharing, cooperating, using persuasion, negotiation and occasionally, strategic coercion (Green & Rechis, 2006). Children acquire these skills within a social setting in which they feel safe, can trust themselves ('I'm okay') and can trust those around them ('You're okay').

At the heart of social skills is empathy. This has been aptly described as emotional resonance with others (Frith, 2004). It is the ability to appreciate how others feel and to respond in a caring way to alleviate their distress (Swick, 2005). It has two aspects (Stephan & Finlay, 1999):

- cognitive empathy, which is the ability to see the world from other perspectives
- emotional empathy, which is sensitivity to others' feelings.

Empathy is the cornerstone of our social development, giving rise to social understanding and a quest for justice and, in turn, to prosocial behaviour (Findlay et al., 2006). Hoffman (1990) sees it as the major cohesive force of society. The capacity to be empathic generates high levels of peer acceptance and the ability to form mutual, harmonious friendships (Clark & Ladd, 2000).

Implication for counselling

The capacity for empathy is inbuilt in humans (Tomasello, 2009). When parents soothe their distressed infant, babies learn emotion regulation skills that they are able to employ independently at a later age (Spinrad et al., 2004). This support helps children to understand their own emotions, teaches them that they deserve to be cared for, and gives them experience of how it feels when someone else understands us (Davidov & Grusec, 2006; Denham et al., 1997). As a result, those who have received empathy are both more understanding of others and more altruistic (Swick, 2005; Young et al., 1999; Zhou et al., 2002).

The implication for counselling, then, is that children who lack empathy were not born that way; instead, their capacity for empathy has been damaged. This means that counsellors must demonstrate empathy and advocate for non-punitive - that is, guidance - methods to be used by parents and teachers even when the children's behaviours are antisocial.

Coping and problem-solving skills

Positive coping and problem-solving skills and emotion regulation abilities protect young people against succumbing to adversity (Arakelyan & Ager, 2021; Khamis, 2019). Coping is relevant for problems that we cannot change, whereas problem solving is applied to those we can. We often think of coping as not feeling symptoms despite being in stressful circumstances. However, this is not coping: It is being out of touch with reality. Instead, *to cope* means that we can use strategies to minimise the impact of the stress on our life. Active coping measures and possessing self-efficacy for their use assist young people to deal with stress (Powell et al., 2021). Taking action both gives individuals experience of being in command of their lives and recruits support from others (Rutter, 1999). In turn, this social support itself will help reduce their distress.

Coping involves managing our emotions, perhaps by distraction, avoidance or soothing ourselves. Self-distraction is a useful strategy but distraction by others (such as engaging young people in an activity to 'take their mind off it') is not helpful (Powell et al., 2021). For those repeatedly exposed to the likes of neighbourhood violence, avoidance seems to be the most effective coping strategy as it can lessen distress and promote safety (DiClemente & Richards, 2022).

Problem-solving strategies include focusing on the problem until it is solved. This will be helpful as long as it does not cause young people to ruminate on problems (Eisenberg et al., 2005).

The least effective strategies are emotional venting, engaging in wishful thinking, worrying, blaming themselves, using drugs or attempting to ignore a problem and hoping it will go away (de Freitas et al., 2022; Halpern, 2004; Hunter & Boyle, 2004; Lewis & Frydenberg, 2002). Even so, aside from the ineffective measures, as long as children have positive coping options, it does not seem to matter precisely which one they use (Rutter, 1985, 1999). However, early exposure to adversity can teach children inflexible and maladaptive coping strategies that generate fresh problems for them (Evans & English, 2002).

Self-efficacy

Self-efficacy is the sixth aspect of my model of resilience. It is our belief about how successful we can be at running our own lives, managing our own thinking, and recruiting social support (Bandura, 1993). It is the source of confidence in ourselves that we can surmount obstacles, which is vital for our well-being and achievement.

Personal self-efficacy is when we believe that we have the skills to take charge of ourselves. Armed with this conviction, we have a greater incentive to invest effort in tasks and to strive for success, are more intrinsically motivated and are more reflective (Bong & Skaalvik, 2003). We approach challenges as something to be mastered rather than as threats to be avoided (Bandura, 1993). In contrast, individuals with low self-efficacy use less adaptive coping strategies that, in turn, generate fresh problems for them. When they subsequently experience failure or setbacks, their faith in their ability is slow to recover because they lack belief that they can do anything about failure (Bandura, 1993).

Our sense of self-efficacy results from the explanations (or 'attributions') that we have drawn about the causes of our previous successes and failures. These attributions have four properties (Weiner, 2000):

- where we locate the *cause* of events: whether we believe them to be due to internal versus external forces
- whether we see these forces as *durable* (e.g. personal traits such as ability) or *temporary* events (e.g. lack of effort)

- whether the causes are *pervasive* (e.g. inability at maths) or *specific* (e.g. not understanding fractions) and
- how *controllable* we believe events to be.

When young people blame their failures on permanent, pervasive and uncontrollable aspects, they are less likely to attempt to manage their own actions because they feel powerless to affect what happens to them anyway. Instead, in order for young people to feel efficacious, they need to explain outcomes as being due to something that is internal, temporary, specific and controllable - namely, strategy use (Robertson, 2000). Specifically, when you hear young people blame their personality for failings (e.g. when they say 'I'm hopeless at this') or when they assume that the problem is permanent ('I'll never be able to do it'), you can affirm their disappointment but then gently correct their statements with something like: 'You're right: It hasn't worked out. ... What would you like to do about that?'.

We can teach attributions via a conversation about exceptions:

> 'Tell me about a time when you failed and were able to see that as a temporary thing, as something you could do something about. ... Tell me about a time when you failed and decided you could fix that'.

Self-regulation

A seventh personal contributor to resilience is self-regulation. This reduces the risk of early adversity being manifested in emotional difficulties (Rodman et al., 2019). As mentioned in Chapter 10, it involves the ability to manage our physical state (arousal), attention, emotions, thoughts and actions. Given that compulsive self-control is unhealthy, the aim is simply for young people to be able to express themselves without infringing on others (see Chapter 10).

Purpose

The final element that promotes resilience is having a purpose in life, serving something bigger than ourselves. Our need for purpose reflects our drive to fulfil our mission in life, to live out our life script, to obey our 'sealed orders' or to arrive at more of a meaningful answer to the question, 'How should I live?'. The drive for purpose means that it is not merely pleasure that motivates us, but gratification - that is, our sense of accomplishment when an activity calls on our strengths to rise to an occasion (Seligman, 2002).

Nevertheless, young clients do not yet have to know their ultimate purpose in life and most people take an indirect route to discovering what fulfils them - rather like swinging from one ornament to another on a Christmas tree (see Figure 11.9). Each new venture builds on the last and lays a foundation for the next ... until ultimately we reach the top of the tree, which is where we are built to be. Our route does not seem obvious at the time, but each new endeavour teaches us skills that we combine into the next and the next, until once at the top and looking back, the route looks predestined. As Dr Martin Luther King said 'You don't need to know what's at the top of the staircase to take the first step' - and young people don't need to know in advance what is at the top of their Christmas tree.

Figure 11.9 The route to purpose

Social resources

The final aspect of resilience reflects the fact that withstanding adversity is not just a characteristic of individuals but a quality of the social support that is available to them (Vindevogel & Verelst, 2020). A warm relationship with parents in particular supports young people to surmount obstacles in life (Anderson et al., 2022; Kaufmann et al., 2000; Propper & Moore, 2006; Wyman et al., 1999).

Meanwhile, students' relationships with their teachers are the strongest influence on their academic self-esteem and sense of belonging in their class and school (Davidson et al., 2010; Goodenow, 1993; Osterman, 2000; Ryan et al., 1994; Tucker et al., 2002; Wentzel, 1998), all of which foster resilience in young people. Meanwhile, peer acceptance protects them from low self-esteem (Letcher et al., 2009; Overbeek et al., 2010), depression (Boulard et al., 2012; De Wit et al., 2011), social anxiety (De Wit et al., 2011), and antisocial behaviour (Dodge et al., 2003; Hay et al., 2004; Johnson et al., 2000; Keiley et al., 2000; Ladd, 2006; Laird et al., 2001; Stormshak et al., 1999; Sturaro et al., 2011; Werner & Crick, 2004). At a more intimate level, friendships provide young people with emotional and cognitive resources for overcoming adversity. These benefits are found across cultures and are particularly valuable for young people whose home life is strained (Schmuck & Schmuck, 2001).

Resilience within a narrative framework

Having asked questions about which of these eight skills clients draw on to rise above difficult circumstances, we will weave these into a story about their identity, upon which many new options for action will become available to them (White, 2016). Landscape of action questions could include (Denborough, 2014; White, 2016, p. 170):

- What is the name of this special skill, knowledge or value that gets you through hard times?
- What is a story about a time when it made a difference to you or others?
- When this resilience is most present for you, how does it affect what you do?
- How does it shape how you are in life?

- What does it make possible in your relationships?
- How does it assist you in going forward with your life?

Landscape of identity questions include (White, 2016, p. 170):

- How does this skill affect what you think about yourself?
- Do you know how you have been able to retain a connection to this resilience through all that has happened in your life?
- How did you sustain this resilience? For example, did Hope or Optimism keep it present for you?
- How was it that you did not just resign yourself to what you were served up in life?
- What told you that life could be different for you?

Conclusion

If a yacht's mast has a hairline fracture, it might still function well in normal weather conditions - but can snap in adverse conditions. Similarly, vulnerable individuals can and do withstand adversity. Yet it is ironic that, at an age when humans are most vulnerable to adversity, we assume that they are the most resilient (Souers & Hall, 2016) - when resilience requires that young people receive support to overcome the challenges that come their way.

References

Adams, C., Blueford, J., Luke, C., & Byrd, R. (2021). At-promise children and adolescents. In R Byrd & C. Luke (Eds.), *Counseling children and adolescents: Cultivating empathic connection* (pp. 138–161). Routledge.

Anderson, A. S., Siciliano, R. E., Henry, L. M., Watson, K. H., Gruhn, M. A. ... Compas, B. E. (2022). Adverse childhood experiences, parenting, and socioeconomic status: Associations with internalizing and externalizing symptoms in adolescence. *Child Abuse and Neglect*, *125*, https://doi.org/10.1016/j.chiabu.2022.105493

Australian Institute of Health and Welfare. (2020). *Australia's children*. AIHW.

Arakelyan, S., & Ager, A. (2021). Annual research review: A multilevel bioecological analysis of factors influencing the mental health and psychosocial well-being of refugee children. *Journal of Child Psychology and Psychiatry*, *62*(5), 484–509. https://doi.org/10.1111/jcpp.13355

Assor, A., & Tal, K. (2012). When parents' affection depends on child's achievement: Parental conditional positive regard, self-aggrandizement, shame and coping in adolescents. *Journal of Adolescence*, *35*(2), 249–260. https://doi.org/10.1016/j.adolescence.2011.10.004

Bakermans-Kranenburg, M. J., van IJzendoorn, M. H., & Kroonenberg, P. M. (2004). Differences in attachment security between African-American and white children: Ethnicity or socio-economic status? *Infant Behavior and Development*, *27*(3), 417–433. https://doi.org/10.1016/j.infbeh.2004.02.002

Bandura, A. (1993). Perceived self-efficacy in cognitive development and functioning. *Educational Psychologist*, *28*(2), 117–148. https://doi.org/10.1207/s15326985ep2802_3

Barr, C. E., Mednick, S. A., & Munk-Jorgensen, P. (1990). Exposure to influenza epidemics during gestation and adult schizophrenia: A 40-year study. *Archives of General Psychiatry*, *47*(9), 869–874. https://doi.org/10.1001/archpsyc.1990.01810210077012

Baumeister, R. F., Smart, L., & Boden, J. M. (1996). Relation of threatened egotism to violence and aggression: The dark side of high self-esteem. *Psychological Review*, *103*(1), 5–33.

Baumeister, R. F., Campbell, J. D., Krueger, J. I., & Vohs, K. D. (2003). Does high self-esteem cause better performance, interpersonal success, happiness, or healthier lifestyles? *Psychological Science in the Public Interest*, *4*(1), 1–44.

Bayless, T. M., Rothfeld, B., Massa, C., Wise, L., Paige, D., & Bedine, M. S. (1975). Lactose and milk intolerance: Clinical implications. *New England Journal of Medicine, 292*(22), 1156–1159. https://doi.org/10.1056/NEJM197505292922205

Bergner, R. M. (1995). *Pathological self-criticism*. Springer. https://doi.org/10.1007/978-1-4757-2410-3_6

Birkeland, M. S., Melkevik, O., Holsen, I., & Wold, B. (2012). Trajectories of global self-esteem development during adolescence. *Journal of Adolescence, 35*(1), 43–54. https://doi.org/10.1016/j.adolescence.2011.06.006

Blum, N. J., & Mercugliano, M. (1997). Attention-deficit/hyperactivity disorder. In M. L. Batshaw (Ed.), *Children with disabilities* (4th ed., pp. 449–470). MacLennan and Petty.

Bong, M., & Skaalvik, E. M. (2003). Academic self-concept and self-efficacy: How different are they really? *Educational Psychology Review, 15*(1), 1–40. https://doi.org/10.1023/A:1021302408382

Bos, A. E., Muris, P., Mulkens, S., & Schaalma, H. P. (2006). Changing self-esteem in children and adolescents: A roadmap for future interventions. *Netherlands Journal of Psychology, 62*(1), 26–33. https://doi.org/10.1007/BF03061048

Boulard, A., Quertemont, E., Gauthier, J. M., & Born, M. (2012). Social context in school: Its relation to adolescents' depressive mood. *Journal of Adolescence, 35*(1), 143–152. https://doi.org/10.1016/j.adolescence.2011.04.002

Boyes, M. E., Tebbutt, B., Preece, K. A., & Badcock, N. A. (2018). Relationships between reading ability and child mental health: Moderating effects of self-esteem. *Australian Psychologist, 53*(2), 125–133. https://doi.org/10.1111/ap.12281

Bracken, B. A., Bunch, S., Keith, T. Z., & Keith, P. B. (2000). Child and adolescent multidimensional self-concept: A five-instrument factor analysis. *Psychology in the Schools, 37*(6), 483–493. https://doi.org/10.1002/1520-6807(200011)37:6%3C483::AID-PITS1%3E3.0.CO;2-R

Branden, N. (1994). *The six pillars of self-esteem*. Bantam.

Branden, N. (2001). *The psychology of self-esteem*. Jossey-Bass.

Bronson, P., & Merryman, A. (2009). *Nurture shock: New thinking about children*. Twelve.

Brown, B. (2010). *The gifts of imperfection*. Hazelden.

Brown, B. (2012). *Daring greatly*. Gotham.

Burns, B. J., Phillips, S. D., Wagner, H. R., Barth, R. P., Kolko, D. J., Campbell, Y., & Landsverk, J. (2004). Mental health need and access to mental health services by youths involved with child welfare: A national survey. *Journal of the American Academy of Child and Adolescent Psychiatry, 43*(8), 960–970. https://doi.org/10.1097/01.chi.0000127590.95585.65

Burns, R. B. (1982). *Self-concept development and education*. Holt, Rhinehart and Winston.

Clark, K. E., & Ladd, G. W. (2000). Connectedness and autonomy support in parent-child relationships: Links to children's socioemotional orientation and peer relationships. *Developmental Psychology, 36*(4), 485–498. https://doi.org/10.1037//0012-1649.36.4.485

Collison, D. R., & Hall, T. (1989). *Why do I feel so awful?* Angus and Robertson.

Covington, M. V., & Müeller, K. J. (2001). Intrinsic versus extrinsic motivation: An approach/avoidance reformulation. *Educational Psychology Review, 13*(2), 157–176. https://doi.org/10.1023/A:1009009219144

Crocker, J. (2002). The costs of seeking self-esteem. *Journal of Social Issues, 58*(3), 597–615. https://doi.org/10.1111/1540-4560.00279

Dahl, R. E. (1999). The consequences of insufficient sleep for adolescents: Links between sleep and emotional regulation. *Phi Delta Kappan, 80*(5), 354–359.

Davidov, M., & Grusec, J. E. (2006). Untangling the links of parental responsiveness to distress and warmth to child outcomes. *Child Development, 77*(1), 44–58. https://doi.org/10.1111/j.1467-8624.2006.00855.x

Davidson, A. J., Gest, S. D., & Welsh, J. A. (2010). Relatedness with teachers and peers during early adolescence: An integrated variable-oriented and person-oriented approach. *Journal of School Psychology, 48*(6), 483–510. https://doi.org/10.1016/j.jsp.2010.08.002

de Freitas, D. F., Mendonça, M., Wolke, D., Marturano, E. M., Fontaine, A. M., & Coimbra, S. (2022). Resilience in the face of peer victimization and perceived discrimination: The role of individual and familial factors. *Child Abuse and Neglect, 125*, 105492. https://doi.org/10.1016/j.chiabu.2022.105492

De Wit, D. J., Karioja, K., Rye, B. J., & Shain, M. (2011). Perceptions of declining classmate and teacher support following the transition to high school: Potential correlates of increasing student mental health difficulties. *Psychology in the Schools, 48*(6), 556–572. https://doi.org/10.1002/pits.20576

Deci, E. L., & Ryan, R. M. (1987). The support of autonomy and the control of behavior. *Journal of Personality and Social Psychology, 53*(6), 1024–1037.

Deci, E. L., Vallerand, R. J., Pelletier, L. G., & Ryan, R. M. (1991). Motivation and education: The self-determination perspective. *Educational Psychologist*, *26*(3 & 4), 325–346. https://doi.org/10.1080/00461520.1991.9653137

Deci, E. L., Koestner, R., & Ryan, R. M. (1999). A meta-analytic review of experiments examining the effects of extrinsic rewards on intrinsic motivation. *Psychological Bulletin*, *125*(6), 627–668.

Deci, E. L., Koestner, R., & Ryan, R. M. (2001). Extrinsic rewards and intrinsic motivation in education: Reconsidered once again. *Review of Educational Research*, *71*(1), 1–27. https://doi.org/10.3102/00346543071001001

Denborough, D. (2014). *Retelling the stories of our lives: Everyday narrative therapy to draw inspiration and transform experience*. Norton.

Denham, S. A., Mitchell-Copeland, J., Strandberg, K., Auerbach, S., & Blair, K. (1997). Parental contributions to preschoolers' emotional competence: Direct and indirect effects. *Motivation and Emotion*, *21*(1), 65–86. https://doi.org/10.1023/A:1024426431247

Diamantopoulou, S., Rydell, A. M., & Henricsson, L. (2008). Can both low and high self-esteem be related to aggression in children? *Social Development*, *17*(3), 682–698. https://doi.org/10.1111/j.1467-9507.2007.00444.x

DiClemente, C. M., & Richards, M. H. (2022). Community violence in early adolescence: Assessing coping strategies for reducing delinquency and aggression. *Journal of Clinical Child and Adolescent Psychology*, *51*(2), 155–169. https://doi.org/10.1080/15374416.2019.1650365

Diener, E., & Diener, M. (1995). Cross-cultural correlates of life satisfaction and self-esteem. *Journal of Personality and Social Psychology*, *68*(4), 653–663.

Diener, M. L., Nievar, M. A., & Wright, C. (2003). Attachment security among mothers and their young children living in poverty: Associations with maternal, child, and contextual factors. *Merrill-Palmer Quarterly*, *49*(2), 154–182. https://www.jstor.org/stable/23096226

Dodge, K. A., Lansford, J. E., Burks, V. S., Bates, J. E., Pettit, G. S., Fontaine, R., & Price, J. M. (2003). Peer rejection and social information-processing factors in the development of aggressive behavior problems in children. *Child Development*, *74*(2), 374–393. https://doi.org/10.1111/1467-8624.7402004

Eisenberg, N., Sadovsky, A., Spinrad, T. L., Fabes, R. A., Losoya, S. H., ... & Shepard, S. A. (2005). The relations of problem behavior status to children's negative emotionality, effortful control, and impulsivity: Concurrent relations and prediction of change. *Developmental Psychology*, *41*(1), 193–211. https://doi.org/10.1037/0012-1649.41.1.193

Ekeland, E., Heian, F., Hagen, K. B., Abbott, J. M., & Nordheim, L. (2004). Exercise to improve self-esteem in children and young people. *Cochrane Database of Systematic Reviews*, (1), CD003683. https://doi.org/10.1002/14651858.CD003683.pub2

Evans, G. W., & English, K. (2002). The environment of poverty: Multiple stressor exposure, psychophysiological stress, and socioemotional adjustment. *Child Development*, *73*(4), 1238–1248. https://doi.org/10.1111/1467-8624.00469

Facompré, C. R., Bernard, K., & Waters, T. E. A. (2018). Effectiveness of interventions in preventing disorganized attachment: A meta-analysis. *Development and Psychopathology*, *30*, 1–11. https://doi.org/10.1017/S0954579417000426

Feldhusen, J. F., Dai, D. Y., & Clinkenbeard, P. R. (2000). Dimensions of competitive and cooperative learning among gifted learners. *Journal for the Education of the Gifted*, *23*(3), 328–342.

Findlay, L. C., Girardi, A., & Coplan, R. J. (2006). Links between empathy, social behavior, and social understanding in early childhood. *Early Childhood Research Quarterly*, *21*(3), 347–359. https://doi.org/10.1016/j.ecresq.2006.07.009

Fraenkel, P., Hameline, T., & Shannon, M. (2009). Narrative and collaborative practices in work with families that are homeless. *Journal of Marital and Family Therapy*, *35*(3), 325–342. https://doi.org/10.1111/j.1752-0606.2009.00119.x

Frith, U. (2004). Emanuel Miller lecture: Confusions and controversies about Asperger syndrome. *Journal of Child Psychology and Psychiatry*, *45*(4), 672–686.

Gecas, V. (1982). The self-concept. *Annual Review of Sociology*, *8*, 1–33.

Gesser, R. M., & Koo, S. C. (1996). Oral inoculation with herpes simplex virus type 1 infects enteric neurons and mucosal nerve fibers within the gastrointestinal tract in mice. *Journal of Virology*, *70*(6), 4097–4102. https://doi.org/10.1128/jvi.70.6.4097-4102.1996

Glaser, D. (2000). Child abuse and neglect and the brain – A review. *Journal of Child Psychology and Psychiatry*, *41*(1), 97–116. https://doi.org/10.1017/S0021963099004990

Goodenow, C. (1993). Classroom belonging among early adolescent students: Relationships to motivation and achievement. *Journal of Early Adolescence*, *13*(1), 21–43. https://doi.org/10.1177/0272431693013001002

Granqvist, P., Sroufe, L. A., Doxier, M., Hesse, E., Steele, M., ... & Duschinsky, R. (2017). Disorganized attachment in infancy: A review of the phenomenon and its implications for clinicians and policy-makers. *Attachment and Human Development*, *19*(6), 534–558. https://doi.org/10.1080/14616734.2017.1354040

Green, V. A., & Rechis, R. (2006). Children's competitive and cooperative interactions in limited resource situations: A literature review. *Journal of Applied Developmental Psychology*, *27*(1), 42–59. https://doi.org/10.1016/j.appdev.2005.12.002

Gregory, A. M., & Sadeh, A. (2012). Sleep, emotional and behavioral difficulties in children and adolescents. *Sleep Medicine Reviews*, *16*(2), 129–136. https://doi.org/10.1016/j.smrv.2011.03.007

Grolnick, W. S. (2003). *The psychology of parental control: How well-meant parenting backfires*. Lawrence Erlbaum.

Hadjivassiliou, M., Grünewald, R. A., Lawden, M., Davies-Jones, G. A. B., Powell, T., & Smith, C. M. L. (2001). Headache and CNS white matter abnormalities associated with gluten sensitivity. *Neurology*, *56*(3), 385–388. https://doi.org/10.1212/WNL.56.3.385

Halpern, L. F. (2004). The relations of coping and family environment to preschoolers' problem behavior. *Journal of Applied Developmental Psychology*, *25*(4), 399–421. https://doi.org/10.1016/j.appdev.2004.06.001

Hamilton, C. E. (2000). Continuity and discontinuity of attachment from infancy to adolescence. *Child Development*, *71* (3), 690–694. https://doi.org/10.1111/1467-8624.00177

Harris, R. (2011). *The confidence gap: A guide to overcoming fear and self-doubt*. Trumpeter.

Hay, D. F., Payne, A., & Chadwick, A. (2004). Peer relations in childhood. *Journal of Child Psychology and Psychiatry*, *45*(1), 84–108. https://doi.org/10.1046/j.0021-9630.2003.00308.x

Hirsch, B. J., & DuBois, D. L. (1991). Self-esteem in early adolescence: The identification and prediction of contrasting longitudinal trajectories. *Journal of Youth and Adolescence*, *20*(1), 53–72. https://doi.org/10.1007/BF01537351

Hoffman, M. L. (1990). Empathy and justice motivation. *Motivation and Emotion*, *14*(2), 151–172. https://doi.org/10.1007/BF00991641

Holt, A., & Birchall, J. (2022). 'Their Mum messed up and Gran can't afford to': Violence towards grandparent kinship carers and the Implications for social work. *The British Journal of Social Work*, *52*(3), 1231–1248. https://doi.org/10.1093/bjsw/bcab156

Hunter, S. C., & Boyle, J. M. E. (2004). Appraisal and coping strategy use in victims of school bullying. *British Journal of Educational Psychology*, *74*(1), 83–107. https://doi.org/10.1348/000709904322848833

Janicki, M. P., McCallion, P., Grant-Griffin, L., & Kolomer, S. R. (2000). Grandparent caregivers I: Characteristics of the grandparents and the children with disabilities for whom they care. *Journal of Gerontological Social Work*, *33*(3), 35–55. https://doi.org/10.1300/J083v33n03_03

Johnson, C., Ironsmith, M., Snow, C. W., & Poteat, G. M. (2000). Peer acceptance and social adjustment in preschool and kindergarten. *Early Childhood Education Journal*, *27*(4), 207–212. https://doi.org/10.1023/B:ECEJ.0000003356.30481.7a

Kamins, M. L., & Dweck, C. S. (1999). Person versus process praise and criticism: Implications for contingent self-worth and coping. *Developmental Psychology*, *35*(3), 835–847.

Kannan, D., & Levitt, H. M. (2013). A review of client self-criticism in psychotherapy. *Journal of Psychotherapy Integration*, *23*(2), 166–178. https://doi.org/10.1037/a0032355

Karlsson, H., Blomström, A., Wicks, S., Yang, S., Yolken, R. H., & Dalman, C. (2012). Maternal antibodies to dietary antigens and risk of nonaffective psychosis in offspring. *American Journal of Psychiatry*, *169*(6), 625–632. https://doi.org/10.1176/appi.ajp.2012.11081197

Kaufmann, D., Gesten, E., Santa Lucia, R. C., Salcedo, O., Rendina-Gobioff, G., & Gadd, R. (2000). The relationship between parenting style and children's adjustment: The parents' perspective. *Journal of Child and Family Studies*, *9*(2), 231–245. https://doi.org/10.1023/A:1009475122883

Keddell, E. (2012). Going home: Managing 'risk' through relationship in returning children from foster care to their families of origin. *Qualitative Social Work*, *11*(6), 604–620. https://doi.org/10.1177/1473325011411010

Keiley, M. K., Bates, J. E., Dodge, K. E., & Pettit, G. S. (2000). A cross-domain growth analysis: Externalizing and internalizing behaviors during eight years of childhood. *Journal of Abnormal Child Psychology*, *28*(2), 161–179. https://doi.org/10.1023/A:1005122814723

Kernis, M. H. (2003). Toward a conceptualization of optimal self-esteem. *Psychological Inquiry*, *14*(1), 1-26. https://doi.org/10.1207/S15327965PLI1401_01

Kernis, M. H., Grannemann, B. D., & Barclay, L. C. (1989). Stability and level of self-esteem as predictors of anger arousal and hostility. *Journal of Personality and Social Psychology*, *56*(6), 1013-1022.

Khamis, V. (2019). Posttraumatic stress disorder and emotion dysregulation among Syrian refugee children and adolescents resettled in Lebanon and Jordan. *Child Abuse and Neglect*, *89*, 29-39. https://doi.org/10.1016/j.chiabu.2018.12.013

Kharrazian, D. (2013). *Why isn't my brain working?* Elephant Press.

Kohn, A. (1999). *Punished by rewards: The trouble with gold stars, incentive plans, A's, praise and other bribes* (2nd ed.). Houghton Mifflin.

Koren-Karie, N., Oppenheim, D., Smadar, D., Sher, E., & Etzion-Carasso, A. (2002). Mothers' insightfulness regarding their infants' internal experience: Relations with maternal sensitivity and infant attachment. *Developmental Psychology*, *38*(4), 534-542.

Ladd, G. W. (2006). Peer rejection, aggressive or withdrawn behavior, and psychological maladjustment from ages 5 to 12: An examination of four predictive models. *Child Development*, *77*(4), 822-846. https://doi.org/10.1111/j.1467-8624.2006.00905.x

LaFontana, K. M., & Cillessen, A. H. N. (2002). Children's perceptions of popular and unpopular peers: A multimethod assessment. *Developmental Psychology*, *38*(5), 635-647. https://doi.org/10.1037//0012-1649.38.5.635

Laird, R. D., Jordan, K. Y., Dodge, K. A., Pettit, G. S., & Bates, J. E. (2001). Peer rejection in childhood, involvement with antisocial peers in early adolescence, and the development of externalizing behavior problems. *Development and Psychopathology*, *13*(2), 337-354. https://doi.org/10.1017/S0954579401002085

Lepper, M. R., & Greene, D. (1975). Turning play into work: Effects of adult surveillance and extrinsic rewards on children's intrinsic motivation. *Journal of Personality and Social Psychology*, *31*(3), 479-486.

Letcher, P., Smart, D., Sanson, A., & Toumbourou, J. W. (2009). Psychosocial precursors and correlates of differing internalizing trajectories from 3 to 15 years. *Social Development*, *18*(3), 618-646. https://doi.org/10.1111/j.1467-9507.2008.00500.x

Letiecq, B. L., Bailey, S. J., & Porterfield, F. (2008). 'We have no rights, we get no help': The legal and policy dilemmas facing grandparent caregivers. *Journal of Family Issues*, *29*(8), 995-1012. https://doi.org/10.1177/0192513X08316545

Leve, L. D., Harold, G. T., Chamberlain, P., Landsverk, J. A., Fisher, P. A., & Vostanis, P. (2012). Practitioner review: Children in foster care – vulnerabilities and evidence-based interventions that promote resilience processes. *Journal of Child Psychology and Psychiatry*, *53*(12), 1197-1211. https://doi.org/10.1111/j.1469-7610.2012.02594.x

Lewis, M., Feiring, C., & Rosenthal, S. (2000). Attachment over time. *Child Development*, *71*(3), 707-720. https://doi.org/10.1111/1467-8624.00180

Lewis, R., & Frydenberg, E. (2002). Concomitants of failure to cope: What we should teach adolescents about coping. *British Journal of Educational Psychology*, *72*(3), 419-431. https://doi.org/10.1348/000709902320634483

Liu, M., Wu, L., & Ming, Q. (2015). How does physical activity intervention improve self-esteem and self-concept in children and adolescents? Evidence from a meta-analysis. *PloS One*, *10*(8), e0134804. https://doi.org/10.1371/journal.pone.0134804

LoCicero, K. A., & Ashby, J. S. (2000). Multidimensional perfectionism in middle school age gifted students: A comparison to peers from the general cohort. *Roeper Review*, *22*(3), 182-185. https://doi.org/10.1080/02783190009554030

Lynch. B. (2013). *MTHFR basics*. Amazon Digital Services.

Lyon, M. R. (2000). *Healing the hyperactive brain: Through the new science of functional medicine*. Focused Publishing.

Mackarness, R. (1990). *Not all in the mind*. Thorsons.

Mäki, M., & Collin, P. (1997). Coeliac disease. *The Lancet*, *349*(9067), 1755-1759. https://doi.org/10.1016/S0140-6736(96)70237-4

Mallick, B. N., & Singh, A. (2011). REM sleep loss increases brain excitability: Role of noradrenalin and its mechanism of action. *Sleep Medicine Reviews*, *15*(3), 165-178. https://doi.org/10.1016/j.smrv.2010.11.001

Marsh, H. W., & Martin, A. J. (2010). Academic self-concept and academic achievement: Relations and causal ordering. *British Journal of Educational Psychology*, *81*(1), 59-77. https://doi.org/10.1348/000709910X503501

Mazzone, L., Postorino, V., Reale, L., Guarnera, M., Mannino, V., Armado, M., ... & Vicari, S. (2013). Self-esteem evaluation in children and adolescents suffering from ADHD. *Clinical Practice and Epidemiology in Mental Health*, *9*, 96–102.

McCallion, P., Janicki, M. P., & Kolomer, S. R. (2004). Controlled evaluation of support groups for grandparent caregivers of children with developmental disabilities and delays. *American Journal on Mental Retardation*, *109*(5), 352-361. https://doi.org/10.1352/0895-8017(2004)109%3C352:CEOSGF%3E2.0.CO;2

Morgan, M. (1983). Decrements in intrinsic motivation among rewarded and observer subjects. *Child Development*, *54*(3), 636–644. https://doi.org/10.2307/1130050

Moss, E., Cyr, C., Bureau, J.-F., Tarabulsy, G. M., & Dubois-Comtois, K. (2005). Stability of attachment during the preschool period. *Developmental Psychology*, *41*(5), 773-783. https://doi.org/10.1037/0012-1649.41.5.773

Motivala, S. J., Sarfatti, A., Olmos, L., & Irwin, M. R. (2005). Inflammatory markers and sleep disturbance in major depression. *Psychosomatic Medicine*, *67*(2), 187-194. https://doi.org/10.1097/01.psy.0000149259.72488.09

Mruk, C. J. (2006). *Self-esteem research, theory, and practice* (3rd ed.). Springer.

Mueller, C. M., & Dweck, C. S. (1998). Praise for intelligence can undermine children's motivation and performance. *Journal of Personality and Social Psychology*, *75*(1), 33–52.

Murray, R. M., Jones, P., O'Callaghan, E., Takei, N., & Sham, P. (1992). Genes, viruses and neurodevelopmental schizophrenia. *Journal of Psychiatric Research*, *26*(4), 225–235. https://doi.org/10.1016/0022-3956(92)90029-N

Murrell, S. A., Meeks, S,. & Walker, J. (1991). Protective functions of health and self-esteem against depression in older adults facing illness or bereavement. *Psychology and Aging*, *6*(3), 352–360.

National Institute of Child Health and Human Development Early Child Care Research Network. (2001). Child-care and family predictors of preschool attachment and stability from infancy. *Developmental Psychology*, *37*(6), 847-862. https://doi.org/10.1037//0012-1649.37.6.847

National Institute of Child Health and Human Development Early Child Care Research Network. (2006). Infant-mother attachment classification: Risk and protection in relation to changing maternal caregiving quality. *Developmental Psychology*, *42*(1), 38–58. https://doi.org/10.1037/0012-1649.42.1.38

Neumeister, K. L. S. (2004a). Understanding the relation between perfectionism and achievement motivation in gifted college students. *Gifted Child Quarterly*, *48*(3), 219–231. https://doi.org/10.1177/001698620404800306

Neumeister, K. L. S. (2004b). Factors influencing the development of perfectionism in gifted college students. *Gifted Child Quarterly*, *48*(4), 259–274. https://doi.org/10.1177/001698620404800402

Neumeister, K. L. S., & Finch, H. (2006). Perfectionism in high-ability students: Relational precursors and influences on achievement motivation. *Gifted Child Quarterly*, *50*(3), 218–251. https://doi.org/10.1177/001698620605000304

Noddings, N. (2003). *Happiness and education*. Cambridge University Press.

Osterman, K. F. (2000). Students' need for belonging in the school community. *Review of Educational Research*, *70*(3), 323-367. https://doi.org/10.3102/00346543070003323

Overall, N. C., & Simpson, J. A. (2015). Attachment and dyadic regulation processes. *Current Opinion in Psychology*, *1*, 61–66. https://doi.org/10.1016/j.copsyc.2014.11.008

Overbeek, G., Zeevalkink, H., Vermulst, A., & Scholte, R. H. J. (2010). Peer victimization, self-esteem, and ego resilience types in adolescents: A prospective analysis of person-context interactions. *Social Development*, *19*(2), 270–284. https://doi.org/10.1111/j.1467-9507.2008.00535.x

Palagini, L., & Rosenlicht, N. (2011). Sleep, dreaming, and mental health: A review of historical and neurobiological perspectives. *Sleep Medicine Reviews*, *15*(3), 179-186. https://doi.org/10.1016/j.smrv.2010.07.003

Parker, W., & Adkins, K. K. (1995). Perfectionism and the gifted. *Roeper Review*, *17*(3), 173-176. https://doi.org/10.1080/02783199509553653

Pauletti, R. E., Menon, M., Menon, M., Tobin, D. D., & Perry, D.G. (2012). Narcissism and adjustment in preadolescence. *Child Development*, *83*(3), 831-837. https://doi.org/10.1111/j.1467-8624.2011.01731.x

Percy, M., & Propst, E. (2008). Celiac disease: Its many faces and relevance to developmental disabilities. *Journal of Developmental Disabilities*, *14*(2), 105–110.

Perlmutter, D., & Loberg, K. (2013). *Grain brain*. Little, Brown & Co.

Peterson, C. (2014). *Looking forward through the life span: Developmental psychology* (6th ed.). Pearson.

Philpott, W. H., & Kalita, D. K. (2000). *Brain allergies: The psychonutrient and magnetic connections* (2nd ed.). Keats Publishing.

Pinxten, M., De Fraine, B., Van Damme, J., & D'Haenens, E. (2010). Causal ordering of academic self-concept and achievement: Effects of type of achievement measure. *British Journal of Educational Psychology, 80*(4), 689-709. https://doi.org/10.1348/000709910X493071

Porter, L. (2016). *Young children's behaviour: Guidance approaches for early childhood educators* (4th ed.). Routledge.

Posada, G., Jacobs, A., Carbonell, O. A., Alzate, G., Bustamante, M. R., & Arenas, A. (1999). Maternal care and attachment security in ordinary and emergency contexts. *Developmental Psychology, 35*(6), 1379–1388.

Powell, T., Wegmann, K. M., & Backode, E. (2021). Coping and post-traumatic stress in children and adolescents after an acute onset disaster: A systematic review. *International Journal of Environmental Research and Public Health, 18*(9), 4865. https://doi.org/10.3390/ijerph18094865

Propper, C., & Moore, G. A. (2006). The influence of parenting on infant emotionality: A multi-level psychobiological perspective. *Developmental Review, 26*(4), 427–460. https://doi.org/10.1016/j.dr.2006.06.003

Purser, D. (2015). *The 85% solution: MTHFR is overpowering our medical system – chances are you have it too*. GSH BioTech.

Raval, V., Goldberg, S., Atkinson, L., Benoit, D., Myhal, N., Poulton, L., & Zwiers, M. (2001). Maternal attachment, maternal responsiveness and infant attachment. *Infant Behavior and Development, 24*(3), 281-304. https://doi.org/10.1016/S0163-6383(01)00082-0

Robertson, J. S. (2000). Is attribution training a worthwhile classroom intervention for K-12 students with learning difficulties? *Educational Psychology Review, 12*(1), 111–134. https://doi.org/10.1023/A:1009089118008

Rodman, A. M., Jenness, J. L., Weissman, D. G., Pine, D. S., & McLaughlin, K. A. (2019). Neurobiological markers of resilience to depression and anxiety following childhood maltreatment: The role of neural circuits supporting the cognitive control of emotion. *Biological Psychiatry, 86*(6), 464–473. https://doi.10.1016/j.biopsych.2019.04.033

Rubinstein, R. P. (1977). Changes in self-esteem and anxiety in competitive and noncompetitive camps. *Journal of Social Psychology, 102*(1), 55–57. https://doi.org/10.1080/00224545.1977.9713238

Rutter, M. (1985). Resilience in the face of adversity: Protective factors and resistance to psychiatric disorder. *British Journal of Psychiatry, 147*(6), 598–611. https://doi.org/10.1192/bjp.147.6.598

Rutter, M. (1999). Resilience concepts and findings: Implications for family therapy. *Journal of Family Therapy, 21*(2), 119-144. https://doi.org/10.1111/1467-6427.00108

Ryan, R. M., & Deci, E. L. (1996). When paradigms clash: Comments on Cameron and Pierce's claim that rewards do not undermine intrinsic motivation. *Review of Educational Research, 66*(1), 33-38. https://doi.org/10.3102/00346543066001033

Ryan, R. M., & Deci, E. L. 2000). Self-determination theory and the facilitation of intrinsic motivation, social development, and well-being. *American Psychologist, 55*(1), 68–78.

Ryan, R. M., & Deci, E. L. (2017). *Self-determination theory: Basic psychological needs in motivation, development and wellness*. Guilford.

Ryan, R. M., Stiller, J. D., & Lynch, J. H. (1994). Representations of relationships to teachers, parents, and friends as predictors of academic motivation and self-esteem. *Journal of Early Adolescence, 14*(2), 226–249. https://doi.org/10.1177/027243169401400207

Salmivalli, C., Kaukiainen, A., Kaistaniemi, L., & Lagerspetz, K. M. J. (1999). Self-evaluated self-esteem, peer-evaluated self-esteem, and defensive egotism as predictors of adolescents' participation in bullying situations. *Personality and Social Psychology Bulletin, 25*(10), 1268–1278. https://doi.org/10.1177/0146167299258008

Santos, A. J., Vaughn, B. E., Peceguina, I., Daniel, J. R., & Shin, N. (2014). Growth of social competence during the preschool years: A 3-year longitudinal study. *Child Development, 85*(5), 2062–2073. https://doi.org/10.1111/cdev.12246

Sapon-Shevin, M. (1999). *Because we can change the world: A practical guide to building cooperative, inclusive classroom communities*. Allyn and Bacon.

Schmuck, R. A., & Schmuck, P. A. (2001). *Group processes in the classroom* (8th ed.). McGraw-Hill.

Seifer, R., LaGasse, L. L., Lester, B., Bauer, C. R., Shankaran, S., Bada, H. S., Wright, L. L., Smeriglio, V. L., & Liu, J. (2004). Attachment status in children prenatally exposed to cocaine and other substances. *Child Development, 75*(3), 850–868. https://doi.org/10.1111/j.1467-8624.2004.00710.x

Seligman, M. E. P. (2002). *Authentic happiness*. Simon and Schuster.
Shi, L., Sidwell, R. W., & Patterson, P. H. (2003). Maternal influenza infection causes marked behavioral and pharmacological changes in the offspring. *The Journal of Neuroscience*, *23*(1), 297–302. https://doi.org/10.1523/JNEUROSCI.23-01-00297.2003
Siegle, D., & Schuler, P. A. (2000). Perfectionism differences in gifted middle school students. *Roeper Review*, *23*(1), 39–44. https://doi.org/10.1080/02783190009554060
Sigelman, C. K., De George, L., Cunial, K., Kohler, M., Ballam, N., & Rider, E. A. (2022). *Life span human development* (4th ANZ ed.). Cengage.
Snell, E. K., Adam, E. K., & Duncan, G. J. (2007). Sleep and body mass index and overweight status of children and adolescents. *Child Development*, *78*(1), 309–323. https://doi.org/10.1111/j.1467-8624.2007.00999.x
Souers, K., & Hall, P. (2016). *Fostering resilient learners: Strategies for creating a trauma-sensitive classroom*. ASCD.
Spear, P. G., & Straus, S. E. (2007). Alphaviruses: Herpes simplex virus and varicella-zoster virus. In N. C. Engleberg, V. DiRita & T. S. Dermody (Eds.), *Schaechter's mechanisms of microbial disease* (4th ed., pp. 406–414). Lippincott, Williams and Wilkins.
Spinrad, T. L., Stifter, C. A., Donelan-McCall, N., & Turner, L. (2004). Mothers' regulation strategies in response to toddlers' affect: Links to later emotion self-regulation. *Social Development*, *13*(1), 40–55. https://doi.org/10.1111/j.1467-9507.2004.00256.x
Sroufe, L. A. (2005). Attachment and development: A prospective, longitudinal study from birth to adulthood. *Attachment and Human Development*, *7*(4), 349–367. https://doi.org/10.1080/14616730500365928
St Aubyn Crump, V. (2009). *Allergies: New Zealand's growing epidemic*. David Bateman.
Stephan, W. G., & Finlay, K. (1999). The role of empathy in improving intergroup relations. *Journal of Social Issues*, *55*(4), 729–743. https://doi.org/10.1111/0022-4537.00144
Stormshak, E. A., Bierman, K. L., Bruschi, C., Dodge, K. A., Coie, J. D., & The Conduct Problems Prevention Research Group. (1999). The relation between behavior problems and peer preference in different classroom contexts. *Child Development*, *70*(1), 169–182. https://doi.org/10.1111/1467-8624.00013
Sturaro, C., van Lier, P. A. C., Cuijpers, P., & Koot, H. M. (2011). The role of peer relationships in the development of early school-age externalizing problems. *Child Development*, *82*(3), 758–765. https://doi.org/10.1111/j.1467-8624.2010.01532.x
Swick, K. (2005). Preventing violence through empathy development in families. *Early Childhood Education Journal*, *33*(1), 53–59. https://doi.org/10.1007/s10643-005-0022-6
Tabrizian, I. (2003). *Nutritional medicine: Fact and fiction* (4th ed.). Nutrition Review Service Publications.
Tafarodi, R. W., & Vu, C. (1997). Two-dimensional self-esteem and reactions to success and failure. *Personality and Social Psychology Bulletin*, *23*(6), 626–635. https://doi.org/10.1177/0146167297236006
Tomasello, M. (2009). *Why we cooperate*. Boston Review.
Tomsone, V., Logina, I., Millers, A., Chapenko, S., Kozireva, S., & Murovska, M. (2001). Association of human herpesvirus 6 and human herpesvirus 7 with demyelinating diseases of the nervous system. *Journal of Neurovirology*, *7*(6), 564–569. https://doi.org/10.1080/135502801753248150
Trzesniewski, K. H., Donnellan, M. B., Moffitt, T. E., Robins, R. W., Poulton, R., & Caspi, A. (2006). Low self-esteem during adolescence predicts poor health, criminal behavior, and limited economic prospects during adulthood. *Developmental Psychology*, *42*(2), 381–390. https://doi.org/10.1037/0012-1649.42.2.381
Tucker, C. M., Zayco, R. A., Herman, K. C., Reinke, W. M., Trujillo, M., Carraway, K., Wallack, C., & Ivery, P. D. (2002). Teacher and child variables as predictors of academic engagement among low-income African American children. *Psychology in the Schools*, *39*(4), 477–488. https://doi.org/10.1002/pits.10038
Valentine, J. C., DuBois, D. L., & Cooper, H. (2004). The relation between self-beliefs and academic achievement: A meta-analytic review. *Educational Psychologist*, *39*(2), 111–133. https://doi.org/10.1207/s15326985ep3902_3
Vansteenkiste, M., Timmermans, T., Lens, W., Soenens, B., & Ven den Broeck, A. (2008). Does extrinsic goal framing enhance extrinsic goal-oriented individuals' learning and performance? An experimental test of the match perspective versus self-determination theory. *Journal of Educational Psychology*, *100*(2), 387–397.
Vindevogel, S., & Verelst, A. (2020). Supporting mental health in young refugees: A resilience perspective. In J. S. Song & P. Ventevogel (Eds.), *Child, adolescent and family refugee mental health: A global perspective* (pp. 53–65). Springer.
Waldinger, R. J., Toth, S. L., & Gerber, A. (2001). Maltreatment and internal representations of relationships: Core relationship themes in the narratives of abused and neglected preschoolers. *Social Development*, *10*(1), 41–58. https://doi.org/10.1111/1467-9507.00147

Wang, Z., Li, W., Cui, N., Sun, X, Rong, T. ... Wang, G. (2022). Association between child maltreatment and sleep disturbances among preschoolers. *Child Abuse and Neglect*, *127*, 105525. https://doi.org/10.1016/j.chiabu.2022.105525
Waters, E., Hamilton, C. E., & Weinfield, N. S. (2000a). The stability of attachment security from infancy to adolescence and early adulthood: General introduction. *Child Development*, *71*(3), 678–683. https://doi.org/10.1111/1467-8624.00175
Waters, E., Merrick, S., Treboux, D., Crowell, J., & Albersheim, L. (2000b). Attachment security in infancy and early adulthood: A twenty-year longitudinal study. *Child Development*, *71*(3), 684–689. https://doi.org/10.1111/1467-8624.00176
Weiner, B. (2000). Interpersonal and intrapersonal theories of motivation from an attributional perspective. *Educational Psychology Review*, *22*(1), 1–14. https://doi.org/10.1023/A:1009017532121
Weinfield, N. S., Sroufe, L. A., & Egeland, B. (2000). Attachment from infancy to early adulthood in a high-risk sample: Continuity, discontinuity, and their correlates. *Child Development*, *71*(3), 695–702. https://doi.org/10.1111/1467-8624.00178
Wentzel, K. R. (1998). Social relationships and motivation in middle school: The role of parents, teachers, and peers. *Journal of Educational Psychology*, *90*(2), 202–209.
Werner, N. E., & Crick, N. R. (2004). Maladaptive peer relationships and the development of relational and physical aggression during middle childhood. *Social Development*, *13*(4), 495–514. https://doi.org/10.1111/j.1467-9507.2004.00280.x
West, K. K., Mathews, B. L., & Kerns, K. A. (2012). Mother-child attachment and cognitive performance in middle childhood: An examination of mediating mechanisms. *Early Childhood Research Quarterly*, *28*(2), 259–270. https://doi.org/10.1016/j.ecresq.2012.07.005
White, M. (2016). *Narrative therapy classics*. Dulwich Centre Publications.
Wood, K. J., & Care, E. (2002). The relationship between perfectionism and intelligence in a group of adolescents. *The Australasian Journal of Gifted Education*, *11*(1), 22–29.
Woteki, C. E., Weser, E., & Young, E. A. (1977). Lactose malabsorption in Mexican-American adults. *The American Journal of Clinical Nutrition*, *30*(4), 470–475. https://doi.org/10.1093/ajcn/30.4.470
Wyman, P. A., Cowen, E. L., Work, W. C., Hoyt-Meyers, L., Magnus, K. B., & Fagen, D. B. (1999). Caregiving and developmental factors differentiating young at-risk urban children showing resilient versus stress-affected outcomes: A replication and extension. *Child Development*, *70*(3), 645–659. https://doi.org/10.1111/1467-8624.00047
Yasko, A. (2010). Biomolecular nutrigenomics: Neutrigenomic DNA testing and RNA-based nutrition. In K. Siri & T. Lyons (Eds.), *Cutting-edge therapies for autism 2010-2011* (pp. 59–62). Skyhorse.
Young, S. K., Fox, N. A., & Zahn-Waxler, C. (1999). The relations between temperament and empathy in 2-year-olds. *Developmental Psychology*, *35*(5), 1189-1197.
Zhou, Q., Eisenberg, N., Losoya, S. H., Fabes, R. A., Reiser, M., Guthrie, I. K., Murphy, B. C., Cumberland, A. J., & Shepard, S. A. (2002). The relations of parental warmth and positive expressiveness to children's empathy-related responding and social functioning: A longitudinal study. *Child Development*, *73*(3), 893-915. https://doi.org/10.1111/1467-8624.00446
Zuchowski, I., Gair, S., Henderson, D., & Thorpe, R. (2019). Convenient yet neglected: The role of grandparent kinship carers. *The British Journal of Social Work*, *49*(3), 615–632. https://doi.org/10.1093/bjsw/bcy085
Zuppardo, L., Serrano, F., Pirrone, C., & Rodriguez-Fuentes, A. (2021). More than words: Anxiety, self-esteem and behavioral problems in children and adolescents with dyslexia. *Learning Disability Quarterly*, 1–15. https://doi.org/10.1177/07319487211041103

12 Grief

It is inevitable that counsellors will be consulting with clients who are grieving over losses such as death or migration, but also will be seeing individuals who are grieving over the losses that their emotional difficulties - such as disordered eating or loneliness - bring into their lives. For all these losses, counsellors need to be literate about grief. Painful as it is, grief is necessary for us to adapt to new circumstances (Harris & Winokeur, 2021). Therefore, when supporting individuals who are grieving, our role as counsellors is to facilitate growth, as opposed to mending loss (Altmeier, 2011).

The grief response

Grief is the constellation of thoughts, intense feelings and personal experiences that we go through when we have lost something we treasure or someone we love (Worden, 1996). In the case of deaths, the rituals of mourning that surround it differ across cultures, but the experience of grief itself is universal. It is the price tag we pay for loving others (Jones, 2020).

As illustrated in Figure 12.1, grief touches us in many ways (Harris & Winokeur, 2021):

- *emotionally*: with sadness, anger and numbness - common emotions during grief
- *cognitively*: inability to focus, difficulties remembering or keeping track of tasks and commitments, being disorganised
- *physically* through symptoms such as headaches, illness or insomnia, or being 'tired but wired' or what Harris and Winokeur (2021, p. 101) term 'restless exhaustion'
- *socially*, with social networks neglected during prolonged grieving, or changed social expectations of the bereaved person, being treated by others as fragile or as a 'victim'
- *spiritually*, as seen in questioning religious beliefs and searching for meaning
- *financially*, through changes in survivors' financial status
- *practically*, through changes in behaviour that occur to survivor's daily routines as a result of the loss.

Therefore, grief counsellors need to understand these many facets of grief, focusing not only on the emotional but on all its other aspects as well.

DOI:10.4324/9781003323938-14

Figure 12.1 The many aspects of grief

The development of children's understandings about death

When children suffer a loss through the death of or a separation from a family member or close friend, their reactions are as profound and as varied as adults'. However, for children, this might be the first time they have experienced such intense sadness, and they may not know what the feeling is. Given that they lack experience of loss, of emotions, and of coping strategies, they are less likely to understand their own feelings (Willis, 2002).

In general, children's response to a loss is determined by their age at the time. From a young age, children have a notion that death is the absence of life. However, until the age of 7 or 8 years, they do not have a mature understanding of three elements of death (Peterson, 2014):

- *Irreversibility*. Young children are not aware that death is irreversible.
- *Non-functionality*. Adults realise that death involves the cessation of the processes of breathing, thinking and apprehending sensations; young children do not realise this.
- *Universality*. Young children might realise that all animals are mortal but believe that this is not so for humans, or they believe that people who are special in some way do not die.

Physically healthy children grasp these three elements of death by the age of eight, whereas children who are terminally ill and those who have experienced the death of a friend or relative do so earlier (Peterson, 2014).

Infants. While babies or toddlers will understand very little about death or other losses, they can sense when other people are feeling bereaved and can miss the person from whom they have become separated. In reaction, they can display erratic, sad or withdrawn behaviour. They can also be confused by the disruption to their routines engendered by a family bereavement (Willis, 2002) or marriage break-up.

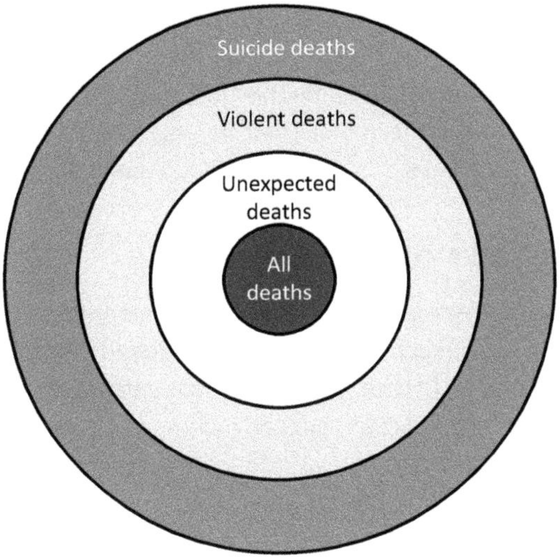

Figure 12.2 Layers of grief related to mode of death

Source: adapted from Jordan & McIntosh, (2011, p. 34).

Toddlers can experience a death (especially of a nuclear family member) as abandonment and feel bewildered at the dead person's sudden absence or at their remaining parent's distraction with his or her own grief and will might miss out on the extra nurturing they need. Confused, they might wander off.

3 to 4 years. Children of this age think that death is temporary and therefore can appear to ignore the death callously. Adults looking on can think that they are 'fine' or might not understand how they can be merrily playing when someone has died. At first, it can seem that they are callously ignoring the death but then they later become bewildered when the dead person does not return.

5 to 8 years. This is the age of magical thinking. Children in this age group who once said in anger, 'I wish you were dead', are likely to think that they caused the other person's death. This guilt and terror can be paralysing. In their guilt, they might try to be especially good to bring the person back to life.

9+ years. Older children can express sorrow in the same way that adults do. They can become apathetic, withdrawn, hostile, angry and might cry a lot. This is healthy and normal. It is important that adults do not censor these feelings but allow children to express them. Older children and adolescents might want to relate to their peers after a death of someone they love, but they still rely heavily on their parents as well. They can begin to worry if their parents' marriage is unhappy at the time, in case their parents might separate, bringing on another loss for them.

Adolescence. Hooyman and Kramer (2006) report that the grieving process of adolescents resembles that of children but that their grieving can be mistaken for the normal developmental angst of adolescence, as a result of which they do not receive the support that they need when they are bereaved. Consequently, adolescents are often the 'forgotten mourners' (Hooyman & Kramer, 2006). Although the facts of physical death are completely grasped during middle childhood (by the age of 6 to 8 years), adolescents intensify their inquiries into what happens after death, which is a concern that remains with them for all of their adult lives (Peterson, 2014).

Additionally, like children, a death of someone close might be the first significant loss that adolescents have experienced so far in life. Their innocent belief that only good things happen to good people and their sense of safety can be suddenly shattered.

Types of losses that give rise to grief

Losses can be primary, secondary or tertiary losses. A *primary* loss is any major loss that one experiences that triggers grief, such as the death of a loved one, the ending of a romantic relationship, or parental divorce. In turn, this type of loss can lead to *secondary* or compounding losses which include such changes as reduced income or loss of financial security, moving house, changing school, changed parental working hours, the need for children to enter child care or out-of-school-hours care, and losing touch with extended family members.

Tertiary or existential losses are our reactions to what the primary loss means for us and our place in the world. It includes changes in our view of the world or of others; a loss of innocence that the world is a reliable, safe and secure place; a loss of trust; reduced faith in justice; and changes to our views of ourselves - that is, our identity (Harris & Gorman, 2011). Wanganeen (2010) defines some of these tertiary losses as relating to our sense of power (including safety, control, self-esteem, confidence and trust) while others relate to our sense of beauty (or transcendence, as described in Chapter 10), such as faith, self-image, personal identity and cultural identity.

Death losses

Young people's experience of the death of someone they love can have profound implications, often being their first encounter with intense sadness, and often bringing with it secondary losses that compound their grief and tertiary losses which can provoke an existential crisis at a life stage when young people are already searching for the meaning of life (Hooyman & Kramer, 2006).

The death of a parent

The loss of a parent during childhood is a developmental crisis. It forces children to confront the concept of death perhaps before they would have naturally, at the same time as losing someone who made their world safe. In addition, the loss of a parent can lead to multiple other changes, such as the need for the surviving parent to increase their working hours, or to changed care or schooling arrangements. Often the surviving parent becomes absorbed in their own grief - in which case the young person has, in effect, lost both parents.

Children can worry about who will take care of them now, especially when the surviving parent is so immersed in grief that they are not available for support (Wolchik et al., 2006; Worden, 1996). Children will also see their surviving parent expressing strong emotion, which might be the first time that they have witnessed this, and it can be unsettling and even disturbing for them (Worden, 1996). They can even believe that they have to act strong in order to protect the surviving parent (Worden, 1996).

Following the death of a parent, older siblings might take over the parenting of younger siblings, with the result that rather than separating from their family progressively through adolescence, instead they become enmeshed in the family, acting as a surrogate parent. Others withdraw and separate too sharply from the family, some engage in risky behaviours and others become angry and demand 'Why me?' (Hooyman & Kramer, 2006). They can be fearful about the future and can develop health complaints (Hooyman & Kramer, 2006). Many of these reactions are normal and will only raise concerns if they are excessive in intensity or duration.

Over time, children will begin to forget who their parent was, which means that something of who they are themselves is lost. Therefore, without idealising their deceased parent, it is important that families keep alive the stories of the parent who has died, maintain contact between the children and extended family members on their deceased parent's side and give children access to photos and personal items of their parent.

If their parent's death was a suicide, it will be very important to tell children that their parent wasn't thinking straight at the time of the suicide. Their body was playing tricks on their mind. They became absorbed in ending whatever emotional pain they were experiencing and were not able to think how much sadness their death would cause. Some parents even feel so worthless that they think that others will be 'better off' without them. Remind the child that there was nothing anyone could have done to prevent this: No one knew their parent was so full of despair. If someone could have done something, they would have.

In their study, Brent et al. (2009) found that depression was common in adolescents during the first nine months following the death of a parent, but longer than this for adolescents whose parent had died by suicide. In the long term, those who have lost a parent between 6 months and 18 years of age have a 50 per cent greater chance of dying from any causes during adolescence and young adulthood, compared with the general population (Li et al., 2014).

The death of a sibling

The death of our children is the most painful loss of all. In their own despair, parents can be so distressed that they do not notice the extent of their surviving children's suffering at the loss of their brother or sister. The parents' own emotional absence can mean that the children lose not only their sibling but their parents as well.

A Swedish study by Rostila et al. (2013) found that individuals whose sibling had died from suicide were at increased risk of suicide up to 18 years later. In contrast, when the sibling died of natural causes, surviving siblings were at no increased risk of suicide (Rostila et al., 2013).

Parents can often place high expectations on surviving siblings, as if they are having to live for two, which adds extra pressure for them. And, fearing another loss, the parents can become overly protective, making it difficult for surviving young people to develop appropriate autonomy (Hooyman & Kramer, 2006).

Loss of a friend

Children can lose friends because of temporary disagreements; as the final result of drifting apart; through physical separation, such as when a friend moves to a different school or leaves the neighbourhood; or through death. The most common causes of the death of young people are vehicular accidents, suicide and - in the U.S. - homicide. All of these are sudden and wrenching. Friends cannot prepare for these losses, and they shake adolescents' belief in a predictable and safe world (Hooyman & Kramer, 2006). They can be wracked afterwards with remorse about any carelessness that led to an accident, with guilt at not seeing and doing something to prevent their friend's suicide, or anxiety about their own safety in the face of a traumatic death of a friend (Hooyman & Kramer, 2006). In the case of a friend's death by suicide, many experience traumatic grief (Melhem et al., 2004).

Suicide

Experiencing the suicide of someone we love is like an emotional tsunami (Grad, 2011). It provokes particular anguish, attracting all the feelings associated with any death but, in addition, painful feelings of rejection or abandonment (Cvinar, 2005), even for non-fatal attempts. The loss is compounded by its sudden or traumatic nature.

Four features distinguish grief over the death by suicide from other deaths (Harvey, 1998, in Cvinar, 2005; Jordan & McIntosh, 2011):

- a greater struggle to find meaning in the suicide loss of a loved one
- greater feelings of guilt and responsibility for not recognising the warning signs or for having contributed to the deceased's suffering or decision to end their life
- greater feelings of rejection and abandonment by, and anger towards, the deceased
- stigma (feeling ashamed or tainted). When they feel shame, survivors often isolate themselves from the very social supports that could assist their grieving (Cvinar, 2005).

If surviving family members have similar emotional difficulties to the person who died by suicide, this places them at increased risk for poor adjustment (Knieper, 1999; Sakinofsky, 2007). The degree of social support that survivors receive seems to be the crucial factor in their ultimate adjustment (Cvinar, 2005).

Homicide

Deaths by homicide are a particularly traumatic loss, complicated by the police investigations. If the police are able to identify the perpetrator, there will be a series of court hearings where the details of the murder are described, and family members might also choose to attend parole hearings. Meanwhile, many face the media pack outside the courtroom and speculation, innuendo and victim blaming in the media. In other words, not only do they lose their loved one in horrific circumstances, but they lose their privacy as well.

Death of a pet

The inevitability of outliving our pets does not make their death any easier to cope with. When our pet dies, we lose a family member, and we lose who we are with that animal: It is probably the only affection that is truly uncomplicated, reciprocated and unconditional. We cherish being able to love in this innocent way. For children, the death of the family pet can be their first encounter with death and therefore needs the same sensitive handling as human deaths.

Ending of a romantic relationship

Adolescence is an important time for learning how to be intimate with others. When adolescents' romantic relationship ends, this will be their first experience of having a broken heart. If they were already emotionally unstable, it can bring on the risk of suicide. In my experience, many young people confuse the *depth* of feeling with the *length* of feeling, assuming that when they love someone deeply, it will last forever, and then are wretched when the relationship ends. They do not realise that 'The one who got away' will always seem to be the 'love of their life' - because they don't live with them long enough for the mundane to tarnish their feelings.

Moreover, many adolescents suffer from a 'personal fable' (Sigelman et al., 2022) in which they believe that they are so unique that no one has felt such deep love as they do, and that no one in the history of civilisation has ever been as agonised over the breakup of a romantic relationship. As a result, they distance themselves from the social supports that could help them to grieve.

Perinatal loss

Of any age group, adolescents are most likely to experience the loss of a child through abortion or relinquishment for adoption (Hooyman & Kramer, 2006). Females grieve the loss of their role as a mother, in addition to grieving the loss of their child (Hooyman & Kramer, 2006). Miscarriage and stillbirth are also a higher risk for this age group because of poor prenatal care. In the latter instance, for the bereaved couple, there is no absence to signal the loss, making it difficult for others to comprehend its importance to them (Pomeroy & Garcia, 2009). These are disenfranchised losses, seen as voluntary, and passed off as being better for all concerned and, as a result of a lack of support, unresolved grief can linger (Hooyman & Kramer, 2006). If the two young parents are no longer in a relationship, they are not even available to support each other.

Parental separation and divorce

Their parents' separation presents children with many challenges to add to the normal demands of growing up. Over the course of some months or years, they must acknowledge the reality of their parents' separation; disengage from their parents' conflict so that they can get on with their own lives; resolve their grief, anger and self-blame about the divorce; accept that their parents' separation is permanent; and form realistic expectations for their own future adult relationships (King, 1992). They will need to navigate the loss of their hopes and dreams for their family at the same time as missing their non-custodial parent.

A separation or divorce can set in train a series of additional or secondary losses, such as moving house, school or neighbourhood; changes in a parent's employment status and children's care and schooling arrangements; financial hardship; and subsequent repartnering of one or both parents. These additional changes add to the adjustments that children need to make to the separation itself. Therefore, where possible, advise parents to space these changes apart to give children time to adjust.

Children's healthy adjustment is helped when they have other people to support them, their relationships with both parents are warm before and after the separation, the parents can get on with their own life and do not remain angry with their former spouse, the separation does not lead to poverty and other secondary losses, the two parents can still cooperate in the children's interests following their separation, and their separation ends any conflict which might have been present during their relationship. It seems that when children experience persistent emotional difficulties following their parents' divorce, these problems were brewing before the separation (D'Onofrio et al., 2007) or are not due to their parents' separation itself, but to the accompanying acrimony, parenting problems and socioeconomic difficulties (Amato, 2000; D'Onofrio et al., 2007).

It can be difficult for children's parents to know what to tell them about their separation and they might ask you to help their child to understand. Children need to know that their parents have left each other but that they have not left the children; parents leave each other because they stop being best friends; it is not the children's fault; and both their parents still love them, even though they don't love each other enough to live together anymore.

If the children have been abandoned by the absent parent, you will need to explain this in a way which fits the facts as the children see them - because to pretend otherwise will be useless and hurtful. You might explain that some people are 'lazy' about showing how much they love other people. Or, for adolescents, you could explain that some people are irresponsible about their relationships. This verifies the children's experience of being abandoned at the same time as not vilifying a parent whom they have lost. Children need to be told over and over again that being abandoned is not because they are unlovable. It is a statement about the absent parent's inability to cope with their own feelings, not about the children's worth.

Intermittent parental absence

Families can cycle through grief on each occasion when one of the parents departs to work away from home for weeks and then returns home during work leave. This fly-in-fly-out (FIFO) lifestyle involves missing the parent who has left, adjusting to his or her absence, then having to adjust again on his return and find ways to include the FIFO parent in family life, which means missing him again when he leaves. Particularly unsettling for the children, they do cope when their parents do and when the parents maintain their roles as family leaders, rather than giving children the role of looking after the parent who remains at home.

Circumstances of losses

The circumstances of loss affect how individuals grieve. These circumstances differ on six dimensions, as illustrated in Figure 12.3. The first of these is a distinction between single versus multiple losses within a short period of time. Successive or multiple losses can throw the mourner's life into chaos, with the practical implications becoming too much to handle. The magnitude of the situation can make reorganising one's life too complex, practically and emotionally. This is known as 'bereavement overload' (Kastenbaum, 1969, cited by Freeman, 2005). In these cases, counsellors can support clients to work slowly and methodically through each loss and its secondary and tertiary effects.

Single	Multiple
Finite	Ongoing
Validated	Disenfranchised
Certain	Ambiguous
Anticipated	Sudden
Individual	Communal

Figure 12.3 Circumstances of losses

Next in Figure 12.3, many losses are a one-off or finite event, such as a death - whereas others are ongoing, as in the case of the chronic illness or disability of oneself or a family member, for example. With these ongoing or 'living' losses, the sand constantly shifts under our feet, resulting in the need for repeated adjustments over time, a sense of not being able to plan for the future (given that the situation could change) and therefore constantly feeling in a state of disequilibrium.

Third, whereas many losses are recognised and validated by others as being legitimate, others are *disenfranchised* or invisible to those around us, perhaps because the *relationship* is not recognised by society (such as the death of a gay or lesbian partner of someone who has not 'come out'); the griever is thought to be incapable of grieving, as in the cases of young children or individuals with an intellectual disability; the *loss* is stigmatised, such as an abortion, or a death by suicide or overdose; or the loss itself is not *recognised* as a genuine loss, as in the case of the death of a pet or a miscarriage. There are four reasons that such losses are not socially acknowledged (Cordaro, 2012; Pomeroy & Garcia, 2009; Worden, 2009). All these disenfranchised losses represent an 'empathic failure' or the inability of others to understand the meaning of the loss to the bereaved person (Cordaro, 2012). The main support, therefore, that counsellors can provide for disenfranchised losses is to validate clients' grief (Cordaro, 2012). Naming the grief as disenfranchised breaks the silence about the loss and gives it legitimacy (Jordan & Neimeyer, 2003). This ends the conspiracy of silence and opens up opportunities to mourn meaningfully (Cordaro, 2012).

Fourth are ambiguous - in contrast with certain - losses when loved ones are physically absent but psychologically present, as is the case with missing persons or adoptees' biological parents and siblings. A second type of ambiguous loss is when people are physically present, but psychologically absent - as in the case of parents' chronic mental illnesses, drug addiction, acquired head injuries or workaholic patterns. Parents whose children undergo a gender transition also experience an ambiguous loss of the son or daughter they gave birth to, even though their child is still alive and present.

With ambiguous loss, family members can withdraw from one another in their preoccupation with the loss. As Boss (1999, p. 11) puts it, 'The family becomes a system with nobody in it'. Therefore, the main role of counsellors is to validate their feelings as being directly related to the uncertainty about the loss (Pomeroy & Garcia, 2009). Counsellors can also support family members to discuss with each other how they perceive the loss, so that their differing modes of grieving can be aired and honoured (Pomeroy & Garcia, 2009).

A fifth circumstance is whether losses are sudden or anticipated. Sudden, traumatic or unfair losses include deaths from accidents or cardiac arrests or the death of a young person. Another is when children are not aware in advance of their parents' imminent separation. Whereas the parents will have done some grieving beforehand, the children's grief might only begin once the separation takes place.

Anticipated losses include deaths by terminal illnesses or in very old age. Walker and colleagues (in Pomeroy & Garcia, 2009) note that counsellors whose clients are anticipating the death of a loved one can assist them to acquire information about the illness and its likely course; express their full range of emotions; guide them to be less isolated, perhaps by joining a support group or an online chat room; support them to complete any 'unfinished business' with the dying person; and help the family maintain open communication among themselves and with the person who is dying.

Finally, some losses are experienced by *individuals*, whereas others are experienced by whole *communities*. When whole communities are under siege - during war time, as refugees, or in the wake of natural disasters - everyone is suffering and therefore individuals cannot be as much support to each other. Further, individuals are reluctant to single themselves out by seeming to be in more need than others. As a result, they can lack the social support that they require for recovery. Moreover, when whole communities experience multiple disasters in succession, some individuals will move away from the area, leaving those behind with a less rich support network.

Australia's stolen generations represent a profound example of communal - and personal - loss. Many lost their culture, language, families, personhood, identity, history, country, home and love of life (Raphael & Delaney, 2011). And the grief for Aboriginal and Torres Strait Islander communities continues today, with the loss of so many of their young men in particular through incarceration, drug abuse or death by suicide or violence. Accordingly, Wanganeen (2010) developed an Indigenous model of grief, which she termed the seven phases of healing (see Figure 12.4). The first phase focuses on the individual's current grief reactions. Next, there is a focus on prior losses from childhood, ancestral losses since

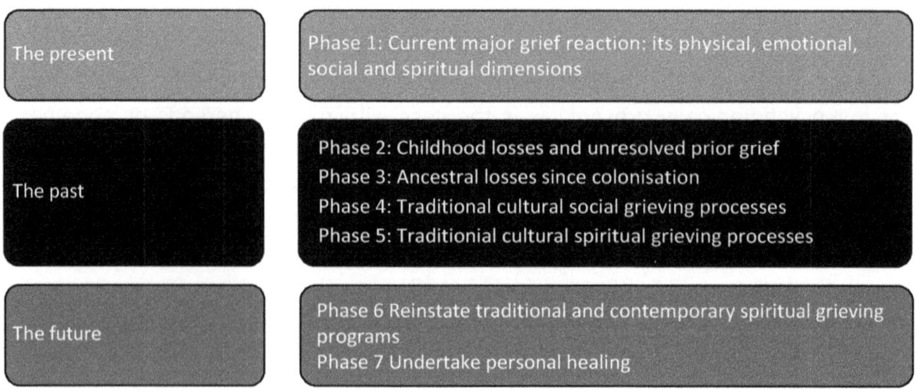

Figure 12.4 Wanganeen's seven phases of healing

Source: Wanganeen (2010).

colonisation and traditional social and spiritual grieving processes. Third is the focus on the future, by reinstating spiritual grieving and undertaking a personal healing journey.

Box 12.1 The seasons of healing

This program was designed for Aboriginal and Torres Strait Islander peoples and equates the tasks of grieving with the seasons of the year, noting that (Graham, 2004):

- No season lasts forever.
- Each season has easy days and hard days.
- Seasons can change from year to year.
- Each season is different from the others, but all are important and useful.
- People have to find ways to live with the different seasons.
- Each person is affected differently by the seasons.
- The change between seasons is often slow and hard to notice.

Tasks of grieving a death

Grieving over a loved one's death involves five tasks (Howarth, 2011; Lowenstein, 2006; Worden, 2009).

- Accept the reality of the loss.
- Process the emotional impact of the loss.
- Find an enduring connection to the deceased.
- Embark on a new life while adjusting to a world from which the deceased person is missing.
- Find meaning in the loss.

These tasks cannot be rushed, of course, but must happen at individuals' pace.

Acceptance of the reality of the loss

At the time of the loss, it is helpful if young children can attend the funeral and wake because it is frightening for them to be separated from their parents and, if kept away, they might assume that they are to blame for the person's death and are being punished for it. They also need to be clear that dead people no longer feel, think or sense. Otherwise they can become distressed at the burial or cremation.

Counsellors can assist children by giving them space to talk about their loved one's death and the events surrounding it. They might need to tell their story many times. When discussing the death, it is vital to given them facts and honest answers to their questions; otherwise they might fill in missing details with their imagination, which can be even more frightening than reality. For this, you will need information from their parents about the circumstances and cause of the death so that you can be honest about the specific events.

Always give concrete facts in words that the children can understand. It will be important to use the words 'died' and 'dead' rather than euphemisms such as 'passed on' (because that provokes the question of passed on to *where*) or 'gone to sleep' because children can develop a fear of going to sleep in case they might die during the night.

You will need to explain to young children that the person they loved died because their body grew very old or they became very *very* sick from an illness or an accident - so sick that nothing could be done to make them better. In the case of an illness-related death of a baby or child, you might say that the baby's body hadn't been made properly and therefore the baby could not live in that body anymore. Remember to tell children that the dead person did not want to leave them. You can then ask them to speculate about what the child's experience of them as a sibling might have been, and how they can carry those skills onwards even though their sibling has died (White, 2016).

If the children ask where the person goes, it will be best to suggest that they ask their parents so that this information is in line with their religious views. But do not introduce superstitious concepts at this time, such as that the dead person is looking down on them. This freaks young children out, worrying for ever more about behaving childishly in case they might attract the censure of a dead parent. But you *can* comment that the love that they felt for that person lives on in their heart and memories, which will always be there.

Young children will need repeated small doses of information ('drip feeding') and to have their questions answered over and over again so that they learn that the facts have not changed. It is not unusual for them to repeat the same question in an effort to receive a different answer (Willis, 2002). This can signal that, naturally, they do not like the facts or that they are unclear because we have cloaked our answers in euphemisms which are confusing or frightening them.

Some children's books can help you to find appropriate words to use when you are talking with children about death and marital separations - see the Resources section.

Box 12.2 Questions for young people about their story of loss

- Who died?
- How did they die?
- When was it: a short or long time ago?
- How did you find out that he or she had died? Who told you?
- What was your immediate reaction after hearing of the death?
- How do you feel now?
- Did you see your loved one after the death?
- What was that like for you to see (or not see) him or her?
- Was there a memorial or other service?
- Were you involved in that?
- What parts were really difficult?
- What parts were less difficult than expected?
- What memories of the person who has died do you feel good about?
- Who was and is able to support you right now?
- What other types of losses have you had in the past?
- How have you dealt with them?

Source: Hooyman and Kramer (2006, p. 175)

Process the emotional impact of the loss

The second task of grieving is to deal with the emotional impact of the loss (Willis, 2002). Those who have suffered a profound loss commonly experience a range of emotions, not in any particular sequence, but can revisit earlier feelings in a two-steps-forward-one-step-back process (Geldard et al., 2017; Henderson & Thompson, 2016). Their emotions often occur in combinations and in waves that advance and recede.

In the immediate aftermath of a loss, survivors can feel *shock* and *numbness*. This suspension of feeling is the brain's way of protecting them from having to process everything at once and gets survivors through the days immediately following the death. Survivors can experience incredulity that someone can be alive one minute ... and dead the next. Although they do not deny the reality of the death, even adolescents (and adults) find it hard to get their head around its permanence and irreversibility.

After the initial shock come the many aspects of *despair*, when survivors can experience a range of intense emotions, including

- *Yearning and searching*. This restlessness can involve phoning friends or relatives of the dead person, as if to get closer to him or her, for example.
- *Sadness*, which incorporates hopelessness, tearfulness, a lack of energy, loss of appetite, sleep disturbances and poor concentration. Across the age ranges, the bereaved will feel lonely, which is a longing for intimacy.
- *Anxiety*: survivors experience distressing chains of thought that are difficult to interrupt (Rainer, 2013). There might also be somatic complaints and, in children, separation distress, behavioural regression (such as bedwetting) and school refusal.
- *Guilt* at anything one might have done or not done to contribute to the loss or death, at not saying certain things to the deceased before death. Guilt can be common in the sense of wishing that the relationship with the deceased had been different, but not in a sense of being to blame for that (Friedman & James, 2008). There can be also feelings of relief – that the deceased is not suffering anymore, for example – which, itself, can give rise to guilt.
- *Anger* at the deceased and at anyone or anything who might have contributed to their death. This can be especially felt in a death by suicide.

Young people might express strong emotions that are usually censored, such as sadness or anger (Harris & Winokeur, 2021). They might need to learn the names of their feelings and to be reassured that, although these are intense, they are not 'going crazy'. To normalise their feelings, Marsten et al. (2016, p. 62) ask of those in grief:

- Does it make sense that Sadness would show up, given your loss?
- Does Sadness ever try to get you down by keeping you all to itself?
- How much of a place would you say Sadness deserves in your life at the moment?
- How much of a place would Sadness lay claim to?

In other words, sadness is not something to conquer, but something to make space for, to the degree that the young person thinks is reasonable. Harris's (2007) idea about feelings being storm clouds that pass could also be helpful (see Chapter 4).

Box 12.3 Themes underlying children's grief

Phase	*Underlying theme*	*Manifestations*
Shock	I am stunned by this loss.	Lack of emotion. Difficulty engaging with others. Poor concentration. Deterioration in schoolwork.
Disbelief	The person can't be dead.	Report seeing or hearing the deceased. Carry on conversations with thedeceased.
Yearning, searching	I must find the deceased.	Wander off or run away. Phone relatives.
Sadness	I am sad, hopeless and lonely because I have lost someone on whom I depended.	Persistent low mood, tearfulness. Low energy, lack of activity. Disrupted sleep and appetite. Poor concentration and schoolwork.
Anger	I am angry because a person I need has abandoned me. I am angry at the changes this has brought into my life.	Aggression, meltdowns, defiance. Conflict with parents, siblings, teachers and peers. Drug or alcohol use. Poor concentration and schoolwork.
Anxiety	I am anxious about losing someone else. I am anxious about dying.	Separation distress, school refusal, regressed behaviour such as bedwetting. Somatic complaints.
Guilt and bargaining	It is my fault that the person died.	Suicidal ideation.
Adjustment	I loved and lost the person who died and now I must carry on without that person while cherishing his/her memory.	Return to prior routines.

Sources: adapted from Moore and Carr (2001, in Henderson & Thompson, 2016, p. 641)

You can reassure children in grief that their feelings are their mind's way of 'getting their attention' - that is, of telling them that something important needs their focus (Harris & Winokeur, 2021). It can also be useful to validate their conflicted feelings by asking them what they miss about their loved one, and also what they do not miss (Worden, 2009). It can be healing to respectfully acknowledge that there were some aspects of the relationship that were not so positive.

Tyrrell (2019) said that, just as athletes need to rest in order to get the best from their bodies, so too those in grief need to give themselves some respite from their grieving. Accordingly, the dual process model (see Figure 12.5) describes how those in grief need to move back and forth between processing the emotions associated with their loss and solving the everyday challenges that it has wrought (Stroebe & Schut, 1999). This oscillation is necessary because it is impossible to grieve unremittingly (Stroebe & Schut, 1999).

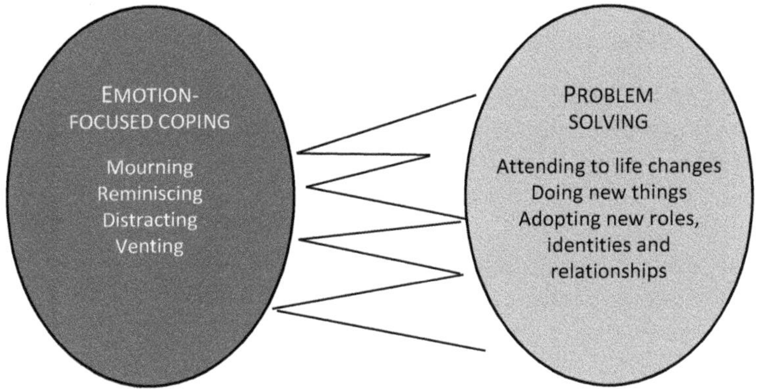

Figure 12.5 The dual process model of grieving

Source: adapted from Stroebe & Schut (1999, p. 213).

Some therapeutic activities to assist young people to process their feelings include the following (Lowenstein, 2006; Wakenshaw, 2002).

- *Trace young children's body outline* on a large sheet of paper and have them choose colours for areas where they feel various emotions.
- *Dice.* Make up some large dice with pictures on each face of their family members and pets (including the one who has died), and when they roll the dice, invite them to tell you about that family member.
- *Play.* Use play telephones or puppet play to talk with young children about their experience of loss.
- *Symbols.* Use the sandpit with figurines and ask the children to create something they have been thinking about, then talk with them about their creation. Dollhouses and pictures of their family can generate similar discussions.
- *Mind map.* Have the children construct a mind map in which they place the loss in the centre of a page and then brainstorm all the outcomes and issues that it has raised for them (Harris & Winokeur, 2021). This concrete representation of their concerns can allow them to become clear about which ones are most important and need their immediate attention.
- *Letters.* Help young people to write a letter to the person who has died - see Box 12.4. The process of writing a letter to the deceased can avoid ruminating on feelings, in the knowledge that these are documented (Rubin et al., 2012).
- *Journaling.* Keeping a journal of the grief experience can help clients to better understand their thoughts and feelings (Worden, 2009).

Never tell children to cheer up, that things will feel better soon, or that big boys don't cry. And remember that empathy never begins with the words *At least*, as in: 'At least she isn't suffering anymore'.

Box 12.4 A letter to someone special

Over the course of a few days or weeks, you might provide young people with the following sentence stems for them to complete (as relevant). Adolescents could fill in their own answers, while you could scribe young children's answers.

Dear
Since your death I have been feeling ...
And I want you to know that ...
I am really glad that we ...
I am sorry that we never got a chance to ...
I will miss never being able to ... with you ever again.
I feel sad that you won't be there when I ...
What I miss most is ...
If you were here now, I would tell you ...
I think if you were here now, you would tell me ...
I feel good knowing that ...
One day I will tell my children that you were ...
Thank you for ...
Love ...

Source: Lowenstein (2006, p. 119)

Remembrance

This is the third task of grieving. Metcalf (2017) believes that the bereaved can only resolve their grief once they acknowledge that the person they have lost is still a 'timeless influence' on their lives and will always have an impact on them. As Delaney (2016) says, death ends a life, not a relationship. Therefore counsellors can reassure clients that they do not have to 'let go' of those who have died, but instead could say 'hello' to them (White, 2016). This, says Metcalf, relieves clients of the pressure from well-meaning people to 'move on'. Indeed, we can give them permission for Sorrow to stay a little while longer (Denborough, 2014).

For children, you might use any of the strategies given in Box 12.5; for older children and adolescents, you might ask questions such as (Metcalf, 2017, p. 133; White, 2016):

- Tell me about (the person you have lost). What difference did they make in your life? What did you love about them? What did they teach you? What else?
- If we looked through their eyes, what would (the deceased) say they appreciated about you?
- What difference will it make to you when you someday begin appreciating those qualities in yourself? What might you begin doing today, just on a small scale that (the deceased) might appreciate as well?
- What do you think (the deceased's) reaction would be to see you appreciate those qualities in yourself?

- What difference would feeling this way make to the steps that you could take to get back into life?
- Keep in mind that each time you do those small actions that (the deceased) appreciated, you bring alive the things that he/she loved about you, and you honour his/her life.

Box 12.5 Ways to encourage remembrance

- *Mementos*. Children might keep a memento on them at all times, which they can bring out and talk about at those times when they are keenly feeling their loss.
- *Electronic memorials*. Survivors can turn the deceased's Facebook page into a memorial for them (Harris & Winokeur, 2021).
- *Bracketing*. You can suggest that clients have a 'grief drawer' or box containing memorabilia and photos of the deceased person and take these out when they need to focus on their feelings. They might light a candle while doing this work, blowing out the candle and shutting the drawer or box when they are ready to move away from emotional processing. This is called 'bracketing the experience' (Harris & Winokeur, 2021). It allows clients to engage with their grief consciously, rather than carrying it with them throughout their daily life.
- *Rituals and ceremonies*. They might plant a tree or dedicate a park bench to the person they have lost, cook their favourite food and have a feast in their honour, or go on a memory outing where they visit and take photos of the places the deceased loved best.
- *Art and music*. Artistic and musical expressions of clients' feelings and their relationship with the deceased can facilitate the expression of grief and allow clients to experience feelings that may be too overwhelming to discuss directly (Worden, 2009).

Adjusting to life without the deceased

The next task of grieving involves adjusting to an environment from which the deceased person is missing. When the deceased is a parent or sibling, throughout their lives, young people will have to negotiate a relationship or place in their lives for that person as they pass through various milestones without them in attendance, such as graduating from high school, getting married and so on (Worden, 1996).

Finding meaning in the loss

Harris and Winokeur (2021) say that the final task of those who are bereaved is to re-think their assumptions that the world is safe, unchanging, predictable, benevolent and under our control. These beliefs represent a 'fundamental illusion' that allows us to feel safe in our world. Instead, we need to find a way of living with the reality that there are no guarantees in life and we have little control over events (Harris & Winokeur, 2021). Despite this, the bereaved need to restore a sense of the world as meaningful and their own lives as purposeful (Neimeyer, 2000). This is referred to as *meaning making*. It is a highly individual process that will depend

Box 12.6 Questions about adjustment

- Of the people you associate with nowadays, who would you say has a similar influence on your life as (the person you have lost)?
- If you invited into your friendship group more of those likeminded people, or even looked for people like that, what do you think would be the result?
- What difference might that make to you?
- What might others notice about you as you repopulated your friendship group?
- Who do you know at the moment to whom you could get closer, to add to your group who could contribute to your life in some of the way that (the person you lost) did?
- Have you gotten close to others like (the person you have lost) before?
- How would you begin to do this, just until we meet again? What would be the first thing you would do?

Source: Metcalf (2017, p. 126)

on the person's cultural worldview, spirituality, beliefs about death and personal values. It comprises the following four aspects (Gillies & Neimeyer, 2006; Oliver & Abel, 2017).

Sense making: Whilst the bereaved will logically understand why a death occurred - for example, because cancer destroys healthy cells - the meaning might still be unclear. They will be asking questions such as 'Why them and not someone else? ... Why now and not in 20 years' time? ... Why did they have to suffer when others have quick, painless deaths?'.

Benefit finding. This is being able to identify benefits or 'silver linings' to having lost a loved one. Although no one cherishes the experience, coping with bereavement can be a growth experience that allows survivors to get in touch with their own inner strength and develop skills that they did not know they had.

Identity reconstruction. As we reconstruct the meaning of our lives in the absence of someone whom we have lost, we necessarily reconstruct ourselves (Gillies & Neimeyer, 2006), perhaps as 'sadder but wiser' and 'simultaneously strengthened and softened by the experience of grief' (Hibberd, 2013, p. 678).

Life significance. By seeing their life as significant or purposeful, those who have been bereaved can regain a connection to their valued goals (Hibberd, 2013). This can manifest in involvement in community causes, such as drug education campaigns, increased road safety, or fundraising for cancer research, suicide awareness or pool safety (reflecting the causes of the loved one's death). In this way, their death is seen not to have occurred in vain.

Davis et al. (1998) found that people who found meaning were better adjusted six months after the death, whereas those who search for meaning but do not find it tend to adjust less well (Neimeyer, 2000).

Peer education

Children and adolescents do not grieve in isolation but within the social context of their family, friends, peers, cultural setting and community (Di Ciacco, 2008). Therefore, Hooyman and

Kramer (2006) recommend enlisting the support of the young person's school community and peer group. Yet the peers of young children will not necessarily understand when their classmate is sad for a prolonged period. To raise the issue of grief, teachers could read the group the book *Lifetimes* (Mellonie & Ingpen, 1983) and ask some questions about death such as:

- What things make people die?
- What do people feel when someone they love dies?
- Is it true that a dead body cannot move, breathe or feel anything?
- Can a dead person come back to life? ... Not even if we wish it really really hard?
- If someone you love dies, does that mean you will die soon too?
- Are children who are sad allowed to cry?
- What can children do to feel better when they are sad?

Sometimes, their loss causes adolescents to see themselves as different from everyone else, believing that no one can understand what they are going through or perceiving that they are now more mature than their age mates (Hooyman & Kramer, 2006). As a result, they can withdraw from peer support. Accordingly, bereavement is regarded as a 'social network crisis' (Hooyman & Kramer, 2006, p. 151). They might benefit from support groups of other bereaved adolescents, in person or online.

Avoid parent protection

When there has been a loss in the family, even young children will watch their parents closely and might take on the job of looking after them. This can be encouraged when someone tells a child that it 'makes' their parent sad to see them crying, that they have to be strong, that they are the man of the house now or that they have to look after others in the family. Not only do these messages interfere with children's grieving, but taking care of others leads to a further loss: of their own childhood.

Some children try to behave extra well to protect their parents from further upset. Some don't tell their parents about their own grief, in case it makes their parents feel worse - and because their children say nothing, the parents think that they are coping okay. The result is that the children do not get the support they need. Other children develop behavioural difficulties, which can be understood in one of two ways. The first is that the behaviour is a sign that the children are grieving and therefore it will go away as they begin to resolve their feelings. A second reframe that I have used is that the children's behaviour distracts their parents from their own grief. In that case, parents will need to explain that they are still here for the children and can look after them, even when terribly sad themselves. Although everyone in the family will feel sad - sometimes very sad - they will cope and, eventually, they will find new ways of being happy. To back up this message, the parents will have to show the children that they are looking after themselves.

Highlight young people's resilience

Grieving young people often lose sight of their own resources. To counteract this, comment on their strengths and efforts to cope. At the same time as being empathic to their pain,

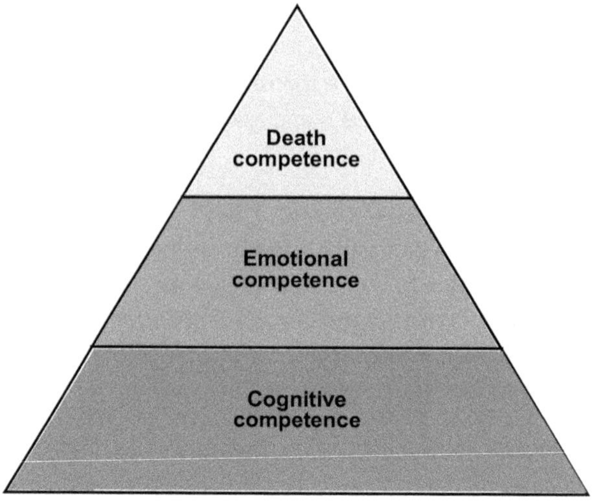

Figure 12.6 A hierarchical model of death competence

Source: adapted from Gamino and Ritter (2011, p. 30).

it is also important to highlight the parts of them that are 'normal' so they do not come to see themselves as fragile, different or damaged - but instead can use their strengths, interests and passions to experience life in ways that are not connected to their loss (Berg & Steiner, 2003). They need to be able to trust that they can be stronger than their sorrows (Byrnes, 2014) and will survive and even thrive in future (Eppler, 2008).

Death competence

Gamino and Ritter (2011) use the term *death competence* to describe the specialised skills needed by grief counsellors. As illustrated in Figure 12.6, it has three aspects. The first is cognitive competence, which refers to counsellors' expert knowledge and skill set (Gamino & Ritter, 2011). Second is emotional competence, which is counsellors' capacity to withstand hearing graphic discussions of trauma, anguish and suffering. This capacity requires psychological resilience, adequate strategies for ongoing self-care, and timely support from other colleagues (Gamino & Ritter, 2011). Finally, death competence is the ability to maintain therapeutic perspective (Gamino & Ritter, 2011). This requires counsellors to be able to handle their own death anxiety; reflect on their own losses and gain awareness of how they healed; have potency, which is 'knowing what they are doing, and doing it with confidence' (Roos, 2002, in Gamino & Ritter, 2011, p. 26); and be able to recover from the death by suicide of clients.

Conclusion

Grieving encompasses a wide range of emotions and behaviours and is a highly individual process, unique in every case. Painful as grief is, humans naturally heal - just as a rose bush naturally produces flowers. In the meantime, young people need our patience to grieve in their own way in their own time (Lowenstein, 2006).

References

Altmeier, E. M. (2011). Best practices in counseling grief and loss: Finding benefit from trauma. *Journal of Mental Health Counseling, 33*(1), 33–45. https://doi.org/10.17744/mehc.33.1.tu9wx5w3t2145122

Amato, P. R. (2000). The consequences of divorce for adults and children. *Journal of Marriage and Family, 62*(4), 1269–1287. https://doi.org/10.1111/j.1741-3737.2000.01269.x

Berg, I. K., & Steiner, S. (2003). *Children's solution work*. Norton.

Boss, P. (1999). *Ambiguous loss: Learning to live with unresolved grief*. Harvard University Press.

Brent, D., Melhem, N., Donohoe, M. B., & Walker, M. (2009). The incidence and course of depression in bereaved youth 21 months after the loss of a parent to suicide, accident, or sudden natural death. *The American Journal of Psychiatry, 166*(7), 786–794. https://doi.org/10.1176/appi.ajp.2009.08081244

Byrnes, I. S. (2014). *The art of saying goodbye*. TEDx Stanford. https://youtu.be/Dkffpibi-Dc

Cordaro, M. (2012). Pet loss and disenfranchised grief: Implications for mental health counseling practice. *Journal of Mental Health Counseling, 34*(4), 283–294. https://doi.org/10.17744/mehc.34.4.41q0248450t98072

Cvinar, J. G. (2005). Do suicide survivors suffer social stigma? A review of the literature. *Perspectives in Psychiatric Care, 41*(1), 14–21. https://doi.org/10.1111/j.0031-5990.2005.00004.x

D'Onofrio, B. M., Turkheimer, E., Emery, R. E., Maes, H. H., Silberg, J., & Eaves, L. J. (2007). A children of twins study of parental divorce and offspring psychopathology. *Journal of Child Psychology and Psychiatry, 48*(7), 667–675. https://doi.org/10.1111/j.1469-7610.2007.01741.x

Davis, C. G., Nolen-Hoeksema, S., & Larson, J. (1998). Making sense of loss and benefiting from the experience: Two construals of meaning. *Journal of Personality and Social Psychology, 75*(2), 561–574.

Delaney, S. (2016). *Grief: It's complicated most of the time*. https://youtu.be/4GDTbtePHUU

Denborough, D. (2014). *Retelling the stories of our lives: Everyday narrative therapy to draw inspiration and transform experience*. Norton.

Di Ciacco, J. (2008). *The colours of grief: Understanding a child's journey through loss from birth to adulthood*. Jessica Kingsley Publishers.

Eppler, C. (2008). Exploring themes of resiliency in children after the death of a parent. *Professional School Counseling, 11*(3), 189–196. https://doi.org/10.1177/2156759X0801100305

Freeman, S. J. (2005). *Grief and loss: Understanding the journey*. Brooks/Cole Cengage.

Friedman, R., & James, J. W. (2008). The myth of the stages of dying, death and grief. *Skeptic, 14*(2), 37–42.

Gamino, L. A., & Ritter, H. (2011). Death competence: An ethical imperative. *Death Studies, 36*(1), 23–40. https://doi.org/10.1080/07481187.2011.553503

Geldard, D., Geldard, K., & Yin Foo, R. (2017). *Basic personal counselling: A training manual for counsellors* (8th ed.). Cangage.

Gillies, J., & Neimeyer, R. A. (2006). Loss, grief, and the search for significance: Toward a model of meaning reconstruction in bereavement. *Journal of Constructivist Psychology, 19*(1), 31–65. https://doi.org/10.1080/10720530500311182

Grad, O. (2011). The sequelae of suicide: Survivors. In R. C. O'Connor, S. Platt & J. Gordon (Eds.), *International handbook of suicide prevention: Research, policy and practice* (pp. 561–576). Wiley-Blackwell.

Graham, A. (2004). Life is like the seasons. *Childhood Education, 80*(6), 317–321. https://doi.org/10.1080/00094056.2004.10521278

Harris, D. L., & Gorman, E. (2011). Grief from a broader perspective: Nonfinite loss, ambiguous loss, and chronic sorrow. In D. L. Harris (Ed.), *Counting our losses: Reflecting on change, loss, and transition in everyday life* (pp. 1–14). Routledge.

Harris, D., & Winokeur, H. (2021). *Principles and practice of grief counselling* (3rd ed.). Springer.

Harris, R. (2007). *The happiness trap: Stop struggling, start living*. Exisle.

Henderson, D. A., & Thompson, C. L. (2016). *Counseling children* (9th ed.). Cengage.

Hibberd, R. (2013). Meaning reconstruction in bereavement: Sense and significance. *Death Studies, 37*(7), 670–692. https://doi.org/10.1080/07481187.2012.692453

Hooyman, N. R., & Kramer, B. J. (2006). *Living through loss: Interventions across the lifespan*. Columbia University Press.

Howarth, R. A. (2011). Concepts and controversies in grief and loss. *Journal of Mental Health Counseling, 33*(1), 4–10. https://doi.org/10.17744/mehc.33.1.900m56162888u737

Jones, L. (2020). Grief and loss in displaced and refugee families. In J. S. Song & P. Ventevogel (Eds.), *Child, adolescent and family refugee mental health: A global perspective* (pp. 123–149). Springer.

Jordan, J. R., & McIntosh, J. L. (2011). Is suicide bereavement different? A framework for rethinking the question. In J. R. Jordan & J. L. McIntosh (Eds.), *Grief after suicide: Understanding the consequences and caring for the survivors* (pp. 19–42). Routledge.

Jordan, J. R., & Neimeyer, R. A. (2003). Does grief counselling work? *Death Studies, 27*(9), 765–786. https://doi.org/10.1080/713842360

King, H. E. (1992). The reactions of children to divorce. In C. E. Walker & M. C. Roberts (Eds.), *Handbook of clinical child psychology* (2nd ed., pp. 1009–1024). Plenum.

Knieper, A. J. (1999). The suicide survivor's grief and recovery. *Suicide and Life-Threatening Behavior, 29*(4), 353–364. https://doi.org/10.1111/j.1943-278X.1999.tb00530.x

Li, J., Vestergaard, M., Cnattingius, S., Gissler, M., Bech, B. H., Obel, C., & Olsen, J. (2014). Mortality after parental death in childhood: A nationwide cohort study from three Nordic countries. *PLoS Medicine, 11*(7), e1001679. https://doi.org/10.1371/journal.pmed.1001679

Lowenstein, L. (2006). *Creative interventions for bereaved children*. Champion Press.

Marsten, D., Epston, D., & Markham, L. (2016). *Narrative therapy in wonderland: Connecting with children's imaginative know-how*. Norton.

Melhem, N. M., Day, N., Shear, M. K., Day, R., Reynolds, C. F. III, & Brent, D. (2004). Traumatic grief among adolescents exposed to a peer's suicide. *American Journal of Psychiatry, 161*(8), 1411–1416. https://doi.org/10.1176/appi.ajp.161.8.1411

Mellonie, B., & Ingpen, R. (1983). *Beginning and endings with lifetimes in between: A beautiful way to explain life and death to children*. Bantam.

Metcalf, L. (2017). *Solution focused narrative therapy*. Springer.

Neimeyer, R. A. (2000). Searching for the meaning of meaning: Grief therapy and the process of reconstruction. *Death Studies, 24*(6), 541–558. https://doi.org/10.1080/07481180050121480

Oliver, B., & Abel, N. (2017). Special populations of children and adolescents who have significant needs. In J. Ziomek-Daigle (Ed.), *Counseling children and adolescents: Working in school and clinical mental health settings* (pp. 371–407). Routledge.

Peterson, C. (2014). *Looking forward through the life span: Developmental psychology* (6th ed.). Pearson.

Pomeroy. E. C., & Garcia, R. B. (2009). *The grief assessment and intervention workbook: A strengths perspective*. Brooks/Cole Cengage.

Rainer, J. (2013). *Life after loss: Contemporary grief counseling and therapy*. PESI Publishing.

Raphael, B., & Delaney, P. (2011). Loss and grief: 'Closing the gap' for Aboriginal people [online]. *Grief Matters: The Australian Journal of Grief and Bereavement, 14*(3), 67–69. https://search.informit.com.au/documentSummary;dn=822081986870009;res=IELHEA

Rostila, M., Saarela, J., & Kawachi, I. (2013). Suicide following the death of a sibling: A nationwide follow-up study from Sweden. *British Medical Journal Open, 3*(4), 1–6. https://doi.org/10.1136/bmjopen-2013-002618

Rubin, S. S., Malkinson, R., & Witztum, E. (2012). *Working with the bereaved: Multiple lenses on loss and mourning*. Routledge.

Sakinofsky, I. (2007). The aftermath of suicide: Managing survivors' bereavement. *Canadian Journal of Psychiatry, 52*(6), 129S–136S.

Sigelman, C. K., De George, L., Cunial, K., Kohler, M., Ballam, N., & Rider, E. A. (2022). *Life span human development* (4th ANZ ed.). Cengage.

Stroebe, M., & Schut, H. (1999). The dual process model of coping with bereavement: Rationale and description. *Death Studies, 23*(3), 197–224. https://doi.org/10.1080/074811899201046

Tyrrell, M. (2019). *Grief counselling: Three techniques therapists can use*. https://youtu.be/v_2QeHCnYzcIn

Wakenshaw, M. (2002). *Caring for your grieving child*. New Harbinger.

Wanganeen, R. (2010). Seven phases of healing. In N. Purdie, P. Dungeon & W. Walker (Eds.), *Working together: Aboriginal and Torres Strait Islander mental health and wellbeing principles and practice* (pp. 267–284). Australian Department of Health and Ageing.

White, M. (2016). *Narrative therapy classics*. Dulwich Centre Publications.

Willis, C. A. (2002). The grieving process in children: Strategies for understanding, educating, and reconciling children's perceptions of death. *Early Childhood Education Journal, 29*(4), 221–226. https://doi.org/10.1023/A:1015125422643

Wolchik, S. A., Tein, J.-Y., Sandler, I. N., & Ayers, T. S. (2006). Stressors, quality of the child-caregiver relationship, and children's mental health problems after parental death: The mediating role of self-system beliefs. *Journal of Abnormal Child Psychology*, *34*(2), 212–229. https://doi.org/10.1007/s10802-005-9016-5

Worden, J. W. (1996). *Children and grief: When a parent dies*. Guilford.

Worden, J. W. (2009). *Grief counseling and grief therapy: A handbook for the mental health practitioner* (4th ed.). Springer.

13 Depression

Globally, depression is the leading cause of disability (Üstün et al., 2004; Bernaras et al., 2019) and is now the second-most costly illness around the world (having been ranked fourth in 1990) (Young et al., 2008, p. 251). Major depression raises by 4½ times the risk of heart attacks; is associated with poor repair of damaged DNA, which is a gateway to cancer; and raises the risk of suicide, particularly in young people (Colbert, 2003).

There is a distinction between depression and grief, which is characterised by sadness in response to loss, 'when the irreversible happens' (Smith, 2015, p. 224). It is part of the human condition to feel sad when we lose someone or something that we value. In these cases, sadness is warranted. It is the natural outcome of being alive (Smith, 2015). However, in susceptible individuals, sorrow can transform into situational depression following a loss or changes in life, particularly multiple losses (Bleiberg & Markowitz, 2008; Fox et al., 2010; McFarlane et al., 1994).

In comparison, the despair of depression is much more than everyday sadness. It has three aspects (Bleiberg & Markowitz, 2008; Burton et al., 2015; de Haan et al., 2020):

- *emotional despair*, in which the underlying emotion is sadness
- *cognitive* symptoms: rumination (recurrent gloomy thoughts), diminished ability to think or concentrate and indecisiveness
- *physical* symptoms: the common pattern is slowing down, disturbed appetite with weight loss, insomnia or sleeping too much, fatigue and loss of energy. A less common pattern is agitation.

Prevalence in the young

Depression is said to be the 'common cold' of mental illness in that virtually everyone has an encounter with at least minor depression at some time of their life, with 16 per cent of individuals experiencing a serious episode (Bleiberg & Markowitz, 2008). Prevalence rates for depression in children vary from 4 per cent in Spain to 10 per cent in Australia and 25 per cent in Colombia (Bernaras et al., 2019). Another worldwide sample of people aged 6 to 18 years found an incidence of 13.4 per cent (Polanczyk et al., 2015).

However, Horwitz and Wakefield (2007, in Smith, 2015) say that the high rates of depression come about because the condition is over-diagnosed, as if it is 'abnormal' to be sad or grieving over life's disappointments. These writers argue that we need to consider the

DOI: 10.4324/9781003323938-15

context and that seeing sadness - or any emotional pain - as something that cannot be borne without medication ill-equips us to cope. Denial of our truth that we are simply *sad* robs us of the opportunity to find meaning in disappointments and to adjust to a new version of ourselves in their aftermath (Smith, 2015).

Causes

Bernaras et al. (2019) note that depression is a complex disorder influenced by many factors, with no single theory fully explaining its etiology or persistence.

Genetics

Parental depression places children at risk of the same condition (Lindberg et al., 2020). However, although a family history of depression doubles or triples the chances of experiencing depression, the reverse of this statistic is that 60 to 70 per cent of the factors giving rise to depression are *not* genetic (Burton et al., 2015).

Health

Depressed individuals commonly have so little energy that they generally have poor health habits which, in turn, cause other diseases (Colbert, 2003). Accordingly, depression accompanies hormonal difficulties (including thyroid hormones, cortisol and decreased growth hormone), sleep disorders, obesity and inflammatory illnesses. In reverse, serious illness can lead to or exacerbate depression (Collison & Hall, 1989).

Obese children, and girls in particular, are at double the risk of experiencing depressive symptoms (Lindberg et al., 2020; Rao et al., 2020; Roberts et al., 2000). These effects could be the result of the social prejudice that overweight individuals experience. But obesity is also related to poverty (Elmore & Crouch, 2020; Lindberg et al., 2020; Wang et al., 2015) which, in turn, is linked to insufficient exercise and an impoverished diet - resulting specifically in deficiencies of vitamins B_{12} and D (Esnafoglu & Ozturan, 2020), plus zinc and magnesium, whose significance for the manufacture of serotonin is illustrated in Figure 11.2 (see page 150). In addition, Vitamin D in particular modulates immunity and, hence, inflammation (Berk et al., 2013; Bock & Stauth, 2008), which is directly implicated in depression (Colasanto et al., 2020).

The cytokine model of depression upholds that poor digestion of proteins leads to the production of inflammatory cytokines (cells that are part of the immune system) and that this inflammation affects both the body and the brain (Kharrazian, 2013). Indeed, people with inflammatory bowel disease show similar lesions in the brain to those with multiple sclerosis (Kharrazian, 2013). This link is also apparent in the fact that other inflammatory conditions such as asthma, eczema, hay fever and periodontal disease are also linked to depression (Berk et al., 2013).

A second source of inflammation is a deficiency of probiotic flora in the gut - particularly bifidobacteria (Adams et al., 2011). These flora improve the absorption of DHA (one of the Omega-3 fatty acids) and amino acids which are vital for brain function, in addition to their renowned ability to decrease allergic responsiveness to foods and reduce gut inflammation (Lyon, 2000).

A third source of inflammation is damage to the wall of the small intestine, which will produce a leaky gut. In turn, this leads to persistent digestive, immune and inflammatory disturbances (Berk et al., 2013).

Adverse childhood experiences

Those who have endured trauma - especially four adverse childhood experiences (ACEs) and particularly interpersonal maltreatment - are especially vulnerable to depression (de Haan et al., 2020; Elmore & Crouch, 2020; Vibhakar et al., 2019).

Parenting style

As with all the emotional difficulties covered in this text, depression is said to be a potential outcome of parents who fail to offer emotional warmth and support, thereby communicating to their children that they are not accepted as they are (Bernaras et al., 2019). Children of controlling parents are more angry, negative, withdrawn, depressed, anxious, unhappy and hostile when frustrated (Baumrind, 1967, 1971; Garber et al., 1997; Ispa et al., 2004; Loukas, 2009; McDowell et al., 2003; Snyder et al., 2003; Strayer & Roberts, 2004). In contrast, those raised under guidance are less vulnerable to depression (Criss et al., 2009; Dearing, 2004; Garber et al., 1997) and are more resilient in adversity (Kaufmann et al., 2000; Propper & Moore, 2006; Wyman et al., 1999).

Distorted thinking

Beck (2011) described that people with depression are convinced of three thoughts: I'm no good, my world is bleak and my future is hopeless. Thus, according to cognitive theory, what distinguishes sadness (the emotion) from depression is individuals' distorted interpretation of events. Kennerley et al. (2017) describe that these patterns of thinking are maintained when sufferers reduce their activity and, in turn, engage less with others, and therefore derive less pleasure from life - see Figure 13.1. They also enact self-fulfilling prophecies that they will not derive enjoyment from activities, whereupon their negative beliefs produce behaviour that confirms those beliefs.

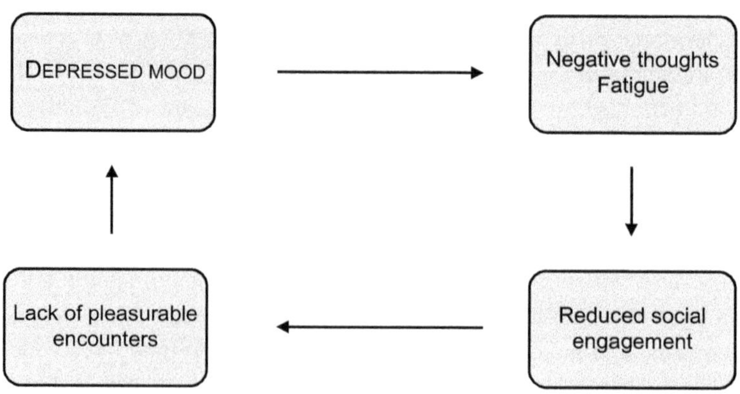

Figure 13.1 The depressive cycle

Sources: Kennerley et al. (2017, p. 79).

Interventions

Play therapy and psychotherapy for depression have been shown to be as effective as doing nothing (Zhou et al., 2020). Instead, some research shows that the most successful therapies for depression are a combination of anti-depressant medications and cognitive therapy (Stark et al., 2012). However, another review focusing on young people found that counselling was more effective than medication and that a combination of the two proved no more effective than each on its own (Cox et al., 2014). Moreover, one-third of sufferers of chronic depression are helped by neither medication nor cognitive therapy (Young et al., 2008). And cognitive therapy has been found to have only short-term benefits and higher drop-out rates than interpersonal therapy (which gives clients skills to deal with relationship conflict) (Zhou et al., 2020).

Support for resilience

While the primary objective is to reduce depressive symptoms, counsellors also need to focus on young people's social and emotional well-being in general (Stark et al., 2012). Young people who are depressed will need particular focus on mastery, finding a purpose, developing their self-esteem and building relationships with others (Chang et al., 2018; Ryff & Singer, 1996).

Coping

Stark et al. (2012) report that young people need to experience the benefits of coping skills before committing to using them. To that end, when young clients look despondent, these writers suggest that counsellors ask them to rate their mood and then have them engage in a fun activity for five minutes (such as playing hula hoops with the counsellor), exerting energy (say, with a game of tag) or practising relaxation. Then they rate their mood again. Inevitably it will have improved, upon which the counsellor asks what this tells them about how to cope next time they feel down (Stark et al., 2012).

Problem-solving skills

Problem solving is for those occasions when we can change a negative circumstance. Because they have low self-efficacy, depressed individuals typically think that they cannot solve problems and, because of doomsday thinking, believe that even if they solved one problem, another would just take its place (Stark et al., 2012). Solution-focused questioning can ask them to think of a time when they managed to solve a problem, how they did that and what this tells them about their skills as a problem solver. Highlighting their successes (using positive blame and relationship questions) will make it harder for them to dismiss these as mere flukes.

Using the anagram SOLVED (adapted from Spirito et al., 2012), the basic steps for problem solving are (Gordon, 2000):

S *State* or *specify* the problem. Use I-messages to express your needs.
O Generate *options* for solving the problem, using brainstorming.
L Consider the *likely* outcomes of these options.
V Choose the solution that seems *viable* (or, for younger children, the *very* best one) – that is, one that is realistic, which means that it is achievable by the child and in the circumstances and has the best chances of working.
E *Enact* it: carry it out and evaluate how it is working.

D *Do* it again. If subsequently the solution fails, this simply signals that the previous plan did not capture the original problem, or the solution was too ambitious. You will need to repeat the process to generate a different strategy until one is found that the individuals can achieve and which meets their needs.

The last step, signalled by the capital D, implies that not every solution will work, but that this does not mean that clients do not know how to solve problems - but simply that sometimes solutions which appear in advance to be the best turn out not to work all that well. This simply triggers another round of problem solving.

Emotion regulation

In Chapter 4, I outlined the ACT method of defusing from unhelpful thoughts, which can be especially useful to regulate depressive thinking. You might give older children a list of the defusion metaphors for them to select one that suits them. For younger children you might introduce them to a list of dysfunctional thinking patterns - see Box 13.1 and use the simplified acronym for ACT (Accept, Choose, Take action) (Walser & Hayes, 2006). Or you could lend them a stuffed toy llama and explain that its name is a reminder for them to use aspects of ACT (Turrell & Bell, 2016):

L Labelling the thoughts, feelings or urges.
L Letting go of the struggle to control these thoughts, feelings and sensations.
A Acceptance: allowing what is inside to be present. This does not mean that we have to like it but just recognise that it is there.
M Mindfulness: being present in the moment, rather than fretting about the past or worrying about the future.
A Approach what matters.

Then in future sessions you can review with them whether the llama is doing a good job of looking after them.

Box 13.1 Common unhelpful thinking patterns of children

Pattern	*Theme*	*Self-talk*	*Emotion*
Robot thinking	It's not my fault.	I can't help it.	Sense of failure.
I'm awful	Everything's my fault.	I can't do anything right. I'm no good.	Low self-esteem. Fear of risks.
You're awful	Everything's your fault.	I'd be able to do this if you weren't so bossy/stupid, etc.	Belligerence. Anger.
Fairy tale thinking	It's not fair.	I wish things would get better.	Hurt, victimhood. helplessness.
Defeatist thinking	I can't stand it.	I can't cope.	Anxiety, fear, over-reaction to threats.
Doomsday thinking	Everything is dreadful.	Things are always awful. They will never get any better.	Depression.

Source: adapted from Roush (1984, in Kaplan & Carter, 1995, p. 396)

Box 13.2 Recognising doomsday thinking

I was working with a gifted 6-year-old who was refusing to go to school on the grounds that it was 'always awful'. On a scale of 1 to 10, she assured me that every day was a zero. I expressed surprise at this because on some days she had library, and some days computer and some days music. If the days were all different, how could their rating be the same? To explain this, together we went through the list in Box 13.1 to see if she recognised any thinking pattern that she used a lot, and she identified that she was a doomsday thinker.

She went away for two weeks with the task of rating each school day on a calendar. She returned after that period to report in some surprise that, in fact, none of the days were zeros; instead, she had rated them as 4s, 5s and 6s. 'So I am a doomsday thinker.... But,' she declared, 'I don't think I'll ever be able to stop it'. Being gifted, she immediately recognised the thought pattern and confessed, 'You know, I just doomsday thought about my doomsday thinking'.

Relaxation is another strategy for emotion regulation. It assists mild depression but on its own is not enough to relieve symptoms. Nevertheless, given that it is a simple intervention with no cost, it can complement other forms of treatment (Jorm et al., 2008). This is especially relevant for adolescents, who might not have access to counselling and for whom medications have limited benefits (Jorm et al., 2008).

Gratitude journal

People who are emotionally robust find some benefit from writing a gratitude journal, where once a week they list three things that they are grateful for (Sheldon & Lyubomirsky, 2004). However, at the heart of some people's depression is despair that they so feel badly when they have so much going for them. They already chastise themselves for being ungrateful. Therefore, intuitive though it may seem, I would advise against suggesting a gratitude journal for clients with depression.

Narrative interventions

In contrast to the idea that young people need to learn resilience skills, the narrative assumption is that they will already know these because they have used them at other times in their life. Instead, narrative counsellors will externalise The Blues (or any other label clients give their state), ask about the tricks it plays to rob their life of joy, ask preference questions about whether they wish to continue to allow it to do that, and develop a rich story of the times when they have resisted its influence. Scaling questions can be ideal for those whose depression causes them to see their world in all-or-nothing terms. The aim of the narrative approach is to allow clients to develop an identity as someone who can rise above a depressed state.

Health interventions

Nevertheless, in my experience, talk therapy is not enough. The mediocre success of cognitive methods and medication could be because these methods overlook the physical health components of depression that prime individuals to react in a gloomy way to negative events (Collison & Hall, 1989). Even if the depression were entirely 'mental', being physically robust would give sufferers the resources they need to do the necessary emotional work of recovery and to participate in active remedies, such as exercise. Therefore, I believe that we need to support clients with depression to get enough sleep, become active, eat healthily and, if needed, lose weight.

In one study, a solution-focused intervention improved the lifestyle behaviours of young people aged 6 to 13 years and was especially effective for those aged under six (Kreier et al., 2013). This intervention employed the standard solution-focused questions about how clients could overcome barriers to maintaining a healthy diet and exercise regime, the miracle question to uncover clients' goals, exception questions to identify when they had achieved these goals even partially and how they did that, coping questions about how they prevent things from getting worse, scaling questions and implementation questions ('What plan are you going to try, and how will you know that it's working?' (Kreier et al., 2013).

Medication

The orthodox biochemical treatment for depression is anti-depressant medication. However, selective serotonin reuptake inhibitors (SSRIs) and the newer selective norepinephrine reuptake inhibitors (SNRIs) seem only moderately effective (Bernaras et al., 2019; Cox et al., 2014; Goldney, 2011; Hetrick et al., 2012) and increase suicidal ideation from 0.2 per cent without medication to 1 per cent while taking it (Walter et al., 2020). Cipriani et al. (2016) conclude that they are of little benefit for depression in young people, given both their ineffectiveness at improving symptoms and their undesirable side effects.

Another medication that has been used is agomelatine (Valdoxan), which works on melatonin, the sleep hormone, to normalise sleep patterns (Bobrov et al., 2010; Tiuvina & Smirnova, 2012). Medvedev (2013) reported that, in combination with other anti-depressant medication, adults with severe depression who also took Valdoxan had significantly reduced depressive symptoms. Studies with adolescents show that Valdoxan was as effective but with fewer side effects than SSRIs (Arango et al., 2022). Liver enzymes need monitoring to ensure that the medication is having no ill effects on the liver, for which adolescents are at no greater risk than adults or those using SSRIs (Arango et al., 2022).

These medications are like a cast for a broken leg: They can give clients a breather while they heal, but are not intended to be a permanent fix, especially in young people where side effects are less understood than in adults. Meanwhile, clients who are prescribed medication can take this to mean that they 'are' depressed, which can become part of their identity and cause them to feel hopeless about the possibilities for change. In that case, you can frame medications as a form of support so that their body gets the rest it needs to do the emotional healing that needs to happen.

There does appear to be a two-fold increased risk of suicide attempts for young people using SSRIs as prescribed, perhaps because the medications can increase agitation (Fergusson et al., 2005), or perhaps because of their folate-deficient biochemical profile (Walsh, 2012) – see below. Also, medications themselves can be the means of further suicide attempts.

Nutrient supplementation

Walsh (2012) identified six main biochemical profiles of people with depression, two of which are most relevant here. First, those who under-methylate (comprising 38 per cent) have low serotonin, dopamine and norephineprine activity at brain synapses. They thrive on the methylating agents SAMe (pronounced *sammy*) and methionine, plus calcium and vitamins B_6 and D, but must avoid folate. A second group (comprising 20 per cent) exhibit folate deficiency depression and commonly also experience anxiety. They thrive on (among other specific nutrients) folic or folinic acid, zinc, vitamins B_6, B_{12}, C and E and nutrients to reduce dopamine synaptic activity (Walsh, 2012). Walsh found that people with folate-deficiency depression are especially prone to worsened symptoms when taking SSRIs because they already have high serotonin levels. Integrated medical practitioners (see Resources) can test the biochemical profile of their patients, and prescribe anti-depressant medications and supplements accordingly.

If clients cannot or are not willing to use medications, they might choose instead (under medical advice) to take natural products such as 5-HTP, zinc and magnesium which, as you can see from Figure 11.2 (page 150), are the raw ingredients that the brain uses to produce serotonin. (5HTP is not recommended for folate deficiency depression, however [Walsh, 2012]). Being ingredients only, these will have no side effects or withdrawal difficulties (other than returned sadness if one is still deficient in essential nutrients). Another well-researched natural herb for mild depression is Hypericum perforatum (commonly known as St John's Wort).

Improved diet

Ortega et al. (2022) report that there are specific groups of foods and nutrients with promising antidepressant effects, most of them included in the likes of a Mediterranean diet (with its high intake of fruit, vegetables, whole grain, fish, olive oil; and low intake of fats, dairy, antioxidants and animal products (Li et al., 2017). Many with depression will need to repair a leaky gut, by experimenting (at least for six months and strictly) with a gluten-free diet and rebalancing their gut flora (Perlmutter & Loberg, 2013).

When young people who are depressed are also overweight, a weight-loss diet can be beneficial because a reduction in fat tissue mass will reduce inflammation and improve brain function (Berk et al., 2013). Among the many available, my favourite is the Nutripoints diet (Vartabedian et al., 1990) (see Chapter 16).

It can also pay to discuss with clients their substance use, as the overuse of drugs or alcohol can interfere with their health and well-being.

Exercise

With acute physical pain, the pain signals that there is tissue injury, in which case rest and recuperation are required, whereas with chronic physical pain, according to Chinese medicine, this is tissue crying out for energy, in which case the best course of action is movement. So it is, I believe, with acute versus chronic emotional pain. With acute distress, we need to nurture ourselves and give ourselves some space to recuperate, whereas with chronic pain – as occurs in depression – we need to mobilise ourselves.

Physical activity has been shown to reduce both depression and anxiety symptoms across the age range and with both mild and serious symptoms (Bailey et al., 2018; Blumenthal et al.,

1999; Dale et al., 2019; Wegner et al., 2020; Zhu et al., 2019). Some researchers have found exercise to produce better effects than anti-depressants (Collison & Hall, 1989). Moreover, those who exercise are less likely to relapse (Babyak et al., 2000). This confirms Glasser's (1998) advice that we need to *do* more in order to feel better physically and emotionally, rather than waiting for our feelings to improve first (see Chapter 10).

One mechanism is that exercise down-regulates systemic inflammation (Berk et al., 2013; Gutin, 2011; Lavoie et al., 2010). Second, it can result in a loss of weight, which would be beneficial for young people whose depression is linked to being obese. A third mechanism contributing to reduced depression is that that the social aspects of participating in extracurricular activities are also beneficial. Fourth, the mere fact that we are committing to something that we decided to do will improve self-efficacy, which is a major substrate of depression.

Sleep

While depression interferes with sleep (Gregory & Sadeh, 2012), in reverse, a lack of sleep causes depression (Bernaras et al., 2019; Bronson & Merryman, 2009). Whereas a cognitive-behaviourist might advise clients about sleep hygiene practices, solution-focused counsellors will ask about what was happening at those times when they have managed to sleep well, what was different about those times and what it would take for them to recreate those conditions. You could lightheartedly threaten clients with an ordeal (Haley, 1984), such as having to do housework or schoolwork for 30 minutes if they lie awake for more than 15 minutes - and their desire to avoid this will cause them to come up with a better solution of their own.

Activity scheduling

As part of a solution-focused approach, counsellors and clients might co-design tasks to increase clients' engagement in activities. They can devise a range of activities that are simply pleasant, that provide a sense of mastery and success, or which involve social engagement (Dobson & Dobson, 2017). To avoid procrastination, clients might set a timer so that the activities last only ten minutes, for example, on the grounds that it is easier to start something that is going to be brief. Recording activities can sustain a change in behaviour, even if it is not especially accurate (Alberto & Troutman, 2013; Bandura, 1986).

Relationships

Young people's friendships protect them from depression (Ju & Lee, 2018). Therefore, our questions can be about how young people could connect to their peers. It can help to link clients to extracurricular activities where they can meet others who share the same passion. These 'tribes' can validate each other's interests and inspire each member to shine (Robinson & Aronica, 2009).

Purpose

Humans are happiest when we are pursuing goals in life that are meaningful to us, whereas a purposeless life breeds resentfulness, listlessness and resignation (Csikszentmihályi, 1990; Seligman, 2011). Purpose and joy go hand in hand and, therefore, it can assist people who are feeling depressed to find a cause bigger than themselves to become passionate about (see Chapter 11).

Prevention

There is evidence that prevention programs are effective at reducing depressive episodes in school students (Merry et al., 2012). Therefore, if you work within a school you could advocate for and deliver programs that target depression in young people. Hetrick et al. (2016) concludes that there are not enough data to know which elements are most effective in preventive programs, which gives room for innovation. You could base the program content on the model of resilience introduced in Chapter 11.

Conclusion

When people are severely depressed, they will be frightened of their own feelings. We will not be able immediately to cure their original despair, but we can remove this second layer of feeling by taking their feelings seriously but not being intimidated by them. In this chapter, I have advocated for a dual approach to improve young people's physical well-being while using narrative therapy to enhance their self-efficacy. Both aspects aim to re-engage them in activities that bring them joy.

References

Adams, J. B., Johansen, L. J., Powell, L. D., Quig, D., & Rubin, R. A. (2011). Gastrointestinal flora and gastrointestinal status in children with autism – comparisons to typical children and correlation with autism severity. *Gastroenterology*, *11*. http://www.biomedcentral.com/1471-230X/11/22

Alberto, P. A., & Troutman, A. C. (2013). *Applied behavior analysis for teachers* (9th ed.). Pearson.

Arango, C., Buitelaar, J. K., Fegert, J. M., Olivier, V., Pénélaud, P. F., Marx, U., & Wolańczyk, T. (2022). Safety and efficacy of agomelatine in children and adolescents with major depressive disorder receiving psychosocial counselling: A double-blind, randomised, controlled, phase 3 trial in nine countries. *The Lancet Psychiatry*, *9*(2), 113–124.

Babyak, M. A., Blumenthal, J. A., Herman, S., Khatri, P., Doraiswarmy, M., & Krishnan, K. R. (2000). Exercise treatment for major depression: Maintenance of therapeutic benefit at 10 months. *Psychosomatic Medicine*, *62*, 633–638.

Bailey, A. P., Hetrick, S. E., Rosenbaum, S., Purcell, R., & Parker, A. G. (2018). Treating depression with physical activity in adolescents and young adults: A systematic review and meta-analysis of randomised controlled trials. *Psychological Medicine*, *48*(7), 1068–1083. https://doi.org/10.1017/S0033291717002653

Bandura, A. (1986). *Social foundations of thought and action*. Prentice Hall.

Baumrind, D. (1967). Child care practices anteceding three patterns of preschool behavior. *Genetic Psychology Monographs*, *75*, 43–88.

Baumrind, D. (1971). Harmonious parents and their preschool children. *Developmental Psychology*, *4*(1), 99–102.

Beck, J. S. (2011). *Cognitive behaviour therapy: Basics and beyond* (2nd ed). Guilford.

Berk, M., Williams, L. J., Jacka, F. N., O'Neil, A., & Maes, M. (2013). So depression is an inflammatory disease, but where does the inflammation come from? *BMC Medicine*, *11*(1), 1–16. https://doi.org/10.1186/1741-7015-11-200

Bernaras, E., Jaureguizar, J., & Garaigordobil, M. (2019). Child and adolescent depression: A review of theories, evaluation instruments, prevention programs, and treatments. *Frontiers in Psychology*, *10*, 543. https://doi.org/10.3389/fpsyg.2019.00543

Bleiberg, K. L., & Markowitz, J. C. (2008). Interpersonal psychotherapy for depression. In D. H. Barlow (Ed.), *Clinical handbook of psychological disorders: A step-by-step treatment manual* (4th ed., pp. 306–327). Guilford.

Blumenthal, J. A., Babyak, M. A., Moore, K. A., Craighead, E., Herman, S., & Krishnan, K. R. (1999). Effects of exercise training on older patients with major depression. *Archives of Internal Medicine, 159*, 2349–2356.

Bobrov, A. S., Petrun'ko, O. V., Khamarkhanova, A. A., & Shvetsova, A. V. (2010). Clinical predictors of the therapeutic response to valdoxan in moderate and severe depression. *Zhurnal nevrologii i psikhiatrii imeni SS Korsakova, 110*(9), 14–21.

Bock, K., & Stauth, C. (2008). *Healing the new childhood epidemics: Autism, ADHD, asthma, and allergies*. Ballantine.

Bronson, P., & Merryman, A. (2009). *Nurture shock: New thinking about children*. Twelve.

Burton, L., Westen, D., & Kowalski, R. (2015). *Psychology* (3rd ed.). Wiley.

Chang, C. W., Yuan, R., & Chen, J. K. (2018). Social support and depression among Chinese adolescents: The mediating roles of self-esteem and self-efficacy. *Children and Youth Services Review, 88*, 128–134. https://doi.org/10.1016/j.childyouth.2018.03.001

Cipriani, A., Zhou, X., Del Giovane, C., Hetrick, S. E., Qin, B., Whittington, C., & Xie, P. (2016). Comparative efficacy and tolerability of antidepressants for major depressive disorder in children and adolescents: a network meta-analysis. *The Lancet, 388*(10047), 881–890. https://doi.org/10.1016/S0140-6736(16)30385-3

Colasanto, M., Madigan, S., & Korczak, D. J. (2020). Depression and inflammation among children and adolescents: A meta-analysis. *Journal of Affective Disorders, 277*, 940–948. https://doi.org/10.1016/j.jad.2020.09.025

Colbert, D. (2003). *Deadly emotions: Understanding the mind-body-spirit connection that can heal or destroy you*. Thomas Nelson.

Collison, D. R., & Hall, T. (1989). *Why do I feel so awful?* Angus and Robertson.

Cox, G. R., Callahan P., Churchill R., Hunot V., Merry S. N., Parker A. G., & Hetrick S. E. (2014). Psychological therapies versus antidepressant medication, alone and in combination for depression in children and adolescents. *Cochrane Database of Systematic Reviews 2014, 11*, CD008324. https://doi.org/10.1002/14651858.CD008324.pub3

Criss, M. M., Shaw, D. S., Moilanen, K. L., Hitchings, J. E., & Ingoldsby, E. M. (2009). Family, neighborhood, and peer characteristics as predictors of child adjustment: A longitudinal analysis of additive and mediation models. *Social Development, 18*(3), 511–535. https://doi.org/10.1111/j.1467-9507.2008.00520.x

Csikszentmihályi, M. (1990). *Flow: The psychology of optimal experience*. Harper Perennial.

Dale, L. P., Vanderloo, L., Moore, S., & Faulkner, G. (2019). Physical activity and depression, anxiety, and self-esteem in children and youth: An umbrella systematic review. *Mental Health and Physical Activity, 16*, 66–79. https://doi.org/10.1016/j.mhpa.2018.12.001

de Haan, A., Landolt, M. A., Fired, E. I., Kleinke, K., Alisic, E., & Meiser-Stedman, R. (2020). Dysfunctional posttraumatic cognitions, posttraumatic stress and depression in children and adolescents exposed to trauma: A network analysis. *Journal of Child Psychology and Psychiatry, 61*(1), 77–87. https://doi.org/10.1111/jcpp.13101

Dearing, E. (2004). The developmental implications of restrictive and supportive parenting across neighborhoods and ethnicities: Exceptions are the rule. *Journal of Applied Developmental Psychology, 25*(5), 555–575. https://doi.org/10.1016/j.appdev.2004.08.007

Dobson, D., & Dobson, K. S. (2017). *Evidence-based practice of cognitive-behavioural therapy* (2nd ed.). Guilford.

Elmore, A. L., & Crouch, E. (2020). The association of adverse childhood experiences with anxiety and depression for children and youth, 8 to 17 years of age. *Academic Pediatrics, 20*(5), 600–608. https://doi.org/10.1016/j.acap.2020.02.012

Esnafoglu, E., & Ozturan, D. D. (2020). The relationship of severity of depression with homocysteine, folate, vitamin B12, and vitamin D levels in children and adolescents. *Child and Adolescent Mental Health, 25*(4), 249–255. https://doi.org/10.1111/camh.12387

Fergusson, D., Doucette, S., Glass, K. C., Shapiro, S., Healy, D., Hebert, P., & Hutton, B. (2005). Association between suicide attempts and selective serotonin reuptake inhibitors: Systematic review of randomised controlled trials. *British Medical Journal, 359, 330*(7488), 396. https://doi.org/10.1136/bmj.330.7488.396

Fox, J. K., Halpern, L. F., Ryan, J. L., & Lowe, K. A. (2010). Stressful life events and the tripartite model: Relations to anxiety and depression in adolescent females. *Journal of Adolescence, 33*(1), 43–54. https://doi.org/10.1016/j.adolescence.2009.05.009

Garber, J., Robinson, N. S., & Valentiner, D. (1997). The relation between parenting and adolescent depression: Self-worth as a mediator. *Journal of Adolescent Research, 12*(1), 12–33. https://doi.org/10.1177/0743554897121003

Glasser, W. (1998). *The quality school: Managing students without coercion* (rev. ed.). Harper Perennial.

Goldney, R. D. (2011). Antidepressants and suicide prevention. In R. C. O'Connor, S. Platt & J. Gordon (Eds.), *International handbook of suicide prevention: Research, policy and practice* (pp. 457–471). Wiley-Blackwell.

Gordon, T. (2000). *Parent effectiveness training* (2nd ed.). Three Rivers Press.

Gregory, A. M., & Sadeh, A. (2012). Sleep, emotional and behavioral difficulties in children and adolescents. *Sleep Medicine Reviews, 16*(2), 129–136. https://doi.org/10.1016/j.smrv.2011.03.007

Gutin, B. (2011). Diet vs exercise for the prevention of pediatric obesity: The role of exercise. *International Journal of Obesity, 35*(1), 29–32. https://doi.org/10.1038/ijo.2010.140

Haley, J. (1984). *Ordeal therapy*. Jossey-Bass.

Hetrick, S. E., Cox, G. R., Witt, K. G., Bir, J. J., & Merry, S. N. (2016). Cognitive behavioural therapy (CBT), third-wave CBT and interpersonal therapy (IPT) based interventions for preventing depression in children and adolescents. *Cochrane Database of Systematic Reviews*, (8). https://doi.org/10.1002/14651858.CD003380.pub4

Hetrick, S. E., McKenzie, J. E., Cox, G. R., Simmons, M. B., & Merry, S. N. (2012). Newer generation antidepressants for depressive disorders in children and adolescents. *Cochrane Database of Systematic Reviews*, (11). https://doi.org/10.1002/14651858.CD004851.pub3

Ispa, J. M., Fine, M. A., Halgunseth, L. C., Harper, S., Robinson, J., Boyce, L., Brooks-Gunn, J., & Brady-Smith, C. (2004). Maternal intrusiveness, maternal warmth, and mother-toddler relationship outcomes: Variations across low-income ethnic and acculturation groups. *Child Development, 75*(6), 1613–1631. https://doi.org/10.1111/j.1467-8624.2004.00806.x

Jorm, A. F., Morgan, A. J., & Hetrick, S. E. (2008). Relaxation for depression. *Cochrane Database of Systematic Reviews*, (4). https://doi.org/10.1002/14651858.CD007142.pub2

Ju, S., & Lee, Y. (2018). Developmental trajectories and longitudinal mediation effects of self-esteem, peer attachment, child maltreatment and depression on early adolescents. *Child Abuse and Neglect, 76*, 353–363. https://doi.org/10.1016/j.chiabu.2017.11.015

Kaplan, J. S., & Carter, J. (1995). *Beyond behavior modification: A cognitive-behavioral approach to behavior management in the school* (3rd ed.). Pro-Ed.

Kaufmann, D., Gesten, E., Santa Lucia, R. C., Salcedo, O., Rendina-Gobioff, G., & Gadd, R. (2000). The relationship between parenting style and children's adjustment: The parents' perspective. *Journal of Child and Family Studies, 9*(2), 231–245. https://doi.org/10.1023/A:1009475122883

Kennerley, H., Kirk, J., & Westbrook, D. (2017). *An introduction to cognitive behaviour therapy* (3rd ed.). Sage.

Kharrazian, D. (2013). *Why isn't my brain working?* Elephant Press.

Kreier, F., Genco, Ş. M., Boreel, M., Langkemper, M. P., Nugteren, I. C., Rijnveld, V., ... & Keessen, M. (2013). An individual, community-based treatment for obese children and their families: The solution-focused approach. *Obesity Facts, 6*(5), 424–432. https://doi.org/10.1159/000355909

Lavoie, M. E., Rabasa-Lhoret, R., Doucet, E., Mignault, D., Messier, L., Bastard, J. P., & Faraj, M. (2010). Association between physical activity energy expenditure and inflammatory markers in sedentary overweight and obese women. *International Journal of Obesity, 34*(9), 1387–1395. https://doi.org/10.1038/ijo.2010.55

Li, Y., Lv, M. R., Wei, Y. J., Sun, L., Zhang, J. X., Zhang, H. G., & Li, B. (2017). Dietary patterns and depression risk: A meta-analysis. *Psychiatry Research, 253*, 373–382. https://doi.org/10.1016/j.psychres.2017.04.020

Lindberg, L., Hagman, E., Danilesson, P., Marcus, C., & Persson, M. (2020). Anxiety and depression in children and adolescents with obesity: A nationwide study in Sweden. *BMC Medicine, 18*(1), 1–9. https://doi.org/10.1186/s12916-020-1498-z

Loukas, A. (2009). Examining temporal associations between perceived maternal psychological control and early adolescent internalizing problems. *Journal of Abnormal Child Psychology, 37*(8), 1113–1122. https://doi.org/10.1007/s10802-009-9335-z

Lyon, M. R. (2000). *Healing the hyperactive brain: Through the new science of functional medicine*. Focused Publishing.

McDowell, D. J., Parke, R. D., & Wang, S. J. (2003). Differences between mothers' and fathers' advice-giving style and content: Relations with social competence and psychological functioning in middle childhood. *Merrill-Palmer Quarterly*, *49*(1), 55–76. https://www.jstor.org/stable/23096194

McFarlane, A. H., Bellissimo, A., Norman, G. R., & Lange, P. (1994). Adolescent depression in a school-based community sample: Preliminary findings on contributing social factors. *Journal of Youth and Adolescence*, *23*(6), 601–620. https://doi.org/10.1007/BF01537632

Medvedev, V. E. (2013). Use of valdoxan (Agomelatin) in the combined treatment of moderate and severe nonpsychotic depression. *Neuroscience and Behavioral Physiology*, *43*(7), 878. https://doi.org/10.1007/s11055-013-9822-0

Merry, S. N., Hetrick, S. E., Cox, G. R., Brudevold-Iversen, T., Bir, J. J., & McDowell, H. (2012). Cochrane Review: Psychological and educational interventions for preventing depression in children and adolescents. *Evidence-Based Child Health: A Cochrane Review Journal*, *7*(5), 1409–1685. https://doi.org/10.1002/ebch.1867

Ortega, M. A., Fraile-Martínez, Ó., García-Montero, C., Alvarez-Mon, M. A., Lahera, G., Monserrat, J., & Alvarez De Mon, M. (2022). Nutrition, epigenetics, and major depressive disorder: Understanding the connection. *Frontiers in Nutrition*, 867150. https://doi.org/10.3389/fnut.2022.867150

Perlmutter, D., & Loberg, K. (2013). *Grain brain*. Little, Brown & Co.

Polanczyk, G. V., Salum, G. A., Sugaya, L. S., Caye, A., & Rohde, L. A. (2015). Annual research review: A meta-analysis of the worldwide prevalence of mental disorders in children and adolescents. *Journal of Child Psychology and Psychiatry*, *56*(3), 345–365. https://doi.org/10.1111/jcpp.12381

Propper, C., & Moore, G. A. (2006). The influence of parenting on infant emotionality: A multi-level psychobiological perspective. *Developmental Review*, *26*(4), 427–460. https://doi.org/10.1016/j.dr.2006.06.003

Rao, W. W., Zong Q-Q., Zhang, J-W., An, F-R., Jackson, T. & Xiang, Y-T. (2020). Obesity increases the risk of depression in children and adolescents: Results from a systematic review and meta-analysis. *Journal of Affective Disorders*, *267*, 78–85. https://doi.org/10.1016/j.jad.2020.01.154

Roberts, R. E., Kaplan, G. A., Shema, S. J., & Strawbridge, W. J. (2000). Are the obese at greater risk for depression? *American Journal of Epidemiology*, *152*(2), 163–170. https://doi.org/10.1093/aje/152.2.163

Robinson, K., & Aronica, L. (2009). *The element: How finding your passion changes everything*. Penguin.

Ryff, C. D., & Singer, B. (1996). Psychological well-being: Meaning, measurement, and implications for psychotherapy research. *Psychotherapy and Psychosomatics*, *65*(1), 14–23. https://doi.org/10.1159/000289026

Seligman, M. E. P. (2011). *Flourish: A visionary new understanding of happiness and well-being*. Free Press.

Sheldon, K. M., & Lyubomirsky, S. (2004). Achieving sustainable happiness: Prospects, practices, and prescriptions. In P. A. Linley & S. Joseph (Eds.), *Positive psychology in practice* (pp. 127–145). Wiley.

Smith, T. W. (2015). *The book of human emotion: An encyclopedia of feeling from anger to wanderlust*. Profile Books.

Snyder, J., Brooker, M., Patrick, M. R., Snyder, A., Schrepferman, L., & Stoolmiller, M. (2003). Observed peer victimization during early elementary school: Continuity, growth, and relation to risk for child antisocial and depressive behavior. *Child Development*, *74*(6), 1881–1898. https://doi.org/10.1046/j.1467-8624.2003.00644.x

Spirito, A., Esposito-Smythers, C., Weismoore, J., & Miller, A. (2012). Adolescent suicidal behavior. In P. C. Kendall (Ed.), *Child and adolescent therapy: Cognitive-behavioral procedures*. (4th ed., pp. 234–256). Guilford.

Stark, K. D., Streusand, W., Arora, P., & Patel, P. (2012). Childhood depression: The ACTION treatment program. In P. C. Kendall (Ed.), *Child and adolescent therapy: Cognitive-behavioral approaches* (4th ed., pp. 190–233). Guilford.

Strayer, J., & Roberts, W. (2004). Empathy and observed anger and aggression in five-year-olds. *Social Development*, *13*(1), 1–13. https://doi.org/10.1111/j.1467-9507.2004.00254.x

Tiuvina, N. A., & Smirnova, V. N. (2012). A comparative evaluation of the efficacy of valdoxan (agomelatine) in recurrent depression and bipolar affective disorder. *Zhurnal nevrologii i psikhiatrii imeni SS Korsakova*, *112*(11 Pt 2), 53–60.

Turrell, S. L., & Bell, M. (2016). *ACT for adolescents: Treating teens and adolescents in individual and group therapy*. Context Press.

Üstün, T. B., Ayuso-Mateos, J. L., Chatterji, S., Mathers, C., & Murray, C. J. L. (2004). Global burden of depressive disorders in the year 2000. *British Journal of Psychiatry, 184*(5), 292–386. https://doi.org/10.1192/bjp.184.5.386

Vartabedian, R. E., Matthews, K., & Barnes, J. A. (1990). *Nutripoints: The breakthrough nutritional program*. Grafton.

Vibhakar, V., Allen, L. R., Gee, B., & Meiser-Stedman, R. (2019). A systematic review and meta-analysis on the prevalence of depression in children and adolescents after exposure to trauma. *Journal of Affective Disorders, 255*, 77–89. https://doi.org/10.1016/j.jad.2019.05.005

Walser, R. D., & Hayes, S. C. (2006). Acceptance and Commitment Therapy in the treatment of posttraumatic stress disorder: Theoretical and applied issues. In V. C. Follette & J. I. Rusek (Eds.), *Cognitive-behavioral therapies for trauma* (2nd ed., pp. 146–172). Guilford.

Walsh, W. J. (2012). Nutrient power: Heal your biochemistry and heal your brain. Skyhorse.

Walter, H. J., Bukstein, O. G., Abright, R., Keable, H., Ramtekkar, U., Ripperger-Suhler, J., & Rockhill, C. (2020). Clinical practice guideline for the assessment and treatment of children and adolescents with anxiety disorders. *Journal of the American Academy of Child and Adolescent Psychiatry, 59*(10), 1107–1124. https://doi.org/10.1016/j.jaac.2020.05.005

Wang, H., Leung, G. M., & Schooling, C. M. (2015). Life course body mass index and adolescent self-esteem: Evidence from Hong Kong's 'Children of 1997' birth cohort. *Obesity, 23*(2), 429–435. https://doi.org/10.1002/oby.20984

Wegner, M., Amatriain-Fernández, S., Kaulitzky, A., Murillo-Rodriguez, E., Machado, S., & Budde, H. (2020). Systematic review of meta-analyses: Exercise effects on depression in children and adolescents. *Frontiers in Psychiatry, 11*, 81. https://doi.org/10.3389/fpsyt.2020.00081

Wyman, P. A., Cowen, E. L., Work, W. C., Hoyt-Meyers, L., Magnus, K. B., & Fagen, D. B. (1999). Caregiving and developmental factors differentiating young at-risk urban children showing resilient versus stress-affected outcomes: A replication and extension. *Child Development, 70*(3), 645–659. https://doi.org/10.1111/1467-8624.00047

Young, J. E., Rygh, J. L., Weinberger, A. D., & Beck, A. T. (2008). Cognitive therapy for depression. In D. H. Barlow (Ed.), *Clinical handbook of psychological disorders: A step-by-step treatment manual* (4th ed., pp. 250–305). Guilford.

Zhou, X., Teng, T., Zhang, Y., Del Giovane, C., Furukawa, T. A., Weisz, J. R., ... & Xie, P. (2020). Comparative efficacy and acceptability of antidepressants, psychotherapies, and their combination for acute treatment of children and adolescents with depressive disorder: A systematic review and network meta-analysis. *The Lancet Psychiatry, 7*(7), 581–601. https://doi.org/10.1016/S2215-0366(20)30137-1

Zhu, X., Haegele, J. A., & Healy, S. (2019). Movement and mental health: Behavioral correlates of anxiety and depression among children of 6–17 years old in the U.S. *Mental Health and Physical Activity, 16*, 60–65. https://doi.org/10.1016/j.mhpa.2019.04.002

14 Stress and anxiety

Anxiety has multiple dimensions, spanning behavioural, physical, cognitive and emotional elements (Kendall, 2012). Behaviourally, the common pattern is avoidance of settings where one expects to feel anxious; physically, somatic symptoms span abdominal sensations and pain, perspiration, heart palpitations and trembling; cognitively, sufferers experience excessive worry; and emotionally, they feel fear and self-consciousness (Kendall, 2012). While it is normal to be 'nervous' when facing challenges, people with anxiety anticipate and worry excessively, and about events that might never happen - either in general, or in particular circumstances only (such as examination stress).

Anxiety disorders are the most common form of emotional difficulties in young people, with a global prevalence of 6.5 per cent (Anna-Kaisa et al., 2022). Around 16 per cent of individuals will experience an anxiety condition during their lifetime (Somers et al., 2006). Although onset can be sudden, anxiety conditions tend to be chronic and to lead to other emotional difficulties, including depression, panic disorders and suicidal ideation and attempts (Walter et al., 2020).

Stress

For its part, strictly speaking, stress is a physical response of the body, while worry is the thinking that accompanies it, and anxiety is the emotional response. But we tend to lump all three together and call them 'stress'. When it comes to exposure to stress, dose matters ... and timing matters.

Stress occurs when we believe that the demands on us exceed our personal capacity to cope and our social supports for resilience. This definition implies that there are four causes of stress: stressful conditions that impose excessive demands on our resources, underestimation of our coping skills (low self-efficacy), inadequate coping skills and insufficient social support.

Around one-third of adolescents are stressed, many chronically so, to the point that their health is at risk (Schrami et al., 2011). Stressed adolescents experience higher demands, less control and less social support than those who are not stressed (Schrami et al., 2011). As a result, they have low self-esteem, poor eating habits, psychosomatic complaints and sleep deprivation (De Wit et al., 2011; Schrami et al., 2011). Their poor emotional well-being also impairs their capacity to learn (Roeser et al., 1998).

DOI: 10.4324/9781003323938-16

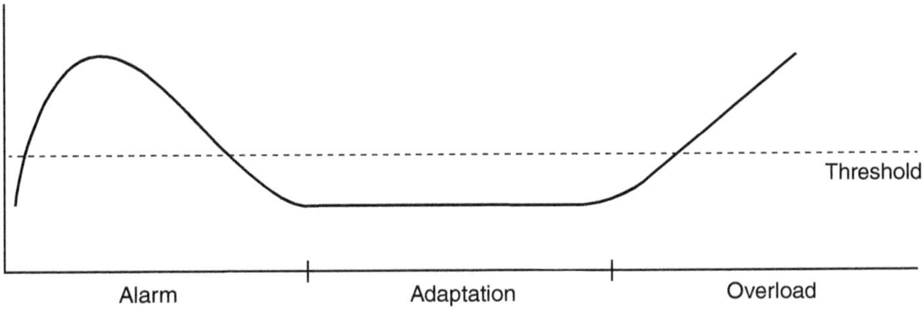

Figure 14.1 Stages of adaptation to stress

Source: Pitman & Porter (2015, p. 56).

The stress response

Hans Selye (pronounced *Sell-y-ay*) described how, over time, we adapt to stress. His model identified three phases of reactions to physical or emotional stressors (illustrated in adapted form in Figure 14.1). The first is an *alarm* phase, when the HPA axis (see below) and sympathetic nervous system are activated, producing heightened arousal and vigilance to either fight, flee or cope with a stressor (the fight-flight response).

If exposure to stressors persists, individuals rally their defences to adapt, during which phase they produce adrenaline and cortisol. Chronic exposure to these stress hormones leads to 'wear and tear' that causes disturbances in the body. Nevertheless, unlike during the previous phase and the one to follow, these disturbances might not produce identifiable symptoms because the body is working hard to suppress these. Finally, however, the individual's defences become overloaded, overwhelmed or exhausted. Symptoms now surface and become numerous (Greenberg, 1990; Mackarness, 1990). Because of the abundance of histamine receptors in the brain, during this phase, symptoms will include problems of the nervous system (such as fatigue or mood disturbances) (Wilson, 2001).

Sources of stress

Every young person experiences everyday stressors such as having to learn new skills, and atypical stressors such as changing schools, moving house or dealing with being bullied. Some, however, endure chronic stress, in which category I include children with chronic illnesses, those in chronic poverty and those who are under extreme pressure to achieve.

Chronic illness

Between 5 and 7 per cent of young people suffer severe chronic health conditions such as allergies, asthma, epilepsy, arthritis, diabetes, chronic fatigue (post-viral) syndrome, AIDS and cancer (Ashton & Bailey, 2004; Clay et al., 2004; Fiese et al., 2009; Kaffenberger, 2006; Shiu, 2001, 2004). Resulting school absences lead to academic delays (Boyle et al., 2007)

Box 14.1 Emotional signs of stress in children

Fight

- aggression
- disruptive or antisocial behaviour (e.g. damage to property)
- negative peer interactions
- explosive anger

Flight

- social withdrawal
- sadness or depression

Freeze

- hypervigilance (scanning the setting to detect potential threats), anxiety, fearfulness
- distress
- compulsive compliance

Sources: Cummings (1998); Cummings et al. (2003, 2006); El-Sheikh & Harger (2001); El-Sheikh et al. (2006); Katz & Woodin (2002); Maughan & Cicchetti (2002); Peterson & Zill (1986); Sternberg et al. (2006a, 2006b)

and disrupt their peer relationships, leading to social isolation (Shiu, 2001). Emotionally, compared to those in good health, chronically ill young people have slightly lower self-esteem as a result of their impaired functioning and reduced peer acceptance (Pinquart, 2013). Their misunderstandings of their condition and its treatment, early encounters with pain and perhaps even the prospect of death, and awareness of the observable strain on their family members can lead to anxieties and fears that surpass those of healthy children (McCarthy, 1987). Without support to promote their coping and resilience, the children's anxiety and grief can lead to emotional adjustment difficulties (Last et al., 2007) while illness-related fatigue can deplete their resources for coping with everyday challenges.

Chronic poverty

Children are the most likely of any social group to be experiencing poverty (with the elderly being the next most probable). In 2017–18 in Australia, 17.6 per cent of people aged under 15 years (or over one in six) were living below the poverty line, which is assessed to be one-half of the median household income (Davidson et al., 2020). This figure is considerably higher among Aboriginal children (Gilding, 1997). It means that Australia has one of the highest poverty rates of developed nations, with the U.S., Japan and Korea only slightly higher (Davidson et al., 2020).

Persistent poverty brings with it substandard housing, frequent moves and homelessness; a disrupted and low-quality education; chaotic neighbourhoods with access to a delinquent subculture (Ingoldsby et al., 2006); reduced recreational opportunities; poor health care;

exposure to the justice system; and stress for parents. In turn, these adversities affect all domains of young people's development (except for motor skills): delayed development overall (Duncan & Brooks-Gunn, 2000) and particularly language skills (Evans et al., 1999; Justice et al., 2019); emotional maladjustment and specifically difficulties with emotion regulation (Dearing et al., 2006); elevated rates of aggression (Demosthenous et al., 2002; Kaiser et al., 2000; Qi & Kaiser, 2003); double the rates of antisocial behaviour (Brody et al., 2001; Fergusson et al., 2004; Ingoldsby et al., 2006; Lee & Zhang, 2022); and chronic health conditions such as obesity, asthma, fatigue and headaches (Schreier et al., 2013) – see www.louiseporter.com.au.

Lacking sufficient income generates multiple stressors that can compromise parenting and thereby detract from young people's well-being (Fisher et al., 2021). This is not inevitable, however. Many parents experiencing material hardship can and do compensate for their stress by nurturing their children and investing in them emotionally (Flouri, 2006; Gershoff et al., 2007; Robinson et al., 2002; Romano et al., 2005; Ruberry et al., 2018; Saitadze & Lalayants, 2021; Sirin, 2005; White, 1982). In other words, it is not family *status* but family *processes* that predict family functioning and, in turn, children's adjustment (Barnes et al., 2005; Raffaele & Knoff, 1999).

Affluenza

Children whose parents value status, image, impression management, acquisition and competition ('winners' and 'losers') can place immense pressure on children to be outstanding and to be who the adults want them to be (Levine, 2008; Luthar & Latendresse, 2005b). These 'project children' are caught in the glare of their parents' headlights, being the focus of their parents' ambitions. The parents are overly concerned with how their children 'do' rather than with who their children 'are' (Levine, 2008). Meanwhile, the parents' own busy schedules limit their time with their children and lead to outsourcing their nurturing functions.

These parents link their own self-esteem to their children's accomplishments and impose on their children goals that are not the children's own (Soenens et al., 2015). However, humans cannot be fulfilled by living out others' version of who we should be (McKay et al., 2010). As a result, the children are subsequently poorly adjusted and more distressed emotionally compared with children whose parents prioritise the children's personal needs (Kasser et al., 1995; Kasser & Ryan, 1993). These trophy children feel isolated from their parents, lack parental support, have low self-efficacy, develop external motivation, display socially prescribed perfectionism and a conditional self-esteem (see Chapter 11), have weak resilience, are more anxious and depressed and lack purpose (Kasser & Ryan, 1993; Levine, 2008; Luthar & Becker, 2002; Luthar & Latendresse, 2005a, 2005b; Pope, 2001; Soenens et al., 2015). They ache for meaning.

Types of anxiety conditions

Anxiety conditions must be distinguished from everyday fears (such as of large animals, the unknown, or illness), which are normal at specific developmental stages (Walter et al., 2020). True anxiety conditions have multiple dimensions, spanning behavioural, physical, cognitive and emotional elements (Kendall, 2012). Behaviourally, the common pattern is avoidance of settings where one expects to feel anxious; physical symptoms span abdominal sensations and pain, perspiration, heart palpitations and trembling; cognitively, sufferers experience excessive worry; and emotionally, they feel fear and self-consciousness (Kendall, 2012; Legerstee et al., 2011). While it is normal (and, indeed self-preserving) to have fear, those whose anxiety becomes immobilising are sending 'false alarm' signals: They are over-reacting given the degree of threat and developing a fear of being afraid (Burton et al., 2015; Craske & Barlow, 2008). And they make 'catastrophic misappraisals' of their bodily sensations, believing that they are about to die or lose all control of themselves (Craske & Barlow, 2008). This causes them to avoid situations where these sensations arise and, in turn, their avoidance means that they do not learn that there was nothing to be afraid of - see Figure 14.2.

Anxiety disorders are the most common form of emotional difficulties in young people, with a global prevalence of 6.5 per cent (Anna-Kaisa et al., 2022). Across the age range, around 16 per cent of individuals will experience an anxiety condition during their lifetime (Somers et al., 2006). Although onset can be sudden, anxiety conditions tend to be chronic and to lead to other emotional difficulties, including depression, panic disorders and suicidal ideation and attempts (Walter et al., 2020).

Separation distress

Uncertainty in new situations commonly leads to distress in infants and children. This is developmentally normal and therefore should not be considered an 'anxiety condition'. Neither should it really be termed separation distress, because it is provoked *both* by separating from a parent *and* from being in an unfamiliar setting. The quality of the setting influences whether children's protest at separation turns into despair (Ahnert et al., 2004).

In other words, there are two issues for the children: leaving their home base and being in the current setting. In terms of leaving their home base, I have experienced children who do not want to leave a parent because they are the only child or youngest of many and they assume that their mother needs their company and I have seen it in children who are the eldest in a clutch of children who believe that their mother needs their help during the day with the younger siblings. In terms of feeling unsafe in the setting, this can be because they *are*

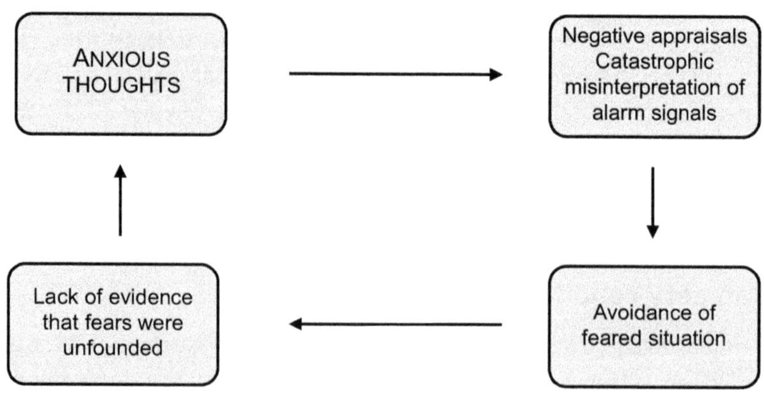

Figure 14.2 The anxiety cycle

Source: adapted from Kennerley et al. (2017, p. 79).

unsafe (for example, they are being bullied or the peer group has a high rate of aggression), or because they simply *feel* unsafe because of a general anxiety condition.

Children's distress peaks between 10 and 18 months of age (Honig, 2002), with toddlers aged 12 to 20 months showing higher levels of the stress hormone, cortisol, for the first two weeks in a new setting, with lesser elevations enduring even for some months thereafter (Ahnert et al., 2004; Bernard et al., 2015). Their experience of distress will depend on their prior experience with separations, the coping strategies they have developed and their age (Robbins, 1997; Rutter, 1985; Waters, 1996). Infants adjust more easily when separations from their parents begin prior to six months of age, before stranger anxiety appears (at around seven months) (Harrison & Ungerer, 2002). Older children are not necessarily better equipped to separate than their younger counterparts, however, with preschool-aged children possibly more stressed by their first exposure to out-of-home care than are infants (Bernard et al., 2015; Robbins, 1997).

Some youngsters can be distressed from the outset, while others will be settled during their initial days in a new location, but then become distressed after that. This can come about for cognitive reasons as they develop the understanding that their attendance is a regular event; because there has been a change in the family such as the birth of a new sibling; or because of changes in their educational setting, such as moving up to a new group or classroom (Greenman & Stonehouse, 2007; Kostelnik et al., 2015).

Social anxiety

After major depression, alcohol abuse and phobias, social anxiety is the fourth most prevalent emotional disturbance, affecting 12 per cent of individuals across the life span (Turk et al., 2008). Those with generalised social fears have debilitating and overwhelming fear of interacting with others, which results in restricted relationships, reduced educational and occupational attainment and, commonly, other emotional problems (Turk et al., 2008). Less broadly affected are those with specific performance fears, such as eating or speaking in public (Turk et al., 2008). Children and adolescents with learning difficulties commonly develop social anxiety in which the underlying fear is of being embarrassed, humiliated or rejected (Kendall, 2012; Zuppardo et al., 2021), although what causes young people to anticipate these toxic emotions varies between individuals.

Performance anxiety

The most common performance anxieties are public speaking and exam stress. Worry about being inadequate leads to anxiety that produces symptoms that make it difficult to perform adequately. In turn, being less successful than expected confirms the need to be anxious about having to perform.

School refusal

One manifestation of general anxiety and, specifically, social anxiety is school refusal, or extended non-attendance at school (Finning et al., 2019). (This is in contrast to truancy, which is concealed from parents.) It is typically accompanied by extreme emotional upset (Heyne et al., 2018) and somatic symptoms such as abdominal pain, nausea, muscular or joint pain, dizziness, fatigue and palpitations (Li et al., 2021), accompanied by determined resistance to parents' attempts to persuade them to go to school (Heyne et al., 2018).

The proximal causes are that students either *are* not safe at school, or do not *feel* safe there. As a result, students develop a combination of the following three patterns (Elliott & Place, 2019; Gonzálvez et al., 2018, 2019, 2020; Ingul et al., 2019).

- Avoidance of social circumstances at school that generate anxiety, such as being isolated, anticipated negative evaluation by peers, conflict with or perceived injustices by teachers and lack of supervision at breaks.
- Anxiety about academic performance, which arises either from actual learning difficulties or from expecting too much of oneself, as seen in socially prescribed perfectionism (see Chapter 11).
- An attempt to escape prolonged bullying, in which case we have to consider the possibility of post-traumatic stress rather than pure anxiety being the underlying emotion (Elliott & Place, 2019).

The peak age of school refusal is 11 to 13 years, at which age separation distress at leaving parents is unlikely; instead it is about anxiety about being at school (Elliott & Place, 2019).

A fifth pattern of simply preferring to do home-based activities such as watching TV or playing video games could be more relevant to truancy because it is not characterised by the emotional and physical symptoms of school refusal (Gonzálvez et al., 2018).

School qualities and the transition to high school have been linked to school refusal (Ingul et al., 2019). High schools are typically larger than primary schools, with looser relationships with teachers at a time when young people continue to need support; are competitive at an age when they are self-conscious; and are more controlling when youth need more autonomy (Roeser et al., 1998). All of these changes are in the opposite direction to what they young people need and limit the availability of both adult and peer social support (Roeser et al., 1998; Wang & Eccles, 2012; Zimmer-Gembeck et al., 2006).

Families are often blamed for school refusal but there is no longitudinal research linking family function to school refusal (Ingul et al., 2019). Any family dysfunction can be the result of dealing with intransigent refusal to attend school, rather than its cause.

Panic

In panic disorders, individuals acquire a fear or dread of their own physical sensations of arousal, and their behaviour (such as refusing to leave the house, as in severe agoraphobia) is an attempt to escape or avoid altogether these physical sensations (Craske & Barlow, 2008). Most sufferers (72 per cent) report an identifiable stressor around the time of the onset of the condition (Craske & Barlow, 2008).

Obsessive compulsive disorder

One manifestation of anxiety is obsessive-compulsive disorder, affecting around one per cent of the population (Franklin & Foa, 2008). Obsessions are persistent irrational thoughts that constantly intrude on thinking and cause distress (Franklin & Foa, 2008). Compulsions are repeated actions taken in response to the obsessive thoughts, with the aim of reducing the anxiety triggered by the obsessive thoughts. The actions are intended to restore safety, in the superstition that this effort will avoid a bad outcome (such as infection). The feared outcome does not happen, which sufferers attribute to their performance of the ritual, but of course the outcome would not have happened anyway. The condition can lead to social withdrawal, both to avoid contamination and to allow time to carry out the rituals (Franklin & Foa, 2008).

In some cases, obsessive thoughts are instigated by toxins activating brain centres, which gives the sufferer the sense that these thoughts are automatic and uncontrollable. One infective instigator of obsessive-compulsive disorder in children is a streptococcus infection (Franklin & Foa, 2008). This is a known as PANDAS: Pediatric Autoimmune Neuropsychiatric Disorders Associated with Streptococcal infection. This condition typically improves with antibiotic treatment, although it can take some time for the strep infection to clear.

Causes

In anxiety conditions, the underlying emotion is fear, while the underlying thought is excessive worry (Legerstee et al., 2011). While it is normal (and, indeed self-preserving) to have fear, those whose anxiety becomes immobilising are sending 'false alarm' signals: They are over-reacting given the degree of threat and developing a fear of being afraid (Burton et al., 2015; Craske & Barlow, 2008). They also make 'catastrophic misappraisals' of their bodily sensations, believing that they are about to die or lose all control of themselves (Craske & Barlow, 2008).

Beneath these difficulties are emotion regulation problems, limited problem-solving skills and low self-efficacy for solving the academic or social problems that are giving rise to their anxiety (Ingul et al., 2019). Avoidance of or escape from a feared situation reduces the fear but does not give the person the opportunity to learn that there was nothing fearful about it in the first place. As Hayes (2004) observes, individuals define their environment as scary and then act as if the scariness is inherent in the setting, rather than something that they have constructed in their own mind.

Mothers who suffer depression during pregnancy and after childbirth are more likely to have children who are anxious (Rogers et al., 2020). This could be because the mother's zinc levels are low, meaning that she has too little to donate to her infant and therefore both suffer depression as a result (see Figure 11.2, page 150).

Emotion regulation

Young people with anxiety lack understanding of how to regulate and change their emotions, especially anger, sadness and worry; and they typically believe that they cannot successfully manage emotionally provocative situations (Kendall, 2012). That is, they have weak self-regulation skills and low self-efficacy. In turn, young people's low self-efficacy with respect to improving their academic achievement or social inclusion translates into low self-efficacy about overcoming their anxieties (Elliott & Place, 2019).

Interventions

One study found that cognitive-behavioural interventions (CBT) were more effective than person-centred counselling for young people's anxiety in that the youth were more likely to achieve full recovery and to sustain this a year later (Silk et al., 2018). Nevertheless, as with other presenting issues, the research evidence indicates using CBT combined with family interventions - in the case of anxiety, to improve parent-child relationships, strengthen family problem solving and communication skills, reduce parental anxiety and guide parents to use emotion coaching with their children (Walter et al., 2020). Although this advice comes from a deficit framework, it can inform the aspects of intervention that we can focus on for anxious young people and their families.

Defusion

In anxiety conditions, people are attempting to avoid their feelings by escaping or avoiding the situations where they occur, or fighting the feelings. They want to get rid of anxiety not because it feels bad, but because it interferes with living a vital life (Hayes, 2004). It is not working for them. In that case, they need to replace it with a different strategy that does allow them to live their best life, the core one of which is to defuse from their thinking, using the steps given in Chapter 4.

Externalise

Using externalisation (see Chapter 3), you might explain to young children that Fear is sneaking up on them, and ask preference questions about whether that is how they would like to live (in Fear's shadow) or whether they would like to find a way to come into the sunshine.

Marsten et al. (2016) externalised worry to enable the client to experience life more abundantly even when Worry visited. They asked:

- Is it possible that Worry has been taking advantage of your sensitivity lately?
- Before Worry showed up, did you think of your sensitivity differently?

Landscape of action questions about the counter-narrative could be:

- How did you get yourself to school when Worry wanted you to stay home?
- Given everything that Worry has going for it, how did you manage to overcome it?

'Next step' questions invite clients to speculate about their future, now that they have changed how they view themselves (Madigan 2019):

- Where do you think you will head next, now that you know that you can tame Worry?
- Do you think this change will allow you to make friends now at school?

Reframing

Young children who come to counselling because of anxiety are often embarrassed in that they know that their peers can cope with situations which cause them alarm. They think that there is something 'wrong' with them. Sometimes, therefore, reframing the problem is a good place to start. For example, if they tell me that they are not brave enough, I ask what they mean by the word *brave*, and almost certainly I will receive the response that it means to be unafraid. But that is *boldness*, not courage, I tell them. *Bravery* is when someone is afraid of something and does it anyway. Many people also believe that everyone else can do things because they are not afraid, when the truth is that everyone is fearful. Some, however, 'feel the fear and do it anyway' (Jeffers, 2007).

Set aside time to worry

When young people's thinking is realistic - such as worrying over just having failed a subject at school - you cannot suggest that they stop worrying because worry is adaptive when it helps us generate strategies for solving a problem. However it becomes dysfunctional when rumination continues after a solution has been planned. In that case, you can suggest that they restrict their worrying to specific worry times (such as 7:00 to 7:15 pm) (Dobson & Dobson, 2017). If the worry tries to intrude at other times, they can simply tell it to be quiet now, because it will get its turn at 7 o'clock.

Parenting styles

According to the research, the parents of anxious young people are often anxious themselves and over-protective, assuming that their child cannot help feeling as they do and cannot be expected to overcome their feelings (Kendall, 2012). When problems such as Anxiety seem to run in families, the two generations who share the same issue can come to realise that Worry plays the same tricks on the child as it did on the parent: It has not learned a single new trick in all the years between them. In that case, they can form a team to outwit Worry, armed with the parent's life experience and the child's sense of mischief (Marsten et al., 2016).

Educational remediation

When young people are anxious about their school performance because they are genuinely achieving below average, counsellors can advocate for them to receive additional tutoring.

Health

Anxiety conditions can have a physical basis. Perhaps because of long exposure to stress or repeated bouts of low blood sugar levels, the body produces too much adrenaline, which activates anxiety. A second possibility is an imbalance of the nutrients need to manufacture key neurotransmitters. The brain chemical, dopamine, gets converted into norephinephrine (pronounced nor-ep-in-*eff*-rin) in the presence of copper (see Figure 11.2, page 150). If there is too much copper in the child's system (relative to zinc, magnesium, molybdenum or selenium), too much dopamine gets converted into norephinephrine. The other name for this neurotransmitter is noradrenaline, which means that it contributes to activating the stress reaction. When in excess, the person experiences anxiety.

Medication

Within two weeks of initiation of treatment with selective serotonin reuptake inhibitors (SSRIs), the primary symptoms of anxiety improve (Walter et al., 2020). Nevertheless, there are some side effects, with the most serious being agitation, seizures and an increase in suicidal ideation – from 0.2 per cent without medication to 1 per cent while taking it (Walter et al., 2020). Numerically, this is clearly a small risk, but potentially very significant in the life of affected individuals. SSRIs also need to be withdrawn slowly to avoid discontinuation effects.

Selective serotonin and norepinephrine reuptake inhibitors (SNRIs) also improve primary anxiety symptoms, although with perhaps more side effects including those for the SSRIs plus high blood pressure, kidney and liver failure and severe skin reactions (Walter et al., 2020). As detailed in Chapter 11, a narrative approach to using medication is to ask clients how the medication assists them in living their life (White, 2016).

Prior to or instead of using these medications, under medical advice some clients and their parents might choose to use nutrients such as zinc and magnesium to offset high copper levels, which are implicated in the creation of too much norepinephrine (see Figure 11.2 on page 150).

Somatic ('bottom up') approaches

The measures discussed so far are 'top-down' methods that work from the head to the body. Working in the reverse direction is also important via attending to the basics of diet, exercise and sleep, and management of PTSD symptoms and any drug or alcohol use. In anxiety conditions, breathing exercises, relaxation, yoga (James-Palmer et al., 2020) and mindfulness exercises can allow clients to notice emotions and experiences without being 'drawn in' by them or actively trying to change them (Laifer et al., 2017). Although research into the benefits of mindfulness for the reduction of anxiety symptoms in young people is scant (Ruiz-Íñiguez et al., 2019), it allows clients to be open, curious and kind towards the workings of their mind.

Conclusion

Anxiety traps individuals into worrying about the future, whereas the present is where everything happens (Zimmerman, 2018). People with anxiety conditions feel out of control of their feelings and are afraid of being afraid. Counselling can support them to accept the first layer of feeling and be relieved of the second layer, the feelings *about* their feelings.

References

Ahnert, L., Gunnar, M. R., Lamb, M. E., & Barthel, M. (2004). Transition to child care: Associations with infant-mother attachment, infant negative emotion, and cortisol elevations. *Child Development*, *75*(3), 639–650. https://doi.org/10.1111/j.1467-8624.2004.00698.x

Anna-Kaisa, V., Virpi, K.-K., Mervi, R., Elisa, R., Terhi, L., Marjo, K., André, S., & Eila, K. (2022). Review: Economic evidence of preventive interventions for anxiety disorders in children and adolescents – A systemic review. *Child and Adolescent Mental Health*, *27*(4), 378–388. https://doi.org/10.1111/camh.12505

Ashton, J., & Bailey, J. (2004). Slipping through the policy cracks: Children with chronic illness in early childhood settings. *Australian Journal of Early Childhood*, *29*(1), 50–58. https://doi.org/10.1177/183693910402900110

Barnes, J., Belsky, J., Broomfield, K. A., Dave, S., Frost, M., Melhuish, E., & The National Evaluation of Sure Start Research Team (2005). Disadvantaged but different: Variation among deprived communities in relation to child and family well-being. *Journal of Child Psychology and Psychiatry*, *46*(9), 952–962. https://doi.org/10.1111/j.1469-7610.2004.00392.x

Bernard, K., Peloso, E., Laurenceau, J. P., Zhang, Z., & Dozier, M. (2015). Examining change in cortisol patterns during the 10-week transition to a new child care setting. *Child Development*, *82*(6), 456–471. https://doi.org/10.1111/cdev.12304

Boyle, M. H., Georgiades, K., Racine, Y., & Mustard, C. (2007). Neighborhood and family influences on educational attainment: Results from the Ontario child health study follow-up 2001. *Child Development*, *78*(1), 168–189. https://doi.org/10.1111/j.1467-8624.2007.00991.x

Brody, G. H., Ge, X., Conger, R., Gibbons, F. X., Murry, V. McB., Gerrard, M., & Simons, R. L. (2001). The influence of neighborhood disadvantage, collective socialization, and parenting on African American children's affiliation with deviant peers. *Child Development*, *72*(4), 1231–1246. https://doi.org/10.1111/1467-8624.00344

Burton, L., Westen, D., & Kowalski, R. (2015). *Psychology* (3rd ed.). Wiley.

Clay, D. L., Cortina, S., Harper, D. C., Cocco, K. M., & Drotar, D. (2004). Schoolteachers' experiences with childhood chronic illness. *Children's Health Care*, *33*(3), 227–239. https://doi.org/10.1207/s15326888chc3303_5

Craske, M. G., & Barlow, D. H. (2008). Panic disorder and agoraphobia. In D. H. Barlow (Ed.), *Clinical handbook of psychological disorders: A step-by-step treatment manual* (4th ed., pp. 1–64). Guilford.

Cummings, E. M. (1998). Stress and coping approaches and research: The impact of marital conflict on children. In B. B. R. Rossman & M. S. Rosenberg (Eds.), *Multiple victimization of children: Conceptual, developmental, research, and treatment issues* (pp. 31–50). Haworth Press.

Cummings, E. M., Goeke-Morey, M. C., & Papp. L. M. (2003). Children's responses to everyday marital conflict tactics in the home. *Child Development*, *74*(6), 1918–1929. https://doi.org/10.1046/j.1467-8624.2003.00646.x

Cummings, E. M., Schermerhorn, A. C., Davies, P. T., Goeke-Morey, M. C., & Cummings, J. S. (2006). Interparental discord and child adjustment: Prospective investigations of emotional security as an explanatory mechanism. *Child Development*, *77*(1), 132–152. https://doi.org/10.1111/j.1467-8624.2006.00861.x

Davidson, P., Saunders, P., Bradbury, B., & Wong, M. (2020). Poverty in Australia 2020: Part 1, Overview. *ACOSS/UNSW Poverty and Inequality Partnership Report No. 3*. ACOSS.

De Wit, D. J., Karioja, K., Rye, B. J., & Shain, M. (2011). Perceptions of declining classmate and teacher support following the transition to high school: Potential correlates of increasing student mental health difficulties. *Psychology in the Schools*, *48*(6), 556–572. https://doi.org/10.1002/pits.20576

Dearing, E., McCartney, K., & Taylor, B. A. (2006). Within-child associations between family income and externalizing and internalizing problems. *Developmental Psychology*, *42*(2), 237–252. https://doi.org/10.1037/0012-1649.42.2.237

Demosthenous, H. T., Bouhours, T., & Demosthenous, C. M. (2002). Socioeconomic status and youth aggression in Australia. *Youth Studies Australia*, *21*(4), 11–15. http://hdl.handle.net/10072/37555

Dobson, D., & Dobson, K. S. (2017). *Evidence-based practice of cognitive-behavioural therapy* (2nd ed.). Guilford.

Duncan, G. J., & Brooks-Gunn, J. (2000). Family poverty, welfare reform, and child development. *Child Development*, *71*(1), 188–196. https://doi.org/10.1111/1467-8624.00133

El-Sheikh, M., Buckhalt, J., Mize, J., & Acebo, C. (2006). Marital conflict and disruption of children's sleep. *Child Development*, *77*(1), 31–43. https://doi.org/10.1111/j.1467-8624.2006.00854.x

El-Sheikh, M., & Harger, J. (2001). Appraisals of marital conflict and children's adjustment, health, and physiological reactivity. *Developmental Psychology*, *37*(6), 875-885. https://doi.org/10.1037//0012-1649.37.6.875

Elliott, J. G., & Place, M. (2019). Practitioner review: School refusal: Developments in conceptualisation and treatment since 2000. *Journal of Child Psychology and Psychiatry*, *60*(1), 4–15. https://doi.org/10.1111/jcpp.12848

Evans, G. W., Maxwell, L. E., & Hart, B. (1999). Parental language and verbal responsiveness to children in crowded homes. *Developmental Psychology*, *35*(4), 1020–1023. https://doi.org/10.1037/0012-1649.35.4.1020

Fergusson, D., Swain-Campbell, N., & Horwood, J. (2004). How does childhood economic disadvantage lead to crime? *Journal of Child Psychology and Psychiatry, 45*(5), 956–966. https://doi.org/10.1111/j.1469-7610.2004.t01-1-00288.x

Fiese, B. H., Everhart, R. S., & Wildenger, L. (2009). Wheezing, sleeping, and worrying: The hidden risks of asthma and obesity in school-age children. *Psychology in the Schools, 46*(8), 728–738. https://doi.org/10.1002/pits.20411

Fisher, M., Scanlon, C., Deojee, B., Hutton, V., & Sisko, S. (2021). Classism. In V. Hutton & S. Sisko (Eds.), *Multicultural responsiveness in counselling and psychology: Working with Australian populations* (pp. 103–123). Springer. https://doi.org/10.1007/978-3-030-55427-9_4

Finning, K., Ukoumunne, O. C., Ford, T., Danielson-Waters, E., Shaw, L., Romero De Jager, I., & Moore, D. A. (2019). The association between anxiety and poor attendance at school: A systematic review. *Child and Adolescent Mental Health, 24*(3), 205–216. https://doi.org/10.1111/camh.12322

Flouri, E. (2006). Parental interest in children's education, children's self-esteem and locus of control, and later educational attainment: Twenty-six year follow-up of the 1970 British birth cohort. *British Journal of Educational Psychology, 76*(1), 51–55. https://doi.org/10.1348/000709905X52508

Franklin, M. E., & Foa, E. B. (2008). Obsessive-compulsive disorder. In D. H. Barlow (Ed.), *Clinical handbook of psychological disorders: A step-by-step treatment manual* (4th ed., pp. 164–215). Guilford.

Gershoff, E. T., Aber, J. L., Raver, C. C., & Lennon, M. C. (2007). Income is not enough: Incorporating material hardship into models of income associations with parenting and child development. *Child Development, 78*(1), 70–95. https://doi.org/10.1111/j.1467-8624.2007.00986.x

Gilding, M. (1997). *Australian families: A comparative perspective*. Longman.

Gonzálvez, C., Inglés, C. J., Fernández-Sogorb, A., Sanmartin, M. V., & García-Fernández, J. M. (2018). Profiles derived from the school refusal assessment scale - revised and its relationship to anxiety. *Educational Psychology, 40*(6), 767–780. https://doi.org/10.1080/01443410.2018.1530734

Gonzálvez, C., Díaz-Herrero, A., Sanmartín, R., Vincent, M., Pérez-Sánchez, A. M., & García-Fernández, J. M. (2019). Identifying risk profiles of school refusal behaviour: Differences in social anxiety and family functioning among Spanish adolescents. *International Journal of Environmental Research and Public Health, 16*(19), 3731. https://doi.org/10.3390/ijerph16193731

Gonzálvez, C., Díaz-Herrero, A., Sanmartín, R., Vincent, M., Fernández-Sogorb, A., & García-Fernández, J. M. (2020). Testing the functional profiles of school refusal behavior and clarifying their relationship with school anxiety. *Frontiers in Public Health, 8*, 598915. https://doi.org/10.3389/fpubh.2020.598915

Greenberg, J. (1990). *Comprehensive stress management* (3rd ed.). William C. Brown.

Greenman, J., & Stonehouse, A. (2007). *Prime times: A handbook for excellence in infant and toddler programs* (2nd ed.). Redleaf Press.

Harrison, L. J., & Ungerer, J. A. (2002). Maternal employment and infant-mother attachment security at 12 months postpartum. *Developmental Psychology, 38*(5), 758–773. https://doi.org/10.1037//0012-1649.38.5.758

Hayes, S. C. (2004). Acceptance and commitment therapy, relational frame theory, and the third wave of behavioral and cognitive therapies. *Behavior Therapy, 35*(4), 639–665. https://doi.org/10.1016/S0005-7894(04)80013-3

Heyne, D., Gren-Landell, M., Melvin, G., & Gentle-Genitty, C. (2018). Differentiation between school attendance problems: Why and how? *Cognitive and Behavioral Practice, 26*(1), 8–34. https://doi.org/10.1016/j.cbpra.2018.03.006

Honig, A. S. (2002). Secure relationships: Nurturing infant/toddler attachment in early care settings. National Association for the Education of Young Children.

Ingoldsby, E. M., Shaw, D. S., Winslow, E., Schonberg, M., Gilliom, M., & Criss, M. M. (2006). Neighborhood disadvantage, parent-child conflict, neighborhood peer relationships, and early antisocial behavior problem trajectories. *Journal of Abnormal Child Psychology, 34*(3), 303–319. https://doi.org/10.1007/s10802-006-9026-y

Ingul, J. M., Havik, T., & Heyne, D. (2019). Emerging school refusal: A school-based framework for identifying early signs and risk factors. *Cognitive and Behavioral Practice, 26*(1), 46–62. https://doi.org/10.1016/j.cbpra.2018.03.005

James-Palmer, A., Anderson, E. Z., Zucker, L., Kofman, Y., & Daneault, J-F. (2020). Yoga as an intervention for the reduction of symptoms of anxiety and depression in children and adolescents: A systematic review. *Frontiers in Pediatrics, 8*, 78. https://doi.org/10.3389/fped.2020.00078

Jeffers, S. (2007). *Feel the fear ... and do it anyway*. Ballantine.

Justice, L. M., Jiang, H., Purtell, K. M., Schmeer, K., Boone, K., Bates, R., & Salsberry, P. J. (2019). Conditions of poverty, parent-child interactions, and toddlers' early language skills in low-income families. *Maternal and Child Health Journal*, *23*, 971–978. https://doi.org/10.1007/s10995-018-02726-9

Kaffenberger, C. J. (2006). School reentry for students with a chronic illness: A role for professional school counselors. *Professional School Counseling*, *9*(3), 223–230. https://www.jstor.org/stable/42732674

Kaiser, A. P., Hancock, T. B., Cai, X., Foster, E. M., & Hester, P. P. (2000). Parent-reported behavioral problems and language delays in boys and girls enrolled in Head Start classrooms. *Behavioral Disorders*, *26*(1), 26–41. https://doi.org/10.1177/019874290002600104

Kasser, T., & Ryan, R. M. (1993). A dark side of the American dream: Correlates of financial success as a central life aspiration. *Journal of Personality and Social Psychology*, *65*(2), 410–422.

Kasser, T., Ryan, R. M., Zax, M., & Sameroff, A. J. (1995). The relations of maternal and social environments to late adolescents' materialistic and prosocial values. *Developmental Psychology*, *31*(6), 907–914.

Katz, L. F., & Woodin, E. M. (2002). Hostility, hostile detachment, and conflict engagement in marriages: Effects on child and family functioning. *Child Development*, *73*(2), 636–652. https://doi.org/10.1111/1467-8624.00428

Kendall, P. C. (2012). Anxiety disorders in youth. In P. C. Kendall (Ed.), *Child and adolescent therapy: Cognitive-behavioral procedures* (3rd ed., pp. 143–189). Guilford.

Kennerley, H., Kirk, J., & Westbrook, D. (2017). *An introduction to cognitive behaviour therapy* (3rd ed.). Sage.

Kostelnik, M. J., Soderman, A. K., Whiren, A. P., Ripiper, M., & Gregory, K. M. (2015). *Guiding children's social development and learning: Theory and skills* (8th ed.). Cengage.

Laifer, A. L., Wirth, K. A., & Lang, A. J. (2017). Mindfulness and acceptance and commitment therapy in the treatment of trauma. In *APA handbook of trauma psychology: Trauma practice, Vol. 2* (pp. 253–273). American Psychological Association.

Last, B. F., Stam, H., Onland-van Nieuwenhuizen, A.-M., & Grootenhuis, M. A. (2007). Positive effects of a psycho-educational group intervention for children with chronic disease: First results. *Patient Education and Counseling*, *65*(1), 101–112. https://doi.org/10.1016/j.pec.2006.06.017

Lee, K., & Zhang, L. (2022). Cumulative effects of poverty on children's social-emotional development: Absolute poverty and relative poverty. *Community Mental Health Journal*, *58*, 930–943. https://doi.org/10.1007/s10597-021-00901-x

Legerstee, J.S., Garnefski, N., Verhulst, F.C., & Utens, E.M.W.J. (2011). Cognitive coping in anxiety-disordered adolescents. *Journal of Adolescence*, *34*(2), 319–326. https://doi.org/10.1016/j.adolescence.2010.04.008

Levine, M. (2008). *The price of privilege*. Harper.

Li, A., Guessoum, S. B., Ibrahim, N., Lefèvre, H., Moro, M. R., & Benoit, L. (2021). A systematic review of somatic symptoms in school refusal. *Psychosomatic Medicine*, *83*(7), 715–723. https://doi.org/10.1097/PSY.0000000000000956

Luthar, S. S., & Becker, B. E. (2002). Privileged but pressured?: A study of affluent youth. *Child Development*, *73*(5), 1593–1610. https://doi.org/10.1111/1467-8624.00492

Luthar, S. S., & Latendresse, S. J. (2005a). Children of the affluent: Challenges to well-being. *Current Directions in Psychological Science*, *14*(1), 49–53. https://doi.org/10.1111/j.0963-7214.2005.00333.x

Luthar, S. S., & Latendresse, S. J. (2005b). Comparable 'risks' at the socioeconomic extremes: Preadolescents' perceptions of parenting. *Development and Psychopathology*, *17*(1), 207–230. https://doi.org/10.1017/S095457940505011X

Mackarness, R. (1990). *Not all in the mind*. Thorsons.

Madigan, S. (2019). *Narrative therapy* (2nd ed.). American Psychological Association.

Marsten, D., Epston, D., & Markham, L. (2016). *Narrative therapy in wonderland: Connecting with children's imaginative know-how*. Norton.

Maughan, A., & Cicchetti, D. (2002). Impact of child maltreatment and interadult violence on children's emotion regulation and socioemotional adjustment. *Child Development*, *73*(5), 1525–1542. https://doi.org/10.1111/1467-8624.00488

McCarthy, M. (1987). Chronic illness and hospitalization. In J. T. Neisworth & S. J. Bagnato (Eds.), *The young exceptional child: Early development and education* (pp. 231–259). Macmillan.

McKay, M., Forsyth, J. P., & Eifert, G. H. (2010). *Your life on purpose: How to find what matters and create the life you want*. New Harbinger.

Peterson, J. L., & Zill, N. (1986). Marital disruption, parent-child relationships, and behavior problems in children. *Journal of Marriage and Family*, *48*(2), 295–307. https://doi.org/10.2307/352397

Pinquart, M. (2013). Self-esteem of children and adolescents with chronic illness: A meta-analysis. *Child: Care, Health and Development*, *39*(2), 153–161. https://doi.org/10.1111/j.1365-2214.2012.01397.x
Pitman, M., & Porter, L. (2014). *Bioresonance explained*. Life Works Health Clinic.
Pope, D. C. (2001). *Doing school: How we are creating a generation of stressed out, materialistic, and miseducated students*. Yale University Press.
Qi, C. H., & Kaiser, A. P. (2003). Behavior problems of preschool children from low-income families. *Topics in Early Childhood Special Education*, *23*(4), 188–216. https://doi.org/10.1177/02711214030230040201
Raffaele, L. M., & Knoff, H. M. (1999). Improving home-school collaboration with disadvantaged families: Organizational principles, perspectives, and approaches. *School Psychology Review*, *28*(3), 448–466. https://doi.org/10.1080/02796015.1999.12085977
Robbins, J. (1997). Separation anxiety: A study on commencement at preschool. *Australian Journal of Early Childhood*, *22*(1), 12–17. https://doi.org/10.1177/183693919702200104
Robinson, N. M., Lanzi, R. G., Weinberg, R. A., Ramey, S. L., & Ramey, C. T. (2002). Family factors associated with high academic competence in former Head Start children at third grade. *Gifted Child Quarterly*, *46*(4), 278–290. https://doi.org/10.1177/001698620204600404
Roeser, R. W., Eccles, J. S., & Sameroff, A. J. (1998). Academic and emotional functioning in early adolescence: Longitudinal relations, patterns, and prediction by experience in middle school. *Development and Psychopathology*, *10*(2), 321–352. https://doi.org/10.1017/S0954579498001631
Rogers, A., Obst, S., Teague, S. J., Rosen, L., Spry, E. A., & Hutchinson, D. (2020). Association between maternal perinatal depression and anxiety and child and adolescent development: A meta-analysis. *JAMA Pediatrics*, *174*(11), 1082–1092. https://doi.org/10.1001/jamapediatrics.2020.2910
Romano, E., Tremblay, R. E., Boulerice, B., & Swisher, R. (2005). Multilevel correlates of childhood physical aggression and prosocial behavior. *Journal of Abnormal Child Psychology*, *33*(5), 565–578. https://doi.org/10.1007/s10802-005-6738-3
Ruberry, E. J., Klein, M. R., Kiff, C. J., Thompson, S. F., & Lengua, L. J. (2018). Parenting as a moderator of the effects of cumulative risk on children's social-emotional adjustment and academic readiness. *Infant and Child Development*, *27*(3), e2071. https://doi.org/10.1002/icd.2071
Ruiz-Íñiguez, R., Germán, M. A. S., Burgos-Julián, F. A., Díaz-Silveira, C., & Montero, A. C. (2019). Effectiveness of mindfulness-based interventions on anxiety for children and adolescents: A systematic review and meta-analysis. *Early Intervention in Psychiatry*, *14*(3), 263–274. https://doi.org/10.1111/eip.12849
Rutter, M. (1985). Resilience in the face of adversity: Protective factors and resistance to psychiatric disorder. *British Journal of Psychiatry*, *147*(6), 598–611. https://doi.org/10.1192/bjp.147.6.598
Saitadze, I., & Lalayants, M. (2021). Mechanisms that mitigate the effects of child poverty and improve children's cognitive and social-emotional development: A systematic review. *Child and Family Social Work*, *26*(3), 289–308. https://doi.org/10.1111/cfs.12809
Schraml, K., Perski, A., Grossi, G., & Simonsson-Sarnecki, M. (2011). Stress symptoms among adolescents: The role of subjective psychosocial conditions, lifestyle, and self-esteem. *Journal of Adolescence*, *34*(5), 987–996. https://doi.org/10.1016/j.adolescence.2010.11.010
Schreier, H., & Chen, E. (2013). Socioeconomic status and the health of youth: A multi-level, multi-domain approach to conceptualizing pathways. *Psychological Bulletin*, *139*(3), 606–654. https://doi.org/10.1037/a0029416
Shiu, S. (2001). Issues in the education of students with chronic illness. *International Journal of Disability, Development and Education*, *48*(3), 269–281. https://doi.org/10.1080/10349120120073412
Shiu, S. (2004). Maintaining the thread: Including young children with chronic illness in the primary classroom. *Australian Journal of Early Childhood*, *29*(1), 33–38. https://doi.org/10.1177/183693910402900107
Silk, J. S., Tan, P. Z., Ladouceur, C. D., Meller, S., Siegle, G. J., McMakin, D. L., & Ryan, N. D. (2018). A randomized clinical trial comparing individual cognitive behavioral therapy and child-centered therapy for child anxiety disorders. *Journal of Clinical Child and Adolescent Psychology*, *47*(4), 542–554. https://doi.org/10.1080/15374416.2016.1138408
Sirin, S. R. (2005). Socioeconomic status and academic achievement: A meta-analytic review of research. *Review of Educational Research*, *75*(3), 417–453. https://doi.org/10.3102/00346543075003417
Soenens, B., Wuyts, D., Vansteenkiste, M., Mageau, G. A., & Brenning, K. (2015). Raising trophy kids: The role of mothers' contingent self-esteem in maternal promotion of extrinsic goals. *Journal of Adolescence*, *42*, 40–49. http://dx.doi.org/10.1016/j.adolescence.2015.04.001

Somers, J. M., Goldner, E. M., Waraich, P., & Hsu, L. (2006). Prevalence and incidence studies of anxiety disorders: A systematic review of the literature. *Canadian Journal of Psychiatry*, *51*(2), 100–113.

Sternberg, K. J., Baradaran, L. P., Abbott, C. B., Lamb, M. E., & Guterman, E. (2006a). Type of violence, age, and gender differences in the effects of family violence on children's behavior problems: A mega-analysis. *Developmental Review*, *26*(1), 89–112. https://doi.org/10.1016/j.dr.2005.12.001

Sternberg, K. J., Lamb, M. E., Guterman, E., & Abbott, C. B. (2006b). Effects of early and later family violence on children's behavior problems and depression: A longitudinal, multi-informant perspective. *Child Abuse and Neglect*, *30*(3), 283–306. https://doi.org/10.1016/j.chiabu.2005.10.008

Turk, C. L., Heimberg, R. G., & Magee, L. (2008). Social anxiety disorder. In D. H. Barlow (Ed.), *Clinical handbook of psychological disorders: A step-by-step treatment manual* (4th ed., pp. 123–163). Guilford.

Walter, H. J., Bukstein, O. G., Abright, R., Keable, H., Ramtekkar, U., Ripperger-Suhler, J., & Rockhill, C. (2020). Clinical practice guideline for the assessment and treatment of children and adolescents with anxiety disorders. *Journal of the American Academy of Child and Adolescent Psychiatry*, *59*(10), 1107–1124. https://doi.org/10.1016/j.jaac.2020.05.005

Wang, M. T., & Eccles, J. S. (2012). Social support matters: Longitudinal effects of social support on three dimensions of school engagement from middle to high school. *Child Development*, *83*(3), 877–895. https://doi.org/10.1111/j.1467-8624.2012.01745.x

Waters, J. (1996). *Making the connection: Parents and early childhood staff*. Lady Gowrie Child Centre (Melbourne).

White, K. R. (1982). The relation between socioeconomic status and academic achievement. *Psychological Bulletin*, *91*(3), 461–481. https://doi.org/10.1037/0033-2909.91.3.461

White, M. (2016). *Narrative therapy classics*. Dulwich Centre Publications.

Wilson, J. L. (2001). Adrenal fatigue: The 21st century stress syndrome. Smart Publications.

Zimmer-Gembeck, M. J., Chipuer, H. M., Hanisch, M., Creed, P. A., & McGregor, L. (2006). Relationships at school and stage-environment fit as resources for adolescent engagement and achievement. *Journal of Adolescence*, *29*(6), 911–933. https://doi.org/10.1016/j.adolescence.2006.04.008

Zimmerman, J. (2018). *Neuro-narrative therapy: New possibilities for emotion-filled conversations*. Norton.

Zuppardo, L., Serrano, F., Pirrone, C., & Rodriguez-Fuentes, A. (2021). More than words: Anxiety, self-esteem and behavioral problems in children and adolescents with dyslexia. *Learning Disability Quarterly*, 1–15. https://doi.org/10.1177/07319487211041103

15 Trauma

Children have been cast as passive recipients or victims of traumatising events, which has a negative effect on their self-efficacy and contributes to feelings of impotence and helplessness (White, 2016). Instead, all children produce responses to these adverse events that can be highlighted so that they can be used to shape identities for themselves that include more than their victimhood. There is the story of the injustice, which must be heard - but there is also the story of the skills and knowledge they used to deal with it (Denborough, 2014).

Types of traumatic experiences

Traumatic experiences are of the following five types.

- Impersonal trauma, such as natural or man-made disasters such as nuclear reactor explosions, tsunamis, floods, fires or earthquakes, motor vehicle accidents, war or contracting a serious medical condition.
- Interpersonal trauma, including assaults by a stranger, prolonged bullying, or witnessing domestic violence, suicide or homicide.
- Intrafamilial trauma, which refers to abuse by family members or those known to the individual.
- Intergenerational trauma that is passed from adults to children and which can cause individuals to be vulnerable to subsequent forms of trauma.
- Systemic trauma refers to cultural attitudes, behaviours, systems and institutions that give rise to trauma and maintain it.

Post-traumatic stress

There are significant differences in the long-term effects of experiencing a single traumatic event, versus enduring multiple traumatic events. Acute stress occurs in the immediate aftermath of a traumatic event, whereas post-traumatic stress is a long-term response that can occur when individuals have experienced or witnessed a shocking event that held a threat or risk of death or serious injury, or a threat to the physical integrity of self or others (Resick et al., 2008). Current estimates indicate that 57 to 75 per cent of individuals will

DOI: 10.4324/9781003323938-17

experience a potentially traumatic event in their lifetime (AIHW, 2020; Steger & Park, 2012). As for young people, the Adverse Childhood Experiences (ACE) study found that (Souers & Hall, 2016, p. 20):

- 45 per cent of school students have experienced at least one ACE.
- 22 per cent have experienced multiple ACEs.
- One in 16 (6%) have experienced four or more ACEs.

Rates of PTSD in the young are vastly underestimated and might be higher than for adults (36 per cent versus the adult rate of 24 per cent) (Dyregrov & Yule, 2006). Post-traumatic stress is more likely to occur in those who have experienced prior trauma, perhaps because they are primed by shame and guilt, which are implicated in the condition (Resick et al., 2008). Although most post-traumatic stress remits over time, the average duration of the condition is 14 years (Mustanski et al., 2016).

Sources of trauma

The main sources of trauma affecting young people that I discuss here are child abuse, witnessing domestic violence, natural disasters, the intergenerational trauma of First Nations peoples and the refugee experience.

Child abuse

Child maltreatment comprises acts of commission against children: physical, sexual and emotional (verbal) abuse; and acts of omission where caregivers fail to provide appropriate protection and care, as in neglect and witnessing domestic violence (Delima & Vimpani, 2011). Children are seldom exposed to only one form of abuse, with physical and sexual abuse and family violence exposure commonly co-occurring (Herrenkohl & Herrenkohl, 2007), and all held in place by verbal or emotional abuse.

Sexual abuse involves the exploitation and coercion of children by someone more powerful than them. As many as 16.5 per cent of children are physically or emotionally abused or neglected (Afifi et al., 2006) with the actual rate suspected to be higher still. Prevalence estimates vary considerably, with one study reporting rates of 15 per cent for girls and 7 per cent for boys (Kim & Cicchetti, 2006) and others finding similar rates for both genders (Bromberg & Johnson, 2001; Rossman et al., 1998). Another study reported that almost one-third of females and 14 per cent of males experience coerced sexual activity prior to the age of 18 (Shrivastava et al., 2017). The peak age of onset of sexual abuse appears to be 7 to 8 years for females and prior to puberty for males (Webster, 2001) and commonly persists for more than two years.

Approximately 20 per cent of adult males and eight per cent of females report having some sexual attraction to children, with as many as seven per cent of males and three per cent of females saying that they would engage in sexual activity with children if they could avoid detection (Bromberg & Johnson, 2001; Vizard et al., 1995). The factor that translates this high level of sexual interest in children into actual abuse is not the mental illness or prior abuse history of the perpetrator, but simply children's powerlessness. Children trust adults to keep them safe, are not capable of assessing adults' motives, and are taught to obey adults (Briggs & McVeity, 2000).

Abuse conveys to children that they are worthless, unloved and unwanted, which descriptors become part of their identity (Haynes-Seman & Baumgarten, 1998; Khoury et al., 2022; Rossman et al., 1998). When young people are subjected to pervasive and repeated physical, sexual or psychological violations, the unpredictability and lack of control over these repeated assaults and the toxic relationship with the perpetrator take an additional toll.

Childhood emotional neglect can be even more insidious than active abuse because shaming children for wanting or needing care can blind them to their own emotional needs (Webb & Musello, 2013). As De Bellis (2001) observes, the trauma of abuse and neglect are not only the maltreatment itself but also the traumatised relationship that victims have with the perpetrator.

Compounding other hardships that families experience, neglect and abuse of children produce a cascade of neurological and emotional damage (Anda et al., 2006; Morris et al., 2007; Pears et al., 2010; Teisl & Cicchetti, 2008). These effects are so profound that Van der Kolk (2005) argues that the term *post-traumatic stress disorder* does not adequately capture the outcomes of childhood abuse and that, instead, we need to create a category of *developmental trauma disorder*. This acknowledges the effects of repeated early trauma on brain structure and function (De Bellis et al., 2015; Kaufman & Charney, 2001; Teicher, 2002; Teicher et al., 2010), which set the stage for unfocused or dysregulated responses to subsequent stress (van der Kolk, 2005). In turn, emotional dysregulation affects all aspects of abused children's competence (see www.louiseporter.com.au).

The excess cortisol production arising from child abuse causes young people to be more reactive to stressors and less able to regulate their emotional reactions, producing a range of devastating emotional symptoms. Their social competence is impaired, with maltreated children displaying fewer prosocial behaviours and more negative behaviour directed at peers and adults, largely because they do not trust others (George & Main, 1979). Academically, long-term elevated cortisol levels contribute to hypervigilance, which detracts from processing capacity to develop skills, resulting in delays in social, motor and cognitive skills. There is also an indication that the structural changes in the brain (such as decreased volume of the corpus callosum) and functional changes (such as reduced hippocampal activity) disrupt arousal and impair working memory, attention and reasoning.

The resulting symptoms are a problem for affected young people, their families and society as a whole, not least because they manifest in antisocial behaviour later in life and contribute to the intergenerational transmission of adversity (Delima & Vimpani, 2011; Smith & Farrington, 2004). Moreover, these conditions are less responsive to drug treatments or therapy (Nemeroff, 2016).

Child abuse in schools

Emotional abuse by teachers is a global phenomenon (Scharpf et al., 2022), with 10 to 15 per cent of students suffering repeated verbal abuse from their teachers from as early as their first year of school and persisting for many years through to adolescence (Brendgen et al., 2006; Delfabbro et al., 2006; Hyman & Perone, 1998). Defined by adult survivors as 'abuse of the spirit' (Nesbit & Philpott, 2002, p. 33), emotional abuse by teachers encompasses emotionally distancing; hostile practices including mockery, insults, discrimination, and threats of punishment; and not stepping in to prevent children from being belittled by their peers (Krugman & Krugman, 1984; McEachern et al., 2008; Nesbit & Philpott, 2002; Piekarska, 2000).

Although some of these practices are considered normative in certain cultures (Shumba, 2002), their effects on children are uniformly negative. Human psychology is the same everywhere. Emotional abuse by teachers lowers students' academic achievement (Brendgen et al., 2006; Delfabbro, et al., 2006; Scharpf et al., 2022) and produces stress in students, with more serious cases leading to symptoms characteristic of post-traumatic stress syndrome, which affects 1 to 2 per cent of the student population (Hyman, 1995; Hyman & Perone, 1998; Krugman & Krugman, 1984; Scharpf et al., 2022).

Affected students can display a sudden onset of excessive worry about school, deterioration in self-esteem, somatic complaints (headaches and stomach aches), sleep disturbances and depression (Hyman, 1995; Krugman & Krugman, 1984). Motivated by a desire to hide, one coping strategy is compulsive compliance and keeping one's head down to avoid being a target of teachers' vitriol (Piekarska, 2000) (while still having to witness it being directed at other students). These students appear to be coping, but commonly have emotional meltdowns at home, having held it together all day at school (Krugman & Krugman, 1984).

Opposite strategies, motivated by a desire to escape, in the short term include truancy and simulation of illness in order to stay home from school. In the longer term, students might escape by dropping out of school or through high-risk behaviours such as alcohol and drug use and, if supported by similarly disenchanted peers, adolescent delinquency (Brendgen et al., 2006, 2007; Delfabbro et al., 2006; Piekarska, 2000). Oppositional and aggressive retaliation towards teachers is also common (Hyman, 1995; McEachern et al., 2008), but this attracts sanctions against the young person, often imposed by the teacher who is mistreating them (Piekarska, 2000).

Witnessing parental violence

Spousal abuse (or intimate partner violence) takes many forms and occurs in at least one in five families across all social classes (Gilding, 1997), affecting children's adjustment by disrupting parenting (Maughan & Cicchetti, 2002). Children's reactions to witnessing their parent being attacked can be similar to those of being abused themselves (Bogat et al., 2006), with young adolescents actually more disturbed by their parent's victimisation than by their own (Sternberg et al., 2006). When child abuse occurs together with partner violence, the children have even more extreme emotional difficulties (such as anxiety, depression and post-traumatic stress) and behavioural problems including aggression and delinquency and are slower to recover from stressful events (Cummings, 1998; Kimball, 2016; Maughan & Cicchetti, 2002; Sternberg et al., 2006).

Adolescents in violent families can have difficulty trusting adults and, in turn, their peers, and thus establishing and maintaining peer relationships; they can experience both low self-efficacy because they cannot control their parents' behaviour and low self-esteem if they blame themselves for it (Buehler et al., 2007). If the parents separate, the violence does not necessarily end, with some young people experiencing handovers as occasions for further abuse of their mothers, fear that their father will eventually kill their mother, and some even have to step in to prevent their father's suicide (Shorey & Baladram, 2023).

Survivors of natural disasters

There is a dose-related stress response in young people who have been through natural disasters such as fires, floods or cyclones. Like adults, children can experience anxiety, depression, behavioural difficulties and post-traumatic stress in response to exposure to these disasters (Terranova et al., 2015). However, objective hardship itself is not as vital as is the distress of those around them, which means that most children readjust once their families and communities regain stability.

First Nations peoples

The combined effect of colonisation and government policies (such as child removal), have contributed to intergenerational trauma within Australian and Torres Strait Islander communities (Dudgeon et al., 2014; Sisko, 2021). This form of trauma is defined as the subjective experiencing and remembering of events in the mind of an individual or the life of a community, passed from adults to children as 'collective emotional and psychological injury ... over the life span and across generations' (Muid et al., cited by Atkinson et al., 2014, p. 294). Intergenerational trauma causes the next generation to absorb some of the psychological burdens of the one that went before (St Vil & St Vil, 2019). These effects are seen in 30 per cent of Aboriginal adolescents reporting high or very high levels of emotional distress, compared with 11 per cent of non-Indigenous adolescents (Lopez-Carmen et al., 2019), with double the rate of suicide of non-Indigenous young people (ABS, 2021).

Refugees and asylum seekers

In 2022, more than 103 million individuals were forcibly displaced, nearly half of whom were under the age of 18 (UNHCR, 2022). *Refugees* have been forced to flee their country because of persecution, war or violence and have had their refugee status recognised by the United Nations High Commission for Refugees (UNHCR) whereas *asylum seekers* might have the same reasons for fleeing their countries but have not yet been recognised as refugees by the UNHCR.

There are three sets of challenges for refugees. First is their experience of atrocities, violence and persecution in their home country that caused them to flee. Unaccompanied children – who number one-third of minors (Hanes et al., 2019) – have typically experienced higher levels of traumatic events than their accompanied peers, with their journey especially hazardous and incurring additional separation, losses, bereavement, persecution and threat (Hodes & Vostanis, 2019).

Second are the privations they endure while in transit and in refugee camps in neighbouring states that themselves are in disarray and therefore ill-equipped to meet their needs (Bali, 2005; Scharpf et al., 2021; Stark et al., 2015). As a result, Hanes et al. (2019) found that most children in camps presented with socioemotional difficulties, malnutrition, Vitamin D deficiency, dental decay and skin and blood conditions.

Australia is the only country in the world to detain children compulsorily while their family's application for refugee status is being processed (Bessant, 2002). These prison-like detention centres deprive children of adequate nutrition and care, social interaction and education, and expose them to despair, intimidation, violence and abuse (Bessant, 2002). The children are under the guard of officers who have not been trained to care for children and whom the children may associate with the militia in their home country who perpetrated violence against their communities (Rayner, 2005).

Third are the circumstances once refugees settle in a host country (Bennouna et al., 2020; Bryant et al., 2021; Hodes & Vostanis, 2019; Kim et al., 2019; Scharpf et al., 2021). Recovery is quicker when resettlement stressors are low (Hodes & Vostanis, 2019). The children and their families need access to housing, education, language classes, and physical and mental health care; parental employment; financial support; and social and cultural support (Arakelyan & Ager, 2021; Bryant et al., 2021; Fazel & Betancourt, 2018; Jones, 2020; Scharpf et al., 2021).

Refugees were persecuted at home and subjected to persecution because of their identity, race, ethnicity, religion, politics or nationality (Kim et al., 2019). Subsequent exposure to racism within their host country is a major impediment to full inclusion (Babacan et al., 2021). Yet popular language used about refugees places them in a 'not us' category (Maher & Smith, 2014): They are not wealthy, not born here, not legal entrants, not genuine refugees (having allegedly jumped a non-existent queue), not native English speakers, not Christian - and, accordingly, a threat to Australian social cohesion (Babacan et al., 2021).

Leaving a place of violence and insecurity for one that is safe can enhance refugees' well-being considerably and, despite enduring multiple challenges, many display remarkable resilience (Fazel & Betancourt, 2018). Their well-being can be assisted or hindered by a range of factors: those within the individual child, family factors, the community and the political level, each of which dynamically interacts with and affects the others (Arakelyan & Ager, 2021) - as illustrated in Figure 15.1. This implies that support needs to be available at these multiple levels.

In terms of the individual, following their exodus from their homeland, as many as one-third experience prolonged grief over the loss of culture, familiar landscape, living conditions and deceased or missing loved ones (Bryant et al., 2021; Jones, 2020) while also worrying

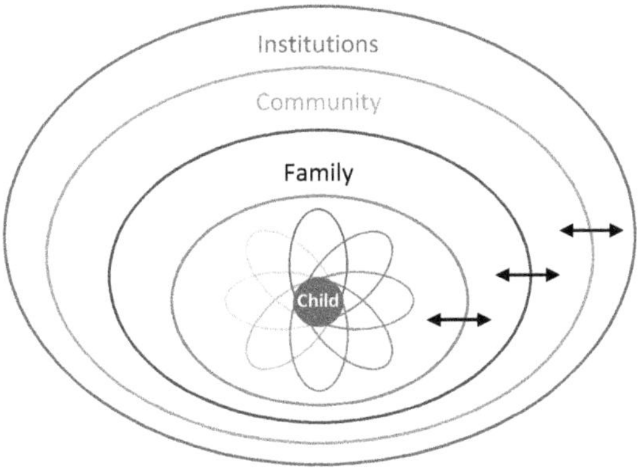

Figure 15.1 Protective factors for refugees

Source: adapted from Arakelyan & Ager (2021, p. 486).

about loved ones left behind. In a dose-related manner, exposure to violence and severe prolonged trauma can have long-term outcomes for the children in the forms of anxiety, depression, self-harm and PTSD (Arakelyan & Ager, 2021; Hodes & Vostanis, 2019; Hubbard et al., 1995; Khamis, 2019; Sourander, 1998; Thomas & Lau, n.d.). In half of cases, PTSD can persist for three years and, in one-third of cases, for 12 years (Kinzie et al., 1989; Sack et al., 1999) with, ultimately, the psychological effects potentially being lifelong (Fazel & Betancourt, 2018). Children can be responding to their parents' stress levels, while adolescents can be responding to the duration of their own victimisation and feelings of responsibility to protect their siblings (Arakelyan & Ager, 2021; Hodes & Vostanis, 2019).

In terms of family resources, children's emotional adjustment is heavily dependent on their mother's well-being and on family cohesion (Almqvist & Broberg, 1999; Green et al., 1991; Thomas & Lau, n.d.; Scharpf et al., 2021). Parents with emotional maladjustment can convey their anxiety to their children, or be overly protective of or excessively dependent on their children, thereby contributing to the children's own maladjustment (Bennouna et al., 2020; Bryant et al., 2021).

Meanwhile, in terms of their own community, because so many are affected by their traumatic histories, they are each less available to support others, with the result that everyone struggles alone (Jones, 2020). Finally, at the level of institutions, schools need the political will to identify and plug service gaps and to cater for children's learning disabilities, which can result from interrupted education or emotional difficulties (Rousseau & Gagnon, 2020).

Mechanisms for neurobiological effects of trauma

The brain is the only organ of the body that is not fully developed at birth and continues to undergo important structural changes until early adulthood. This means that trauma at any stage during the developmental period can lead to both structural and functional changes to the brain (Cabrera et al., 2020; Delima & Vimpani, 2011).

The nervous and endocrine (hormonal) systems act together to coordinate the function of all bodily systems. The key regulators of the system are the hypothalamus and pituitary glands in the brain, which serve as the link between the endocrine and nervous systems. Taking the endocrine system first, many hormones function as part of a cascade, targeting the tissue of another endocrine gland (Hinson et al., 2010). This functional grouping is called an axis – for example, the hypothalamo-pituitary-adrenal axis (HPA axis) – see Figure 15.2.

In response to stress, the hypothalamus sends hormones to the pituitary gland which, in turn, signals to the adrenal glands to produce adrenaline and cortisol. These are released into the bloodstream to produce a surge of energy for muscles to allow flight from stressors. After the threat has passed, feedback loops allow the system to return to balance. However, in individuals with constant exposure to stress, there is a failure in this feedback loop, such that the HPA axis remains activated (McCrory et al., 2011). An opposite pattern is also possible, wherein individuals who have endured chronic stress become hyporeactive, with exhausted adrenal glands producing insufficient cortisol, one result being that they are less sensitive to threat and, therefore, will take more risks (Carpenter et al., 2007, 2011).

Hormones are transported in the blood stream and therefore can deliver their messages throughout the body (Hinson et al., 2010). This means that symptoms of stress can occur

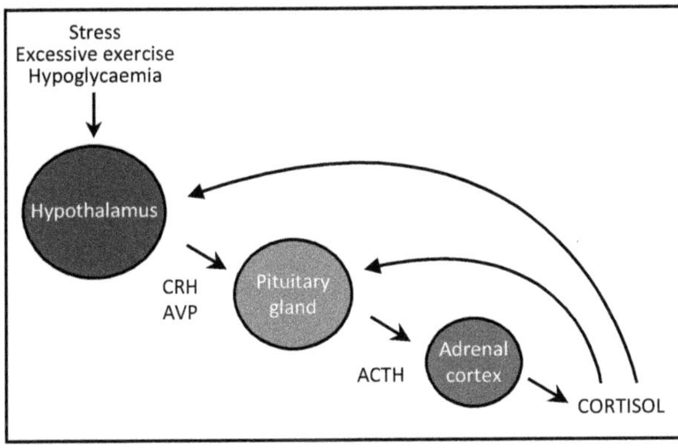

Figure 15.2 The HPA axis

throughout the metabolic and immune systems (Delima & Vimpani, 2011; Tyrka et al., 2013). Meanwhile, the presence of corticosteroids (principally cortisol) will impair learning, concentration and memory as the brain instead is in fight-flight mode (Cabrera et al., 2020; De Bellis, 2001; Wilson et al., 2011).

In contrast, the nervous system communicates electrically, resulting in fast and targeted messaging (Cabrera et al., 2020). As illustrated in Figure 15.3, it comprises the central and autonomic nervous systems, the latter controlling automatic functions of the body such as breathing and digestion. Its subsection, the sympathetic nervous system, governs our activation, while the parasympathetic governs calming.

Together, both chronic activation of the sympathetic nervous system and long-term production of cortisol are toxic to the brain and body. A history of early-life stress increases individuals' risk for several medical conditions, including asthma, cardiovascular disease, diabetes, fibromyalgia (a post-traumatic pain syndrome), chronic fatigue (post-viral) syndrome, premature ageing and metabolic syndrome (comprising central obesity, high cholesterol levels, increases in blood pressure and insulin resistance) (Cameranesi et al., 2022; Clemens et al., 2018; Nemeroff, 2016; Tyrka et al., 2013).

As well as affecting brain function, stress also alters brain structures. Neuroimaging findings indicate that childhood maltreatment inhibits cell growth in the frontal brain regions that

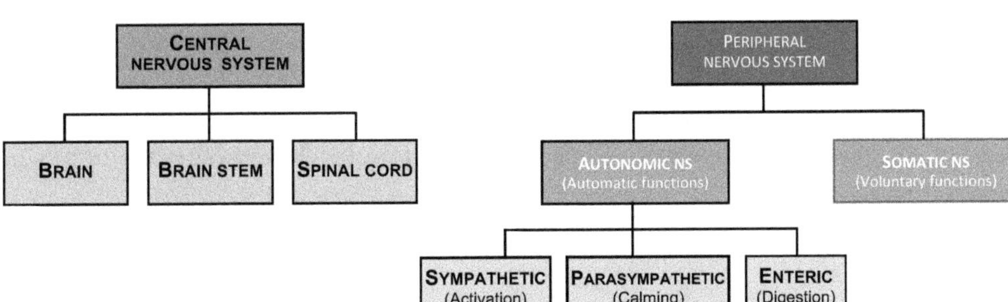

Figure 15.3 The branches of the nervous system

are necessary for the regulation of emotions and impulses (Delima & Vimpani, 2011; Rodman et al., 2019; Teicher & Samson, 2016; Tyrka et al., 2013). This could account for stressed children's difficulties with acquiring self-regulation skills (Tremblay et al., 1995).

Post-traumatic growth

Steger and Park (2012, p. 176) note that 60 to 70 per cent of individuals experience at least one trauma in their lifetimes, yet just 6.8 per cent develop post-traumatic stress disorder. The remainder manage to 'bounce back' – that is, to be resilient and might even grow from the experience. Growth refers to positive changes in individuals from their struggle to cope in the aftermath of a traumatic event (Tedeschi & Calhoun, 2004). Even though survivors feel an increased sense of vulnerability and psychological distress after a trauma, many also experience improved relationships, new possibilities for life, a greater appreciation of life, a greater sense of personal strength and resilience, and spiritual development, in the sense of having 'a more fully developed, satisfying and meaningful' philosophy of life (Tedeschi & Calhoun, 2004, p. 407). They discover friends they did not know they had, and they experience a greater sense of compassion towards others.

To achieve such growth, trauma survivors first need social support for their disclosures about the trauma; otherwise, silence forces shame underground and their experience becomes a personal problem rather than a social need for acceptance and connection with others (Brown, 2007). Second, they need to cognitively process the event so that they can make sense of it and of its significance for their world view (Tedeschi & Calhoun, 2004); third, they need to problem solve so that they can act on their choices; and last, they need self-efficacy – that is, the self-belief that they can put those choices into action (Brown, 2007).

Principles of trauma-informed practice

Four fundamental domains are disrupted by stress or trauma, signified by the acronym SELF: *safety*, regulation of *emotions*, grieving over *loss*, and envisioning a *future* (Levenson et al., 2021). Accordingly, because traumatised clients will have felt unsafe during the traumatic experiences and in their aftermath, we need to promote their safety; counsellors need to establish trust because their victimisation has meant that clients have been betrayed; clients need choices because they had no control over the traumas they experienced; and we need to recognise young people's resilience, highlight their strengths and foster their agency or self-efficacy (Kezelman & Stavropolous, 2020). Finally, interventions must engage both young people and their parents (or other caregivers) in service planning and provision (Chipalo, 2021; Hodes & Vostanis, 2019; Weiner et al., 2009). These qualities cannot be confined to the counselling relationship alone but must permeate all elements of the culture of organisations such as schools (Butler & Critelli, 2019).

Interventions

With young trauma survivors, trauma-focused cognitive-behavioural methods (TF-CBT) reduce PTSD symptoms more than pure CBT (Bastien et al., 2020; Xiang et al., 2021) and are sustained after treatment ceases (Mannarino et al., 2012). (For an excellent description of this approach, see Runyon et al., 2019.) However, one study found it less effective with children with more severe PTSD (Mannarino et al., 2012); another found that TF-CBT was no more effective than the waiting list (Bastien et al., 2020); and others found that pure CBT was no more effective than other forms of counselling (Xiang et al., 2021). Furthermore, cognitive methods will need significant modification for preschool-aged children and might not be as useful for them compared to adolescents (Lee & Brown, 2022; McGuire et al., 2021; Xiang et al., 2021). Meanwhile, the duration of treatment - commonly from 12 to 28 weeks - (Chipalo, 2021) could be prohibitive.

Solution-focused approaches

As an alternative to these orthodox treatments, Berg and Steiner (2003) start with three core assumptions: First, that, no matter how badly they have been treated, traumatised children still have areas where they function well; second, we should begin by talking about these areas first; and, third, we should ask children for their ideas about how they want their life circumstances to be better. It is important, these authors say, not to see maltreated children as damaged, fragile or helpless victims because this will cause us to try to rescue and take over their care. Despite the seriousness of their problems, we need to convey that in many ways they are like other children - and are capable of achieving their preferred future (Zatloukal & Furman, 2022).

Reframing

Sometimes, young people who have been traumatised display this in behaviours that are considered 'misbehavior', 'inappropriate', 'challenging' or 'disruptive'. The implication is that they need to act more responsibly. However, on occasion I have reframed this as their experience with adversity has caused them to grow up too quickly. They watch over their parents or siblings, or keep family secrets. All this responsibility has put too much on their plate, leaving no energy for growing up. So my reframe is that they will have to grow down, before they can grow up. We then look at which responsibilities they can relinquish, so that they have the energy needed to shape their own lives.

A profound reframe is that the intensity of their pain about their trauma is a testament to the determination with which survivors have held onto what was precious to them (White, 2004, 2016). It reflects their refusal to relinquish their prized purposes, beliefs and values, their aspirations, moral visions of how things should be in the world and their commitments to how they choose to live their life (White, 2016). They will not let the matter drop and remain on guard against those who would dismiss their experience (White, 2016).

Narrative therapy

Michael White (2016) argues that individuals who have been traumatised are in no fit shape to re-experience or process the trauma itself because doing so would simply reinforce the negative conclusions that they have drawn about themselves. It would escalate their shame, vulnerability, hopelessness, desolation and sense of futility. Instead, we need to 'reposition their territory of identity' - that is, redefine their identity via highlighting their knowledges and skills. Only from this strong place will they be able to talk about and process their trauma.

Madigan (2019) asserts that many individuals who have been maltreated during childhood have often not so much lost their identity as never been able to develop it. Their traumatic experiences violated, disqualified or disrespected what mattered to and defined them (White, 2004, 2016). Accordingly, it will be important to discover their accomplishments despite what they have endured.

Deconstruction

The first step with traumatised young people is to use narrative conversations to deconstruct the power-over tactics that they suffered under threat from someone more powerful than them and review the context of imbalanced gender relations (Madigan, 2019). Some questions might include (White, 2016, p. 171):

- At what point did you first become conscious of the fact that what you were being put through was not okay?
- What does this say about your position on justice and injustice?

Finding exceptions

Trauma survivors are viewed - and see themselves - as 'messed up', 'damaged' or 'ruined for life'. This victimhood deprives them of a sense of agency and increases their reliance on health professionals (Yuen, 2007). To counter this and instead construct an identity based on their strengths, narrative conversations help young people to identify how they have responded to their traumatic experiences. Yuen (2007) asks:

> 'What did you do when you were scared? ... How did you show or not show it on your face when you were scared? ... Even though you could not stop the abuse, how did you try to protect yourself or others? ... Where did you hide? ... How did you comfort yourself and your siblings? ... How did they comfort you?'.

Then she asks what the children did to lessen the effects: 'Afterwards, how did you help yourself feel better?' The next set of questions is about their practical skills for living: 'Did you use imagining skills? ... How did you manage to focus on keeping warm?'.

Next, she asks about acts of resistance: 'What did you do to resist or oppose the abuse?' Finally, she asks about significant helpers: 'Did you have a friend, pet or stuffed toy that helped you get through? ... How did they comfort you?'.

These skills are used to construct a narrative about identity so that young people's skills (not their victimhood) begin to define them. Yuen (2007) asks, 'How did you know to do that? ... What name would you give this skill? ... What do you think of your younger self for being able to use these clever strategies? ... What would others think of you at that age? ... How do you feel about this skill that you have?'.

Highlighting strengths

Next, White (2016, p. 146) and Yuen (2007, p. 15) ask:

- Can you tell me some stories of your life that reflect these learnings about getting through things that are difficult?
- What is a good name for this capacity to hold onto goals that are important to you?
- Why is that skill important to you?
- When did this skill first become important in your life?
- Who wouldn't be surprised that you value (...)?
- What do you think this says about the kind of person you are?
- What does this say about what you want for your life?

White's (2016) list of how individuals respond to traumatic experiences is extensive. He notes that survivors have acted to preserve life when it was under threat; find support in hostile environments; establish domains of safety in unsafe places; hold onto possibilities for life in contexts that discount these; nurture others in circumstances that degrade care; find connections in settings that are isolating; refuse to visit trauma onto others; heal in conditions that are unfavourable to this; achieve self-acceptance in conditions that are rejecting (White, 2016, p. 132). They have also mourned when bitterness and anger would be both righteous and understandable. Even symptoms such as becoming invisible, remaining silent, or having a relationship with anger or drugs are efforts to survive an abusive context (Madigan, 2019). By talking about these modes of responding to adversity, young people can experience being at one with positive conclusions about their identity (White, 2016). Their skills are evidence that adults do not need to teach them 'coping skills' but instead build their extraordinary resilience into a story about their identity.

Re-membering

Because children often construct these resilient responses in collaboration with others, there are opportunities to repopulate their social networks and reconnect their stories with the lives of others, through letters to or honouring ceremonies of those who helped them in the past (White, 2016). White (2016, p. 104) asks:

- What do you think your teacher/neighbour/aunt noticed about you that (the abusing adult) was blind to?
- What is it about you that told your (neighbour) this?
- What did this (teacher) know about you that you can know about yourself?

Connectedness to school and a good friendship network are also protective against adversity (Farineau et al., 2013; Scharpf et al., 2021), as is maintaining cultural links and involvement in a religion (Fazel & Betancourt, 2018), perhaps because of the social support or because it allows them to extract meaning from their experiences (Bennouna et al., 2020). Therefore, interventions can focus on ways to build stable social networks and friendships around distressed young people.

Definitional ceremonies

Definitional ceremonies provide people with the opportunity to tell the stories of their lives to an audience of witnesses (White, 2004, 2007). The aim is to make visible to clients the change in their definition of themselves - that is, their identity (White, 2007). This is especially vital when childhood abuse or other trauma prevented them from developing their own identity apart from their victimhood.

For these ceremonies, counsellors invite an audience of former clients who have insider experience of a similar problem (such as being bullied) and who have volunteered for the audience role. In part one, they listen as clients describe their predicament and their responses to it. In part two, the counsellor interviews the witnesses, whose job is not to empathise or give opinions but to reflect to the counsellor (in the child's hearing) four key aspects of the client's story (Denborough, 2014; White, 2004):

- what they heard that captured their attention
- what metaphors this evoked for them and what these suggested to them about who the client is as a person and what is important to them
- what struck a chord with them and their own experience, and
- what they were experiencing as a result of being a witness to the clients' story.

The purpose is not for applause, evaluation or interpretation, but to represent what clients give value to (White, 2007). This allows the values that the client stands for to be more visible and richly known. In part three, clients then outline how the witnesses' reflections have affected them.

Lenz and colleagues (2012) introduce a slight variation by having as witnesses insiders whom the client nominates. The session begins (accompanied by balloons or other celebratory paraphernalia) with clients talking about the transformation that has occurred for them during counselling. Next, the witnesses reflect on how the story resonates with them; third, clients reflect on how they experience the witnesses' testimonies. Counsellors then present clients with a certificate of achievement to commemorate the event.

A variant on this is *insider witness ceremonies*, where the counsellor and their supervisor record a session in which they talk about the client's values and identity shifts (Carlson & Epston, 2017). Shortly afterwards, the counsellor plays the recording to the client, with pauses for processing time and for clients to give their reactions to what they have heard being said about them. In this way, clients can take custody of 'the regard of another' (Carlson & Epston, 2017, p. 19).

Academic remediation

Disadvantaged students and those with a disrupted education will frequently have delays in reading, which leads to progressive declines in their academic attainment (McGee et al., 2002; Spira & Fischel, 2005). This is because, in the junior primary years, children are learning to read, whereas thereafter they are reading to learn. Therefore, if they cannot read proficiently by middle primary school, they have a distinct risk of failing across all subject areas. In turn, academic failure in itself has a negative effect on traumatised children's long-term emotional well-being, over and above the effects of the adversity they have experienced (Forsman et al., 2016).

You can advocate, therefore, for these students to receive remedial tutoring, preferably at school - because private tutoring will be beyond the budget of impoverished families. For those with attention deficits in particular, this tutoring will need to be sustained for at least two academic years (Volpe et al., 2009). Improvements in students' reading skills have been found to improve their social skills as well (Rutherford et al., 2008), perhaps because they feel more efficacious in general or because peers no longer define them as less worthy.

Validate

I have explained to young abused children that, sometimes, some people forget to be kind to children. Having already spoken with and gained a commitment from the adult with whom I am consulting, I then promise them that their teacher, foster parent or other caregiver will *never* forget to be kind to them. This validates their feelings of having been mistreated and secures them a sense of safety, without denigrating their abuser whom, if a member of their family, they will love.

Resilience

As detailed in Chapter 11, recovery requires attending to health needs: the basics of diet, exercise and sleep, and management of PTSD symptoms through the likes of breathing exercises and mindfulness. This last is vital for survivors of trauma because their hypervigilance makes it difficult for them to focus on anything other than threats (McLean & Follette, 2016). However, meditation as part of a mindfulness intervention can have negative effects for one-third to one-half of those practising it, including an increase in depression or anxiety, dysregulated arousal and dissociation (Britton et al., 2021). The conclusion has to be that meditation is not suitable for everyone.

Grounding techniques are aimed at helping those experiencing agitation to reconnect through all five senses with their body and with the present moment and place (Sanderson, 2010). They can be useful during counselling sessions if clients experience episodes of distress or dissociation (Briere & Scott, 2015; Harris, 2006). We can orient clients to the immediate, external environment by reminding them that they are with us in the room right now (not in the past traumatic circumstances). Among other measures, we might ask them to notice one thing they feel (such as their weight in their chair), one thing they can hear and one that they can see.

Forgiveness

When our needs have not been met during a childhood of adversity, the appropriate response is to mourn (Rosenberg, 2003). The alternative emotions of feeling anger or seeking revenge are righteous in the sense that it is right to feel distressed about being betrayed. However, survivors' anger is best honoured by channeling it into determining how their needs can be met in future.

Next, there needs to be a public condemnation of perpetrators' wrongdoing (if only through definitional ceremonies within narrative therapy). Third, clients might choose to forgive. However, a desire to forgive is the prerogative of victims, and cannot be preached or imposed (Mani, 2005; Robertson, 2006). Forgiveness can take any of three forms (Bennett, 2003).

- *Retributive* forgiveness, which victims offer only to those perpetrators who admit their wrongdoing and who submit to punishment for it.
- *Reparative* forgiveness, where victims forgive perpetrators who attempt to make amends.
- *Restorative* or altruistic forgiveness, when we forgive voluntarily as a gift, regardless of whether perpetrators have 'earned' this by their remorse.

Forgiveness does not expect us to deny, stifle or repress our feelings, and it does not excuse or condone the wrong that we have suffered. Instead it guides us to transform our anger into grief which, while still intense and painful, is more authentic and - potentially - more constructive (Rosenberg, 2003). To that end, Seligman (2002, pp. 79-81) details a five-step process for forgiveness, guided by the acronym REACH:

R	*Recall* the hurt, as objectively as possible. Take slow, calming breaths and visualise or recount the events.
E	*Empathise* with your own grief at your unmet needs. Mourn. In this way, the expression, 'I feel ... because I need' can replace the accusation, 'I am angry because you ...'.
A	*Altruistically forgive*, not because perpetrators 'deserve' forgiveness because of their remorse or attempts at making amends, but in recognition that we cannot hurt perpetrators by refusing to forgive them, whereas we can hurt ourselves by holding onto bitterness. Remaining embittered is like cutting ourselves and hoping that someone else bleeds.
C	*Commit* yourself publicly to forgive. Write in your diary (journal), write a forgiving letter to the perpetrator (but *do not send it*), or tell a trusted friend what you have done.
H	*Hold* onto forgiveness. Forgiveness cannot and should not erase the memory of past wrongs, but it will change the meaning of the trauma in your life now. You will not have to dwell vengefully on the past, but instead can neutralise the effects of those memories on you now. Perhaps you can periodically re-read your documents to remind yourself that you have forgiven.

Conclusion

In this chapter, of necessity I have spoken about various types of stressors as if they are separate. However, many individuals endure intersecting traumatic experiences, such as poverty plus First Nation status; poverty accompanied by parental drug abuse; or the infliction of multiple forms of childhood maltreatment, for example. Nevertheless, a narrative approach aims to ensure that victimisation does not become the dominant element of survivors' identity.

References

Afifi, T. O., Brownridge, D. A., Cox, B. J., & Sareen, J. (2006). Physical punishment, childhood abuse and psychiatric disorders. *Child Abuse and Neglect*, *30*(10), 1093-1103. https://doi.org/10.1016/j.chiabu.2006.04.006

Almqvist, K., & Broberg, A. G. (1999). Mental health and social adjustment in young refugee children 3 ½ years after their arrival in Sweden. *Journal of the American Academy of Child and Adolescent Psychiatry*, *38*(6), 723-730. https://doi.org/10.1097/00004583-199906000-00020

Anda, R. F., Felitti, V. J., Bremner, J. D., Walker, J. D., Whitfield, C., Perry, B. D., Dube, S. R., & Giles, W. H. (2006). The enduring effects of abuse and related adverse experiences in childhood: A convergence of evidence from neurobiology and epidemiology. *European Archives of Psychiatry and Clinical Neuroscience*, *256*(3), 174–186. https://doi.org/10.1007/s00406-005-0624-4

Arakelyan, S., & Ager, A. (2021). Annual research review: A multilevel bioecological analysis of factors influencing the mental health and psychosocial well-being of refugee children. *Journal of Child Psychology and Psychiatry*, *62*(5), 484–509. https://doi.org/10.1111/jcpp.13355

Atkinson, J., Nelson, J., Brooks, R., Atkinson, C., & Ryan, K. (2014). Addressing individual and community transgenerational trauma. In P. Dudgeon, H. Milroy & R. Walker (Eds.), *Working together: Aboriginal and Torres Strait Islander mental health and wellbeing principles and practice* (pp. 289–306). Commonwealth of Australia.

Australian Bureau of Statistics. (2021). *Causes of Death, Australia*. ABS. https://www.abs.gov.au/statistics/health/causes-death/causes-death-australia/latest-release

Australian Institute of Health and Welfare. (2020). *Australia's children*. AIHW.

Babacan, A., Jacobs, R., Kemp, A., Paradies, Y., Piyarathne, A., Wang, C., Zwi, K., Woodland, L., & Hutton, V. (2021). Racism. In V. Hutton & S. Sisko (Eds.), *Multicultural responsiveness in counselling and psychology: Working with Australian populations* (pp. 53–102). Springer. https://doi.org/10.1007/978-3-030-55427-9_3

Bali, S. (2005). Migration and refugees. In B. White, R. Little & M. Smith (Eds.), *Issues in world politics* (3rd ed., pp. 173–193). Palgrave Macmillan.

Bastien, R. J. B., Jongsma, H. E., Kabadayi, M., & Billings, J. (2020). The effectiveness of psychological interventions for post-traumatic stress disorder in children, adolescents and young adults: A systematic review and meta-analysis. *Psychological Medicine*, *50*(10), 1598–1612. https://doi.org/10.1111/jcpp.13094

Bennett, C. (2003). Is amnesty a collective act of forgiveness? *Contemporary Political Review*, *2*(1), 67–76. https://doi.org/10.1057/palgrave.cpt.9300072

Bennouna, C., Stark, L., & Wessells, M. G. (2020). Children and adolescents in conflict and displacement. In J. S. Song & P. Vindevogel (Eds.), *Child, adolescent and family refugee mental health: A global perspective* (pp. 17–36). Springer.

Berg, I. K., & Steiner, S. (2003). *Children's solution work*. Norton.

Bessant, J. (2002). Australia's child asylum seeker. *Alternative Law Journal*, *27*(4), 165–170. https://doi.org/10.1177/1037969X0202700403

Bogat, G. A., DeJonghe, E., Levendosky, A. A., Davidson, W. S., & von Eye, A. (2006). Trauma symptoms among infants exposed to intimate partner violence. *Child Abuse and Neglect*, *30*(2), 109–125. https://doi.org/10.1016/j.chiabu.2005.09.002

Brendgen, M., Wanner, B., & Vitaro, F. (2006). Verbal abuse by the teacher and child adjustment from kindergarten through grade 6. *Pediatrics*, *117*(5), 1585–1598. https://doi.org/10.1542/peds.2005-2050

Brendgen, M., Wanner, B., Vitaro, F., Bukowski, W. M., & Tremblay, R. E. (2007). Verbal abuse by the teacher during childhood and academic, behavioral, and emotional adjustment in young adulthood. *Journal of Educational Psychology*, *99*(1), 26–38. https://doi.org/10.1037/0022-0663.99.1.26

Briere, J. N., & Scott, C. (2015). *Principles of trauma therapy: A guide to symptoms, evaluation, and treatment* (2nd ed.). Sage.

Briggs, F., & McVeity, M. (2000). *Teaching children to protect themselves*. Allen and Unwin.

Britton, W. B., Lindahl, J. R., Cooper, D. J., Canby, N. K., & Palitsky, R. (2021). Defining and measuring meditation-related adverse effects in mindfulness-based programs. *Clinical Psychological Science*, 9(6), 1185–1204. https://doi.org/10.1177/2167702621996340

Bromberg, D. S., & Johnson, B. T. (2001). Sexual interest in children, child sexual abuse, and psychological sequelae for children. *Psychology in the Schools*, *38*(4), 343–355. https://doi.org/10.1002/pits.1023

Brown, B. (2007). *I thought it was just me (but it isn't)*. Gotham.

Bryant, R. A., Edwards, B., Creamer, M., O'Donnell, M., Forbes, D., Felmingham, K. L., & Hadzi-Pavlovic, D. (2021). Prolonged grief in refugees, parenting behaviour and children's mental health. *Australian and New Zealand Journal of Psychiatry*, 55(9), 863–873. https://doi.org/10.1177/0004867420967420

Buehler, C., Lange, G., & Franck, K. L. (2007). Adolescents' cognitive and emotional responses to marital hostility. *Child Development*, *78*(3), 775–789. https://doi.org/10.1111/j.1467-8624.2007.01032.x

Butler, L. D., & Critelli, F. M. (2019). Traumatic experience, human rights violations, and their intersection. In L. D. Butler, F. M. Critelli & J. Carello (Eds.), *Trauma and human rights: Integrating approaches to address human suffering* (pp. 11–53). Springer.
Cabrera, C., Torres, H., & Harcourt, S. (2020). The neurological and neuropsychological effects of child maltreatment. *Aggression and Violent Behavior*, *54*, 101408. https://doi.org/10.1016/j.avb.2020.101408
Cameranesi, M., Shooshtari, S., & Piotrowski, C. C. (2022). Investigating adjustment profiles in children exposed to intimate partner violence using a biopsychosocial resilience framework: A Canadian population-based study. *Child Abuse and Neglect*, *125*, 105453. https://doi.org/10.1016/j.chiabu.2021.105453
Carlson, T. S., & Epston, D. (2017). Insider witnessing practice: Performing hope and beauty in narrative therapy: Part two. *Journal of Narrative Family Therapy*, *1*(19), 39.
Carpenter L. L., Carvalho J. P., Tyrka A. R., Wier L. M., Mello A. F., Mello M. F., Anderson G. M., Wilkinson C. W., & Price L. H. (2007). Decreased adrenocorticotropic hormone and cortisol responses to stress in healthy adults reporting significant childhood maltreatment. *Biological Psychiatry*, *62*(10), 1080–1108. https://doi.org/10.1016/j.biopsych.2007.05.002
Carpenter, L.L., Shattuck, T. T., Tyrka, A. R., Geracioti, T. D., & Price, L. H. (2011). Effect of childhood physical abuse on cortisol stress response. *Psychopharmacology*, *214*, 367–375. https://doi.10.1007/s00213-010-2007-4
Chipalo, E. (2021). Is trauma focused-cognitive behavioral therapy (TF-CBT) effective in reducing trauma symptoms among traumatized refugee children? A systematic review. *Journal of Child and Adolescent Trauma*, *14*(4), 545–558. https://doi.org/10.1007/s40653-021-00370-0
Clemens, V., Huber-Lang, M., Plener, P. L., Brähler, E., Brown, R. C., & Fegert, J. M. (2018). Association of child maltreatment subtypes and long-term physical health in a German representative sample. *European Journal of Psychotraumatology*, *9*. https://doi.org/10.1080/20008198.2018.1510278
Cummings, E. M. (1998). Stress and coping approaches and research: The impact of marital conflict on children. In B. B. R. Rossman, & M. S. Rosenberg (Eds.), *Multiple victimization of children: Conceptual, developmental, research, and treatment issues* (pp. 31–50). Haworth Press.
De Bellis, M. D. (2001). Developmental traumatology: The psychobiological development of maltreated children and its implications for research, treatment, and policy. *Development and Psychopathology*, *13*, 539–564. https://doi.org/10.1017/S0954579401003078
De Bellis, M. D., Hooper, S. R., Chen, S. D., Provenzale, J. M., Boyd, B. D., Glessner, C. E., & Woolley, D. P. (2015). Posterior structural brain volumes differ in maltreated youth with and without chronic post-traumatic stress disorder. *Development and Psychopathology*, *27*(4 pt 2), 1555–1576. https://doi.org/10.1017/S0954579415000942
Delfabbro, P., Winefield, T., Trainor, S., Dollard, M., Anderson, S., Metzer, J., & Hammarstrom, A. (2006). Peer and teacher bullying/victimization of South Australian secondary students: Prevalence and psychosocial profiles. *British Journal of Educational Psychology*, *76*(1), 71–90. https://doi.org/10.1348/000709904X24645
Delima, J., & Vimpani, G. (2011). The neurobiological effects of childhood maltreatment: An often overlooked narrative related to the effects of early childhood trauma? *Family Matters*, *11*, 42–52.
Denborough, D. (2014). *Retelling the stories of our lives: Everyday narrative therapy to draw inspiration and transform experience*. Norton.
Dudgeon, P., Wright, M., Paradies, Y., Garvey, D., & Walker, I. (2014). Aboriginal social, cultural and historical contexts. In P. Dudgeon, H. Milroy & R. Walker (Eds.), *Working together: Aboriginal and Torres Strait Islander mental health and wellbeing principles and practices* (2nd ed., pp. 3–24). Commonwealth of Australia.
Dyregrov, A., & Yule, W. (2006). A review of PTSD in children. *Child and Adolescent Mental Health*, *11*(4), 176–184. https://doi.org/10.1111/j.1475-3588.2005.00384.x
Farineau, H. M., Stevenson Wojciak, A., & McWey, L. M. (2013). You matter to me: Important relationships and self-esteem of adolescents in foster care. *Child and Family Social Work*, *18*(2), 129–138. https://doi.org/10.1111/j.1365-2206.2011.00808.x
Fazel, M., & Betancourt, T. S. (2018). Preventive mental health interventions for refugee children and adolescents in high-income settings. *The Lancet Child and Adolescent Health*, *2*(2), 121–132. https://doi.org/10.1016/S2352-4642(17)30147-5
Forsman, H., Brännström, L., Vinnerljung, B., & Hjern, A. (2016). Does poor school performance cause later psychosocial problems among children in foster care? Evidence from national longitudinal registry data. *Child Abuse and Neglect*, *57*, 61-71. https://doi.org/10.1016/j.chiabu.2016.06.006

George, C., & Main, M. (1979). Social interactions of young abused children: Approach, avoidance, and aggression. *Child Development*, *50*(2), 306–318. https://doi.org/10.2307/1129405

Gilding, M. (1997). *Australian families: A comparative perspective*. Longman.

Green, B. L., Korol, M., Grace, M. C., Vary, M. G., Leonard, A. C., Gleser, G. C., & Smitson-Cohen, S. (1991). Children and disaster: Age, gender, and parental effects on PTSD symptoms. *Journal of the American Academy of Child and Adolescent Psychiatry*, *30*(6), 945–951. https://doi.org/10.1097/00004583-19911 1000-00012

Hanes, G., Chee, J., Mutch, R., & Cherian, S. (2019). Paediatric asylum seekers in Western Australia: Identification of adversity and complex needs through comprehensive refugee health assessment. *Journal of Paediatrics and Child Health*, *55*(11), 1367–1373. https://doi.org/10.1111/jpc.14425

Harris, R. (2006). Embracing your demons: An overview of acceptance and commitment therapy. *Psychotherapy in Australia*, *12*(4), 70–76.

Haynes-Seman, C., & Baumgarten, D. (1998). The victimization of young children. In B. B. R. Rossman & M. S. Rosenberg (Eds.), *Multiple victimization of children: Conceptual, developmental, research, and treatment issues* (pp. 67–86). Haworth Press.

Herrenkohl, T. I., & Herrenkohl, R. C. (2007). Examining the overlap and prediction of multiple forms of child maltreatment, stressors, and socioeconomic status: A longitudinal analysis of youth outcomes. *Journal of Family Violence*, *22*, 553–562. https://doi.org/10.1007/s10896-007-9107-x

Hinson, J., Raven, P., & Chew, S. (2010). *The endocrine system* (2nd ed.). Churchill Livingstone Elsevier.

Hodes, M., & Vostanis, P. (2019). Practitioner review: Mental health problems of refugee children and adolescents and their management. *Journal of Child Psychology and Psychiatry*, *60*(7), 716–731. https://doi.org/10.1111/jcpp.13002

Hubbard, J., Realmuto, G. M., Northwood, A. K., & Masten, A. S. (1995). Comorbidity of psychiatric diagnoses with posttraumatic stress disorder in survivors of childhood trauma. *Journal of the American Academy of Child and Adolescent Psychiatry*, *34*(9), 1167–1173. https://doi.org/10.1097/00004583-19950 9000-00014

Hyman, I. A. (1995). Corporal punishment, psychological maltreatment, violence, and punitiveness in America: Research, advocacy, and public policy. *Applied and Preventive Psychology*, *4*(2), 113–130. https://doi.org/10.1016/S0962-1849(05)80084-8

Hyman, I. A., & Perone, D. C. (1998). The other side of school violence: Educator policies and practices that may contribute to student misbehavior. *Journal of School Psychology*, *36*(1), 7–27. https://doi.org/10.1016/S0022-4405(97)87007-0

Jones, L. (2020). Grief and loss in displaced and refugee families. In J. S. Song & P. Vindevogel (Eds.), *Child, adolescent and family refugee mental health: A global perspective* (pp. 123–149). Springer.

Kaufman, J., & Charney, D. (2001). Effects of early stress on brain structure and function: Implications for understanding the relationship between child maltreatment and depression. *Development and Psychopathology*, *13*(3), 451–471. https://doi.org/10.1017/S0954579401003030

Kezelman, C., & Stavropolous, P. (2020). *Organisational guidelines for trauma-informed service delivery*. Blue Knot Foundation. https://www.blueknot.org.au/Resources/Publications/Practice-Guidelines/Organisational-Guidelines

Khamis, V. (2019). Posttraumatic stress disorder and emotion dysregulation among Syrian refugee children and adolescents resettled in Lebanon and Jordan. *Child Abuse and Neglect*, *89*, 29–39. https://doi.org/10.1016/j.chiabu.2018.12.013

Khoury, J. E., Tanaka, M., Kimber, M., MacMillan, H. L., Afifi, T. O., ...Gonzalez, A. (2022). Examining the unique contributions of parental and youth maltreatment in association with youth mental health problems. *Child Abuse and Neglect*, *124*. https://doi.org/10.1016/j.chiabu.2021.105451

Kim, I., Berthold, S. M., & Critelli, F. M. (2019). Refugees and asylum seekers. In L. D. Butler, F. M. Critelli & J. Carello (Eds.), *Trauma and human rights: Integrating approaches to address human suffering* (pp. 221–240). Palgrave Macmillan. https://doi.org/10.1007/978-3-030-16395-2

Kim, J., & Cicchetti, D. (2006). Longitudinal trajectories of self-system processes and depressive symptoms among maltreated and nonmaltreated children. *Child Development*, *77*(3), 624–639. https://doi.org/10.1111/j.1467-8624.2006.00894.x

Kimball, E. (2016). Edleson revisited: Reviewing children's witnessing of domestic violence 15 years later. *Journal of Family Violence*, *31*, 625–637. https://doi.org/10.1007/s10896-015-9786-7

Kinzie, J. D., Sack, W., Angell, R., Clarke, G., & Ben, R. (1989). A three-year follow-up of Cambodian young people traumatized as children. *Journal of the American Academy of Child and Adolescent Psychiatry*, *28*(4), 501–504. https://doi.org/10.1097/00004583-198907000-00006

Krugman, R. D., & Krugman, M. K. (1984). Emotional abuse in the classroom: The pediatrician's role in diagnosis and treatment. *American Journal of Diseases of Children*, *138*(3), 284–286. https://doi.org/10.1001/archpedi.1984.02140410062019

Lee, A. H., & Brown, E. (2022). Examining the effectiveness of trauma-focused cognitive behavioral therapy on children and adolescents' executive function. *Child Abuse and Neglect*, *126*, 105516. https://doi.org/10.1016/j.chiabu.2022.105516

Lenz, A. S., Zamarripa, M. X., & Fuentes, S. (2012). A narrative approach to terminating therapy. *Journal of Professional Counseling: Practice, Theory and Research*, *39*(2), 2–13. https://doi.org/10.1080/15566382.2012.12033883

Levenson, J. S., Craig, S. L., & Austin, A. (2021). Trauma-informed and affirmative mental health practices with LGBTQ+ clients. *Psychological Services*, *20*(S1), 134–144. https://doi.org/10.1037/ser0000540

Lopez-Carmen, V., McCalman, J., Benveniste, T., Askew, D., Spurling, G., Langham, E., & Bainbridge, R. (2019). Working together to improve the mental health of indigenous children: A systematic review. *Children and Youth Services Review*, *104*, 104408. https://doi.org/10.1016/j.childyouth.2019.104408

Madigan, S. (2019). *Narrative therapy* (2nd ed.). American Psychological Association.

Maher, M., & Smith, S. (2014). Asylum seeker and refugee children belonging, being and becoming: The early childhood educator's role. *Australasian Journal of Early Childhood*, *39*(1), 22–29. https://doi.org/10.1177/183693911403900104

Mani, R. (2005). Rebuilding an inclusive political community after war. *Security Dialogue*, *36*(4), 511–526. https://doi.org/10.1177/0967010605060452

Mannarino, A. P., Cohen, J. A., Deblinger, E., Runyon, M. K., & Steer, R. A. (2012). Trauma-focused cognitive-behavioral therapy for children: sustained impact of treatment 6 and 12 months later. *Child Maltreatment*, *17*(3), 231–241. https://doi.org/10.1177/1077559512451787

Maughan, A., & Cicchetti, D. (2002). Impact of child maltreatment and interadult violence on children's emotion regulation and socioemotional adjustment. *Child Development*, *73*(5), 1525–1542. https://doi.org/10.1111/1467-8624.00488

McCrory, E., De Brito, S. A., & Viding, E. (2011). Impact of childhood maltreatments: A review of neurobiological and genetic factors. *Frontiers in Psychiatry*, *2*, 1–15. https://doi.org/10.3389/fpsyt.2011.00048

McEachern, A.G., Aluede, O. & Kenny, M.C. (2008). Emotional abuse in the classroom: Implications and interventions for counselors. *Journal of Counseling and Development*, *86*(1), 3–10. https://doi.org/10.1002/j.1556-6678.2008.tb00619.x

McGee, R., Prior, M., Williams, S., Smart, D., & Sanson. A. (2002). The long-term significance of teacher-rated hyperactivity and reading ability in childhood: Findings from two longitudinal studies. *Journal of Child Psychology and Psychiatry*, *43*(8), 1004–1017. https://doi.org/10.1111/1469-7610.00228

McGuire, A., Steele, R. G., & Singh, M. N. (2021). Systematic review on the application of trauma-focused cognitive behavioral therapy (TF-CBT) for preschool-aged children. *Clinical Child and Family Psychology Review*, *24*, 20–37. https://doi.org/10.1007/s10567-020-00334-0

McLean, C., & Follette, V. M. (2016). Acceptance and commitment therapy as a nonpathologizing intervention approach for survivors of trauma. *Journal of Trauma and Dissociation*, *17*(2), 138–150. https://doi.org/10.1080/15299732.2016.1103111

Morris, A. S., Silk, J. S., Steinberg, L., Myers, S. S., & Robinson, L. R. (2007). The role of the family context in the development of emotion regulation. *Social Development*, *16*(2), 361–388. https://doi.org/10.1111/j.1467-9507.2007.00389.x

Mustanski, B., Andrews, R., & Puckett, J. A. (2016). The effects of cumulative victimization on mental health among lesbian, gay, bisexual, and transgender adolescents and young adults. *American Journal of Public Health*, *106*(3), 527–533. https://doi.org/10.2105/AJPH.2015.302976

Nemeroff, C. B. (2016). Paradise lost: The neurobiological and clinical consequences of child abuse and neglect. *Neuron*, *89*. https://doi.org/10.1016/j.neuron.2016.01.019

Nesbit, W. C., & Philpott, D. F. (2002). Confronting subtle emotional abuse in classrooms. *Guidance and Counselling*, *17*(2), 32–38.

Pears, K. C., Fisher, P. A., Bruce, J., Kim, H. K., & Yoerger, K. (2010). Early elementary school adjustment of maltreated children in foster care: The roles of inhibitory control and caregiver involvement. *Child Development*, *81*(5), 1550–1564. https://doi.org/10.1111/j.1467-8624.2010.01491.x

Piekarska, A. (2000). School stress, teachers' abusive behaviors, and children's coping strategies. *Child Abuse and Neglect*, *24*(11), 1443–1449. https://doi.org/10.1016/S0145-2134(00)00201-5

Rayner, M. (2005). The lost children: Child refugees. In J. Bessant, R. Hill & E. Watts (Eds.), *Violations of trust: How social and welfare institutions fail children and young people* (pp. 117–132). Ashgate.

Resick, P. A., Monson, C. M., & Rizvi, S. L. (2008). Posttraumatic stress disorder. In D. H. Barlow (Ed.), *Clinical handbook of psychological disorders: A step-by-step treatment manual* (4th ed., pp. 65–122). Guilford.
Robertson, G. (2006). Crimes against humanity: The struggle for global justice (3rd ed.). Penguin.
Rodman, A. M., Jenness, J. L., Weissman, D. G., Pine, D. S., & McLaughlin, K. A. (2019). Neurobiological markers of resilience to depression and anxiety following childhood maltreatment: The role of neural circuits supporting the cognitive control of emotion. *Biological Psychiatry*, *86*(6), 464–473. https://doi.org.10.1016/j.biopsych.2019.04.033
Rosenberg, M. B. (2003). Nonviolent communication: A language of life (2nd ed.). Puddle Dancer Press.
Rossman, B. B. R., Hughes, H. M., & Hanson, K. L. (1998). The victimization of school-age children. In B. B. R. Rossman & M. S. Rosenberg (Eds.), *Multiple victimization of children: Conceptual, developmental, research, and treatment issues* (pp. 87–106). Haworth Press.
Rousseau, C., & Gagnon, M. M. (2020). Intervening to address the impact of stress and trauma on refugee children and adolescents resettled in high-income countries. In J. S. Song & P. Vindevogel (Eds.), *Child, adolescent and family refugee mental health: A global perspective* (pp. 151–164). Springer.
Runyon, M. K., Risch, E., & Deblinger, E. (2019). Trauma-focused cognitive behavioral therapy: An evident-based approach for helping children overcome the impact of child abuse and trauma. In L. J. Farrell, T. H. Ollendick & P. Muris (Eds.), Innovations in CBT for childhood anxiety, OCD, and PTSD: Improving access and outcomes (pp. 525–549). Cambridge University Press. https://doi.org/10.1017/9781108235655.026
Rutherford, L. E., DuPaul, G. J., & Jitendra, A. K. (2008). Examining the relationship between treatment outcomes for academic achievement and social skills in school-age children with attention-deficit hyperactivity disorder. *Psychology in the Schools*, *45*(2), 145–157. https://doi.org/10.1002/pits.20283
Sack, W. H., Him, C., & Dickason, D. (1999). Twelve-year follow-up study of Khmer youths who suffered massive war trauma as children. *Journal of the American Academy of Child and Adolescent Psychiatry*, *38*(9), 1173–1179. https://doi.org/10.1097/00004583-199909000-00023
Sanderson, C. (2010). *Introduction to counselling survivors of interpersonal trauma*. Jessica Kingsley.
Scharpf, F., Kaltenbach, E., Nickerson, A., & Hecker, T. (2021). A systematic review of socio-ecological factors contributing to risk and protection of the mental health of refugee children and adolescents. *Clinical Psychology Review*, *83*, 101930. https://doi.org/10.1016/j.cpr.2020.101930
Scharpf, F., Kızıltepe, R., Kirika, A., & Hecker, T. (2022). A systematic review of the prevalence and correlates of emotional violence by teachers. *Trauma, Violence, and Abuse*, 1–17. https://doi.org/10.1177/15248380221102559
Seligman, M. E. P. (2002). *Authentic happiness*. Simon & Schuster.
Shorey, S., & Baladram, S. (2023). 'Does it really get better after Dad leaves?': Children's experiences with domestic violence: A qualitative systematic review. *Trauma, Violence, and Abuse*, 1–18. https://doi.org/10.1177/15248380231156197
Shrivastava, A. K., Karia, S. B., Sonavane, S. S., & De Sousa, A. A. (2017). Child sexual abuse and the development of psychiatric disorders: A neurobiological trajectory of pathogenesis. *Industrial Psychiatry Journal*, *26*, 4–12. https://doi.org/10.4103/ipj.ipj_38_15
Shumba, A. (2002). The nature, extent and effects of emotional abuse on primary school pupils by teachers in Zimbabwe. *Child Abuse and Neglect*, *26*(8), 783–791. https://doi.org/10.1016/S0145-2134(02)00351-4
Sisko, S. (2021). Cultural responsiveness in counselling and psychology: An introduction. In V. Hutton & S. Sisko (Eds.), *Multicultural responsiveness in counselling and psychology: Working with Australian populations* (pp. 3–21). Springer. https://doi.org/10.1007/978-3-030-55427-9_1
Smith, C. A., & Farrington, D. P. (2004). Continuities in antisocial behavior and parenting across three generations. *Journal of Child Psychology and Psychiatry*, *45*(2), 230–247. https://doi.org/10.1111/j.1469-7610.2004.00216.x
Souers, K., & Hall, P. (2016). *Fostering resilient learners: Strategies for creating a trauma-sensitive classroom*. ASCD.
Sourander, A. (1998). Behavior problems and traumatic events of unaccompanied refugee minors. *Child Abuse and Neglect*, *22*(7), 719–727. https://doi.org/10.1016/S0145-2134(98)00053-2
Spira, E. G., & Fischel, J. E. (2005). The impact of preschool inattention, hyperactivity, and impulsivity on social and academic development: A review. *Journal of Child Psychology and Psychiatry*, *46*(7), 755–773. https://doi.org/10.1111/j.1469-7610.2005.01466.x
St Vil, C., & St Vil, N. M. (2019). Black trauma in the US and the pursuit of human rights: A brief history. In L. D. Butler, F. M. Critelli & J. Carello (Eds.), *Trauma and human rights: Integrating approaches to address human suffering* (pp. 99–124). Palgrave Macmillan. https://doi.org/10.1007/978-3-030-16395-2

Stark, L., Plosky, W. D., Horn, R., & Canavera, M. (2015). 'He always thinks he is nothing': The psychosocial impact of discrimination on adolescent refugees in urban Uganda. *Social Science and Medicine*, *146*, 173–181. http://dx.doi.org/10.1016/j.socscimed.2015.10.045

Steger, M. F., & Park, C. L. (2012). The creation of meaning following trauma: Meaning making and trajectories of distress and recovery. In R. A. McMackin, E. Newman, J. M. Fogler & T. M. Keane (Eds.), *Trauma therapy in context: The science and craft of evidence-based practice* (pp. 171–191). American Psychological Association. https://psycnet.apa.org/doi/10.1037/13746-008

Sternberg, K. J., Baradaran, L. P., Abbott, C. B., Lamb, M. E., & Guterman, E. (2006). Type of violence, age, and gender differences in the effects of family violence on children's behavior problems: A mega-analysis. *Developmental Review*, *26*(1), 89–112. https://doi.org/10.1016/j.dr.2005.12.001

Tedeschi, R. G., & Calhoun, L. G. (2004). A clinical approach to posttraumatic growth. In P. A. Linley & S. Joseph (Eds.), *Positive psychology in practice* (pp. 405–419). Wiley.

Teicher, M. H. (2002). Scars that won't heal: The neurobiology of child abuse. *Scientific American*, *286*(3), 68–75. https://www.jstor.org/stable/26059603

Teicher, M. H., & Samson, J. A. (2016). Annual research review: Enduring neurobiological effects of childhood abuse and neglect. *Journal of Child Psychology and Psychiatry*, *57*(3), 241–266. http://doi.org/10.1111/jcpp.12507

Teicher, M. H., Rabi, K., Sheu, Y. S., Seraphin, S. B., Andersen, S. L., Choi, J., & Tomoda, A. (2010). Neurobiology of childhood trauma and adversity. In R. A. Lanius, E. Vermetten, & C. Pain (Eds.), *The impact of early life trauma on health and disease: The hidden epidemic* (pp. 112–122). Cambridge University Press.

Teisl, M., & Cicchetti, D. (2008). Physical abuse, cognitive and emotional processes, and aggressive/disruptive behavior problems. *Social Development*, *17*(1), 1–23. https://doi.org/10.1111/j.1467-9507.2007.00412.x

Terranova, A. M., Morris, A. S., Myers, S., Kithakye, M., & Morris, M. D. S. (2015). Children's adjustment following a hurricane: Risk and resilience in the face of adversity. *Early Education and Development*, *26*(4), 534–548. https://doi.org/10.1080/10409289.2015.994463

Thomas, T., & Lau, W. (n.d.) Psychological well being of child and adolescent refugee and asylum seekers: Overview of major research findings of the past ten years. Retrieved 21/09/08 from www.hreoc.gov.au/HUMAN_RIGHTS/children_detention

Tremblay, R. E., Boulerice, B., Arseneault, L., & Niscale, M. J. (1995). Does low self-control during childhood explain the association between delinquency and accidents in early adolescence? *Criminal Behaviour and Mental Health*, *5*(4), 439–451. https://doi.org/10.1002/cbm.1995.5.4.439

Tyrka, A. R., Burgers, D. E., Philip, N. S., Price, L. H., & Carpenter, L. L. (2013). The neurobiological correlates of childhood adversity and implications for treatment. *Acta Psychiatrica Scandinavica*, *128*(6), 434–447. https://doi.org/10.1111/acps.12143

UNHCR. (2022). *Refugee data finder*. https://www.unhcr.org/refugee-statistics/

van der Kolk, B. A. (2005). Developmental trauma disorder: Toward a rational diagnosis for children with complex trauma histories. *Psychiatric Annals*, *35*(5), 401–409. https://doi.org/10.3928/00485713-20050501-06

Vizard, E., Monck, E., & Misch, P. (1995). Child and adolescent sex abuse perpetrators: A review of the research literature. *Journal of Child Psychology and Psychiatry*, *36*(5), 731–756. https://doi.org/10.1111/j.1469-7610.1995.tb01326.x

Volpe, R. J., DuPaul, G. J., Jitendra, A. K., & Tresco, K. E. (2009). Consultation-based academic interventions for children with attention deficit hyperactivity disorder: Effects on reading and mathematics outcomes at 1-year follow-up. *School Psychology Review*, *38*(1), 5–13. https://doi.org/10.1080/02796015.2009.12087845

Webb, J., & Musello, C. (2013). *Running on empty: Overcome your childhood emotional neglect*. Morgan James Publishing.

Webster, R. E. (2001). Symptoms and long-term outcomes for children who have been sexually assaulted. *Psychology in the Schools*, *38*(6), 533–547. https://doi.org/10.1002/pits.1041

Weiner, D. A., Schneider, A., & Lyons, J. S. (2009). Evidence-based treatments for trauma among culturally diverse foster care youth: Treatment retention and outcomes. *Children and Youth Services Review*, *31*(11), 1199–1205. https://doi.org/10.1016/j.childyouth.2009.08.013

White, M. (2004). Working with people who are suffering the consequences of multiple trauma: A narrative perspective. *International Journal of Narrative Therapy and Community Work*, *1*, 44–75.

White, M. (2007). *Maps of narrative practice*. Norton.

White, M. (2016). *Narrative therapy classics*. Dulwich Centre Publications.

Wilson, K. R., Hansen, D. J., & Li, M. (2011). The traumatic stress response in child maltreatment and resultant neuropsychological effects. *Aggression and Violent Behavior*, *16*(2), 87–97. https://doi.org/10.1016/j.avb.2010.12.007

Xiang, Y., Cipriani, A., Teng, T., Del Giovane, C., Zhang, Y., Weisz, J. R., ... & Xie, P. (2021). Comparative efficacy and acceptability of psychotherapies for post-traumatic stress disorder in children and adolescents: A systematic review and network meta-analysis. *BMJ Mental Health*, *24*(4), 153–160. https://doi.org/10.1136/ebmental-2021-300346

Yuen, A. (2007). Discovering children's responses to trauma: A response-based narrative practice. *International Journal of Narrative Therapy and Community Work*, *2007*(4), 3–18.

Zatloukal, L., & Furman, B. (2022). The solution-focused approach to trauma therapy. *Journal of Constructivist Psychology*, 1–21. https://doi.org/10.1080/10720537.2022.2035863

16 Self-destructive behaviours

In this chapter I discuss four self-destructive behaviour patterns: disordered eating, self-harm, suicide and substance use. Although manifesting in vastly different ways, these conditions share many similarities. First, all typically emerge in the early to middle adolescent years and second, all can be chronic. Third, they are often accompanied by other emotional difficulties such as depression and anxiety that complicate treatment and imperil recovery (Bayes & Madden, 2011; Simic et al., 2022). Fourth, in each their own way, they are addictive, with short-term gains outweighing the long-term physical, emotional and social costs.

Fifth, recovery involves some distressing experiences (such as withdrawal from drugs, force feeding for anorexia or confrontation with painful emotions), which leads to a high dropout rate from treatment. Sixth, clients often lack self-efficacy – that is, the belief that they can make any difference to their symptoms.

Seventh, the conditions all have a myriad of complex causes, each of which on its own can be unresponsive to treatment. Eighth, they all lead to severe conflict with parents. Ninth, individuals with these conditions tend to postpone seeking treatment, or treatment is unavailable, leading to protracted delays, by which time the conditions can be dire (Kazdin et al., 2017). Tenth, self-destructive behaviours derail adolescents' development, stalling them at the age when their symptoms become intrusive, impairing the successful transition to adulthood (Nawi et al., 2021), narrowing their ability to pursue their life goals (Juarascio et al., 2013) and limiting the emotional and social maturation that young people can use for recovery. Finally, all these conditions attract considerable stigma, with clients experiencing shame not only for their actions, but for who they are.

Disordered eating

The three main eating disorders are *anorexia nervosa, bulimia nervosa* and *binge eating*. Anorexia involves adherence to strict dietary regimes out of exaggerated fears of weight gain, accompanied by behaviours that interfere with weight gain, such as excessive exercise (Martin et al., 2012; Rienecke, 2017). Severity is classified medically, according to clients' Body Mass Index (Hay et al., 2014). This is calculated by dividing their weight by their height squared:

$$\frac{\text{Weight (Kg)}}{\text{Height}^2\text{ (metres)}}$$

DOI: 10.4324/9781003323938-18

Box 16.1 Interpretation of BMI calculations

Adults' BMI	*Children's BMI*	*Interpretation*
Under 18		Very underweight
Under 20	Below 5th PR[a]	Underweight
19 - 25	5th - 85th PR	Healthy range for women
20 - 26	5th - 85th PR	Healthy range for men
26 - 30	85th - 95th PR	Overweight
Over 30	Above 95th PR	Obese

Sources: Cabot (2004, p. 201); Cabot & Jasinska (2011, p. 130)

[a] A PR (or percentile ranking) of 70 means that the person attained levels similar to 70 per cent of the population; a PR of 5 means that they attained similar levels to 5 per cent of the population.

Bulimia involves extreme weight control behaviours such as purging through the use of laxatives, or episodes of binge eating and self-induced vomiting. Given that purging is not a regular occurrence, many sufferers are overweight (Hay et al., 2014). Over time, individuals commonly migrate back and forth between bulimia and anorexia (Fairburn et al., 2008). The third category is binge eating, which can either be a distinct condition on its own or an aspect of bulimia.

A fourth category, avoidant-restrictive food intake disorder (ARFID) involves substantially restricted intake of particular foods, resulting in malnourishment, loss of weight and significant health problems (Norris et al., 2016). Individuals might restrict their food out of fear of 'dangerous' or 'bad' foods, to avoid nausea or abdominal pain, in reaction to the sensory input (particularly taste or texture) of particular foods, or as a response to stressful meal times (Norris et al., 2016).

A fifth category includes those on strict 'fad' diets and *orthorexia nervosa*, which is a fixation with eating only clean or pure (organic) foods. This can start out as simply being health conscious but can degenerate into an obsession with being healthy that instead causes ill health because of a severely limited range of food intake. It can lead to social isolation in that affected individuals might not wish to eat in restaurants or consume any food prepared by others for fear of not being able to conform to their diet.

Disordered eating is found everywhere where food is abundant. In the past decade, the incidence of eating disorders doubled in Australia (Morris et al., 2022). Although this increase is at least partly because of better recognition of the conditions (Herpertz-Dahlmann, 2017), disordered eating represents the second leading mental illness in females aged 10 to 24 years (Bailey et al., 2014).

Its outcomes can be dire. Bulimia has twice the normal death rate, and anorexia six times higher than usual (Bailey et al., 2014), half from cardiac arrest and half from suicide (Datta et al., 2022). This makes anorexia the second-most fatal of all mental illnesses after opioid addiction (Onnink et al., 2022). Aside from mortality, the conditions deplete vitality, decrease the quality of sufferers' lives and cause significant physical health problems. Also of concern is that these conditions are persistent, with their average duration being ten years, and recovery not necessarily complete even then (Dobrescu et al., 2020; Stewart et al., 2022).

Self-harm

Self-harm refers to the deliberate self-destruction of tissue. It encompasses both direct acts such as cutting, hitting, biting, poisoning or burning oneself, and the abuse of medications; and indirect health-harming behaviours such as eating large amounts of food in a short time frame with the intent of hurting oneself (El Nagar et al., 2022), and reckless behaviour such as running into traffic, or jumping from heights (Laye-Gindhu & Schonert-Reichl, 2005).

This behaviour is concerning, first because of its prevalence. In any 12-month period, 8 per cent of Australian 12- to 17-year-olds report engaging in self-harm behaviour, with an incidence of 11.6 per cent for 16- to 17-year-olds (Zubrick et al., 2016). Second, it is chronic: Only 20 per cent of cases involve single episodes, with the remainder being repeated incidents (Bean et al., 2022). Third, especially for females and younger adolescents, deliberate self-harm seems to be a gateway to future suicide attempts (Greydanus, 2011; Lee et al., 2019), especially when they have major depression (Zubrick et al., 2016). Some might not intend to die, but the lethality of methods is increasing, which can lead to accidental fatality.

Researchers have identified various motivations for volitional self-harm, driven by a desire to end pain but not to end life (Hawton et al., 2015; Laye-Gindhu & Schonert-Reichl, 2005; Miller et al., 2021; Osuch et al., 1999; Stänicke et al., 2018; Van Vliet & Kalnins, 2011):

- affect (emotion) modulation: to distract from feelings of loneliness, depression; or to release anger, hostility or tension
- to feel alive: to counteract the emptiness or numbness with feeling *something*
- desolation: to move the pain from 'the heart' to somewhere else
- to experience a sense of control
- in response to negative feelings towards the self: using self-harm to inflict punishment on oneself
- to communicate one's distress or to hurt or frighten others (but *not* to 'seek attention' or to be manipulative)
- to produce positive feelings of a rush and calmness
- to protect others from their difficult feelings by not taking their anger out on them
- to differentiate oneself from one's peers (as being more screwed up than them) or to connect with peers who also self-harm
- as part of the process of searching for identity.

Suicidal ideation

Around the age of six years, children learn that they (and others) can and will die. At times of despair, they might declare that they wish they were dead, which alarms their parents considerably. However, it is usually because they lack the language to say, 'I feel despondent'. Despondency, of course, is a cause for concern – but not a matter for alarm. Then by the age of eight years, children become aware that they can die by their own hand, and some express a wish to kill themselves. Again, typically this is a communication that something is wrong in their lives that needs addressing – but at that young age is seldom a statement of intent to kill themselves. By early adolescence (the age of 10 years onwards), transient suicidal thoughts become increasingly common, with *persistent* suicidal ideation a sign of severe emotional and social disturbance (Buddeberg et al., 1996).

Globally, after accidents, suicide is the second leading cause of death in children and adolescents (Lim et al., 2019; Ougrin et al., 2021). In Australia it is the leading cause of death of young people, with over half of these deaths being of people aged 16 to 17 years (ABS, 2021). Of those who attempt suicide, 24 to 27 per cent make a repeated attempt within one year, with the greatest risk being within six months (Hawton & Fagg, 1988; Hulten et al., 2001).

Substance abuse

Around 14 per cent of the total health burden in young men globally is caused by alcohol and drug abuse (Nawi et al., 2021). The line between drug use and drug abuse depends on the context, the frequency and the purpose for which a drug is used (McWhirter et al., 2013). However, when discussing youth, use can often *be* abuse given their developing brains' susceptibility to damage from drugs and given that early heavy use is likely to signal chronic problematic use throughout life (McWhirter et al., 2013).

Goodman (2008, in Marsh et al., 2013) identifies the following characteristics of addiction:

- *Chronic course*, beginning in adolescence.
- *Persistence*, despite negative consequences of the addiction.
- *Loss of control* over the behaviour.
- *Progression* from craving to loss of control, to narrowing of one's behavioural repertoire, to harmful consequences.
- *Tolerance*. As the behaviour is repeated, its power to reward is diminished.
- *Withdrawal*. Individuals experience physical or psychological discomfort when the behaviour is discontinued.
- *Behavioural substitution*: When one addiction stops, another substitutes.
- *Priorities change*: As the addiction takes over, other aspects of life are neglected, such as education, employment and leisure activities.
- *Recurrent emotional and social difficulties*. These include low self-esteem, self-centredness, denial, rationalisation, conflict over dependence versus control, relationship problems and contact with the justice system.

During adolescence, brain cells - particularly in the frontal cortex and corpus callosum - continue to build myelin (the coating that speeds signal transmission) (Moss, 2008). This is known as white matter and, in the brains of binge drinkers, becomes less dense in a dose-dependent manner (McQueeny et al., 2009; Moss, 2008). The constituents of marijuana also alter the myelination of the brain circuits that govern higher cognitive function and emotion regulation, which has permanent effects on cognitive skills - specifically on verbal fluency, executive function, decision making, processing speed and attention (Kwan et al., 2020). Frequent and early use (at ages 15 and 16 years) of cannabis is linked to a higher rate of depression in adulthood (Hengartner et al., 2020), increased anxiety and a three- to four-fold increase in psychosis, that, moreover, has an earlier onset and reduced response to treatment (Kwan et al., 2020). Compared to single-substance use, the risks to polyusers' physical and mental health is greater, with polysubstance use also associated with risky sexual behaviours, lower educational attainments, early parenthood and criminal behaviour (Carbonneau et al., 2022).

At the time of alcohol intoxication, the main social effects are disinhibition - that is, people behave in ways they ordinarily would not. This contributes to elevated rates of aggression and risk-taking behaviours; 10 per cent of deaths; 73 per cent of violent crimes; half of all rapes, domestic assaults, and car crashes; and one-third of vehicular and pedestrian deaths (Collison & Hall, 1989; Myers, 2005; Porter, 1980).

Common stressors of individuals with self-destructive behaviour

In this section, I discuss the life circumstances and events that can put individuals at risk of developing self-destructive behaviours. Nevertheless, this is not a list of causes nor an attempt to allocate blame, nor even to locate solutions - but to give counsellors an understanding of the burdens under which clients are functioning so that we can 'cut them a little slack' and fully appreciate what they are up against.

As illustrated in Figure 16.1, there are distal (or background influences) on self-destructive patterns, and proximal influences, which are those occurring close in time to the onset of the conditions. These factors lead to behaviours whose outcomes themselves are a risk for suicide, such as drug or alcohol use, aggression and violence, conflict within relationships and depressive episodes (Conner & Ilgen, 2011).

Trauma

Those who have endured emotional or sexual abuse are at increased risk of self-destructive patterns (Afifi et al., 2020; Andersen, 2019; Deas & Brown, 2006; Hay et al., 2014; Mishra et al.,

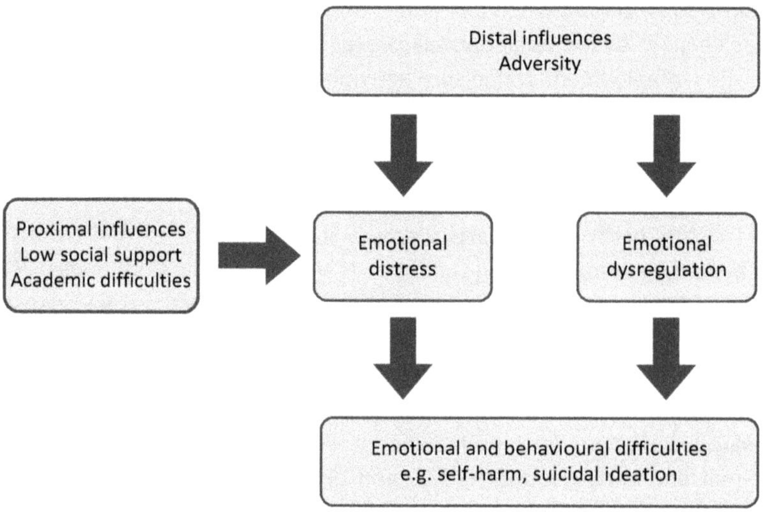

Figure 16.1 Influences on self-destructive behaviours

2022; Nawi et al., 2021). Almost six out of every ten young females who die by suicide have been abused (Lee et al., 2019). Each additional adverse childhood experience (ACE) confers an 11 per cent increase in risk of self-harm (Russell et al., 2019) and increases the risk of suicide two- to eight-fold (Dube et al., 2001).

Maltreatment teaches children that they are unworthy of being cared for and leads to high levels of distress at the same time as reduced environmental support to learn adaptive coping strategies (Fisher et al., 2012; Selekman, 2006). Moreover, as discussed in Chapter 15, early life adversity leads to lasting changes in the response of the HPA axis, which later in life result in abnormal hormonal responses to further stress (Mann & Currier, 2011).

Family malfunction

The core family characteristics that protect young people from drug use in particular and self-destructive behaviours in general are high levels of warmth and cohesion within the family, the ability to resolve conflict, and adequate parental knowledge of their child's activities and whereabouts (Ballester et al., 2018; Bogenschneider et al., 1998; Chiang et al., 2022; Gomes et al., 2021; Nawi et al., 2021; Trucco, 2020; Valente et al., 2017). It is about *connection*.

Relationship difficulties, violence and conflict within the family are common experiences of those who harm themselves (Fortune et al., 2016; Hawton et al., 2015; Miner et al., 2016). Young people who have lost a parent to traumas such as suicide or sudden injury are at increased risk of dying by suicide themselves (Hua et al., 2019; Fergusson et al., 2003). Other risk factors are when their parent has a mental illness or addiction, or was abused in childhood themselves (Ballester et al., 2018; Fortune et al., 2016; Miner et al., 2016), with young people whose fathers are antisocial or alcoholic being most at risk of drug abuse (Carbonneau et al., 2022).

In turn, families' responses to their child's behaviours can become problematic: Some become overly protective and, in an effort to keep their daughters or sons safe, greatly restrict their opportunities for autonomy. Others become angry, lecture them or treat their behaviours as 'manipulative' or 'attention seeking'. A third group under-react altogether because they are distant from their children and remain so even in the face of this threat to their well-being, or because parents are attempting not to rupture their relationship with their child (Fortune et al., 2016).

Social context

Poverty. Self-destructive behaviours are observed in families with low income, low parental education and parental unemployment, the common variable being that the families are stressed (Manhica et al., 2020; Platt, 2011; Zubrick et al., 2016). In Aotearoa/New Zealand, young people from the lowest socioeconomic levels were found to be 31 times more likely to die by suicide compared with advantaged youth (Beautrais et al., 2016). Nevertheless, economic pressures exert an influence only when these affect parents' well-being and parenting skills (Fortune et al., 2016).

Minority status. Gay or bisexual males and those questioning their sexual orientation are at a three-fold risk for suicide attempts (Garofalo et al., 1999; Goodenow et al., 2006; O'Reilly et al., 2021; Raifman et al., 2020). Young people with intersecting marginal identities report high rates of suicidality (Standley & Foster-Fishman, 2021).

The suicide rate for Aboriginal and Torres Strait Islander males is 2.8 times higher and, for females, 1.9 times higher than for non-indigenous Australians (NSW Department of Health, 2004). Similarly, New Zealand Māori are at much higher risk than non-Māori, at 16.9 per 100,000 in 2020 compared with 10 for non-Māori, with the highest rates being for 15- to 24-year-olds (NZ Parliament, 2022). This is potentially because of their lower socioeconomic status, cultural alienation and identity confusion, increased victimisation by violence and other traumas, and purposelessness (Glenn et al., 2019).

Individual mental health

It is common for those with self-destructive behaviours to have other accompanying mental health issues such as depression, anxiety and obsessive-compulsive conditions (Bayes & Madden, 2011; Epstein et al., 2020; Fisher et al., 2012; Selekman, 2006). Negative emotionality contributes to depression, drug and alcohol abuse and deficient self-regulation; in turn, these add to the risks of suicide (Conner & Ilgen, 2011), especially when young people are in the grip of an acute severe depressive episode (Fergusson et al., 2003; Rihmer, 2011).

Pain (physical or emotional) has three aspects: current pain (how we feel now), past pain (how long we've been feeling like this and therefore how depleted we are by our pain), and future or anticipated pain. The use of drugs can be an attempt to self-medicate to deal with emotional pain (Benedini & Fagan, 2020), while people who are suicidal anticipate that the pain will go on forever. They do not see how it can end and dying seems like their only way for it to end.

Emotion regulation. Self-destructive behaviours are predominantly an effort to regulate or avoid upsetting feelings of rejection, imperfection and failure (Juarascio et al., 2013). In disordered eating, socially prescribed perfectionism is played out on our bodies, using self-deprivation and starving to justify our existence (Martin, 2007).

Conditional self-esteem. Martin (2007, p. 5) says that disordered eating is based in 'a fundamental distrust that we deserve to be on this earth in the shape we are in'. Low worth, self-criticism and self-hatred are common in those who self-harm (Van Vliet & Kalnins, 2011). For self-harm, some researchers assert that chronic parental criticism and invalidation of young people leads to shame (Adrian et al., 2018; Bean et al., 2022), while the idealised images that pervade social media (Gültzow et al., 2020) and the presence of online bullying all add to individuals' conditional sense of worth.

Low self-efficacy. Hopelessness about the future and rumination (dwelling on distress) are also linked to depression and thence to suicide ideation and attempts, perhaps because they interfere with problem solving (O'Connor, 2011; Wasserman et al., 2021) and reflect low self-efficacy.

Substance use. After depression, both acute and chronic substance use is the second most common condition that is linked to suicide (Buddeberg et al., 1996; Conner & Ilgen, 2011;

Rihmer, 2011; Tuisku et al. 2014), especially when individuals have early onset, severe and multiple drug use (Conner & Ilgen, 2011).

Impulsivity. For up to 40 per cent of first suicide attempts, there is little ideation or planning (sometimes less than 30 minutes) but instead their suicide is an impulsive response to immediate events such as failing an exam or being bullied (Conner & Ilgen, 2011; Nock et al., 2013; Uddin et al., 2019). These attempts are more likely to be lethal if the means are readily to hand (Wasserman et al., 2021).

Compulsiveness. Anorexia has been thought to be due to sufferers exercising too much control over their food intake, when instead they exercise too little control over their obsessive ruminations about their weight. Similarly, whereas some attribute self-harm to insufficient impulse control (Madge et al., 2011; Peh et al., 2017), instead Miller et al. (2021) see it as a compulsion, whereby the mental and physical urge is satisfied only by the act of hurting oneself. Self-injury can become an obsession - as can suicide. The continuous repetition of self-critical thoughts, pessimistic predictions of the future and the desire to die becomes compulsive and leads to a wish to end consciousness (Kerkhof & van Spijker, 2011), with dying being seen as the only option to achieve this.

Control. Given that maltreated children will have experienced being out of control of the abuse, some self-destructive behaviours such as self-harm and disordered eating are attempts to exercise control.

Shame. Shame is an intensely painful feeling or belief that we are flawed and therefore unworthy of acceptance and belonging (Brown, 2007). It is the most toxic of human emotions. Whereas guilt is self-reproach (a thought) or remorse (the accompanying emotion) for our actions, shame is about being judged for who we are by an external audience (real or imagined) (Brown, 2007; Jacquet, 2015). Guilt is hearing our own conscience, whereas shame is about being seen by others to be defective, with the implied threat of rejection (Elison et al., 2014; Smith, 2015).

Body image. David Elkind (1967) described adolescence as a time of extreme self-consciousness in which young people are sensitised to what others think of them. Taken to its extreme in the forms of anorexia and bulimia, individuals become preoccupied by their body image, judging their self-worth largely or even exclusively on the criterion of weight, which results in dieting to lose weight even when their weight is within a healthy range (Harter, 2006; Hoare & Cosgrove, 1998; Monteleone et al., 2020).

Interoception. This is the processing of data from our internal organs (Feldman Barrett, 2020). People with disordered eating tend to focus too much on the signals that their body produces, do not trust these signals and perceive normal signals as being malevolent. The result is that they do not feel safe in their own bodies (Monteleone et al., 2020).

Individual physical health

Primed by early life adversity to react to subsequent stressors, and making deleterious lifestyle choices such as poor diet, smoking and heavy drinking, adults who attempt suicide are twice as likely as usual to die from natural causes such as respiratory disorders, circulatory, endocrine (hormonal) and neurological disease (Hawton & Fagg, 1988).

Low cholesterol levels are linked to suicidality (Lester, 2002; Plana et al., 2010; Wu et al., 2016), possibly because cholesterol is needed to transport the fat-soluble vitamins (particularly Vitamin D) to the brain, where they are needed to generate neurotransmitters, especially serotonin, whose deficiency is implicated in depression.

In an early study, Hawton and Fagg (1988) found that adults who attempted suicide were more likely to be in poor physical health, leading to more than double the usual death rate from natural causes such as respiratory disorders, circulatory, endocrine (hormonal) and neurological disease. Some of this would be due to lifestyle, such as smoking, alcoholism and poor sleep (Hawton & Fagg, 1988), while much is likely due to the cascading effects on the immune and metabolic system from changes to the responsiveness of the HPA axis (see Chapter 15).

Campbell-McBride (2010) contends that eating disorders are not 'all in the mind' but instead can be triggered and maintained by physical ill health. The mechanism can be that when individuals severely restrict their food intake, they experience protein malnutrition. In turn, this causes the body to become deficient in hormones, enzymes, neurotransmitters and zinc (Campbell-McBride, 2010; Hay et al., 2014) - see Figure 11.2, page 150. Vitamin B deficiency is almost inevitable also on a vegan diet, while a low-fat diet causes a deficiency of the fat-soluble vitamins (A, D, E and K). This deficiency impairs a range of metabolic functions as well as the immune system.

Consequently, malnutrition leads to constant infections, for which antibiotics are administered. Now gut dysbiosis results, with large populations of unhealthy bacteria producing biotoxins that cross the blood-brain barrier, interfering with all brain functions including perception and, hence, self-perception (Campbell-McBride, 2010). The damage to the gut means that it can no longer digest efficiently - and the typical therapeutic diet, which is high in carbohydrates so that sufferers gain weight quickly, both feeds these bacteria and harms the gut lining further (Campbell-McBride, 2010).

Ultimately, the starved body can breach a 'tipping point' where hormones and digestive enzymes are now so depleted that eating literally does cause nausea. In that case, any individuals (however healthy emotionally) would find it difficult to recover physically. They are now in a state of metabolic fatigue.

Peer influence

Family difficulties make the peer group even more important to young people. In the face of parental absence, many teens seek refuge in a 'second family' in the form of gangs, the rave/dance club culture or drug users (Selekman, 2006). In turn, self-destructive behaviours are learned from peers and can be a way to fit in with them. However, it could simply be that youth seek out like-minded peers.

A lack of true (unconditional) friendship has a particularly important role in disordered eating (Lukas et al., 2022). Prolonged bullying and social exclusion are also risk factors for self-harming behaviours in general (Epstein et al., 2020; Fortune et al., 2016; Koyanagi et al., 2019), while the disruption of interpersonal relationships through loss, rejection or exclusion is a core instigator of a first suicide attempt (Lee et al., 2019). A sense of having been humiliated, that one is a burden to others and loneliness are common (Gijzen et al., 2021; O'Connor,

2011; Stewart et al., 2019). Nevertheless, it seems that suicidal individuals are no less isolated than others in that they have similar social networks - but they feel less engaged with them (Gijzen et al., 2021).

Connection to school

Positive student-teacher relationships, strong bonds to school, and high academic self-efficacy and self-esteem protect adolescents against drug use (Santibáñez et al., 2020; Trucco, 2020). In reverse, disaffection with school increases the risk of later suicide or death by non-natural causes in those who are self-harming (Asarnow & Mehlum, 2019) and exposes individuals to an antisocial peer group and hence to a range of risky behaviours (Fergusson et al., 2003; Hawkins et al., 2001; Zubak et al., 2018). In turn, substance use is likely to impair young people's academic achievement (Zubak et al., 2018).

Principles of interventions

Self-destructive behaviours require a trauma-informed approach that takes account of both current and past exposure to trauma (Asarnow & Mehlum, 2019). In addition, it is vital that adolescent clients are heard (Ganci et al., 2021). Young people often believe that goals which they find important are overlooked in the focus on behaviour change alone (such as weight gain for anorexia or cessation of drug use) (Simic et al., 2022). With lives in the balance, counsellors will also need to collaborate with other professionals, such as medical practitioners and psychiatrists, as the physical management of these conditions must occur alongside psychological interventions.

Neutrality

We must be neutral on the question of whether clients should change their behaviour. We can express bias (as in, 'It breaks my heart to think of you so despondent that this seems to be your only option') at the same time as being neutral (on the issue of what they should do): 'But of course I understand that it is your life, that you get to decide how to live it, and what you want to do next'. For clients who are contemplating suicide, our statement can be stronger still: We can safely express our personal conviction that killing themselves is tragic, and state that it is our personal and professional obligation to do what we can to prevent that.

Triangulation of data

Triangulation of data means gaining information from more than one source and checking one against the other. Therefore, you will need to interview clients' families about their concerns for their daughter or son, and to liaise with their medical practitioners because clients themselves might minimise the seriousness of their predicament (NSW Department of Health, 2004). Corroboration from other informants can supplement your own clinical judgement, which improves the chances of keeping clients safe (Granello, 2010).

Plan for setbacks

Between 20 and 50 per cent of individuals with any addictive behaviour patterns will relapse (Bailey et al., 2014). This can be because of the physical discomforts of withdrawal or resumed food intake, or because the behaviours have worked to avoid or soothe distressing feelings that resurface during recovery (Robinson et al., 2013).

Ways of reframing relapses are given in Chapter 2, most useful of which might be that they provide extra information about the tricks and tactics the problem uses to take over clients' life (Morgan, 1999). We need also to challenge all-or-nothing thinking, where clients who have relapsed see the relapse as a sign that they are a 'total' failure (rather than having made a single mistake). Scaling can be vital here.

Recovering individuals run the risk of losing their friendship group once they turn their back on disordered eating or drug use. In order to avoid relapses, intervention, then, has to plan how they can establish a new basis of friendship with the current peer group, or build new friendships based on healthy behaviours.

Interventions

Trucco (2020) observes that despite overwhelming evidence that social factors are vital for initiating and maintaining self-destructive behaviours, most theory focuses on individual factors. Accordingly, most therapy does too. Yet there is an ethical and political problem with theories that locate these conditions within individuals, overlooking their social and cultural context (Ellis, 2022).

Cognitive-behavioural and dialectical behaviour therapy that include the family show some evidence of effectiveness with self-harm and suicidal ideation, especially when the therapy is long term (Asarnow & Mehlum, 2019; Glenn et al., 2019; Kothgassner et al., 2021; Yue & Ougrin, 2018). However, poor engagement and compliance are common, with 77 per cent of adolescents withdrawing from treatment (Yue & Ougrin, 2018). Moreover, success rates of these methods are still low and recidivism rates high (Bean et al., 2022).

Suicide risk assessment

Mental health professionals have a fundamental duty to protect individuals from self-harm through a comprehensive assessment of their risk (Jobes & O'Connor, 2009). Nevertheless, a focus on problems can cause clients not to disclose the depth of their despair for fear of being medicated or hospitalised against their will (Sharry et al., 2002). Also, risk status can change and even clients themselves might not know their intentions in any given moment. Given that suicide risk is not static, assessment must therefore be an ongoing monitoring of clients' well-being in general and ideation, plans and intent specifically. To understand a client's predicament, Hawkes et al. (1998, in Sharry et al., 2002) recommend using a solution-focused interview as a starting point, and if (based on awareness of risk factors, such as those illustrated in Figure 16.2) concerns surface about client safety, counsellors will conduct a risk assessment and negotiate a safety plan with clients.

Scaling to assess risk

To assess suicide risk, Sharry et al. (2002, p. 396) recommend the following scaling questions.

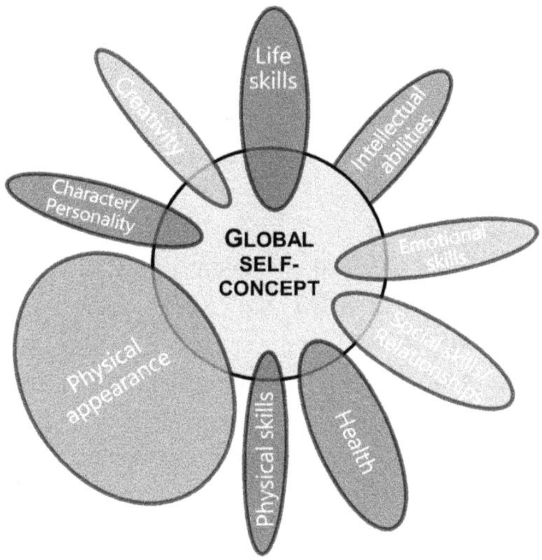

Figure 16.2 The potential self-concept rankings of a person with disordered eating

- On a scale between 1 and 10, when 10 is you can absolutely guarantee me you will be able to keep yourself safe until we meet again and 1 is that after our meeting you think you are definitely going to end your life, where would you say you are now?
- On a scale of 1 to 10, how confident are you that you will be able to get through the weekend without attempting to harm yourself, where 1 means you feel you have no chance and 10 means you are totally confident? ... What makes you that confident? ... What needs to happen to make you more confident ... to move one point forward on the scale?
- Suppose over the weekend your mood drops two points on the scale, what will you do to ensure you get back on track? What would help you to get back up to 6 on the scale?

Box 16.2 A suicide risk assessment

1. Ask clients if they have thought about killing themselves.
    - Are you thinking about suicide?
    - Have things been so bad lately that you've thought that you would rather not be here?
    - How persistent are your suicidal thoughts?
    - On a scale of 1 to 10, how badly do you want to die?
    - Do you see suicide as a good solution for yourself, or a bad solution?
    - Do you think of suicide as a brave, strong thing to do or a weak thing to do?

    If clients have thought about suicide often, have a high score on the scale, see suicide as a good solution and a strong act, they are at high risk.
2. Ask family members if they are concerned that the client might die by suicide. Note that the client is at high risk if family members dismiss their despair or believe that they are just putting on an act.

3. Check the client's plan for suicide.
   - Have you made a plan to kill yourself?
   - How are you thinking of doing it? If they have access to the means and knowledge to carry it out and the chosen method is irreversible (e.g. shooting themselves or jumping from a height), the risk is greater.
   - Do you intend to do it soon?
   - Where do you plan to do it? If the client plans to attempt suicide in an isolated location, there will be a low chance of discovery and rescue, and hence a greater likelihood of fatality.
   - Have you made arrangements for pets, given away any possessions or said goodbye?
   - Have they thought about harming someone else (in a murder-suicide)?
   - The more detailed and feasible the plan, and the lower the chance of being rescued, the greater the risk.
4. Check clients' emotional well-being.
   - Are clients experiencing hopelessness, entrapment, humiliation, shame, guilt, agitation or despair?
   - Do they have a diagnosed mental illness, especially depression?
   - Are they in the midst of an acute severe depressive episode?
   - Are they emerging from depression? (This is a high-risk time because although they still feel depressive, they now have enough energy to act on those feelings.)
   - Do they have a history of aggression or impulsivity? (These make their risk status less predictable.)
   - Have they experienced trauma, such as torture, war or being a refugee?
   - Are they questioning their gender identity or sexual orientation?
5. Check their history of suicide.
   - Have they made previous attempts at suicide or self-harm, particularly in the past six months?
   - Within the last 28 days, have they been discharged from hospital after a previous suicide attempt or incident of self-harm?
   - How do they feel about surviving previous attempts?
   - Do they have any family members or friends who have died by suicide?
6. Enquire about their physical health.
   - Are they likely, given their food intake, to be malnourished?
   - Do they have insomnia?
   - Have they experienced decreased appetite and weight loss recently?
7. Enquire about recent or upcoming changes in their lives.
   - Have they moved or migrated recently, resulting in a loss of country, identity and perhaps local social support? (Jobes & O'Connor, 2009).
   - Have they recently lost their home?
   - Is there a recent or upcoming anniversary of a traumatic event or loss?
   - Is there an impending criminal court case or a parental divorce or custody battle in their near future?

- Are they experiencing or at risk of academic failure?
- Have they recently acquired a serious physical illness or disability?
- Have they recently lost a baby or child to abortion, adoption or death?

8. Ask clients about their social supports.
   - Who do you talk to when you're feeling distressed?
   - Who have you told about your thoughts about killing yourself?
   - How do they respond when you tell them?
   - Have you had any sudden and recent changes in social support, such as the breakup of a romantic relationship?
   - Do you have cultural or religious supports? (These can be a protective factor but can also impede their reaching out for help.)
   - Are you willing to access ongoing counselling support?
9. Enquire about their previous history of coping with distress. The purpose of these questions is to discover if clients believe that there are other options for resolving their distress besides suicide.
   - How have you managed stressful situations in the past?
   - What did you do that pulled you out of previous attacks of despair?
   - What does this tell you about your capacity to cope now?
   - How do you cope with these feelings?
   - Do you worry about losing control of yourself? (Kanel, 2018, p. 73)
10. Enquire about their medication and drug use.
    - Illicit drug use, because the availability of drugs makes a suicide by overdose possible.
    - Use of alcohol, especially to excess.
    - Sudden cessation of drug use, as the drugs might have been masking painful emotions.
    - Recent commencement of anti-depressant medication. This is because, without mood stabilisers, for those with depression or bipolar disorder, anti-depressants can trigger rapid cycling between depression and mania (Rihmer, 2011).
11. Ask about their reasons to live.
    - What has been stopping you from killing yourself?
    - Do you have a reason for living?
    - What needs to happen for you to no longer to want to die?
    - You came here for help. What does this tell you about your desire to live?
12. Assess their risk of harm to others.
    Someone who is distraught over the ending of their romantic relationship might plan to kill their former partner and then themselves, either out of retribution or to pursue the romantic myth that they are 'meant' to be together - if not in this life, then in the afterlife.
    - Have you been thinking of harming anyone else?
    - What reasons do you have for thinking this?
    - What needs to happen to keep them safe?

Sources: Kanel (2018); Marsh et al. (2003); NSW Department of Health (2004); Rihmer, (2011)

Normalise suicidal ideation

It can be helpful to *low-risk* clients to let them know that thinking about one's death does not make it happen, and that wondering if suicide is an option is a common human response to stressful or traumatic circumstances (Kanel, 2018). This does not reduce their distress, but it can remove that second layer of feeling - namely, panicking about their distress.

Solution-focused therapy

With all self-destructive behaviours, interventions to date will have been around getting the young person to stop the behaviour. The young person is in front of you, which means that these attempts have not worked. Therefore, you will need to do something different.

Formulate goals

Self-destructive patterns are a strategy for meeting a need. Therefore, a solution-focused approach rests on identifying a different, less harmful strategy for meeting that need - that is, to open up other options. To that end, you will start with the standard question, 'You must have good reasons for not eating / cutting yourself / wanting to kill yourself / using drugs. ... Can you tell me about those?' (Berg & Steiner, 2003).

Having found out how the habit helps, Metcalf (2017) advises counsellors to then ask clients about their best hopes for their future:

- It seems really tough for you right now. What would have to change to make things just a little bit better?

Use of the miracle question or its variants (see Chapter 2) allows clients to imagine their preferred future, even though they might not yet know the mechanics of how to achieve that. Follow-up questions will enable them to describe this in detail (Sharry et al., 2002). This will allow clients to feel less hopeless about their future possibilities.

Berg and Steiner (2003, p. 212) demonstrate how a client's hopelessness can quickly be transformed into goals and, in turn, to a plan to make those goals a reality:

Client	I just feel like I'm never good at anything, so why bother? Nobody gives a damn, nobody cares about me anyway.
Counsellor	So what is important to you is that you want to do better at school, you want somebody to care about you and you also want to be good at something, is that right?
Client	Yeah, doesn't everybody?...
Counsellor	Just suppose you have these things, become better at school, find something you are good at, and have somebody who cares about you ... what would you be doing then that you are not doing right now?

For clients with disordered eating who learn visually, you might present the flower model of the self-concept (see Figure 11.3, page 156). Then you might invite them to draw two versions of their self-concept, with the size of each petal depicting first, how much each aspect contributes now to their overall self-concept, and in their second diagram, how important they would like each aspect to be. The next step will be to enquire about a time when their

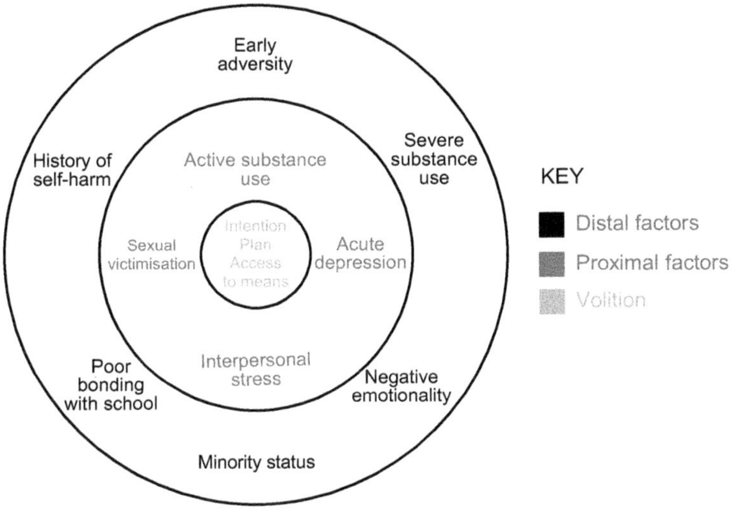

Figure 16.3 Risk factors for suicide

self-concept more resembled their second diagram, and what needs to happen to regain that balance.

Identify exceptions

The fact that clients can report that they are depressed (for example) indicates that there was a comparison time when they were not (Sharry et al., 2002). You can ask about these times or when they have experienced some of their goals, even a little bit, how that came about and what they did specifically to achieve that.

For any of the self-destructive patterns, solution-focused approaches can incorporate ACT's concept of mindful acceptance of feelings by noting times when clients were willing to sit with their feelings without using escape measures, and the concept of defusion by asking about times when they did not buy into their pathological self-critic, and how they managed to do so. In this way, in addition to examining exceptions to the behaviour, we can ask them to consider exceptions to the avoidance of feelings.

Identify strengths

Once this exception has been identified, counsellors help clients to explore it in detail, asking about what they and others notice about how things are different then and which strengths and resources they used to bring them about. The 'What else?' question is very useful here to highlight details. Sharry et al. (2002) note that, when counsellors explore clients' skills, it will emerge that they use many of the methods that other therapies believe they need to 'learn'. This means that counsellors do not have to engage in psychoeducation - although they might, with clients' consent, suggest some ways that clients can build on their present tools, such as by presenting them with a list of ACT's defusion metaphors and having them select one that resonates most with them.

Scaling

Suicidal individuals believe that they have just two options: to live on in pain, or to end the pain by dying. Scaling can be especially useful for these clients and any who think in black-and-white terms that self-destructive behaviours are the only solution to their distress.

Highlight strengths

We need to reverse the logic that grim problems are scary and instead allow young people's strengths to scare their problems. You can highlight their strengths by asking about other habits they managed to quit or other ways that they have enacted their values. For example, I asked an adolescent Ice addict about his values and he said that he had been living with other users who had children and would use in front of the children, whereas he said that, no matter how strong the cravings, he would never do that. I then asked what it was about him that allowed him to stand by his values with such conviction, and what it would take for him to enact his values about getting clean.

Box 16.3 A case study with avoidant-restrictive food intake

Freeman et al. (1997) detail a young child's avoidant-restrictive food intake and how they learned from the child that he possessed a tiger strength inside him. They established that the tiger grew stronger with being fed and, given that it was his friend, they asked the child if he thought he ought to feed it. They asked the parents to buy the child a tiger costume to wear every second day to meals, so that the tiger could eat and stay strong.

Narrative therapy

Clients with self-destructive behaviours see themselves as damaged and broken – and powerless to do anything about that. I have quoted elsewhere the classic statement from narrative therapy that *The person is not the problem: The problem is the problem* (Winslade & Monk, 2007, p. 2). However, Lock et al. (2004) take this a step further when they state that neither one is the problem: The problem is individuals' relationship to the problem – that is, what they think it says about who they are. Being totalitarian, the conditions come to define the total person, overlooking all other aspects of their identity, to the point that they are not even said to 'have' the conditions, but to *be* anorexic or to *be* an addict.

Externalisation

Externalisation begins by settling on a name for the problem and personifying it as if it were a separate, external, entity (Lock et al., 2004). For this purpose, verbs (such as cutting) are transformed into nouns, such as The Cutting (Hannen & Woods, 2012). Or, clients might name the motivation for self-harm, such as The Despair, The Numbness, The Fury, or Perfectionism. This last is a bully, which makes it easy to externalise - because everyone knows how a bully operates: It steals our joy. Depending on their experience of it, clients might prefer to call it the 'Joy thief' or, in ACT terms, Radio triple F (broadcasting our fears, flaws and failings).

Instead of clients 'having' anorexia, narrative therapy sees anorexia as *having them* (Lock et al., 2004). Just as people can 'have' malaria, a parasitic infection that invades their body, so too anorexia is a parasite that overtakes the body and mind of its host.

Enquire about the problem's pattern of entry

Next, using this client language, the counsellor will ask what the Problem wants for them. This opens the way for a discussion of Anorexia's tactics, its rhetorical strategies (how it talks to them and what it says), the moves it makes, and its attempts to cover its tracks and deny its true role. It pretends to be a saviour and sufferers' only 'true friend', the only one who understands them - but instead it steals life and vitality and joy by belittling, judging, shaming and controlling them, just as a parasite feeds off its host. Anorexia is the most devious of all, telling individuals that their body is inferior, that they are weak and that this can only be remedied by depriving and torturing their body in cruel and exacting ways (Lock et al., 2004). It seduces people by promising to make their bodies 'good enough' to earn social acceptance (Lock et al., 2004). Once sufferers have been beguiled by it, anorexia and the other addictions act as a ventriloquist, taking away their own voice and replacing it with the addiciton's own (Lock et al., 2004).

Deconstruction

Next, deconstruction focuses not only on the social forces that might be contributing to self-destructive behaviours ('In what ways do systems of oppression cause the voice of Despair to be louder?'), but also on the oppressive nature of the patterns themselves. Deconstruction contests their right to take control of sufferers.

To that end, landscape of action questions ask clients to identify how the behaviour insinuates itself into their life, relationships with family and friends, school, and physical well-being (White, 2016). Clients might report that it isolates them from others, makes them secretive, and causes them to think that everyone is constantly evaluating them (White, 2016). Their answers will identify how it takes over their voice and - worse - causes them to believe that its voice is their own.

This questioning is aimed at helping clients to direct their resistance towards the whisperings of Anorexia, Addiction or Self-harm. We can begin by asking,

> Is *anorexic/addict* a term that you gave to yourself or was it given to you by someone else? ... Do you think of it as a complete description of you? ... Why do you think it is not a complete picture of you?... What does it leave out? ... Are any of these qualities things that you would rather be? ... Are you happy that Addiction hides these qualities from you and others?

Unique outcomes

Next, counsellors will ask clients about the times when the problem did not dominate them and they were able to stand up to it and live their best life. These questions examine the evidence that clients might be able to regain 'government of themselves'. Together, counsellors and clients will build these 'unique outcomes' into a counter-story of courage and resistance, giving this new story the name that clients themselves allocate to it.

- Can you tell me about a time when even a little of what you value was part of your life?
- Tell me about the times when the voice of Despair is quieter.
- What do you do to defend yourself against Loneliness/Despair/Hopelessness/Shame/ Guilt?
- How do you get through the times when it seems to you that hurting yourself/taking drugs/suicide is your only way out?
- Cutting has been very skilled at cutting off escape routes for you. Can you tell me about a time when you managed to outsmart it and not hurt yourself when it was urging you to?
- What have you done to frustrate (Self-harm's) plans and best efforts to take over your life?
- What threatens (Addiction's) power over your life?
- What could (It) do to reassert itself against those threats?

Over the course of the sessions, these 'unique outcomes' will be accumulated into a new story which, again, the client names - perhaps as 'Regaining my voice', for example.

Box 16.4 Narrative questions for self-destructive patterns

Landscape of action questions

- What does (The Cutting/Anorexia/Drugs/Self-hate- hereafter referred to as It) want for your life?
- What does (It) require you to do to yourself?
- Does (It) want you to feel heard?
- Does (It) want you to be connected to others/to have friends, or does it want you all to itself?
- What techniques does (It) use to get you on its side?
- What tricks does (It) use to get its own way with you?
- What does (It) like to hear you saying or doing?
- What does (It) work in league with?
- What makes (Its) work easier or more difficult?
- What does (It) promise you when you are reluctant to listen to it?
- What practices does (It) force you to do, that it relies on for its survival?
- Does this Self-hate set itself up as an authority on what other people think of you?
- How does it do this, and how does this affect your relationships with others?
- How did Anorexia recruit you to do these things to yourself: to police your body so that it becomes a specific shape so that you can be considered worthy?
- What does (It) have you doing to yourself that might be against your better judgement?

- What feeds Anorexia?
- What starves it?

Landscape of identity questions

Landscape of identity questions will ask clients how their self-destructive behaviour affects their attitude to and relationship with themselves:

- What does Anorexia have you believing about yourself?
- Do your doubts about your ability to come out from under Addiction's oppression mean that you are weak, or do your doubts mean that your voice needs your commitment so that it becomes louder than Addiction's lies?
- What gives you the strength to withstand your despair at those times?
- What might it mean to you that you were able to resist (the problem)?
- What identity were you embodying when you resisted (It)?
- What skills empowered you to defend yourself against Self-harm's influence?
- What skills empowered you to take back agency in your life?

Preference questions

- Does your policing of your body/harming yourself / taking drugs/enrich your life?
- Do you want to think of yourself as someone who is very sick, or as someone with a voice that deserves to be heard?
- How would you prefer your relationship to (Despair) to be?
- Are you content to submit to its claims on your life, or would you prefer to take your life over and make it your own?
- Why do you think you prefer to speak with your own voice, instead of Anorexia's / The Cutting's/Addiction's voice?
- Do you consider the times when you resisted (Its) claims on your life to be significant for how you want to live your life, or are they trivial and unimportant?
- When you die, do you want to be remembered for being the thinnest person you could be, or as someone who lived life to the full, who gave to her family, friends and community?
- Do you want to go along with society's values that define us by how we look, or do you want to define yourself on your own terms?
- You feel relief when you cut yourself. If Cutting were a destiny that you were allocated at birth and other infants were not, would you have any questions about this being your fate?
- Is this okay for you? Why not?
- What stories might your parents share about why you are not happy that Cutting is your fate?

Sources: Combs & Freedman (2012); Lock et al. (2004); White (2007, 2016); Winslade & Monk (2007)

A common narrative technique for clients to express their preferences is to write a letter to the problem, so that they can confront it and its influence in their lives – see Box 16.5. This client gave self-harm the name, 'Persistent pain' (Hoffman & Kress, 2008).

A variation of this technique is to have clients write a letter *from* the Problem, detailing what it wants for them and how it gangs up on them to prevent them from living their best life (Hoffman & Kress, 2008). A third method is for clients to draw the problem and, as sessions progress, to draw how they plan to defeat it. In addition to being able to read and re-read their letter, they can use their drawing as a visual reminder of their alternative story (Hoffman & Kress, 2008).

Box 16.5 A letter to the Problem

Dear Persistent Pain,

I am tired of you controlling my life. I want to wear short sleeve shirts. I want to act like everyone else. I am tired of hurting myself and pushing others away because I am afraid of what they will think if they know the truth about my relationship with you. I will make you stop hurting me. You're nasty and you make me feel ugly. It is you that is the problem. I want you to leave me alone. I want to be free of you.

Source: Hoffman & Kress (2008, p. 167)

Re-member social networks

Clients' self-harm isolates them in order to keep their actions a secret. A key intervention will be to repopulate their social networks, not only to avoid loneliness but also to provide a team that can stand with them in their resistance to the problem. Therefore, once clients are resisting The Problem's attempts to keep it all to itself, you can ask what they can do to reconnect with peers and family:

- Who helped you to defend yourself against being sucked in by (Despair)?
- Who is your greatest support at times when you feel most depressed? What do they do that is helpful?

A crisis response plan

For clients at low risk of suicide, counsellors can gain their commitment to return for another therapy session and make an appointment sooner than they otherwise might, have them agree to discard any drugs to which they have access, and have a responsible adult dispense their prescribed medications. A crisis response plan will entail being sure that clients and family have a list of the names and numbers of people and agencies to call in an emergency. Contingency planning takes the form of: If (x happens), the client will ... the family will ... and the service provider will ... (NSW Department of Health, 2004) and these agreements are documented. You will need their consent to communicate with their medical practitioners in case of an emergency.

Arrange a suicide watch

Some authors recommend a no-suicide pact, which is an agreement that the client will not take action to end their life until they return for another counselling session. However, there is no evidence that these work (Kroll, 2000). Breaking their word is probably the least of clients' problems at the time they attempt to end their lives. And if the attempt is not fatal, a pact can even increase their guilt afterwards.

Instead, for anyone at medium to high risk (who has thoughts, a plan and an intent to carry it out), ensure that the person is never left alone by arranging a 'suicide watch' roster of family and friends. This will involve having someone scheduled in four or six-hour shifts around the clock to be with the at-risk individual.

Health interventions

Physical recovery is vital alongside psychological recovery (Ganci et al., 2021). When people with severe anorexia are being force fed, Lock et al. (2004) advise reframing this, not as hospital staff trying to take over and 'save' their life when all they want to do is die, but instead as an effort to forbid anorexia from murdering them (Lock et al., 2004).

During a feeding regimen, medical practitioners will monitor for the emergence of refeeding syndrome, which is a potentially fatal shift in fluids and electrolytes and resulting clinical complications (Mehanna et al., 2008). They will monitor heart and blood pressure problems, electrolyte imbalances and bone marrow loss, among others and will test for blood cell counts in order to assess progress, as weight gain alone is a weak indicator of clients' true health status (Hay et al., 2014).

Prolonged starvation from addiction or anorexia will also lead to many nutrient deficiencies, which in itself will make physical and emotional recovery difficult. Therefore, under the guidance of an integrated medical practitioner, those attempting to recover will need, first, to supplement their digestive enzymes so that when they resume eating, they are more able to digest their food and less likely to experience nausea. Some could also have unrecognised food intolerances, in which case those foods will need to be eliminated from their diet (see Chapter 11).

Meanwhile blood tests will allow medical practitioners to target which specific nutrients have become deficient and a compounding pharmacy will make up a blend that precisely matches clients' nutritional needs. Particular attention will need to be paid to levels of magnesium because it is depleted by stress, and zinc, which is vital for the production of stomach acid and hence digestion of protein in particular; and both of these minerals are needed for the production of the sleep hormone, melatonin and the main neurotransmitters: serotonin, dopamine and norepinephrine (Kharrazian, 2013; Tabrizian 2003) - see Figure 11.2, page 150).

Sufferers will also likely be tested and, where relevant, treated for conditions such as weak methylation (see Chapter 11) and pyrrole disorder, in which there is poor absorption of zinc and vitamin B_6. This vitamin (pyridoxine) is involved in more bodily functions than almost any other nutrient, affecting both physical and emotional health (Balch, 2006). Its deficiency is common in anorexia, and is responsible for copious symptoms including anaemia, impaired antibody production, fatigue, muscle weakness, vomiting and impaired wound healing, with nervous system symptoms including confusion, depression and insomnia (Balch, 2006).

Diet

Except for those with orthorexia, the Nutripoints diet might be useful for anyone whose self-starvation from disordered eating or drug use has resulted in malnutrition (Vartabedian et al., 1990). In the accompanying manual to this diet, the nutritional value of each food has been calculated, so that by eating foods with high nutritive value in proportion across the food groups, each day the body will have gained at least the recommended daily intake (RDI) of nutrients, while keeping within bounds the dietary components that, although beneficial in small amounts, we often eat to excess - namely total and saturated fat, cholesterol, sodium, sugar, caffeine and alcohol.

The goal is to reach a total number of nutripoints by adding the values across six food groups (or five for vegetarians), in order to achieve an RDI for all nutrients. For people who are malnourished, achieving an RDI is unlikely to be sufficient, but it is a start. Given the beneficial effects of cholesterol on our brain (Perlmutter & Loberg, 2013), the points system inadvisedly penalises high-cholesterol foods such as eggs (at -11.5 points), while people with insulin problems might need to lower their fruit intake. Nevertheless, the diet takes the guesswork out of determining whether you have received enough of each macronutrient each day, allows you to make up for a poor day by topping up with highest-rating foods within a day or two and is positive in that you are aiming for a high number, in contrast with calorie-controlled diets where any intake can be seen to be a negative. Even if clients only used the system to select within a food group for the highest nutrient count, their diet would be improved. For example, they might choose 150 grams of strawberries (with their 19 nutripoints), rather than a plum (at 6 points) or an apple (at 4.5 points); or they could decide on 150g of spinach (at 75 points) in preference to corn on the cob (at 6 points).

Urge surfing

Addictions - whether to substances or to self-harm - 'talk to us' whenever we attempt to give them up: 'Just once more; I deserve it' (Lock et al., 2004). Therefore, counsellors will need to ask users how they can think past the immediate positive effects of their behaviours to their delayed negative outcomes. One possibility is to explain that urges come in waves. When clients can do something to wait out the urge, the wave recedes. Briere and Scott (2015, p. 224) term this 'urge surfing', based on the advice that, 'You can't stop the waves, but you can learn to surf'.

After a brief discussion of this concept, your next questions would be,

'Tell me about the times when you've managed to overcome the urge to use/cut yourself (etc.)? ... What was happening at that time? ... What did you do that made a difference? ... Did you know you could do that? ... How were you able to defy Addiction's urges? ... What gave you the strength to do it?... Where did that strength come from?... Is this what would would prefer to do? ... What would it take for you to do that again?'.

Postsuicide interventions in schools

Adolescents are particularly susceptible to an imitation effect, whereby their knowledge of the suicide of another increases the risk of further suicides in the same location, within a short space of time, or by the same method (Hawton et al., 2020; Niedzwiedz et al., 2014). Given that those who were distant from the deceased can be most at risk of imitation, when a student has died by suicide it is important to put in place a response for the whole school (Hawton et al., 2020). In-person debriefings can occur for students and staff, with social media postings used to disseminate accurate information and thereby to dispel rumours (Callahan, 1996). Information about the grief process, trauma, resilience and how to access available supports will be vital (Niedzwiedz et al., 2014; Torok et al., 2019). Advice to parents on how to talk to their children about suicide deaths is useful and, in Indigenous communities, the involvement of elders can be indispensable (Robertson et al., 2012).

Social media can provide a venue for memorialisation of someone who has died by suicide, although close friends of the deceased can see other peers' postings as intrusive and disingenuous, while the speed and urgency with which information spreads on social media increase the risk of imitation (Hawton et al., 2020; Robertson et al., 2012).

In the aftermath of a suicide, it is vital not to promote an atmosphere of 'romantic tragedy' such that those who have died by suicide are idealised (Callahan, 1996). Callahan advises counsellors to see students individually rather than in groups so that melodrama is not contagious (Morken et al., 2020), to not hold prolonged counselling sessions in order to avoid exacerbating emotional intensity, and to require students to make a counselling appointment outside of class time so that their feelings are not reacted to as if they were a crisis. Nevertheless, of course, for those expressing suicidal intent, a crisis response is essential (Callahan, 1996).

Collaboration with parents

Just as young people with self-destructive behaviours feel shame, so too do their parents. Any presenting issues of families can be a result of living with these conditions, especially long term. Secrecy, concealment and a gradual progression of symptoms make it difficult for parents to know that anorexia or self-harm or addiction have taken up residence in their family (Williams et al., 2020). The confirmation is typically preceded by a lingering stretch of time populated with suspicion, accusations and denials, unease and confusion (Williams et al., 2020).

Once the condition is acknowledged, parents commonly experience guilt, shame, helplessness, shock, self-blame, betrayal and ambiguous loss (Williams et al., 2020). There can also be many changes in family life such as the symptomatic individual becomes central to family life; conflict with that child is exacerbated and it is difficult for parents to trust them; and the family focus narrows to the here-and-now (De La Rie et al., 2005; Fox et al., 2017; Treasure & Nazar, 2016; Whitney & Eisler, 2005; Williams et al., 2020). Moreover, the family becomes isolated, perhaps to respect their child's privacy and perhaps in the hopes that their child will recover soon, in which case disclosure would not be necessary, and perhaps to prevent their child's difficulties coming to define them in the same way that it defines their child.

Siblings also have their own emotional responses to their brother or sister's predicament and need support themselves (Fox et al., 2017; Nilsen et al., 2021), not least because their parents will be occupied dealing with the symptomatic sibling. Nilsen and colleagues found that siblings need information about the condition, its treatment and how their sister or brother is coping.

Parents will often be in despair and will need a moratorium on guilt. You can deconstruct guilt with questions such as (Freeman et al., 1997):

- What does Cutting/Anorexia/Drugs have you thinking about yourselves as parents?
- Have you accused yourself of being too close/not close enough to your child?
- Have you accused yourself of being too involved with your work/not having your own separate life?
- Have you accused yourself of being distracted by the needs of your other children?
- Have you accused yourself for not having other children?

These and many similar questions subtly undermine and put a moratorium on parents' guilt. They can be followed with an outright challenge to guilt with (Freeman et al., 1997):

- Right now, do you feel inclined to explore further your culpability for your child's problem, or do you think it's time to invest in solving it?
- In view of what you have been through, do you think it would be wise to continue the problem-solving tactics that you have been using, or would you prefer to let your child's wisdom show the way?

As the conversation progresses, we can help parents and young people realise that they share the same goals, with questions such as:

- What do your hopes and dreams for your child's recovery tell you about your love for them?
- Is there anyone you know who would not be surprised to learn about this love that you have for your child?
- If your child's voice were to grow louder, and The Cutting's voice to grow silent, what would you want to hear your child saying?
- What effect would this have on (your child)? On you? On your family?

Finally, questions to recruit their support for an alternative story for their daughter or son include (White, 2016):

- What have you witnessed (name of child) doing that could throw some light on how they are defying Anorexia's demands of them?
- What stories from their past can you tell me about where this skill of standing up to The Cutting came from?
- What have you witnessed them doing in the past that gave you a hint that this would be a possibility for them?

Szapocznik and Williams (2000) recognise that many times counsellors cannot get access to the family members of young clients, but we can use a 'one person family therapy' approach by asking relationship questions about how other family members see the problem and the young person, what evidence they would provide about the young person's ability to overcome their self-destructive patterns and what this implies for their identity.

Conclusion

Never in the history of civilisation has the sentence ever been uttered that, 'Taking drugs has improved my quality of life'. Addiction and all other self-harming acts are a self-destructive solution to unhappiness, disconnection and a lack of purpose, one that detracts from all three. The tragedy is that people who are already in pain are rendered more hopeless and distressed by their self-harm, and the lack of emotional robustness that made them vulnerable in the first place makes it difficult for them to recover. It is vital, therefore, that we mine for alternative stories that identify their values and strengths and how they have employed these in the past and could do so again.

The approaches outlined here are in accord with what clients and their families are asking for in treatment for these conditions – namely, a shift from a focus on ceasing the self-destructive behaviour, to a more holistic focus on emotional needs; a collaborative relationship between counsellors, clients and their families; a focus on the person, not on treating the condition; and enhanced family and peer support for clients and their families (Mitrofan et al., 2019).

Narrative approaches view young people as *facing* rather than *being* a problem (Freeman et al., 1997). It is vital not to be intimidated by the gravity of these problems. While taking *clients* seriously, we need to be irreverent about *problems* (Gehart, 2018): We must not over-react and let problems scare us, and instead maintain a sense of calm and faith that individuals can find a way out of their predicament – because, if we do not have faith in their inner wisdom, they certainly cannot.

References

Adrian, M., Berk, M. S., Korslund, K., Whitlock, K., McCauley, E., & Linehan, M. (2018). Parental validation and invalidation predict adolescent self-harm. *Professional Psychology: Research and Practice*, *49*(4), 274–281. https://doi.org/10.1037/pro0000200

Afifi, T. O., Taillieu, T., Salmon, S., Davila, I. G., Stewart-Tufescu, A., Fortier, J., ... & MacMillan, H. L. (2020). Adverse childhood experiences (ACEs), peer victimization, and substance use among adolescents. *Child Abuse and Neglect*, *106*, 104504. https://doi.org/10.1016/j.chiabu.2020.104504

Andersen, S. L. (2019). Stress, sensitive periods, and substance abuse. *Neurobiology of Stress*, *10*, 100140. https://doi.org/10.1016/j.ynstr.2018.100140

Asarnow, J. R., & Mehlum, L. (2019). Practitioner review: Treatment for suicidal and self-harming adolescents – advances in suicide prevention care. *Journal of Child Psychology and Psychiatry*, *60*(1), 1046–1054. https://doi.org/10.1111/jcpp.13130

Australian Bureau of Statistics. (2021). *Causes of death, Australia*. ABS. https://www.abs.gov.au/statistics/health/causes-death/causes-death-australia/latest-release

Bailey, A. P., Parker, A. G., Colautti, L. A., Hart, L. M., Liu, P., & Hetrick, S. E. (2014). Mapping the evidence for the prevention and treatment of eating disorders in young people. *Journal of Eating Disorders*, *2*(5). https://doi.org/10.1186/2050-2974-2-5

Balch, P. A. (2006). *Prescription for nutritional healing* (4th ed.). Avery Trade.

Ballester, L., Valero, M., Orte, C., & Amer, J. (2018). An analysis of family dynamics: A selective substance abuse prevention programme for adolescents. *European Journal of Social Work*, *23*(1), 93–105. https://doi.org/10.1080/13691457.2018.1473842

Bayes, A., & Madden, S. (2011). Early onset eating disorder in male adolescents: A series of 10 inpatients. *Australasian Psychiatry*, *19*(6), 526–530. https://doi.org/10.3109/10398562.2011.603328

Bean, R. A., Keenan, B. H., & Fox, C. (2022). Treatment of adolescent non-suicidal self-inquiry: A review of family factors and family therapy. *The American Journal of Family Therapy*, *50*(3), 264–279. https://doi.org/10.1080/01926187.2021.1909513

Beautrais, A. L., Joyce, P. R., & Mulder, R. T. (2016). Youth suicide attempts: A social and demographic profile. *Australian and New Zealand Journal of Psychiatry*, *32*(3). https://doi.org/10.3109/00048679809065527

Benedini, K. M., & Fagan, A. A. (2020). From child maltreatment to adolescent substance use: Different pathways for males and females? *Feminist Criminology*, *15*(2), 147–173. https://doi.org/10.1177/1557085118810426

Berg, I. K., & Steiner, S. (2003). *Children's solution work*. Norton.

Bogenschneider, K., Wu, M., Raffaelli, M., & Tsay, J. C. (1998). Parent influences on adolescent peer orientation and substance use: The interface of parenting practices and values. *Child Development*, *69*(6), 1672-1688. https://doi.org/10.1111/j.1467-8624.1998.tb06184.x

Briere, J. N., & Scott, C. (2015). *Principles of trauma therapy: A guide to symptoms, evaluation, and treatment* (2nd ed.). Sage.

Brown, B. (2007). *I thought it was just me (but it isn't)*. Gotham.

Buddeberg, C., Buddeberg-Fischer, B., Gnam, G., Schmid, J., & Christen, S. (1996). Suicidal behavior in Swiss students: An 18-month follow-up survey. *Crisis*, *17*(2), 78–86. https://doi.org/10.1027/0227-5910.17.2.78

Cabot, S. (2004). *Magnesium: The miracle mineral*. WHAS.

Cabot, S., & Jasinska, M. (2011). *Infertility: The hidden causes*. WHAS.

Callahan, J. (1996). Negative effects of a school suicide postvention program—a case example. *Crisis*, *17*(3), 108–115. https://doi.org/10.1027/0227-5910.17.3.108

Campbell-McBride, N. (2010). *Gut and psychology syndrome*. Medinform.

Carbonneau, R., Vitaro, F., Brendgen, M., & Tremblay, R. E. (2022). Alcohol, marijuana and other illicit drugs use throughout adolescence: Co-occurring courses and preadolescent risk factors. *Child Psychiatry and Human Development*, *53*(6), 1194–1206. https://doi.org/10.1007/s10578-021-01202-w

Chiang, Y. C., Li, X., Lee, C. Y., Wu, C. C., Chang, H. Y., & Zhang, S. (2022). Effects of social attachment on experimental drug use from childhood to adolescence: An 11-year prospective cohort study. *Frontiers in Public Health*, *10*, 818894. https://doi.org/10.3389/fpubh.2022.818894

Collison, D. R., & Hall, T. (1989). *Why do I feel so awful?* Angus and Robertson.

Conner, K. R., & Ilgen, M. A. (2011). Substance use disorders and suicidal behavior. In R. C. O'Connor, S. Platt & J. Gordon (Eds.), *International handbook of suicide prevention: Research, policy and practice* (pp. 93–107). Wiley-Blackwell.

Datta, N., Matheson, B. E., Citron, K., van Wye, E. M., & Lock, J. D. (2022). Evidence based update on psychosocial treatments for eating disorders in children and adolescents. *Journal of Clinical Child and Adolescent Psychology*. https://doi.org/10.1080/15374416.2022.2109650

De La Rie, S. M., Van Furth, E. F., De Koning, A., Noordenbos, G., & Donker, M. C. (2005). The quality of life of family caregivers of eating disorder patients. *Eating Disorders*, *13*(4), 345–351. https://doi.org/10.1080/10640260591005236

Deas, D., & Brown, E. S. (2006). Adolescent substance abuse and psychiatric comorbidities. *Journal of Clinical Psychiatry*, *67*(S7), 18–23.

Dobrescu, S. R., Dinkler, L., Gillberg, C., Råstam, M., Gillberg, C., & Wentz, E. (2020). Anorexia nervosa: 30-year outcome. *British Journal of Psychiatry*, *216*(2), 97–104. https://doi.org/10.1192/bjp.2019.113

Dube, S. R., Anda, R. F., Felitti, V. J., Chapman, D. P., Williamson, D. F., & Giles, W. H. (2001). Childhood abuse, household dysfunction, and the risk of attempted suicide throughout the life span: findings from the Adverse Childhood Experiences Study. *JAMA*, *286*(24), 3089–3096. https://doi.org/10.1001/jama.286.24.3089

El Nagar, Z. M., Barakat, D. H., Rabie, M. A. E. M., Thabeet, D. M., & Mohamed, M. Y. (2022). Relation of non-suicidal self-harm to emotion regulation and alexithymia in sexually abused children and adolescents. *Journal of Child Sexual Abuse*, *31* (4), 431–446. https://doi.org/10.1080/10538712.2022.2047855

Elison, J., Garofalo, C., & Velotti, P. (2014). Shame and aggression: Theoretical considerations. *Aggression and Violent Behaviour*, *19*(4), 447–453. https://doi.org/10.1016/j.avb.2014.05.002

Elkind, D. (1967). Egocentrism in adolescence. *Child Development*, *38*(4), 1025–1034. https://doi.org/10.2307/1127100

Ellis, É. (2022). A critical, relational approach for working with suicide in family therapy. *Australian and New Zealand Journal of Family Therapy*, *43*(1), 104–117. https://doi.org/10.1002/anzf.1477

Epstein, S., Roberts, E., Sedgwick, R., Polling, C., Finning, K., Ford, T., Dutta, R., & Downs, J. (2020). School absenteeism as a risk factor for self-harm and suicidal ideation in children and adolescents: A systematic review and meta-analysis. *European Child and Adolescent Psychiatry*, *29*, 1175–1194. https://doi.org/10.1007/s00787-019-01327-3

Fairburn, C. G., Cooper, Z., Shafran, R., & Wilson, G. T. (2008). Eating disorders: A transdiagnostic protocol. In D. H. Barlow (Ed.), *Clinical handbook of psychological disorders: A step-by-step treatment manual* (4th ed., pp. 578–614). Guilford.

Feldman Barrett, L. (2020). *Seven and a half lessons about the brain*. Picador.

Fergusson, D. M., Beautrais, A. L., & Horwood, L. J. (2003). Vulnerability and resiliency to suicidal behaviours in young people. *Psychological Medicine*, *33*(1), 61–73. https://doi.org/10.1017/S0033291702006748

Fisher, H. L., Moffitt, T. E., Houts, R. M., Belsky, D. W., & Arseneault, L. (2012). Bullying victimization and risk of self harm in early adolescence: Longitudinal cohort study. *British Medical Journal*, *344*. http://www.bmj.com/content/344/bmj.e2683

Fortune, S., Cottrell, D. & Fyfe, S. (2016). Family factors associated with adolescent self-harm: A narrative review. *Journal of Family Therapy*, *38*(2), 226–256. https://doi.org/10.1111/1467-6427.12119

Fox, J. R., Dean, M., & Whittlesea, A. (2017). The experience of caring for or living with an individual with an eating disorder: A meta-synthesis of qualitative studies. *Clinical Psychology and Psychotherapy*, *24*(1), 103–125. https://doi.org/10.1002/cpp.1984

Freeman, J., Epston, D., & Lobovits, D. (1997). *Playful approaches to serious problems: Narrative therapy with children and their families*. Norton.

Ganci, M., Atkins, L., & Roberts, M. E. (2021). Exploring alternatives for adolescent anorexia nervosa: Adolescent and parent treatment (APT) as a novel intervention prospect. *Journal of Eating Disorders*, *9*, 67. https://doi.org/10.1186/s40337-021-00423-7

Garofalo, R., Wolf, C., Wissow, L. S., Woods, E. R., & Goodman, E. (1999). Sexual orientation and risk of suicide attempts among a representative sample of youth. *Archives of Pediatrics and Adolescent Medicine*, *153*(5), 487–493. https://doi.org/10.1001/archpedi.153.5.487

Gehart, D. (2018). *Mastering competencies in family therapy: A practical approach to theories and clinical case documentation* (3rd ed.). Cengage.

Gijzen, M. W., Rasing, S. P., Creemers, D. H., Smit, F., Engels, R. C., & De Beurs, D. (2021). Suicide ideation as a symptom of adolescent depression: A network analysis. *Journal of Affective Disorders*, *278*, 68–77. https://doi.org/10.1016/j.jad.2020.09.029

Glenn, C. R., Esposito, E. C., Porter, A. C., & Robinson, D. J. (2019). Evidence base update of psychosocial treatments for self-injurious thoughts and behaviors in youth. *Journal of Child and Adolescent Psychiatry*, *48*(3), 357–392. https://doi.org/10.1080/15374416.2016.1591281

Gomes, M. C., Granville-Garcia, A. F., Neves, E. T. B., da Costa Dutra, L., Ferreira, F. M., & Paiva, S. M. (2021). Family and contextual factors associated with licit drug use in adolescence. *Revista de Saúde Pública*, *55*, 95. https://doi.org/10.11606/s1518-8787.2021055003531

Goodenow, C., Szalacha, L., & Westheimer, K. (2006). School support groups, other school factors and the safety of sexual minority adolescents. *Psychology in the Schools*, *43*(5), 573–589. https://doi.org/10.1002/pits.20173

Granello, D. H. (2010). The process of suicide risk assessment: Twelve core principles. *Journal of Counseling and Development*, *88*(3), 363–371. https://doi.org/10.1002/j.1556-6678.2010.tb00034.x

Greydanus, D. E. (2011). Treating self-harm in children and adolescents: A complex conundrum for the clinician. *Psychiatric Times*, *28*(2), 33–33; 36–37.

Gültzow, T., Guidry, J., Schneider, F., & Hoving, C. (2020). Male body image portrayals on instagram. *Cyberpsychology, Behavior and Social Networking*, *23*(5), 281–289. https://doi.org/10.1089/cyber.2019.0368

Hannen, E., & Woods, K. (2012). Narrative therapy with an adolescent who self-cuts: A case example. *Educational Psychology in Practice*, *28*(2), 187–214. https://doi.org/10.1080/02667363.2012.669362

Harter, S. (2006). The development of self-esteem. In M. H. Kernis (Ed.), *Self-esteem: Issues and answers: A sourcebook of current perspectives* (pp. 144–150). Psychology Press.

Hawkins, J. D., Guo, J., Hill, K. G., Battin-Pearson, S., & Abbott, R. D. (2001). Long-term effects of the Seattle social development intervention on school bonding trajectories. *Applied Developmental Science*, *5*(4), 225–236. https://doi.org/10.1207/S1532480XADS0504_04

Hawton, K., & Fagg, J. (1988). Suicide, and other causes of death, following attempted suicide. *The British Journal of Psychiatry*, *152*(3), 359–366. https://doi.org/10.1192/bjp.152.3.359

Hawton, K., Witt, K. G., Taylor Salisbury, T. L., Arensman, E., Gunnell, D., Townsend, E., van Heeringen, K., & Hazel, P. (2015). Interventions for self-harm in children and adolescents. *Cochrane Database of Systematic Reviews*, *12*, CD012013. https://doi.org/10.1002/14651858.CD012013

Hawton, K., Hill, N. T., Gould, M., John, A., Lascelles, K., & Robinson, J. (2020). Clustering of suicides in children and adolescents: A review. *The Lancet Child and Adolescent Health*, *4*(1), 58–67. https://doi.org/10.1016/S2352-4642(19)30335-9

Hay, P., Chinn, D., Forbes, D., Madden, S., Newton, R., Sugenor, L., Touyz, S., & Ward, W. (2014). Royal Australian and New Zealand College of Psychiatrists clinical practice guidelines for the treatment of eating disorders. *Australian and New Zealand Journal of Psychiatry*, *48*(11), 1–62. https://doi.org/10.1177/0004867414555814

Hengartner, M. P., Angst, J., Ajdacic-Gross, V., & Rössler, W. (2020). Cannabis use during adolescence and the occurrence of depression, suicidality and anxiety disorder across adulthood: Findings from a longitudinal cohort study over 30 years. *Journal of Affective Disorders*, *272*, 98–103. https://doi.org/10.1016/j.jad.2020.03.126

Herpertz-Dahlmann, D. (2017). Treatment of eating disorders in child and adolescent psychiatry. *Current Opinion in Psychiatry*, *30*(6), 438–445. https://doi.org/10.1097/YCO.0000000000000357

Hoffman, R. M., & Kress, V. E. (2008). Narrative therapy and non-suicidal-self-injurious behavior: Externalizing the problem and internalizing personal agency. *Journal of Humanistic Counselling, Education and Development*, *47*(2), 157–171. https://doi.org/10.1002/j.2161-1939.2008.tb00055.x

Hoare, P., & Cosgrove, L. (1998). Eating habits, body-esteem and self-esteem in Scottish children and adolescents. *Journal of Psychosomatic Research*, *45*(5), 425–431. https://doi.org/10.1016/S0022-3999(98)00025-7

Hua, P., Bugeja, L., & Maple, M. (2019). A systematic review on the relationship between childhood exposure to external cause parental death, including suicide, on subsequent suicidal behaviour. *Journal of Affective Disorders*, *257*, 723–734. https://doi.org/10.1016/j.jad.2019.07.082

Hulten, A., Jiang, G. X., Wasserman, D., Hawton, K., Hjelmeland, H., De Leo, D., … & Schmidtke, A. (2001). Repetition of attempted suicide among teenagers in Europe: frequency, timing and risk factors. *European Child and Adolescent Psychiatry*, *10*(3), 161–169. https://doi.org/10.1007/s007870170022

Jacquet, J. (2015). *Is shame necessary?: New uses for an old tool*. Pantheon Books.

Jobes, D. A., & O'Connor, S. S. (2009). The duty to protect suicidal clients: Ethical, legal, and professional considerations. In J. L. Werth, Jr., E. R. Welfel & G. A. H. Benjamin (Eds.), *The duty to protect: Ethical, legal, and professional considerations for mental health professionals* (pp. 163–180). American Psychological Association.

Juarascio, A., Shaw, J., Forman, E., Timko, C. A., Herbert, J. D., Butryn, M., & Lowe, M. (2013). Acceptance and commitment therapy for eating disorders: Clinical applications of a group treatment. *Journal of Contextual Behavioral Science*, *2*(3–4), 89–94. https://doi.org/10.1016/j.jcbs.2013.08.001

Kanel, K. (2018). *A guide to crisis intervention* (6th ed.). Cengage.

Kazdin, A. E., Fitzsimmons-Craft, E. E., & Wilfley, D. E. (2017). Addressing critical gaps in the treatment of eating disorders. *International Journal of Eating Disorders*, *50*(3), 170–189. https://doi.org/10.1002/eat.22670

Kerkhof, A., & van Spijker, B. (2011). Worrying and rumination as proximal risk factors for suicidal behaviour. In R. C. O'Connor, S. Platt & J. Gordon (Eds.), *International handbook of suicide prevention: Research, policy and practice* (pp. 199–209). Wiley-Blackwell.

Kharrazian, D. (2013). *Why isn't my brain working?* Elephant Press.

Kothgassner, O. D., Goreis, A., Robinson, K., Huscsava, M. M., Schmahl, C., & Plener, P. L. (2021). Efficacy of dialectical behavior therapy for adolescent self-harm and suicidal ideation: A systematic review and meta-analysis. *Psychological Medicine*, *51*, 1057–1057. https://doi.org/10.1017/S0033291721001355

Koyanagi, A., Oh, H., Carvalho, A. F., Smith, L., Haro, J. M., Vancampfort, D., … & DeVylder, J. E. (2019). Bullying victimization and suicide attempt among adolescents aged 12–15 years from 48 countries. *Journal of the American Academy of Child and Adolescent Psychiatry*, *58*(9), 907–918. https://doi.org/10.1016/j.jaac.2018.10.018

Kroll, J. (2000). Use of no-suicide contracts by psychiatrists in Minnesota. *American Journal of Psychiatry*, *157*(10), 1684–1686. https://doi.org/10.1176/appi.ajp.157.10.1684

Kwan, L. Y., Eaton, D. L., Andersen, S. L., Dow-Edwards, D., Levin, E. D., Talpos, J., Vorhees, C. V., & Li, A. A. (2020). This is your teen brain on drugs: In search of biological factors unique to dependence toxicity in adolescence. *Neurotoxicology and Teratology*, *81*, 106916. https://doi.org/10.1016/j.ntt.2020.106916

Laye-Gindhu, A., & Schonert-Reichl, K. A. (2005). Nonsuicidal self-harm among community adolescents: Understanding the 'whats' and 'whys' of self-harm. *Journal of Youth and Adolescence*, *34*, 447–457. https://doi.org/10.1007/s10964-005-7262-z

Lee, S., Dwyer, J., Paul, E., Clarke, D., Treleaven, S., & Roseby, R. (2019). Differences by age and sex in adolescent suicide. *Australian and New Zealand Journal of Public Health*, *43*(3), 248–253. https://doi.org/10.1111/1753-6405.12877

Lester, D. (2002). Serum cholesterol levels and suicide: A meta-analysis. *Suicide and Life-Threatening Behavior*, *32*(3), 333–346. https://doi.org/10.1521/suli.32.3.333.22177

Lim, K. S., Wong, C. H., McIntyre, R. S., Wang, J., Zhang, Z., Tran, B. X., ... & Ho, R. C. (2019). Global lifetime and 12-month prevalence of suicidal behavior, deliberate self-harm and non-suicidal self-injury in children and adolescents between 1989 and 2018: A meta-analysis. *International Journal of Environmental Research and Public Health*, *16*(22), 4581. https://doi.org/10.3390/ijerph16224581

Lock, A., Epston, D., & Maisel, R. (2004). Countering that which is called anorexia. *Narrative Inquiry*, *14*(2), 275–301. https://doi.org/10.1075/ni.14.2.06loc

Lukas, L., Buhl, C., Schulte-Körne, G., & Sfärlea, A. (2022). Family, friends, and feelings: The role of relationships to parents and peers and alexithymia in adolescents with anorexia nervosa. *Journal of Eating Disorders*, *10*, 143. https://doi.org/10.1186/s40337-022-00661-3

Madge, N., Hawton, K., McMahon, E. M., Corcoran, P., De Leo, D., de Wilde, E. J., & Arensman, E. (2011). Psychological characteristics, stressful life events and deliberate self-harm: Findings from the Child and Adolescent Self-harm in Europe (CASE) Study. *European Child and Adolescent Psychiatry*, *20*(10). https://doi.org/10.1007/s00787-011-0210-4

Manhica, H., Straatmann, V. S., Lundin, A., Agardh, E., & Danielsson, A. K. (2020). Association between poverty exposure during childhood and adolescence, and drug use disorders and drug-related crimes later in life. *Addiction*, *116*, 1747–1756. https://doi.org/10.1111/add.15336

Mann, J., & Currier, D., (2011). Relationships of gene and early-life experience to the neurobiology of suicidal behaviour. In R. C. O'Connor, S. Platt & J. Gordon (Eds.), *International handbook of suicide prevention: Research, policy and practice* (pp. 133–150). Wiley-Blackwell.

Marsh, A., Dale, A., & O'Toole, S. (2013). *Addiction counselling: Content and process* (2nd ed.). IP Communications.

Martin, C. E. (2007). *Perfect girls, starving daughters*. Piatkus.

Martin, C. V., Guterman, J. T., & Shatz, K. (2012, March 21–25). *Solution-focused counseling for eating disorders*. Paper presenting at the *American Counseling Association, San Francisco*.

McQueeny, T., Schweinsburg, B. C., Schweinsburg, A. D., Jacobus, J., Bava, S., Frank, L. R., & Tapert, S. F. (2009). Altered white matter integrity in adolescent binge drinkers. *Alcoholism: Clinical and Experimental Research*, *33*(7), 1278–1285. https://doi.org/10.1111/j.1530-0277.2009.00953.x

McWhirter, J. J., McWhirter, B. T., McWhirter, E. H., & McWhirter, R. J. (2013). *At risk youth: A comprehensive response for counselors, teachers, psychologists, and human service professionals*. Brooks/Cole.

Mehanna, H. M., Moledina, J., & Travis, J. (2008). Refeeding syndrome: What it is and how to prevent and treat it. *British Medical Journal*, *336*(7659), 1495–1498. https://doi.org/10.1136/bmj.a301

Metcalf, L. (2017). *Solution focused narrative therapy*. Springer.

Miller, M., Redley, M., & Wilkinson, P. O. (2021). A qualitative study of understanding reasons for self-harm in adolescent girls. *International Journal of Environmental Research and Public Health*, *18*(7). https://doi.org/10.3390/ijerph18073361

Miner, C. L., Love. H. A. & Paik, S. E. (2016). Non-suicidal self-injury in adolescents: Addressing the function and the family from the perspective of systemic family therapies. *American Journal of Family Therapy*, *44*(4), 211–220. https://doi.org/10.1080/01926187.2016.1150798

Mishra, A. A., Marceau, K., Christ, S. L., Schwab Reese, L. M., Taylor, Z. E., & Knopik, V. S. (2022). Multi-type childhood maltreatment exposure and substance use development from adolescence to early adulthood: A GxE study. *Child Abuse and Neglect*, *126*, 105508. https://doi.org/10.1016/j.chiabu.2022.105508

Mitrofan, O., Petkova, H., Janssens, A., Kelly, J., Edwards, E., & Byford, S. (2019). Care experiences of young people with eating disorders and their parents: Qualitative study. *BJPsychOpen*, *5*, e6, 1–8. https://doi.org/0.1192/bjo.2018.78

Monteleone, A. M., Cascino, G., Martini, M., Patriciello, G., Ruzzi, V., Delsedime, N., Abbate-Daga, G., & Marzola, E. (2020). Confidence in one-self and confidence in one's own body: The revival of an old paradigm for anorexia nervosa. *Clinical Psychology and Psychotherapy*, *28*, 818–827. https://doi.org/10.1002/cpp.2535

Morgan, A. (Ed.) (1999). *Once upon a time... Narrative therapy with children and their families*. Dulwich Centre Publications.

Morken, I. S., Dahlgren, A., Lunde, I., & Toven, S. (2020). The effects of interventions preventing self-harm and suicide in children and adolescents: An overview of systematic reviews. *F1000Research*, *8*, 890. https://doi.org/10.12688/f1000research.19506.2

Morris, A., Elliott, E., & Madden, S. (2022). Early-onset eating disorders in Australian children: A national surveillance study showing increased incidence. *International Journal of Eating Disorders*, *55*, 1838–1842. https://doi.org/10.1002/eat.23794

Moss, H. B. (2008). Alcohol and adolescent brain development. *Alcoholism: Clinical and Experimental Research*, *32*(3), 427–429. https://doi.org/10.1111/j.1530-0277.2007.00606.x

Myers, D. G. (2005). *Social psychology* (8th ed.). McGraw-Hill.

Nawi, A. M., Ismail, R., Ibrahim, F., Hassan M. R., Manaf, M. R. A., Amit, N., Ibrahim, N., & Shafurdin, N. S. (2021). Risk and protective factors of drug abuse among adolescents: A systematic review. *BMC Public Health*, *21*, 2088. https://doi.org/10.1186/s12889-021-11906-2

Niedzwiedz, C., Haw, C., Hawton, K., & Platt, S. (2014). The definition and epidemiology of clusters of suicidal behavior: A systematic review. *Suicide and Life-Threatening Behavior*, *44*(5), 569–581. https://doi.org/10.1111/sltb.12091

Nilsen, J. V., Hage, T. W., Rø, Ø., Halvorsen, I., & Oddli, H. W. (2021). Family-based inpatient treatment for adolescent anorexia nervosa: A thematic analysis of former patients' post-treatment reflections. *Eating Disorders*, *29*(4), 390–407. https://doi.org/10.1080/10640266.2019.1656469

Nock, M. K., Green, J. G., Hwang, I., McLaughlin, K. A., Sampson, N. A., Zaslavsky, A. M., & Kessler, R. C. (2013). Prevalence, correlates, and treatment of lifetime suicidal behavior among adolescents: Results from the National Comorbidity Survey Replication Adolescent Supplement. *JAMA Psychiatry*, *70*(3), 300–310. https://doi.org/10.1001/2013.jamapsychiatry.55

NSW Department of Health. (2004). *Framework for suicide risk assessment and management for NSW health Staff*. Author.

Norris, M. L., Spettigue, W. J., & Katzman, D. K. (2016). Update on eating disorders: Current perspectives on avoidant/restrictive food intake disorder in children and youth. *Neuropsychiatric Disease and Treatment*, *12*, 213–218. http://dx.doi.org/10.2147/NDT.S82538

NZ Parliament. (2022). *Suicide in New Zealand: A snapshot of recent trends*. Parliamentary Library Te Pātaka Rangahau Research Paper, 2022/01.

O'Connor, R. C. (2011). Towards an integrated motivational-volitional model of suicidal behaviour. In R. C. O'Connor, S. Platt & J. Gordon (Eds.), *International handbook of suicide prevention: Research, policy and practice* (pp. 181–198). Wiley-Blackwell.

O'Reilly, L. M., Pettersson, E., Donahue, K., Quinn, P. D., Klonsky, E. D., Lundström, S., … & D'Onofrio, B. M. (2021). Sexual orientation and adolescent suicide attempt and self-harm: A co-twin control study. *Journal of Child Psychology and Psychiatry*, *62*(7), 834–841. https://doi.org/10.1111/jcpp.13325

Onnink, C. M., Konstantinidou, Y., Moskovich, A. A., Karekla, M. K., & Merwin, R. M. (2022). Acceptance and commitment therapy (ACT) for eating disorders: A systematic review of intervention studies and call to action. *Journal of Contextual Behavioral Science*, *26*, 11–28. https://doi.org/10.1016/j.jcbs.2022.08.005

Osuch, E. A., Noll, J. G., & Putnam, F. W. (1999). The motivations for self-injury in psychiatric inpatients. *Psychiatry: Interpersonal and Biological Processes*, *62*(4), 334–346. https://doi.org/10.1080/00332747.1999.11024881

Ougrin, D., Wong, B. H. C., Vaezinejad, M., Plener, P. L., Mehdi, T., Romaniuk, L., … & Landau, S. (2021). Pandemic-related emergency psychiatric presentations for self-harm of children and adolescents in 10 countries (PREP-kids): a retrospective international cohort study. *European Child and Adolescent Psychiatry*, 1–13. https://doi.org/10.1007/s00787-021-01741-6

Peh, C. X., Shahwan, S., Fauxiana, R., Mahesh, M. V., Sambasivam, R., & Subramaniam, M. (2017). Emotion dysregulation as a mechanism linking child maltreatment exposure and self-harm behaviors in adolescents. *Child Abuse and Neglect*, *67*, 383–390. https://doi.org/10.1016/j.chiabu.2017.03.013

Perlmutter, D., & Loberg, K. (2013). *Grain brain*. Little, Brown and Co.

Plana, T., Gracia, R., Méndez, I., Pintor, L., Lazaro, L., & Castro-Fornieles, J. (2010). Total serum cholesterol levels and suicide attempts in child and adolescent psychiatric inpatients. *European Child and Adolescent Psychiatry*, *19*(7), 615–619. https://doi.org/10.1007/s00787-009-0084-x

Platt, S. (2011). Inequalities and suicidal behaviour. In R. C. O'Connor, S. Platt & J. Gordon (Eds.), *International handbook of suicide prevention: Research, policy and practice* (pp. 211–234). Wiley-Blackwell.

Porter, L. (1980). *Evaluation of an alcohol education programme for periodic detainees*. Unpublished Master of Arts (Psychology) thesis. University of Canterbury.

Raifman, J., Charlton, B. M., Arrington-Sanders, R., Chan, P. A., Rusley, J., Mayer, K. H., ... & McConnell, M. (2020). Sexual orientation and suicide attempt disparities among US adolescents: 2009–2017. *Pediatrics, 145*(3), e20191658. https://doi.org/10.1542/peds.2019-1658

Rienecke, R. D. (2017). Family-based treatment of eating disorders in adolescents: Current insights. *Adolescent Health, Medicine and Therapeutics, 8*, 69–79. https://doi.org/10.2147/AHMT.S115775

Rihmer, Z. (2011). Depression and suicidal behavior. In R. C. O'Connor, S. Platt & J. Gordon (Eds.), *International handbook of suicide prevention: Research, policy and practice* (pp. 59–74). Wiley-Blackwell.

Robertson, L., Skegg, K., Poore, M., Williams, S., & Taylor, B. (2012). An adolescent suicide cluster and the possible role of electronic communication technology. *Crisis, 33*(4), 239–245. https://doi.org/10.1027/0227-5910/a000140

Robinson, A. L., Dolhanty, J., & Greenberg, L. (2013). Emotion-focused family therapy for eating disorders in children and adolescents. *Clinical Psychology and Psychotherapy, 22*(1). https://doi.org/10.1002/cpp.1861

Russell, A. E., Heron, J., Gunnell, D., Ford, T., Hemani, G., Joinson, C., ... & Mars, B. (2019). Pathways between early-life adversity and adolescent self-harm: The mediating role of inflammation in the Avon Longitudinal Study of Parents and Children. *Journal of Child Psychology and Psychiatry, 60*(10), 1094–1103. https://doi.org/10.1111/jcpp.13100

Santibáñez, R., Solabarrieta, J., & Ruiz-Narezo, M. (2020). School well-being and drug use in adolescence. *Frontiers in Psychology, 11*, 1668. https://doi.org/10.3389/fpsyg.2020.01668

Selekman, M. D. (2006). *Working with self-harming adolescents: A collaborative, strengths-based therapy approach*. Norton.

Sharry, J., Darmody, M., & Madden, B. (2002). A solution-focused approach to working with clients who are suicidal. *British Journal of Guidance and Counselling, 30*(4), 383–399. https://doi.org/10.1080/0306988021000025690

Simic, M., Stewart, C. S., Konstantellou, A., Hodsoll, J., Eisler, I., & Baudinet, J. (2022). From efficacy to effectiveness: Child and adolescent eating disorder treatments in the real world (part 1): Treatment course and outcomes. *Journal of Eating Disorders, 10*, 27. https://doi.org/10.1186/s40337-022-00553-6

Smith, T. W. (2015). *The book of human emotion: An encyclopedia of feeling from anger to wanderlust*. Profile Books.

Standley, C. J., & Foster-Fishman, P. (2021). Intersectionality, social support, and youth suicidality: A sociological approach to prevention. *Suicide and Life-Threatening Behavior, 51*(1), 203–211. https://doi.org/10.1111/sltb.12695

Stänicke, L. I., Haavind, H., & Gullestad, S. E. (2018). How do young people understand their own self-harm? A meta-synthesis of adolescents' subjective experience of self-harm. *Adolescent Research Review, 3*(2), 173–191. https://doi.org/10.1007/s40894-018-0080-9

Stewart, C. S., Baudinet. J., Munuve, A., Bell, A., Konstantellou, A., Eisler, I., & Simic, M. (2022). From efficacy to effectiveness: Child and adolescent eating disorder treatments in the real world (part 2): 7-year follow-up. *Journal of Eating Disorders, 10*, 14. https://doi.org/10.1186/s40337-022-00535-8

Stewart, J. G., Shields, G. S., Esposito, E. C., Cosby, E. A., Allen, N. B., Slavich, G. M., & Auerbach, R. P. (2019). Life stress and suicide in adolescents. *Journal of Abnormal Child Psychology, 47*(10), 1707–1722. https://doi.org/10.1007/s10802-019-00534-5

Szapocznik, J., & Williams, R. A. (2000). Brief strategic family therapy: Twenty-five years of interplay among theory, research and practice in adolescent behavior problems and drug abuse. *Clinical Child and Family Psychology Review, 3*(2), 117–134. https://doi.org/10.1023/A:1009512719808

Tabrizian, I. (2003). *Nutritional medicine: Fact and fiction* (4th ed.). Nutrition Review Service Publications.

Torok, M., Calear, A. L., Smart, A., Nicolopoulos, A., & Wong, Q. (2019). Preventing adolescent suicide: A systematic review of the effectiveness and change mechanisms of suicide prevention gatekeeping training programs for teachers and parents. *Journal of Adolescence, 73*, 100–112. https://doi.org/10.1016/j.adolescence.2019.04.005

Treasure, J., & Nazar, B. P. (2016). Interventions for the carers of patients with eating disorders. *Current Psychiatry Reports, 18*, 1–7. https://doi.org/10.1007/s11920-015-0652-3

Trucco, E. M. (2020). A review of psychosocial factors linked to adolescent substance use. *Pharmacology Biochemistry and Behavior, 196*, 172969. https://doi.org/10.1016/j.pbb.2020.172969

Tuisku, V., Kiviruusu, O., Pelkonen, M., Karlsson, L., Strandholm, T., & Marttunen, M. (2014). Depressed adolescents as young adults – predictors of suicide attempt and non-suicidal self-injury during an 8-year follow-up. *Journal of Affective Disorders, 152*, 313–319. https://doi.org/10.1016/j.jad.2013.09.031

Uddin, R., Burton, N. W., Maple, M., Khan, S. R., & Khan, A. (2019). Suicidal ideation, suicide planning, and suicide attempts among adolescents in 59 low-income and middle-income countries: A population-based study. *The Lancet Child and Adolescent Health*, *3*(4), 223–233. https://doi.org/10.1016/S2352-4642(18)30403-6

Valente, J. Y., Cogo-Moreira, H., & Sanchez, Z. M. (2017). Gradient of association between parenting styles and patterns of drug use in adolescence: A latent class analysis. *Drug and Alcohol Dependence*, *180*, 272–278. https://doi.org/10.1016/j.drugalcdep.2017.08.015

Van Vliet, K., & Kalnins, G. (2011). A compassion-focused approach to nonsuicidal self-injury. *Journal of Mental Health Counseling*, *33*(4), 295–311. https://doi.org/10.17744/mehc.33.4.j7540338q223t417

Vartabedian, R. E., Matthews, K., & Barnes, J. A. (1990). *Nutripoints: The breakthrough nutritional program*. Grafton.

Wasserman, D., Carli, V., Iosue, M., Javed, A., & Herrman, H. (2021). Suicide prevention in childhood and adolescence: A narrative review of current knowledge on risk and protective factors and effectiveness of interventions. *Asia-Pacific Psychiatry*, *13*(3), e12452. https://doi.org/10.1111/appy.12452

White, M. (2007). *Maps of narrative practice*. Norton.

White, M. (2016). *Narrative therapy classics*. Dulwich Centre Publications.

White, M., & Epston, D. (1990). *Narrative means to therapeutic ends*. Norton.

Whitney, J., & Eisler, I. (2005). Theoretical and empirical models around caring for someone with an eating disorder: The reorganization of family life and inter-personal maintenance factors. *Journal of Mental Health*, *14*(6), 575–585. https://doi.org/10.1080/09638230500347889

Williams, E. P., Russell-Mayhew, S., Moules, N. J., & Dimitropoulos, G. (2020). 'My whole world fell apart': Parents discovering their child has anorexia nervosa. *Qualitative Health Research*, *30*(12), 1821–1832. https://doi.org/10.1177/1049732320939508

Winslade, J., & Monk, G. (2007). *Narrative counseling in schools: Powerful and brief* (2nd ed.). Corwin Press.

Wu, S., Ding, Y., Wu, F., Xie, G., Hou, J., & Mao, P. (2016). Serum lipid levels and suicidality: A meta-analysis of 65 epidemiological studies. *Journal of Psychiatry and Neuroscience*, *41*(1), 56–69. https://doi.org/10.1503/jpn.150079

Yue, S. Y. P., & Ougrin, D. (2018). Self-harm and suicide. In M. Robson & S. Pattison (Eds.), *The handbook of counselling children and young people* (2nd ed., pp. 351–365). Sage.

Zubak, Z., Zenic, N., Ostojic, L., Zubak, I., & Pojskic, H. (2018). A prospective study on the influence of scholastic factors on the prevalence and initiation of illicit drug misuse in adolescence. *International Journal of Environmental Research and Public Health*, *15*(5), 874. https://doi.org/10.3390/ijerph15050874

Zubrick, S. R., Hafekost, J., Johnson, S. E., Lawrence, D., Saw, S., & Buckinghamn, W. J. (2016). Self-harm: Prevalence estimates from the second Australian child and adolescent survey of mental health and wellbeing. *Australian and New Zealand Journal of Psychiatry*, *50*(9), 911–921. https://doi.org/10.1177/0004867415617837

PART III

Social issues

17 Aggression

Aggression has four main functions (Dane et al., 2022). First, it gives perpetrators a competitive edge by gaining them access to resources. This serves a vital survival function; therefore, it is not surprising that it occurs at high rates in our species. Second, it functions as impression management, to gain social status or prestige from onlookers. A third form, proactive or callous actions, involves being hurtful just for fun or to alleviate boredom and signals that perpetrators are out of control of their impulses. Both the second and third types are linked to bullying (Dane et al., 2022). Fourth is reactive aggression in which perpetrators respond to perceived threats or provocation by lashing out at others; this signals that they are out of control of their emotions.

Modes of aggression

Aggression is an act intended to cause harm. As illustrated in Figure 17.1, it can be a reaction to events, can be proactive or can be bullying (which is discussed in Chapter 18). Reactive aggression occurs in retaliation against some real or imagined provocation or threat. Accordingly, this form is also known as defensive or 'hot-blooded' aggression (Card & Little, 2006). It arises from difficulties regulating emotion, specifically anger and frustration (Garofalo et al., 2020; Hubbard, 2001; Prinstein & Cillessen, 2003; Vitaro et al., 2006). Often the outrage that children feel is righteous in that they are reacting to unfair treatment of themselves or a friend. However, by the age of school entry, their peers expect them to possess skills for resolving conflicts by prosocial means.

The second type of aggression is proactive. Being unprovoked, it is also referred to as instrumental or 'cold-blooded' aggression (Card & Little, 2006). It is aimed at obtaining desired goals, such as access to resources (for young children, toys) or to secure or cement aggressors' social dominance (Vitaro et al., 2002). Perpetrators are not angry but are using aggression strategically (Hubbard, 2001; Prinstein & Cillessen, 2003; Vitaro et al., 2002, 2006). By school age, children's frequent use of proactive aggression signals not that they are out of control of their emotions, but that they are failing to regulate their behaviour or *impulses* (Frick et al., 2003).

Trends in aggression

Physical aggression emerges once babies become mobile and can move towards others and continues to grow in frequency. Around 5 per cent of one-year-olds display high levels of

DOI: 10.4324/9781003323938-20

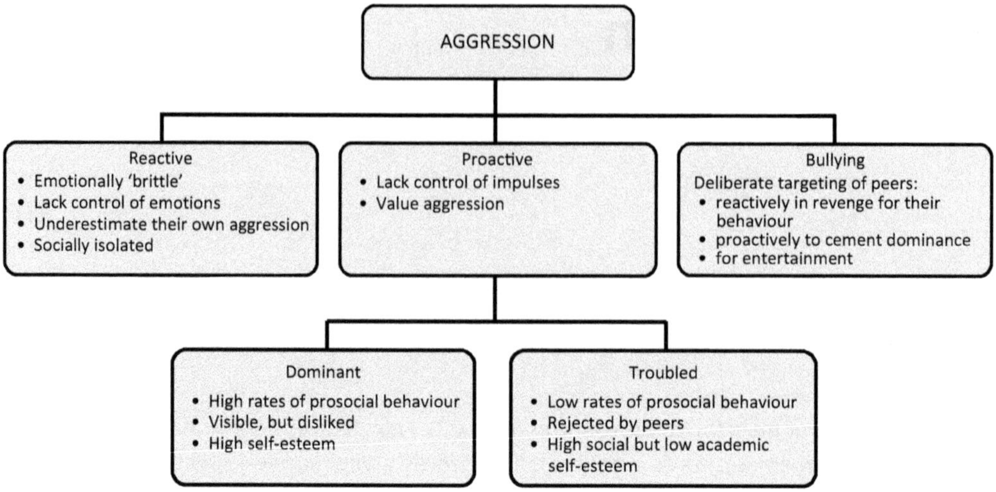

Figure 17.1 Modes of aggression

aggression (Alink et al., 2006; Baillargeon et al., 2007b; Côté et al., 2007) that continue to climb, peaking somewhere between 24 and 42 months of age; following this, aggression begins a steady decline both in frequency and severity as young children learn to manage (from the age of around 3 $^1/_2$ years) their own emotional arousal (Côté et al., 2006; Denham et al., 2002; Frick et al., 2003; Hay et al., 2004; Owens & Shaw, 2003; Prinzie et al., 2006; Rubin et al., 2003; Schaeffer et al., 2003; Shaw et al., 2003; Vitaro et al., 2006).

With a few exceptions (Broidy et al., 2003; Prinzie et al., 2006), studies typically find that this decline is most apparent for girls, with the result that, by 18 months of age, highly physically aggressive boys outnumber girls by a ratio of 5 to 1, which ratio persists throughout life (Baillargeon et al., 2007a, 2007b; Colder et al., 2002). Declining aggression is most pronounced for children raised by guidance methods. In contrast, a slower rate of decline (or even an increase) is seen in children whose parents use controls (rewards and punishments), especially when they use spanking, which raises the risk of behavioural problems at school entry by over 400 per cent (Hyman, 1995; Ohene et al., 2006; Slade & Wissow, 2004; Smith, 2006).

Once of school age, the majority of children exhibit low to moderate levels of all forms of aggression that remain stable or decline steadily through the early and middle school years (Côté et al., 2006; Ingoldsby et al., 2006; Kokko & Pulkkinen, 2005; Nagin & Tremblay, 1999; Patterson et al., 2005; Underwood et al., 2009; Zhou et al., 2007). However, if they experience academic failure, their aggression climbs - see Figure 17.2.

The dual failure model of aggression

As many as 60 per cent of those three-year-olds with severe antisocial behaviours maintain these high rates into the early school years and beyond (Campbell, 1995; Campbell & Ewing, 1990;

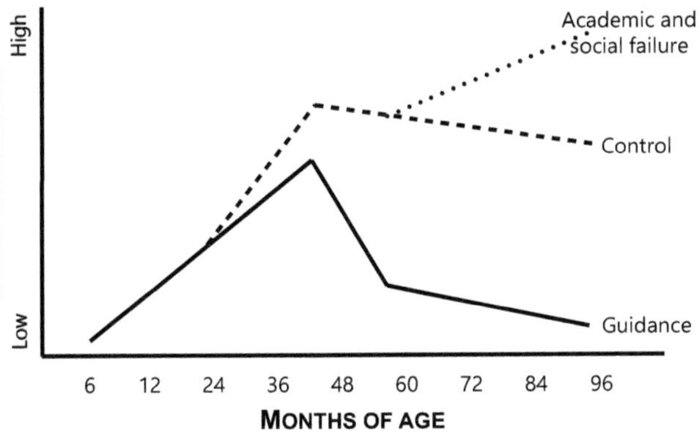

Figure 17.2 Trajectories of aggression

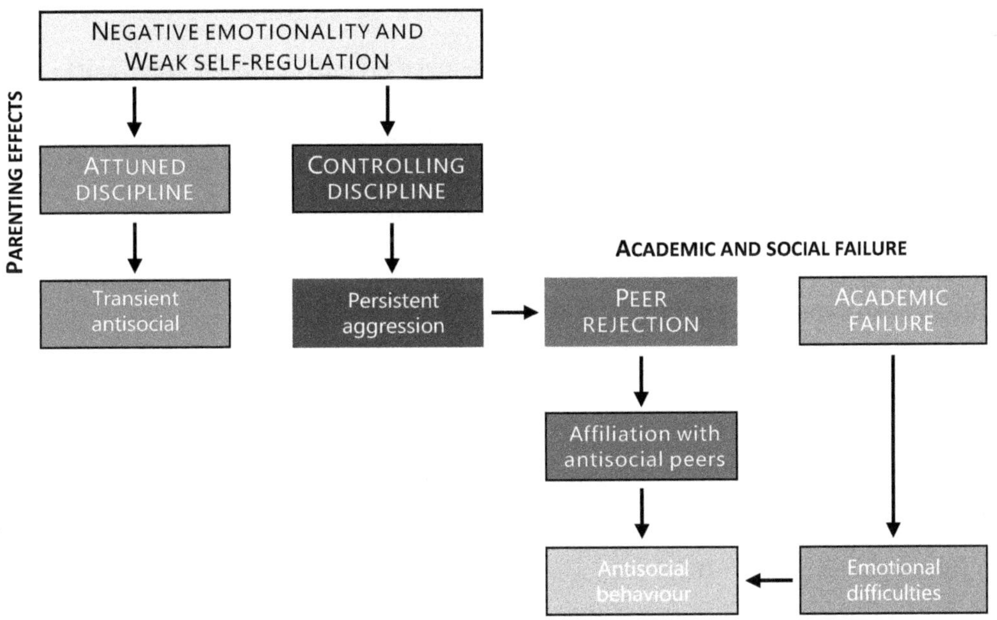

Figure 17.3 The dual failure model of aggression

Campbell et al., 2000, 2006). The dual failure model explains this persistence (Laird et al., 2001) – see Figure 17.3. Parenting effects tip the first domino in this model. Parents who are sensitive and responsive to their children (that is, parents who use guidance) typically produce children who are decreasingly aggressive over the early childhood years (Aunola & Nurmi, 2005; Baumrind, 1967; Crockenberg & Litman, 1990; Denham et al., 2000; Donovan et al., 2000; Feldman & Klein, 2003; Gilliom et al., 2002; Hoeve et al., 2009; Kochanska et al., 2005; Miller-Lewis et al., 2006; Parpal & Maccoby, 1985; Rubin et al., 2003; Smith et al., 2004;

Stayton et al., 1971; Stormshak et al., 2000; Weiss & Schwarz, 1996; Zahn-Waxler et al., 1979). In contrast, some children are rendered emotionally vulnerable by family adversity or controlling parenting and then maintain high levels of aggression past the age of three years (Kingston & Prior, 1995; Kwon et al., 2012; Mesman et al., 2019; Trzesniewski et al., 2006; Underwood et al., 2009; Xie et al., 2002).

When they enter school, their aggression leads to peer rejection (van Lier et al., 2012; Xie et al., 2002) that, for many, causes an escalation of their aggressiveness (Laird et al., 2001). By default, these isolated children come to associate with antisocial peers, who then cement their aggressive patterns.

Second and meanwhile, these early-onset aggressors typically experience academic failure. They commonly have attention difficulties, low reading ability and weak self-regulation skills, while those whose aggression emerges at school entry commonly have delayed language skills (Doctoroff et al., 2006; Harachi et al., 2006; Kingston & Prior, 1995; Martino et al., 2008). These academic difficulties persist throughout the school years (Loveland et al., 2007; Nelson et al., 2004) but, on their own, lead to emotional difficulties, rather than to behavioural problems (van Lier et al., 2012).

Together, however, emotional difficulties and affiliation with antisocial peers lead to high rates of aggression. It is thus dual social and academic failure at school that leads to escalating oppositional and disruptive behaviours (van Lier et al., 2012) - see Figure 17.3. In short, there is no late-onset pattern of aggression but instead, for a minority, a continuation of early childhood aggression into adolescence and (sometimes) adulthood (van Lier et al., 2009).

Social information processing errors

A comprehensively researched model of social skills states that the production of a successful social behaviour depends on a series of thought processes (Dodge & Crick, 1990), illustrated in Figure 17.4. The first three have to do with motivation, which is based on individuals' belief about whether they can trust others to meet their needs (Waldinger et al., 2001). On this basis, they interpret the social behaviour of others. Second, they have to decide on their goals: in essence, whether they want to get their own way, or want to get along with others (Green & Rechis, 2006). Third, they will access a response from their repertoire (such as assertiveness, aggression or problem solving), typically choosing the one that is most familiar to them (Dodge & Crick, 1990). Fourth, they have to be skilful at enacting that chosen response: using self-regulation, producing the relevant action, and noting feedback about whether it worked for them and others (Maszk et al., 1999). All these processes rely on the quality of the social setting and on individuals' emotions before, during and after a social encounter.

Children with high rates of aggression make errors at every step (Asher, 1983; Champion et al., 2003; Katsurada & Sugawara, 1998; Lochman et al., 2012; MacBrayer et al., 2003; Nelson et al., 2012; Salguero et al., 2020; van den Berg & Lansu, 2020; Wang et al., 2020; Yoon et al., 2000):

- *Motivation*: They have been taught to value aggressive behaviour and, therefore, are motivated to employ it.

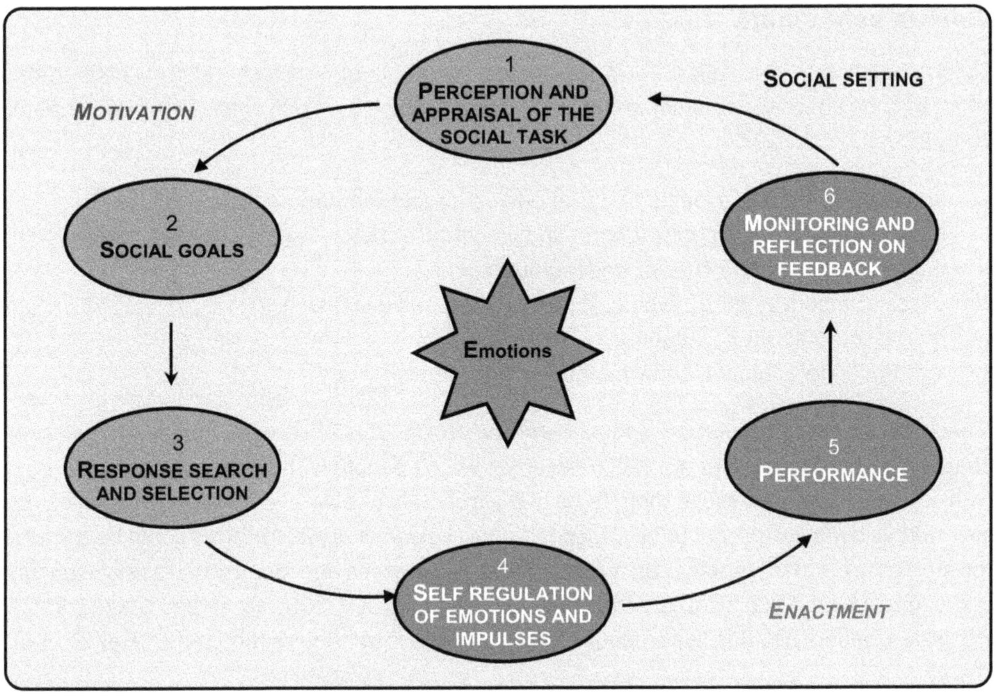

Figure 17.4 A model of social information processing

- *Perceptions*: Children who are habitually aggressive attend to fewer relevant social cues and have what is termed a hostile attribution bias, which means that they perceive others as being more hostile than they actually are.
- *Goals*: Their goal is to be dominant.
- *Response search and selection*: They have an inadequate repertoire of problem-solving skills and are biased towards selecting an aggressive response in the belief that this will work for them.
- *Self-regulation*: They tend to blame others for provoking them, with the result that they are not disposed towards exercising self-control and, even if they were, they have problems regulating their emotions and impulses, ruminate on perceived injustices and become too roused when provoked, with the result that their responses often become disorganised.
- *Performance*: Their performance is impaired by all of the above, including being reactive rather than reasoned.
- *Reflection on feedback*: Their reflection on their own behaviour is inaccurate, resulting in an underestimation of their own aggressiveness and a lack of awareness that their behaviours are unwelcome.

This series of errors means that we cannot teach social skills such as assertiveness (at station 5 in the model) to children with high rates of aggression, because their errors occur prior to that. They might even have the skill to be assertive, but don't use it. This means that we will need to address those prior errors, not the enactment of the skill itself.

Callous behaviours

Callous behaviour is a severe form of antisocial behaviour in which children deliberately inflict pain on another person or animal. It is characterised by (Frick et al., 2003; Waller et al., 2016, 2017):

- impaired emotional aspects of moral reasoning and regulation
- insensitivity to prohibitions (do not show guilt after behaving thoughtlessly)
- deficient attention to cues of impending danger
- a lack of empathy for or even enjoyment of others' distress
- fearlessness about consequences
- emotional detachment, showing little affection.

A lack of emotion regulation and a defensive form of self-esteem are implicated (see Chapter 11) (Lee-Rowland et al., 2020). Whereas young people with antisocial behaviour have high cortisol levels that cause them to be highly reactive to perceived threats, those who display *callous* behaviour seem to be under-reactive (Hawes et al., 2009). This could be because the studies are with older children and adolescents, by which age long-term trauma exposure can lead to a blunted cortisol response (Carpenter et al., 2007, 2011). Given this link to trauma, it is little wonder that this hyporeactive group has the most severe difficulties (Hawes et al., 2009).

For the majority of young people, antisocial behaviour in general and callousness in particular are the outcomes of harsh parenting including physical punishment, accompanied by a lack of parental warmth (Pardini et al., 2007; Waller et al., 2016; Waller & Hyde, 2017). Although callous children start out with similar levels of empathy to their more prosocial counterparts (Hastings et al., 2000), parental instability, high levels of chaos in the home, persistent poverty and other forms of family adversity lead to parental stress and, in turn, to a lack of parental nurturance (Waller et al., 2017). Many have witnessed a parent's violence, such as injuring the family pet (Currie, 2006; Waller et al., 2017). As a result, they are three times more likely to display cruelty towards animals or other forms of callousness (Currie, 2006).

The most crucial time for acquiring callousness is prior to the age of three, when children are developing moral reasoning and empathy (Hyde et al., 2016). If by this age, children have been raised without receiving empathy themselves, they do not learn how to empathise with others. As a result, compared to children with antisocial behaviour but without callousness, those who display callous behaviour are at increased risk of severe and persistent life-course antisocial behaviour, including both proactive and reactive aggression (Hawes et al., 2009; Waller et al., 2016; Waller & Hyde, 2017). Nevertheless, this is not destined: Interventions – particularly with parents' parenting skills – can offset even genetic risk (Waller & Hyde, 2017; Waller et al., 2016).

Aggression directed at parents

Hitting parents during the early childhood years is common because young children lack the language skills to express themselves when frustrated. Past this age, however, it is developmentally abnormal. Against a background of parental conflict and violence, use of harsh discipline and other forms of family adversity, plus child impulsivity and anger, child-to-parent violence is a consequence of parents' violence towards their children (Del Hoyo-Bilbao et al., 2020; Ibabe, 2019; Loinaz Calvo & de Sousa, 2020). The outcome is that those who have been victimised by their parents are 70 per cent more likely to be aggressive towards parents compared to non-victimised children (Gallego et al., 2019).

Aggression directed at teachers

Within a two-year time frame, on average one-half of teachers experience aggression directed at them, although this rate varies between countries (Longobardi et al., 2019). This aggression takes the forms of obscene gestures; verbal insults; teasing, mockery or playing harmful tricks; threats; humiliating a teacher; sexual harassment; property damage; and physical attacks (Chen & Astor, 2009; Espelage et al., 2013; Longobardi et al., 2019; McMahon et al., 2017).

Rates are lower in primary school and higher in secondary schools (Chen & Astor, 2009), indicating that the aggression is not due to students' developmental incapacity to regulate emotion. Instead, it seems to reflect conflict-ridden student-teacher relationships, with students stating that their main reasons for aggression are retaliation against unreasonable demands or unfair treatment, disagreements with the teacher or wanting to get back at teachers who put them down or disrespect them, their families or their culture (Chen & Astor, 2009; Hyman & Perone, 1998).

Interventions

Children or adolescents who are referred to counselling for aggressive behaviour are the quintessential involuntary client. They don't want to be there, and usually have little voice and instead their parents dominate the conversation. I used to have the parents talk with me about their children's difficulties while the children sat outside the room so that they were not humiliated by hearing their parents speak harshly of them, but then I realised that they had heard it all before and need to be there if this negative story is to turn around.

Advocate for behaviour guidance

Fifty years ago, Diana Baumrind (1967) identified four main disciplinary styles. We can reject two of them out of hand - permissiveness and neglect - because of their negative outcomes. That leaves just two styles. Baumrind called the first of these *authoritarian* and the second *authoritative* but these two words are so similar that it is easy to confuse them. Therefore, I have called the first method *controlling*, and Dan Gartrell (2003) named the second method as *guidance*.

Controlling discipline puts adults in control of children's behaviour. It uses rewards (such as praise, treats, stickers or star charts) to get children to do more of what we want, and punishments (reprimands and time out, for example) to discourage behaviours that we do not like. That is, it uses consequences, in the belief that individuals are controlled from the outside.

This style was given the formal title of *Behaviourism* in 1914 (Alberto & Troutman, 2013), although of course it was part of folklore long before that.

Around a decade later, the guidance approach emerged, labelled at the time as humanism. It uses no rewards or punishments, but instead *teaches* children to manage their emotions and impulses so that they can act considerately. It teaches thoughtful behaviour in the same way that we teach children to ride a bicycle or to write their names. When children make mistakes with these developmental tasks, we don't punish them, but just teach them again and give them extra chances to practise. Thus, the core belief of guidance is that children do not need incentives to behave well: *They need skills* (Greene, 2010).

Second, with its humanist roots, guidance believes that every behaviour is an attempt to meet a need (not a response to external consequences). These two beliefs spell the end of consequences - because we do not punish children for being in need, and we do not punish them for not having the chance to learn relevant skills.

To explain children with aggressive behaviour, we need to review children's emotional needs. Figure 10.1 (page 131) shows us that we gain our self-esteem from belonging and from our ability to be in command of our own lives (autonomy).

In my experience, we can divide the population into an 80/20 split. (The proportions differ between cultures and generations, but the exact numbers aren't important: It's the distinction that matters.) That is to say, 80 per cent of children gain most of their self-esteem from having their belonging needs met. These children want you to like them and will behave well most of the time for fear of damaging their relationships. (You might find it useful to think of their self-esteem branch in Figure 10.1 leaning over to the left, because the main source of their self-esteem is belonging.) When they do make the occasional behavioural mistake, they are upset, are remorseful and are willing to make amends. Therefore, these children do not need punishment to 'teach them a lesson' - because they have already learned from what happened.

In contrast are the (roughly) 20 per cent of non-conformist children whose self-esteem comes mainly from being in command of their own lives. (You might find it useful to think of their self-esteem branch in Figure 10.1 leaning over to the right, because the main source of their self-esteem is autonomy.) In adult life, we refer to people with strong autonomy needs as 'control freaks' (although I prefer the term control enthusiasts). In childhood, I call them *spirited*. These children are willing to risk your displeasure to prove to you that you can't make them do stuff. Their mantras are:

- You're not the boss of me!
- You can't make me.
- You can't stop me.

Unlike children with a strong need to belong for whom punishment is unnecessary, spirited children don't profit from punishment. When we we try to control them, their behaviour deteriorates - and rapidly. We get into a 'dance' of escalating coercion on our part being met by escalating defiance on theirs. This is illustrated in Figure 17.5.

In this dance, we insist that children do things our way and they resist. ... So we threaten some form of sanction, and they rebel. ... In response, we administer a punishment, and they retaliate. ... Until, finally, we escalate the punishment, and they escape - if not physically at least

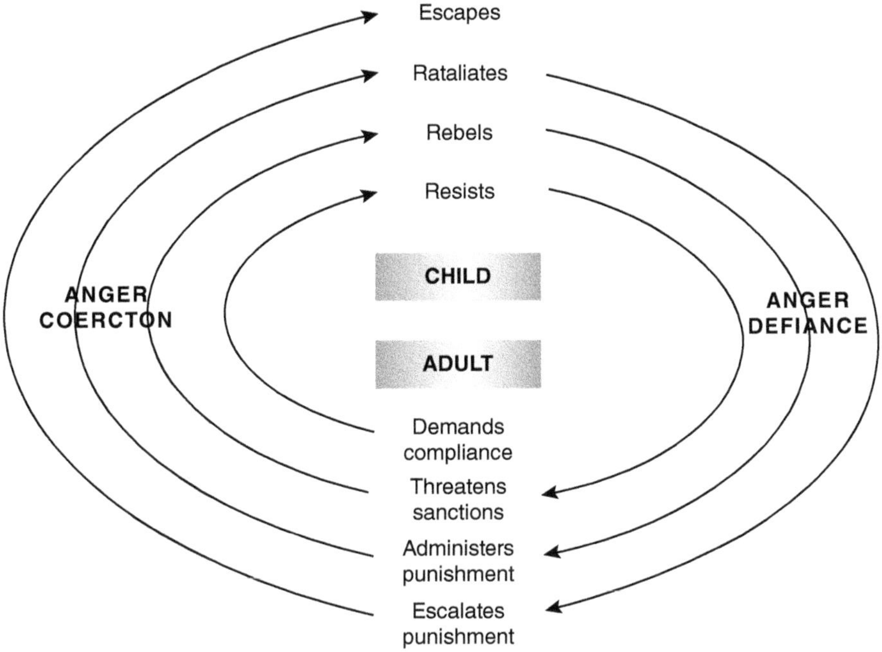

Figure 17.5 The dance of escalating adult coercion and child defiance

Source: Porter (2014, p. 159).

emotionally: They stop listening to us. The interaction becomes increasingly unmanageable – perhaps even to the point of labelling the child as having 'Oppositional-defiance disorder'.

However, the problem is not the dancers: It's the dance. That is, the problem is not the child, and it is not the adults: It's their coercive interaction pattern. Research is very clear on this. Children are not born inherently oppositional; they become so when adults use restrictive control over them (Denham et al., 2000; NICHD Early Child Care Research Network, 2004; Paterson & Sanson, 1999; Sanson et al., 2004; Shaw et al., 2001; Tung & Lee, 2014). That is, aggression is caused when spirited children are met with controlling discipline. This tells us that our response to children's aggressive outbursts cannot be punitive. It simply does not work to prevent future disruptions, teach children skills or cause them to want to listen to us. If punishment were going to work, it would have by now.

Therefore, adults in children's lives need to cease using both rewards (see Chapter 11) and punishments and, instead, support them to exercise self-regulation (see Porter, 2014, 2016).

Health

If young children are being raised in caring homes and yet their aggression has not followed the usual downward trend after the age of three, the logic is that if it is not an external problem, then it must be internal. Particularly if children have constant ear, nose or throat infections, I usually suspect a dairy intolerance, because it is mucous producing (Rank, 1986). If a two-week dairy-free diet (with oat milk being the most nutritious substitute) does not help the irritated nervous system, then gluten is a suspect - see Chapter 11. Weak methylation or other nutrient deficiencies could also be checked by an integration medical practitioner - see Resources.

Academic remediation

Interventions to help children with aggressive behaviours to be more successful academically are vital (Hayden, 2013). This is especially true for their reading skills. Therefore, they need sustained tutoring so that they become less disheartened because they can see themselves as making progress.

Solution-focused therapy

As with other presenting issues, counsellors might reserve narrative methods for severe issues but, for simple outbursts of aggression in young children, solution-focused approaches might be all that is needed. This will rest on awareness that, let's say, children have an aggressive outburst at school three times a week, totalling 15 minutes' duration, whereas their school week totals 30 hours. A simple law of numbers suggests focusing on the 29 hours and 45 minutes when the children are not being aggressive, rather than the 15 minutes when they are. Counsellors will ask how they manage to rein in their frustration or anger at those times, and what it would take for them to do that more often. Scaling questions can also be useful to gauge progress and to avoid the black-and-white thinking (on everybody's part, including the children themselves) that defines the children as an 'aggressive child' when, for 29 hours and 45 minutes per week, they are not (see Chapter 2).

Narrative therapy for childhood aggression

The wonderfulness interview (see Chapter 3) lays the foundation for the development of a preferred identity to replace the identity of 'the aggressive child' (Marsten et al., 2016). Once you know about the child's special qualities, you will move on to gaining a description of the problematic behaviour (who does what, when and how). By way of an example, let's say that during this discussion, the young person chose to call the problem 'Trouble'.

Some *landscape of action* questions about the aggression could be (Denborough, 2014):

- When did Trouble first come into your life?
- When is it most likely to visit?
- Where is it most powerful?
- What are the effects of Trouble at home? At school?
- When Trouble moved into your life, what moved out to make room for it?

Your *deconstruction* questions that identify the oppressive effects of the problem could be (Denborough, 2014):

- What does Trouble want for your life?
- Does it want you to have friends, or to be lonely?

Your *landscape of identity* questions could be (Denborough, 2014):

- What does Trouble plant in your mind about who you are?
- What does Trouble tell you about who you are?

***Preference* questions**

- (To the child): What is it like for you to be talked into believing such negative things about yourself? (White, 2016).
- (To the parents) What do you think it's like for Jaxon to be talked into such negative ideas about who he is? (White, 2016).
- Would you prefer to have a 'good boy' reputation or a 'bad boy' reputation? (Madigan, 2019).
- Is life easier, or harder, when Trouble comes to visit you?
- You said that your apartment is quite small. Is there room in it for all of you and for Trouble as well?
- Why do you want to change the upset that Trouble brings to your life?

You would then ask about times when Trouble is less of a problem than it might have been (the exceptions) and how the young person brought those about. You would ask landscape of action questions about these 'sparkling moments', filling each example with rich descriptions and details so that they become newsworthy.

Landscape of identity questions about the exceptions

- What is the name of your special skill that helps you put Trouble in its place?
- Where did this special skill come from?
- I have a special power (that I can make the end of my finger wobble) (Demonstrate whatever weird skill you have, because children love to be grossed out). What is the name of your super-power?
- Tell me about other times when you've used this super-power?
- Who would be the most surprised to hear that you have this super-power?
- Is this super-power connected to your family (culture/traditions) in some special way?

Conclusion

We cannot teach children to be humane by using inhumane methods (Sapon-Shevin, 1996). That is to say, if we punish children for their behaviours, we are punishing them for not yet having acquired the necessary skills for self-regulation, and we are perpetuating the adverse conditions that failed to teach them these skills. Instead, we need to build these children's sense of themselves as worthy, responsible, capable human beings who can, with support, behave considerately of others (Curwin & Mendler, 1988).

References

Alberto, P. A., & Troutman, A. C. (2013). *Applied behavior analysis for teachers* (9th ed.). Pearson.

Alink, L. R. A., Mesman, J., Koot, H. M., van Zeijl, J., Stolk, M. N., Juffer, F., Bakermans-Kranenburg, M. J., & van Ijzedoorn, M. H. (2006). The early childhood aggression curve: Development of physical aggression in 10- to 50-month old children. *Child Development*, *77*(4), 954-966. https://doi.org/10.1111/j.1467-8624.2006.00912.x

Asher, S. R. (1983). Social competence and peer status: Recent advances and future directions. *Child Development*, *54*(6), 1427–1434. https://doi.org/10.2307/1129805

Aunola, K., & Nurmi, J.-E. (2005). The role of parenting styles in children's problem behavior. *Child Development*, *76*(6), 1144–1159. https://doi.org/10.1111/j.1467-8624.2005.00840.x-i1

Baillargeon, R. H., Normand, C. L., Séguin, J. R., Zoccolillo, M., Japel, C., Pérusse, D., Wu, H.-X., Boivin, M., & Tremblay, R. E. (2007a). The evolution of problem and social competence behaviors during toddlerhood: A prospective population-based cohort survey. *Infant Mental Health Journal*, *28*(1), 12–38. https://doi.org/10.1002/imhj.20120

Baillargeon, R. H., Zoccolillo, M., Keenan, K., Côté, S., Pérusse, D., Wu, H.-X., Boivin, M., & Tremblay, R. E. (2007b). Gender differences in physical aggression: A prospective population-based survey of children before and after 2 years of age. *Developmental Psychology*, *43*(1), 13–26. https://doi.org/10.1037/0012-1649.43.1.13

Baumrind, D. (1967). Child care practices anteceding three patterns of preschool behavior. *Genetic Psychology Monographs*, *75*, 43–88.

Broidy, L. M., Nagin, D. S., Tremblay, R. E., Bates, J. E., Brame, B., Dodge, K. A., ... & Vitaro, F. (2003). Developmental trajectories of childhood disruptive behaviors and adolescent delinquency: A six-site, cross-national study. *Developmental Psychology*, *39*(2), 222–245. https://doi.org/0.1037/0012-1649.39.2.222

Campbell, S. B. (1995). Behavior problems in preschool children: A review of recent research. *Journal of Child Psychology and Psychiatry*, *36*(1), 113–149. https://doi.org/10.1111/j.1469-7610.1995.tb01657.x

Campbell, S. B., & Ewing, L. J. (1990). Follow-up of hard-to-manage preschoolers: Adjustment at age 9 and predictors of continuing symptoms. *Journal of Child Psychology and Psychiatry*, *31*(6), 871–889. https://doi.org/10.1111/j.1469-7610.1990.tb00831.x

Campbell, S. B., Shaw, D. S., & Gilliom, M. (2000). Early externalizing behavior problems: Toddlers and preschoolers at risk for later maladjustment. *Development and Psychopathology*, *12*(3), 467–488. https://doi.org/10.1017/S0954579400003114

Campbell, S. B., Spieker, S., Burchinal, M., Poe, M. D., & The NICHD Early Child Care Research Network (2006). Trajectories of aggression from toddlerhood to age 9 predict academic and social functioning through age 12. *Journal of Child Psychology and Psychiatry*, *47*(8), 791–800. https://doi.org/10.1111/j.1469-7610.2006.01636.x

Card, N. A., & Little, T. D. (2006). Proactive and reactive aggression in childhood and adolescence: A meta-analysis of differential relations with psychosocial adjustment. *International Journal of Behavioral Development*, *30*(5), 466–480. https://doi.org/10.1177/0165025406071904

Carpenter L. L., Carvalho J. P., Tyrka A. R., Wier L. M., Mello A. F., Mello M. F., Anderson G. M., Wilkinson C. W., & Price L. H. (2007). Decreased adrenocorticotropic hormone and cortisol responses to stress in healthy adults reporting significant childhood maltreatment. *Biological Psychiatry*, *62*(10), 1080–1108. https://doi.org/10.1016/j.biopsych.2007.05.002

Carpenter, L.L., Shattuck, T. T., Tyrka, A. R., Geracioti, T. D., & Price, L. H. (2011). Effect of childhood physical abuse on cortisol stress response. *Psychopharmacology*, *214*, 367–375. https://doi.10.1007/s00213-010-2007-4

Champion, K., Vernberg, E., & Shipman, K. (2003). Nonbully victims of bullies: Aggression, social skills, and friendship characteristics. *Journal of Applied Developmental Psychology*, *24*(5), 535–551. https://doi.org/10.1016/j.appdev.2003.08.003

Chen, J. K., & Astor, R. A. (2009). Students' reports of violence against teachers in Taiwanese schools. *Journal of School Violence*, *8*(1), 2–17. https://doi.org/10.1080/15388220802067680

Colder, C. R., Mott, J. A., & Berman, A. S. (2002). The interactive effects of infant activity level and fear on growth trajectories of early childhood behavior problems. *Development and Psychopathology*, *14*(1), 1–23. https://doi.org/10.1017/S0954579402001013

Curwin, R. L., & Mendler, A. N. (1988). Packaged discipline programs: Let the buyer beware. *Educational Leadership*, *46*(2), 68–71.

Côté, S. M., Vaillancourt, T., LeBlanc, J. C., Nagin, D. S., & Tremblay, R. E. (2006). The development of physical aggression from toddlerhood to pre-adolescence: A nation wide longitudinal study of Canadian children. *Journal of Abnormal Child Psychology*, *34*(1), 68–82. https://doi.org/10.1007/s10802-005-9001-z

Côté, S. M., Vaillancourt, T., Barker, E. D., Nagin, D., & Tremblay, R. E. (2007). The joint development of physical and indirect aggression: Predictors of continuity and change during childhood. *Development and Psychopathology*, *19*(1), 37–55. https://doi.org/10.1017/S0954579407070034

Crockenberg, S., & Litman, C. (1990). Autonomy as competence in 2-year-olds: Maternal correlates of child defiance, compliance, and self-assertion. *Developmental Psychology*, *26*(6), 961–971.

Currie, C. L. (2006). Animal cruelty to children exposed to domestic violence. *Child Abuse and Neglect*, *30*(4), 425–435. https://doi.org/10.1016/j.chiabu.2005.10.014

Dane, A. V., Lapierre, K. R., Andrews, N. C. Z., & Volk, A. A. (2022). Evolutionarily relevant aggressive functions: Differentiating competitive, impression management, sadistic and reactive motives. *Aggressive Behavior*, *48*(3), 331–340. https://doi.org/10.1002/ab.22020

Del Hoyo-Bilbao, J., Orue, I., Gámez-Guadix, M., & Calvete, E. (2020). Multivariate models of child-to-mother violence and child-to-father violence among adolescents. *The European Journal of Psychology Applied to Legal Context*, *12*(1), 11–21. https://doi.org/10.5093/ejpalc2020a2

Denborough, D. (2014). *Retelling the stories of our lives: Everyday narrative therapy to draw inspiration and transform experience*. Norton.

Denham, S. A., Workman, E., Cole, P. M., Weissbrod, C., Kendziora, K. T., & Zahn-Waxler, C. (2000). Prediction of externalizing behavior problems from early to middle childhood: The role of parental socialization and emotion expression. *Development and Psychopathology*, *12*(1), 23–45. https://doi.org/10.1017/S0954579400001024

Denham, S. A., Caverly, S., Schmidt, M., Blair, K., DeMulder, E., Caal, S., Hamada, H., & Mason, T. (2002). Preschool understanding of emotions: Contributions to classroom anger and aggression. *Journal of Child Psychology and Psychiatry*, *43*(7), 901–916. https://doi.org/10.1111/1469-7610.00139

Doctoroff, G. L., Greer, J. A., & Arnold, D. H. (2006). The relationship between social behavior and emergent literacy among preschool boys and girls. *Journal of Applied Developmental Psychology*, *27*(1), 1–13. https://doi.org/10.1016/j.appdev.2005.12.003

Dodge, K. A., & Crick, N. R. (1990). Social information-processing bases of aggressive behavior in children. *Personality and Social Psychology Bulletin*, *16*(1), 8–22. https://doi.org/10.1177/0146167290161002

Donovan, W. L., Leavitt, L. A., & Walsh, R. O. (2000). Maternal illusory control predicts socialization strategies and toddler compliance. *Developmental Psychology*, *36*(3), 402–411. https://doi.org/10.1037//0012-1649.36.3.402

Espelage, D., Anderman, E. M., Brown, V. E., Jones, A., Lane, K. L., McMahon. S. D., Reddy, L. A., & Reynolds, C. R. (2013). Understanding and preventing violence directed against teachers. *American Psychologist*, *68*(2), 75–87. https://doi.org/10.1037/a0031.307

Feldman, R., & Klein, P. S. (2003). Toddlers' self-regulated compliance to mothers, caregivers, and fathers: Implications for theories of socialization. *Developmental Psychology*, *39*(4), 680–692. https://doi.org/10.1037/0012-1649.39.4.680

Frick, P. J., Cornell, A. H., Bodin, S. D., Dane, H. E., Barry, C. T., & Loney, B. R. (2003). Callous-unemotional traits and developmental pathways to severe conduct problems. *Developmental Psychology*, *39*(2), 246–260. https://doi.org/10.1037/0012-1649.39.2.246

Gallego, R., Novo, M., Fariña, F., & Arce, R. (2019). Child-to-parent violence and parent-to-child violence: A meta-analytic review. *The European Journal of Psychology Applied to Legal Context*, 11, 51–59. https://doi.org/10.5093/ejpalc2019a4

Garofalo, C., Gillespie, S. M., & Velotti, P. (2020). Emotion regulation mediates relationships between mindfulness facets and aggression dimensions. *Aggressive Behavior*, *46*(1), 60–71. https://doi.org/10.1002/ab.21868

Gartrell, D. (2003). *A guidance approach for the encouraging classroom* (3rd ed.). Delmar.

Gilliom, M., Shaw, D. S., Beck, J. E., Schonberg, M. A., & Lukon, J. L. (2002). Anger regulation in disadvantaged preschool boys: Strategies, antecedents, and the development of self-control. *Developmental Psychology*, *38*(2), 222–235. https://doi.org/10.1037//0012-1649.38.2.222

Green, V. A., & Rechis, R. (2006). Children's competitive and cooperative interactions in limited resource situations: A literature review. *Journal of Applied Developmental Psychology*, *27*(1), 42–59. https://doi.org/10.1016/j.appdev.2005.12.002

Greene, R. W. (2010). *The explosive child*. Harper.

Harachi, T. W., Fleming, C. B., White, H. R., Ensminger, M. E., Abbott, R. D., Catalano, R. F., & Haggerty, K. P. (2006). Aggressive behavior among girls and boys during middle childhood: Predictors and sequelae of trajectory group membership. *Aggressive Behavior*, *32*(4), 279–293. https://doi.org/10.1002/ab.20125

Hastings, P. D., Zahn-Waxler, C., Robinson, J., Usher, B., & Bridges, D. (2000). The development of concern for others in children with behavior problems. *Developmental Psychology*, *36*(5), 531–546. https://doi.org/10.1037/0012-1649.36.5.531

Hawes, D. J., Brennan, J., & Dadds, M. R. (2009). Cortisol, callous-unemotional traits, and pathways to antisocial behavior. *Current Opinion in Psychiatry*, *22*, 357–362. https://doi.org/10.1097/YCO.0b013e32832bfa6d

Hay, D. F., Payne, A., & Chadwick, A. (2004). Peer relations in childhood. *Journal of Child Psychology and Psychiatry*, *45*(1), 84–108. https://doi.org/10.1046/j.0021-9630.2003.00308.x

Hayden, C. (2013). Youth offending and emotional and behavioural difficulties. In T. Cole, H. Daniels, & J. Visser (Eds.), *The Routledge international companion to emotional and behavioural difficulties* (pp. 48–56). Routledge.

Hoeve, M., Dubas, J. S., Eichelsheim, V. I., van der Laan, P. H., Smeenk, W., & Gerris, J. R. M. (2009). The relationship between parenting and delinquency: A meta-analysis. *Journal of Abnormal Child Psychology*, *37*(6), 749–775. https://doi.org/10.1007/s10802-009-9310-8

Hubbard, J. A. (2001). Emotion expression processes in children's peer interaction: The role of peer rejection, aggression, and gender. *Child Development*, *72*(5), 1426–1438. https://doi.org/10.1111/1467-8624.00357

Hyde, L. W., Waller, R., Trentacosta, C. J., Shaw, D. S., Neiderhiser, J. M., Ganiban, J. M., Reiss, D., & Leve, L. D. (2016). Heritable and nonheritable pathways to early callous-unemotional behaviors. *American Journal of Psychiatry*, *173*(9), 903–910. https://doi.org/10.1176/appi.ajp.2016.15111381

Hyman, I. A. (1995). Corporal punishment, psychological maltreatment, violence, and punitiveness in America: Research, advocacy, and public policy. *Applied and Preventive Psychology*, *4*(2), 113–130. https://doi.org/10.1016/S0962-1849(05)80084-8

Hyman, I. A., & Perone, D. C. (1998). The other side of school violence: Educator policies and practices that may contribute to student misbehavior. *Journal of School Psychology*, *36*(1), 7–27. https://doi.org/10.1016/S0022-4405(97)87007-0

Ibabe, I. (2019). Adolescent-to-parent violence and family environment: The perceptions of same reality? *International Journal of Environmental Research and Public Health*, *16*(12), 2215. https://doi.org/10.3390/ijerph16122215

Ingoldsby, E. M., Shaw, D. S., Winslow, E., Schonberg, M., Gilliom, M., & Criss, M. M. (2006). Neighborhood disadvantage, parent-child conflict, neighborhood peer relationships, and early antisocial behavior problem trajectories. *Journal of Abnormal Child Psychology*, *34*(3), 303–319. https://doi.org/10.1007/s10802-006-9026-y

Katsurada, E., & Sugawara, A. I. (1998). The relationship between hostile attributional bias and aggressive behavior in preschoolers. *Early Childhood Research Quarterly*, *13*(4), 623–636. https://doi.org/10.1016/S0885-2006(99)80064-7

Kingston, L., & Prior, M. (1995). The development of patterns of stable, transient, and school-age onset aggressive behavior in children. *Journal of the American Academy of Child and Adolescent Psychiatry*, *34*(3), 348–358. https://doi.org/10.1097/00004583-199503000-00021

Kochanska, G., Aksan, N., & Carlson, J. J. (2005). Temperament, relationships, and young children's receptive cooperation with their parents. *Developmental Psychology*, *41*(4), 648–660. https://doi.org/10.1037/0012-1649.41.4.648

Kokko, K., & Pulkkinen, L. (2005). Stability of aggressive behavior from childhood to middle age in women and men. *Aggressive Behavior*, *31*(5), 485–497. https://doi.org/10.1002/ab.20063

Kwon, K., Kim, E., & Sheridan, S. (2012). Behavioral competence and academic functioning among early elementary children with externalizing problems. *School Psychology Review*, *41*(2), 123–140. https://doi.org/10.1080/02796015.2012.12087516

Laird, R. D., Jordan, K. Y., Dodge, K. A., Pettit, G. S., & Bates, J. E. (2001). Peer rejection in childhood, involvement with antisocial peers in early adolescence, and the development of externalizing behavior problems. *Development and Psychopathology*, *13*(2), 337–354. https://doi.org/10.1017/S0954579401002085

Lee-Rowland, L. M., Lui, J. H., Bortfeld, D., Barry, C. T., & Reiter, S. (2020). Internalizing problems and their impact on the relation between callous-unemotional traits, narcissism, and aggression. *Aggressive Behavior*, *46*(3), 278–286. https://doi.org/10.1002/ab.21888

Lochman, J. E., Powell, N. R., Whidby, J. M., & FitzGerald, D. P. (2012). Aggression in children. In P. C. Kendall (Ed.), *Child and adolescent therapy: Cognitive-behavioral procedures* (4th ed., pp. 27–60). Guilford.

Loinaz Calvo, I., & de Sousa, A. M. (2020). Assessing risk and protective factors in clinical and judicial child-to-parent violence cases. *European Journal of Psychology Applied to Legal Context*, *12*(1), 43–51. http://hdl.handle.net/2445/178390

Longobardi, C., Badenes-Ribera, L., Fabris, M. A., Martinez, A., & McMahon, S. D. (2019). Prevalence of student violence against teachers: A meta-analysis. *Psychology of Violence*, *9*(6), 596. https://doi.org/10.1037/vio0000202

Loveland, J. M., Lounsbury, J. W., & Welsh, D. (2007). The validity of physical aggression in predicting adolescent academic performance. *British Journal of Educational Psychology*, *77*(1), 167–176. https://doi.org/10.1348/000709905X79563

MacBrayer, E. K., Milich, R., & Hundley, M. (2003). Attributional biases in aggressive children and their mothers. *Journal of Abnormal Psychology*, *112*(4), 698–708. https://doi.org/10.1037/0021-843X.112.4.698

Madigan, S. (2019). *Narrative therapy* (2nd ed.). American Psychological Association.

Marsten, D., Epston, D., & Markham, L. (2016). *Narrative therapy in wonderland: Connecting with children's imaginative know-how*. Norton.

Martino, S. C., Ellickson, P. L., Klein, D. J., McCaffrey, D., & Edelen, M. O. (2008). Multiple trajectories of physical aggression among adolescent boys and girls. *Aggressive Behavior*, *34*(1), 61–75. https://doi.org/10.1002/ab.20215

Maszk, P., Eisenberg, N., & Guthrie, I. K. (1999). Relations of children's social status to their emotionality and regulation: A short-term longitudinal study. *Merrill-Palmer Quarterly*, *45*(3), 468–492. https://www.jstor.org/stable/23092582

McMahon, S. D., Martinez, A., Reddy, L. A., Espelage, D. L., & Anderman, E. M. (2017). Predicting and reducing aggression and violence toward teachers: Extent of the problem and why it matters. In P. Sturmey (Ed.), *The Wiley handbook of violence and aggression Volume 3. Societal interventions* (pp. 1335–1350). John Wiley & Sons. https://digitalcommons.sacredheart.edu/socwk_fac

Mesman, G. R., Harper, S. L., Edge, N. A., Brandt, T. W., & Pemberton, J. L. (2019). Problematic sexual behavior in children. *Journal of Pediatric Health Care*, *33*(3), 323–331. https://doi.org/10.1016/j.pedhc.2019.11.002

Miller-Lewis, L. R., Baghurst, P. A., Sawyer, M. G., Prior, M.R., Clark, J. J., Arney, F. M., & Carbone, J. A. (2006). Early childhood externalizing behaviour problems: Child, parenting, and family-related predictors over time. *Journal of Abnormal Child Psychology*, *34*(6), 891–906. https://doi.org/10.1007/s10802-006-9071-6

Nagin, D., & Tremblay, R. E. (1999). Trajectories of boys' physical aggression, opposition, and hyperactivity on the path to physically violent and nonviolent juvenile delinquency. *Child Development*, *70*(5), 1181–1196. https://doi.org/10.1111/1467-8624.00086

National Institute of Child Health and Human Development Early Child Care Research Network. (2004). Affect dysregulation in the mother-child relationship in the toddler years: Antecedents and consequences. *Development and Psychopathology*, *16*(1), 43–68.

Nelson, J. R., Benner, G. J., Lane, K., & Smith, B. W. (2004). Academic achievement of K-12 students with emotional and behavioral disorders. *Exceptional Children*, *71*(1), 59–73. https://doi.org/10.1177/001440290407100104

Nelson, W. M. III, Finch, A. J. Jr, & Ghee, A. C. (2012). Anger management with children and adolescents: Cognitive-behavioral therapy. In P. C. Kendall (Ed.), *Child and adolescent therapy: Cognitive-behavioral procedures* (4th ed., pp. 92–139). Guilford.

Ohene, S. A., Ireland, M., McNeely, C., & Borowsky, I. W. (2006). Parental expectations, physical punishment, and violence among adolescents who score positive on a psychosocial screening test in primary care. *Pediatrics*, *117*(2), 441–447. https://doi.org/10.1542/peds.2005-0421

Owens, E. B., & Shaw, D. S. (2003). Predicting growth curves of externalizing behavior across the preschool years. *Journal of Abnormal Child Psychology*, *31*(6), 575–590. https://doi.org/10.1023/A:1026254005632

Pardini, D. A., Lochman, J. E., & Powell, N. (2007). The development of callous-unemotional traits and antisocial behavior in children: Are there shared and/or unique predictors? *Journal of Clinical Child and Adolescent Psychology*, *36*(3), 319–333. https://doi.org/10.1080/15374410701444215

Parpal, M., & Maccoby, E. E. (1985). Maternal responsiveness and subsequent child compliance. *Child Development*, *56*(5), 1326–1334. https://doi.org/10.2307/1130247

Paterson, G., & Sanson, A. (1999). The association of behavioural adjustment to temperament, parenting and family characteristics among 5-year-old children. *Social Development*, *8*(3), 293–309.

Patterson, G. R., Shaw, D. S., Snyder, J. J., & Yoerger, K. (2005). Changes in maternal ratings of children's overt and covert antisocial behavior. *Aggressive Behavior*, *31*(5), 473–484. https://doi.org/10.1002/ab.20095

Porter, L. (2014). *A comprehensive guide to classroom management: Facilitating engagement and learning in schools*. Routledge.

Porter, L.(2016). *Young children's behaviour: Guidance approaches for early childhood educators* (4th ed.). Routledge.

Prinstein, M. J., & Cillessen, A. H. N. (2003). Forms and functions of adolescent peer aggression associated with high peer status. *Merrill-Palmer Quarterly*, *49*(3), 310–342. https://www.jstor.org/stable/23096058

Prinzie, P., Onghena, P., & Hellinck, W. (2006). A cohort-sequential multivariate latent growth curve analysis of normative CBCL aggressive and delinquent problem behavior: Associations with harsh discipline and gender. *International Journal of Behavioral Development*, *30*(5), 444–459. https://doi.org/10.1177/0165025406071901

Rank, P. (1986). Milk and arteriosclerosis. *Medical Hypotheses*, *20*(3), 317–338. https://doi.org/10.1016/0306-9877(86)90047-2

Rubin, K. H., Burgess, K. B., Dwyer, K. M., & Hastings, P. D. (2003). Predicting preschoolers' externalizing behaviors from toddler temperament, conflict, and maternal negativity. *Developmental Psychology*, *39*(1), 164–176. https://www.jstor.org/stable/42728427

Salguero, J. M., García-Sancho, E., Ramos-Cejudo, J., & Kannis-Dymand, L. (2020). Individual differences in anger and displaced aggression: The role of metacognitive beliefs and anger rumination. *Aggressive Behavior*, *46*(2), 162–169. https://doi.org/10.1002/ab.21878

Sanson, A., Hemphill, S. A., & Smart, D. (2004). Connections between temperament and social development: A review. *Social Development*, *13*(1), 142–170.

Sapon-Shevin, M. (1996). Beyond gifted education: Building a shared agenda for school reform. *Journal for the Education of the Gifted*, *19*(2), 194–214.

Schaeffer, C. M., Petras, H., Ialongo, N., Poduska, J., & Kellam, S. (2003). Modeling growth in boys' aggressive behavior across elementary school: Links to later criminal involvement, conduct disorder, and antisocial personality disorder. *Developmental Psychology*, *39*(6), 1020–1025. https://doi.org/10.1037/0012-1649.39.6.1020

Shaw, D. S., Owens, E. B., Giovannelli, J., & Winslow, E. B. (2001). Infant and toddler pathways leading to early externalizing disorders. *Journal of the American Academy of Child and Adolescent Psychiatry*, *40*(1), 36–43.

Shaw, D. S., Gilliom, M., Ingoldsby, E. M., & Nagin, D. S. (2003). Trajectories leading to school-age conduct problems. *Developmental Psychology*, *39*(2), 189–200. https://doi.org/10.1037/0012-1649.39.2.189

Slade, E. P., & Wissow, L. S. (2004). Spanking in early childhood and later behavior problems: A prospective study of infants and young toddlers. *Pediatrics*, *113*(5), 1321–1330. https://doi.org/10.1542/peds.113.5.1321

Smith, A. B. (2006). The state of research on the effects of physical punishment. *Social Policy Journal of New Zealand*, *27*, 114–127.

Smith, C. L., Calkins, S. D., Keane, S. P., Anastopoulos, A. D., & Shelton, T. L. (2004). Predicting stability and change in toddler behavior problems: Contributions of maternal behavior and child gender. *Developmental Psychology*, *40*(1), 29–42. https://doi.org/10.1037/0012-1649.40.1.29

Stayton, C. J., Hogan, R., & Ainsworth, M. D. S. (1971). Infant obedience and maternal behavior: The origins of socialization reconsidered. *Child Development*, *42*(4), 1057–1069. https://doi.org/10.2307/1127792

Stormshak, E. A., Bierman, K. L., McMahon, R. J., Lengua, L. J., & The Conduct Problems Prevention Research Group. (2000). Parenting practices and child disruptive behavior problems in early elementary school. *Journal of Clinical Child Psychology*, *28*(1), 17–29. https://doi.org/10.1207/S15374424jccp2901_3

Trzesniewski, K. H., Moffitt, T. E., Caspi, A., Taylor, A., & Maughan, B. (2006). Revisiting the association between reading achievement and antisocial behavior: New evidence of an environmental explanation from a twin study. *Child Development*, *77*(1), 72–88. https://doi.org/10.1111/j.1467-8624.2006.00857.x

Tung, I., & Lee, S. S. (2014). Negative parenting behavior and childhood oppositional defiant disorder: Differential moderation by positive and negative peer regard. *Aggressive Behavior*, *40*(1), 79–90.

Underwood, M. K., Beron, K. J., & Rosen, L. H. (2009). Continuity and change in social and physical aggression from middle childhood through early adolescence. *Aggressive Behavior*, *35*(5), 357–375. https://doi.org/10.1002/ab.20313

van den Berg, Y. H. M., & Lansu, T. A. M. (2020). It's not just what you say, it's how you say it too. Adolescent hostile attribution of intent and emotional responses to social comments. *Aggressive Behavior*, *46*(5), 425–436. https://doi.org/10.1002/ab.21910

van Lier, P. A. C., Vitaro, F., Barker, E. D., Koot, H. M., & Tremblay, R. E. (2009). Developmental links between trajectories of physical violence, vandalism, theft, and alcohol-drug use from childhood to adolescence. *Journal of Abnormal Child Psychology*, *37*(4), 481–492. https://doi.org/10.1007/s10802-008-9289-6

van Lier, P. A. C., Vitaro, F., Barker, E. D., Brendgen, M., Tremblay, R. E., & Boivin, M. (2012). Peer victimization, poor academic achievement, and the link between childhood externalizing and internalizing problems. *Child Development*, *83*(5), 1775–1788. https://doi.org/10.1111/j.1467-8624.2012.01802.x

Vitaro, F., Brendgen, M., & Tremblay, R. E. (2002). Reactively and proactively aggressive children: Antecedent and subsequent characteristics. *Journal of Child Psychology and Psychiatry*, *43*(4), 495–505. https://doi.org/10.1111/1469-7610.00040

Vitaro, F., Barker, E. D., Boivin, M., Brendgen, M., & Tremblay, R. E. (2006). Do early difficult temperament and harsh parenting differentially predict reactive and proactive aggression? *Journal of Abnormal Child Psychology*, *34*(5), 685–695. https://doi.org/10.1007/s10802-006-9055-6

Waldinger, R. J., Toth, S. L., & Gerber, A. (2001). Maltreatment and internal representations of relationships: Core relationship themes in the narratives of abused and neglected preschoolers. *Social Development*, *10*(1), 41–58. https://doi.org/10.1111/1467-9507.00147

Waller, R., & Hyde, L. (2017). Callous-unemotional behaviors in early childhood: Measurement, meaning, and the influence of parenting. *Child Development Perspectives*, *11*(2), 120–126. https://doi.org/10.1111/cdep.12222

Waller, R., Trentacosta, C., Shaw, D. S., Neiderhiser, J. M., Ganiban, J. M., Reiss, D., Leve, L. D., & Hyde, L. W. (2016). Heritable temperament pathways to early callous-unemotional behaviour. *British Journal of Psychiatry*, *209*, 475–482. https://doi.org/10.1192/bjp.bp.116.181503

Waller, R., Shaw, D. S., Neiderhiser, J. M., Ganiban, J. M., Natsuaki, M. N., Reiss, D., Trentacosta, C., Leve, L. D., & Hyde, L. W. (2017). Towards an understanding of the role of the environment in the development of early callous behavior. *Journal of Personality*, *85*(1), 90–103. https://doi.org/10.1111/jopy.12221

Wang, Y., Cao, S., Zhang, Q., & Xia, L. X. (2020). The longitudinal relationship between angry rumination and reactive-proactive aggression and the moderation effect of consideration of future consequences-immediate. *Aggressive Behavior*, *46*(6), 476–488. https://doi.org/10.1002/ab.21913

Weiss, L. H., & Schwarz, J. C. (1996). The relationship between parenting types and older adolescents' personality, academic achievement, adjustment, and substance use. *Child Development*, *67*(5), 2101–2114. https://doi.org/10.1111/j.1467-8624.1996.tb01846.x

White, M. (2016). *Narrative therapy classics*. Dulwich Centre Publications.

Xie, H., Swift, D. J., Cairns, B. D., & Cairns, R. B. (2002). Aggressive behaviors in social interaction and developmental adaptation: A narrative analysis of interpersonal conflicts during early adolescence. *Social Development*, *11*(2), 205–224. https://doi.org/10.1111/1467-9507.00195

Yoon, J. S., Hughes, J. N., Cavell, T. A., & Thompson, B. (2000). Social cognitive differences between aggressive-rejected and aggressive-nonrejected children. *Journal of School Psychology*, *38*(6), 551–570. https://doi.org/10.1016/S0022-4405(00)00052-2

Zahn-Waxler, C., Radke-Yarrow, M., & King, R. A. (1979). Child rearing and children's prosocial initiations toward victims of distress. *Child Development*, *50*(2), 319–330. https://doi.org/10.2307/1129406

Zhou, Q., Hofer, C., Eisenberg, N., Reiser, M., Spinrad, T. L., & Fabes, R. A. (2007). The developmental trajectories of attention focusing, attentional and behavioral persistence, and externalizing problems during school-age years. *Developmental Psychology*, *43*(2), 369–385. https://doi.org/10.1037/0012-1649.43.2.369

18 Bullying

Bullying is a specific and targeted form of aggression in which individuals oppress others who are typically younger or weaker than themselves in gratuitous, unjustified, deliberate and repeated attempts to dominate and inflict hurt (Kochenderfer-Ladd & Ladd, 2001; Rigby, 2006; Slee, 1995a, 1995b; Smith & Sharp, 1994).

Distinctions between aggression and bullying

Aggression and bullying are different in both the magnitude of their effects on targets and their underlying psychology. To clarify the differences, first, bullying is distinguished from simple aggression by its repeated and targeted nature. A second way in which aggression and bullying differ is that, with some exceptions such as in revenge for poaching friends (Owens et al., 2000b), bullies typically choose to exercise power over others proactively (without provocation), whereas aggression is typically reactive. Third, with aggression, once perpetrators realise that they have hurt the target, they pull back, whereas bullies crank it up another gear. Hurting the other person is the goal and seeing that they have achieved this emboldens them to persist.

Fourth, with aggression, perpetrators choose the target whereas, with bullying, the target is sanctioned by the group. Fifth and relatedly, the two have very different causes. Aggression gains perpetrators access to resources and status, whereas bullying is a product of unnatural power structures which devalue some group members and thereby make them potential targets.

Finally, in terms of their trajectory or pattern over time, aggression and bullying appear at different ages, and whereas aggression declines with age, bullying tends to increase with age and persist even into adulthood. Persistent childhood bullies are typically bullies in their work and personal lives; this is not true of the majority of early aggressors.

Incidence of bullying

Bullying is so widespread that, 'No study of social behaviour in any school anywhere in the world has shown an absence of bullying' (Noble, 2006, p. 68). It seems to be immune to culture, with rates being similar the world over. Despite difficulties with under-reporting,

DOI: 10.4324/9781003323938-21

estimates tend to settle on (Espelage & Swearer, 2003; Golberg et al., 2007; Nansel et al., 2001; Olweus, 1993):

- up to 10 per cent of young people are victims
- 13 per cent are perpetrators
- 6 per cent are both, with these aggressive victims declining in number from middle to late primary school.

Nevertheless, figures vary widely according to which forms of bullying are counted, with the result that involvement in bullying is likely to be closer to 35 per cent (Modecki et al., 2014). Victimhood is reasonably stable over three to four months (Sapouna et al., 2012), with more prolonged bullying (across three years) experienced by as many as 14 per cent of students, with 4 per cent enduring bullying that persists for at least four years (Kochenderfer-Ladd & Wardrop, 2001).

Forms of bullying

Although early literature focused mainly on direct attacks, recent research has examined its more furtive types. Being covert, these are harder to detect and therefore are safer to use.

Direct attacks

Direct, open or overt bullying comprises direct physical attacks such as pushing, shoving, punching, tripping up, damaging the victim's clothing or possessions, and striking with or without weapons; and direct verbal attacks such as taunting, name calling or using a person consistently as the butt of jokes (O'Moore & Minton, 2004). A final form, extortion, entails the extraction of money or other possessions under threat, or being forced to commit antisocial or illegal acts such as theft or vandalism.

Relational bullying

The intent of relational bullying is to isolate and exclude individual children. Given humans' need to belong, this can be devastating. Methods become increasingly covert and subtle as children mature (Shute et al., 2002) and span surreptitious behaviours such as those listed in Box 18.1.

Verbal relational bullying is often accompanied by non-verbal signals that are aimed at conveying disgust or anger while asserting one's own power or status (Shute et al., 2002). These include stares, 'bitchy' looks, looking someone up and down in a disparaging manner, rolling the eyes, using a sarcastic tone of voice and tossing the head in 'telegraphic' displays of emotion (Shute et al., 2002). Displaying public affection such as huddles, loud talk and extravagant greetings with only the 'in' members of a clique also communicates that some-one is on the outer. These non-verbal means ensure that relational bullying remains covert, allowing perpetrators to disguise their aggressive intentions and conferring total deniability (James & Owens, 2004). The bullying has maximum effect on the victim with minimum risk to the perpetrator, because any reaction or report can be met with accusations that the victim is over-reacting, imagining things or is 'paranoid'. Victims can then suffer further bullying in retaliation for reporting or for appearing unable to be assertive on their own behalf (Newman & Murray, 2005; Scholte et al., 2007).

Box 18.1 Exclusionary manoeuvres

- *Verbal putdowns*: using hurtful nicknames that parody a person's personal characteristics; leaving anonymous messages in notes, emails, phone messages or web sites.
- *Isolation*: ignoring someone briefly or for extended periods, outright prolonged ostracism, hiding from and thus isolating particular peers. Some will manipulate group acceptance by invoking a third party to collude in exclusion, as in, 'We're not playing with her, are we?'.
- *Blocking a child's access to play*: prematurely terminating play once a particular peer enters, restricting children's access to other peers or to play equipment.
- *Placing constraints on the relationship*: 'You can't be my friend unless...'; restricting or threatening to restrict a peer's access to social events, as in, 'You can't come to my birthday party'; dominating or bossing peers during play which playmates either have to submit to, or lose the right to play.
- *Gossiping*: talking about others behind their backs, using code names for victims which they suspect refer to themselves. Sometimes gossiping is discreet but at other times gossip is semi-public, with nearby students hearing and numbers of students laughing and perhaps looking meaningfully at the isolated, unhappy student who is the obvious topic of the conversation (Low et al., 2010).
- *Betrayals of trust*: telling secrets or circulating shared confidences; threatening to expose shared confidences; spreading malicious rumours.

Sources: Crick et al. (2001); Deater-Deckard (2001); James & Owens (2005); Olweus (1993); Ostrov & Keating (2004); Owens et al. (2000a, 2001); Rigby (1996, 1998); Salmivalli et al. (1998); Shute et al. (2002); Slee (1995b); Smith & Sharp (1994); Tattum (1993a)

Sexual harassment

A further form of peer bullying is sexual harassment, which is 'verbal or non-verbal behaviour with sexual content that is unwanted and perceived negatively by the target' (Diehl et al., 2012, p. 521). Sexual harassment spans four main categories: unwanted sexual attention, gender harassment, sexual coercion, and heterosexist harassment (Diehl et al., 2012; Drouet, 1993; Fineran, 2001; Owens et al., 2005). These behaviours appear to have three motives: to signal sexual interest; to express hostility towards females because of their gender (Diehl et al., 2012; Stein, 1995) or at individuals for their gender identity or sexual orientation; or to gain status for perpetrators with their male peers.

Unwanted sexual attention targets individual females. It includes offensive and unrequited behaviours such as sexually toned verbal comments about girls' physical appearance;

circulation of rumours affecting their sexual reputation; and requiring girls to perform favours (not necessarily sexual) at the threat of having sexual rumours spread about them.

Gender harassment is insulting, hostile and degrading sexual behaviours aimed at denigrating and suppressing women as a group and emphasising their inferiority to men (Diehl et al., 2012). This can involve sexist jokes; using acronyms to refer to sexual acts or sex organs; and visual harassment such as using pornography or defacing school posters of females to embarrass or intimidate them.

Sexual coercion is physical touch, pressure to engage in unwanted sexual behaviour, and rape.

Over 80 per cent of females and 50 per cent of males are subjected to sexual harassment at school that is sustained and often public in nature (Stein, 1995). Most perpetrators are males, with the pattern of belittling girls for being female beginning in preschool (Harter et al., 1997) and persisting because teachers either accept it or blame the girls for doing something to provoke it (Stein, 1995). Although rape is seen as deviant, harassment is not and perpetrators justify their taunts on the grounds that these are humorous or are flattering to females, that they are harmless, or that females are 'asking for it' (Lonsway et al., 2008). However, their victims find harassment threatening and nasty, feel helpless and frightened, and may feel obliged to avoid areas in which males congregate (Owens et al., 2005; Stein, 1995). The public nature of the harassment adds to the distress of victims because their humiliation is public; their reputation is damaged, although the perpetrators' status is not – go figure! (Stein, 1995).

Heterosexist harassment focuses on the recipient's gender identity or sexual orientation (Bontempo & D'Augelli, 2002; Fineran, 2001; Murdock & Bolch, 2005; Rivers, 2001). Sexual minority youth often endure not only interpersonal verbal and physical bullying from school peers and teachers, but also mobbing by unknown assailants and continuous sociocultural heterosexist harassment (Espelage et al., 2008; Fineran, 2001; Henning-Stout et al., 2000; Jordan et al., 1997; Malinsky, 1997; Savin-Williams, 1994). In high school, the incidence of verbal slurs has been reported to be *26 times* per day, with teachers responding only 3 per cent of the time (Macgillivray, 2000). The rate of homophobic bullying seems to decline through high school as young people mature and social hierarchies are established (Hatchel et al., 2020).

Cyber bullying

Cyber bullying involves wilful, deliberate, hostile and repeated harassment or threats delivered over the internet (Mason, 2008). It can entail using text messages, emails, social media and personal web pages to defame, humiliate, verbally abuse or threaten the target, circulate rumours, or post malicious comments. Some of these platforms can be anonymous, and with some, the content can disappear, making it almost impossible to save the material as proof of bullying. Other forms involve impersonating peers online to disrupt their friendships or get them into trouble. Some forms also constitute stalking, which is a crime, as are sharing sexually explicit photos of people under the age of consent and disseminating pornographic photos.

Approximately 15 per cent of adolescents experience cyber bullying, which is about half the rate of in-person bullying (Modecki et al., 2014). The source can be individuals, or it can be a blitz attack from numbers of peers. Electronic bullying by others is distinguished from in-person bullying in the following four ways (Chaux et al., 2016; Mason, 2008; Raskauskas & Stoltz, 2007; Stauffer et al., 2012; Wright & Li, 2013).

- It can be anonymous. This fosters disinhibition (Mason, 2008) (just as we can exhibit less gracious behaviour while driving, compared with face-to-face encounters) and its anonymity makes detection less likely and therefore it is less risky to join in (Van Cleemput et al., 2014).
- The invisibility of the victim allows perpetrators to avoid seeing the harm they are doing and gives potential defenders few cues to know whether and how to intervene. Onlookers are also less likely to feel an obligation to help, given that they do not know the victim. Given this moral disengagement, these same bystanders would probably do nothing in face-to-face encounters either (Van Cleemput et al., 2014).
- The target has no respite from and cannot escape the victimisation, which makes it more pernicious than regular bullying because there is no sanctuary anywhere.
- Cyberbullying has a larger reach, potentially being dispersed to a wider audience. This magnifies the target's humiliation, and takes it a step further into *shaming*, which involves exposure of an individual to the judgement and ostracism of the crowd, typically well out of proportion to the alleged wrongdoing (Jacquet, 2015). This is dehumanising and strips individuals of their dignity (Jacquet, 2015).

Adolescents are likely to use cyber aggression against those whom they see as rivals for sexual partners (Lapierre & Dane, 2020). It seems that the majority (94 per cent) of perpetrators who use electronic media to bully also use traditional means as well, while 84 per cent of electronic victims are traditional victims also (Raskauskas & Stoltz, 2007; Wang et al., 2012). Many regard electronic media as entertainment, which allows them to view cyber bullying as a game, which they do 'for fun' (Pornari & Wood, 2010).

Targets of cyberbullying react with a similar range of emotions as those who are the targets of in-person bullying, although depression and suicidal ideation and attempts can be more severe when cyberbullying attacks are frequent (Perwitasari & Wuryaningsih, 2022).

One rarer form (employed by 1 in 20, or 5 per cent of adolescents) is cyber self-bullying, in which adolescents anonymously post denigrating comments about themselves - sometimes multiple times - either out of self-hatred or depression (sometimes resulting from being bullied), as a joke, to recruit sympathy, or to see if anyone comes to their defence (Pacheco et al., 2019; Patchin & Hinduja, 2017). Those who post something mean about themselves are five times more likely to have suicidal thoughts, and nine to 15 times more likely to make suicide attempts (Patchin et al., 2023).

Although schools sometimes argue that they can do nothing about cyber bulling, the school is often where perpetrators meet and select their victims (Raskauskas & Stoltz, 2007). Therefore, both school policy and interventions need to protect targets on this medium as well as in its face-to-face forms.

Causes of bullying

The first reason that bullying persists is because it is embedded in systems (schools, classrooms and families) that inadvertently model, maintain and reinforce domination and intimidation (Pepler et al., 1993; Tattum, 1993b). The rate of bullying in one school can be up to four times higher than in another, which has been attributed to the school ethos and teaching practices.

Second, within classrooms, teachers' values shape the quality of peer relationships (Patrick et al., 2011). Teachers who favour the more academically able students and belittle students who are impulsive, distractible or less able, actively promote hierarchies within classrooms (Mikami et al., 2012). This emphasis on social comparison generates differences in students' perceptions of their worth or prestige (Ames, 1981; Ames & Felker, 1979). Not only does this contribute to the alienation of those young people who are less able (Pomeroy 1999), but also leads to their neglect and rejection by peers (Mikami et al., 2012).

A third cause of bullying is the parenting style under which children are raised. Authoritarian parenting leads to elevated rates of sibling aggression which is transferred to the use of aggression towards peers (Tippett & Wolke, 2015; Vaillancourt et al., 2007). As well as failing to teach young people prosocial means for solving disputes within the family and elsewhere, a controlling parenting style denies young people opportunities to participate in decisions affecting them; in turn, this increases their risk of becoming both bullies (to exert power that is otherwise denied them) and victims (because they lack personal power to defend themselves) (Chaux & Castellanos, 2015).

Parents who use psychological controls - such as love withdrawal, criticism, or the induction of guilt or shame - are actively teaching their children how to use relational bullying with other people (Skripkauskaite et al., 2015). As well as modelling manipulative behaviours, these parents often fail to check older siblings' relational aggression towards their younger brothers or sisters (Brendgen et al., 2005; Casas et al., 2006; Ostrov et al., 2006; Stauffacher & DeHart, 2006).

Fourth are causes arising from within peer groups themselves. Naturally, social success is the main currency of middle childhood and adolescence, which makes some social assertiveness common. But, in an authoritarian climate and hierarchical setting, aggression and bullying occur at elevated rates. This is because these behaviours work primarily to secure social status (Long & Li, 2020; Long & Pellegrini, 2003; Pellegrini, 2004; Xie et al., 2002). Some bullying is a strategy to get revenge or payback for social aggression such as gossiping, or for the poaching of same-sex friends or boyfriends (Reynolds & Repetti, 2010; Xie et al., 2002).

Last, adolescents say that they bully to alleviate boredom or for 'fun'. (Owens, 1997; Owens et al., 2000b; Reynolds & Repetti, 2010; Thornberg, 2010). Sometimes, the reaction of the target is considered amusing, whereas sometimes it is just fun to be haughty and mean (Thornberg, 2010), presumably because it defies adult injunctions against such behaviour.

Actors involved in bullying

Bullying behaviour occurs because group - and, to a lesser extent, school - norms govern the acceptability of aggression to the group (Chang, 2004; Kohm, 2015; Nipedel et al., 2010).

Dominant group members are never the target, which tells us that the group colludes to define some individuals as being part of the in-group and others as outsiders (Duffy & Nesdale, 2009; Hodges et al., 1997; Huitsing & Veenstra 2012).

Instigators. Perpetrators are of two main types: social manipulators with high social skilfulness, and troubled individuals. Social manipulators are outgoing and confident, and enjoy a wide base of peer support. They have high self-efficacy about being able to dominate or make aggression work for them. They are capable of cognitive empathy in that they understand the hurt they are inflicting but lack the emotional empathy or moral reasoning to care about that.

In contrast, troubled bullies have few social skills. They have deficient problem-solving skills and therefore cannot use more prosocial means for solving disputes. They are impulsive, with insufficient self-regulation skills (Jolliffe & Farrington, 2011). In late adolescence, they also have a higher than usual rate of antisocial behaviour (Vassallo et al., 2014).

Colluders or accomplices. Present in 80 to 85 per cent of relational bullying incidents (Craig et al., 2000; Hawkins et al., 2001; Xie et al. 2002), accomplices' most common response is to support the instigator (Tapper & Boulton, 2005). These colluders take an active role either under the direction of the instigator or by spurring that person on. On other occasions, they may themselves be the instigators (Gumpel et al., 2014).

Supporters or reinforcers look on approvingly, but do not actively participate (Olthof et al., 2011). Teachers are often accomplices, sanctioning the continuation of bullying by doing nothing about it (Gumpel et al., 2014). Their silence amounts to tacit support.

Disengaged bystanders or onlookers do not agree with the behaviour but might disengage because no one else is doing anything (the bystander effect), or they think it's not their problem or is none of their business.

Empathic onlookers. Around one-third of onlookers are empathic but nevertheless do nothing to help (Craig et al., 2000; Olweus, 2001). Both individual and group factors account for this: They don't know what to do or fear doing the wrong thing, it might seem too physically dangerous to intervene; they fear being associated with someone who is devalued; or are fearful of becoming future targets themselves (Cowie, 2000; Kohm, 2015; Sentse et al., 2013; Theodore & Chiasson, 2021; Thornberg, 2010). From the target's perspective, however, bystanders' inaction causes them to appear to be colluding with the bullying (Cowie, 2000).

Peer defenders. Peers intervene in just 12 to 25 per cent of incidents (Kohm, 2015), with one study reporting that boys intervene more often than girls simply because they are present more often (Hawkins et al., 2001), but another reporting that girls were more likely to intervene out of their greater distaste for moral transgressions (Caravita et al., 2012). Typically, these altruists are high in both cognitive and emotional empathy and are motivated by a desire to relieve another's pain (Gini et al., 2007; Hoffman, 1981).

Young children are more willing to help victims than are older children and adolescents (Rigby & Johnson, 2006). These defenders typically seek help, comfort the victim, or use problem-solving skills to resolve the dispute (Cowie, 2000). If these assertive responses fail, half of the interventions escalate into aggression (Hawkins et al., 2001) - possibly because, being young, the defenders lack sufficient skills for resolving heated conflict.

Teacher defenders. Between 91 and 97 per cent of teachers report that they take action to deal with aggression and bullying (Bradshaw et al., 2007; Olweus, 1993; Pepler et al., 1998; Slee 1994). However, 25 to 60 per cent of students report that their teachers seldom act to

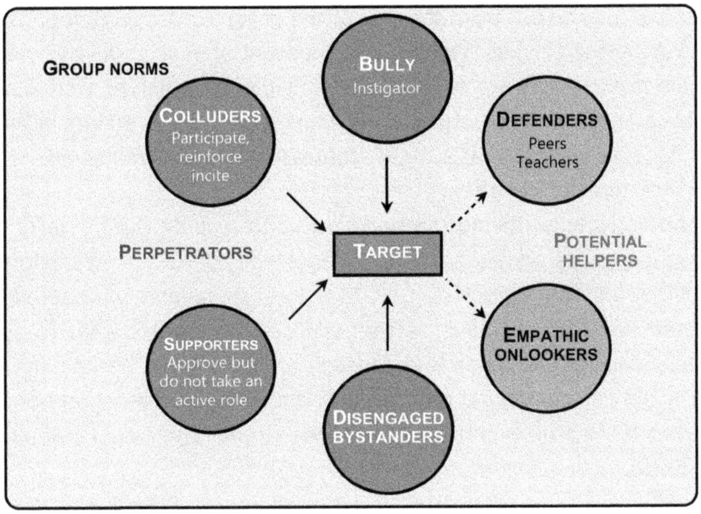

Figure 18.1 The actors involved in bullying

Source: Porter (2016, p. 95).

protect them, and that, when they do, their response is often unsatisfactory (Kosciw et al., 2020). This discrepancy partly reflects the difference between the number of incidents that actually occur, versus the number that teachers witness.

Teachers who believe that bullying is normative are unlikely to intervene and instead expect boys in particular to deal with it on their own (to 'man up') (Kochenderfer-Ladd & Pelletier, 2008). They are more dismissive of incidents that they do not witness and of relational bullying because there is less evidence of tangible harm to its recipient than is the case with physical assaults (Bradshaw et al., 2007; Young et al., 2006).

A profile of targets

Particularly in early childhood, aggressive children initially direct their vitriol towards anyone in their vicinity and then home in on targets whose response is gratifying (Hanish et al., 2005; Perry et al., 1990). At older ages, their behaviour deliberately target peers whom they assess to be deviant because they look different, behave oddly (such as employing ineffective humour), display atypical personality characteristics (being 'nerdy', for example), have a disability or poor motor skills, are economically disadvantaged, or are seen to be deviant by association (such as having a strange mother, an unusual religion, or minority culture) (Bejerot et al., 2015; Chaux & Castellanos, 2015; DeRosier & Mercer, 2009; D'Urso & Symonds, 2021; Thornberg, 2010). Nevertheless, these atypical qualities are merely an after-the-fact excuse for bullying that results from the dehumanisation of targets. Moreover, the group determines which characteristics are salient in defining deviance (Thornberg, 2010).

Children with a strong sense of justice are at increased risk of being bullied (Chaux & Castellanos, 2015; Kochenderfer & Ladd, 1996; Olweus, 1993) because their resulting upset at bullies' meanness is gratifying to perpetrators. Commonly, targets are also isolated and therefore, are easily 'picked off' from the rest of the group (D'Urso & Symonds, 2021; Hodges et al., 1997). Nevertheless, targets typically have appropriate social skills (Smith et al., 2004). Attractive female adolescents are at a 35 per cent elevated risk of victimisation, to make them appear less attractive to the other sex (Gallup et al., 2011; Leenaars et al., 2008; Sainio et al., 2012; Vaillancourt & Sharma, 2011). In contrast, attractive males are at a 25 per cent *reduced* risk of victimisation (Leenaars et al., 2008).

Some respond actively by telling the perpetrator to stop or, during early childhood, will seek help from their peers or teachers (Kochenderfer-Ladd, 2004; Waasdorp & Bradshaw, 2011). In contrast, adolescents are less likely to ask for help, instead generally coping alone (Waasdorp & Bradshaw, 2011). This is partly because they do not want to appear helpless (Theodore & Chiasson, 2021) and partly because students say that the teachers just tell them to ignore it or, in the case of sexual minority adolescents, to stop acting in gender nonconformist ways (that is, to stop being who they are) so that their peers won't pick on them (Kosciw et al., 2020).

A small minority of victims respond with reflexive aggression. They lash out hotly when provoked, with their emotional arousal leading to disorganised behaviour that peers regard as inappropriate for their age and the circumstances. Their fiery reactions escalate conflicts and attract further victimisation, which deepens their sense of isolation and loneliness (Flaspohler et al., 2009; Hanish & Guerra, 2000; Hodges & Perry, 1999; Hodges et al., 1999; Kawabata et al., 2014; LaFontana & Cillessen, 2002; Lamarche et al., 2006; Leadbeater et al., 2006; Mahady Wilton et al., 2000; O'Brennan et al., 2009; Prinstein & Cillessen, 2003; Rosen et al., 2012; Salmivalli & Helteenvuori, 2007; Schwartz, 2000; Unnever, 2005). These aggressive victims are ridiculed and rejected by peers, with adults feeling little sympathy for their plight as victims, believing that they bring it on themselves.

Effects of bullying

At the time, most victims are angry, and some report being upset, sad, depressed, worried, embarrassed and humiliated; for indirect or relational bullying, stress and depression are common reactions (Hunter et al., 2007; Ortega et al., 2012; Vassallo et al., 2014). Victims are often confused about why they have been targeted, and might cover up or deny the reality of their victimisation, or less adaptively, blame themselves for it (Juvonen et al., 2000; O'Brennan et al., 2009; Owens et al., 2000b). Typically, their self-esteem is low but this is a result - not a cause - of the bullying, with the domain most affected being social self-esteem (Erath et al., 2008; Kochenderfer & Ladd, 1996; Kochenderfer-Ladd & Wardrop, 2001; Pan et al., 2020; Wu et al., 2021).

Long-term bullying can lead to anxiety and post-traumatic stress (Crosby et al., 2010; Ferraz de Camargo et al., 2022; Idsoe et al., 2021; Juvonen et al., 2000; Kochenderfer-Ladd & Ladd, 2001; Mateu et al., 2020; Meyer, 2019; Mynard et al., 2000; Olweus, 2001; Rivers, 2001; Smith et al., 2004). In a dose-related manner, bullying increases the risk of suicide by targets (Koyanagi et al., 2019), particularly in those who are lonely, depressed, have attention deficits, are violent, use drugs, are overweight, have asthma or are questioning their gender identity or sexual orientation (Dorol-Beauroy-Eustache & Mishara, 2021). Those missing school for fear of being bullied are three times more likely to attempt suicide (Garofalo et al., 1999).

Socially, protracted bullying can lead in the long term to distrust of others (Juvonen et al., 2000; Kochenderfer-Ladd & Ladd, 2001; Rosen et al., 2009; Ziv et al., 2013). In turn, distrust of peers can lead to withdrawal, social anxiety, social phobia and alienation (Wu et al., 2021; Zimmer-Gembeck & Pronk, 2012) and absenteeism from school. As a result of feeling shame that there must be something wrong with them to attract bullying, they become lonely, isolated and helpless (Wu et al., 2021), leading to deepening isolation as targets are increasingly neglected and rejected over time (Kawabata et al., 2014; Sentse et al., 2013).

Once the victimisation has ceased, some targets of sustained bullying report few long-lasting effects, whereas others experience ongoing maladjustment, commonly enduring emotional effects that are characteristic of post-traumatic stress (Crosby et al., 2010; Ferraz de Camargo et al., 2022; Idsoe et al., 2021; Juvonen et al., 2000; Kochenderfer-Ladd & Ladd 2001; Mateu et al., 2020; Meyer, 2019; Mynard et al., 2000; Olweus, 2001; Rivers, 2001; Smith et al., 2004). The core factors that protect those who have been bullied from these negative outcomes are having strong social skills, being connected to school and achieving well academically (Kim et al., 2020; Vassallo et al., 2014). However, having a high attachment to peers (which is threatened by bullying) increases the risk of depression and other negative outcomes later in life (Vassallo et al., 2014).

Box 18.2 Effects of prolonged victimisation from bullying

Emotional effects

- dysregulated emotions
- feelings of distress, anxiety, isolation, unhappiness and loneliness
- explosive anger
- low self-esteem (especially in the social domain)
- impaired self-efficacy
- depression
- preoccupation with threat
- post-traumatic stress
- self-harm
- suicidal ideation and suicide attempts

Social effects

- fear of going to school
- avoidance of interactions at the time and subsequently, even into adult life
- social phobia
- fear for future relationships

Academic effects

- declining academic performance
- absenteeism
- leaving school altogether

Health effects

- sleeping difficulties
- weight gain
- increased health complaints, possibly because stress undermines immune system functioning
- increased alcohol, nicotine and drug use, either to cope with stress or in an effort to gain entry to a delinquent peer group

Behaviours

- In adolescence, girls who are put down by other girls might delay dating and perceive themselves as being less attractive (Gallup et al., 2011).
- Some seek the comfort and support of a series of short-term sexual or romantic relationships, but these entail additional breakups, conflict and rejection (Gallup et al., 2011).
- Increased risk of the onset of drug use during adolescence (Guo, 2022).

Sources: Buhs et al., (2006); Dempsey & Storch (2008); Egan & Perry (1998); Espelage & Swearer (2003); Fekkes et al., (2006); Field & Carroll (2006); Graham et al., (2006); Hunter & Boyle (2004); Idsoe et al., (2021); Juvonen et al., (2000); Kochenderfer-Ladd & Ladd (2001); Marsh et al., (2004); Martin & Huebner (2007); Murray-Close et al., (2007); Mynard et al., (2000); Nansel et al., (2001); Olweus (1993); O'Moore & Minton (2004); Owens et al., (2000b); Putallaz et al., (2007); Qualter et al., (2015); Rigby (1996, 1999, 2001, 2006); Scholte et al., (2007); Schwartz et al., (2005); Slee (1995a, 1995b); P. K. Smith et al., (2004); Sullivan et al., (2006); Sweeting et al., (2007); Vaillancourt et al., (2013); Vassallo et al., (2014)

Interventions

Tattum (1993a, p. 3) does not mince words when he calls bullying 'the most malicious and malevolent form of antisocial behaviour practised in our schools'. While a perfectly natural human reaction, this view can cause us to demonise its perpetrators, in turn yielding a range of ineffective responses. Punitive responses would model the very 'Might makes right' ethos that aggressive students already endorse. Authoritarian interventions would thus not only be ineffective but also hypocritical, in that they would simply replicate and reinforce the belief that power is the route to social status and that it is acceptable to dominate vulnerable individuals. Therefore, most researchers favour non-punitive (non-behaviourist) approaches to bullying (McGrath & Stanley, 2006). These provide both support and structure (in contrast to punishment) to prevent and respond to bullying.

Given that bullying reflects imbalances of power within the school system, interventions on only one level are unlikely to be effective (Slee, 2020). Therefore, school counsellors will need to lead anti-bullying measures across the entire school. Slee (2006, 2020) proposes that schools enact a five-phase anti-bullying program described by the acronym PEACE:

P	Preparation
E	Education
A	Action
C	Countering strategies
E	Evaluation

Preparation involves collecting data through anonymous surveys about the types and incidence of bullying in the school, writing an anti-bullying policy, formalising their procedures for students to report incidents, and instituting measures to prevent bullying such as building a cohesive school and class community. This will create an atmosphere in which injustice towards others is less tolerated.

Education. The most important goal of education is to increase empathy for targets (Diehl et al., 2014). To achieve this, teachers, parents and students need to receive some straightforward information about the various forms of bullying, its signs and its effects on victims, and procedures to use to deal with it.

Although at high school level, the success of anti-bullying curricula is limited, partly because young people who do not share the school's values will not be won over by rules of the 'Be nice to each other' variety (see, e.g. Orpinas et al., 2003). Indeed, some will even be contemptuous of efforts to include these programs at their level. Neverthless, younger students can be receptive to these curricula, perhaps because both bully and victim roles are not yet stable (Owens et al., 2000a; Salmivalli et al., 2005; Smith & Ananiadou, 2003; Stevens et al. 2000). Even so, education programs will not be enough, because implementation will necessarily be patchy amongst the many other curricular demands and because bullies are not going to be convinced by messages about civility and helping each other (Rapee et al., 2020). Nevertheless, in the context of other measures to enhance social cohesion in classrooms and across the school, raising the awareness of bystanders can mobilise them to be more empathic towards targets and therefore to give less tacit support to bullies (Rigby & Bagshaw, 2006; Salmivalli et al., 2005; Vaillancourt & Hymel, 2006).

Taking action. This involves first-order change - that is, responding appropriately to incidents, which is the surest way of preventing future episodes (Pikas, 2002; Slee, 2020). Given that teachers are unlikely to directly witness relational bullying, they will need to be receptive and responsive to students' reports of this covert form of victimisation, particularly its more subtle forms of intimidation such as exclusion and non-verbal manipulation (Shute et al., 2002). Teachers' interventions will need to provide emotional support for targets and structural support, such as providing structured activities at breaks, supervising playgrounds, or assigning targets a mentor or peer buddy to provide them with company so that their isolation does not make them vulnerable. Peer mediation and conflict resolution methods which have been advocated in the past have been found not to work, and in fact can increase bullying (Cowie, 2000; Cowie & Olafsson, 2000; Kosciw et al., 2020; Slee, 2020; Smith & Daunic, 2002).

Meanwhile, second-order change involves changes to the school system itself (Slee, 2020). This will include limiting competition between students by ceasing classroom reward systems and school awards, because competition causes students to regard each other as rivals (Ryan & Patrick, 2001) and contributes to hostility and ill-feeling amongst classmates (Crockenberg et al., 1976; Deutsch, 1979).

Supporting victims to counter bullying. Adults can recommend that targets of victimisation use coping and problem-solving skills (see Chapter 11). Under the guise of narrative therapy, most young people will be able to suggest their own countering strategies but, sometimes, they will need a few suggestions, from which they can select one that appeals to them. One strategy that I have recommended to young targets of exclusion is what I term 'gate-keeping'. This, I warn them, is very difficult to do but only needs to be done once or twice, and role playing in preparation at home can help. The method is that, when their group finally invites them to join them, the young target declines, saying that s/he has something else to do. In this way, targets become the gatekeepers of when they will and will not join the group, instead of the group having this power over them.

As examples of behavioural strategies, without attempting to engage the bullies in deep conversation or to forge a relationship with them, targets could surprise them by greeting them briefly, asking them how they are, enquiring how their team went on the weekend, or bringing cupcakes or other treats for the whole class (including the perpetrators) to share, and so on. These gestures put the target in charge, rather than passively waiting to see how the perpetrators will treat them today. These measures will not forge friendships - but they will communicate that the target is not easily cowed.

While a longer-term solution is being worked out, it can be useful to separate the perpetrators and target. This reduces opportunities for repeat attacks and also avoids assaults in retribution for disclosing the bullying (Kochenderfer-Ladd & Pelletier, 2008). A simple 'invisibility' strategy is for victims to temporarily avoid those areas where most bullying occurs (Fuller, 2006).

Evaluation of the effectiveness of the program. Once a school's policy and procedures are in place, the final component of Slee's PEACE program is to evaluate whether the practices that were enshrined in its provisions are working to achieve its goals. At the outset someone will need to be allocated responsibility to conduct an evaluation and to be accountable for its completion within a given time frame. Evaluation of *processes* requires staff members to reflect on how satisfied they are with students' safety and well-being and with their own preventive and interventive measures. Assessment of *outcomes* will focus on the effects of preventive and interventive measures on individual students, while checking that certain individuals or groups are not being overlooked by the approaches being used.

A solution-focused approach

Young (2001) details three steps of a solution-focused approach: statement of the problem, recruiting peer support, and review. I reserve this approach for primary-aged children enduring less severe patterns of bullying.

Statement of the problem. In an interview with the target, open the discussion by stating that you, another teacher, or the student's parent is worried about him or her. You can follow this up with the question, 'Are we right to be worried about you?'. Having received assent that the worry is justified, you will need to state that answers to the next three questions will not get anyone into trouble. These questions are:

- 'Who do you find difficult to deal with at the moment?'. Do not ask what the named students are doing, because this can make the conversation deteriorate into problem-saturated talk.
- 'Who else is around when (the named peer) is being difficult?'. This allows you to identify bystanders who could be recruited to help.
- 'Who are your friends?' or, for those who are now completely isolated from their peer group, 'Who would you like to be your friend?'.

Recruit the support group. Meet with the students whom the target has named. Because it is a mixed group of perpetrators, onlookers and potential or actual friends, no one is being accused of anything. Simply explain that the target has been unhappy at school lately and has told you that they are the best people to help. Do not mention bullying or talk about any incidents, because this could degenerate into accusations of fault and blame. Instead, discuss with members of the group times when they have been unhappy at school and express empathy that it is not easy to be so. Then ask for their suggestions of what might help the focus student. As they raise suggestions, you can compliment promising ideas while checking that they are realistic: That could work. Would that be difficult or easy for you to do?'. When in reply students volunteer that it would not be difficult, you might thank them for their kindness and check that they are willing to do it. While not asking them to be friends with the focus student, once a plan is agreed on, you can end this session with a comment that you think their plan will work to make the victim happier at school.

Review. A week or so later, meet with targets to hear what has been better over the past week and ask how they managed to make that happen (e.g. responding to or trusting the friendlier overtures of the former bullies). Also contact students' parents for their feedback about their progress.

Next, meet again with the support group and ask what each member has done over the previous week to help the focus student. There is no need to refer back to their original suggestions, because it does not matter if they employed those particular strategies, only that they did something to make the situation improve for the victim. Congratulate them personally and as a group for a job well done and ask if they would like to continue for another week. Conduct one more review and, if no further problems surface, cease the intervention.

A narrative approach

The solution-focused approach might be useful for primary school and for interventions in the early stages of bullying. However, when a pattern is entrenched, it will likely be necessary to use narrative methods.

Narrative approaches with perpetrators

In narrative work, our questions are aimed at eliciting values, not at preaching these to young people (Marsten et al., 2016). We will avoid using the word *bully* for all its negative connotations and because it is totalising, but in our discussion of the bullying behaviour, an underlying theme will emerge, which clients will give a name. Depending on how the conversation has proceeded and what young people have labelled their pattern of behaviour, and depending on the strengths or wonderfulness that your earlier questions have exposed, you might ask the following questions (Marsten et al., 2016; White, 2016).

Landscape of identity questions about the dominant story

- What does Meanness have you thinking about yourself?
- Does The Boy Code convince you that you have to be a certain kind of male?
- Does The Code tell you that it is better to have gotten in the last punch than to have backed down?
- What does The Code talk you into believing about yourself?
- What seeds does it plant in your mind about who you are?

Preference questions

- Are you happy with Meanness defining you?
- If Meanness told you what matters most, how would that match up with what matters most to you?
- (For reactive bullying): If The Code wants you to get even, why not just follow its instructions?
- Are you happy living by The Code, or do you want something else for your relationships?
- What have you had to give up in order to keep The Codes' rules?
- How well does it suit you to have The Code decide for you what types of relationships to have?
- Do you like having a reputation as a standover guy, or would you like people to see you in some other way?
- You've heard (your teachers/your parents) here today saying troubling things about you. What is it like for you to be talked into such negative beliefs about yourself?
- What does Queen Bee want for your life? Is that the same as what you want for yourself?

Landscape of identity questions about the counter-narrative

- How have you managed to hold onto a wish to be kind to others, when The Code just wants you to be a tough guy?
- What might it take to be satisfied with a humble life, instead of needing to come out on top?

Preference questions about the counter-narrative

- Is it a fleeting wish to be kind to others, or is it a hope that you want to hold onto?
- Were those times when you felt close to your friends something that you want to preserve, or was it just a one-off thing?
- Would you prefer to have a modest heart, or a vengeful one?
- Is this something you want for yourself, or something you want to want?

Narrative approaches with targets

White (2004) notes that bullying behaviour demeans its targets by convincing them that they are too sensitive and weak, should stop reacting, should 'get over it', develop more 'grit' or have better self-esteem. White describes a client who had endured persistent bullying for years - and yet was still attending school. This achievement, said White, was a form of counter-power to Bullying's abuse.

With targets, you would decontextualise bullying as a form of oppression. Marsten et al. (2016, p. 63) ask of victims: 'If it were up to Unfairness, how would it spend your time and energy?'. Next, counsellors would ask how Unfairness has wormed its way into their lives and managed to convince them about their identity, and then mine for instances of 'sparkling moments' or exceptions to these ideas. It might be that a target is described as being too sensitive. We could then ask about instances from her earlier childhood that signify that she is sensitive and frame this as being loving and kind. Then you can ask what she would lose if she gave up being sensitive, and would she like to give that up? (It might be, for instance, that she would have to give up being kind to a sibling and is not willing to do that.)

A re-membering intervention for someone who loves team sports is outlined by Denborough (2014). Having described the bullying and clients' responses to it, counsellors would ask how they could change their relationship to the problem: Do they want to outsmart it, disempower it, undermine it, refuse its influence, come out of its shadow, for example? (Denborough 2014). And, if any of those, what could they do to outsmart Bullying? Who could be on their team to outsmart it? What would the team be called? What tricks would they use to out-trick Bullying?

In the case of a child who had endured bullying for two years, White (2004) conducted an outsider witness (definitional) ceremony (see Chapter 3) to allow the child to get some distance from the identity that Bullying had imposed on him.

Collaboration with parents of perpetrators

Bullying has been found to precede delinquency, but when parents of perpetrators support their children to change their behaviour, this progression becomes less likely (Walters et al., 2020). Therefore, school administrators or counsellors need to advise parents of perpetrators about their child's behaviour, without condemning their daughter or son, or criticising the parents themselves.

Overall, parents can have five potential reactions: punitive, dismissive, defensive, retaliatory and helpless. Taking each scenario in turn, to avoid angry parents punishing their children at home, it will be crucial to communicate that this is a school-based problem that the school intends to solve. In those rare cases where you suspect that the parents might severely punish their child, it could be necessary to provide limited specifics about the incidents.

Second, like their children, parents often view relational aggression as normative and benign, (Murray-Close et al., 2006; Werner & Grant, 2009) which may reduce both their concern over their child's actions and their commitment to collaborating with teachers to resolve the issue.

Third, by avoiding blame of perpetrators, we reduce the risk that their parents will also feel blamed and become defensive to protect themselves. Some might become defensive because, although their child is the perpetrator in the current instance, in the past the role of the protagonists was reversed, in which case parents might assert that their child's behaviour

Box 18.3 Advice for parents of targets

- Accept that social problems are inevitable and normal but, nevertheless, painful (without necessarily being traumatic).
- Do not 'interview for pain' at the end of each school day to discover the hurts that children have suffered during the day.
- Reflect children's hurt without feeling the need to 'fix' it.
- Trust your child's resilience.
- Trust friendship: It cycles between aggression and affection.
- Provide plenty of opportunities for your child to socialise with school peers during extracurricular activities and play dates. Cementing friendships alleviates individuals' isolation and makes them a less ready target for victimisation.
- Adult solutions interfere with children's learning to work things out themselves. Therefore, intervene only in crises.
- Ask children: 'Do I need to be worried?' Do not intervene if they answer 'No' but reserve the right to do so if your concerns escalate.
- If problems persist and you are getting alarmed, let your child know that you are going to take action, but ask their advice about what you could do that would be the least embarrassing for them and most likely to be effective.
- Do not approach the perpetrator yourself. This is intimidating and will backfire if you want to teach young people that intimidation is unjust.
- Unless you are good friends of the perpetrator's parents, do not approach them to ask for their intervention. They might respond the same way as their child by blaming the victim, or could punish their child who, in turn, could escalate the bullying in retaliation for being told on.

Source: Thompson et al. (2002)

is justified by their prior victimisation (Werner & Grant, 2009). As a result, these parents overlook their child's culpability and instead claim victim status only.

Fourth, it will be important to avoid confronting parents with criticism of themselves or their child, because a few will react by 'ganging up' with parents of the other perpetrators to ostracise the victim or the victim's parents (Field & Carroll, 2006). This can only make a bad situation worse.

Finally, some might be experiencing similar antisocial behaviour at home, and feel helpless to respond. In these cases, outside counselling might be useful for them.

Suspension of recalcitrant aggressors

Given the serious effects of severe bullying (as listed in Box 18.2), the physical and psychological health of victims must take precedence over perpetrators' rights. Therefore, in those rare cases where perpetrators have had every chance to cease their harassment but have been unwilling to do so, in order to support their victim, as a last resort, the perpetrator will need to be suspended or expelled from school. When school administrators suspend perpetrators, justice demands that they recommend alternative placements and, in the meantime, provide a home-based curriculum. Although suspension contradicts an inclusive ethos, suspension can be a positive force that impels the parents of perpetrators to instigate problem solving. It is also preferable to the alternative of having victims change schools, which seems unfair given that they are not at fault and therefore should not be the ones to have their education disrupted.

Legal remedies

When a behaviour is illegal in the community, it is equally illegal on school grounds and, therefore, the school will need to invoke the justice system. It would be an error to attempt to protect the school's reputation by failing to report crimes. To do so would teach perpetrators that they are above the law and leave them free to repeat or escalate their offending with impunity.

Victims have the option of resorting to legal remedies - such as provided by anti-stalking legislation or apprehended violence orders (Nicholson, 2006). However, these are likely to be too little too late. Once victims have had to resort to the courts to protect themselves, they have already suffered harm and, potentially, trauma.

Conclusion

The most successful way for schools to prevent bullying is to be supremely effective at responding to incidents, thus avoiding a repetition (Pikas, 2002; Slee, 2020). However, to achieve this, the focus cannot just be on the individuals involved: We cannot change perpetrators' behaviour without changing the hierarchical social relationships that incite and support their actions. This will include ensuring that teacher discrimination against or preference for particular students does not heighten the salience of racial, gender, ability or other differences and thereby generate differences in status between students that the dominant can then exploit.

References

Ames, C. (1981). Competitive versus cooperative reward structures: The influence of individual and group performance factors on achievement attributions and affect. *American Educational Research Journal*, *18*(3), 273-287. https://doi.org/10.3102/00028312018003273

Ames, C., & Felker, D. W. (1979). An examination of children's attributions and achievement-related evaluations in comparative, cooperative, and individualistic reward structures. *Journal of Educational Psychology*, *71*(4), 413-420.

Bejerot, S., Plenty, S., Humble, A., & Humble, M. B. (2015). Poor motor skills: A risk marker for bully victimization. *Aggressive Behavior*, *39*(6), 453-461. https://doi.org/10.1002/ab.21489

Bontempo, D. E., & D'Augelli, A. R. (2002). Effects of at-school victimization and sexual orientation on lesbian, gay, or bisexual youths' health risk behavior. *Journal of Adolescent Health*, *30*(5), 364-374. https://doi.org/10.1016/S1054-139X(01)00415-3

Bradshaw, C. P., Sawyer, A. L., & O'Brennan, L. M. (2007). Bullying and peer victimization at school: Perceptual differences between students and school staff. *School Psychology Review*, *36*(3), 361-382. https://doi.org/10.1080/02796015.2007.12087929

Brendgen, M., Dionne, G., Girard, A., Boivin, M., Vitaro, F., & Pérusse, D. (2005). Examining genetic and environmental effects on social aggression: A study of 6-year-old twins. *Child Development*, *76*(4), 930–946. https://doi.org/10.1111/j.1467-8624.2005.00887.x

Buhs, E. S., Ladd, G. W., & Herald, S. L. (2006). Peer exclusion and victimization: Processes that mediate the relation between peer group rejection and children's classroom engagement and achievement? *Journal of Educational Psychology*, *98*(1), 1–13. https://doi.org/10/1037/0022-0663.98.1.1

Caravita, S. C. S., Gini, G., & Pozzoli, T. (2012). Main and moderating effects of moral cognition and status on bullying and defending. *Aggressive Behavior*, *38*(6), 456–468. https://doi.org/10.1002/ab.21447

Casas, J. F., Weigel, S. M., Crick, N. R., Ostrov, J. M., Woods, K. E., Yeh, E. A. J., & Huddleston-Casas, C. A. (2006). Early parenting and children's relational and physical aggression in the preschool and home contexts. *Journal of Applied Developmental Psychology*, *27*(3), 209–227. https://doi.org/10.1016/j.appdev.2006.02.003

Chang, L. (2004). The role of classroom norms in contextualizing the relations of children's social behaviors to peer acceptance. *Developmental Psychology*, *40*(5), 691–702. https://doi.org/10.1037/0012-1649.40.5.691

Chaux, E., Velásquez, A. M., Schultze-Krumbholz, A., & Scheithauer, H. (2016). Effects of the cyberbullying prevention program media heroes (Medienhelden) on traditional bullying. *Aggressive Behavior*, *42*(2), 157–165. https://doi.org/10.1002/ab.21637

Chaux, E., & Castellanos, M. (2015). Money and age in schools: Bullying and power imbalances. *Aggressive Behavior*, *41*(3), 280–293. https://doi.org/10.1002/ab.21558

Cowie, H. (2000). Bystanding or standing by: Gender issues in coping with bullying in English schools. *Aggressive Behavior*, *26*(1), 85–97. https://doi.org/10.1002/(SICI)1098-2337(2000)26:1%3C85::AID-AB7%3E3.0.CO;2-5

Cowie, H., & Olafsson, R. (2000). The role of peer support in helping victims of bullying in a school with high levels of aggression. *School Psychology International*, *21*(1), 79–95. https://doi.org/10.1177/0143034300211006

Craig, W. M., Pepler, D., & Atlas, R. (2000). Observations of bullying in the playground and in the classroom. *School Psychology International*, *21*(1), 22–36. https://doi.org/10.1177/0143034300211002

Crick, N. R., Nelson, D. A., Morales, J. R., Cullerton-Sen, C., Casas, J. F., & Hickman, S. E. (2001). Relational victimization in childhood and adolescence: I hurt you through the grapevine. In J. Juvonen & S. Graham (Eds.), *Peer harassment in school: The plight of the vulnerable and victimized* (pp. 196–214). Guilford.

Crockenberg, S. B., Bryant, B. K., & Wilce, L. S. (1976). The effects of cooperatively and competitively structured learning environments on inter- and intrapersonal behavior. *Child Development*, *47*(2), 386–396. https://doi.org/10.2307/1128793

Crosby, J. W., Oehler, J., & Capaccioli, K. (2010). The relationship between peer victimization and post-traumatic stress symptomatology in a rural sample. *Psychology in the Schools*, *47*(3), 297–310. https://doi.org/10.1002/pits.20471

D'Urso, G., & Symonds, J. (2021). Risk factors for child and adolescent bullying and victimisation in Ireland: A systematic literature review. *Educational Review*, 1–26. https://doi.org/10.1080/00131911.2021.1987391

Deater-Deckard, K. (2001). Annotation: Recent research examining the role of peer relationships in the development of psychopathology. *Journal of Child Psychology and Psychiatry*, *42*(5), 565–579. https://doi.org/10.1017/S0021963001007272

Dempsey, A. G., & Storch, E. A. (2008). Relational victimization: The association between recalled adolescent social experiences and emotional adjustment in early adulthood. *Psychology in the Schools*, *45*(4), 310–322. https://doi.org/10.1002/pits.20298

Denborough, D. (2014). *Retelling the stories of our lives: Everyday narrative therapy to draw inspiration and transform experience*. Norton.

DeRosier, M. E., & Mercer, S. H. (2009). Perceived behavioral atypicality as a predictor of social rejection and peer victimization: Implications for emotional adjustment and academic achievement. *Psychology in the Schools*, *46*(4), 375–387. https://doi.org/10.1002/pits.20382

Deutsch, M. (1979). Education and distributive justice: Some reflections on grading systems. *American Psychologist*, *34*(5), 391–401.

Diehl, C., Rees, J., & Bohner, G. (2012). Flirting with disaster: Short-term mating orientation and hostile sexism predict different types of sexual harassment. *Aggressive Behavior*, *38*(6), 521–531. https://doi.org/10.1002/ab.21444

Diehl, C., Glaser, T., & Bohner, G. (2014). Face the consequences: Learning about victim's suffering reduces sexual harassment myth acceptance and men's likelihood to sexually harass. *Aggressive Behavior, 40*(6), 489–503. https://doi.org/10.1002/ab.21553

Dorol-Beauroy-Eustache, O. & Mishara, B. L. (2021). Systematic review of risk and protective factors for suicidal and self-harm behaviors among children and adolescents involved in cyberbullying. *Preventive Medicine, 152*, 106684. https://doi.org/10.1016/j.ypmed.2021.106684

Drouet, D. (1993). Adolescent female bullying and sexual harassment. In D. Tattum (Ed.), *Understanding and managing bullying* (pp. 173–188). Heinemann Educational.

Duffy, A. L., & Nesdale, D. (2009). Peer groups, social identity, and children's bullying behavior. *Social Development, 18*(1), 121–139. https://doi.org/10.1111/j.1467-9507.2008.00484.x

Egan, S. K., & Perry, D. G. (1998). Does low self-regard invite victimization? *Developmental Psychology, 34*(2), 299–309.

Erath, S. A., Flanagan, K. S., & Bierman, K. L. (2008). Early adolescent social adjustment: Associations with friendship and peer victimization. *Social Development, 17*(4), 853–870. https://doi.org/10.1111/j.1467-9507.2008.00458.x

Espelage, D. L., Aragon, S. R., Birkett, M., & Koenig, B. W. (2008). Homophobic teasing, psychological outcomes, and sexual orientation among high school students: What influence do parents and schools have? *School Psychology Review, 37*(2), 202–216. https://doi.org/10.1080/02796015.2008.12087894

Espelage, D. L., & Swearer, S. M. (2003). Research on school bullying and victimization: What have we learned and where do we go from here? *School Psychology Review, 32*(3), 365–383. https://doi.org/10.1080/02796015.2003.12086206

Fekkes, M., Pijpers, F. I. M., Fredriks, A. M., Vogels, T., & Verloove-Vanhorick, S. P. (2006). Do bullied children get ill, or do ill children get bullied? A prospective cohort study on the relationship between bullying and health-related symptoms. *Pediatrics, 117*(5), 1568–1574. https://doi.org/10.1542/peds.2005-0187

Ferraz de Camargo, L., Rice, K., & Thorsteinsson, E. (2022). A systematic review and empirical investigation: bullying victimisation and anxiety subtypes among adolescents. *Australian Journal of Psychology, 74*(1), 2145236. https://doi.org/10.1080/00049530.2022.2145236

Field, E., & Carroll, P. (2006). Effective ways to work with parents. In H. McGrath & T. Noble (Eds.), *Bullying solutions: Evidence-based approaches to bullying in Australian schools*. (pp. 209–225). Pearson Longman.

Fineran, S. (2001). Peer sexual harassment in high school. *Journal of School Social Work, 11*(2), 50–69.

Flaspohler, P. D., Elfstrom, J. L., Vanderzee, K. L., Sink, H. E., & Birchmeier, Z. (2009). Stand by me: The effects of peer and teacher support in mitigating the impact of bullying on quality of life. *Psychology in the Schools, 46*(7), 636–649. https://doi.org/10.1002/pits.20404

Fuller, A. (2006). A resilience-based approach to helping victims of bullying and their families. In H. McGrath & T. Noble (Eds.), *Bullying solutions: Evidence-based approaches to bullying in Australian schools* (pp. 161–173). Pearson Longman.

Gallup, A. C., O'Brien, D. T., & Wilson, D. S. (2011). Intrasexual peer aggression and dating behavior during adolescence: An evolutionary perspective. *Aggressive Behavior, 37*(3), 258–267. https://doi.org/10.1002/ab.20384

Garofalo, R., Wolf, C., Wissow, L. S., Woods, E. R., & Goodman, E. (1999). Sexual orientation and risk of suicide attempts among a representative sample of youth. *Archives of Pediatrics and Adolescent Medicine, 153*(5), 487–493. https://doi.org/10.1001/archpedi.153.5.487

Gini, G., Albiero, P., Benelli, B., & Altoè, G. (2007). Does empathy predict adolescents' bullying and defending behavior? *Aggressive Behavior, 33*(5), 467–476. https://doi.org/10.1002/ab.20204

Golberg, M. E., Olweus, D., & Endresen, I. M. (2007). Bullies and victims at school: Are they the same pupils? *British Journal of Educational Psychology, 77*(2), 441–464. https://doi.org/10.1348/000709906X105689

Goodenow, C., Szalacha, L., & Westheimer, K. (2006). School support groups, other school factors and the safety of sexual minority adolescents. *Psychology in the Schools, 43*(5), 573–589. https://doi.org/10.1002/pits.20173

Graham, S., Bellmore, A. D., & Mize, J. (2006). Peer victimization, aggression, and their co-occurrence in middle school: Pathways to adjustment problems. *Journal of Abnormal Child Psychology, 34*(3), 363–378. https://doi.org/10.1007/s10802-006-9030-2

Gumpel, T. P., Zioni-Koren, V., & Bekerman, Z. (2014). An ethnographic study of participant roles in school bullying. *Aggressive Behavior, 40*(3), 214–228. https://doi.org/10.1002/ab.21515

Guo, S. (2022). Childhood and/or adolescence bullying victimization and trajectories of hard drug use from late adolescence to young adulthood. *Victims and Offenders*, *17*(7), 1074–1087. https://doi.org/10.1080/15564886.2021.1982801

Hanish, L. D., & Guerra, N. G. (2000). Predictors of peer victimization among urban youth. *Social Development*, *9*(4), 521–543. https://doi.org/10.1111/1467-9507.00141

Hanish, L. D., Ryan, P., Martin, C. L., & Fabes, R. A. (2005). The social context of young children's peer victimization. *Social Development*, *14*(1), 2–19. https://doi.org/10.1111/j.1467-9507.2005.00288.x

Harter, S., Waters, P., & Whitesell, N. R. (1997). Lack of voice as a manifestation of false self behavior among adolescents: The school setting as a stage upon which the drama of authenticity is enacted. *Educational Psychologist*, *32*(3), 153–173. https://doi.org/10.1207/s15326985ep3203_2

Hatchel, T., Ingram, K. M., Huang, Y., & Espelage, D. L. (2020). Homophobic bullying victimization trajectories: The roles of perpetration, sex assigned at birth, and sexuality. *Aggressive Behavior*, *46*(5), 370–379. https://doi.org/10.1002/ab.21897

Hawkins, D. L., Pepler, D. J., & Craig, W. M. (2001). Naturalistic observations of peer interventions in bullying. *Social Development*, *10*(4), 512–527. https://doi.org/10.1111/1467-9507.00178

Henning-Stout, M., James, S., & Macintosh, S. (2000). Reducing harassment of lesbian, gay, bisexual, transgender, and questioning youth in schools. *School Psychology Review*, *29*(2), 180–191. https://doi.org/10.1080/02796015.2000.12086006

Hodges, E. V. E., Malone, M. J., & Perry, D. G. (1997). Individual risk and social risk as interacting determinants of victimization in the peer group. *Developmental Psychology*, *33*(6), 1032–1039.

Hodges, E. V. E., Boivin, M., Vitaro, F., & Bukowski, W. M. (1999). The power of friendship: Protection against an escalating cycle of peer victimization. *Developmental Psychology*, *35*(1), 94–101.

Hodges, E. V. E., & Perry, D. G. (1999). Personal and interpersonal antecedents and consequences of victimization by peers. *Journal of Personality and Social Psychology*, *76*(4), 677–685.

Hoffman, M. L. (1981). Is altruism part of human nature? *Journal of Personality and Social Psychology*, *40*(1), 121–137.

Huitsing, G. & Veenstra, R. (2012). Bullying in classrooms: Participant roles from a social network perspective. *Aggressive Behavior*, *38*(6), 494–509. https://doi.org/10.1002/ab.21438

Hunter, S. C., & Boyle, J. M. E. (2004). Appraisal and coping strategy use in victims of school bullying. *British Journal of Educational Psychology*, *74*(1), 83–107. https://doi.org/10.1348/000709904322848833

Hunter, S. C., Boyle, J. M. E., & Warden, D. (2007). Perceptions and correlates of peer-victimization and bullying. *British Journal of Educational Psychology*, *77*(4), 797–810. https://doi.org/10.1348/000709906X171046

Idsoe, T., Vaillancourt, T., Dyregrov, A., Hagen, K. A., Ogden, T., & Nærde, A. (2021). Bullying victimization and trauma. *Frontiers in Psychiatry*, *11*, 480353. https://doi.org/10.3389/fpsyt.2020.480353

Jacquet, J. (2015). *Is shame necessary? New uses for an old tool*. Pantheon Books.

James, V., & Owens, L. D. (2004). Peer victimization and conflict resolution among adolescent girls in a single-sex South Australian school. *International Education Journal*, *5*(1), 37–49.

James, V. H., & Owens, L. D. (2005). 'They turned around like I wasn't there': An analysis of teenage girls' letters about their peer conflicts. *School Psychology International*, *26*(1), 71–88. https://doi.org/10.1177/0143034305050895

Jolliffe, D., & Farrington, D. P. (2011). Is low empathy related to bullying after controlling for individual and social background variables? *Journal of Adolescence*, *34*(1), 59–71. https://doi.org/10.1016/j.adolescence.2010.02.001

Jordan, K. M., Vaughan, J. S., & Woodworth, K. J. (1997). I will survive: Lesbian, gay, and bisexual youths' experience of high school. *Journal of Gay and Lesbian Social Services*, *7*(4), 17–33. https://doi.org/10.1300/J041v07n04_02

Juvonen, J., Nishina, A., & Graham, S. (2000). Peer harassment, psychological adjustment, and school functioning in early adolescence. *Journal of Educational Psychology*, *92*(2), 349–359. https://doi.org/10/1037//0022-0663.92.2.349

Kawabata, Y., Tseng, W.-L., & Crick, N. R. (2014). Adaptive, maladaptive, meditational, and bidirectional processes of relational and physical aggression, relational and physical victimization, and peer liking. *Aggressive Behavior*, *40*(3), 273–287. https://doi.org/10.1002/ab.21517

Kim, J., Walsh, E., Pike, K., & Thompson, E. A. (2020). Cyberbullying and victimization and youth suicide risk: The buffering effects of school connectedness. *The Journal of School Nursing*, *36*(4), 251–257. https://doi.org/10.1177/1059840518824395

Kochenderfer, B. J., & Ladd, G. W. (1996). Peer victimization: Cause or consequence of school maladjustment? *Child Development*, *67*(4), 1305–1317. https://doi.org/10.1111/j.1467-8624.1996.tb01797.x

Kochenderfer-Ladd, B. (2004). Peer victimization: The role of emotions in adaptive and maladaptive coping. *Social Development*, *13*(3), 329–349. https://doi.org/10.1111/j.1467-9507.2004.00271.x

Kochenderfer-Ladd, B., & Ladd, G. W. (2001). Variations in peer victimization: Relations to children's maladjustment. In J. Juvonen & S. Graham (Eds.), *Peer harassment in school: The plight of the vulnerable and victimized* (pp. 25–48). Guilford.

Kochenderfer-Ladd, B., & Pelletier, M. E. (2008). Teachers' views and beliefs about bullying: Influences on classroom management strategies and students' coping with peer victimization. *Journal of School Psychology*, *46*(4), 431–453. https://doi.org/10.1016/j.jsp.2007.07.005

Kochenderfer-Ladd, B., & Wardrop, J. L. (2001). Chronicity and instability of children's peer victimization experiences as predictors of loneliness and social satisfaction trajectories. *Child Development*, *72*(1), 134–151. https://doi.org/10.1111/1467-8624.00270

Kohm, A. (2015). Childhood bullying and social dilemmas. *Aggressive Behavior*, *41*(2), 97–108. https://doi.org/10.1002/ab.21579

Kosciw, J. G., Clark, C. M., Truong, N. L., & Zongrone, A. D. (2020). *The 2019 National school climate survey: The experiences of lesbian, gay, bisexual, transgender, and queer youth in our nation's schools*. GLSEN. www.glsen.org/research

Koyanagi, A., Oh, H., Carvalho, A. F., Smith, L., Haro, J. M., Vancampfort, D., & DeVylder, J. E. (2019). Bullying victimization and suicide attempt among adolescents aged 12–15 years from 48 countries. *Journal of the American Academy of Child and Adolescent Psychiatry*, *58*(9), 907–918. https://doi.org/10.1016/j.jaac.2018.10.018

LaFontana, K. M., & Cillessen, A. H. N. (2002). Children's perceptions of popular and unpopular peers: A multimethod assessment. *Developmental Psychology*, *38*(5), 635–647. https://doi.org/10.1037//0012-1649.38.5.635

Lamarche, V., Brendgen, M., Moivin, M., Vitaro, F. Pérusse, D. & Dionne, G. (2006). Do friendships and sibling relationships provide protection against peer victimization in a similar way? *Social Development*, *15*(3), 373–393. https://doi.org/10.1111/j.1467-9507.2006.00347.x

Lapierre, K. R., & Dane, A. V. (2020). Cyberbullying, cyber aggression, and cyber victimization in relation to adolescents' dating and sexual behavior: An evolutionary perspective. *Aggressive Behavior*, *46*(1), 49–59. https://doi.org/10.1002/ab.21864

Leadbeater, B. J., Boone, E. M., Sangster, N. A., & Mathieson, L. C. (2006). Sex differences in the personal costs and benefits of relational and physical aggression in high school. *Aggressive Behavior*, *32*(4), 409–419. https://doi.org/10.1002/ab.20139

Leenaars, L. S., Dane, A. V., & Marini, Z. A. (2008). Evolutionary perspective on indirect victimization in adolescence: The role of attractiveness, dating and sexual behavior. *Aggressive Behavior*, *34*(4), 404–415. https://doi.org/10.1002/ab.20252

Long, J. D., & Pellegrini, A. D. (2003). Studying change in dominance and bullying with linear mixed models. *School Psychology Review*, *32*(3), 401–417. https://doi.org/10.1080/02796015.2003.12086208

Long, Y., & Li, Y. (2020). The longitudinal association between social status insecurity and relational aggression: Moderation effects of social cognition about relational aggression. *Aggressive Behavior*, *46*(1), 84–96. https://doi.org/10.1002/ab.21872

Lonsway, K. A., Cortina, L. M., & Magley, V. J. (2008). Sexual harassment mythology: Definition, conceptualization, and measurement. *Sex Roles*, *58*(9–10), 599–615. https://doi.org/10.1007/s11199-007-9367-1

Low, S., Frey, K. S., & Brockman, C. J. (2010). Gossip on the playground: Changes associated with universal intervention, retaliation beliefs, and supportive friends. *School Psychology Review*, *39*(4), 536–551. https://doi.org/10.1080/02796015.2010.12087740

Macgillivray, I. K. (2000). Educational equity for gay, lesbian, bisexual, transgendered, and queer/questioning students: The demands of democracy and social justice for America's schools. *Education and Urban Society*, *32*(3), 303–323. https://doi.org/10.1177/0013124500323003

Mahady Wilton, M. M., Craig, W. M., & Pepler, D. J. (2000). Emotional regulation and display in classroom victims of bullying: Characteristic expressions of affect, coping styles and relevant contextual factors. *Social Development*, *9*(2), 226–245. https://doi.org/10.1111/1467-9507.00121

Malinsky, K. P. (1997). Learning to be invisible: Female sexual minority students in America's public high schools. *Journal of Gay and Lesbian Social Services*, *7*(4), 35–50. https://doi.org/10.1300/J041v07n04_03

Marsh, H. W., Parada, R. H., Craven, R. G., & Finger, L. (2004). In the looking glass: A reciprocal effects model elucidating the complex nature of bullying, psychological determinants, and the central role of self-concept. In C. E. Sanders & G. D. Phye (Eds.), *Bullying: Implications for the classroom* (pp. 63–109). Elsevier.

Marsten, D., Epston, D., & Markham, L. (2016). *Narrative therapy in wonderland: Connecting with children's imaginative know-how*. Norton.

Martin, K. M., & Huebner, E. S. (2007). Peer victimization and prosocial experiences and emotional well-being of middle school students. *Psychology in the Schools*, *44*(2), 199–208. https://doi.org/10.1002/pits.20216

Mason, K. L. (2008). Cyberbullying: A preliminary assessment for school personnel. *Psychology in the Schools*, *45*(4), 323–348. https://doi.org/10.1002/pits.20301

Mateu, A., Pascual-Sánchez, A., Martinez-Herves, M., Hickey, N., Nicholls, D., & Kramer, T. (2020). Cyberbullying and post-traumatic stress symptoms in UK adolescents. *Archives of Disease in Childhood*, *105*(10), 951–956. http://dx.doi.org/10.1136/archdischild-2019-318716

McGrath, H., & Stanley, M. (2006). A comparison of two non-punitive approaches to bullying. In H. McGrath & T. Noble (Eds.), *Bullying solutions: Evidence-based approaches to bullying in Australian schools* (pp. 189–208). Pearson Longman.

Meyer, C. C. (2019). *Bullying victimisation and traumatic stress severity among High school learners*. Masters dissertation submitted to Faculty of Health Sciences at Nelson Mandela University.

Mikami, A. Y., Griggs, M. S., Reuland, M. M., & Gregory, A. (2012). Teacher practices as predictors of children's classroom social preference. *Journal of School Psychology*, *50*(1), 95–111. https://doi.org/10.1016/j.jsp.2011.08.002

Modecki, K. L., Minchin, J., Harbaugh, A. G., Guerra, N. G., & Runions, K. C. (2014). Bullying prevalence across contexts: A meta-analysis measuring cyber and traditional bullying. *Journal of Adolescent Health*, *55*(5), 602–611. https://doi.org/10.1016/j.jadohealth.2014.06.007

Murdock, T. B., & Bolch, M. B. (2005). Risk and protective factors for poor school adjustment in lesbian, gay, and bisexual (LGB) high school youth: Variable and person-centered analyses. *Psychology in the Schools*, *42*(2), 159–172. https://doi.org/10.1002/pits.20054

Murray-Close, D., Crick, N. R., & Galotti, K. M. (2006). Children's moral reasoning regarding physical and relational aggression. *Social Development*, *15*(3), 345–372. https://doi.org/10.1111/j.1467-9507.2006.00346.x

Murray-Close, D., Ostrov, J. M., & Crick, N. R. (2007). A short-term longitudinal study of growth of relational aggression during middle childhood: Associations with gender, friendship intimacy, and internalizing problems. *Development and Psychopathology*, *19*(1), 187–203. https://doi.org/10.1017/S0954579407070101

Mynard, H., Joseph, S., & Alexander, J. (2000). Peer-victimisation and posttraumatic stress in adolescents. *Personality and Individual Differences*, *29*(5), 815–821. https://doi.org/10.1016/S0191-8869(99)00234-2

Nansel, T. R., Overpeck, M., Pilla, R. S., Ruan, W. J., Simons-Morton, B., & Scheidt, P. (2001). Bullying behaviors among US youth: Prevalence and association with psychosocial adjustment. *JAMA*, *285*(16), 2094–2100. https://doi.org/10.1001/jama.285.16.2094

Newman, R. S., & Murray, B. J. (2005). How students and teachers view the seriousness of peer harassment: When is it appropriate to seek help? *Journal of Educational Psychology*, *97*(3), 347–365. https://doi.org/10.1037/0022-0663.97.3.347

Nicholson, A. (2006). Legal perspectives on bullying. In H. McGrath & T. Noble (Eds.), *Bullying solutions: Evidence-based approaches to bullying in Australian schools* (pp. 17–45). Pearson Longman.

Nipedal, C., Nesdale, D. & Killen, M. (2010). Social group norms, school norms, and children's aggressive intentions. *Aggressive Behavior*, *36*(3), 195–204. https://doi.org/10.1002/ab.20342

Noble, T. (2006). Core components of a school-wide safe schools curriculum. In H. McGrath & T. Noble (Eds.), *Bullying solutions: Evidence-based approaches to bullying in Australian schools* (pp. 67–83). Pearson Longman.

O'Brennan, L. M., Bradshaw, C. P., & Sawyer, A. L. (2009). Examining developmental differences in the social-emotional problems among frequent bullies, victims, and bully/victims. *Psychology in the Schools*, *46*(2), 100–115. https://doi.org/10.1002/pits.20357

O'Moore, M., & Minton, S. J. (2004). *Dealing with bullying in schools: A training manual for teachers, parents and other professionals*. Paul Chapman.

Olthof, T., Goossens, F. A., Vermande, M. M., Aleva, E. A., & van der Meulen, M. (2011). Bullying as strategic behavior: Relations with desired and acquired dominance in the peer group. *Journal of School Psychology*, *49*(3), 339–359. https://doi.org/10.1016/j.jsp.2011.03.003

Olweus, D. (1993). *Bullying at school: What we know and what we can do*. Blackwell.

Olweus, D. (2001). Peer harassment: A critical analysis and some important issues. In J. Juvonen & S. Graham (Eds.), *Peer harassment in school: The plight of the vulnerable and victimized* (pp. 3–20). Guilford.

Orpinas, P., Horne, A. M., & Staniszewski, D. (2003). School bullying: Changing the problem by changing the school. *School Psychology Review*, *32*(3), 431–444. https://doi.org/10.1080/02796015.2003.12086210

Ortega, R., Elipa, P., Mora-Merchán, J. A., Genta, M. L., Brighi, A., Guarini, A., Smith, P. K., Thompson, F., & Tippett, N. (2012). The emotional impact of bullying and cyberbullying on victims: A European cross-national study. *Aggressive Behavior*, *38*(5), 342–356. https://doi.org/10.1002/ab.21440

Ostrov, J. M., & Keating, C. F. (2004). Gender differences in preschool aggression during free play and structured interactions: An observational study. *Social Development*, *13*(2), 255–277. https://doi.org/10.1111/j.1467-9507.2004.000266.x

Ostrov, J. M., Crick, N. R., & Stauffacher, K. (2006). Relational aggression in sibling and peer relationships during early childhood. *Journal of Applied Developmental Psychology*, *27*(3), 241–253. https://doi.org/10.1016/j.appdev.2006.02.005

Owens, L. (1997). Teenage girls: Voices of aggression. In Proceedings of the International School Psychology 20th Annual Colloquium (pp. 219–222). Melbourne, July 1997.

Owens, L., Shute, R., & Slee, P. (2000a). 'Guess what I just heard!': Indirect aggression among teenage girls in Australia. *Aggressive Behavior*, *26*(1), 67–83. https://doi.org/10.1002/(SICI)1098-2337(2000)26:1%3C67::AID-AB6%3E3.0.CO;2-C

Owens, L., Shute, R., & Slee, P. (2000b). 'I'm in and you're out...': Explanations for teenage girls' indirect aggression. *Psychology, Evolution and Gender*, *2*(1), 19–46. https://doi.org/10.1080/14616660050082906

Owens, L., Slee, P., & Shute, R. (2001). Victimization among teenage girls: What can be done about indirect harassment? In J. Juvonen & S. Graham (Eds.), *Peer harassment in school: The plight of the vulnerable and victimized* (pp. 215–241). Guilford.

Owens, L., Shute, R., & Slee, P. (2005). 'In the eye of the beholder...': Girls', boys' and teachers' perceptions of boys' aggression to girls. *International Education Journal*, *5*(5), 142–151.

Pacheco, E., Melhuish, N., & Fiske, J. (2019). Digital self-harm: Prevalence, motivations and outcomes for teens who cyberbully themselves. *Digital self-harm: prevalence, motivations and outcomes for teens who cyberbully themselves*. Netsafe New Zealand. https://www.netsafe.org.nz/digital-self-harm-19/

Pan, Y., Yang, C., Liu, G., Chan, M., Liu, C., & Zhang, D. (2020). Peer victimization and problem behaviors: The roles of self-esteem and parental attachment among Chinese adolescents. *Child Development*, *91*(4), e968–e983. https://doi.org/10.1111/cdev.13319

Patchin, J. W., & Hinduja, S. (2017). Digital self-harm among adolescents. *Journal of Adolescent Health*, *61*(6), 761-766. https://doi.org/10.1016/j.jadohealth.2017.06.012

Patchin, J. W., Hinduja, S., & Meldrum, R. C. (2023). Digital self-harm and suicidality among adolescents. *Child and Adolescent Mental Health*, *28*(1), 52–59. https://doi.org/10.1111/camh.12574

Patrick, H., Kaplan, A., & Ryan, A. M. (2011). Positive classroom motivational environments: Convergence between mastery goal structure and classroom social climate. *Journal of Educational Psychology*, *103*(2), 367–382. https://doi.org/10.1037/a0023311

Pellegrini, A. D. (2004). Bullying during the middle school years. In C. E. Sanders & G. D. Phye (Eds.), *Bullying: Implications for the classroom* (pp. 177–202). Elsevier.

Pepler, D., Craig, W., Ziegler, S., & Charach, A. (1993). A school-based anti-bullying intervention: Preliminary evaluation. In D. Tattum (Ed.), *Understanding and managing bullying* (pp. 76–91). Heinemann Educational.

Pepler, D. J., Craig, W. M., & Roberts, W. L. (1998). Observations of aggressive and nonaggressive children on the school playground. *Merrill-Palmer Quarterly*, *44*(1), 55–76. https://www.jstor.org/stable/23093393

Perry, D. G., Williard, J. C., & Perry, L. C. (1990). Peers' perceptions of the consequences that victimized children provide aggressors. *Child Development*, *61*(5), 1310–1325. https://doi.org/10.1111/j.1467-8624.1990.tb02863.x

Perwitasari, D. R., & Wuryaningsih, E. W. (2022). Why did you do that to me? A systematic review of cyberbullying Impact on mental health and suicide among adolescents. *NurseLine Journal*, *7*(1), 35–47. https://doi.org/10.19184/nlj.v7i1.27311

Pikas, A. (2002). New developments of the shared concern method. *School Psychology International*, *23*(3), 307–326. https://doi.org/10.1177/0143034302023003234

Pomeroy, E. (1999). The teacher-student relationship in secondary school: Insights from excluded students. *British Journal of Sociology of Education*, *20*(4), 465–482. https://doi.org/10.1080/01425699995218

Pornari, C. D., & Wood, J. (2010). Peer and cyber aggression in secondary school students: The role of moral disengagement, hostile attribution bias, and outcome expectancies. *Aggressive Behavior*, *36*(2), 81–94. https://doi.org/10.1002/ab.20336

Porter, L. (2016). *Aggression and bullying in childhood and adolescence: Causes and solutions*. Small Poppies International.

Prinstein, M. J., & Cillessen, A. H. N. (2003). Forms and functions of adolescent peer aggression associated with high peer status. *Merrill-Palmer Quarterly*, *49*(3), 310–342. https://www.jstor.org/stable/23096058

Putallaz, M., Grimes, C. L., Foster, K. J., Kupersmidt, J. B., Coie, J. D., & Dearing, K. (2007). Overt and relational aggression and victimization: Multiple perspectives within the school setting. *Journal of School Psychology*, *45*(5), 523–547. https://doi.org/10.1016/j.jsp.2007.05.003

Qualter, P., Murphy, S. M., Abbott, J., Gardner, K. J., Japel, C., Vitaro, F., Boivin, M., & Tremblay, R. E. (2015). Developmental associations between victimization and body mass index from 3 to 10 years in a population sample. *Aggressive Behavior*, *41*(2), 109–122. https://doi.org/10.1002/ab.21580

Rapee, R. M., Shaw, T., Hunt, C., Bussey, K., Hudson, J. L., Mihalopoulos, C., & Cross, D. (2020). Combining whole-school and targeted programs for the reduction of bullying victimization: A randomized, effectiveness trial. *Aggressive Behavior*, *46*(3), 193–209. https://doi.org/10.1002/ab.21881

Raskauskas, J., & Stoltz, A. D. (2007). Involvement in traditional and electronic bullying among adolescents. *Developmental Psychology*, *43*(3), 564–575.

Reynolds, B. M., & Repetti, R. L. (2010). Teenage girls' perceptions of the functions of relationally aggressive behaviors. *Psychology in the Schools*, *47*(3), 282–296. https://doi.org/10.1002/pits.20470

Rigby, K. (1996). *Bullying in schools: And what to do about it*. A.C.E.R.

Rigby, K. (1998). Gender and bullying in schools. In P. T. Slee & K. Rigby (Eds.), *Children's peer relations* (pp. 47–59). Routledge.

Rigby, K. (1999). Peer victimisation at school and the health of secondary school students. *British Journal of Educational Psychology*, *69*(1), 95–104. https://doi.org/10.1348/000709999157590

Rigby, K. (2001). Health consequences of bullying and its prevention in schools. In J. Juvonen & S. Graham (Eds.), *Peer harassment in school: The plight of the vulnerable and victimized* (pp. 310–331). Guilford.

Rigby, K. (2006). What international research tells us about bullying. In H. McGrath & T. Noble (Eds.), *Bullying solutions: Evidence-based approaches to bullying in Australian schools* (pp. 3–15). Pearson Longman.

Rigby, K., & Bagshaw, D. (2006). Using educational drama and bystander training to counteract bullying. In H. McGrath & T. Noble (Eds.), *Bullying solutions: Evidence-based approaches to bullying in Australian schools* (pp. 133–145). Pearson Longman.

Rigby, K., & Johnson, B. (2006). Expressed readiness of Australian schoolchildren to act as bystanders in support of children who are being bullied. *Educational Psychology*, *26*(3), 425–440. https://doi.org/10.1080/01443410500342047

Rivers, S. (2001). The bullying of sexual minorities at school: Its nature and long-term correlates. *Educational and Child Psychology*, *18*(1), 32–46.

Rodkin, P. C., & Hodges, E. V. E. (2003). Bullies and victims in the peer ecology: Four questions for psychologists and school professionals. *School Psychology Review*, *32*(3), 384–400. https://doi.org/10.1080/02796015.2003.12086207

Rosen, L. H., Underwood, M. K., Beron, K. J., Gentsch, J. K., Wharton, M. E., & Rahdar, A. (2009). Persistent versus periodic experiences of social victimization: Predictors of adjustment. *Journal of Abnormal Child Psychology*, *37*(5), 693–704. https://doi.org/10.1007/s10802-009-9311-7

Rosen, P. J., Milich, R., & Harris, M. J. (2012). Dysregulated negative emotional reactivity as a predictor of chronic peer victimization in childhood. *Aggressive Behavior*, *38*(5), 414–427. https://doi.org/10.1002/ab.21434

Ryan, A. M., & Patrick, H. (2001). The classroom social environment and changes in adolescents' motivation and engagement during middle school. *American Educational Research Journal*, *38*(2), 437–460. https://doi.org/10.3102/00028312038002437

Sainio, M., Veenstra, R., Huitsing, G., & Salmivalli, C. (2012). Same- and other-sex victimization: Are the risk factors similar? *Aggressive Behavior*, *38*(6), 442–455. https://doi.org/10.1002/ab.21445

Salmivalli, C., & Helteenvuori, T. (2007). Reactive, but not proactive aggression predicts victimization among boys. *Aggressive Behavior*, *33*(3), 198–206. https://doi.org/10.1002/ab.20210

Salmivalli, C., Kaukiainen, A., & Lagerspetz, K. (1998). Aggression in the social relations of school-aged girls and boys. In P. T. Slee & K. Rigby (Eds.), *Children's peer relations* (pp. 60–75). Routledge.

Salmivalli, C., Ojanen, T., Haanpää, J., & Peets, H. (2005). 'I'm OK but you're not' and other peer-relational schemas: Explaining individual differences in children's social goals. *Developmental Psychology*, *41*(2), 363-375. https://doi.org/10/1037/0012-1649.41.2.363

Sapouna, M., Wolke, D., Vannini, N., Watson, S., Woods, S., Schneider, W., Enz, S., & Aylett, R. (2012). Individual and social network predictors of the short-term stability of bullying victimization in the United Kingdom and Germany. *British Journal of Educational Psychology*, *82*(2), 225–240. https://doi.org/10.1111/j.2044-8279.2011.02022.x

Savin-Williams, R. C. (1994). Verbal and physical abuse as stressors in the lives of lesbian, gay male, and bisexual youths: Associations with school problems, running away, substance abuse, prostitution, and suicide. *Journal of Consulting and Clinical Psychology*, *62*(2), 261–269.

Scholte, R. H. J., Engles, R. C. M. E., Overbeek, G., de Kemp, R. A. T., & Haselager, G. J. T. (2007). Stability in bullying and victimization and its association with social adjustment in childhood and adolescence. *Journal of Abnormal Child Psychology*, *35*(2), 217–228. https://doi.org/10.1007/s10802-006-9074-3

Schwartz, D. (2000). Subtypes of victims and aggressors in children's peer groups. *Journal of Abnormal Child Psychology*, *28*(2), 181–192. https://doi.org/10.1023/A:1005174831561

Schwartz, D., Gorman, A. H., Nakamoto, J., & Toblin, R. L. (2005). Victimization in the peer group and children's academic functioning. *Journal of Educational Psychology*, *97*(3), 425–435. https://doi.org/10.1037/0022-0663.97.3.425

Sentse, M., Dijkstra, J. K., Salmivalli, C., & Cillessen, A. H. N. (2013). The dynamics of friendships and victimization in adolescence: A longitudinal social network perspective. *Aggressive Behavior*, *39*(3), 229–238. https://doi.org/10.1002/ab.21469

Shute, R., Owens, L., & Slee, P. (2002). 'You just stare at them and give them daggers': Nonverbal expressions of social aggression in teenage girls. *International Journal of Adolescence and Youth*, *10*(4), 353–372. https://doi.org/10.1080/02673843.2002.9747911

Skripkauskaite, S., Hawk, S. T., Branje, S. J. T., Koot, H. M., van Lier, P. A. C., & Meeus, W. (2015). Reactive and proactive aggression: Differential links with emotion regulation difficulties, maternal criticism in adolescence. *Aggressive Behavior*, *41*(3), 214–226. https://doi.org/10.1002/ab.21583

Slee, P. T. (1994). Life at school used to be good: Victimisation and health concerns of secondary school students. *Youth Studies Australia*, *13*(4), 20–23.

Slee, P. T. (1995a). Peer victimisation and its relationship to depression among Australian primary school students. *Journal of Personality and Individual Differences*, *18*(1), 57–62. https://doi.org/10.1016/0191-8869(94)00114-8

Slee, P. T. (1995b). Bullying: Health concerns of Australian secondary school students. *International Journal of Adolescence and Youth*, *5*(4), 215–224. https://doi.org/10.1080/02673843.1995.9747767

Slee, P. T.(2006). The P.E.A.C.E. Pack: A whole-school program for reducing school bullying. In H. McGrath & T. Noble (Eds.), *Bullying solutions: Evidence-based approaches to bullying in Australian schools* (pp. 85–99). Pearson Longman.

Slee, P. T. (2020). School prevention: How to develop an anti-bullying program. In B. A. Gerrard, M. J. Carter & D. Ribera (Eds.), *School-based family counseling: An interdisciplinary practitioner's guide* (pp. 283–311). Routledge.

Smith, P. K., & Ananiadou, K. (2003). The nature of school bullying and the effectiveness of school-based interventions. *Journal of Applied Psychoanalytic Studies*, *5*(2), 189–209. https://doi.org/10.1023/A:1022991804210

Smith, P. K., & Sharp, S. (1994). The problem of school bullying. In P. K. Smith & S. Sharp (Eds.), *School bullying: Insights and perspectives* (pp. 1-19). Routledge.

Smith, P. K., Talamelli, L., Cowie, H., Naylor, P., & Chauhan, P. (2004). Profiles of non-victims, escaped victims, continuing victims and new victims of school bullying. *British Journal of Educational Psychology*, *74*(4), 565–581. https://doi.org/10.1348/0007099042376427

Smith, S. W., & Daunic, A. P. (2002). Using conflict resolution and peer mediation to support positive behavior. In B. Algozzine & P. Kay (Eds.), *Preventing problem behaviors: A handbook of successful prevention strategies* (pp. 142–161). Corwin Press.

Stauffacher, K., & DeHart, G. B. (2006). Crossing social contexts: Relational aggression between siblings and friends during early and middle childhood. *Journal of Applied Developmental Psychology*, *27*(3), 228–240. https://doi.org/10.1016/j.appdev.2006.02.004

Stauffer, S., Heath, M. A., Coyne, S. M., & Ferrin, S. (2012). High school teachers' perceptions of cyberbullying prevention and intervention strategies. *Psychology in the Schools*, *49*(4), 353–367. https://doi.org/10.1002/pits.21603

Stein, N. (1995). Sexual harassment in school: The public performance of gendered violence. *Harvard Educational Review*, *65*(2), 145–162. https://doi.org/10.17763/haer.65.2.7080h5t354300557

Stevens, V., De Bourdeauhuij, I., & Van Oost, P. (2000). Bullying in Flemish schools: An evaluation of anti-bullying intervention in primary and secondary schools. *British Journal of Educational Psychology*, *70*(2), 195–210. https://doi.org/10.1348/000709900158056

Sullivan, T. N., Farrell, A. D., & Kliewer, W. (2006). Peer victimization in early adolescence: Association between physical and relational victimization and drug use, aggression, and delinquent behaviors among middle school students. *Development and Psychopathology*, *18*(1), 119–137. https://doi.org/10.1017/S095457940606007X

Sweeting, H., Young, R., West, P., & Der, G. (2007). Peer victimization and depression in early-mid adolescence: A longitudinal study. *British Journal of Educational Psychology*, *76*(3), 577–594. https://doi.org/10.1348/000709905X49890

Tapper, K., & Boulton, M. J. (2005). Victim and peer group responses to different forms of aggression among primary school children. *Aggressive Behavior*, *31*(3), 238–253. https://doi.org/10.1002/ab.20080

Tattum, D. (1993a). What is bullying? In D. Tattum (Ed.) *Understanding and managing bullying* (pp. 3–14). Heinemann Educational.

Tattum, D. (1993b). Short, medium and long-term management strategies. In D. Tattum (Ed.), *Understanding and managing bullying* (pp. 59–75). Heinemann Educational.

Theodore, P. S., & Chiasson, J. (2021). Evolving strategies to counter school bullying of gender and sexually diverse students. In M. C. Lytle & R. A. Sprout (Eds.), *Supporting gender identity and sexual orientation diversity in K-12 schools* (pp. 71–96). American Psychological Association. https://doi.org/10.1037/0000211-005

Thompson, M., Cohen, L. J., & Grace, C. O. N. (2002). *Mom, they're teasing me: Helping your child solve social problems*. Ballantine.

Thornberg, R. (2010). School children's social representations on bullying causes. *Psychology in the Schools*, *47*(4), 311–327. https://doi.org/10.1002/pits.20472

Tippett, N., & Wolke, D. (2015). Aggression between siblings: Associations with the home environment and peer bullying. *Aggressive Behavior*, *41*(1), 14–24. https://doi.org/10.1002/ab.21557

Unnever, J. D. (2005). Bullies, aggressive victims, and victims: Are they distinct groups? *Aggressive Behavior*, *31*(2), 153–171. https://doi.org/10.1002/ab.20083

Vaillancourt, T., & Sharma, A. (2011). Intolerance of sexy peers: Intrasexual competition among women. *Aggressive Behavior*, *37*(6), 569–577. https://doi.org/10.1002/ab.20413

Vaillancourt, T., & Hymel, S. (2006). Aggression and social status: The moderating roles of sex and peer-valued characteristics. *Aggressive Behavior*, *32*(4), 396–408. https://doi.org/10.1002/ab.20138

Vaillancourt, T., Miller, J. L., Fagbemi, J. Côté, S., & Tremblay, R. E. (2007). Trajectories and predictors of indirect aggression: Results from a nationally representative longitudinal study of Canadian children aged 2-10. *Aggressive Behavior*, *33*(4), 314–326. https://doi.org/10.1002/ab.20202

Vaillancourt, T., Hymel, S., & McDougall, P. (2013). The biological underpinnings of peer victimization: Understanding why and how the effects of bullying can last a lifetime. *Theory into Practice*, *52*(4), 241–248. https://doi.org/10.1080/00405841.2013.829726

Van Cleemput, K., Vandebosch, H., & Pabian, S. (2014). Personal characteristics and contextual factors that determine 'helping', 'joining in', and 'doing nothing' when witnessing cyberbullying. *Aggressive Behavior*, *40*(5), 383–396. https://doi.org/10.1002/ab.21534

Vassallo, S., Edwards, B., Renda, J., & Olsson, C. A. (2014). Bullying in early adolescence and antisocial behavior and depression six years later: What are the protective factors? *Journal of School Violence*, *13*(1), 100–124. https://doi.org/10.1080/15388220.2013.840643

Waasdorp, T. E., & Bradshaw, C. P. (2011). Examining student responses to frequent bullying: A latent class approach. *Journal of Educational Psychology*, *103*(2), 336–352. https://doi.org/10.1037/a0022747

Walters, G. D., Kremser, J., & Runell, L. (2020). Moderating the bullying perpetration-delinquency relationship with parental support and knowledge: A prospective analysis of middle school students. *Aggressive Behavior*, *46*(3), 244–253. https://doi.org/10.1002/ab.21885

Wang, J., Iannotti, R. J., & Luk, J. W. (2012). Patterns of adolescent bullying behaviors: Physical, verbal, exclusion, rumor, and cyber. *Journal of School Psychology*, *50*(4), 521–534. https://doi.org/10.1016/j.jsp.2012.03.004

Werner, N. E., & Grant, S. (2009). Mothers' cognitions about relational aggression: Associations with discipline responses, children's normative beliefs, and peer competence. *Social Development*, *18*(1), 77–98. https://doi.org/10.1111/j.1467-9507.2008.00482.x

White, M. (2004). Working with people who are suffering the consequences of multiple trauma: A narrative perspective. *International Journal of Narrative Therapy and Community Work*, *1*, 44–75.

White, M. (2016). *Narrative therapy classics*. Dulwich Centre Publications.

Wright, M. F., & Li, Y. (2013). Normative beliefs about aggression and cyber aggression among young adults: A longitudinal investigation. *Aggressive Behavior*, *39*(3), 161–170. https://doi.org/10.1002/ab.21470

Wu, X., Qi, J., & Zhen, R. (2021). Bullying victimization and adolescents' social anxiety: Roles of shame and self-esteem. *Child Indicators Research*, *14*(2), 769–781. https://doi.org/10.1007/s12187-020-09777-x

Xie, H., Swift, D. J., Cairns, B. D., & Cairns, R. B. (2002). Aggressive behaviors in social interaction and developmental adaptation: A narrative analysis of interpersonal conflicts during early adolescence. *Social Development*, *11*(2), 205–224. https://doi.org/10.1111/1467-9507.00195

Young, E. L., Boye, A. E., & Nelson, D. A. (2006). Relational aggression: Understanding, identifying, and responding in schools. *Psychology in the Schools*, *43*(3), 297–312. https://doi.org/10.1002/pits.20148

Young, S. (2001). Solution focused anti-bullying. In Y. Ajmal & I. Rees (Eds.), *Solutions in schools* (pp. 86–96). BT Press.

Zimmer-Gembeck, M. J., & Pronk, R. E. (2012). Relation of depression and anxiety to self- and peer-reported relational aggression. *Aggressive Behavior*, *38*(1), 16–30. https://doi.org/10.1002/ab.20416

Ziv, Y., Leibovich, I., & Shechtman, Z. (2013). Bullying and victimization in early adolescence: Relations to social information processing patterns. *Aggressive Behavior*, *39*(6), 482–492. https://doi.org/10.1002/ab.21494

19 Dating violence

Intimate partner violence within an adolescent sexual relationship is referred to as dating violence. This term might seem to minimise the violence, however, which would be a mistake, because it is more common in adolescent than in adult relationships (Ellsberg et al., 2018).

Forms of intimate partner violence

There is a more marked imbalance of power and consequently more severe violence within adult compared to adolescent relationships (Espelage et al., 2018). Aside from this difference, both share the same range of controlling behaviours (Cuccì et al., 2019; Orpinas et al., 2012):

- Coercive control, such as dictating what a partner can and cannot do, limiting a partner's use of the phone, restricting contact with family and friends, menacing, stalking, deliberately provoking jealousy and threatening to end the relationship.
- Verbal and emotional abuse, including put-downs, insults and ridicule in public.
- Physical assaults, such as shoving, hitting, hair pulling, slapping and damaging a partner's personal items.
- Sexual assault, including unwanted touch, refusing to use a condom, coerced sex and rape.
- Cyber violence: the use of technology for aggression. This takes the forms of abuse, threats or humiliation through the dissemination of private material, making constant phone calls or sending text messages, getting angry if a partner does not respond, accessing partners' social media accounts, and controlling current or former partners by electronically stalking and monitoring their location, activities and relationships (Cava et al., 2020; Lozano-Martínez et al., 2022).

Violence against partners is often seen to be an escalation of conflict, as if it is a quantitative change in conflict resolution skills, when instead it is qualitative (Jenkins, 1990).

Prevalence

In the United States, just over 20 per cent of adolescent females and 10 per cent of males are perpetrators or victims of physical or sexual assault within their romantic relationships,

DOI: 10.4324/9781003323938-22

with 40 per cent experiencing emotional or verbal abuse (Cascardi & Jouriles, 2018; Ellis & Dumas, 2018; Orpinas et al., 2012). Both males and females are perpetrators, with the aggression often mutual (Cascardi & Jouriles, 2018; Cuccì et al., 2020; Orpinas et al., 2012), although it could have different effects for males and females (Ellsberg et al., 2018). As would be expected, victimisation within a romantic relationship reduces adolescents' sense of well-being and satisfaction with life, increases their stress and anxiety, and can contribute to poor academic achievement, low self-esteem, substance abuse and disordered eating (Cuccì et al., 2019).

Histories of perpetrators and targets of dating violence

Explanations of causes of violence are located within the perpetrator, their interactions with others, their childhood history, or their culture (Jenkins, 1990).

Personal explanations. A hostile and distrustful attitude to women, the desire to dominate women and low attachment to multiple sex partners lead to violence against them (Bosson et al., 2015; Swartout et al., 2015). Perpetrators lack self-regulation (have 'anger issues') and often blame others for provoking them; they also fail to consider the outcomes of their actions (Derefinko et al., 2011; Jenkins, 1990).

Having been hit themselves, many young men think of violence as normative (Reyes et al., 2015, 2016). Nevertheless, perpetrators do not necessarily see violence as justifiable or acceptable in advance but, having been violent, justify their actions afterwards (Cascardi & Jouriles, 2018). Some people (victims and perpetrators alike) excuse violence on grounds such as that the perpetrator was drunk at the time and, therefore, out of control. However, perpetrators manage to damage only items that are precious to the victim, while breaking none of their own stuff; they hurt only the victim, rather than anyone else in the room; and they hit the victim where it won't show. These are not the actions of someone who is out of control. But, rather than pointing this out, you can simply ask, 'I wonder: Do you hurt her because you are drunk? ... Or do you get drunk so that you can hurt her?'.

Interactions with others. Many perpetrators of dating violence have been physical bullies or employ aggression in their peer relationships, with the result that they lack experience with high-quality friendships and, in turn, the skills to form high-quality dating relationships (Ellis & Dumas, 2018; Orpinas et al., 2012). Meanwhile, support from peers for hostile attitudes to females sanctions aggression against them (Bosson et al., 2015; Reed et al., 2008), while having peers with antisocial behaviours - such as drug use, unsafe sex, fighting and vandalism - and those who use dating violence is a more powerful predictor of perpetration than is childhood adversity (Ellis & Dumas, 2018; Van Ouytsel et al., 2017).

Childhood history. Witnessing violence between their parents or, more significantly, being assaulted themselves, teaches young people that aggression is normal within relationships (Calvete et al., 2018; Reyes et al., 2015). Particularly when subjected to emotional abuse or harsh parenting, young people's exposure to violence fails to teach them that they are safe, that they deserve to be nurtured, how to be empathic, how to respect women, and how to regulate their impulses and their emotions in general and anger in particular; meanwhile, they learn to be disconnected, expect rejection and develop a hostile attribution bias (Calvete et al., 2018; Cascardi & Jouriles, 2018; Cuccì et al., 2019; Ellis & Dumas, 2018; Johansson et al., 2020).

Yet Jenkins (1990) argues that many individuals with adverse early experiences are *not* violent towards their partners, in which case adversity does not explain it. And as for female victims, adversity-related symptoms of depression and anxiety lead to a poor choice of romantic partner and thereby increase the likelihood that females will be subjected to intimate partner violence (Cascardi & Jouriles, 2018).

Culture. Sexist attitudes to females entrench toxic masculinity, in which men simultaneously feel entitled to get their needs met at the expense of others and conversely make others responsible for their resulting antisocial behaviour (Jenkins, 1990). However, rather than being deviant in some way, male perpetrators are simply conforming *too much* to sexist attitudes that men are superior to women and children, and therefore are 'entitled' to disregard their welfare (Jenkins, 1990).

For female perpetrators, no personal factors predict their use of dating violence, which suggests that personal qualities are less powerful than family, peer and relationship factors (King et al., 2015). Myths about romantic love play a part, such as (Cava et al., 2020, p. 3):

- Love can surmount all difficulties.
- Love is suffering.
- Jealousy is a sign of love.
- One needs romantic love to be happy.
- We have a single soul mate who is our one true love.

And, like people of all ages, some young people confuse belonging *with*, with belonging *to*. Some of these myths cause victims to excuse violence on the grounds that it is inspired by jealousy and therefore is a sign of love (Lozano-Martínez et al., 2022; Reed et al., 2008).

'Causes' or 'restraints to responsibility'?

Perpetrators can draw on their adverse histories as excuses that allow them to see themselves as passive victims of circumstance (Jenkins, 1990). Jenkins argues instead that these explanations are *restraints*: They restrain perpetrators from actively taking responsibility for regulating their own feelings or actions, for their relationships, and (in the case of those who are parents) for their parenting. The gender stereotypes are a recipe for men's social and emotional incompetence and the expectation that their partner should protect them from themselves by avoiding conflict or not being sexually alluring. The upshot of these beliefs is that perpetrators of violence have all the status in the relationship, but none of the responsibility (Jenkins, 1990).

Dating violence prevention

Schools are places where young people learn social (including sexual) norms (Ellsberg et al., 2018). Lundgren and Amin (2015) report that school-based and community-based education programs making violence unacceptable and exposing myths about dating violence and rape are more effective than placing the responsibility on young people to protect themselves. To shift the perceptions of both males and females, these programs need to focus on adolescent relationships and on broader themes of gender inequality (Ellsberg et al., 2018).

However, changes in attitudes do not necessarily translate into changed behaviour, few programs have focused on young people aged under 15, and few have tested program efficacy with vulnerable groups such as migrants or sexual minorities (Lundgren & Amin, 2015). Furthermore, the most successful programs are long term and multifaceted, which will be beyond the reach of most child and youth counsellors.

Nevertheless if choosing to implement such a program, counsellors or school personnel could be guided by the *Me and You: Building healthy relationships* program (Peskin et al., 2018). This comprises thirteen lessons on (among other topics) personal rules for safe relationships, the link between thoughts and emotions, communication skills, cyber control and how to identify and leave unhealthy dating relationships. As is the case with anti-bullying programs, many such programs prove effective by changing the attitudes of bystanders (Ellsberg et al., 2018).

Interventions

The goal with intimate partner (or dating) violence is to prevent further harm coming to the victim. Working with a couple when there is the threat of ongoing violence presents a danger to the victim and therefore the perpetrator must have individual counselling first (Corey et al., 2019).

Narrative therapy for dating violence

Jenkins (1990) believes that most abusive men are so guilty or remorseful that they think about their abuse only briefly in its aftermath and move on quickly to finding excuses and justifications. Yet he also believes that perpetrators want caring relationships but have been failing to take responsibility for acting in ways that promote these. Therefore, he invites the man to address his violence, to 'help me understand' why he has come to counselling.

White (2016) begins by discussing with perpetrators their responsibility for the violence, and survivors' experience of it and its short- and long-term traumatic effects on them. His goal is for perpetrators to 'take responsibility to mend what might be mended' (White, 2016, p. 19).

Externalisation

Counsellors will not externalise 'violence' as this would allow men to elude responsibility for their actions, but Jenkins (1990) does externalise the feelings that precede it, such as hurt, insecurity, fear or frustration (depending on what perpetrators disclose). More important, he externalises patterns of avoiding responsibility through questions such as:

- Who has tended to worry most about your violence in the past?
- What has (your partner) needed to do in order to live with your violence?
- Who has worked hardest to try to prevent your outbursts?

Deconstruction

White (2016, pp. 19–20) then goes on to deconstruct the conditions that contribute to men's abusive behaviour. He questions taken-for-granted realities and practices and how they came to produce a toxic masculinity that threatens the safety of men's loved ones. These conversations render these assumptions strange, or 'exoticise the domestic' (White, 2016, p. 28). White lists the following deconstruction questions.

- If a man wanted to dominate another person, particularly a woman or a child, what sort of attitudes would be necessary in order to justify this?
- What sort of strategies or techniques of power could make this feasible?
- How has your violence prevented you in the past from achieving the kind of relationship you want?
- Can you handle a relationship in which (your partner) says what she really thinks, or do you need her to say what she thinks you want to hear? (Jenkins, 1990).

Landscape of action questions about the problem

In the men's answers, the ways that they dominate others become clear to them, upon which the counsellor will ask landscape of action questions that detail how they have acted (Jenkins, 1990; Madigan, 2019; White, 2016):

- Which of these attitudes and methods have you given life to?
- Are there certain ways that you live because of this thinking?
- In what specific ways have these ideas about being a man shaped your life?
- How did you get recruited to these attitudes and techniques?

Landscape of identity questions

In the clients' answers, counsellors will ask what these actions have taught clients about who they are (Jenkins, 1990; Madigan, 2019; White, 2016):

- What effect has violence had on how you feel about yourself?
- How do these ways of living have you relating to yourself?
- How do they have you relating to others?

Landscape of action questions about exceptions

Counsellors will ask about exceptions by asking clients to think about just one occasion in their lives when they found themselves standing outside their beliefs about what it is to be a man, or used some strategies to accept responsibility and to keep others safe. Then counsellors will ask some landscape of action questions about how clients managed to do this, and then landscape of identity questions about what this tells them about who they are and what is important to them. Some landscape of action questions about an alternative to violence could be (Jenkins, 1990; Madigan, 2019; White, 2016):

- Your ideas about being a man would work well for you if you wanted a slave - but you're telling me that you want a partner. Have you noticed any times when you have stood up to the old-fashioned ideas and have been able to handle (your partner) having her own ideas and opinions?

- If you were to decide to take a further step along a different way of being a man, what do you imagine this would require you to do now and in the future?
- If I asked (a best friend, a parent, a grandparent), what would they say would make it easier or harder for you to take that next step?

Landscape of identity questions about the counter-narrative

- Are you becoming more, or less, sucked in by these ideas about what it is to be a man?
- What does it say about you that you had the courage to walk in the door today?
- What does it say about you that you have the strength to face up to your violence?
- What does it tell you about who you can be that you are willing to give her space while she decides if she can trust you again?
- How did you do that: You didn't text her even once? How did you stand up to your insecure feelings?

Preference questions

Preference questions are interspersed among the landscape of action and identity questions and aim to enquire whether clients see the outcomes of these exceptions as desirable, or of no consequence (White, 2016). The intent is to invite clients to argue for non-violent relationships (Jenkins, 1990). Specific preference questions could be (Jenkins, 1990; Madigan, 2019; White, 2016):

- What effect has violence had on your relationship?
- Is that the kind of relationship you want?
- Do you want your relationship to include violence, or do you want your partner to feel safe with you?
- Are you sure? How important is this to you?
- Is it important for you to earn genuine trust and respect, or would you settle for a pretence?
- Do you want to continue to subject your life to these ideas about how men must be?
- To what extent do you want to continue to live your life as an instrument of power and terror?
- To what extent do you want to cooperate with these tactics that so devastate the lives of others?
- Do these ways of living bring you closer to yourself and others, or further away?
- Is (your partner) feeling more safe or less safe over time in this relationship? Is she gaining more respect for you over time, or less over time? Is she more loving over time, or less? What will happen if this trend continues?
- Are there downsides to living this way for others? For yourself?
- In light of your understanding of the real effects of these strategies on others, do you want to continue with these strategies as a framework for your life?

Facilitate planning new action

The difference between a goal and dream is that a goal has a plan. Therefore, rather than wishing for relationship repair, perpetrators need a plan for contributing to their partner's sense of safety. This might entail accepting that the relationship has ended, or leaving their partner alone until she makes contact. Many men will want to race ahead by making contact with their partner, apologising and asking for forgiveness - all before they have proven to themselves that they can quit being dominated by old blueprints of manhood. In that case, counsellors can ask:

- Are you ready to take action to prove to yourself that you can handle her having her own ideas? That you can stand up to your feelings?
- What evidence is there that you are ready?

With respect to learning how to withdraw from conflict to avoid an escalation, Jenkins (1990) asks:

- What warning signs would you pick up in yourself?
- How could you prove to yourself and to your family that they are safe from violence, no matter what they say or do?
- How could you prove to yourself and them that you can handle disappointment or frustration without resorting to violence?
- In which situations are you more likely to think that you are right and they are wrong? How will you prepare yourself for those times?
- How would you know if (a family member) were feeling scared of you?

Counselling adolescent victims of dating violence

Denborough (2014) talks female victims of intimate partner violence through 'getting their life back from the hostile voices' that came to define their identity. He calls this process a *migration of identity*. He notes that, at the time of separation, women hold high hopes for a future life free of terror and despair, but that the realities of being alone can seduce them back into an abusive relationship. However, like any migration, he says, there is always a 'betwixt and between' phase of disorientation and confusion. Therefore, he has clients map their journey, graphing how they feel before, during and in the months after the separation, so that they can see that the 'trough' of disorientation gradually abates, and that the overall trend is upwards. Another analogy he uses is that passing through various stages of separation is like passing through the various seasons (Denborough, 2014). These analogies allow survivors not to be overtaken by despondency during the disorientation phase.

Denborough (2014) also predicts that there will be times when the hostile voices of their abuser which clients have absorbed into their own identity use tricks to have them believe the negative stories of who they are. He helps clients to predict these backlashes and plan what they will do to prevent being sucked in by the voice of abuse.

Restorative justice

It is important to call out individuals who have harmed others. However, asking them to accept responsibility must be within the context of seeing them at their best, whereas blame is about seeing them at their worst (Marsten et al., 2016). Restitution needs to be offered willingly on a platform of self-worth that allows them to admit responsibility and remorse for their *behaviour*, but not from having been shamed as a person (Brown, 2007). Shaming young people for their actions as a tool of discipline silences them, teaches them that they are unworthy, and threatens them with rejection, thereby disconnecting them emotionally, spiritually and intellectually from others (Brown, 2007). In contrast, guilt or remorse (given freely) can motivate restitution. As Brené Brown (2007, p. 14) states, 'Recognizing we've *made a mistake* is far different from believing we *are a mistake*'.

With this distinction in mind, the issue in restorative justice is not to restore the authority of the rules, but to focus on the harm done to individuals and to the community, such as a school (Winslade & Monk, 2007). That is, accountability is to the victim, not to the authorities.

In restorative justice conferences, the facilitator invites those in attendance to name (externalise) the problem, then victims or their advocates map its effects on them (Winslade & Monk, 2007). Next, exceptions to the problem are listed and, finally, the perpetrator is asked which story (the problem-based one or the exception-based one) they would like to go forward with from the meeting. Then a plan is formulated, based on several principles: what can be mended, must be mended; the victim needs to be asked what would achieve this; invitations to take responsibility have to be issued broadly within the perpetrator's network of relationships; and the existence of a positive story about the offender is not taken as an excuse or used to minimise the offence (Winslade & Monk, 2007).

Conclusion

Violence towards others occurs against a background of toxicity. While supporting victims, we need to recognise the adversity experienced by perpetrators so that they can mourn and heal and, ultimately, conduct themselves in ways that promote supportive relationships, both for their own sake and for their partners.

References

Bosson, J. K., Parrott, D. J., Swan, S. C., Kuchynka, S. L., & Schramm, A. T. (2015). A dangerous boomerang: Injunctive norms, hostile sexist attitudes, and male-to-female sexual aggression. *Aggressive Behavior*, *41*(6), 580–593. https://doi.org/10.1002/ab.21597

Brown, B. (2007). *I thought it was just me (but it isn't)*. Gotham.

Calvete, E., Fernández-González, L., Orue, I., & Little, T. D. (2018). Exposure to family violence and dating violence perpetration in adolescents: Potential cognitive and emotional mechanisms. *Psychology of Violence*, *8*(1), 67–75. https://doi.org/10.1037/vio0000076

Cascardi, M., & Jouriles, E. N. (2018). Mechanisms underlying the association of exposure to family of origin violence and adolescent dating violence. In D. Wolfe & J. R. Temple (Eds.), *Adolescent dating violence: Theory, research, and prevention* (pp. 159–188). Academic Press. https://doi.org/10.1016/B978-0-12-811797-2.00007-4

Cava, M. J., Buelga, S., Carrascosa, L., & Ortega-Barón, J. (2020). Relations among romantic myths, offline dating violence victimization and cyber dating violence victimization in adolescents. *International Journal of Environmental Research and Public Health*, *17*(5), 1551. https://doi.org/10.3390/ijerph17051551

Corey, G., Corey, M. S., & Corey, C. (2019). *Issues and ethics in the helping professions* (10th ed.). Cengage.

Cuccì, G., O'Leary, K. D., Olivari, M. G., Bonanomi, A., & Confalonieri, E. (2019). Adolescent dating violence perpetration, emotion dysregulation, and parenting styles. *Journal of Family Psychology*, *33*(1), 12–22. https://doi.org/10.1037/fam0000464

Cuccì, G., Confalonieri, E., Olivari, M. G., & Borroni, E. (2020). Adolescent romantic relationships as a tug of war: The interplay of power imbalance and relationship duration in adolescent dating aggression. *Aggressive Behavior*, *46*(6), 498–507. https://doi.org/10.1002/ab.21919

Denborough, D. (2014). *Retelling the stories of our lives: Everyday narrative therapy to draw inspiration and transform experience*. Norton.

Ellis, W. E., & Dumas, T. M. (2018). Peers over parents? How peer relationships influence dating violence. In D. Wolfe & J. R. Temple (Eds.), *Adolescent dating violence: Theory, research, and prevention* (pp. 105–133). Academic Press. https://doi.org/10.1016/B978-0-12-811797-2.00005-0

Ellsberg, M., Ullman, C., Blackwell, A., Hill, A., & Contreras, M. (2018). What works to prevent adolescent intimate partner and sexual violence? A global review of best practices. In D. Wolfe & J. R. Temple (Eds.), *Adolescent dating violence: Theory, research, and prevention* (pp. 381–414). Academic Press. https://doi.org/10.1016/B978-0-12-811797-2.00016-5

Espelage, D., Anderman, E. M., Brown, V. E., Jones, A., Lane, K. L., McMahon. S. D., Reddy, L. A., & Reynolds, C. R. (2013). Understanding and preventing violence directed against teachers. *American Psychologist*, *68*(2), 75–87. https://doi.org/10.1037/a0031.307

Espelage, D. L., Hong, J. S., & Valido, A. (2018). Associations among family violence, bullying, sexual harassment, and teen dating violence. In D. Wolfe & J. R. Temple (Eds.), *Adolescent dating violence: Theory, research, and prevention* (pp. 85–102). Academic Press. https://doi.org/10.1016/B978-0-12-811797-2.00004-9

Jenkins, A. (1990). Invitations to responsibility: The therapeutic engagement of men who are violence and abusive. Dulwich Centre Publications.

Johansson, A, Rötkönen, N., & Jern, P. (2020). Is the association between childhood maltreatment and aggressive behavior mediated by hostile attribution bias in women? A discordant twin and sibling study. *Aggressive Behavior*, *47*(1), 28–37. https://doi.org/10.1002/ab.21928

King, D. M., Hatcher, S. S., & Bride, B. (2015). An exploration of risk factors associated with dating violence: Examining the predictability of adolescent female dating violence perpetration. *Journal of Human Behavior in the Social Environment*, *25*(8), 907–922. https://doi.org/10.1080/10911359.2015.1040907

Latzman, N. E., Vivolo-Kantor, A. M., Niolon, P. H., & Ghazarian, S. R. (2015). Predicting adolescent dating violence perpetration: Role of exposure to intimate partner violence and parenting practices. *American Journal of Preventive Medicine*, *49*(3), 476–482. https://doi.org/10.1016/j.amepre.2015.06.006

Lozano-Martínez, J., Castillo-Reche, I. S., Morales-Yago, F. J., & Ibáñez-López, F. J. (2022). Control violence begins in adolescent dating: A research from students' perception. *International Journal of Environmental Research and Public Health*, *19*(15), 8974. https://doi.org/10.3390/ijerph19158974

Lundgren, R., & Amin, A. (2015). Addressing intimate partner violence and sexual violence among adolescents: Emerging evidence of effectiveness. *Journal of Adolescent Health*, *56*(1), S42–S50. http://dx.doi.org/10.1016/j.jadohealth.2014.08.012

Madigan, S. (2019). *Narrative therapy* (2nd ed.). American Psychological Association.

Marsten, D., Epston, D., & Markham, L. (2016). *Narrative therapy in wonderland: Connecting with children's imaginative know-how*. Norton.

Orpinas, P., Nahapetyan, L., Song, X., McNicholas, C. & Reeves, P.M. (2012). Psychological dating violence perpetration and victimization: Trajectories from middle to high school. *Aggressive Behavior*, *38* (6), 510–520. https://doi.org/10.1002/ab.21441

Peskin, M. F., Markham, C. M., Gabay, E. K., Shegog, R., Cuccaro, P. M., Temple, J. R., & Emery, S. T. (2018). Using intervention mapping to develop 'Me and you: Building healthy relationships', a healthy relationship intervention for early middle school students. In D. Wolfe & J. R. Temple (Eds.), *Adolescent dating violence: Theory, research, and prevention* (pp. 467–501). Academic Press. https://doi.org/10.1016/B978-0-12-811797-2.00019-0

Reed, E., Silverman, J. G., Raj, A., Rothman, E. F., Decker, M. R., Gottlieb, B. R., & Miller, E. (2008). Social and environmental contexts of adolescent and young adult male perpetrators of intimate partner violence: A qualitative study. *American Journal of Men's Health*, *2*(3), 260–271. https://doi.org/10.1177/1557988308318863

Reyes, H. L. M., Foshee, V. A., Fortson, B. L., Valle, L. A., Breiding, M. J., & Merrick, M. T. (2015). Longitudinal mediators of relations between family violence and adolescent dating aggression perpetration. *Journal of Marriage and Family*, *77*(4), 1016–1030. https://doi.org/10.1111/jomf.12200

Reyes, H. L. M., Foshee, V. A., Niolon, P. H., Reidy, D. E., & Hall, J. E. (2016). Gender role attitudes and male adolescent dating violence perpetration: Normative beliefs as moderators. *Journal of Youth and Adolescence*, *45*, 350-360. https://doi.org/10.1007/s10964-015-0278-0

Swartout, K. M., Swartout, A. G., Brennan, C. L., & White, J. W. (2015). Trajectories of male sexual aggression from adolescence through college: A latent growth curve analysis. *Aggressive Behavior*, *41*(5), 467-477. https://doi.org/10.1002/ab.21584

Van Ouytsel, J., Ponnet, K., & Walrave, M. (2017). The associations of adolescents' dating violence victimization, well-being and engagement in risk behaviors. *Journal of Adolescence*, *55*, 66-71. https://doi.org/10.1016/j.adolescence.2016.12.005

White, M. (2016). *Narrative therapy classics*. Dulwich Centre Publications.

Winslade, J., & Monk, G. (2007). *Narrative counseling in schools: Powerful and brief* (2nd ed.). Corwin Press.

20 Sexual assault by juveniles

Between one-fifth and one-third of child sexual abuse (including rape) is committed by young people (Hackett et al., 2013), with 12 to 15 per cent of perpetrators being aged under 10 years (Vizard et al., 2007). Of instances of child sexual abuse, juveniles are the perpetrators in 38 per cent of cases where victims are aged under six, in 42 per cent of cases where they are six to 11 years old, and in 31 per cent of cases where the victim is aged 12 to 17 years (Mesman et al., 2019).

Our view of childhood as a time of innocence can cause us to overlook sexual offending by young people. Yet these statistics are testament to the relevance of the saying, *I wouldn't have seen it if I hadn't believed it*.

Sexualised play

Children's sexual behaviours range on a continuum from normal (experimental), to inappropriate, problematic, abusive and violent (McAlinden, 2018). Taking the benign end of the continuum first, young children will naturally be curious and will explore their own and the opposite sex's bodies (Kostelnik et al., 2015). When sexual play is between consenting children who are similar to each other in age and status, it can be perfectly natural (Johnson, 2002).

However, play can start out as being merely experimental but then degenerate into being controlling and exploitive (McAlinden, 2018) and can physically injure or be abusive of a play partner (Mesman et al., 2019). In turn, that play partner could repeat coercive sexual play with another child (Cantwell, 1988). Signs of an unhealthy interest in sexual play are given in Box 20.1.

The nature of child sexual abuse by juveniles

The most common sexual assaults are touching others' genitals; over half of perpetrators or attempt to penetrate their victim. Fifteen per cent of young perpetrators act with an accomplice (McAlinden, 2018) and in one-fifth of cases the sexual assault is accompanied by physical violence (Hackett et al., 2013).

A profile of perpetrators

Most perpetrators (92 to 98 per cent) are male (Hackett et al., 2013), with the majority committing their first sexual offence before 15 years of age. Adolescent sexual offending

DOI: 10.4324/9781003323938-23

Box 20.1 Signs of unhealthy sexual play in early childhood

- differences in age, status or power of the play partners
- the deliberate use of grooming strategies
- lack of mutuality
- furtiveness about the sexual play, in contrast with openness or lack of self-consciousness
- participants are anxious, tense, guilty or shameful about their sexual play or, alternatively, lack emotion about it
- sexualised play that is part of an overall pattern of behavioural difficulties, especially social difficulties and poor impulse control
- disproportional, preoccupied or compulsive interest in sexual play compared with other play interests
- eroticism in sexual play (in contrast with curiosity) - as eroticism signals an advanced understanding or knowledge about sexual behaviour
- purposeful self-stimulation rather than a mere attempt at self-soothing
- inability to re-direct the children to other forms of play - that is, they do not stop when directed to do so
- approaches to unfamiliar children rather than friends as sexual play partners
- coercion of partners
- pressure on the partner to maintain secrecy
- complaints from other peers about the nature of a child's play
- penetration of any bodily orifice
- oral-genital contact
- recruitment of third parties to participate with a dyad
- children's heightened knowledge of sexual matters compared with peers from a similar economic, social and cultural background.

Sources: Davies et al. (2000); Essa & Murray (1999); Hornor (2004); McAlinden (2018); Mesman et al. (2019)

occurs within a broader pattern of serious antisocial or delinquent behaviour and academic disengagement (Lavoie et al., 2002; Ronis & Borduin, 2007). Many (42 per cent) have criminal histories prior to their sexual offence, and one-third have learning difficulties (Hackett et al., 2013).

Half of juvenile offenders have been sexually abused themselves; half have not (Hackett et al., 2013). Many have been physically abused or neglected, or witnessed domestic violence - or all of these (Vizard et al., 2007). Early-onset offenders typically experience significantly more adversity and at younger ages (Vizard et al., 2007).

Seventeen per cent of all child abuse cases involve the abuse of a younger sibling by an older brother (McAlinden, 2018). In fact, sibling incest is five times more common than adult-child incest (McAlinden, 2018; Vizard, 2013). Perpetrators of sibling incest fit two patterns:

The first is simple experimentation and curiosity within a family that supervises the children inadequately and fails to be open about sexuality and teach the children about boundaries (McAlinden, 2018). Second, it can occur against a background of sexual abuse of the perpetrator (McAlinden, 2018).

The few offenders who are female are almost all victims of sexual abuse themselves, molest fewer victims, use less physical violence, and mostly abuse non-related boys aged under 10 years (Masson et al., 2015; Vizard et al., 2007).

Child sex offenders differ from adult offenders in that they have a lower recidivism rate, better response to treatment, and have less knowledge about sexual boundaries and concepts of consent (Craig, 2020). The use of violence during the abuse and the abuse of both male and female victims are risk factors for recidivism (Hackett et al., 2013). While few child perpetrators of sexual abuse grow up to be adult sexual offenders, they are more likely than non-abusers to offend in other ways (Vizard, 2013). This risk is reduced when young perpetrators are socially anchored to their family and community (Bateman & Milner, 2015).

A profile of victims

Victims are usually known to the abuser, being related in 25 per cent of cases. Many are rendered vulnerable by having unmet emotional and social needs, but others are vulnerable precisely because they have no such risks and therefore are invisible.

Box 20.2 The frequency of victimisation by juveniles

- In one study, 76.8 per cent of perpetrators had three victims; 15 per cent had four to nine victims; and a few had so many victims that it was impossible to calculate precisely (Masson et al., 2015).
- Vizard et al. (2007) found that their 280 young sexual offenders had abused 684 identified victims.
- In Shaw et al.'s study (2000), 36 per cent of victims were abused once; 25 per cent were abused two to five times; 6 per cent were abused six to ten times; and 31 per cent were abused more than ten times.

Grooming practices

Sexually abusive actions by young offenders are typically about power and control, not about sexual gratification (McAlinden, 2018). Their grooming practices - aimed at access, compliance and secrecy - differ a little from adults', in that the children (especially siblings) already engage in social and leisure activities together and are already trusted companions, whereas adults often have to inveigle their way into children's lives (McAlinden, 2018). As a result, grooming by young perpetrators can be very quick (McAlinden, 2018).

Both adult and young perpetrators use latent coercion or manipulation; befriend the child (perhaps by buying gifts for children or drugs and alcohol for adolescents); isolate them from adult supervision; and use verbal threats and physical violence to secure compliance and secrecy. Young offenders are careful to pick as victims children who won't tell and many use online grooming to minimise the risk of being caught (McAlinden, 2018).

Effects of sexual abuse by juveniles

The effects of child-on-child sexual abuse are virtually identical to those of abuse by an adult, except that victims of juvenile perpetrators seem to have more sexual problems as a consequence (Shaw et al., 2000).

Disclosure

Young victims might believe their abuser that the sexual behaviour is normal, might fear losing the friendship, or not expect adult support and therefore do not report the abuse (McAlinden, 2018). This can make it more difficult to extricate themselves than when the abuser is an adult (McAlinden, 2018). And it can make it difficult for them to name what has happened to them as being abusive and, therefore, to engage in therapy (McAlinden, 2018). If children disclose at all, they tend to tell another peer of their own age who, however, is likely to be too young to know how to recruit help (McAlinden, 2018).

In the case of incest, the sibling relationship makes disclosure less likely but, when discovered, a common reaction of the parents is to keep silent about it, or for the family to implode, bringing further negative outcomes for victims (McAlinden, 2018).

Adolescent rape

By late adolescence, 3 per cent of males engage in increasing frequency and high severity of sexual aggression (including rape), which persists throughout their lifetime (Swartout et al., 2015). Many perpetrators of rape have histories of physical abuse, domestic violence, and have been exposed to sexually explicit material that objectifies sexual partners and normalises violence (Craig, 2020; McAlinden, 2018; Mesman et al., 2019).

Compared to their heterosexual peers, sexual minority youth are over 3.5 times more likely to be raped, over 2.5 times more likely to have experienced sexual dating violence and over twice as likely to have experienced physical dating violence (Smithee et al., 2019).

Rape is about power - not sex - and is an attempt to demean the victim. It is about the feelings of entitlement that men can act as they wish, without regard for victims' feelings or needs. Our societies have a long history of validating men's beliefs that they do not have to be held to account for the harm they do. After all, there is no eleventh commandment, '*Thou shalt not rape*'.

There is a problematic belief that women's clothing or actions - such as agreeing to ride home with their date - reveal their consent, despite the woman's protests (Ward, 2000). Myths that it is not rape unless it is violent, that women say 'No' when they mean 'Yes' and that men cannot be expected to control their sexual urges cause perpetrators and victims alike to minimise the significance of non-consensual sex (McAlinden, 2018).

As for pack rape, this is typically part of perpetrators' overall antisocial lifestyle of drug use and criminality. Also of concern is a pattern where perpetrators work in groups to groom female adolescents to engage in sexually exploitive situations such as group sex, prostitution or pornography, all the while believing that they are in a relationship with their pimps (McAlinden, 2018). They do not see themselves as being victimised, having given what is termed 'survival consent' in exchange for money or drugs, or 'coerced consent' where they have been manipulated into taking part by a gang or party culture that requires them to exchange sex to gain or maintain group membership (McAlinden, 2018).

Effects of sexual assault and rape

As the primary event, sexual assault leads to secondary losses: loss of health; loss of intimacy in romantic relationships; changes in relationships with friends and family; avoiding social situations; and disruption to employment. Other losses are tertiary: a loss of sense of self, of safety, of self-esteem, of honour, of physical integrity. Rape can reaffirm assumptions by women and those in marginalised communities (such as gay men) that they are devalued (Boyd, 2011). As such, it is not only physical violence but also mental violence (Boyd, 2011). Recovery is possible but is compromised when others minimise or dismiss victims' claims of rape or fail to offer support.

Child protection training

School-based counsellors might wish to deliver programs aimed at preventing child sexual abuse. However, these have three weaknesses. The first is that they lack evidence that they empower children to resist abuse (Bevill & Gast, 1998). Most were built on the concepts of an adult stranger-perpetrator and unassertive child victim, when instead most perpetrators are known to children, and some are other youth. This gives rise to the saying that teaching children to keep themselves safe by looking out for strangers is like teaching them to cross the road while looking out for bicycles.

The second weakness is that training is more efficient, but less effective, when delivered in groups as opposed to individually (Johnson et al., 2005). Third, the programs can make young children overly suspicious - even terrified - of adults (Bonner et al., 1992; Johnson et al., 2005; Jordan, 1993). Perhaps even more damning than these shortcomings is that, by the time children are having to fend off an attack, assertiveness skills will be too little too late. Instead, the first aspect of child protection is to immunise children against being in abusive situations in the first place by allowing them to be assertive in everyday ways at home and at school - that is, by ensuring that they have a voice.

The Daniel Morcombe Foundation teaches children the three Rs of safety: *Recognise, react* and *report*. That is, *recognise* when you feel unsafe or something does not feel right, *react* by running away, and *report* your concerns to the adults in your safety network. Based on the core principle that *It's my body; I get to choose*, the first aspect of teaching young children to keep safe is to *recognise* their feelings and to notice when their feelings are telling them that something is wrong. The guiding rule here is: *If you don't feel safe, you aren't safe*. You might ask young children where in their bodies they experience unsafe feelings, for example, when they are at the top of a high playground slide. You can then highlight the difference between these excited-scared emotions and bad-scared feelings. Children need to be able to take safe risks, have fun and enjoy the challenge of being 'good-scared' but to take steps to protect themselves when they are feeling 'bad-scared'.

The second safety behaviour is to *react*. To encourage this, I let children know that police, ambulance and fire trucks are allowed to speed and go through red lights - that is, break the rules - in an emergency. In just the same way, if they are ever in danger, they do not have to be polite to someone who is scaring them: They can scream loudly and run away.

Third, you will need to ensure that children know how to *report* and seek adult help by approaching school staff, phoning their parents or calling emergency services. They will need a backup plan for occasions when the first person whom they would approach is not available. Formal protectiveness training programs get children to draw around their hand and on each finger place a photo or write the names of people they could approach for help. You then explain that they have to persist and talk to every person on their list until they find someone who is available to assist them.

To encourage disclosure of abuse, we need to teach young children the difference between good secrets and bad secrets. Good secrets always have an end date - such as keeping a secret about what you are giving Mum for her birthday. In contrast, bad secrets are ones where someone threatens you so that you won't tell. They tell lies to convince children that speaking up will get them into trouble when, the truth is, they are the ones who are doing the wrong thing.

School administrators can also advise parents about internet safety for their children and recommend to parents that their children have a code word that any honest adult will know. If someone comes to collect the child from school, for example, but does not know the code word, it means that they do not have their parents' permission to take the child. Another strategy is for parents to teach their children that if they get lost within a shop, they must wait by the checkout. If they get lost in a shopping centre or mall, they need to go to a pharmacy. The reasoning here is that pharmacists will largely be ethical, their shops are always well populated, and there is a pharmacy in every shopping centre. Whenever they are in a new shopping centre, parents will need to show their child where the pharmacy is.

Given that 19 per cent of child sexual abuse occurs at school (Bromberg & Johnson, 2001), schools can also have their own code word, such as advising students that if they come to the front office and ask for, say, 'Angela', this is code for needing help. (The school will have to choose a different name if someone called Angela is actually on staff!) Office staff will know to discreetly take the young person somewhere safe from where they can call the school counsellor, their parents or other authorities as needed.

Interventions

Counselling for juvenile sexual offenders will need multiple facets, with a principal focus being the effect of their actions on their victims. It will be vital that perpetrators take responsibility without excusing their actions or minimising the effects.

Under a narrative therapy approach, landscape of action questions could be:

- What has been the effect of your sexual behaviour on (the victim)? On the victim's family? On witnesses? On your family?

- What effect or influence does your sexual behaviour have on your life, on the people who are important to you, on your relationships?
- What influence do you have on your sexual behaviour?
- What would (the victim) say needs to happen for them to feel safe?
- What is the first thing you will notice that will tell you that they are feeling safer?
- What difference will that difference make to your relationships with your (siblings, mother, father)?

Landscape of identity questions could be (Bateman & Milner, 2015):

- Do you like being labelled as a 'sex offender'?
- Does this label describe all of you, or are there other aspects of your identity that the label overlooks?
- What does your sexually harmful behaviour have you thinking about yourself?
- What does it say about you that you are ashamed of having done this?
- What would it say about you if you were not ashamed?

Counsellors will need to ask clients about times when they could have abused a child, but did not – and what stopped them from doing so. Such a question could be framed as, 'Can you tell me about times when you've demonstrated safe/respectful sexual behaviour?' (Bateman & Milner, 2015). Preference questions will ask them: 'Would you prefer your life with your troubling sexual behaviour, or would you like to be free of it?' The identity question then would be: 'What does this say about what is important to you as a person?' (Bateman & Milner, 2015).

Scaling questions can be useful:

> 'If on the scale of 1 to 10, with 1 being you can't be bothered doing anything about (the harmful sexual behaviour) and 10 being you are willing to do whatever it takes, where are you on the scale? ... What would need to happen for your rating to move further up the scale? ... On a scale from 1 to 10, how confident are you that you can adhere to the agreed safety plan?'.
>
> (Bateman & Milner, 2015, p. 77)

If the young person denies the offence, you do not need to get caught up in who to believe, but can ask questions such as, 'What needs to happen for you not to be open to this sort of allegation in the future? ... What needs to happen so this (victim) can feel safe?' (Bateman & Milner, 2015).

It will seem unfair if perpetrators have to take responsibility for their own sexually harmful acts, when someone who molested them has not (Bateman & Milner, 2015). Therefore, at the same time as working with them to ensure others' safety, young offenders will need support to heal from their own traumatic history and to deal with associated difficulties such as depression, anxiety and drug use. Any learning difficulties will need remediation, not least because educational success will enable employment, which protects young people from association with antisocial peers and therefore a recurrence of abuse (Ha et al., 2016).

Meanwhile, two practical steps that they can take to contribute to the safety of their victims is to meet with representatives of those they have harmed in what White (2016) terms 'escape from secrecy meetings'. At this meeting, they would admit their responsibility for the abuse, and develop a contingency plan should the targets again feel unsafe. Second, they can write a detailed letter of apology to their victims – see Box 20.3.

Box 20.3 Elements of a letter of apology for child sexual abuse

- Reason for writing: This is a statement of concern for the victim's feelings about the abuse. *I am writing to you because I feel (...) about how I treated you.*
- Apology for specific actions and their effects: *I am sorry for (touching your private parts) and for threatening to (...) if you told anyone.*
- Statement of responsibility: *I am fully responsible for this. It is not your fault. I knew it was a trick and you did not know this. I knew how to stop it, but you didn't. I should have been a better (friend/brother) to you. Children don't have to be pushed around by someone bigger than them. I think that you were very brave to tell. This is the best thing to do when someone is hurting you. Now you are getting some help, and so am I.*
- Statement of understanding of the impact of the abuse itself, of secrecy, of being made responsible for others. *You must have felt confused when I (told you it was okay). I betrayed you by violating your body and your privacy ... by taking advantage of your trust ... by not being sensitive to your feelings ... by telling lies about it after you told what I was doing to you ... by making you responsible for what would happen to me after you told ... by dumping my problems onto you and making you carry them for me.*
- Statement of what the perpetrator is doing about it. *I am seeing a counsellor to make sure I never do this again. I am learning to face up to what I did. I have decided to leave home/move neighbourhoods/change schools so that you feel safe.*
- Statement about accepting consequences. *I know that I have committed a crime as well as betraying you. I can handle whatever consequences that I have to face for doing this. It is not your responsibility.*
- Statement of future intent. *I will never sexually abuse you or anyone else ever again. I am not asking you to forgive me. I believe that you have every right to feel angry and betrayed. I don't need you to keep secrets for me or look after me anymore.*

Source: Jenkins (1990, pp. 224-227)

Collaboration with families of perpetrators

In many cases, the family will be ashamed and will feel to blame for getting into such a mess; instead, we must take an interest in how they can get out of it (Bateman & Milner, 2015). We will need to start with the wonderfulness interview, asking about qualities of the offending young people that makes them proud as parents, how they have managed to carry on in the face of the accusations, and what this says about them as parents (Bateman & Milner, 2015).

When the harmful sexual behaviour has been between siblings, the family needs to construct a plan to increase safety within the home (Bateman & Milner, 2015). For example, a basic rule will be that when there are two or more people in a room, the door stays open.

Conclusion

Given their likely combination of victim and abuser status, young people with sexually harmful behaviour will need help to explore what a safe future would look like for the victim and family and what they are already doing that is working towards this, as well as counselling for their own victimisation.

References

Bateman, J., & Milner, J. (2015). *Children and young people whose behaviour is sexually concerning or harmful: Assessing risk and developing safety plans*. Jessica Kingsley.

Bevill, A. R., & Gast, D. L. (1998). Social safety for young children: A review of the literature on safety skills instruction. *Topics in Early Childhood Special Education*, *18*(4), 222–234. https://doi.org/10.1177/027112149801800405

Bonner, B. L., Kaufman, K. L., Harbeck, C., & Brassard, M. R. (1992). Child maltreatment. In C. E. Walker & M. C. Roberts (Eds.), *Handbook of clinical child psychology* (2nd ed., pp. 967–1008). John Wiley and Sons.

Boyd, C. (2011). *The impacts of sexual assault on women*. Australian Centre for the Study of Sexual Assault.

Bromberg, D. S., & Johnson, B. T. (2001). Sexual interest in children, child sexual abuse, and psychological sequelae for children. *Psychology in the Schools*, *38*(4), 343–355. https://doi.org/10.1002/pits.1023

Cantwell, H. B. (1988). Child sexual abuse: Very young perpetrators. *Child Abuse and Neglect*, *12*(4), 579–582. https://doi.org/10.1016/0145-2134(88)90075-0

Craig, E. (2020). Child's play or sexual abuse? Reviewing the efficacy of the justice framework in dealing with child on child sexual abuse in the United Kingdom. *Journal of Child Sexual Abuse*, *29*(6), 734–748. https://doi.org/10.1080/10538712.2020.1719448

Davies, S. L., Glaser, D., & Kossoff, R. (2000). Children's sexual play and behavior in pre-school settings: Staff's perceptions, reports, and responses. *Child Abuse and Neglect*, *24*(10), 1329–1343. https://doi.org/10.1016/S0145-2134(00)00184-8

Essa, E. L., & Murray, C. I. (1999). Sexual play: When should you be concerned? *Childhood Education*, *75*(4), 231–234. https://doi.org/10.1080/00094056.1999.10522023

Ha, T., Kim, H., Christopher, C., Caruthers, A., & Dishion, T. J. (2016). Predicting sexual coercion in early adulthood: The transaction among maltreatment, gang affiliation, and adolescent socialization of coercive relationship norms. *Development and Psychopathology*, *28*(3), 707–720. https://doi.org/10.1017/S0954579416000262

Hackett, S., Phillips, J., Masson, H., & Balfe, M. (2013). Individual, family and abuse characteristics of 700 British child and adolescent sexual abusers. *Child Abuse Review*, *22*(4), 232–245. https://doi.org/10.1002/car.2246

Hornor, G. (2004). Sexual behavior in children: Normal or not? *Journal of Pediatric Health Care*, *18*(2), 57–64. https://doi.org/10.1016/S0891-5245(03)00154-8

Jenkins, A. (1990). *Invitations to responsibility: The therapeutic engagement of men who are violence and abusive*. Dulwich Centre Publications.

Johnson, B. M., Miltenberger, R. G., Egemo-Helm, K., Jostad, C. M., Flessner, C., & Gatheridge, B. (2005). Evaluation of behavioral skills training for teaching abduction-prevention skills to young children. *Journal of Applied Behavior Analysis*, *38*(1), 67–78. https://doi.org/10.1901/jaba.2005.26-04

Johnson, F. C. (2002). Child maltreatment: Recognition, reporting and risk. *Pediatrics International*, *44*(5), 554–560. https://doi.org/10.1046/j.1442-200X.2002.01642.x

Jordan, N. H. (1993). Sexual abuse prevention programs in early childhood education: A caveat. *Young Children*, *48*(6), 76–79.

Kostelnik, M. J., Soderman, A. K., Whiren, A. P., Ripiper, M., & Gregory, K. M. (2015). *Guiding children's social development and learning: Theory and skills* (8th ed.). Cengage.

Lavoie, F., Hébert, M., Tremblay, R., Vitaro, F., Vézina, L., & McDuff, P. (2002). History of family dysfunction and perpetration of dating violence by adolescent boys: A longitudinal study. *Journal of Adolescent Health, 30*(5), 375–383. https://doi.org/10.1016/S1054-139X(02)00347-6

Masson, H., Hackett, S., Phillips, J., & Balfe, M. (2015). Developmental markers of risk or vulnerability? Young females who sexually abuse – characteristics, backgrounds, behaviours and outcomes. *Child and Family Social Work, 20*(1), 19–29. https://doi.org/10.1111/cfs.12050

McAlinden, A. M. (2018). *Children as 'risk': Sexual exploitation and abuse by children and young people*. Cambridge University Press.

Mesman, G. R., Harper, S. L., Edge, N. A., Brandt, T. W., & Pemberton, J. L. (2019). Problematic sexual behavior in children. *Journal of Pediatric Health Care, 33*(3), 323–331. https://doi.org/10.1016/j.pedhc.2019.11.002

Ronis, S. T., & Borduin, C. M. (2007). Individual, family, peer and academic characteristics of male juvenile sexual offenders. *Journal of Abnormal Child Psychology, 35*(2), 153–163. https://doi.org/10.1007/s10802-006-9058-3

Shaw, J. A., Lewis, J. E., Loeb, A., Rosado, J., & Rodriguez, R. A. (2000). Child on child sexual abuse: Psychological perspectives. *Child Abuse and Neglect, 24*(12), 1591–1600. https://doi.org/10.1016/S0145-2134(00)00212-X

Smithee, L. C., Sumner, B. W., & Bean, R. A. (2019). Non-suicidal self-injury among sexual minority youth: An etiological and treatment overview. *Children and Youth Services Review, 96*, 212–219. https://doi.org/10.1016/j.childyouth.2019.11.055

Swartout, K. M., Swartout, A. G., Brennan, C. L., & White, J. W. (2015). Trajectories of male sexual aggression from adolescence through college: A latent growth curve analysis. *Aggressive Behavior, 41*(5), 467–477. https://doi.org/10.1002/ab.21584

Vizard, E. (2013). Practitioner review: The victims and juvenile perpetrators of child sexual abuse – assessment and intervention. *Journal of Child Psychology and Psychiatry, 54*(5), 503–515. https://doi.org/10.1111/jcpp.12047

Vizard, E., Hickey, N., French, L., & McCrory, E. (2007). Children and adolescents who present with sexually abusive behaviour: A UK descriptive study. *The Journal of Forensic Psychiatry and Psychology, 18*(1), 59–73. https://doi.org/10.1080/14789940601056745

Ward, T. (2000). Sexual offenders' cognitive distortions as implicit theories. *Aggression and Violent Behavior, 5*(5), 491–507. https://doi.org/10.1016/S1359-1789(98)00036-6

White, M. (2016). *Narrative therapy classics*. Dulwich Centre Publications.

21 Social inclusion of gender and sexual minorities

The West's history of pathologising sexual minority status (seeing it as a disorder) casts a long shadow, contributing still to social and institutional discrimination against and marginalisation of sexual minority youth and adults.

Terms

Sexuality refers to 'the quality of being sexual and includes an individual's capacities for sexual feelings, thoughts and behaviours' (Sigelman et al., 2022, p. 412). It is not limited to romance and intercourse but, more broadly, is about relationships, life choices, dispositions, play, and family (Robinson, 2002).

Heteronormativity is the cultural bias which upholds that heterosexuality is the only 'normal' sexual orientation; cisnormativity is the assumption that all people are born cisgender – that is, that their gender identity matches the biological sex that they were born with. This is in contrast with transgender, which refers to individuals who experience their gender differently from what is associated with the sex they were assigned at birth (Tebbe & Budge, 2022). Some trans individuals will identify as one or the other gender, whereas others (who are termed non-binary) might identify with neither gender or with a blend (Tebbe & Budge, 2022). It is not uncommon for the gender identity of transgender individuals to change over time, which is referred to as gender fluidity (Knutson et al., 2019). Intersex people are born with any of several sex characteristics including chromosomal makeup or sex organs that do not fit typical binary notions of male or female bodies.

Although terminology changes rapidly, at present non-binary (*enbee*) is commonly used to refer to those who identify themselves outside of the male-female dichotomy, although terms such as genderqueer or gender expansive seem preferable because this language focuses on who people are, rather than who they are not (Knutson et al., 2019).

In this chapter, I employ the terms sexual minorities and LGBTQI+ (for lesbian, gay, bisexual, transgender, sexually questioning, intersexual, plus non-binary people). The 'plus' also includes individuals identifying as queer, in a conscious choice to distance themselves from what they see as categorical notions of gender and sexuality (Barnett et al., 2021). I recognise, however, that the acronym lumps all sexual minorities together as if they share the same challenges, which is not the case (Barnett et al., 2021). Also, the categories can intersect, with

DOI: 10.4324/9781003323938-24

someone perhaps identifying as transgender (gender identity) and as gay (sexuality), for example (Barnett et al., 2021).

Gender identity

Gender identity is a person's 'deeply felt internal and individual experience of gender, which may or may not correspond with the sex assigned at birth' (Elze, 2019, p. 181). It incorporates individuals' sense of their body as well 'other expressions of gender, including dress, speech and mannerisms' (Elze, 2019, p. 181). Gendered narratives in society assert that there is a 'right' way to be female (feminine) and male (masculine). Pressure to conform to these prescribed patterns of masculinity or femininity leads to low self-esteem and relationship anxiety in gender minorities, because it conveys to them that they are not accepted as they are. Social pressure also foreshadows decreased peer acceptance (Yunger et al., 2004).

Nevertheless society as a whole is more tolerant of females than of males who are unconventional in their sex roles (Hatchel et al., 2020). Girls are allowed to be tomboyish, but homophobic attitudes imposed on boys disallow any attraction towards 'feminine' skills or interests (Kerr & Cohn, 2001). For males, a 'boy code' states that not only 'boys will be boys' but, more insistently, that boys *must* be boys (Kerr & Cohn, 2001).

Sexual orientation

Individuals' sexual orientation is their 'capacity for profound emotional, affectional and sexual attraction to, and intimate and sexual relations with, individuals of a different gender or the same gender or more than one gender' (Elze, 2019, p. 181). From their earliest years, children absorb messages that heterosexuality is not just a statistical majority, but is the norm: natural, unquestioned and, indeed, compulsory (Robinson, 2002). In the early years in particular, there is almost complete silence about alternatives, with gay or lesbian individuals and families seldom discussed and rarely represented in children's literature.

Although their sexual orientation will emerge during adolescence, children as young as five or six years of age can already have some awareness of their sexual preferences, with children's first sexual attraction occurring by the age of ten (Carver et al., 2004; Maguen et al., 2002; Peterson & Rischar, 2000). Many individuals who identify as being gay or lesbian in adult life were aware during childhood that they did not conform to heterosexual expectations.

It is important that we do not communicate heterosexist attitudes to children, not least because they will grow into adults who might be part of a sexual minority. In a large U.S. study, whereas in 2009, 7.7 per cent of adolescents reported same-sex sexual contact, in 2017, this figure was 13.1 per cent, with 2.5 per cent of adolescents in 2009 and 5.2 per cent in 2017 identifying exclusively as lesbian or gay (Raifman et al., 2020).

Specific challenges for sexual minority youth

Sexual minority individuals face the challenge of developing a healthy self-identity within a society which views their gender identification or sexual orientation as 'abnormal'. Specific sections within this community also face their own unique challenges.

Minority stress and intersectionality

Like other marginalised groups, sexual minority youth are subject to minority stress, which is a conflict between their internal self and the expectations of society (Craig et al., 2013). It reflects a lack of connection to the dominant culture. Having grown up in a homophobic culture, many internalise the negative attitudes surrounding them (Saenz, 2020), which can leave deep scars on the soul.

Sexual minority youth experience more child abuse and family, school and community violence than their straight counterparts (Elze, 2019). This means that the challenges arising from their gender identity or sexual orientation intersect with the challenges of surviving adversity. Their class, race, First Nations affiliation, gender, location (small town versus city), church membership and age all also affect how young people approach their sexuality (Hulko & Hovanes, 2017). For example, LGBTQI+ individuals from minority cultures are less likely to 'come out' to their parents or professionals (Hulko & Hovanes, 2017). Meanwhile, people in stigmatised cultural groups (such as Arabs) can find that their culture or religion pathologises and rejects them for being in a sexual minority, while their host culture rejects them for their ethnic identity (Chaney et al., 2020).

Identity formation

Identity formation is a continuous developmental process that occurs within sexual minority individuals' social context. Cass (1979) described that, for many, identity formation goes through phases of *confusion* about how come they don't conform to heterosexual norms and wondering what is wrong with them; *comparison*, when they feel alienated from the mainstream; *tolerance* when they begin to acknowledge their gender or sexual needs via exploring the sexual minority community; *acceptance* and ownership to who they are; *pride* arising from identifying with the sexual minority community that accepts them for who they are; and, finally identity *integration* when they incorporate their sexual status as one of their identities rather than the predominant one.

Although this model was first conceptualised as being linear, these phases can occur simultaneously and cyclically, and individuals can foreclose at any point, not progressing beyond (Cass, 1979). Furthermore, the phases might not apply to all cultures, or all subgroups of the LGBTQI+ community. For example, bisexual individuals adopt multiple personas rather than a single identity (Hulko & Hovanes, 2017).

Public identity disclosure ('coming out')

Adolescents' disclosure of their LGBTQI+ identity can send ripples - indeed, tidal waves - through their family, which reverberate back onto the adolescent (Mills-Koonce et al., 2018). It carries some risks of destabilisation of their family and bringing shame on it from their cultural group (Chaney et al., 2020).

The timing of coming out to oneself and to others has changed across the generations (Hulko & Hovanes, 2017). The gap between self-awareness and public disclosure used to be an average of ten years (Savin-Williams & Diamond, 2000). However, the average age at which young people publicly declare their sexual orientation has dropped since the 1970s from

20 to 14 years (Russell & Fish, 2016). Adolescents with a close relationship with their parents are likely to come out at a younger age.

Although we talk of 'coming out' as a liberating act, Steelman (2016) notes that it exposes sexual minority youth to societal discrimination. Yet despite this increased risk of school victimisation and family rejection, those who come out during high school report greater well-being (Russell & Fish, 2016), as a result of being able to be true to themselves. If they believe that they have to hide their true selves from their parents, they cut themselves off from parental support, and will be unable to be public with their sexual identities outside of home for fear of being detected by the family (Mills-Koonce et al., 2018).

Whereas members of a cultural minority can expect support from their families for their group membership, sexual minority youth face the possibility of rejection from their families (Craig et al., 2013). And, more than being rejected for disclosing their gender identity or sexual orientation, these young people find that they now lack support from their family for the everyday challenges that adolescent life poses. Moreover at a young age they are still dependent for emotional and financial support from their families (LaSala, 2013). A lack of both can lead to physical ejection from the family home, resulting in homelessness (McConnell et al., 2016). In that case, it might pay to wait until they have the financial resources to function independently (Mills-Koonce et al., 2018). A young disclosure age also runs the risk that parents will invalidate their child's disclosure ('How can you know something so important, when you are still so young?') (Mills-Koonce et al., 2018).

Nevertheless, family support does increase as parents become more familiar with their child's sexual minority status and observe their child's acceptance within their peer group (McConnell et al., 2016). And, in testament to young people's resilience, their distress improves through adolescence, even when they lack family support (McConnell et al., 2016).

Social isolation

During late adolescence, peer and community support can compensate for a lack of family support, improving the well-being of sexual minority youth (McConnell et al., 2016; Puckett et al., 2019). However, community support is not available to those who are unable to disclose their gender identity or sexual orientation (Puckett et al., 2019), while those living in rural and regional communities will lack access to role models, gay spaces such as gay nightclubs, or support services at the same time as facing more pressures to conform to the (typically) conservative ethos of a small town (Hulko & Hovanes, 2017). On the other hand, young people can use the internet to explore information, identities and lifestyles that otherwise would be inaccessible to them (Craig & McInroy, 2014). This can help them achieve acceptance of and explore their sexual identity in an affirming setting before enacting this in their offline (real) life. They can rehearse their offline coming out disclosures, and limit their online disclosures to selected friends. At the same time, the internet can expose them to cyber bullying, developmentally inappropriate content, and to grooming.

Young people's religion can be a source of belonging for them, but this might be denied them once they come out – and could even expose them to further institutional homophobic preachings and practices that invalidate and shame them (Austin & Craig, 2015). The net result can be that, while some ethnic groups discourage youth from seeking professional support because it signals that they do not trust God to take care of the issue, neither can sexually diverse youth approach religious leaders for support (Chaney et al., 2020).

Bullying

Compared to straight adolescents, gay, lesbian, bisexual and sexually questioning adolescents experience more frequent and more severe verbal and physical abuse, micro-aggressions, cyber bullying, social exclusion, humiliation, violence and sexual harassment (Barnett et al., 2021; Bontempo & D'Augelli, 2002; Chan et al., 2022; Fineran, 2001; Murdock & Bolch, 2005; Mustanski et al., 2016; Rivers, 2001; Smithee et al., 2019). In one U.S. study, over one-third had experienced anti-gay harassment in the previous six months; and nearly 5 per cent reported being the targets of physical violence (Huebner et al., 2004). These sexual minority adolescents often endure not only interpersonal verbal and physical bullying from school peers (and teachers), but also mobbing by unknown assailants and continuous sociocultural heterosexist harassment about their gender identity or sexual orientation (Espelage et al., 2008; Fineran, 2001; Henning-Stout et al., 2000; Jordan et al., 1997; Malinsky, 1997; Savin-Williams, 1994). Sexual prejudice repudiates who they are, with the result that victims suffer more compared to those who endure random assaults (Parrott & Peterson, 2008; Russell & Fish, 2016). Cumulative victimisation can lead to depression and post-traumatic stress (Mustanski et al., 2016). And if LGBTQI+ youth live in a small town with only one school available to them, they cannot escape the bullying by changing schools (Hulko & Hovanes, 2017).

Box 21.1 Some U.S. statistics on bullying of sexual minority students

- 98.5% heard anti-LGBTQI+ language at school.
- 56.6% heard such language from teachers and school staff.
- 59.5% felt unsafe at school.
- 75.4% avoided school functions because of feeling uncomfortable or unsafe.
- Almost 20% had to change schools because of feeling uncomfortable or unsafe.
- 70% were verbally harassed at school on the grounds of their sexual orientation.
- In any one year, 28% were physically harassed because of their sexual orientation.
- In any one year, 48.7% were harassed electronically because of their sexual orientation.
- In any one year, 57.3% were sexually harassed at school.
- 55.3% did not report this harassment to school staff for fear that it would make it worse.
- 60.4% of those who did report the incident stated that school staff did not intervene and instead told them to ignore it.

Source: Byrd, Chan and Luke (2021)

During adolescence, the combination of a homophobic school climate, low teacher support and elevated levels of victimisation contributes to a hostile learning environment for victims and onlookers alike, reducing their sense of safety within school and resulting for victims in declining academic performance, anxiety conditions and increased risky behaviours (Bontempo & D'Augelli, 2002; Darwich et al., 2012; Fineran, 2001; Jones et al., 2017; Jordan et al., 1997; Macgillivray, 2000; Murdock & Bolch, 2005). Many of these adolescents report being lonely at school and absent themselves out of fear for their safety (Carver et al., 2004; Hansen, 2007; Malinsky, 1997; Rivers & Noret, 2008). As many as 28 per cent drop out of school as a result of continual attacks (Goodenow et al., 2006; Savin-Williams, 1994).

Emotional difficulties

A disproportionate percentage of the sexual minority community experience significant mental health concerns including depression, anxiety, self-harm and suicidality (Barnett et al., 2021; Fortune et al., 2016; O'Reilly et al., 2021; Puckett et al., 2019; Russell & Fish, 2016; Ryan et al., 2010; Tebbe & Budge, 2022). Bisexual individuals appear to have more emotional adjustment difficulties than solely same-sex attracted youth, while those questioning their sexuality report higher levels of depression compared to other sexual minorities (Russell & Fish, 2016). For their part, trans individuals can experience lower levels of well-being and social support compared to other sexual minorities, while those who describe themselves as 'queer' because they do not neatly fit in the categories of gay, lesbian or bisexual, find it harder to assimilate within these communities and struggle to find an authentic sexual identity for themselves (Ryan et al., 2010).

Compared to heterosexual youth, sexual minority adolescents are more than three times more likely to attempt suicide (Garofalo et al., 1999; Goodenow et al., 2006; Raifman et al., 2020; Russell & Fish, 2016; Savin-Williams, 1994), with non-binary trans individuals experiencing still higher rates (Jadva et al., 2021), perhaps as high as 50 per cent (Tebbe & Budge, 2022). Their elevated risk is not the result of their gender identity or sexual orientation as such, but of not being integrated into the dominant culture and lacking social support (Fineran, 2001; Henning-Stout et al., 2000). Sexually diverse youth are especially vulnerable to mental health difficulties if they internalise homonegativity (Petrou & Lemke, 2017), if they are bullied and if they lack family support (Hansen, 2007; Martin-Storey & Crosnoe, 2012; Mustanski et al., 2016; Savin-Williams, 1994; Simons et al., 2013).

Romantic relationships

Forming romantic and sexual relationships is a key developmental task of adolescence. However, sexual minority youth experience a number of barriers to doing so, such as limited access to potential partners, internalisation of negative attitudes to dating same-sex partners, and social mores against demonstrating affection in public (Russell & Fish, 2016). Yet, having a partner improves their self-esteem and reduces internalised homophobia (Russell & Fish, 2016).

Many sexual minority youth have internalised the societal belief that they cannot have long-lasting relationships (Sue & Sue, 2016). In turn, these obstacles can direct them to public venues such as gay clubs where there can be increased risky behaviours such as unsafe sex or substance use (Russell & Fish, 2016). Men who have sex with men make up 5 per cent of the population, yet in the U.S. account for 50 per cent of all cases of HIV, with the rate of HIV infection there rising by 12 per cent per year (LaSala, 2013).

Children of sexual minority parents

In addition to discussing the needs of sexual minority youth, we need also to remind ourselves that nearly half of women and one-fifth of men who identify as LGBTQI+ themselves have children (Herbstrith, 2021). The only data of which I am aware is about children raised by lesbian parents, however, which is what I report here.

In terms of outcomes, young people raised by lesbian mothers have similar emotional well-being, behavioural issues, quality of life, and gender identities and sexual orientation to all other young people (Allen & Burrell, 1997; Golombok et al., 2003; Gottman, 1989; MacCallum & Golombok, 2004; van Gelderen et al., 2012; van Rijn-van Gelderen et al., 2015; Wainright et al., 2004). This makes sense because in all families, the well-being of the children is reliant on the quality of relationships within the family, not on its structure (van Rijn-van Gelderen et al., 2015). It is adversity - not diversity - that derails young people's emotional development.

Having lesbian parents seems to produce in children a greater awareness of discrimination and more accepting attitudes to nonconformity to gender roles (Siegel et al., 2022; Wainright et al., 2004). Nevertheless, lesbian mothers are concerned about their children being harassed, which fears are well founded, with 41 per cent of adolescents reporting being stigmatised because of their mother's sexual orientation (Bos & Gartrell, 2010) and one-quarter feeling unsafe at school (Kosciw et al., 2016, in Herbstrith, 2021). This can contribute to emotional and behavioural difficulties during adolescence and into early adulthood (Bos et al., 2021; Koh et al., 2019; van Gelderen et al., 2012; van Rijn-van Gelderen et al., 2015).

In schools, these young people are exposed to educators who lack knowledge about this community and its issues and who regard their family as not legitimate and to be in violation of social values (Herbstrith, 2021). The invisibility of these families is apparent in simple micro-aggressions such as not having enrolment and permission forms that allow for same-gender parents; having a school policy on inclusion that is silent about the inclusion of sexual minority students and families; and the curriculum and resources containing no mention of sexually diverse individuals and families.

If their gay parents have chosen to protect themselves by not coming out to the school, the children will have to be vigilant to keep their parents' sexual orientation a secret (Herbstrith, 2021). In contrast, those lesbian mothers who have a warm relationship with their children, and are forthright about their lifestyle and provide positive role models (such as by being active in the gay community) make their children less vulnerable to stigma (Bos & Gartrell, 2010). Peer support is also protective (van Gelderen et al., 2012).

Interventions

Counselling for sexual minority youth will need to take account of minority stress - that is, must start with an understanding that social attitudes to these young people, rather than their own maladjustment, is the main cause of their disquiet about their gender identity or sexual orientation (Bochicchio et al., 2022). Open-ended questions (such as those listed in Box 9.1 (see page 115) can assist sexually diverse youth to deconstruct the oppressive influences of their culture.

Second, given the complex issues that sexual minorities face, you will need to assess for substance use and suicidal ideation, particularly at the time of coming out, because the risk of suicide is highest at this time if their families are unsupportive (Bochicchio et al., 2022). And their relationship history is bound to have an effect on future relationships and therefore must not be overlooked (Barnett et al., 2021).

Third, diversity competence is vital for members of marginalised groups because it is affirming (Oh et al., 2019). Finally, your practice will need to be trauma-informed (Elze, 2019; see Chapter 15). Meanwhile, of course, sexual minority youth can experience distress over the same life events - such as academic stress or their parents' divorce - that any young people find challenging.

The use of validating language

It is vital to affirm and validate clients' diverse gender identities and sexual orientations via the use of their preferred pronouns. Some will use *they, them* and *their* to refer to themselves in the singular, with other pronouns such as *ze* or *zie*, *zir* and *zirself* not yet in common usage. Gender fluidity requires counsellors to check in regularly with clients about their current identities and which pronouns they prefer (Knutson et al., 2019).

Deadnaming is when we use the name clients were given at birth, when they have selected a different name to be known by (Knutson et al., 2019). A simple work-around is to have on intake forms spaces to record both a legal and a preferred name, with space for preferred pronouns and for self-identification of gender, adding to the male and female boxes: MTF (male to female), FTM (female to male), transgender, non-binary, gender fluid, gender expansive and an open category (Knutson et al., 2019). At the same time, it will be important not to pressure clients to adopt labels for themselves when they are not ready (Chaney et al., 2020).

Narrative therapy

Narrative therapy is uniquely equipped for working with sexual minority youth because it explicitly deconstructs oppressive cultural narratives that fuel discrimination (Jordan, 2020; Saltzburg, 2007), exposing heterosexism and its propaganda, misconceptions and falsehoods (Farrukh & Qamar, 2023) and how these affect clients' identities and their families' thoughts about their sexual minority children (Saltzburg, 2007).

The issue is not individuals' gender identity or their sexual orientation - these are not problems. Therefore these do not need to be externalised (Steelman, 2016). What does need to be externalised, however, is oppression - so that clients can separate from and take an active stand against heterosexist discourses and practices that they might have internalised and which limit and blame them (Nylund, 2017; Steelman, 2016). Deconstruction questions might include:

- How do you feel, as a (gay, lesbian, trans, intersex, questioning, queer person) to have society dictate who you can and cannot be?
- Tell me about a time when you have been able to resist the homophobic attitudes around you, and feel good about yourself?

The narrative goal is for sexual minority clients to write their own identity. When their rights to telling their own story have been violated by oppression or discrimination, or when the voice of abuse strengthens the story that who they is not good enough, they will need to develop new storylines for their identity (Denborough, 2014). For gay and lesbian youth, Steelman (2016) advises that their sexual orientation should be discussed as an addition to their personality, not the only or most important part, as if it were a welcomed houseguest who occupies one room of the house but does not take over all of it.

Box 21.2 Narrative questions for sexual minority youth

Landscape of action questions

Questions on the following themes could be useful for gay or lesbian youth (Steelman, 2016) - although for trans individuals, their gender identity is the foundation of their personality, in which case these questions will be inappropriate.

- How old were you when gay crept into your life?
- How old were you when you told your parents about gay?
- So gay was in your life for four years without your parents noticing?

Landscape of identity questions

- Having spoken about their social supports, you might ask: What do these supportive people have you believing about yourself?
- What would (name of person) say about who you are and what you stand for?
- What does it tell you about you that you have such good friendships in your life?
- What can you do to bring those positive influences into your life more often?
- (To a parent): What was (child) like before gay became known? Is he still those things? (Steelman, 2016).
- It seems to me that when you were 13 you kind of let gay take up more room in the house rather than allowing equal space for all parts of you. Does that sound about right?
- Do (name some other qualities) still live with you, or did gay make them move out?
- So what can your parents do to acknowledge gay just as they noticed (other qualities) before?
- Even though gay isn't all that you are, what tricks does it use to convince you and your parents that it is all that you are?
- What can you do to stick up for gay without letting it overpower all of the other parts of you?
- What can you do to help your parents acknowledge gay without its overpowering the other valuable parts of you as well?

Collaboration with parents

Family acceptance improves the well-being of sexual minority youth in general and specifically protects against depression, substance abuse, and suicidal ideation and attempts (Ryan et al., 2010). Therefore, the engagement in counselling of the families of LGBTQI+ youth is vital.

The goal of narrative therapy with families is to help them to accept their LGBTQI+ children without echoing the voices of homophobia and heterosexism (Saltzburg, 2007). To that end, Saltzburg (2007, p. 63) suggests some questions:

- What arguments does homophobia make to justify marginalising and victimising LGBTQI+ people in the name of morality and family values?
- How does this argument make sense to you in light of the violence and discrimination carried out against sexual minorities?
- How did homophobia become such a loud voice in your life?
- How do homophobia and heterosexism argue against the worth of your child?
- What effect does this have on how you are thinking about your child? And on your relationship with them?
- What does homophobia say that others are thinking about your child and you?

Interventions will be based on the age-old wisdom that parents want their children to be happy, safe, healthy and connected to the family, which is what their daughters and sons want also (LaSala, 2013). Parents' worries for their child can be reframed as an expression of how much they love them, want them to find happiness and want to know that they will be okay (LaSala, 2013).

The young people's stories can be re-authored to assist parents to identify the ways in which their daughter or son has not changed because of gender identity or sexual orientation and that they can still connect to their future of optimism and possibilities (Saltzburg, 2007). Their feeling that their child is now stigmatised and that therefore they are alone leads to questions such as (Saltzburg, 2007, p. 65):

- How does heterosexism talk you into thinking that you are alone, with no one like you or your child?
- How does heterosexism convince you that there are no common threads connecting you to other parents?

Next, counsellors will enquire about the people who love and care about them, and ask (Saltzburg, 2007, p. 65):

- What might these loved ones say about your child and yourself?
- How might they coach you to stand up to the voices of homophobia and heterosexism?

The parents' feelings that they now have nothing to offer their daughter or son in the way of life advice can be addressed with questions such as (Saltzburg, 2007, p. 66):

- What other times in your life have you felt new to parenting or unsure about what to do to care for your child?

- How were you able to overcome your fear of not knowing, to remind yourself that you do know?
- What steps did you take to do this?

Definitional ceremonies can link parents of sexual minority adolescents, and re-membering practices allow them to consider the criteria for membership of the family's club, downgrading the membership of judgemental individuals and giving lifelong membership to those supportive individuals who inspire and embrace them (Saltzburg, 2007).

Advocacy

There is a lack of support in the fabric of institutions that figure in the lives of sexual minority youth, such as schools and extracurricular clubs (Russell & Fish, 2016). Therefore, counsellors can champion social justice at the school or community level. Framing gender and sexuality issues as issues of equity, advocates can encourage school personnel to employ gender-neutral terms; to challenge homophobic and transphobic 'jokes'; adopt anti-bullying policies that explicitly mention heterosexist bullying; provide queer-affirming curricula and include HIV prevention information within sex education classes; and, just as they do for cultural minorities, display symbols (such as a rainbow flag) or posters that signify that their classroom and this school is a safe place for minorities of all stripes (Theodore & Chiasson, 2021).

Counsellors can also advocate for the establishment of Gender and Sexuality Alliances (formerly Gay-straight Alliances) or support groups at schools. These are clubs where sexual minority adolescents can discuss issues of and advocacy for LGBTQI+ youth. These clubs help youth feel safe at school, regardless of whether they are even members (Hulko & Hovanes, 2017; Theodore & Chiasson, 2021). Such measures not only cause sexual minority youth to feel safer – but also to *be* safer (Chan et al., 2022; Crisp & McCave, 2007; Toomey et al., 2011).

Conclusion

People suffer mental anguish when their culture's dominant narratives conflict with their lived experience (Jordan, 2020). While sexual minority youth will attend counselling for the same issues that all young people experience, they can also attend for issues explicitly relating to their minority status. In these cases, gender-affirmative practices are vital as you support them to process their presenting concerns.

References

Allen, M., & Burrell, N. (1997). Comparing the impact of homosexual and heterosexual parents on children: Meta-analysis of existing research. *Journal of Homosexuality*, *32*(2), 19–35. https://doi.org/10.1300/J082v32n02_02

Austin, A., & Craig, S. L. (2015). Empirically supported interventions for sexual and gender minority youth. *Journal of Evidence-Informed Social Work*, *12*(6), 567–578. http://dx.doi.org/10.1080/15433714.2014.884958

Barnett, M., Fotheringhamn, F., Hutton, V., & O'Loughlin, K. (2021). Heterosexism and cisgenderism. In V. Hutton & S. Sisko (Eds.), *Multicultural responsiveness in counselling and psychology: Working with Australian populations* (pp. 153–178). Springer. https://doi.org/10.1007/978-3-030-55427-9_6

Bochicchio, L., Reeder, K., Ivanoff, A., Pope, H., & Stefancic, A. (2022). Psychotherapeutic interventions for LGBTQ+ youth: A systematic review. *Journal of LGBT Youth*, 1–28. https://doi.org/10.1080/19361653.2020.1766393

Bontempo, D. E., & D'Augelli, A. R. (2002). Effects of at-school victimization and sexual orientation on lesbian, gay, or bisexual youths' health risk behavior. *Journal of Adolescent Health*, *30*(5), 364–374. https://doi.org/10.1016/S1054-139X(01)00415-3

Bos, H., Carone, N., Rothblum, E. D., Koh, A., & Gartrell, N. (2021). Long-term effects of homophobic stigmatization during adolescence on problem behavior in emerging adult offspring of lesbian parents. *Journal of Youth and Adolescence*, *50*, 1114–1125. https://doi.org/10.1007/s10964-020-01364-1

Bos, H., & Gartrell, N. (2010). Adolescents of the USA National Longitudinal Lesbian Family Study: Can family characteristics counteract the negative effects of stigmatization? *Family Process*, *49*(4), 559–572. https://doi.org/10.1111/j.1545-5300.2010.01340.x

Byrd, R., Chan, C., & Luke, C. (2021). LGB children and adolescents. In R. Byrd & C. Luke (Eds.), *Counseling children and adolescents: Cultivating empathic connection* (pp. 226–245). Routledge.

Carver, P. R., Egan, S. K., & Perry, D. G. (2004). Children who question their heterosexuality. *Developmental Psychology*, *40*(1), 43–53. https://doi.org/10.1037/0012-1649.40.1.43

Cass, V. (1979). Homosexual identity formation: A theoretical model. *Journal of Homosexuality*, *4*(3), 219–235. https://doi.org/10.1300/J082v04n03_01

Chan, A. S. W., Wu, D., Lo, I. P. Y., Ho, J. M. C., & Yan, E. (2022). Diversity and inclusion: Impacts on psychological wellbeing among lesbian, gay, bisexual, Transgender, and queer communities. *Frontiers in Psychology*, *13*, 82. https://doi.org/10.3389/fpsyg.2022.726343

Chaney, M. P., Dubaybo, F., & Chang, C. Y. (2020). Affirmative counseling with LGBTQ+ Arab Americans. *Journal of Mental Health Counseling*, *42*(4), 281–302. https://doi.orgl10.17744/mehc.42.4.01

Craig, S. L., Austin, A., & Alessi, E. (2013). Gay affirmative cognitive behavioral therapy for sexual minority youth: A clinical adaptation. *Clinical Social Work Journal*, *41*(3), 258–266. https://doi.org/10.1007/s10615-012-0427-9

Craig, S. L., & McInroy, L. (2014). You can form a part of yourself online: The influence of new media on identity development and coming out for LGBTQ youth. *Journal of Gay and Lesbian Mental Health*, *18*, 95–109. https://doi.org/10.1080/19359705.2013.777007

Crisp, C., & McCave, E. L. (2007). Gay affirmative practice: A model for social work practice with gay, lesbian and bisexual youth. *Child and Adolescent Social Work Journal*, *24*, 403–421. https://doi.org/10.1007/s10560-007-0091-z

Darwich, L., Hymel, S., & Waterhouse, T. (2012). School avoidance and substance use among lesbian, gay, bisexual, and questioning youths: The impact of peer victimization and adult support. *Journal of Educational Psychology*, *104*(2), 381–392. https://doi.org/10.1037/a0026684

Denborough, D. (2014). *Retelling the stories of our lives: Everyday narrative therapy to draw inspiration and transform experience*. Norton.

Elze, D. E. (2019). The lives of lesbian, gay, bisexual, and transgender people: A trauma-informed and human rights perspective. In L. D. Butler, F. M. Critelli & J. Carello (Eds.), *Trauma and human rights: Integrating approaches to address human suffering* (pp. 179–206). Palgrave Macmillan. https://doi.org/10.1007/978-3-030-16395-2

Espelage, D. L., Aragon, S. R., Birkett, M., & Koenig, B. W. (2008). Homophobic teasing, psychological outcomes, and sexual orientation among high school students: What influence do parents and schools have? *School Psychology Review*, *37*(2), 202–216. https://doi.org/10.1080/02796015.2008.12087894

Farrukh, H., & Qamar, T. (2023). Narrative therapy with intersex individual: A clinical case study. *South Asian Journal of Social Sciences and Humanities*, *4*(1), 1–18. https://doi.org/10.48165/sajssh.2023.4101

Fineran, S. (2001). Peer sexual harassment in high school. *Journal of School Social Work*, *11*(2), 50–69.

Fortune, S., Cottrell, D. & Fyfe, S. (2016). Family factors associated with adolescent self-harm: A narrative review. *Journal of Family Therapy*, *38*(2), 226–256. https://doi.org/10.1111/1467-6427.12119

Garofalo, R., Wolf, C., Wissow, L. S., Woods, E. R., & Goodman, E. (1999). Sexual orientation and risk of suicide attempts among a representative sample of youth. *Archives of Pediatrics and Adolescent Medicine*, *153*(5), 487–493. https://doi.org/10.1001/archpedi.153.5.487

Golombok, S., Perry, B., Burston, A., Murray, C., Mooney-Somers, J., Stevens, M., & Golding, J. (2003). Children with lesbian parents: A community study. *Developmental Psychology*, *39*(1), 20–33. https://doi.org/10.1037/0012-1649.39.1.20

Goodenow, C., Szalacha, L., & Westheimer, K. (2006). School support groups, other school factors and the safety of sexual minority adolescents. *Psychology in the Schools*, *43*(5), 573–589. https://doi.org/10.1002/pits.20173

Gottman, J. S. (1989). Children of gay and lesbian parents. *Marriage and Family Review*, *14*(3–4), 177–196. https://doi.org/10.1300/J002v14n03_09

Hansen, A. L. (2007). School-based support for GLBT students: A review of three levels of research. *Psychology in the Schools*, *44*(8), 839–848. https://doi.org/10.1002/pits.20269

Hatchel, T., Ingram, K. M., Huang, Y., & Espelage, D. L. (2020). Homophobic bullying victimization trajectories: The roles of perpetration, sex assigned at birth, and sexuality. *Aggressive Behavior*, *46*(5), 370–379. https://doi.org/10.1002/ab.21897

Henning-Stout, M., James, S., & Macintosh, S. (2000). Reducing harassment of lesbian, gay, bisexual, transgender, and questioning youth in schools. *School Psychology Review*, *29*(2), 180–191. https://doi.org/10.1080/02796015.2000.12086006

Herbstrith, J. C. (2021) Using a systems approach to creating equitable educational environments for gender and sexually diverse families. In M. C. Lytle & R. A. Sprott (Eds.), *Supporting gender identity and sexual diversity in K-12 schools* (pp. 121–142). American Psychological Association.

Huebner, D. M., Rebchook, G. M., & Kegeles, S. M. (2004). Experiences of harassment, discrimination, and physical violence among young gay and bisexual men. *American Journal of Public Health*, *94*(7), 1200–1203. https://doi.org/10.2105/AJPH.94.7.1200

Hulko, W., & Hovanes, J. (2017). Intersectionality in the lives of LGBTQ youth: Identifying as LGBTQ and finding community in small cities and rural towns. *Journal of Homosexuality*, *65*(4), 427–455. http://dx.doi.org/10.1080/00918369.2017.1320169

Jadva, V., Guasp, A., Bradlow, J. H., Bower-Brown, S., & Foley, S. (2021). Predictors of self-harm and suicide in LGBT youth: The role of gender, socio-economic status, bullying and school experience. *Journal of Public Health*, 1–7. https://doi.org/10.1093/pubmed/fdab383

Jones, A., Robinson, E., Oginni, O., Rahman, Q., & Rimes, K. A. (2017). Anxiety disorders, gender nonconformity, bullying and self-esteem in sexual minority adolescents: Prospective birth cohort study. *Journal of Child Psychology and Psychiatry*, *58*(11), 1201–1209. https://doi.org/10.1111/jcpp.12757

Jordan, F. (2020). Changing the narrative for LGBTQ Adolescents: A literature review and call for research into narrative therapy to improve family acceptance of LGBTQ teens. *Counseling and Family Therapy Scholarship Review*, *3*(1), 6. https://doi.org/10.53309/RAQX6953

Jordan, K. M., Vaughan, J. S., & Woodworth, K. J. (1997). I will survive: Lesbian, gay, and bisexual youths' experience of high school. *Journal of Gay and Lesbian Social Services*, *7*(4), 17–33. https://doi.org/10.1300/J041v07n04_02

Kerr, B. A., & Cohn, S. J. (2001). *Smart boys: Talent, manhood, and the search for meaning*. Great Potential Press.

Knutson, D., Koch, J. M., & Goldbach, C. (2019). Recommended terminology, pronouns, and documentation with transgender and non-binary populations. *Practice Innovations*, *4*(4), 214–224. http://dx.doi.org/10.1037/pri0000098

Koh, A. S., Bos, H. M., & Gartrell, N. K. (2019). Predictors of mental health in emerging adult offspring of lesbian-parent families. *Journal of Lesbian Studies*, *23*(2), 257–278. https://doi.org/10.1080/10894160.2018.1555694

LaSala, M. C. (2013). Out of the darkness: Three waves of family research and the emergence of family therapy for lesbian and gay people. *Clinical Social Work Journal*, *41*, 267–276. https://doi.org/10.1007/s10615-012-0434-x

MacCallum, F., & Golombok, S. (2004). Children raised in fatherless families from infancy: A follow-up of children of lesbian and single heterosexual mothers at early adolescence. *Journal of Child Psychology and Psychiatry*, *45*(8), 1407–1419. https://doi.org/10.1111/j.1469-7610.2004.00324.x

Macgillivray, I. K. (2000). Educational equity for gay, lesbian, bisexual, transgendered, and queer/questioning students: The demands of democracy and social justice for America's schools. *Education and Urban Society*, *32*(3), 303–323. https://doi.org/10.1177/0013124500323003

Maguen, S., Floyd, F. J., Bakeman, R., & Armistead, L. (2002). Developmental milestones and disclosure of sexual orientation among gay, lesbian, and bisexual youths. *Journal of Applied Developmental Psychology*, *23*(2), 219–233. https://doi.org/10.1016/S0193-3973(02)00105-3

Malinsky, K. P. (1997). Learning to be invisible: Female sexual minority students in America's public high schools. *Journal of Gay and Lesbian Social Services*, *7*(4), 35–50. https://doi.org/10.1300/J041v07n04_03

Martin-Storey, A., & Crosnoe, R. (2012). Sexual minority status, peer harassment, and adolescent depression. *Journal of Adolescence*, *35*(4), 1001–1011. https://doi.org/10.1016/j.adolescence.2012.02.006
McConnell, E. A., Birkett, M., & Mustanski, B. (2016). Families matter: Social support and mental health trajectories among lesbian, gay, bisexual, and transgender youth. *Journal of Adolescent Health*, *59*(6), 674–680. https://doi.org/10.1016/j.jadohealth.2016.07.026
Mills-Koonce, W. R., Rehder, P. D., & McCurdy, A. L. (2018). The significance of parenting and parent–child relationships for sexual and gender minority adolescents. *Journal of Research on Adolescence*, *28*(3), 637–649. https://doi.org/10.1111/jora.12404
Murdock, T. B., & Bolch, M. B. (2005). Risk and protective factors for poor school adjustment in lesbian, gay, and bisexual (LGB) high school youth: Variable and person-centered analyses. *Psychology in the Schools*, *42*(2), 159–172. https://doi.org/10.1002/pits.20054
Mustanski, B., Andrews, R., & Puckett, J. A. (2016). The effects of cumulative victimization on mental health among lesbian, gay, bisexual, and transgender adolescents and young adults. *American Journal of Public Health*, *106*(3), 527–533. https://doi.org/10.2105/AJPH.2015.302976
Nylund, D. (2017). Queer informed narrative therapy: Radical approaches to counselling with transgender persons: Discourse in practice. *Social Justice and Counseling*, 159–170. https://doi.org/10.4324/9781315753751-16
Nylund, D., & Temple, A. (2017). Queer informed narrative therapy: Radical approaches to counseling with transgender persons. In C. A. Audet & D. Paré (Eds.), *Social justice and counseling: Discourse in practice* (pp. 159–170). Routledge.
Oh, S., Kim, N., Bennett, C. M., & Taylor, D. D. (2019). Multiculturally competent intake interview with LGBTQI++ clients. *Journal of Gay and Lesbian Mental Health*, *23*(2), 186–204. https://doi.org/10.1080/19359705.2019.1568943
O'Reilly, L. M., Pettersson, E., Donahue, K., Quinn, P. D., Klonsky, E. D., Lundström, S., & D'Onofrio, B. M. (2021). Sexual orientation and adolescent suicide attempt and self-harm: A co-twin control study. *Journal of Child Psychology and Psychiatry*, *62*(7), 834–841. https://doi.org/10.1111/jcpp.13325
Parrott, D. J., & Peterson, J. L. (2008). What motivates hate crimes based on sexual orientation? Mediating effects of anger on antigay aggression. *Aggressive Behavior*, *34*(3), 306–318. https://doi.org/10.1002/ab.20239
Peterson, J. S., & Rischar, H. (2000). Gifted and gay: A study of the adolescent experience. *Gifted Child Quarterly*, *44*(4), 231–246. https://doi.org/10.1177/001698620004400404
Petrou, P., & Lemke, R. (2017). Victimization and life satisfaction of gay and bisexual individuals in 44 European countries: the moderating role of country-level and person-level attitudes towards homosexuality. *Culture, Health and Sexuality*, *20*(6), 640–657. https://doi.org/10.1080/13691058.2017.1368710
Puckett, J. A., Matsuno, E., Dyar, C., Mustanski, B., & Newcomb, M. E. (2019). Mental health and resilience in transgender individuals: What type of support makes a difference? *Journal of Family Psychology*, *33*(8), 954. https://doi.org/10.1037/fam0000561
Raifman, J., Charlton, B. M., Arrington-Sanders, R., Chan, P. A., Rusley, J., Mayer, K. H., & McConnell, M. (2020). Sexual orientation and suicide attempt disparities among US adolescents: 2009–2017. *Pediatrics*, *145*(3), e20191658. https://doi.org/10.1542/peds.2019-1658
Rivers, I., & Noret, N. (2008). Well-being among same-sex- and opposite-sex-attracted youth at school. *School Psychology Review*, *37*(2), 174–187. https://doi.org/10.1080/02796015.2008.12087892
Rivers, S. (2001). The bullying of sexual minorities at school: Its nature and long-term correlates. *Educational and Child Psychology*, *18*(1), 32–46.
Robinson, K. H. (2002). Making the invisible visible: Gay and lesbian issues in early childhood education. *Contemporary Issues in Early Childhood*, *3*(3), 415–434.
Russell, S. T., & Fish, J. N. (2016). Mental health in lesbian, gay, bisexual and transgender (LGBT) youth. *Annual Review of Clinical Psychology*, *28*(12), 465–487. https://doi.org/10.1146/annurev-clinpsy-021815-093153
Ryan, C., Russell, S. T., Huebner, D., Diaz, R., & Sanchez, J. (2010). Family acceptance in adolescence and the health of LGBT young adults. *Journal of Child and Adolescent Psychiatric Nursing*, *23*(4), 205–213. https://doi.org/10.1111/j.1744-6171.2010.00246.x
Saenz, S. R. (2020). Sexuality and gender in psychiatry: Ethical and clinical Issues. *FOCUS: The Journal of Lifelong Learning in Psychiatry*, *18*(3), 304–306. https://doi.org/10.1176/appi.focus.20200019
Saltzburg, S. (2007). Narrative therapy pathways for re-authoring with parents of adolescents coming-out as lesbian, gay, and bisexual. *Contemporary Family Therapy*, *29*, 57–69. https://doi.org/10.1007/s10591-007-9035-1

Savin-Williams, R. C. (1994). Verbal and physical abuse as stressors in the lives of lesbian, gay male, and bisexual youths: Associations with school problems, running away, substance abuse, prostitution, and suicide. *Journal of Consulting and Clinical Psychology*, *62*(2), 261–269.

Savin-Williams, R. C., & Diamond, L. M. (2000). Sexual identity trajectories among sexual-minority youths: Gender comparisons. *Archives of Sexual Behavior*, *29*(6), 607–627. https://doi.org/10.1023/A:1002058505138

Siegel, M., Legler, M., Neziraj, F., Goldberg, A. E., & Zemp, M. (2022). Minority stress and positive identity aspects in members of LGBTQ+ parent families: Literature review and a study protocol for a mixed-methods evidence synthesis. *Children*, *9*(9), 1364. https://doi.org/10.3390/children9091364

Sigelman, C. K., De George, L., Cunial, K., Kohler, M., Ballam, N., & Rider, E. A. (2022). *Life span human development* (4th ANZ ed.). Cengage.

Simons, L., Schrager, S. M., Clark, L. F., Belzer, M., & Olson, J. (2013). Parental support and mental health among transgender adolescents. *Journal of Adolescent Health*, *53*(6), 791–793. https://doi.org/10.1016/j.jadohealth.2013.07.019

Smithee, L. C., Sumner, B. W., & Bean, R. A. (2019). Non-suicidal self-injury among sexual minority youth: An etiological and treatment overview. *Children and Youth Services Review*, *96*, 212–219. https://doi.org/10.1016/j.childyouth.2018.11.055

Steelman, S. M. (2016). Externalizing identities: An integration of narrative therapy and queer theory. *Journal of Family Psychotherapy*, *27*(1), 79–84. https://doi.org/10.1080/08975353.2016.1136549

Sue, D. W., & Sue, D. (2016). *Counseling the culturally diverse: Theory and practice* (7th ed.). Wiley.

Tebbe, E. A., & Budge, S. L. (2022). Factors that drive mental health disparities and promote well-being in transgender and nonbinary people. *Nature Reviews Psychology*, *1*(12), 694–707. https://doi.org/10.1038/s44159-022-00109-0

Theodore, P. S., & Chiasson, J. (2021). Evolving strategies to counter school bullying of gender and sexually diverse students. In M. C. Lytle & R. A. Sprout, (Eds.), *Supporting gender identity and sexual orientation diversity in K-12 schools* (pp. 71–96). American Psychological Association. https://doi.org/10.1037/0000211-005

Toomey, R. B., Ryan, C., Diaz, R. M., & Russell, S. T. (2011). High school gay-straight alliances (GSAs) and young adult well-being: An examination of GSA presence, participation, and perceived effectiveness. *Applied Developmental Science*, *15*(4), 175–185. https://doi.org/10.1080/10888691.2011.607378

van Gelderen, L., Bos, H. M., Gartrell, N., Hermanns, J., & Perrin, E. C. (2012). Quality of life of adolescents raised from birth by lesbian mothers: The US National Longitudinal Family Study. *Journal of Developmental and Behavioral Pediatrics*, *33*(1), 17–23. https://doi.org/10.1097/DBP.0b013e31823b62af

van Rijn-van Gelderen, L., Bos, H. M., & Gartrell, N. K. (2015). Dutch adolescents from lesbian-parent families: How do they compare to peers with heterosexual parents and what is the impact of homophobic stigmatization? *Journal of Adolescence*, *40*, 65–73. http://dx.doi.org/10.1016/j.adolescence.2015.01.005

Wainright, J. L., Russell, S. T., & Patterson, C. J. (2004). Psychosocial adjustment, school outcomes, and romantic relationships of adolescents with same-sex parents. *Child Development*, *75*(6), 1886–1898. https://doi.org/10.1111/j.1467-8624.2004.00823.x

Yunger, J. L., Carver, P. R., & Perry, D. G. (2004). Does gender identity influence children's psychological well-being? *Developmental Psychology*, *40*(4), 572. https://doi.org/10.1037/0012-1649.40.4.572

Resources

This chapter lists some resources that can support counsellors and young people to understand and address various presenting issues.

Solution-feocused therapy

Tyrrell, M. The miracle question: https://youtu.be/pAVetl4I3_w
Tyrrell, M. Scaling questions. https://youtu.be/3rB4zDVGgQM

Narrative therapy

Dulwich Centre Foundation. Acts of resistance; acts of reclaiming. https://youtu.be/ftCAmkYnAY4?si=3dVQsY5mLs-jLXmy
Madigan, S. Narrative therapy with Stephen Madigan. https://youtu.be/j6tdvnL2hKw?si=SdZodpL.pbOuFqWG4
Madigan, S. Narrative therapy with children. https://youtu.be/XMst5HoOS6c?si=n7FOGTZIIa4T4OTN
White, M. Trauma. https://youtu.be/ZEmordU3Q18?si=RrF375bVafG-dQuF

For those with access to psychotherapy.net:

Madigan, S. Narrative family therapy. https://www.psychotherapy.net/video/narrative-family-therapy
Madigan, S. Narrative therapy with children. https://www.psychotherapy.net/video/madigan-narrative-therapy-children

Acceptance and commitment therapy

Hayes, S. Mental brakes to avoid mental breaks: https://youtu.be/GnSHpBRLJrQ
Harris, R. Turning off the struggle switch: https://youtu.be/rCp1l16GCXI

DOI: 10.4324/9781003323938-25

Ethics

The ACA Code of ethics and practice provides can be found online at: https://www.theaca.net.au/documents/ACA%20Code%20of%20Ethics%20and%20Practice%20Ver15.pdf

For members, PACFA's Code of ethics can be found online at: https://www.pacfa.org.au/wp-content/uploads/2017/11/PACFA-Code-of-Ethics-2017.pdf

Confidentiality

Grande, T. L. *Explaining the limits of confidentiality to clients.* https://youtu.be/IWKseYFhp1Y

Privacy legislation

- Federal: Privacy Act 1988 (Commonwealth).
- ACT: Health Records (Privacy and Access) Act 1997
- NSW: Health Records (Privacy and Access) Act 1997 (NSW); Health Records Information Privacy Act 2002 (NSW)
- VIC: Health Records Act 2001
- WA: Regulation 8, Public Service Regulation 1988
- QLD: Information Privacy Act 2009
- SA: No specific legislation; Information Privacy Principles
- Tasmania: Personal Information Protection Act 2004
- NT: Information Act 2002

Legislation on child abuse and child protection

- ACT: Children and Young People Act 2008
- NSW: Children and Young Persons (Care and Protection) Act 1998
- VIC: Children, Youth and Families Act 2005
- WA: Children and Community Services Act 2004
- QLD: Child Protection Act 1999
- SA: Children's Protection Act 1993
- Tasmania: Children, Young Persons and their Families Act 1997
- NT: Care and Protection of Children Act 2007

Child protection

www.danielmorcombefoundation.com.au

https://aifs.gov.au/resources/resource-sheets/mandatory-reporting-child-abuse-and-neglect

NSW: https://reporter.childstory.nsw.gov.au/s/

CALM Santa Barbara (2014). Recognizing and reporting child abuse. https://youtu.be/VDTOnxrDliM

Touch

Zur Institute (2022). *Guidelines for clinically appropriate and ethical touch in therapy.* https://www.zurinstitute.com/clinical-updates/touch-in-therapy/

Negligence (Tort law)

Although discussing medical negligence, this video lists the four tests that would be used to determine negligence: https://youtu.be/B7O_VeOXJ14?

Compassion fatigue

Cunningham, A. *Drowning in empathy: The cost of vicarious trauma.* https://youtu.be/Zsaorjlo1Yc

Barnett, J. E. (2014). Distress, therapist burnout, self-care, and the promotion of wellness for psychotherapists and trainees: Issues, implications, and recommendations. [Web article]. Retrieved from https://societyforpsychotherapy.org/distress-therapist-burnout-self-care-promotion-wellness-psychotherapists-trainees-issues-implications-recommendations/

Adversity

Office for the Victims of Crime. *Through our eyes: Children, violence and trauma.* https://www.youtube.com/watch?v=z8vZxDa2KPM

Burke Harris, N. *How childhood trauma affects health across a lifetime.* https://youtu.be/95ovIJ3dsNk

Rothschild, B. *Safe recovery from trauma.* https://youtu.be/QQz5yVkBm5w

Rothschild, B. (2013). *Key 5: To share your shame.* https://www.youtube.com/watch?v=QJrzZrNtUM8

Snipes, D. E. *Neurobiological impact of psychological trauma on the HPA axis.* https://youtu.be/qLxgQdxedL4

Tyrrell, M. (2014). *Three easy questions for diagnosing PTSD.* https://youtu.be/3qnXWQJy6Bg

Grief

Amirpoor, S. Anticipated losses: https://youtu.be/vJk_t8yc3ts

Byrnes, I. S. The art of saying goodbye: https://youtu.be/Dkffpibi-Dc This is about the communal grief of young people losing their friends to cystic fibrosis.

Judy's House: *Lessons learned from grieving children.* https://youtu.be/vum6c4tluXk

Lynn, K. *When someone you love dies, there is no such thing as moving on.* https://youtu.be/kYWICGbbDGI

McInerny, N. *We don't 'move on' from grief.* https://youtu.be/khkJkR-ipfw

Scishow. *The truth about the five stages of grief.* https://youtu.be/9LudhllbeXs

Villanueva Tepper, T. *Grief: What everyone needs to know.* https://youtu.be/BwPoqQPynEc

Tyrrell, M. *Three techniques for good grief counselling.* https://youtu.be/v_2QeHCnYzcIn

Park, B. *How to comfort a grieving teen*. https://youtu.be/ySeZLAqcnuo
Winch, G. *How to fix a broken heart*. https://youtu.be/kOGQSJrpVhM
Grief out loud: Teens talk about loss: https://youtu.be/qgrRoJyljeQ
Grief and loss for First Nations peoples. https://youtu.be/eXuYGTvSacU

Anxiety and depression

Tyrrell, M. *Three instantly calming CBT techniques for anxiety*. https://youtu.be/JiDaTi_iQrY
Tyrrell, M. *Two vital techniques I use for depression*. https://youtu.be/KDOrrJwlJas
Winch, G. *How to practice emotional first aid*. https://youtu.be/F2hc2FLOdhI

Life purpose

Leipzig, A. *How to know your life purpose in five minutes*. https://youtu.be/vVsXO9brK7M

Bullying

www.caper.com.au
Gibbs, B. (2015). *How to stop a bully*. https://youtu.be/7oKjW1OIjuw?si=PzNdpIz8iO4qNuND

Addiction

Bower Place (2019). *Malcolm Robinson discusses addiction*. https://www.google.com.au/url?sa=t&rct=j&q=&esrc=s&source=web&cd=&cad=rja&uact=8&ved=2ahUKEwi_reDQ-bj6AhUv-DgGHd3_DAoQwqsBegQIBRAB&url=https%3A%2F%2Fwww.facebook.com%2FBowerPlace55%2Fvideos%2Fmalcolm-robinson-discusses-addiction%2F2369083026507952%2F&usg=AOvVaw3o9XdXNP6ckOFNXxqjO9V7

Suicide

Brennan, R. *Understanding and forgiving suicide*. https://youtu.be/reWmwCJ6VwA
Carr, J. *Attempted suicide: Overlooked and under-served* https://youtu.be/kjX6TLbvlqE

Suicide risk assessment

Grande, T. L. Ideation without intent or a plan. https://www.youtube.com/watch?v=eqIM3n7ujVA
Grande, T. L. Ideation and a plan without intent: https://www.youtube.com/watch?v=4gtDUCVAxxY
Grande, T. L. Ideation with a plan and intent. https://www.youtube.com/watch?v=OXEKrRJeB5I
Screening Tool for Assessing Risk of Suicide (STARS): https://suicideriskassessment.com.au/wp-content/uploads/2019/04/SAK-screener-computerised-updated.pdf
https://www.griffith.edu.au/griffith-health/australian-institute-suicide-research-prevention/systematic-tailored-assessment-for-responding-to-suicidality

National Drug and Alcohol Research Centre (NDARC) and University of NSW (2015): https://suicideriskassessment.com.au/wp-content/uploads/2019/04/SAK-screener-computerised-updated.pdf

Western Australian Clinical Training Network. https://youtu.be/wNF1FIKHKEU

Integrated medical practitioners

www.biobalance.org.au

Index

Pages in *italics* refer to figures and pages in **bold** refer to boxes.

For Product Safety Concerns and Information please contact our EU representative GPSR@taylorandfrancis.com
Taylor & Francis Verlag GmbH, Kaufingerstraße 24, 80331 München, Germany

www.ingramcontent.com/pod-product-compliance
Ingram Content Group UK Ltd.
Pitfield, Milton Keynes, MK11 3LW, UK
UKHW050232200926
475702UK00020B/2984
* 9 7 8 1 0 3 2 3 4 8 0 8 7 *